The Psychology of Reading and Language Comprehension

Marcel Adam Just

Patricia A. Carpenter

Carnegie-Mellon University

Allyn and Bacon, Inc.
Boston   London   Sydney   Toronto

Managing Editor: William Barke
Production Coordinator/Copy Editor: Susan Freese
Production Services: TKM Productions
Text Designer: Denise Hoffman
Cover Coordinator: Linda K. Dickinson

Library of Congress Cataloging-in-Publication Data

Just, Marcel Adam.
  The psychology of reading and language comprehension.

  Bibliography: p.
  Includes index.
  1. Reading comprehension.   2. Psycholinguistics.
3. Cognition.   4. Reading, Psychology of.   I. Carpenter,
Patricia A. (Patricia Ann)   II. Title.
BF456.R2J87   1987   153.6   86-3314
ISBN 0-205-08760-4

Printed in the United States of America

10   9   8   7   6   5   4   3   2   90   89   88   87

**To
Adam and Allan**

Contents

Preface

Why We Wrote this Book

Written language is a relatively new development, barely 5,000 years old, and a very junior offspring of the 100,000-year-old spoken form of language. When writing systems first developed in some societies, the skills of reading and writing were looked upon with awe; decoding a written message enabled a reader to communicate magically with others from whom he was removed in time and space. In our contemporary world, communicating over distance is now commonplace, but the process of reading retains some of its mystique, although for somewhat different reasons. We wrote this book to examine this mystique and explain the psychological processes involved in reading.

Scientific research attempts to unravel some of the mysteries of nature; psychological research, in particular, tries to unravel some of the mysteries of human thinking. In the past fifteen years, researchers have substantially advanced the frontiers of our knowledge about reading, producing significant new discoveries. Several years ago, we decided to integrate our own research on reading within a broad theoretical framework, a theory of human thought capable of explaining reading as it occurs in a variety of situations. The opportunity to write a book came in 1982, when we were invited to spend a year's leave at the Netherlands Institute for Advanced Study. We then had some important new results, the outline of a theory, and the opportunity to put them all together.

The Goals of this Book

We have addressed this book to a wide range of readers: researchers in the psychology of reading and language, senior undergraduates and graduate students in psychology and education, teachers of reading, and educators, in general. This book is intended to be used in a course on the psychology of reading or the psychology of language comprehension, or in a graduate seminar on either of these topics. Our experience in teaching both undergraduate and graduate courses on the psychology of reading and language for the last ten years persuaded us that the central issues can be effectively communicated in a common format to all of these potential users. Even though the book presents a thorough account of the psychological processes that occur in reading, we have tried to make it understandable to someone who has had as little as one course in cognitive psychology.

Another goal of this book is to extend the theoretical framework to a fairly wide scope, covering the kinds of topics that are of general interest to psychologists and educators. We have developed a precise theory and used it as rigorously as possible to organize and explain a very broad and diverse field.

The Underlying Approach and Assumptions

The main feature of this book is its unified approach based on a comprehensive theoretical framework, which integrates new and old results on different facets and types of reading. The theory is outlined in the first chapter and is then described in considerable detail in Chapter 9; in addition, it is referred to throughout the book. The theory is described in terms of a model called READER, which can perform the act of reading comprehension. In several of the chapters that deal with a particular component process of reading, we describe how the READER model executes that process. For example, in Chapter 3 on lexical access, we describe how the READER model accesses the meaning of a word in its own internal lexicon and compare the model's behavior to human behavior. Thus, throughout the discussions of the various component processes involved in reading, we do not have to describe one kind of theory to account for one set of results and then describe another type of theory to account for another set of results. The unified framework provided by our theory encompasses all of the components of reading.

The theoretical framework also makes the extensive coverage of the literature coherent. The references to many hundreds of journal articles are introduced within the shared framework, providing supporting evidence, detail, and illustration. Even though the book paints a picture that is large and detailed, we have tried to make all of the pieces of the picture fit together.

One reason that the picture of reading is so large is that *reading* is a generic term for a large family of different tasks—from the first laborious steps in word decoding by a first-grader to the fluent, rapid reading of a skilled reader. Our approach to this diversity was to initially focus our research on a prototypical reading situation. The experiments and theory were then extended to other instructionally relevant situations, such as the acquisition of reading, speed reading, learning from reading, individual differences among normal readers, and special problems of dyslexic readers. The organization of the book reflects this approach; the first nine chapters primarily describe the component processes in conventional skilled reading, while the last six describe several specialized types of reading.

Instructional and Classroom Implications

Because reading plays such a central role in education, we have considered several different kinds of instructional implications. We do not prescribe how reading should be taught, but we do provide information that will be useful to the reading instructor.

The most obvious type of instructional implication concerns the acquisition of reading skills by children and adults in a classroom. This issue is directly addressed in several chapters: Chapter 4, Vocabulary Acquisition; Chapter 11, Beginning Reading; and Chapter 14, Speed Reading. For example, we consider how children learn the perceptual skills in reading, as well as how they acquire vocabulary. We also examine how readers at high skill levels can increase their fluency and optimize their reading speed for acquiring certain types of information.

A second type of instructional implication concerns the learning of content by reading or studying text. Much of the knowledge a literate person possesses has been acquired through reading, either in school, at work, or at leisure. In two chapters—Chapter 8, Understanding an Extended Text, and Chapter 13, Learning from Text—we consider the acquisition of knowledge through reading. These chapters explore how the reading comprehension processes determine what information is ultimately retained. We also consider how people acquire information from different types of texts.

A third type of instructional implication concerns the wide differences in reading ability among individuals. Educators are almost always faced with students who learn to read at different rates and attain different levels of skill. To deal with such differences effectively, it is important to understand the psychological processes that differentiate people with different levels of reading ability. In Chapter 15, Individual Differences, we examine several possible sources of individual differences and describe a new approach, based on the operational capacity of working memory, that permits the measurement and prediction of reading ability among college students. And in Chapter 12, Dyslexia, we examine a psychological disability that is specific to reading and describe the reading processes that are impaired. Our treatment of these three types of instructional implications provides a firm basis for understanding what processes occur during reading and during the learning of reading, a basis that seems central to instruction in a classroom situation.

The Scientific Basis of the Approach

Our theory is based on what is known about reading, particularly on the data from psychological experiments that examine human performance in reading tasks. Among the experiments that are described are many from our own laboratory; however, this book is not a compendium of our work. We have been doing research on reading and language comprehension for over fifteen years, and the time came to synthesize our own experimental results and theoretical proposals within a broader framework. Within this framework, we do describe a number of previously unpublished results from our laboratory as they bear on the issues that arise. For example, the main research on speed reading (Chapter 14) that we report is a study from our own lab; this chapter draws heavily on our study of the eye fixations and comprehension of a group of speed readers reading scientific and narrative texts. We also draw on our own research in the discussion of Chinese orthography (Chapter 10), in which we describe the comprehension and eye fixations in the reading of Chinese scientific texts. Similarly, Chapter 12 on dyslexia describes our study of several academically successful students who have severe reading difficulty. And Chapters 2 and 3 present new data on word perception as it occurs during reading. All of these research results, as well as many others from other laboratories, reveal important, new information about the characteristics of reading.

Our approach has treated reading as a language comprehension process that has a great deal in common with oral language comprehension. To be sure, reading contains an important visual-perceptual component that distinguishes it from oral comprehension, and written language is somewhat different than spoken language. But the main processes in reading are fundamentally language comprehension processes. Reading is intimately tied to oral language processing, both in how it is acquired by children and in how it is processed by skilled adults. Viewed from this perspective, the theory we present is not just a theory of reading. It also forms a large part of a theory of language comprehension.

Acknowledgements

We hope that the citations throughout this book point out the intellectual debts that we owe to other researchers. In addition, we have many colleagues and students to thank for their participation in the research enterprise in our laboratory. Robert Thibadeau helped make the theory both more precise and more accurate and was central in the development of the computer-simulation model. Michael Masson collaborated in the studies of speed reading, from inception to description, and Rosalind Wu collaborated in the study of reading in Chinese. Meredyth Daneman played a central role in research on the role of working memory in reading. These co-workers are an integral part of the research team that made the new discoveries.

Those colleagues and students who read and commented on parts of the book throughout its development have our gratitude for their time and patience. Their constructive comments were responsible for significant improvements from early versions of the manuscript. We thank Isabelle Beck, Robert Calfee, Ruth Day, Tony Jorm, Walter Kintsch, Brian MacWhinney, Jay McClelland, Bob Nagy, Lance Rips, Jay Samuels, and Bob Siegler for their comments. We are especially grateful to John B. Carroll, Mike Kamil, David Kieras, and Ed Shoben, who provided many valuable comments on the entire book. We also thank Sue MacNealy, Jacqui Woolley, and particularly Claire Progar for their assistance in preparing the manuscript.

Institutions, as well as individuals, helped us in writing this book. The Netherlands Institute for Advanced Study, in Wassenaar, Holland, generously provided us with a year of time for writing and thinking that made this book possible. The National Institute of Mental Health, the National Institute of Education, and the Office of Naval Research have supported our research through research grants for many years. In addition, Carnegie-Mellon University provided the scientific and educational support that enabled us to pursue our research and writing. Most of all, we are grateful for our good fortune to be located at a time and place in which scientific research is valued, supported, and used constructively.

The order of the authorship of this book was decided by the toss of a coin. There are some chapters in which MAJ was the senior author (namely, Chapters 3, 5, 6, 7, 8, and 9) and some chapters in which PAC was the senior author (namely, Chapters 2, 4, 10, 11, 12, and 15). But on the whole, the book is a reflection of our joint work.

Part One

Cognitive Processes in Reading

1

An Introduction and Overview of the Theory

An expert can make a complex skill look easy. But the apparent effortlessness of a chess master or concert pianist does not deceive us. We know that mastering a complex skill requires many thousands of hours of study, and practice and performing it requires the exquisite orchestration of many subskills.

What we sometimes fail to appreciate is that skilled reading is an intellectual feat no less complex than chess playing. Reading is a complex cognitive skill, consisting of a collection of psychological processes that together produce an understanding of a text. Readers of this book are, in many ways, as expert at reading as chess masters are expert at chess. But because of the deceptively effortless look and feel of reading, and the fact that there are relatively many "reading masters" in our society, reading skill is not given as much credit for complexity as other forms of expertise. Its complexity is also one reason why not everyone learns to read, and certainly not everyone becomes an expert reader.

This book describes the psychological processes that comprise the unheralded expertise of skilled reading. This book has two major parts. The first one is a detailed analysis of normal, skilled reading. Then, in the second part, this analysis is applied to variations in reading, including reading in foreign writing systems, beginning reading, reading disabilities, speed reading, reading for learning, and differences in reading ability among individuals.

Overview   Our main purpose in this chapter is to introduce some issues that are explored in a cognitive analysis of reading. In the first section, called **The Focus on Processes,** we will explain what is entailed by a process approach and give examples of the processes used in reading. One of the research tools introduced is the analysis of readers' eye fixations, both where they look and how long they spend on various words or sentences in a text. In the second section, **The Cognitive Approach,** we will give a more general description of the features that are characteristic of many cognitive theories, the present theory included. One such characteristic is a concern with how information is mentally represented while it is being processed. Another feature that is common to many cognitive theories is a concern with how people organize and use their knowledge to execute a complex skill, like reading or chess playing. In the third section, **A Theory of Reading,** we will preview the theory. Then we will show how the theory enables us to characterize different types of reading (such as speed reading) and reading problems.

The Focus on Processes

Although reading involves many processes, a reader normally only becomes aware of them if one or another process encounters some difficulty. For example, a reader might read something and say, "I understand the ideas behind the text, but the grammar is atrocious." Or in another case, the reader might judge, "The wording and grammar seem fine, but I have no idea what this text is about." Or the reader might understand most of the text, except for some particular words. These difficulties make the reader aware of a few of the numerous processes that make up reading. The analysis of such processes and how they operate together is the major subject matter examined in this book.

Since this book presents a theory of the psychological processes in reading, the concept of a psychological process is central to the approach. The noun *process* refers to a set of operations that accomplish some goal. For example, one process in the petroleum industry refines crude oil to produce gasoline and other byproducts. The process has a beginning state, an end state, and some intervening transformations.

In the case of reading, the beginning state includes the printed words on the page, the reader's initial knowledge of the topic, and the reader's knowledge of the language. The end state includes the new knowledge that the reader has acquired from the text. The intervening transformations are all of the processes and structures that make up reading.

While petroleum-refining processes operate on crude oil to produce gasoline, reading processes operate on symbols to produce new symbols, the new information. Because the reading processes operate on symbols rather than on physical materials, they are called information processes. The symbols that are operated upon are the other side of the process coin, and they also must be described as part of the theory.

The component processes in reading can be described by specifying their various characteristics, including:

- what information in the text starts the process;
- how long the process takes;
- what information was used during the process;
- the likely sources of mistakes; and
- what the reader has learned when the process is finished.

We will examine both perceptual processes and comprehension processes. The perceptual processes visually register written language, transforming from printed symbols to language. The comprehension processes interpret language, transforming from linguistic symbols to a more abstract symbolic representation —that is, from language to thought. Obviously, both perception and comprehension are crucial to reading, and they operate together.

One of the goals of recent research has been to discover the nature of the cooperation among different processes. We will describe how various processes can influence one another, how some circumstances can make one process dominate another, and how the results from different processes are pooled so that the reader understands the text.

To describe the psychological processes occurring in a person's mind is easier said than done, because there is no way to look inside to determine what is happening. The processes can only be inferred by observing what the reader does. Unfortunately, there is not much to observe when a person is reading silently. If we were analyzing a more physical skill, like piano playing, we could record and analyze the temporal patterning and force of the finger movements during the performance of a Beethoven sonata. But what can we analyze while someone reads *War and Peace*?

One naturally occurring behavior that can be recorded and analyzed is the reader's eye fixations on the words of the text. Experiments that examine the patterns of eye fixations have recently made several new discoveries about the ongoing reading processes. We will present a small sample of some eye-fixation data below, along with a brief description of what they indicate about reading.

What Eye Fixations Can Tell Us about Reading

It has long been known that a reader's eyes do not sweep smoothly along the lines of print (Javal, 1879). Rather, the eyes make a series of pauses, or fixations, punctuated by brief jumps from one place to another. The fixations vary in duration, but the average fixation lasts a quarter of a second, or 250 milliseconds (thousandths of a second). The average jump lasts between 10 and 20 milliseconds.

Recent computer-based instruments allow researchers to measure and record the eyes' behavior, indicating precisely which word is being fixated at any given time. The reader's pattern of eye fixations shows which words are fixated, how long they are fixated, and which words are refixated. If the reader is fluent and the text is not difficult, most of the fixations are forward fixations, progressing from earlier words in the text to later words. But if the reader encounters difficulty or is not fluent, he will tend to make regressive fixations back to earlier parts of the text. The time that a reader spends on various parts of a text and the places where he fixates or rereads the text are excellent indices of the ongoing psychological processes.

The time a reader spends on a word or phrase can indicate when a process occurs and how its duration is influenced by characteristics of the text, the reader, and the task. To give a concrete example, Figure 1.1 represents some typical data based on the eye fixations of a college student who was reading the first few sentences of a passage about flywheels in order to recall the gist of the passage (Just & Carpenter, 1980). Consecutive fixations on the same word have been aggregated into units called *gazes*. The duration of the gaze is measured in milliseconds, so a number like 1,566 above the first word indicates that the reader spent 1,566 milliseconds on that

Flywheels are one of the oldest mechanical devices known to man. Every

internal-combustion engine contains a small flywheel that converts the jerky

motion of the pistons into the smooth flow of energy that powers the drive shaft.

Figure 1.1   The time a college reader spent on the words in the opening two sentences of a technical article about flywheels. The times, indicated above the fixated word, are in milliseconds. This reader read the sentences from left to right with one regressive fixation to an earlier part. *Source:* Adapted from Just & Carpenter, 1980, p. 330. Copyright 1980 by the American Psychological Association. Adapted by permission.

word before fixating any other word. As illustrated in Figure 1.1, the reader made mostly forward gazes, from earlier words to later words.

The distribution of the gazes in this sample is fairly typical of the way college students read this kind of passage in order to summarize or answer questions about it. One interesting characteristic of the data is that they illustrate that even skilled readers fixate a high proportion (over 80 percent) of the content words, such as nouns, adjectives, verbs, and adverbs. They fixate a smaller proportion of the function words, like *the* and *a,* producing an overall average of 65 percent of all words being fixated. The proportion of words that are fixated is even higher if the text is especially difficult or if the reader is unskilled. These findings are contrary to the common misconception that readers directly fixate only one out of every three or four words.

The usefulness of eye-fixation data can be emphasized by contrasting a reader to a listener. A reader, unlike a listener, can skip over portions of the text; a reader can pause on a particular word or reread an earlier word or an entire sentence. In short, readers can take in information at a pace that matches their internal comprehension processes. Even the time that readers spend on individual words and short phrases depends in part on the perception and comprehension processes required to recognize and process the word and phrase. For example, as the data presented in Figure 1.1 show, this reader spent a very long time when she first looked at the topic of a new paragraph—flywheels (over 1,500 milliseconds in the first line). But she spent considerably less time (just over 1,000 milliseconds) on the second encounter with the word *flywheel* in the second line (Just & Carpenter, 1980). In general, readers spend less time on a topically related word as they become more familiar with the concept.

The relation between the eye-fixation behavior and text properties can indicate the nature of the ongoing reading processes. To analyze gaze durations, we typically compute the average time that a group of readers spends on a particular word and compare the duration to some contrasting condition, such as the time spent on the same word in a different context, or the time spent on a different kind of word, or the time spent on the same word by different types of readers. We can illustrate the analysis with a brief example of syntactic processing. In a number of eye-fixation studies, readers spent more time on a word that was syntactically unexpected (Carpenter & Just, 1983; Frazier & Rayner, 1982). For example, consider this sentence:

> *The pickpocket stood before the black-robed judge*
> *entered the courtroom to convene the jury.*

Most readers initially misinterpret *before the black-robed judge* as a prepositional phrase meaning "in front of the black-robed judge." Consequently, they don't expect to encounter the verb *entered;* when they do, they spend additional time on it (compared to the time taken on a control sentence in which *before* is replaced by an unambiguous conjunction, such as *while*). The pause on *entered* provides evidence that the sentence was initially misinterpreted. It also provides evidence that readers were trying to determine the syntactic role of *entered* while they were still fixating it. Thus, eye-fixation analyses can suggest which interpretation is given to an ambiguous sentence and where various computations are made.

In spite of our enthusiasm for eye-fixation research, this is not a book about eye fixations in reading but about the psychological processes in reading. Eye fixations provide only one type of data. Other types include the time taken to read part or all of a text, the ability to answer questions about the text, the ability to recall the text, and the nature of any misinterpretations. All of these kinds of data are drawn on throughout the book. But we have singled out eye-fixation data for discussion in this chapter for two reasons. First, the technique provides one of the few ways to study reading processes as they occur. Second, the eye-fixation patterns convey something of the rapid, dynamic nature of reading processes.

Levels of Language and Types of Processes

Reading is fundamentally the comprehension of language. The various levels of language, including words, phrases, sentences, and entire texts, are operated on by some of the component processes of reading. The different processes associated with these various levels provide one of the organizational devices of the book. To illustrate this approach, we will describe some of the levels of language and the processes associated with them.

A good place to begin is the word or **lexical** level. The lexical level is prominent in reading because individual words are usually the focus of early reading instruction when children are taught word recognition and vocabulary. Individual words continue to be a critically important level of psychological organization in adult reading. The word level is associated with several reading processes, including encoding the printed word and accessing its meaning in a mental dictionary or lexicon, a process referred to as **lexical access.** Lexical access provides the conventional meaning of the word, including its common interpretations and part of speech.

While the word level is important, it is obviously not sufficient for comprehension. Individual words must be put together to form a larger structure that indicates the relations among the concepts in a phrase or clause. Determining how the words of a clause fit together is the purpose of the syntactic and semantic analyses. **Semantic analysis** focuses on meaning relations among the sentence elements, or, roughly speaking, determining who is doing what to whom. **Syntactic analysis** focuses on the grammatical relations among the words in a phrase or clause, such as determining which word is the subject of the verb and whether the verb is past or present tense.

Syntactic and semantic analyses collaborate to determine the semantic relations. For example, the syntactic analysis in English uses word order, among other cues, to determine the grammatical relations among the words in a phrase or sentence. Different word orders in two otherwise identical sentences can result in very different syntactic and semantic representations. For example, in the following sentences, interchanging the words *dog* and *the* completely changes the meaning:

> *The little girl's father fed her dog the biscuits.*
> *The little girl's father fed her the dog biscuits.*

Beyond understanding individual clauses and sentences, readers also have to interrelate these elements to make sense of a text, whether they are following the plot of a short story, the argument of a newspaper editorial, or the description in a biology textbook. Such interrelating requires understanding the causal, temporal, and other relations among concepts. And such understanding draws on knowledge of the world, as well as knowledge of particular types of text genres. For example, consider how a reader might recognize the complication in the following vignette:

> *John hoped to buy the new jacket that evening. As he was daydreaming about its dashing appearance, he opened the afternoon mail to find a bank notice stating that his account was overdrawn. And here it was, still two more weeks until the end of the month.*

To understand this text, a reader has to know about money, banking practices, purchasing, and pay schedules to infer that the second and third sentences present a complication for the goal stated in the first sentence: buying a new jacket. Even a simple story may require lots of unstated information to fit the parts together.

More generally, language must be related to the concepts to which it refers. While working through a text, the reader must construct a representation of the individual concepts and the situation to which the text is referring (that is, a representation of the referential world). We will call this the **referential representation.** For example, a reader who was reading about the original design of Washington, D.C., might construct a mental representation of its layout, with the capitol buildings at the center and a set of radiating lines for the major streets. To construct the referential representation, the reader draws on the text, as well as any previous knowledge of the topic. The referential level of processing is central because the main purpose of written text is often to impart new information about a referent. This characteristic is true not only of descriptive texts, but also of expository texts and narratives.

While reading involves language comprehension, it also has an important perceptual component, the most prominent of which is word recognition. We will use the term **word recognition** in this chapter to refer to the combination of two processes that will be discussed separately in subsequent chapters. The two components of word recognition are:

1. encoding the visual pattern of a printed word and
2. accessing its meaning in the internal dictionary (lexical access).

Word recognition is an impressive perceptual skill. Skilled readers can identify and discriminate among tens of thousands of words, even if a single word is shown briefly and without context. But reaching this state usually requires formal instruction and thousands of hours of practice. Children who enter first grade already comprehend spoken language, but they generally don't recognize printed words. Somehow, word recognition must be combined with language comprehension to produce reading. Each of the linguistic and perceptual processes associated with these various levels will be the topic of Chapters 2 through 8.

The Cognitive Approach

The theory of reading to be presented is a *cognitive* theory. Cognitive theories have been developed to describe many aspects of normal human thinking, such as problem solving (Newell & Simon, 1972), perceiving and manipulating visual images (Just & Carpenter, 1985; Kosslyn, 1980; Shepard, 1975), and writing (Hayes & Flower, 1980). Most cognitive approaches, including the current theory of reading, share a number of characteristics, which we will briefly introduce before giving more detailed explanations of how they apply to the theory of reading.

Characteristics of the Cognitive Approach

The most prominent characteristic of a cognitive approach is the focus on the processes underlying a cognitive skill, a focus we discussed in the preceding section. But to describe how information is processed, the theory must also specify how the information itself is mentally represented. Processes and representations are inextricably linked, like the proverbial two sides of a coin. Having already considered what it means to describe a process, we will briefly consider what it means to describe a representation.

To describe a mental representation is to specify what information it contains and what form that information takes. For example, a person may represent the fact that a figure is round, and that information could take the form of a visual image, a verbal statement, or an algebraic expression. In the case of reading, many different types of information are relevant, including visual information (such as the appearance of particular letters and the spelling of a word), semantic information about the meaning of words and phrases, and information about the structure of a story. So the theory must describe the representations of several different types of information.

Cognitive approaches have also been concerned with the role played by knowledge and its representation. This issue is sometimes studied by exploring what experts know about their field—for example, what are the differences between the moves made by a master chess player and a novice? Or how do the planning processes differ for a professional author and a freshman writing a composition?

The importance of knowledge is especially evident in reading. Every reader knows it is easier to read a text on a familiar topic than on an unfamiliar topic, even if the wording, grammar, and style are otherwise fairly similar. To explain this well-known effect, a cognitive theory must describe how the knowledge is represented in the reader's mind and what role the knowledge plays in the comprehension processes.

Reading also requires other kinds of knowledge, particularly linguistic knowledge. For example, the reader must know the meanings of specific words and the grammatical structure of English. This knowledge may not always be something that a reader can describe. Grammatical knowledge, for example, is often difficult to describe, although it is demonstrably present. Readers demonstrate grammatical knowledge when they have difficulty processing ungrammatical constructions, like *the was happy* or *the consists.* Their difficulty indicates that, at some level, they know the word *the* signals a noun phrase, not a verb phrase. The various types of linguistic knowledge used in reading must be described as part of the theory of comprehension.

A theory of a complex cognitive skill can be quite cumbersome to describe because there are so many components to identify, explain, and relate. Furthermore, English and other natural languages are not well suited to describing information-processing operations. In some disciplines, like physics, the theories are usually expressed in the language of mathematics. In cognitive psychology, theories are often expressed in the language of computer-simulation models. Just as cardiac physiologists sometimes build hydraulic models of how they think the human heart operates, so do cognitive theorists build computer programs as models of how they think the human mind operates.

A computer-simulation model allows a theorist to put all of the components of the theory together to see how they operate in concert and what predictions they make. The computer model typically performs some task, such as generating a chess move or recognizing a spoken phrase. Then some aspect of the program's performance, such as the quality of the chess move or the accuracy of its speech recognition, can be compared to human performance. Computer models are used in cognitive psychology because some aspects of human information processing resemble aspects of some (unconventional) types of computer programs. Of course, no one suggests that the human mind is a digital computer. But some computer simulation models provide good characterizations of certain aspects of human thought.

Computer simulations are particularly useful in the area of reading. In the past, reading theories were rather piecemeal affairs; there was one theory about how a word was recognized and another about how a sentence was processed. Theorists seldom put the various parts together, in part, because there was no formalism that could accommodate the large number of different processes involved in something as complex as reading. Computer simulations provide the integrative formalism. They provide a medium for storing lots of information and making lots of computations. Having described some of the general features of cognitive approaches, we will now consider the role these features play in reading.

The Representation of Knowledge

As reading teachers have long known, comprehension is better if the reader has some forehand knowledge about the topic (Smith, 1963). It has often been recommended that students be familiarized with a topic before they read about it, and this practice has been institutionalized in elementary school reading programs. Recently, researchers in artificial intelligence and psychology have been exploring how knowledge improves comprehension. It quickly became apparent that to improve comprehension, knowledge must be more than a set of isolated facts. To be useful, the facts must be organized.

The organizational aspect of knowledge is captured in a knowledge representation called a **schema** (Bartlett, 1932; Minsky, 1975; Schank, 1982). A schema is a framework containing a set of slots, with each slot labeled to indicate what type of information it can contain. A schema is a little like a questionnaire that consists of a set of blanks, with labels to indicate where respondents should fill in their name, the date, and so on. For example, the schema for a familiar, complex concept, such as the KITCHEN in a house, would have slots for the major categories of information about a kitchen, such as its appliances, furniture, layout, and users, as depicted in Figure 1.2. Each slot indicates some typical fillers that can be used as default

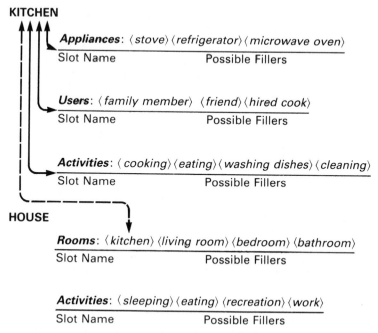

Figure 1.2 A schema for a concept, such as **KITCHEN,** contains slots for various kinds of information, such as *appliances, users,* and *activities.* Each slot has possible fillers that can serve as default values. For example, *appliances* has the possible fillers *stove, refrigerator, microwave oven,* and so on. The schema may be connected to other schemata, such as the schema for HOUSE.

(fallback) values should the situation fail to provide any. In the kitchen schema, the *appliances* slot might have the defaults of *stove* and *refrigerator;* more opulent kitchens might also have a *dishwasher, microwave oven,* and *toaster.*

The schema also indicates relations among slots. For example, one slot might indicate possible pieces of furniture, while another slot might indicate how they are arranged. This generic schema is the basis of a more specific representation the reader constructs when reading about or visiting a particular kitchen. A reader can fill in the slots with values based on information in the text. He can also fill a slot with a default value if the text fails to provide a filler. If a text described a country-style kitchen with a round, oak eating table in the middle, this information could be incorporated into the slots for the layout and furniture in a schema for that particular kitchen. The labeled, organized slots and their default values constitute the schema for a concept.

A schema is connected to other schemata (the plural of schema) by a variety of relations, such as part-whole or subordinate-superordinate relations. For example, the schema for a kitchen may be connected to the schema for a house (of which it is a part) or to the schema for a room (of which it is an instance). A schema also may be connected to schemata for related concepts. For example, the schema for a home kitchen may be connected to the schema for a restaurant kitchen.

Schemata play several roles in reading. First, the slots and their default values can help the reader identify the referent of a term in the text. If the text mentions a woman going to the kitchen to get *glasses,* the reader can infer that this word refers to drinking glasses and not eyeglasses. The schema can also provide information that interrelates different parts of the text. If the text said that the woman then *turned on the faucet,* the reader can infer the relation between *glasses* and *turning on the faucet,* even if the text never explicitly described it. These background inferences are easily made with the help of the schema, and a text that explicitly described them would be extremely tedious. On the other hand, if a story permits no schema to be evoked or constructed, readers rate the story difficult to comprehend and recall it poorly. However, if before reading the story they are given a title that indicates the appropriate schema, then their comprehension and recall are much better (Bransford & Johnson, 1973).

Schema representations for other levels   As these examples have illustrated, schemata are useful in representing what a reader might know or learn about a particular topic. The notion of a schema is also useful for expressing various types of knowledge about language, such as the structure of a child's story or a simple fable. A schema for a fable would have a labeled slot for each of its components, including a slot for the setting, the characters, one or more episodes that are composed of an initiating event and a resolution, and the moral. The schema might also indicate something of the normal temporal and causal relations among the components. For example, it would indicate that initiating events precede resolutions and that morals come at the ends of fables.

The story schema would be used during comprehension, much as we suggested that the schema for some particular content would be used. As a child reads or hears a fable, she recognizes that a particular part of the fable corresponds to a schema slot (such as the resolution) and fills in the value from the fable. For example, in the well-known Aesop fable about the tortoise and the hare, the child would recognize that the resolution of the race episode occurred when the hare woke up and saw that the tortoise had crossed the finish line. Thus, the schema provides a system for organizing the information from a story.

As important as schemata are to comprehension, their role is even more apparent in learning and memory. In recalling a story, a child might retrieve each of the familiar slots in her schema with the specific content extracted from a given story (Rumelhart, 1975). A schema can also be used to mentally reorganize information if a story describes events in an unusual sequence (Mandler, 1978; Stein & Trabasso, 1981). When readers recall a story about a familiar situation, like eating at a restaurant, they sometimes recall facts that are commonly true of that situation but were not mentioned in the story, indicating the use of default slot fillers (Bower, Black, & Turner, 1979). If readers are given a story from another culture, particularly one with unfamiliar concepts, then recall is distorted in systematic ways. Readers tend to rearrange the story, delete information, and add other information in a manner that makes the story more consistent with their own culture (Bartlett, 1932; Kintsch & Greene, 1978). Thus, schema-based knowledge of language and knowledge of the world play a vital role in text comprehension.

The Representation of Information

The linguistic, conceptual, and perceptual information that is needed for reading must be internally represented so that it can be accessed by various processes. Almost all theories of language processing have proposed that information is represented in units called **propositions.** A proposition is a symbolic structure that includes a predicate and one or more arguments. For example, consider a very simple sentence:

> *Bernard carved a melon.*

A proposition can represent the fact that Bernard is the person performing the action (who is called the *agent*):

> (**AGENT** :IS *Bernard*)

The predicate of the proposition is the relation :IS and the arguments are the two concepts, AGENT and Bernard. This notation is equivalent to saying, "The agent is Bernard." A proposition is the smallest unit of knowledge that can be true or false. In this instance, it is sensible to ask whether it is true that the agent is Bernard. But it is not sensible to ask whether a smaller unit—such as the single argument *Bernard*—is true or false. Of course, readers do not internally represent information using parentheses, colons, and capital letters, or this particular word order. These aspects of the notation have no theoretical significance. What is theoretically important is the idea that the reader has internal symbols arranged in some structure to represent the denoted concepts and their relation.

One of the main uses of propositional notation in language research has been to represent the meaning or semantic content of a text. The content of the sentence *Bernard carved a melon* could be represented as a set of propositions—one indicating that the action is carving (ACTION :IS carve); a second indicating that

Bernard is the do-er of the action (the AGENT); the third indicating that a melon is being acted upon (the OBJECT):

    (**ACTION** :IS *carve*)
    (**AGENT** :IS *Bernard*)
    (**OBJECT** :IS *melon*)

Propositions can be used as building blocks to represent more complex sentences. By conjoining propositions and embedding them, one inside another, it is possible to construct representations of entire texts.

    Propositional representations can be used to symbolize other levels of linguistic information besides the semantic level. The same notation can represent grammatical information, such as the fact that the grammatical subject of a sentence is *Bernard* or that a verb is in the past tense. Propositions can also be used to represent conceptual information, such as the information in a schema for a kitchen. Moreover, propositions can also represent visual information, such as the letters that make up a word or the visual features that make up a letter. A set of propositions can express the fact that a *T* consists of a vertical line of some length, whose top bisects a shorter horizontal line. Because propositions can represent many different kinds of information, they have proven to be extremely useful. Some variant of propositional notation is used in almost all language theories in psychology, linguistics, and artificial intelligence.

Activation

Many cognitive theories use a mechanism called **activation** to explain how a mental structure can be at different states of accessibility at different times (Anderson, 1976; Collins & Loftus, 1975; McClelland & Rumelhart, 1981; Morton, 1969). This concept explains the familiar intuition that a given piece of knowledge (such as one's mother's maiden name) is sometimes activated (for example, when asked to recall it), while at other times, it is still in one's mind but in a dormant state.

    The mental structures proposed in our reading theory, propositions, are each assumed to have an **activation level** that corresponds roughly to its accessibility or its credibility at that instant in time. A proposition's activation level can be increased or decreased as a function of the rest of the knowledge state (using a process that we will describe later). When a proposition's activation level rises to a predetermined threshold value, that proposition becomes fully accepted as being true and becomes part of the representation of the text. In the convention we have used, the activation level of a proposition is represented numerically by a number between 0 and 1; the threshold level has the value 1. We can illustrate the use of activation levels and a threshold in the domain of word recognition.

    Consider the following situation. Suppose a word is briefly flashed to a reader (perhaps by a malfunctioning neon sign). If the flash is sufficiently brief, the reader will not recognize the word. However, if it is flashed a second and third time, even though the flashes are equally brief, the reader will eventually recognize the word.

    The phenomenon can be explained by using the activation mechanism. When the word was initially flashed, activation was directed to a number of candidates that matched some of the features of the letters. Suppose the sign actually said

DANGER. The first flash may have been sufficient to activate certain letters in particular positions. These letters, in turn, may have activated a number of perceptual representations that are compatible with the partial information, such as *BADGER, DANCER,* and *DANGER.* Each of these alternative interpretations can be expressed as a proposition, and their activation level can be represented by a number. The number is higher if the candidate is more consistent with the partial information and lower if it is less consistent. After the first flash, no interpretation has reached threshold, so the activation level is represented by some number that is less than the threshold value.

The candidate interpretations and their activation levels can be represented as follows:

Proposition	Activation Level
(WORD-1 :IS *DANGER*)	.7
(WORD-1 :IS *DANCER*)	.6
(WORD-1 :IS *BADGER*)	.5

The second time the neon sign flashes, more features will be perceived and more correct letters will be activated; in turn, they will activate various perceptual representations. Eventually, with enough flashes, the correct word's activation level will reach the threshold value of 1, and it will become the accepted interpretation.

The activation mechanism provides a way for processes to collaborate during word recognition. Two different processes may activate the same proposition and, consequently, help it reach threshold faster. For example, in the case of the malfunctioning neon sign, suppose that the reader sees that the sign is perched on a closed lane of a highway where the reader knows there was a recent rock slide. That knowledge might add extra activation to the *DANGER* candidate so that the word would be recognized even sooner. This is an example of a context effect, a case in which context facilitates word recognition.

The activation mechanism operates at other levels besides word encoding. In the current model, the internal representations of several structures (such as phrases, clauses, and referents) are assumed to have activation levels that increase or decrease as a result of various comprehension processes. For example, activation levels can express the varying degrees of confidence a reader might have in different inferences. Suppose that the reader encounters a description of a girl stirring some soup. The proposition that the girl is stirring soup would have a high activation level, since the text explicitly provided the information. By contrast, the inference that the girl used a spoon would not have as high a level of activation; although spoons are typically associated with stirring, other instruments can be used. So the activation levels can reflect the degree to which the inferences are believed.

In this section, we have described some of the features commonly found in cognitive theories and shared by the theory of reading described in this book. First, the theory assumes that information used in reading is internally represented in a propositional format; this includes visual information, linguistic information, and conceptual information. Propositions are created by various perceptual and linguistic processes, and they can be retrieved from long-term memory. Second, each proposition has an associated activation level that can be raised, lowered, or left unchanged.

A Theory of Reading

Reading is characterized by two prominent properties that have a shaping influence on a theory of reading. First, reading is inherently sequential; a reader takes in the text one word at a time, not all at once. Nevertheless, the information from many words must be interrelated. A theory of reading must explain how and when different parts are interrelated as a reader progresses through a text. A second property of reading is that it involves several component processes, which we have already enumerated. A theory of reading must describe how the different component processes are coordinated.

Thus, the theory must account for the sequential integration over the processing of many separate words and the vertical integration over several different component processes. In this section, we discuss these two issues, provide an overview of our theory and the computer-simulation model, and, finally, describe how the theory helps in analyzing the differences among readers and reading tasks.

Interpretation is Immediate

Comprehenders deal with the sequential nature of language by trying to interpret each successive word of a text as soon as they encounter it, integrating the new information they have gleaned with what they already know about the text and its subject matter. We will refer to this processing strategy as the **immediacy of interpretation.** A listener tries to follow on the heels of a speaker; a reader tries to digest each piece of the text as he encounters it (Just & Carpenter, 1980).

The immediacy of interpretation can be contrasted with a different strategy for dealing with the sequential nature of language, namely, a wait-and-see strategy. A reader can always increase the probability of correctly interpreting a given word or phrase if she postpones interpreting it until she sees what follows in the sentence. Wait-and-see strategies have been proposed by several researchers (Kimball, 1973; Marcus, 1980), and this contrast between immediacy and wait-and-see makes the properties of each strategy clearer, even though the evidence is overwhelming that readers don't wait-and-see unless they have to. Comprehenders who use the immediacy strategy still use the context that follows a piece of text to help interpret that piece, but they do so by elaborating or amending an already existing interpretation, rather than waiting for the context before making any interpretation.

The immediacy of interpretation entails all levels of comprehension: encoding the word, accessing its meaning, associating it with its referent, and determining its semantic and syntactic status in the sentence and the discourse. The cognitive system attempts the multiple levels of interpretation as soon as it gets access to the word. It is important to note that although the attempt at interpretation is immediate, the text can force postponement by withholding essential information. In such cases, the postponement is out of necessity rather than strategic choice. The default strategy is to interpret immediately.

The eye-fixation behavior of a reader is completely consistent with an immediacy strategy and inconsistent with a wait-and-see strategy. When a reader encounters a difficult word—for example, one that is very long, infrequent, or syntactically anomalous—she pauses on that very word before moving on to the rest of the text

(Carpenter & Just, 1983; Just & Carpenter, 1980, 1984). This finding suggests that the reader is processing that word at that time, rather than using a wait-and-see strategy. Perceptual processes are usually enabled as soon as the word is encoded. If it is possible to execute all of the other component processes of comprehension immediately (i.e., without the benefit of information to follow), then they *are* executed immediately.

Immediacy and wait-and-see can also be contrasted as applied to the interpretation of a syntactically ambiguous sentence. For example, suppose a reader waits-and-sees for two subsequent words before interpreting an earlier word. She would collect a total of three successive words in some temporary storage buffer before interpreting the first of the three words. Consider what this wait-and-see strategy predicts about the interpretation of the following sentence:

> *The old train the young.*

The interpretation of the first word, *The,* would wait until the first three words (*The old train*) were available to the cognitive system. Similarly, the reader would not decide on the syntactic status of *old* or *train* until she knew the two words that followed each of them; in this case, the last two words, *the young,* would have indicated that *old* is not an adjective and *train* is not a noun. So the reader would have avoided misinterpreting this phrase if she really used a wait-and-see strategy.

But most readers experience a startle effect with the *old train* sentence. Their initial tendency is to interpret *The old train* as "The antiquated locomotive" and not as "The elders instruct." The fact that readers are startled by such sentences shows that they do not wait-and-see the next word or two before interpreting the current word.

On some occasions, the interpretation of a newly encountered word cannot be made immediately; for this reason, immediacy refers only to the *attempt* at immediate interpretation. For example, suppose that the following sentence occurred at the very beginning of a narrative text:

> *As he entered the classroom, the nervous student noticed that there were no empty seats left.*

In this sentence, it is impossible to determine the referent of the pronoun *he* at the time it is first encountered, because the referent of *he* is not mentioned until later in the sentence. The immediacy strategy dictates that a reader try to interpret each word as far as possible. But if some information critical to the interpretation is lacking, then she has no choice but to wait-and-see. In this sentence, the reader probably interprets the *he* as some male human, but, of necessity, must postpone the determination of who it refers to. Thus, readers use a wait-and-see strategy only when it is unavoidable.

How Processes are Coordinated

Language comprehension, in general, and reading, in particular, involves a variety of processes. According to our theory, reading comprehension consists of several levels of representation and their associated processes, including perceptual pro-

cesses to encode words, lexical processes to access word meaning, syntactic and semantic processes to organize word meanings into larger units such as phrases and
clauses, and processes to construct a representation of the story or text, as well as
the events and objects it describes. A theory must describe not only the individual
processes but also how they are coordinated. The current theory proposes that in
skilled reading, many of these processes require little cognitive effort and can occur
at the same time, in parallel.

Highly practiced processes become automatic; that is, they occur even if the
reader does not consciously initiate them (Posner & Snyder, 1975; Shiffrin &
Schneider, 1977). The most striking example of an automatic process in reading is
word recognition. The automaticity has been strikingly demonstrated in the *Stroop
task*. In this task, a person is shown a long list of color terms, such as the words *blue,
red*, and *green*. Each term is printed in an ink color that is different from the term's
referent. For instance, the word *blue* might be printed in red ink, the word *red*, in
green ink, and the word *green*, in blue ink. If subjects are asked to read the words
aloud and ignore the ink colors, they have no difficulty. But if they are asked to
name the ink colors and ignore what the words say, then they are much slower;
moreover, they mistakenly tend to say the word, rather than the ink color (Jensen
& Rohwer, 1966). The interference demonstrates how the process of recognizing a
familiar word is so automatic that it cannot be suppressed, even when the reader
does not intend to read the word.

In reading, the processes that are most likely to become automatic are perceptual processes, such as recognizing words and programming eye movements. Within each level, there are constellations of processes that may be automatic. Word
recognition, for example, involves computations that operate on letters, syllables,
and entire words. These perceptual processes become highly automatic, often in
the early stages of learning to read. Once such a process is automatic, it may be difficult to become aware of either the process or the resulting representation. For example, during the proofreading of an essay, it is difficult to be continually aware of
the individual letters or words; it is much easier to attend to the semantic content. It
is plausible that highly practiced linguistic processes, such as those associated with
syntactic and semantic analysis, are also automatic, but no experiments have been
conducted to test this hypothesis.

As processes become highly practiced, it becomes increasingly possible to execute them at the same time, in parallel. This was demonstrated in a training study in
which people were reading while simultaneously copying a list of words being
dictated by an experimenter (Spelke, Hirst, & Neisser, 1976). Initially, it was difficult
for the subjects to perform both tasks at once, and the copying task slowed their
reading considerably. But with six weeks of practice, the readers were back up to
normal reading speed, although they could not remember what they had copied.
With even more training and the instruction to remember what they were copying,
the subjects read at normal speed and remembered what they had copied. Thus,
with sufficient practice, two complex skills like reading and copying might be able
to coexist as peacefully as walking and chewing gum.

In reading, many but not all of the processes both within and between levels
may also be executed in parallel. For example, after encoding a word, the reader
may simultaneously be determining its syntactic role, computing its referent, and

inferring its relation to other concepts in the sentence and discourse. The reader tries to determine an interpretation that is simultaneously compatible with the constraints originating from many levels.

Our theory's answer to the question of coordination is that many component processes of reading are sufficiently automatic to be executed in parallel. But this is only a partial answer, because the theory must also explain how the results of the various component processes are integrated. The theory proposes that all the processes deposit their partial and final results in a common workspace, called **working memory.** Working memory constitutes what is usually thought of as short-term memory, a repository of currently activated information. The common workspace provided by working memory makes it possible for several processes to collaborate. For example, a syntactic process can collaborate with a semantic process to determine that an ambiguous word like *hammer* refers to an object rather than an action in a particular context. The collaborative processes can converge on the most appropriate interpretation by coactivating the representation of that interpretation. By operating in parallel on shared information in working memory, the component processes in reading coordinate the simultaneous constraints they impose on an interpretation.

The Simulation Model: READER

The theory that we have developed to describe skilled reading has been expressed as a computer-simulation model (Just & Carpenter, 1980; Thibadeau, Just, & Carpenter, 1982). The simulation, called READER, provides a single, integrated model of the various processes of skilled reading. The model ensures that individual processes and structures function properly together.

The model's goals   READER was designed to simulate how human readers comprehend a technical passage and, in particular, to account for the time they take to read successive words and phrases in the passage. The basic data came from studies in which human readers were asked to read a technical passage (such as the text describing flywheels shown in Figure 1.3) and then summarize or answer questions

---

Flywheels are one of the oldest mechanical devices known to man. Every internal-combustion engine contains a small flywheel that converts the jerky motion of the pistons into the smooth flow of energy that powers the drive shaft. The greater the mass of a flywheel and the faster it spins, the more energy can be stored in it. But its maximum spinning speed is limited by the strength of the material it is made from. If it spins too fast for its mass, any flywheel will fly apart. One type of flywheel consists of round sandwiches of fiberglas and rubber providing the maximum possible storage of energy when the wheel is confined in a small space as in an automobile. Another type, the "superflywheel," consists of a series of rimless spokes. This flywheel stores the maximum energy when space is limited.

Figure 1.3   The *Flywheels* passage that READER processes.

about it (Carpenter & Just, 1981; Just & Carpenter, 1980). The studies analyzed how the distribution and duration of eye fixations reflected various perceptual and comprehension processes. Those studies indicated how much time readers took to process the successive words of a text.

The results from the eye-fixation studies were used to constrain the simulation model, such that words that receive longer gazes from human readers also require more processing by READER. As the simulation processes a passage word by word, it continually updates its representation of the phrase, sentence, text, and situation. When it has finished, READER has constructed a representation of the text that it can use to summarize the passage or answer questions about it. In fact, READER's summary is very similar to the type of summary produced by human readers.

Production systems   The model is written in an information-processing organization called a **production system,** in which each unit of a process is expressed as a **production.** Each production states an action to be performed and the conditions under which that action should be taken. The idea can be illustrated with a simple production system for hammering nails into a board. A production is written with a condition on the left and an arrow pointing to the action on the right.

Production A: *If nail is above surface*   →   *Then hit nail with hammer.*
Production B: *If nail is even with surface* →   *Start next nail.*
Production C: *If all of the nails are used* →   *Quit.*

Reading these productions also gives an idea of how such a system operates. When the condition of a production is satisfied, the action is taken and the production is described as *firing.* In this example, as long as one nail was started and its head was above the surface, Production A would repeatedly fire, producing repeated blows of the hammer on the nail. Production A would not fire when the blows made the nailhead even with the board's surface. At that time, Production B's condition would be satisfied, so it would fire and a new nail would be started. Then Production A's condition might again be satisfied, initiating a new round of nail-pounding cycles. When all of the nails were used, Production C would halt the system.

The same general condition-action format is used in the READER model's productions, although they deal with mental representations rather than nails and boards. For example, a production that detects noun phrases might look roughly like this:

If the word the *occurs*   →   *Assume a noun phrase is starting*

If READER encountered the word *the* in a text, this production would fire, leading READER to infer that it is currently processing a noun phrase.

The model operates in cycles that have two phases. In the first phase of each cycle, the conditions of all the productions are compared against the current state of knowledge. This first phase determines which of the productions are satisfied (that is, which have all of their conditions matched in the current state of knowledge). In the second phase, the actions of the satisfied productions are performed. The actions modify working memory, often by introducing new knowledge structures or bringing the activation level of some knowledge structure to threshold. Then a new cycle begins, and the new knowledge structures may satisfy different productions. The system moves from state to state until it succeeds in performing its task.

One of the strengths of a production system is that it nicely expresses the generally automatic nature of skilled reading. The sequence of mental processes in a production system is self-scheduling. The contrast between self-scheduling and centrally organized systems can be clarified by considering an analogy to organizations that can be used to build a house.

The conventional way of building a house does not follow a self-scheduling system but rather has a central executive (the general contractor) who schedules and coordinates the processes. The general contractor first calls an excavator to dig out the space for the foundation; then the cement contractor is asked to pour the foundation; then carpenters are told to put up the frame; then an electrician does the wiring; and so on. By contrast, a self-scheduling system takes a very different approach to the organizational issue. The experts are assembled at the building site and expected to keep watch on the building's progress so that each one performs his task as soon as conditions permit. Each expert self-schedules his activities. Similarly, for skilled readers, the processes are automatically evoked when the appropriate conditions arise. The decision of what to do next is not determined by a central executive but by the dynamically changing knowledge state.

The production-system organization is also convenient for expressing the immediacy of interpretation. For example, when a reader recognizes a word, the process that is to compute the word's syntactic role is evoked automatically. The appropriate condition (having recognized a word) automatically initiates the syntactic analysis. This feature means that immediacy of processing is a naturally emergent property of a production system. As soon as the enabling information is available, the enabled process begins to operate, rather than wait for some control signal to initiate it.

Another strength of a production system is that it makes it easy to show how reading processes can vary depending on the particular text, the reader's knowledge about the topic, and the reader's momentary reading goals. Both the reader's goals and indices to various related information can be activated. Thus, they would be part of the activated knowledge that influences reading. Consequently, the reader's enduring interests, as well as any short-term goals, can influence which productions are satisfied and hence determine the nature of the reading.

Applications of the Approach

Even though it is good scientific strategy to begin with a particular group of readers and a fairly narrow range of reading tasks, a reading theory must eventually accommodate the obvious variation that exists among readers and tasks. In this book, our strategy has been to start with a baseline condition—a model of skilled readers who are reading a technical passage to summarize or answer questions about it. This baseline is then used to explore how reading processes change in various situations or among readers. In this section, we will illustrate some of the advantages of establishing a model before exploring the diverse field of reading.

Reading, in spite of the single term, actually refers to a large family of tasks and resulting constellations of processes. Consider the different meanings of the term *reading* in the following situations:

- a student *reading* a textbook in preparation for an exam;
- a six-year-old *reading* the first-grade primer;
- a dyslexic *reading* a textbook;
- a Chinese student *reading* a Chinese text; and
- a graduate of a speed-reading course *reading* at 700 words per minute.

Obviously, these readers and reading situations differ in important ways. To understand reading, we need a way to characterize the differences and organize the results of the studies of these different types of readers and situations. That is what our approach provides. We will briefly illustrate this point in two domains—reading disabilities and speed reading.

Dyslexia   The most striking poor readers are those bright children and adults who have a very specific reading problem. If their reading comprehension lags markedly behind other measures of their intellectual ability, such as their ability to learn by listening, they are called **dyslexic.** In brief, the dyslexics' reading provides a strong contrast with the rapid, automatic processes that are characteristic of skilled readers. Dyslexics' reading problems are evident as soon as they begin to read aloud. Words that comparable students recognize with little difficulty can stump dyslexics. They take longer, make more errors, and sometimes give up entirely. Although their listening comprehension may be slightly poorer than that of normal readers, their main problems reside in visual word recognition. It is so slow, effortful, and inaccurate that it interferes with understanding.

While the dyslexics' major difficulty lies in recognizing words, the problem is not specifically visual. Most dyslexics, including the ones we studied, have perfectly adequate vision. They can perceive letters and even fairly complex shapes accurately. But they do not develop the internal representations of words, syllables, and letter clusters that are essential for the rapid word recognition necessary for skilled reading. In Chapter 12, we will describe research on how dyslexics read and discuss the nature of their problem more fully.

Speed reading   At the other end of the continuum are reports of those lucky individuals who read at fantastically rapid rates, 500 and even sometimes 1,000 words per minute. These people supposedly can go through Sunday's *New York Times* in a fraction of the time taken by the rest of us mortals. Even scholarly journals have reported studies of people who make only three or four fixations on a page, devoting a total of one or two seconds, whereas a normal reader would devote at least a couple of minutes. Reflecting how valued the skill is, students and businessmen are willing to pay $300–$400 or more for lessons, and commercial speed-reading courses are available near many university campuses.

Some commercial speed-reading companies, as well as some researchers, have speculated that these amazingly rapid rates are the ultimate achievement of true expertise. The reader is able to recognize more than words. Rather, whole lines or parts of a page can be recognized at a single glance. Or so they say.

The experimental study of speed-reading rate and comprehension suggests a very different and more modest interpretation of the phenomenon. To begin with, the studies of readers who make three or four fixations are often worthless. One difficulty is that the experiments often neglect to determine what the reader has learned; without an assessment of comprehension, the high speed alone is not very impressive. In Chapter 14, we describe some of our own research on the eye fixations of speed readers and on what they do and do not learn from the text.

Speed readers do enjoy some advantages, but all of the data suggest that these are conceptual advantages. For instance, they learn how to "put together a good story" with the bits and pieces that they happen to fixate. And contrary to the myth of recognizing whole lines or parts of the page, a speed reader cannot report information that was three characters away from the word that he fixated! Thus, a skill that, on the surface, looks as though it has a perceptual basis turns out to be conceptual. This is not to say that speed reading is not a valuable skill. Some people acquire the ability to read rapidly and not lose too much in comprehension, and rapid reading is certainly appropriate for some situations.

We will discuss both dyslexia and speed reading in detail in later chapters. These introductory remarks merely demonstrate some of the ways in which reading varies. In addition, this discussion provides modest support for the approach of this book: (1) to describe the processes that constitute *normal reading* and (2) to consider applications of the approach to other reading situations.

Summary

A cognitive approach focuses on the way information is mentally represented and on the processes that manipulate the information. The information that a reader uses includes his representation of the portions of the text he has already read, his previous knowledge of the content area, and his knowledge of the language and the text genre. Knowledge can be represented in a framework called a schema, consisting of a frame with labeled slots and some default values for the slots.

Reading is a multicomponent skill that deals with the sequence of words, phrases, and sentences that make up a text. Readers try to interpret each word of a text as they encounter it, using a strategy we have called the immediacy of interpretation.

Our theory specifies how the component processes in reading are coordinated in time, along with how they communicate with each other. The theory suggests that reading processes can operate in parallel (simultaneously) with each other and that they communicate by placing all their partial and final results in a common working memory.

Finally, we pointed out that the term *reading* is actually a label for a wide variety of reading-related activities. In particular, it is interesting that the prototypical situation to which the term *reading* applies has changed over the past few centuries as the nature of education has changed. The current prototypical referent of *reading* might be a person silently processing a written text to gain new information to use, analyze, or be entertained with. However, in the eighteenth and nineteenth centuries, *reading* referred to reciting aloud a limited number of very familiar religious texts, such as excerpts from the Bible (Darnton, 1984; Resnick & Resnick, 1977). Moreover, not many adults could read, even in the sense of prompted recitation. Only a very small proportion of the population was able to understand an unfamiliar text. Thus, a book on reading written two hundred years ago would have focused on a different type of reading. And very few people would have been able to read it.

Suggested Readings

As background reading on the cognitive approach described in this chapter, we recommend an introductory-level book on cognitive psychology, particularly those sections that deal with language comprehension, mental representations, memory, and knowledge. Among the suitable books are those by Anderson (1985), Glass, Holyoak, and Santa (1986), Lindsay and Norman (1977), Reed (1982), Reynolds and Flagg (1983), and Wood (1983).

For a more advanced treatment of particular cognitive theories, we recommend J. R. Anderson (1983), who discusses production systems in considerable detail, as well as the articles collected in two volumes edited by McClelland and Rumelhart (McClelland & Rumelhart, 1986; Rumelhart & McClelland, 1986), which describe models of parallel computation and use them to account for a variety of phenomena in language comprehension.

2

Eye Fixations
and Word Encoding

The perceptual processes involved in reading include both those related to eye fixations and those that encode printed words. These perceptual processes are a part of understanding language by eye but not a part of understanding language by ear. Although central to reading, these perceptual processes are so rapid and automatic that skilled readers are generally unaware of their precise nature.

Not only are these processes somewhat mysterious to the skilled reader, but they remain major research topics in psychology and education, in spite of the fact that eye fixations and word recognition have been studied since the turn of the century. However, there is now something new to report. Innovative studies done in the 1970s and 1980s used several new experimental techniques to uncover important facts about perceptual processes during reading.

The perceptual aspects of fluent word-recognition skill described in this chapter should not be viewed in isolation from other important factors in reading. Later chapters will describe the influence of the different writing systems on the perceptual processes (Chapter 10), children's acquisition of the perceptual skills in reading (Chapter 11), and the prominent role of word perception in certain kinds of reading difficulties (Chapters 12 and 15).

Overview In the first section, **Eye Fixations during Reading,** we will describe some of the characteristics of fixations: their locations, durations, and distribution on the words of a text, as well as the perceptual and cognitive processes that influence them. We will also describe some recent experiments that show that readers seldom encode the words to the right of the one they are fixating.

In the second part of the chapter, we will address word recognition. To recognize a word, a reader must translate the printed symbols on the page into a mental concept. This translation involves two processes. First, the reader must encode the word, generating the perceptual representation of the visual word form. And second, the reader must access the word's meaning in the internal lexicon. These two processes are often jointly referred to as *word recognition,* but they are separable processes; thus, we will consider them individually in this book. In the second section, **Word Encoding,** we will first describe the process and representations in word encoding, citing evidence from reading studies. We will also discuss how context affects word encoding. Finally, we will consider the relation of word- and letter-perception tasks to reading.

Eye Fixations during Reading

The subjective impression of most readers is that their eyes move smoothly over the print, scanning across letters, words, and phrases. But this impression is incorrect. Over one hundred years ago, a French opthalmologist named Javal discovered that the eyes do not scan smoothly across the lines of print. Rather, they make a series of discrete fixations with fast movements in between; Javal named these movements *saccades.* The movements themselves take relatively little time, usually less than 15 milliseconds, although their duration depends on their length. Also, little visual information is acquired during the movements. Instead, the visual information necessary for reading is acquired primarily during the fixations. Consequently, reading researchers wisely focus most of their attention on the fixations, rather than the movements per se. (Several techniques can be used to determine where a reader is fixating. One technique is described in an appendix at the end of this chapter.)

Fixations occupy from 90 to 95 percent of the time in reading. The average fixation lasts about 250 milliseconds, although there is a great deal of variability in the durations. The average duration tends to be longer if the reading task is more difficult. Most of a reader's fixations are **forward fixations,** from earlier words to later words in the text. **Regressive fixations** (fixations to earlier parts of the text) are more likely if the text is difficult or if the reader encounters some local linguistic or conceptual problem.

Poor readers make many more forward fixations and more regressions than good readers. This point is illustrated in Figure 2.1, which shows the words a good reader and a poor reader fixated while reading (Buswell, 1937). For the poor reader—a man who never finished high school and seldom read for entertainment—reading was both time consuming and difficult. His eye fixations were numerous, with many regressions, and were longer than average in duration. By contrast, the good reader read much faster. Her eye fixations were fewer, with few regressions, and tended to be shorter in duration.

Although a poor reader's deficiencies in reading skill are apparent in his pattern of eye fixations, the eye fixations are only manifestations of problems in the underlying perceptual and cognitive processes. The movement and placement of the eye is not the source of reading problems. Some early training programs misguidedly attempted to improve the comprehension of poor readers by training them to make the same types of patterns of fixations as those made by good readers—namely, a pattern of shorter fixations and fewer regressive fixations. These programs did not address the underlying perceptual and cognitive processes that were the source of the poor reader's problems. Not surprisingly, the programs

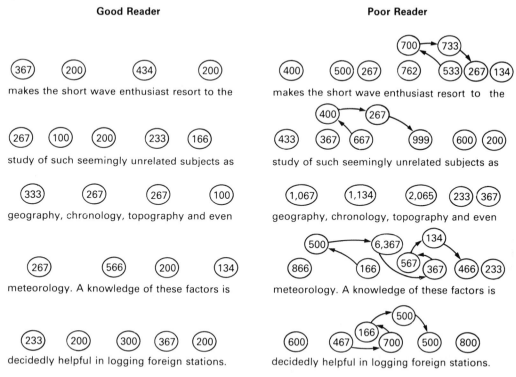

Figure 2.1   The comparison between a good reader's gazes (on the left) and a poor reader's gazes (on the right) shows that the good reader directly fixated fewer words and spent less time on them. The number written over the fixated word represents the gaze duration on that word (in milliseconds). The arrows indicate regressions to earlier words. Otherwise, the sequence of gazes is from left to right. *Source:* Adapted from Buswell, 1937, Plates III and IV, pp. 6, 7.

were unsuccessful (Tinker, 1958). There are only a few isolated cases of people who have been found to have reading problems that originate with the neuromotor control of eye fixations. Almost all reading problems are due to difficulties in recognizing written words and comprehending language. These are the skills that must be learned.

The Gaze-contingent Paradigm

The precise relation between eye fixations and reading processes has been difficult to study because eye fixations are so brief and saccadic movements are rapid. Only recently have researchers developed techniques to analyze eye fixations as they occur during reading. This section describes one such technique; subsequent sections will present data produced by this technique on the nature of eye fixations during reading.

The recent progress made in studying eye fixations during reading is due partially to the development of a new experimental technique we call the **gaze-con-**

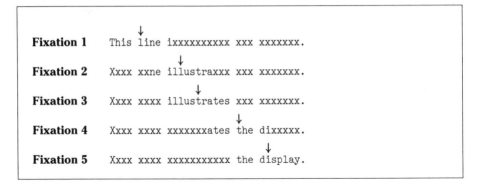

Figure 2.2   The displays during five consecutive fixations in a gaze-contingent paradigm. The computer controls what is displayed on the screen, making it contingent on where the reader is fixating. In this example, only five characters on either side of the fixated character (indicated by an arrow) are displayed normally; characters beyond that area are replaced by x's or altered in other ways.

tingent paradigm. In this paradigm, the reader reads a text displayed on a computer-controlled screen. At the same time, the reader's eye fixations are tracked by the same computer that controls the screen. The computer can make the content of the display depend on where the reader is looking (Rayner, 1975; Reder, 1973).

In some applications of the technique, a normal word is displayed at the location that the reader is directly fixating, but the upcoming text will be altered. For example, a few of the letters in the upcoming word can be replaced by visually similar letters, or one or more upcoming words can be replaced by a row of x's. When the reader begins to make a new eye movement, the computer determines where his next fixation will land (based on the initial speed of the eye movement) and can change the display accordingly. The change is usually made during the eye movement, a time when the visual system takes in less information, so the reader does not notice the change taking place. Figure 2.2 presents some examples of how a display would change between a reader's successive fixations.

This technique allows a researcher to explore the role played by various kinds of information in the upcoming text. The upcoming visual information may be presented in its normal form, eliminated completely, or altered in specific ways. This allows the researcher to compare the number and duration of eye fixations in these various conditions to determine how the change in the not-yet-fixated visual information influences the reading process.

Information Available from the Parafovea

In part, readers make eye fixations because of perceptual limitations on their ability to perceive words that are several letters away from the point of fixation. Visual acuity is best when the word falls on the **fovea,** the place on the back surface of the eye (the retina) that has the best resolution of visual detail in normal light. Figure 2.3 shows a cross-section of the eye and the various regions of the retina. The fovea

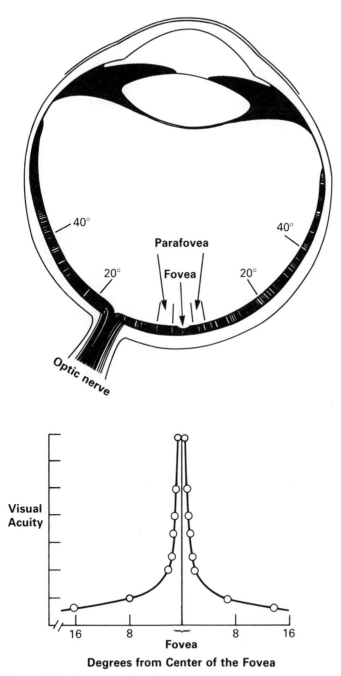

Figure 2.3 A cross-section of an eye, indicating the position of the *fovea,* a 1- to 2-degree retinal area with the best acuity. Surrounding the fovea is the *parafovea,* which has lower acuity. As the accompanying graph depicts, visual acuity decreases very rapidly as a letter is projected further from the fovea, in the parafovea or periphery. *Source:* The bottom figure is from Alpern, 1962, Figure 2, p. 4. Used with permission of Academic Press and the author.

subtends a small area, about 1 to 2 degrees of visual angle, or three to six letters at normal viewing distance. The area immediately adjacent to the fovea is called the **parafovea,** and beyond that is the **periphery.**

Although the three areas have distinct names, they are functionally continuous. A reader's accuracy in identifying a letter gets steadily worse as the letter's projection on the retina is further and further from the center of the fovea. The disadvantage of the parafovea relative to the fovea is even greater if the target letter is flanked by other letters, as are most letters in a text (Bouma, 1970). In the absence of foveal information, information solely from the parafovea is not sufficient for reading. People with damage to the part of the brain that processes foveal information find reading impossible (Teuber, Battersby, & Bender, 1960).

Several studies using the gaze-contingent paradigm on normal readers have demonstrated the limitations of parafoveal processing. The information from the parafovea is often insufficiently detailed to allow the reader to identify unpredictable words (Rayner & Bertera, 1979; Rayner, Inhoff, Morrison, Slowiaczek, & Bertera, 1981). In these studies, the gaze-contingent paradigm was used to thwart the normal perception of foveal information. The letters at and around the reader's point of fixation (at the fovea) were replaced by a mask, an array of stripes, and only the letters in the parafovea or periphery were displayed normally. When the reader fixated a new location, the word that had previously been displayed there was replaced by the mask, and the mask in the previously fixated location was changed back to the normal text. Consequently, readers could see letters and words only in the parafovea. The readers were presented with a series of simple, unrelated sentences and were asked to read and report them one at a time.

The reading rate dropped precipitously from a rapid 300 words per minute in the control condition, which had no mask, to under 50 words per minute when three to five foveal letters were replaced by a mask, as shown in Figure 2.4. Readers also made many errors when reporting sentences with large masks (see Figure 2.4), further indicating the difficulty of reading with only parafoveal information. Readers often misidentified content words, such as *person, conductor, metal,* and *rusted,* reporting instead a visually similar word, such as *program, coordinator, medals,* and *raised,* respectively. This result indicates that information from the parafovea may be adequate for indicating the approximate length of a word and its beginning and ending letters; such information is not adequate for accurate recognition of content words. The poor recognition of words in the parafovea, together with the extremely slow reading rates, suggests that readers do not identify upcoming content words in the parafovea during normal reading.

Evidence against parafoveal word recognition A gaze-contingent experiment that manipulates the information in the parafovea can indicate whether readers generally recognize the word to the right of the fixated word. In a reading task that appeared normal to the readers, college students read and recalled short passages containing a critical word, like the word *flame* in the sentence below (McConkie, Zola, Blanchard, & Wolverton, 1982):

> *Dr. Koppof was able to demonstrate that the* flame *which had been so disconcerting to the natives of the region originated from a neighboring tribe.*

While the reader was making his rightward saccade from a preceding word (like *that* or *the*) to the critical word, the critical word was changed to a physically similar

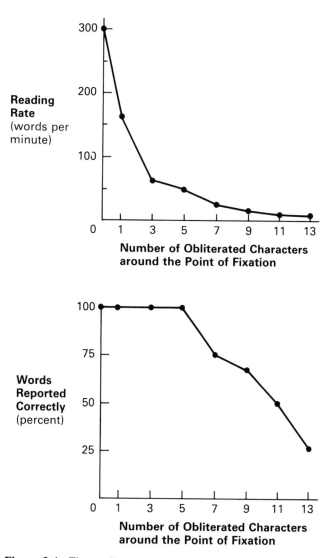

Figure 2.4 The reading rate (top graph) decreases precipitously when readers must rely on information outside of the fovea. When five or more characters around the point of fixation are obliterated, the reading rate decreases to below 50 words per minute. Readers had difficulty accurately reporting the sentence (bottom graph) when many of the letters around the point of fixation were obliterated and only the letters in the parafovea and periphery were normal. *Source:* Based on data from Rayner, Inhoff, Morrison, Slowiaczek, & Bertera, 1981, p. 172.

word that made equally good sense in the passage. In the example above, *flame* was changed to *blare* for the entire duration of the fixation at that location. Making the change during a saccade minimized the chance that a reader would notice that the display was being changed. If the reader had already recognized the critical word as *flame* before fixating it, he should show some surprise when he directly fixates it and finds that it has been altered to *blare*. However, there was no evidence of surprise. The pattern and duration of the eye fixations in this condition were no different than those of a control group of readers for whom the display had not been changed. There was no evidence that the readers had recognized the critical word while fixating a prior word, even if they had fixated within a few character spaces of it. In other words, there was no evidence of recognition of a word in the parafovea in this reading task.

Another experiment using this paradigm found that readers did not even notice a nonword in a text until they fixated on it or immediately to the left of it (Rayner, 1975), again demonstrating a lack of word recognition (or nonrecognition) in the parafovea. Readers were given short texts that contained a nonword in a target location, such as:

The rebels guarded the pyctce *with their guns.*

The presence of a nonword in a text usually elicits long fixations and extra fixations when the nonword is detected, compared to a control condition in which a normal word is presented (in this case, *palace*). But the readers who were shown the sentence with the nonword did not have markedly longer fixations until they directly fixated on or within two character spaces of the nonword, as shown in Figure 2.5. Thus, readers showed almost no evidence of noticing even a bizarre nonword until they directly fixated it.

Although readers seem not to identify the words to the right of the one they are fixating, they nevertheless do obtain some visual information about these words. Rayner's (1975) study determined whether readers differentially acquired information from different portions of a critical word on the right, using the

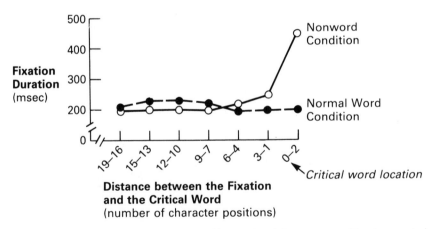

Figure 2.5   Readers do not show any evidence of noticing a nonword (such as *pyctce*) until they directly fixate it or are within two character spaces of it. The graph shows the average duration of fixations at varying distances to the left of the critical word and on the critical word itself. Two conditions are shown: (1) when the critical word was a nonword (such as *pyctce*) and (2) when it was a normal word (such as *palace*). *Source:* Adapted from Rayner, 1975, Figure 1, p. 76. Used with permission of Academic Press and the author.

approach of the McConkie et al. experiment (1982) described above. While a reader was making his rightward saccade to a critical word, changes were made to some combination of the initial, interior, or final letters of the word, as shown in Table 2.1. The assumption was that if a reader had encoded some particular information about a critical word before fixating it and that information was changed while he was making a saccade to it, then he should be surprised when he fixates the word (Rayner, 1975). Rayner found that whether a change was noticed depended not only on the nature of the change but also on the distance between the critical word and the location of the prior fixation.

Readers showed evidence of having parafoveally acquired different types of information at different distances. At a distance of 10 to 12 letters from the critical word, readers showed sensitivity to changes in the initial and final letters (such as *qcluec* changed to *palace*) and to major changes in the internal letters (such as *pyctce* changed to *palace*). But readers had to be closer to the critical word before showing sensitivity to more subtle changes. The readers had to have fixated no more than four to six letters to the left of the critical word in order to have noticed minor changes in the visual features of the internal letters (such as *pcluce* changed to *palace*).

Because of a technical problem with Rayner's equipment, the display changes were sometimes made while the readers' eyes were stationary, rather than only during their saccades. Thus, readers may have noticed a flicker or a motion during the display change, rather than the discrepancy in the perceptual information. Consequently, this study may overestimate the readers' sensitivity to these various types of information.

Taken together, these studies suggest that readers generally do not recognize content words (such as nouns, adjectives, or verbs) before directly fixating them. Readers apparently do obtain some information about upcoming words, such as their lengths (McConkie & Rayner, 1975) and possibly the identities of the initial letters.

Left-right asymmetry in perception The area from which readers obtain information is larger to the right of the point they fixate than to the left. The gaze-contingent paradigm was used to obliterate the letters in areas to the left or right of

Table 2.1 Types of displays used to determine the visual information encoded from words to the right of the fixated one

Example of Original Display	**Relation to Final Critical Word** (in this example, *palace*)
1. *qcluec*	different initial and final letters, similar interior letters
2. *pyctce*	same initial and final letters, dissimilar interior letters
3. *pcluce* or *police*	same initial and final letters, similar interior letters

Source: Based on data from Rayner, 1975.

the point of fixation (Rayner, Well, & Pollatsek, 1980). By noting how close to the point of fixation the obliterations had to be before they disrupted the normal pattern of eye fixations, the experimenters could infer the area from which information was being encoded. The results indicated that the area over which readers process information is asymmetrical; readers process information much farther to the right of fixation than to the left.

The asymmetry is related to the left-to-right direction of written English. Readers of Hebrew (which is written from right to left) show the opposite effect; they process information farther to the left than to the right (Pollatsek, Bolozky, Well, & Rayner, 1981). For people who are bilingually fluent in Hebrew and English, the direction of the asymmetry depends on which language they are reading. Thus, the asymmetry appears to be a part of a well-learned perceptual skill, rather than being determined physiologically.

The area from which readers obtain information is determined not just by the sheer distance from the location of fixation but also by the word boundary. An obliteration on a preceding word did not disrupt performance, even if the distance between the obliteration and the point of fixation was as little as two character spaces (Rayner, Well, & Pollatsek, 1980). Like the language specificity of the asymmetry described above, this influence of word boundaries indicates that the constraints on perception during reading are determined as much by the reading process itself as by physiological limitations.

Fixation placement within a word   For words that receive only one fixation, the location of that fixation tends to be on the first half of the word, about one-third of the way into the word (O'Regan, 1975; Rayner & Pollatsek, 1981). This location is exactly what one would expect, given the asymmetry of the area from which visual information is encoded in English. Because readers encode fewer letters to the left of the point of fixation than to the right, they need to be closer to the beginning of the word to maximize the number of letters of the word that can be encoded.

A second but related reason that readers might fixate about one-third of the way into a word is that the beginning letters of English words are more informative about a word's identity (Bruner & O'Dowd, 1958). For example, it is easier to guess the words in the following sentences from their initial letters than from their final letters:

Final letters:	*_he ____tion _f ____tions ___ies _n ___ding.*
Initial letters:	*Th_ loca____ o_ fixat____ var___ i_ read___.*
Actual sentence:	*The location of fixations varies in reading.*

The Control of Eye Fixations

Researchers are beginning to unravel how perceptual, cognitive, and motor processes influence the decisions made during reading, including how long to stay in the current location, in which direction to move next, and how far to move. In this section, we describe an older theory about the control of eye fixations, reviewing the data that invalidated it and providing some new answers to classic questions about perceptual processes in reading.

The oculomotor theory Until recently, some psychologists thought that the locations and durations of eye fixations in reading were not directly influenced by perceptual and comprehension processes but by the characteristics of the oculomotor system, the motor system that controls eye position. The **oculomotor theory** proposed that the eyes were driven along by some semiautomatic motor process that tended to let the eyes remain stationary for about 250 milliseconds before advancing them by some average amount, usually about seven character spaces. The theory assumed that the visual information taken in could be stored internally until it was processed later. The theory proposed that fixations were generally longer if the text was very difficult and shorter if it was easy. The central proposal of the theory, from our viewpoint, was that perceptual and comprehension processes exerted no moment-by-moment influence on eye fixations during reading (Bouma & de Voogd, 1974; Kolers, 1976).

The oculomotor theory developed, in part, because of the finding that saccadic eye movements are *ballistic,* which means that the eyes' path is decided some time before the movement begins. Neither the saccade's path nor the time of its onset can be modified once the decision has been made. The duration of the interval between the decision and the start of the movement was estimated from nonreading tasks to be approximately 200 milliseconds (Westheimer, 1954). However, 250 milliseconds is the average duration of an individual eye fixation in reading. If a saccade had to be planned at least 200 milliseconds before it was executed, there would be little or no time during a given fixation for information to influence either the duration of that fixation or the direction and length of the following saccade.

Evidence against the oculomotor theory Three recent developments have disproved the oculomotor theory. First, recent research estimating the duration of the interval between the decision about a movement and the start of the movement have revised the estimate downward from 200 milliseconds to 150 milliseconds and even less, perhaps 100 milliseconds (Becker & Jurgens, 1979; Morrison, 1984; Rayner & Pollatsek, 1981). Thus, only a very brief fixation is unlikely to be influenced by what is encoded during that fixation.

Second, several studies have demonstrated that a reader makes longer fixations or additional fixations immediately upon encountering an unexpected difficulty, such as a word that is inconsistent with the reader's current interpretation of the sentence (Carpenter & Daneman, 1981; Frazier & Rayner, 1982; Just & Carpenter, 1978). These results are best explained by assuming that the durations and locations of eye fixations are responsive to cognitive processes.

The third development came from experiments that directly examined whether events that occurred during a given fixation influenced its duration and the location of the next fixation. The influence was demonstrated in a study that used the gaze-contingent paradigm to control how many letters were displayed to the reader on either side of the place he was fixating (Rayner & Pollatsek, 1981). The number of such letters displayed varied from fixation to fixation so that it was unpredictable. Sometimes, only a few letters were visible; at other times, many letters were visible. When the number of displayed letters was small, the very next eye movement was shorter than average. When the number of displayed letters was larger, the very next eye movement was longer than average. Thus, contrary to the oculomotor theory, the amount of visual information presented during a given fixation influenced the location of the very next fixation.

Also contrary to the oculomotor theory, the duration of a fixation was influenced by events occurring during that fixation (Morrison, 1984; Rayner & Pollatsek, 1981). In several experiments, the gaze-contingent paradigm was used to delay the onset of the display after each eye movement, so that the reader could not see any information for a short time during the first part of a new fixation. The duration of the delay was unpredictable, changing from fixation to fixation. The duration of the delay influenced the duration of the eye fixation. Most of the fixations were lengthened by an amount that compensated for the initial delay before the words were shown. Only the very short fixations were not affected by the delay and seemed to be impervious to the perceptual processing. Together, these experiments disproved the oculomotor theory because they showed that for most fixations, the perceptual processes did influence the duration of the current fixation and the location of the next.

Another erroneous belief associated with earlier theories was that vision was suppressed during the first 50 milliseconds of a fixation to the extent that no word encoding could occur during that period. According to this older view, the information acquired during a fixation was encoded too late to influence the control of that fixation or of the ensuing saccade. However, it has been found that people can read a text normally even if the words are presented *only* during the first 50 milliseconds of a fixation (Rayner, Inhoff, Morrison, Slowiaczek, & Bertera, 1981; Rayner & Pollatsek, 1981). The gaze-contingent paradigm was used to display the sentence for only a brief time—either 10, 30, 50, or 150 milliseconds—at the beginning of each new fixation, and then it was replaced by a striped mask. If the sentence was presented for at least 50 milliseconds at the beginning of each fixation, the pattern of eye fixations was essentially normal. Thus, the first 50 milliseconds of a fixation can provide sufficient visual information for normal reading.

The Location of Gazes in a Text

The gaze   Up to this point, we have primarily addressed the nature of individual eye fixations and how they are influenced by reading processes. However, we have found that a more useful measure for studying reading is the **gaze.** The gaze is either a single fixation or group of consecutive fixations on a unit of the text—usually a single word, but sometimes a phrase or sentence. The duration of the gaze is the sum of the consecutive fixations on that unit. The most important feature of the gaze, as a unit of analysis, is that its location and duration turns out to be more closely linked to reading processes than is the duration of individual fixations. What's more, because gazes are defined for units such as words and phrases, they are more easily related to the theoretical constructs that are part of a theory of reading.

A gaze may correspond to a single fixation or many consecutive fixations on a particular unit of text. Thus, a long gaze duration can result from either multiple fixations, a single long fixation, or some combination of more and longer fixations. In fact, long gazes are usually a result of multiple fixations. It seems to be easier for readers to vary the number of fixations they make than to make a large change in their durations. In this section, we will show how the location and duration of gazes are closely related to perceptual and comprehension processes.

A study of eye fixations in normal reading College readers fixate a majority of the words in a text, often fixating adjacent words or skipping no more than one word between two fixated words, so even fluent readers densely sample the text. For instance, in one of our studies (Just & Carpenter, 1980)—which we will refer to throughout the book—14 college students read 15 different short passages, each about 135 words long, excerpted from *Newsweek* and *Time* magazines. The passages were on a variety of topics about scientific discoveries, technical inventions, and biological mechanisms. The passage about flywheels, presented in the introductory chapter, was one example. Other passages described the use of levers in building the Egyptian pyramids, toxins produced by insects, why infants smile, and the development of an artificial blood. Most of the students were unfamiliar with the information in the passages. The content and style of these passages was representative of what college students read to learn about technical topics.

Each passage was presented on a computer-controlled screen; the reader's eye fixations were monitored with a remote camera. The readers were told to read normally, not to study, and to summarize orally what they had read immediately after they finished reading each passage. The main point of the study was to analyze how various features of eye fixations relate to features of the text, characteristics of the readers, or variation in the task (such as instructions to recall or answer questions).

Which words are fixated? In our study, readers fixated over 80 percent of the content words (adjectives, adverbs, nouns, and verbs) and about 40 percent of the function words (such as conjunctions, articles, and prepositions). To analyze the location of fixations, we counted the lengths of the runs of successive unfixated words. If the reader fixated two adjacent words, then the length of the run of unfixated words was zero. If the reader skipped one word, then the length of the run was one, and so on. The scoring can be illustrated with the following sequence of gazes, numbered from 1 to 7, with their location indicated above the fixated word:

1   2   3   4   5   6   7

Thousands of people asked that the serum be made available immediately.

In this hypothetical example, the reader fixated adjacent words three times (*people asked, asked that,* and *available immediately*). There were two instances of a single unfixated word occurring between two fixated words (*of, the*) and one case of two successive unfixated words (*be made*).

Using this counting procedure for the data from the 14 students reading 15 passages, it was found that readers usually fixated adjacent words or skipped only one word between fixated words (Carpenter & Just, 1983). The number of occurrences of each pattern per 100 words of text is shown in Figure 2.6. The sum of all the y-values of the points plotted is approximately 68, indicating that about 68 percent of the words are fixated. Of the 68 words per hundred that were fixated, 41 of them (or 60 percent) were preceded by a skipping over zero words. This means that when readers moved their eyes forward in the text from one word to another, they

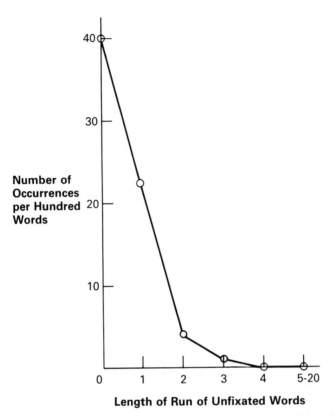

Length of Run of Unfixated Words

Figure 2.6   Readers usually fixate adjacent words (run length = 0) or skip no more than one word (run length = 1) between successively fixated words. The graph shows the frequency of runs of unfixated words of varying lengths per one hundred words of text. *Source:* Carpenter & Just, 1983, Figure 17.1, p. 279. Used with permission of Academic Press.

fixated the very next word most of the time (60 percent); they skipped only one word 33 percent of the time; they skipped two words only 6 percent of the time; and they almost never skipped more than two words. Even though these were college readers, they fixated on or immediately adjacent to most of the words.

College students fixated almost as frequently on reading material that was slightly less technical, such as an article from *Reader's Digest*. Across a number of studies, the exact proportion of fixated words did not vary widely when the reading rates were normal (around 240 words per minute) and a comprehension test was administered. However, readers fixated fewer words when the texts were simple and the comprehension test was undemanding (Buswell, 1937). In such a case, readers were more likely to fixate every two words, presumably because the cognitive load imposed by the task was lower and the necessity for accurate perception was lessened. Readers also fixated fewer words when they were skimming or speed reading at rates twice or three times as fast as normal reading. In those cases, readers typically skipped two or more consecutive words. (The eye fixations during rapid reading are discussed further in Chapter 14 on speed reading and skimming.)

Some of the words that are not fixated directly are still processed to some extent. The evidence for this claim is that certain words are more likely to be skipped than others. If readers did not process the skipped words, then all words would be equally likely to be skipped. But readers were much more likely to skip the more frequent and linguistically constrained words, such as function words (like the conjunctions, *and, but,* and determiners, *the, an, a*) than the less frequent and usually more informative content words (nouns, verbs, adjectives, and adverbs). One complication in making this comparison is that short words are less likely to be fixated than long words. Although function words tend to be much shorter than content words, word length was not the only determinant of which words were skipped. Readers were more likely to skip three-letter function words (such as *the, and*) than three-letter content words (such as *ant, run*) (Carpenter & Just, 1983). This finding is similar to that of O'Regan (1979), who found readers were more likely to skip the word *the* than a three-letter verb. This selectivity implies that readers had more information about those words than just their length, even though the words were not fixated. Readers may skip some short function words because they were processed during the prior fixation on the adjacent word.

We offer the following tentative account of the frequent skipping of short function words and the frequent fixation of content words. Suppose that a reader's current fixation happens to be near the right-hand edge of a word, and just to the right lies a short function word. To make the example more concrete, suppose that the reader has fixated on the terminal letter *e* in *possible* in the phrase *it is possible to*. Our tentative account is that while the processing of *possible* is being executed, the reader may sometimes encode the initial letters of the immediately adjacent word (in this example, *to*). Because a word like *to* is short, all of its letters may be encoded within the fovea. Moreover, because it is short and because it is a frequently occurring word, the recognition of *to* may plausibly be executed in parallel with the processing of the currently fixated word, *possible*. The processing of the two words would proceed in parallel until the processing of the fixated word is completed. A short frequent word like *to* may well be recognized before the completion of processing of *possible*. This applies to many function words (like *to, of, the,* or *and*) and even some content words. If the processing of such an adjacent word is completed before the concurrent processing of the currently fixated word, then the adjacent word could be skipped.

To the extent that such processing of a nonfixated word occurs, it is contrary to our strong position (elaborated below) that only the currently fixated word is being processed. We might have to qualify the strong position when a fixation lies on the right-hand boundary of a word that is followed by a short, frequent word. Of course, we should not assume that all of the short, frequent words that are skipped under such circumstances are being recognized. Many readers have had the experience of completing a passage of text that did not make sense, only to reread it and discover that they had failed to read a critical word. Similarly, some short, frequent words that are skipped may simply not be processed.

Now consider the case in which a reader fixates on the right edge of a word, and the adjacent word to the right is longer and less frequent (a description that applies to most content words and to some function words). In this case, the adjacent word will not be recognized while the reader is processing the fixated word, for two reasons. First, the sheer length of the adjacent word (which can be detected parafoveally) might be enough to prevent the completion of the recognition process. Even if the processing of the adjacent word to the right is initiated, its relative infrequency would make its processing take sufficiently long that it would not be completed before the processing of the currently fixated word. In either case, the adjacent word would then be fixated, and its processing would start over. Thus, following a fixation at the right edge of a word, a longer, less frequent adjacent word (like a content word) would be unlikely to be skipped, whereas a shorter, more-frequent word (like many function words) would be more likely to be skipped.

We do not want to leave the impression that the decision of whether to fixate an adjacent word is based solely on the events occurring during the preceding fixation. It is also influenced by more global factors, such as the reader's attentiveness—whether he is reading carefully, carelessly, or skimming. In addition, the decision of where to fixate may be influenced by the local difficulty of processing a phrase or sentence. A reader spends more time on the exact same words if they occur in a more difficult text or if they occur in a sentence that signals that they are important.

Immediacy and the Eye-Mind Hypothesis

In Chapter 1, we described our finding that readers try to interpret each word of a text as they encounter it, rather than use a wait-and-see strategy. The **immediacy** of interpretation pervades all levels of comprehension, such as encoding a word, accessing its meaning, and determining its referent and semantic and syntactic status in the sentence. Therefore, it is difficult to limit the discussion of immediacy to just one chapter. Because the immediacy of interpretation is so clearly manifested in the eye-fixation behavior, we have chosen to discuss it in the current chapter, with the proviso that most of what follows applies to processes described in subsequent chapters, as well.

People probably use the strategy of immediate interpretation when they are listening, as well as when they are reading. Immediacy is not a strategy that is specific to the comprehension of written language. Immediacy refers to the way in which the cognitive system (not the visual system) deals with continuous prose. However, there is an interesting and important way that immediacy of interpretation manifests itself in the eye-fixation behavior of readers, thanks to the **eye-mind hypothesis.**

The eye-mind hypothesis proposes that not only is the interpretation of each word immediate, but also that the interpretation of the word occurs while the word is being fixated. The implication of the eye-mind hypothesis is that the cognitive system has access to visual information very soon after it is fixated. According to the eye-mind hypothesis, there is no appreciable delay (beyond a possible few tens of milliseconds) between what is fixated and what is available for cognitive processing.

Now we can relate the eye-mind hypothesis to the immediacy of interpretation. If the eye-mind hypothesis is correct, then readers must be using the strategy of immediate interpretation. After all, if the processing of a word occurs while the word is being fixated and before the next word is considered, then, by definition, the interpretation is immediate rather than wait-and-see. The empirical evidence described below and elsewhere in the book clearly supports the eye-mind hypothesis and hence demonstrates that readers use the immediacy strategy.

Evidence for immediacy and eye-mind   The clearest evidence for the immediacy strategy and the eye-mind hypothesis is that the time spent looking at a word is strongly influenced by the characteristics of that word (Carpenter & Just, 1983; Just & Carpenter, 1980). Later in this chapter, we will present the data indicating that the gaze duration on a word is directly related to the word's length (measured in number of letters), an effect we attribute to the encoding of the visual form of the word. Thus, each word is encoded while it is being fixated. In Chapter 3, on lexical access, we will present the data indicating that the gaze duration on a word is related to the word's normative frequency in the language, an effect we attribute to the accessing of the word's meaning in the mental lexicon. Readers spend longer on a rare word like *sable* than on a common word like *table*. Thus, the meaning of each is being accessed while the word is being fixated. In the chapters on semantic and syntactic processing (Chapters 5 and 6), we present data indicating that gaze durations are unusually long on a word that is semantically or syntactically difficult or anomalous. This result indicates that the semantic and syntactic analyses of each word occurs while the word is being fixated. Thus, the evidence indicates immediacy at several levels of interpretation, such as the lexical (Carpenter & Just, 1983; Just & Carpenter, 1980), syntactic (McDonald & Carpenter, 1981), and text levels (Dee-Lucas, Just, Carpenter, & Daneman, 1982). That is, when an increase in the processing load at any of these levels is introduced by a given word, there is an increased gaze duration on that word. All these results constitute strong support for the eye-mind hypothesis and the immediacy of interpretation.

The result that gaze durations increase on the word that increases the processing load demonstrates that the interpretation of the word starts while the word is still being fixated. But does the reader continue to fixate that word until he has finished processing it before he advances and fixates the next word? Or does some of the processing of a difficult word spill over onto the fixation of the next word? There are several results indicating little, if any, spillover.

One straightforward result concerns some extremely difficult technical terms, such as *thermoluminescence,* that occasionally appeared in our *Time* and *Newsweek* passages. There was approximately one such novel word in each passage, and as the eye-mind hypothesis predicts, the gaze duration on each of these words was elevated. In fact, when they encountered such words, readers spent an average of 686 *extra* milliseconds beyond what would have been predicted by the words' length and infrequency (Thibadeau, Just, & Carpenter, 1982). The interesting result pertinent to spillover is that the readers spent no extra time on the word following the novel word, indicating that the readers continued to fixate these novel words until the processing of the word had been completed. The linkage between the comprehension processes and the eye-fixation behavior appears to be extremely close.

Additional tests for spillover of word encoding and lexical access confirm that there is little, if any, spillover. These tests examined whether the gaze duration on a given word is influenced by the characteristics of the preceding word. If the eye-mind hypothesis were incorrect—say, with the eye being exactly one word ahead of the mind—then the processing of word *N − 1* would occur during the gaze on word *N*, and the gaze duration should be a function of the properties of word *N − 1*. However, analyses of the time readers spend on the words of the *Time* and *News-week* passages show that gaze durations are almost totally uninfluenced by the length or frequency of the preceding word (Carpenter & Just, 1983). The time spent on a word is strongly influenced by the length and frequency of that word itself.

The preceding results indicate that when a reader is fixating a given word, *N*, he is probably not processing the preceding word, *N − 1*. A similar analysis indicates that when he is fixating word *N*, he is not doing much processing of the word to the right, *N + 1*, either. The gaze duration on word *N* is almost totally uninfluenced by the length and frequency of word *N + 1* (Carpenter & Just, 1983). These analyses indicate the strong relation between what is being processed and what is being fixated, supporting the eye-mind assumption.

Why immediacy works   There are two aspects of language use that minimize the costs and maximize the benefits of immediacy. One reason that the costs are minimal is that it generally *is* possible to compute the correct interpretation of a word on the first encounter. Wait-and-see theorists focus on contrived sentences presented without context, in which a reader has so little knowledge that he has no choice but to wait-and-see. However, most authors try to avoid misleading a reader. Normal context makes it possible for a reader to interpret a word correctly on the first encounter an overwhelming proportion of the time. Readers use the context and their knowledge of relative frequencies of alternative interpretations to choose the most likely interpretation. The benefit of immediacy is that it reduces the memory load that would be imposed by storing multiple interpretations of an ambiguity or by retaining information in an unprocessed form while waiting-and-seeing.

A second reason the costs of immediacy are minimal is that readers can easily repair the occasional misinterpretations that do occur. Some incorrect interpretations can be detected on the basis of a subsequent syntactic or semantic anomaly. Studies of how readers detect and repair incorrect interpretations have found that readers are relatively efficient in recovering. For example, while reading the sentence *The thirsty boy watched the pitcher carefully,* most readers initially interpret *pitcher* to mean a "jug"; if the sentence continued *The thirsty boy watched the pitcher carefully throw the ball,* they would look back and reinterpret the word *pitcher* to mean a "ballplayer." The inconsistencies are detected very early, generally, as soon as the reader encounters the first word that reveals the inconsistency of his interpretation. Thus, immediacy of interpretation makes inconsistencies evident at the earliest possible time.

In summary, the immediacy strategy suggests that a reader tries to interpret each piece of the text as he encounters it (Just & Carpenter, 1980). The phrase "tries to interpret" refers to several cognitive processes, such as encoding the word, accessing its meaning, associating it with its referent, and determining its semantic and syntactic status in the sentence and the discourse. "Encounter" refers to the time when the cognitive system (not the visual system) first has access to the word. If a word imposes a processing difficulty of any sort (for example, because it is particularly long or infrequent or syntactically anomalous), then the reader spends more time on that word, indicating that the processing occurs during the fixation on the word. Although the *attempt* at interpretation is immediate, the text can force postponement of the actual interpretation by not providing some vital information. When vital information is lacking, a reader will postpone the interpretation, but he will do so because of necessity, rather than strategic choice. The preferred strategy is to interpret immediately.

Word Encoding

Word recognition has a rich recent history in psychological research. In fact, most of the research on reading between 1950 and 1970 focused on word recognition, treating it as a perceptual skill in isolation from the many other component processes in reading. In a typical experiment, words or letters were presented very briefly, and people were timed or their accuracy was scored while they indicated what letters or words they had seen.

Much of the interest in this type of experiment was due to the fact that word recognition is an impressive perceptual skill. After thousands of hours of practice in reading, every skilled reader who walks into a psychology laboratory is a master at recognizing words. A reader's ability to recognize rapidly a word like *dreadful* is comparable to a chess master's ability to recognize rapidly that the bishop will take the knight. Both skills are based on acquiring thousands of complex perceptual patterns in long-term memory (Chase & Simon, 1973). The readers' skill is apparent if their excellent ability to recognize and report words is contrasted with their relatively poor ability to recognize nonwords. This contrast was at the heart of numerous studies (Henderson, 1982), and we, too, will discuss it in a following section. However, word recognition is more than just a perceptual skill. It is part of reading. When it is considered in the context of reading, some traditional questions take on new importance, while others become insignificant. So, in this chapter, we will describe the process of word encoding as it occurs in reading; only in the last section will we consider how the more traditional research relates to reading.

Distinguishing *Word Encoding* and *Lexical Access*

To recognize a word, the reader must translate the printed symbols on the page into a mental concept. This translation involves two processes:

1. encoding the word as a visual percept and
2. accessing the word's meaning (lexical access).

In reading, word encoding and lexical access generally occur rapidly, automatically, and close together in time. However, there are several ways in which the two processes can be distinguished from each other.

One way to distinguish them is to describe situations in which only one of the two processes occurs. An interesting example of lexical access without word encoding occurs in the tip-of-the-tongue state, when a person accesses a word meaning but is unable to think of the corresponding word. This state can be induced by giving someone the definition of an infrequent word and asking her to produce the defined word. For example, what word is defined by the following?

> *A small boat, not the* junk, *used in the river and harbor traffic of China and Japan.*

If the defined word is infrequent, some people will not be able to retrieve the word, even though they know it. They have accessed the meaning without encoding its perceptual form. (For those readers who were in the tip-of-the-tongue state, the defined word was *sampan.*)

The other form of dissociation, word encoding without lexical access, occurs when a reader encounters a word that is totally unfamiliar (such as *gallimaufry*). Even though many readers cannot access any meaning for this word, they still form a word-percept, a representation of the word's perceptual form. Forming this representation is an instance of word encoding without any accompanying lexical access. (For those readers who performed encoding without lexical access, *gallimaufry* means "a hodgepodge.")

Another way to distinguish word encoding from lexical access is to demonstrate that some properties of words affect only encoding, while other properties affect only lexical access; in addition, these two properties have additive effects on task performance. The performance that is sometimes measured is the decision time in a task requiring subjects to decide whether a string of letters is a word (such as *table*) or a nonword (such as *rable*). This is called the **lexical decision task.** Degrading the print quality of a word, which is presumed to affect encoding, makes the decision take longer; and presenting an infrequent word (such as *sable* instead of *table*), which is presumed to affect lexical access, also makes the decision take longer. If a word is both degraded and infrequent, the effect on decision time is the sum of the two individual effects, suggesting that the two properties influence different processes (Becker & Killion, 1977; Stanners, Jastrzembski, & Westbrook, 1975).

Another pair of variables that are thought to affect word encoding and lexical access, respectively, are the length of a word and the frequency of the word. They have additive effects on the gaze durations on each word of a text, an important result discussed later in this chapter, as well as in Chapter 3 on lexical access (Carpenter & Just, 1983). These results suggest that word encoding and lexical access are distinct processes.

The READER Model's Word-encoding Process

The input to the word-encoding mechanism is the representation of individual letters and their serial position in the word, while the output is the representation of the visual form of the word. For convenience, we call the representation of the visual form a **word-percept.** This symbolic structure represents the pattern formed by the constellation of letters in the word, without any regard to meaning. The representation is of a general pattern, not sensitive to type case. For example, *Man* and *man* would be associated with the same word-percept, just as for a chess master, two board configurations differing only in the style of the chess pieces would be associated with the same stored pattern. During word encoding, the representations of individual letters activate the word-percept, as described below. Consider the following example of what the input and output for the word *man* might be:

Input: (**LETTER-1** :IS *m*), (**LETTER-2** :IS *a*), (**LETTER-3** :IS *n*)
Output: (**WORD-PERCEPT** :IS *man*)

Letter position and word length are probably represented less precisely than this numerical notation suggests, particularly for the internal letters of longer words. Readers can easily recognize words with an extra letter (such as *approppriate*) or a missing letter (such as *indvidual*), in spite of the fact that few of the letters are in the correct position if numbered from the beginning. Consequently, the numerical notation should be interpreted as only an approximation.

An important parenthetical comment is necessary here. We are discussing only the *visual* word-percept in this chapter. However, the visual letters sometimes give rise to an auditory word-percept or what is called the *speech code*. That code is discussed in Chapter 3 on lexical access.

The activation process   Like many of READER's other processes, word encoding occurs when productions direct activation from one type of representation to another, in this case, from the letter representation to the word-percept. Each letter representation activates word-percepts that contain that letter at the corresponding serial position. The letters are processed one at a time, usually starting from the outside letters and progressing inward, with a bias for starting with the leftmost letters. Consider, for example, how the word *man* might be encoded. The initial *m* activates short patterns that begin with *m*, such as *mat, mew, man,* and *mid*. Then, the terminal *n* activates patterns that end with *n*, such as *man* and *min* and also *tin* and *can*. In the READER model, the activation is directed from the *m* and *n* to the candidate words by the following production:

| *If you see a letter in a given serial position* | → | *Then increase the activation level of word-percepts that contain that letter at that position* |

At this point, word-percepts such as *man, men,* and *min* have received activation from two letters, and so they have higher levels of activation than other candidates, such as *tin* or *mat*. Then, by means of the same production, the medial *a* activates word-percepts with a medial *a*, such as *man* and also *tan, can,* and *mat*. This further increments the activation level of the word-percept *man* until its activation level reaches a threshold and it becomes the accepted word-percept. The other competing word-percepts are deactivated. At this point in the process, the representation of the visual form of the word is available for the next step, accessing the word's meaning.

The model makes no attempt to explain how the letter representations (the inputs to the word-encoding process) are arrived at in the first place. The model assumes that the letter representations are available in working memory, placed there by an earlier pattern-recognition process that uses the constellation of lines, curves, and intersections to activate the letter representations (Gibson, 1969; Rumelhart & Siple, 1974). Although an activation-based mechanism like READER's can account for the process, we have left the generation of letter representations outside the scope of the model.

There are two controversial aspects of this proposed word-encoding process: First, the process is sequential, operating on one letter at a time; and second, the units it operates on are single letters rather than larger groups, such as consonant clusters or syllables. We will discuss each of these issues in turn.

Evidence for a Sequential Word-encoding Process

The effect of word length   If a fluent reader processes the letters of a word one by one, then word-encoding time should increase with the length of the word. It does! This finding constitutes important support for the sequential encoding process.

In several of our reading studies in which we monitored eye fixations, readers spent an average of about 30 extra milliseconds on a word for each additional letter in the word (Carpenter & Just, 1981; Just & Carpenter, 1980). That means, for example, that readers spent about 90 milliseconds longer on a seven-letter word than on a four-letter word, all other things being equal. Figure 2.7 shows the average amount of time readers spent on words of different lengths in the experiment described in the first part of the chapter in which college students read short technical passages from *Time* and *Newsweek* (Just & Carpenter, 1980). We have separated the words that occur frequently in the language from those that occur only moderately frequently, or infrequently. As the graph shows, frequency also affects the time readers spend on a word, a result of the way word meanings are accessed. The result relevant to word encoding is that within each frequency range, the gaze du-

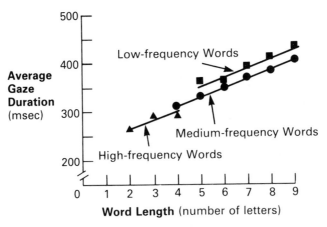

Figure 2.7   The amount of time that readers spend on a word (the average gaze duration) increases linearly with the word's length, measured in number of letters. The increase is about 30 milliseconds per letter. The result holds for words of low, medium, or high frequency. *Source:* Adapted from Carpenter & Just, 1983, Figure 17.2, p. 288. Used with permission of Academic Press.

ration increases with word length. This result suggests that the duration of the word-encoding process increases with word length.

The word-length effects are extremely robust. Readers spend more time on longer words, whether they are reading simple narratives or difficult expository articles, short passages or very long texts. So the most straightforward prediction of this model receives strong support in many reading situations.

Longer words take more time than shorter words in many kinds of tasks, such as recognizing a briefly presented word (McGinnies, Comer, & Lacey, 1952), deciding whether a string of letters is a word or a nonword (the lexical decision task) (Whaley, 1978), and pronouncing a word (Forster & Chambers, 1973). However, length effects have not always been found in nonreading tasks, including lexical decision tasks (see Henderson, 1982, for a brief summary). Since our main purpose is to analyze normal reading, we give more weight to the fact that length effects are found in reading.

Before we take the word-length effect as firm evidence for the sequential word-encoding process, we can try to rule out an alternative interpretation. It might be tempting to speculate that longer words take more time to process because they are so wide that some of their letters are likely to be projected outside the fovea. As a result of the decrease in visual acuity, it might take longer to perceive the letters. A reader might make additional eye fixations to place all of the parts of the word in foveal view. Longer words certainly do receive more fixations, and some of the word-length effect may be due to acuity limitations. However, three pieces of evidence argue against the interpretation that acuity accounts for all or even most of the word-length effect.

First, the word-length effect occurs even for short words (two, three, four, and five letters long), which are generally within foveal vision. If acuity were the main determinant of processing time, one would not expect a systematic increase in processing time with word length for such short words.

Second, the same word-length effect was found in an experiment in which eye movements were much less likely (Just, Carpenter, & Woolley, 1982). In that experiment, each successive word of a text was presented one after another, centered at the same position on the screen. The reader pressed a button to remove one word and bring up the next, so his response time was a measure of the time needed to process each word. On average, readers took longer to press the button on longer words (independently of the word-frequency effect), even though they were probably never making more than one fixation on a word.

The third source of evidence against the role of acuity is a study described in Chapter 10 in which people read Chinese texts (Just, Carpenter, & Wu, 1983). In the Chinese orthography, all of the characters are approximately the same size, although the number of brush strokes that make up each character varies. The amount of time that Chinese readers spent on each character increased linearly with the number of brush strokes, even though the characters did not differ in size. This result is analogous to the readers of English texts increasing their time on each word with the number of letters in the word. The result obtained in the Chinese study cannot be explained in terms of the physical size of characters, because there was no such variation. Both the Chinese and English results *can* be explained in terms of an encoding mechanism that operates component by component. All three sources of evidence argue against a visual-acuity explanation of the word-length effect and suggest that longer words take longer to process because there are more components to encode.

Another argument against the sequential word-encoding process is that it is too slow to account for word recognition. However, the sequential encoding process is very fast—somewhere around a letter every 30 milliseconds. Readers do not dwell on each individual letter long enough to say the letter's name or sound (a process that would take more time than pronouncing the entire word). The proposed sequential encoding process is fast enough to be compatible with all the known performance characteristics of human readers.

Serial-position effects   If letters are encoded one at a time, in what order are they processed? Several word-perception studies have found that the first and last letters of a briefly presented word are reported more accurately than the internal letters. The way such studies are currently done is to present a word and then interrogate the subject about the letter at one of the locations. The interrogation is a multiple-choice test, where the choice is between two alternative letters, either of which would be possible in the word (Reicher, 1969). For example, the word *road* might be briefly presented and the subject would be asked immediately whether an *o* or an *e* occurred in the second position, since these make up the words *road* and *read*. This type of experiment eliminates the possibility that the subject's response is a guess based on knowledge of English words. In a number of studies with four-letter words (like *road*), subjects were most accurate in reporting on the first letter, least accurate on the third letter, and similarly accurate on the second and fourth letters (Rumelhart & McClelland, 1982). Thus, not all letter positions are processed identically. A straightforward explanation of this result is that the word-encoding process starts by operating on the first letter, letting it activate corresponding word-percepts, then operating on the last letter, and so on. The serial-position effects in perceiving the letters of a word support a sequential encoding process.

Nonsequential models   Although we have argued for a very rapid, sequential encoding process, a limited capacity *parallel* model could account for the data, although not quite as simply. The difficulty of discriminating sequential models (sometimes called *serial* models) from parallel models has been encountered in memory research (Murdock, 1971; Townsend, 1974), and the difficulties exist here, as well.

According to a parallel model, all of the letters are encoded simultaneously, but the speed of the encoding is slower for larger words, presumably due to some capacity limitation that slows down processing as the number of letters increases. Thus, one would have to assume that three letters strain the capacity more than two letters, and so on, for a wide range of lengths. One relevant facet of our gaze-duration data is that the word-length effect was linear with the number of letters. That is, the extra amount of time taken by a five-letter word compared to a four-letter word was about the same as the extra time taken by a nine-letter word compared to an eight-letter word. Such a linear increase, at 30 extra milliseconds for each extra letter, is not naturally predicted by the parallel model, although it is not incompatible with it either. By contrast, a linear increase is precisely what a sequential process would predict. Similarly, a parallel model could explain the serial-position effects by assuming that visual masking factors lower the perceptibility of the interior letters, so that their processing would take longer than that of the exterior letters.

Between the extremes of serial and parallel mechanisms lie some hybrid models, such as the cascade model proposed by McClelland (1979). The cascade model proposes that operations are initiated sequentially, but the processes are also permitted to operate in parallel. READER's architecture permits such hybrid combinations, as well. In the case of word encoding, however, the word-length effect, the linearity of the word-length effect, and the serial-position effect all seem to favor the sequential word-encoding process.

Criticisms of the sequential encoding hypothesis A sequential, letter-by-letter encoding process has been suggested before by others (such as Sperling, 1963; and Gough, 1972). Many details of the previous proposals differ from ours, but the basic sequentiality is the same. These proposals were not well received, so it is worth evaluating what made them unpopular.

First, it is intuitively unpalatable to think that skilled readers process a word letter by letter. It is much more flattering to think that skilled readers recognize entire words. Moreover, the parallel encoding of an entire word seems more consistent with the subjective impression of a seemingly instantaneous recognition process. Although no one has explicitly articulated these arguments, it is important to recognize that our intuitions about extremely brief perceptual processes are not necessarily accurate; these processes occur below the level of conscious awareness. No one can subjectively discriminate between a sequential process that takes 30 milliseconds per letter and a parallel process.

A second line of argument against sequential word encoding was based on experiments showing that in various word-perception tasks, young children showed strong word-length effects and adults did not (Samuels, LaBerge, & Bremer, 1978). The beginning readers were characterized as processing the letters of a word sequentially, whereas the adults were characterized as processing the word as a whole. However, our finding of word-length effects when skilled adults actually read a text rather than isolated words weakens this line of argument.

The most prominent argument against a sequential word-encoding process has been based on the finding that readers recognize a word more accurately than a string of random letters (McClelland & Rumelhart, 1981; Reicher, 1969). A string of random letters can only be processed by letter by letter, because there is no higher-order unit that relates the letters. Since words are processed faster than nonwords, the argument goes, they are not being processed letter by letter. The fallacy in this argument is the assumption that there exists only one sequential process (the one used on nonwords) and that any more rapid process is not sequential. Contrary to this assumption, words may be encoded differently from nonwords, and both encoding processes can be sequential.

The Unit of Encoding

The second controversial aspect of the proposed word-encoding mechanism is that it operates on single letters rather than larger groups, such as consonant clusters or syllables. The reason for our proposal was the linearity of the word-length effect on gaze duration. However, we acknowledge the possibility that letters could also activate familiar subword percepts, such as frequently co-occurring letter pairs, letter triplets, or syllables (see Gibson & Levin, 1975; Mason, 1975).

These various alternatives have been difficult to disentangle from each other and from letter-by-letter encoding because the units overlap each other in English. For example, consider the letters *ed*. Are they encoded as two separate letters, as a pair of letters, as a syllable, or as a morpheme (a unit that has its own meaning)? The letters *ed* frequently constitute a syllable (as in *edible* and *editor*) but not always (*edge* or *edict*). When *ed* occurs at the end of a word, it is usually the past-tense morpheme (*walked*), although sometimes it is not (*red*).

The *ed* example illustrates the overlap between various types of descriptions. Partly because of this overlap, the evidence for one type of unit over another has been conflicting and unconvincing. However, it is certainly possible that letters may activate many kinds of intermediate subword percepts. Therefore, our proposal of letters as the units of encoding should not be interpreted as an argument against these other possibilities. Another point to keep in mind is that some of the grouping of letters into subword units may occur during lexical access rather than at word encoding.

One of our eye-fixation studies (Just, Carpenter, & Masson, 1982; see Chapter 14) also happened to shed some interesting light on the role of experience on the units of word encoding. The text in that study was a long narrative about an American frontiersman named John Colter. The average gaze duration increased with word length, as in all our previous studies, except that six-letter words had a much shorter gaze duration than expected. A careful look at the data showed that the shorter gaze was attributable entirely to the word *Colter,* which occurred very frequently in the text. Although the first few occurrences of *Colter* received the amount of gaze we would expect on a six-letter word, the many subsequent occurrences of the word received an unexpectedly short gaze duration. One possible explanation of the shorter-than-predicted gaze duration on this word is that the readers did not encode all six of the letters in *Colter*. The word *Colter* may have become sufficiently predictable from the first two letters and the shape and length of the word that it was unnecessary to encode the entire word before guessing what it referred to. This is similar to the feeling students report when reading literature that contains many foreign words, such as the Russian names found in a Dostoyevsky novel; namely, they code some of these names in terms of their first few letters. An alternative possibility is that all of the letters in *Colter* were processed, but the connections between the letters and the word-percept became so strong after repeated encounters that the activation level of the word-percept reached threshold much sooner. Either alternative could lead to the faster encoding of repeated words.

One uncertainty about the letter as the unit of encoding stems from the difficulty in assessing the word-length effect. Word length can be measured using several scales: the number of characters, the number of syllables, the number of subword units (prefixes, suffixes, subunits of a compound word), or combinations of these. Some previous studies have suggested that performance is most closely related to length as measured in syllables (such as Whaley, 1978), yet others have suggested that length should be measured in letters (such as Gough, 1972). Our gaze-duration data were more closely related to the number of letters than the number of syllables. Although we await further experimental verification, we tentatively accept the letter rather than the syllable as the normative unit of encoding during normal reading.

The Role of Word Shape

There have been repeated suggestions in the literature that words are not encoded in terms of letters or syllables but that the entire shape of the word is the input to the word-encoding process. Such suggestions propose **whole-word** models of word encoding, as opposed to our proposed **letter-mediated** process. According to the whole-word models, readers activate word-percepts on the basis of the global features of a word, such as its overall shape or contour (Smith, 1971). The shape of a word depends on its length and the pattern of ascending letters (like *d, h,* and *l*) and descending letters (like *p, q,* and *y*). A whole-word model predicts that readers should have great difficulty processing a text in which the word-shape cues are missing (BECAUSE ALL THE WORDS ARE PRINTED IN UPPER CASE) or if the cues are incongruous (BeCaUsE tHe WoRdS aRe iN aLtErNaTiNg CaSeS). However, readers take only slightly longer (about 10 percent) to read such texts, suggesting that word shape can play a minor role in reading. One reason why word shape is unlikely to play a large role in word recognition is that shape is seldom unique to a word, even when the word is in lower case. For example, *lint, hint, tint, list, find,* and *fist* all have a similar overall shape.

One finding that at first glance looks like evidence for the role of word shape is that readers sometimes confuse words with similar shapes, such as *list* and *lint*. However, such confusion could be due to similarities between individual letters, rather than overall shape. If *list* is confused with *lint* more than with *lilt*, it could be because *s* is more confusable with *n* than with *l*. The relative importance of word shape and the identity of a substituted letter was evaluated in a study of proofreading for spelling errors (Paap, Newsome, & Noel, 1984). This study found that the critical determinant of detecting misspellings was the similarity of the substituted letter to the original letter, rather than the similarity of the overall word shape. Word shape played a very small role in proofreading.

Word shape is more important in tasks that emphasize visual form over meaning. A typical study that has been used to demonstrate the role of word shape is a visual search task. In one such study, subjects repeatedly searched through a list of words that were printed in mixed upper and lower cases, looking for a particular set of targets, like *cAnAdA* and *sPaIn* (Brooks, 1977). After lots of practice, the subjects became quite fast at identifying the targets. Then the shape of the targets was changed—for example, to *CaNaDa* and *SpAiN*. This change slowed down the search, indicating that the particular visual shapes of the targets were important. However, the very characteristics of this task that make the role of word shape so important are also characteristics that make the task very different from reading. One characteristic is the deemphasis of meaning. In the search task, the word's meaning played little or no role. Meaning was further deemphasized because the words were presented in a list, rather than in a text. Second, the subjects were given lots of practice with the same visual shapes. Again, in normal reading, the reader can see lots of words and different fonts (types of print), such as **BOLD,** *italics,* CAPITALIZED. Although the type font can vary, it does not change the interpretation the reader gives to a word. In reading tasks, it is the identity of the word's constituent letters, not the overall visual shape of the word, that determines meaning.

Word shape may play a larger role in the recognition of those few words and logos that occur only in one particular visual configuration. Consider how much harder it is to recognize the logos *ibm* and *gm* than *IBM* and *GM,* not to mention e. e. cummings.

Context Effects in Letter Perception

Readers recognize a word like *school* much faster and more accurately than a nonword like *solcho,* which uses the same letters. Over 100 years ago, Cattell (1885) discovered that if he briefly presented a string of letters, people accurately reported a maximum of three or four individual letters. On the other hand, they also accurately reported two short words that contained more than three or four letters. It was unclear why the letters composing a word were easier to process than a nonword string.

This finding has intrigued researchers, because it suggests an apparent paradox: Words are perceived better than the individual letters that comprise them. Of course, reporting a string of letters places a greater burden on short-term memory than does reporting two words. Researchers have refined their techniques to eliminate the memory burden by asking the viewer to report which letter was present at a particular location (Sperling, 1963). When the memory burden is minimized, it is clear that the viewer can perceive many more than three or four letters. Even so, letters that make up a word are still reported slightly more accurately than letters that do not. Because of this apparent paradox, letter perception has been the focus of numerous studies (see Henderson, 1982). In this section, we will describe one of the major theoretical explanations of the phenomenon and then discuss how it is related to reading.

A letter in a word is perceived better than a letter in a nonword and better than an isolated letter (Reicher, 1969; Wheeler, 1970). This phenomenon has been labeled the **word-superiority effect.** However, it is important to remember that the result refers to the perception of a letter. The most common procedure used to study the effect is illustrated in Table 2.2. First, a string of letters is briefly flashed to the viewer. The string may be one of three types: a word, a nonword, or a single letter surrounded by *X*'s. This string is followed by a visual mask (a display of *X*'s that is intended to interfere with any further encoding of useful information from the display) and then by two alternative letters that are placed above or below the location of one of the letters in the initial display. The viewer must choose which of the two alternative letters was shown in that location. The study found that readers chose more accurately if the letter was part of a word than if it was part of a nonword or presented in isolation.

Before explaining this effect, we can rule out two alternative theories. First, the advantage is not due to choosing a letter that completes a word; the two response alternatives both make up an acceptable word in the word condition. Sec-

Table 2.2 Sequence of events in the three conditions of a letter-detection task that demonstrates the word-superiority effect

	Type of Condition		
What the subject is shown:	**Word**	**Nonword**	**Letter**
1. The stimulus	LINT	TINL	XIXX
2. A mask	XXXX	XXXX	XXXX
3. The alternatives	I	I	I
	E	E	E

ond, the advantage cannot be due in any large part to accessing the meaning of a word. Pseudowords like *lant* that can be pronounced and follow the conventions of English spelling have an advantage in comparison to nonword strings like *tnla*, even though pseudowords do not have a meaning to be accessed (McClelland & Rumelhart, 1981).

Context facilitates letter perception   One of the most convincing explanations of the word-superiority effect has been the proposal that words facilitate the recognition of their constituent letters by feeding back activation from the word-percept level to the letter level, improving the perceptibility of individual letters (McClelland & Rumelhart, 1981). For example, information from the display *LINT* activates word-percepts, such as *lint, lent,* and *tint.* Activation from these representations is then fed back to their associated letters, raising their activation level to threshold that much sooner. By contrast, a random string of letters, like *tinl,* will not strongly activate any word-percepts. Hence, the letter representations will not receive any extra activation increment from a word-percept, and so they will require more time to reach threshold. This model can also explain why letters in pseudowords have an advantage over letters in random strings. The pseudowords are more likely to activate word-percepts that have similar letters, so at least some of the letters will receive activation from word-percepts.

Not only does context facilitate letter perception, but the earlier the context appears, the more helpful it is to the viewer. In a number of experiments, McClelland and Rumelhart found that viewers recognized a target letter in a word more accurately if the other letters in the word were shown slightly before the target, rather than slightly after. Perception of the target letter improved if the context was present for a longer time, even though the target letter was always present for the same amount of time.

The evidence of such top-down influence (from the word-percept level down to the letter level) in an experimental task makes it plausible that a top-down influence could occur in normal reading, as well. Context effects can often be explained in terms of feedback from higher levels influencing lower levels. However, before we assume that this particular top-down influence plays a role in reading, we should consider some other context effects and how these tasks do and do not resemble reading.

All week, the weather was amazing. Even flowers in the park withered and became leathery under the sun's thermal rays. Children wearing no clothes bathed near the southern shore of the lake, while their mothers discussed other problems of psychotherapy and anesthesia. Panthers in the zoo surveyed the scene in a fatherly manner. As shadows lengthened, the air became ethereal and clouds began gathering on the horizon. "Bother," mumbled Alice, who was one of the sunbathers. "I've hardly begun my thesis on the theory of medieval atheism, and I'd rather go and buy the earthenware jug I saw on Friday."

Figure 2.8   A sample passage to read and search for *t*'s. *Source:* Drewnowski & Healy, 1977, p. 647. Used with permission of the Psychonomic Society and the authors.

Context obscures letter perception   In many everyday situations, a word context can make a letter harder to perceive than when it is presented out of context. Two such situations include proofreading for a misspelled word and searching for a particular letter. Try such a letter search yourself by reading the story in Figure 2.8 and circling each occurrence of the letter *t*.

Most people miss the *t* more often if it is part of a frequently occurring word (like *the*) than if it is part of a less-frequent word (like *thesis*). The passage contains a total of 12 *t*'s in *the* and 24 *t*'s in other words, such as *earthenware*. If all the *t*'s were detected with the same ease, readers should circle the same proportion of *t*'s in *the* as in other words. But in most experiments, readers detected a much smaller proportion of the *t*'s in *the* (Drewnowski & Healy, 1977, 1982; Healy & Drewnowski, 1983). Why should the letter *t* be harder to detect when it occurs in a frequently used word? Drewnowski and Healy argued that very frequent words (like *the*) are processed as a unit. Moreover, once the unit is lexically accessed, the representations of its constituent letters are less accessible to conscious attention. So this is a case in which a letter is harder to detect when it is in the context of a word, particularly a frequently occurring word.

The *t* search task presents an apparent contradiction to the word-superiority effect. In the word-superiority effect, the word context facilitates the perception of a constituent letter, while in the *t* search task, the word context obscures its constituent letters. The resolution to the paradox lies in two differences between the search task and word-superiority task, both of which make it more difficult to attend to the letter level in the search task. First, in a search or proofreading task, the location of the target letter or misspelled word is obviously unknown, so readers must direct their attention to successive locations in the text. By contrast, in the word-superiority task, the viewers can direct their attention to a single four-letter word. It seems likely that when attention can be focused on a smaller area, it is easier to attend to the individual constituents in that area. A second difference between the two tasks is that readers in the search and proofreading tasks have less total attention available to direct to the letter level because some of their attentional resources are automatically engaged in understanding the text. Even though most people who are proofreading or searching for a target sacrifice some level of understanding, they nevertheless are performing some linguistic and conceptual computations. If the textlike qualities of the stimulus words are eliminated by presenting the words in random order or in a vertical list, then the detection of the target letters is no longer affected by their linguistic context (Drewnowski & Healy, 1977). This suggests that if comprehension processes are impossible (because of the random arrangement of words), then it is easier to direct attention to individual letters. In the word-superiority task, there is no text to process, and so the viewer may have more attentional capacity to direct to the letter level.

Differences between Reading and Nonreading Tasks

Because it is such an impressive perceptual skill, word recognition has been a topic of great interest and has been studied using many different tasks, including:

1. recognizing a word that is very briefly presented;
2. identifying which letter was presented in a word or nonword;
3. pronouncing a word;
4. deciding whether a string of letters is a word or nonword;
5. searching for a particular letter, syllable, or word; and
6. proofreading—that is, searching for various kinds of errors.

In this section, we will explore how these tasks differ from normal reading and consider how the differences may influence word recognition.

Some of these tasks differ from normal reading in the quality of graphic information. In normal reading, words are presented under normal lighting conditions, for an unlimited amount of time, in clear type. In some word-perception tasks, words are presented so that there is little contrast between the word and background, or they are presented for only a few tens of milliseconds, or they are visually degraded. These manipulations are often used to explore the effects of higher-level factors, such as the word context. Since the perceptual information is impoverished, such studies may overestimate the importance of the top-down influences when compared to normal reading conditions.

A second difference is the presence or absence of linguistic context. In normal reading, words are recognized among other words. However, in word-recognition studies, words are typically presented alone, without a syntactic and semantic context. Obviously, such studies cannot indicate the role of the linguistic context and how it might interact with perceptual processes.

As we mentioned with respect to the word-superiority task, the presence of a context may have subtle effects on the nature of the processing. Reading a text involves a number of processes that engage the reader's attention. This is not true of a task that only requires a reader to identify a single isolated word or letter. One consequence of the absence of a text in this latter task is that it may allow the reader to attend to aspects of the word, such as particular letters, that might usually receive little or no conscious attention in normal reading.

This difference in the presence or absence of context has a parallel in the nature of the subject's goals. In reading, the reader's goal is typically to understand the text, although she may also want to remember the information, analyze it, enjoy it, and so on. The understanding process can impose significant cognitive demands that may interact with perceptual and lexical processes. By contrast, in laboratory tests of word perception, the goal is typically not language comprehension but only letter or word identification. Consequently, the degree to which various processes are involved may vary considerably between those tasks that involve understanding and those that do not.

A third way in which typical word-recognition tasks differ from normal reading is that they often introduce additional processes that are not part of normal reading. It is always possible that these additional processes will alter the perceptual processes from the way they are normally executed in reading. For example, consider the task of proofreading. Although proofreading can be considered to be a form of reading, searching for misspellings is an additional process that is not normally part of reading. Such a task undoubtedly influences the reading process by consuming some of the reader's attention that might ordinarily be devoted to understanding the meaning of a text. A similar point can be made about the lexical decision task, in which subjects are presented a string (such as *nurse* or *resun*) and asked to decide whether it is a word or nonword. Making this decision is not a normal part of reading. A reader who looks at a text assumes that each string of letters is a word, even if it is unfamiliar or perhaps misspelled. Researchers who use these tasks sometimes assume that the basic perceptual processes in word recognition are so automatic that they are not fundamentally altered by the additional processes. This assumption may be correct, but it still must be examined, task by task.

A fourth difference between some of these tasks and normal reading is a gross disparity in speed. For example, the average time spent on each word in a lexical decision task (600–800 milliseconds) is considerably longer than the time spent on a comparable word during normal reading (200–400 milliseconds) and also longer than the time spent to perceive and pronounce the word (Theios & Muise, 1977). Another example of speed disparity is that in some search tasks that require people to read through texts, the rate slows down to 125 words per minute, compared to a rate of about 240 words per minute in normal reading. If the processing rate in an experimental task is much different than that in normal reading, it may change the usual nature of the collaboration among the component processes. For example, running is more than just a fast form of walking; the nature of the coordination between the two feet is fundamentally different in the two forms of locomotion, such that walkers but not runners always have one foot on the ground. Similarly, reading might change if it is done much faster or slower than normal. Moreover, a gross decrease in speed might encourage the addition of processes that are not a part of normal reading, while a gross increase in speed might encourage the deletion of processes that are a part of normal reading. It is important to check that experimental tasks that proceed at a much different speed than normal reading are not introducing qualitative changes in the processing.

Do all of these differences mean that nonreading tasks cannot help us understand perceptual processes in reading? No, not at all. We have cited results from one or another of these paradigms to support theoretical interpretations of various reading phenomena. Such paradigms can be invaluable sources of converging evidence. Their differences from normal reading can sometimes be a strength; in particular, these tasks are useful for exploring one process in isolation from others. However, the question remains whether the process of interest operates the same way in reading as in the nonreading task and how the differences between the experimental tasks and reading might alter the process. The most confidence should be placed in results that are robust, that occur in many different tasks, and, especially, that occur in real reading tasks.

Summary

As a skilled reader progresses through a text at an overall rate of approximately 240 words per minute, he fixates a large proportion of the content words in a text (approximately 80 percent) and a smaller proportion of the function words (approximately 40 percent). As his eyes land on a given word, he takes in the information from that word. He does very little, if any, processing of adjacent words, unless he happens to fixate immediately to the left of a short, familiar function word. Almost all of his comprehension processes concern the word he is fixating and its relation to the preceding text.

This chapter focused on the word-encoding process, during which the letters of a word are encoded sequentially, proceeding from the first letters to the last letters and ending with the interior letters. The time taken to encode a word increases linearly with word length. The perceptual representations of words receive activation from the letter representations. The encoding process increases the activation level of the word-percept until it reaches a threshold level. A letter that occurs in the context of a word is easier to perceive because activation from the word-percept contributes to the activation level of the letter representation. Some of the perceptual processes that occur in reading can be examined in experimental studies of nonreading tasks, but generalizations from nonreading tasks must take task differences into account.

Suggested Readings

Some of the initial research on the nature of reading at the turn of the century pioneered the use of eye fixations as an experimental technique. Many of these works are classics because they present interesting hypotheses and consider rather far-ranging phenomena. The references that we have found most interesting and useful are Huey (recent edition, 1968), Dearborn (1906), Judd and Buswell (1922), and Buswell (1922, 1937).

Several new techniques have been developed to study comprehension processes as they occur. These techniques and what they have uncovered about comprehension are described in an edited volume by Kieras and Just (1984). This volume also gives a more detailed description of how eye fixations have been used to study comprehension processes (Just & Carpenter, 1984). Examples of the recent burst of research activity on the nature of eye fixations in reading can be found in the volume edited by Rayner (1983).

Word encoding (or more generally, word recognition) is one of the most researched topics of psychology that has any relation to reading. For those who want to read more extensive discussions and results of the research on word recognition, we recommend Gibson and Levin (1975) and the more recent book by

Henderson (1982). They are also good bibliographic sources for this topic. The papers by McClelland and Rumelhart (1981; Rumelhart & McClelland, 1982) present the most convincing explanation of the word-superiority effect and elegantly demonstrate how clever experimental studies in conjunction with a computer simulation can lay bare the processes underlying an effect.

Appendix

Description of the Eye Tracker

Figure 2.9 saves us a thousand words of description by showing our laboratory. The reader sits in a chair and reads from a computer-controlled videoscreen about 20 inches in front of him. Off to the side of the screen is the optical part of the tracker, consisting of a light source, a mirror, and a camera. These remote sensors register where the subject is looking without being close to his eyes. The main principle on which the tracker operates is the easily observable phenomenon that if a light is shined on the eyes (say, by an immobile flashlight), it will be reflected back from the front surface of the eyeball (the *cornea*). As the eye rotates in its socket, the light's reflection also moves. The reflection can be calibrated such that the position of the reflection reveals which location in the viewing field is being fixated. All of the calibration and computation is done by computers. What follows is a more precise and technical description of the instrumentation.

The eye tracker (Applied Science Laboratories Model 1998, processor-based system with a head-tracking mirror) is especially suited to monitoring eye fixations in reading. The system has three main components. The first component is the sensor, a videocamera fitted with a sensitive vidicon tube that is focused on one of the subject's eyes. The eye is illuminated by a low-intensity, infrared light source that is coaxial with the camera lens. The light that is reflected from the cornea and pupil is registered by the videocamera. The second main component is an electronic device that preprocesses the signal produced by the camera, converts it into a digital format, and recognizes the outline of the pupil and the corneal reflection. The third component is a minicomputer that uses the digital representation of the video image to compute the subject's point of regard.

In addition to these three components of the eye tracker, a laboratory computer (DEC MicroVAX II) collects the eye-fixation data from the tracker and stores it. The MicroVAX also controls the stimulus display; most reading experiments use a display of 11 rows of double-spaced text, with a maximum of 80 characters per row. The entire system operates at 60 cycles per second, such that the sensor camera produces 60 video fields per second. The tracker computes the reader's location of fixation on each of the fields and communicates the data (in the form of x and y coordinates) to the MicroVAX.

The eye tracker relates the position of the pupil and the corneal reflection to a particular location of fixation. If a person's head is fixed in one position and he moves his eyes around to look at various places, then the corneal reflection of a fixed light source will move around in monotonic relation to the fixated points in space. The minicomputer's program contains a function that maps from the position of the corneal reflection to the location of fixation. This function was developed by the manufacturer in a generalized form, with individualized parameters computed for each reader. These parameters are obtained during a brief calibration procedure by having the program note the position of the corneal reflection as the reader fixates nine predefined locations distributed around the viewing screen.

Head movements, as well as eye movements, can cause a change in the position of the corneal reflection. Consequently, the tracker must use a second reference point to distinguish between the two types of movement. The second reference point is provided by the position of the pupil (actually, the center of the pupil), which indicates head movements. The program uses these two reference points to determine the location of fixation even if the subject moves his head. The tracker allows head movement within about one square inch, beyond which the pupil falls outside of the viewing field of the camera. The allowable head movement is increased considerably (to about 36 square inches) by a servo-controlled mirror through which the camera views the eye. Whenever the program detects the pupil moving across a boundary of the camera's viewing field, it repositions the mirror to recenter the pupil in the field.

The system is accurate to about 1 degree of visual angle in the horizontal axis (approximately the width of three characters) and about 1.5 degrees in the vertical (approximately 1.5 times the height of each character). Because the vertical

Figure 2.9 Eye-fixation laboratory. A student reading from the computer-controlled display. The video camera on the left remotely registers the light reflections from the reader's eye. A computer uses this information to determine where the reader is fixating.

accuracy is not quite sufficient to distinguish fixations on adjacent lines of the display, the text is displayed on every second line. The visual angle of the print is roughly similar to that of common reading situations. A videotape recording is usually made of the text with superimposed cross hairs indicating the location of fixation. The reader sits in an armchair, usually using a headrest (not shown in the photograph).

To determine the gaze duration on a word, all of the consecutive coordinates that are located on the word must be pooled. Since each pair of coordinates corresponds to 16.7 milliseconds of looking time, the gaze duration is computed by multiplying 16.7 milliseconds by the number of pairs of consecutive coordinates located on the word.

3

Lexical Structure and Lexical Access

How would you feel if you dressed yourself the way you dressed a salad? Or dressed a salad the way you dressed a turkey? Why do lights go *out* but never *in*?

Somehow, the sight of a printed word eventually leads a reader to think of an interpretation of the word. But these word games illustrate that the sight of a printed word is not the sole determinant of its interpretation. Many words have multiple meanings, and context can determine which meaning a word conveys. The problem that a reader faces as he encounters a given word in a text is first to encode the word and then access its meaning in his internal lexicon, using a process called **lexical access.** The **internal lexicon** is a person's mental representation of word meanings. This chapter discusses the structure of the information stored in the internal lexicon and the processes that access that information.

Even though there is much more to reading than just understanding individual words, the understanding of individual words in a text plays an important role in comprehension. Several phenomena in reading originate at the level of interpreting individual words:

1. Words that are frequently used in the language are accessed faster than those that are infrequently used. This phenomenon is called the *word-frequency effect.* But why should the time needed to access a word meaning in the internal lexicon be affected by frequency of usage?
2. Ambiguous words like *bank,* which have several homonymous meanings, are generally interpreted appropriately. How does a reader deal with such lexical ambiguity?
3. Novel words that are composed of familiar stems and affixes (e.g., *unreconstructed*) can easily be understood. How are words decomposed and meaning components synthesized?
4. When a word is preceded by an appropriate context, it is usually processed faster than when it occurs in a neutral sentence. What process is facilitated by the context?

Overview   In the first section of this chapter, we will discuss **The Content and Structure of the Lexicon.** Concepts that correspond to the meanings of words or parts of words are stored in the mental lexicon, which is hypothesized to be configured as a large knowledge network.

In the second section, **Lexical Access,** we will describe a mechanism for accessing the meaning of a word. This mechanism is based on the activation of concepts, providing direct access from the printed form of a word to its meaning. The proposed mechanism accounts for the finding that frequently used words are accessed faster than those that are used less often.

In the third section, **Lexical Ambiguity,** we will describe how the appropriate meanings of ambiguous words are selected. The selection process takes the preceding context into consideration, as well as the relative frequencies of the multiple meanings of the word.

In the fourth section, **Context Effects,** we will discuss how an earlier context may decrease the time a reader requires to access a word meaning. And finally, in the fifth section, **Speech Codes in Silent Reading,** we will examine speech recoding, involving the representation of the sounds of words during reading.

The Content and Structure of the Lexicon

Each reader has a great deal of knowledge associated with most of the words she knows. The knowledge includes a representation of the word itself, specifically, its pronunciation and spelling. But the central knowledge that is stored about a word is the representation of the associated concept, including its properties and its relation to other concepts. We will refer to this information as the **word meaning** or the **word-concept.**

The term *word-concept* refers to the meaning of a word, while *word-precept* refers to the perceptual representation of a written word. For example, the word-concept corresponding to the word *pencil* might indicate that it refers to an instrument used for writing or drawing; that it is a manmade physical object, usually cylindrical in shape; and that it functions by leaving a trail of graphite along a writing surface. The word-concept might also indicate that a *pencil* is one of a class of writing instruments and a close relative of the *pen, eraser,* and *sharpener.* Beyond the physical and functional properties of pencils, a reader also knows where they can be purchased, approximately how much they cost, and what their usual life expectancy is. If the reader is a historian, she might also know that Johann Faber was one of the developers of the wood-encased pencil.

A reader also has syntactic information about the word, which indicates its part of speech (such as adjective, noun, or adverb) and possible syntactic roles. For example, the syntactic information about *pencil* might indicate that it is a noun but also links the entry to the corresponding verb that refers to writing or drawing with a pencil.

Word Knowledge and *World* Knowledge

We can distinguish the knowledge that is specific to language from general knowledge about the world. But does this distinction imply a separation of the two kinds of knowledge in long-term memory? In one view, the lexicon is simply the reader's knowledge of the world. In another view, the lexicon contains only the information pertinent to language use but also provides pointers to the knowledge of the world, stored in a separate organization of information.

The boundary between *word* knowledge and *world* knowledge is hard to specify. As an example, consider how we normally interpret each of the sentences below:

> *Our store sells alligator shoes.*
> *Our store sells horse shoes.*

The word *shoes* is interpreted very differently in the two sentences because of our knowledge that alligators don't wear shoes of any kind, while horses do. Moreover, people sometimes wear shoes made of alligator hide but almost never of horse hide. Is this knowledge included in the lexicon with the entries for *alligator, horse,* and *shoe*? A priori, one would think that such knowledge is not part of the meaning of each of these words but rather part of the reader's knowledge of the world. Yet, as Bolinger (1965) pointed out, this knowledge is necessary to interpret the sentences correctly. A reader must have access to both word knowledge and world knowledge, even though there could be an internal distinction between them.

Features in the Lexicon

An entry in the mental lexicon is the representation of a word meaning. This representation has several components, the most significant of which is the top-level entry point for all the different information that makes up the word meaning. In an earlier section, we described some of the other possible components of the meaning of *pencil* informally, using sentences such as *A reader knows how much a pencil costs.* A somewhat more formal way to specify the content of a lexical entry is to provide a list of features that define a word. A **feature** is an attribute-value pair, indicating the value that the concept occupies along a continuous or discrete dimension. In most notations, the name of the dimension is not written out. For example, the meaning of *father* may be paraphrased by two features: [+ male] and [+ parent]. The feature [+ male] indicates the value of the concept FATHER along the dimension of sex, which is not written out.

Characterizing concepts in terms of features works very well for certain types of words, such as those listed in Table 3.1. Note that these words come from domains that are relatively well structured by physical, social, or biological dimensions, which then serve as the basis of semantic features. Other types of words (like *money* or *honesty* or *car*), which do not come from well-structured domains, are more difficult to characterize as a set of features.

It is difficult to determine or agree upon the underlying features of most words. No methodology directly reveals the meaning components of a word. A linguist can use his trained intuition to discern the meaning components of a word, but even

Table 3.1   Some examples of word meanings with separable features

Domain	Words	Examples of Features
Spatial terms	*tall, deep*	1. Spatial extent 2. Direction from reference point
Motion verbs	*ascend, descend*	1. Vertical motion 2. Direction of motion
Kinship terms	*son, grandmother*	1. Gender 2. Generation

linguists do not always agree on the features. Alternative methods are based on the performance of untrained subjects. One such technique requires subjects to sort words into separate groups, allowing the subjects to formulate the criteria for sorting in any way they wish. If all the words in one group share a particular feature, then the sorting suggests that the feature is accessible (Anglin, 1970; Miller & Johnson-Laird, 1976).

While this method can reveal which features have the potential of being used in the sorting task, it does not guarantee that the feature is normally accessed during comprehension, which is very unlike the sorting task. For example, although readers are capable of sorting concrete nouns into two groups, depending on whether the referent can be purchased in a department store, readers probably do not access this feature of a word's meaning during normal comprehension. Despite the difficulty in confirming what is or is not a feature of a word, it is generally accepted that certain words are comprehended by accessing various features or meaning components. The features are most obvious for words that are part of a well-structured taxonomy, such as the kinship terms *father, uncle, son,* and *grandfather.*

Defining features and characteristic features   Not all concepts have defining features (necessary and sufficient features). Using the concept GAME as an example, Wittgenstein (1953) pointed out that games do not have a defining feature. Solitaire, football, chess, and so forth are all games but not because they all share a particular feature. Not all games are competitive, not all are played with other people, and not all are played for enjoyment. Rather, each game has some subset of the features associated with the concept GAME. Some concepts appear to be represented in terms of a prototype that possesses the characteristic feature (Rosch, 1975). For instance, when asked to think of a bird, people think of robinlike creatures more often than penguinlike creatures. (The results would probably be different if the subjects in the experiment had been Antarctic residents rather than U.S. college students.)

Characteristic features and defining features (if there are any) are both used in deciding whether a description of a familiar concept is accurate. McNamara and Sternberg (1983) examined how the presence of these different types of features affected the rated accuracy of a description. For example, readers rated the following description of a diamond as accurate: "sparkles, made of carbon, mined in Africa." Different descriptions mentioned defining features (such as "made of carbon"), characteristic features (such as "mined in Africa"), or both. Descriptions that contained defining features were rated as more accurate. Moreover, the ratings were influenced by the number and importance of both defining and characteristic features.

Representation and Activation of Features

Semantic network representation The format in which the semantic features of a word are represented is usually presumed to be a network, consisting of nodes (corresponding to concepts and features) that are interconnected by links. Labels on the links indicate the nature of the relation between the nodes they connect (Collins & Loftus, 1975; Collins & Quillian, 1969; Quillian, 1968). Figure 3.1 illustrates how the concepts ROBIN, BIRD, and ANIMAL might be represented in a network. The superset-subset relation that exists between concepts (like ROBIN and BIRD) is denoted by *is a*. Other types of relations include *has, can,* and *is*. The meaning of a word such as *robin* consists of all the nodes and labeled relations that are linked to the top-level ROBIN node. For example, one of the features of the meaning of ROBIN is that it has a red breast. The network illustrated in the figure is an example of a *hierarchical* network representation, with the ordering in the hierarchy defined by set-inclusion relations (*is a*) among the nodes of the network. In this example, higher-order concepts (like ANIMAL) include lower-order concepts (like BIRD and ROBIN).

More recently proposed semantic networks have been *heterarchical,* such that there is no single relation (like set inclusion) that orders all the concepts. An example of a heterarchical network is shown in Figure 3.2 (with the labels specifying the various types of links omitted). Although it is possible to represent relations among animals with a hierarchical network, a heterarchical network is more appropriate for representing concepts from ill-structured domains.

There is a trade-off between how much information is stored in a network and how much must be computed during comprehension. For example, readers know that ducks can breathe. It is possible that this fact is explicitly stored (as well as the facts that hamsters, goldfish, alligators, and many other creatures breathe) and that it is accessed when it is needed. But it is also possible that readers store only the fact that animals breathe; thus, since a duck is an animal, they infer that ducks can breathe. To minimize the amount of information stored, properties would be stored with the highest node for which they are applicable. Although a number of studies have attempted to determine which features are stored redundantly, there is no conclusive empirical guidance on this issue. Perhaps people directly store facts that are needed frequently and infer facts that are needed infrequently.

Many different types of network representations have been proposed, and the importance of the differences is difficult to evaluate. In some instances, one proposed network representation is a minor notational variant of another. In other instances, two proposed representations seem isomorphic but differ as to which kinds of computations they would make straightforward and which lengthy. Empirical results alone generally don't dictate a choice among a number of plausible network representations. Consequently, researchers usually choose a representation based on theoretical considerations. For example, in the case of the READER

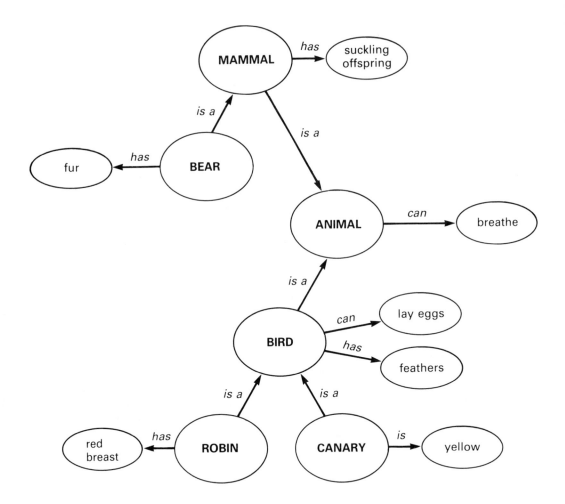

Figure 3.1   A depiction of the hierarchical relations among the concepts of ANIMAL, BIRD, ROBIN, and the like in semantic memory. Concepts are linked to their superordinates with *is a* relations. Properties of the concept are linked by relations such as *has, is,* and *can.*

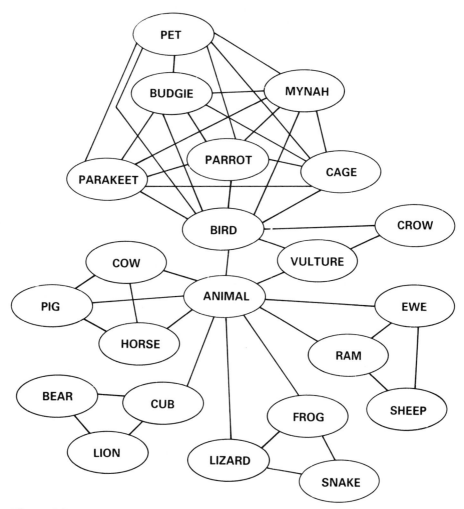

Figure 3.2 A depiction of a heterarchical network. (The labels on the links have been deleted.)

model, the choice of representation was dictated by two theoretical considerations: (1) compatibility with the activation-directing processes that underlie its comprehension and (2) a desire for homogeneity of representation across different levels of comprehension.

Just as several different network representations are formally equivalent to each other, so, too, are network representations formally equivalent to meaning representations in terms of sets of features. A semantic network, consisting of nodes linked by relations, can be recast as a set of concepts, each associated with a set of features (Hollan, 1975). The terminology that theorists use sometimes differs, depending on whether they think of word meanings being represented as a network or as sets of concepts with features. Within this chapter, we have already used the word *feature* in the context of describing word meaning. In the context of a semantic network, we tend to use the term *meaning component* instead of *feature*.

Activation levels   Many networks, including the one used in the READER model, assume that each node in the semantic network has an **activation level.** The activation level is a quantity that denotes the concept's degree of activity at a particular point in time. The nature of the activity is not specified but may be analogous to the firing rate of a neuron. The higher the activation level, the greater its availability for interaction with other nodes. The activation level of a node when it is in its resting state is called the **base activation level.**

A node can have its activation level temporarily raised above its base level (Anderson, 1976; Collins & Loftus, 1975). When this occurs, the node is said to have been activated. Activation of one node can produce activation of other nodes to which it is linked in the network. Then the newly activated nodes can activate their neighbors and so on. The degree to which one node A activates another node B depends on the activation level of A. The higher the activation of A, the more it will activate B. Moreover, the link between A and B can weight the size of A's effect on B, either magnifying or reducing it. In addition, some links are inhibitory, such that activation of one node produces a lowering of activation of the node to which it is linked. The mechanism by which activation is propagated through the network varies somewhat from theory to theory. For now, we will assume an amorphous spreading of activation; later, we will describe the mechanism used in READER.

There is a uniform activation threshold in the system, such that the nodes become available to certain processes only after their activation levels reach the threshold. In this sense, the activation level of a node is a measure of its availability. A node can be activated to threshold by a single source of activation, or several different sources of activation can converge on a node to bring it to threshold.

The activating of nodes is an important mechanism by which symbolic processing occurs in READER and in several other current models of human thought (e.g., Anderson, 1983; McClelland & Rumelhart, 1986). Semantic networks and activation levels and processes draw on an analogy to neural networks, in which an increase in the electrical activity of one neuron can cause an increase or decrease in the activity of contiguous neurons.

The mechanism of one node activating another has been used to explain many psychological phenomena, particularly those concerned with retrieving information from memory (Collins & Loftus, 1975; Smith, Shoben, & Rips, 1974). In the area of reading, it has also been invoked to explain context effects in lexical access. A predictive context, such as *I like my coffee with cream and . . .* might make it faster to access the meaning of a word like *sugar* if the preceding context raises the activation level of the concept SUGAR above its base level.

Lexical Access

Just having a mental lexicon doesn't automatically provide a reader with word meanings. The meanings of the words of a text must be accessed in the lexicon and made available to the other comprehension processes. But how is the meaning of one particular word found among many thousands of other word meanings in the lexicon? Two main forms of access have been proposed: *search* and *direct access.* Although the READER model proposes direct access, we will first briefly contrast search and direct access to clarify the nature of each.

Search models imply that the stored word meanings are examined, one at a time, until the desired word meaning is encountered. According to a pure search model, there is no indexing scheme to indicate how to find a particular word meaning in the internal lexicon. The search proceeds similarly, regardless of which word is being accessed, until the desired word meaning is found. A familiar example of a search process is trying to find a particular book on a bookshelf in which the books are randomly arranged; there is no way of knowing where to find the desired item. Most search models of lexical access do not assume that word meanings are randomly arranged but rather that they are organized in some way. The objective of researchers who believe in search models is often to determine the organizational scheme in which the word meanings are arranged. It has been proposed that entries in the mental lexicon may be organized by frequency—for example, from most frequently used to least frequently used. Thus, a search model of lexical access might propose that the word meanings are examined in a fixed order, starting with the most frequent.

Direct access to the lexicon implies that the user has an indexing scheme that allows him to evoke any lexical entry directly. An example of direct access is going to the correct place in one's own library to find a book, without having to scan the contents of the shelves. Someone who is familiar with a library already knows the locations of many items. In lexical access, the indexing scheme need not necessarily indicate locations, as long as it can indicate a pathway to the meaning of any word in the internal lexicon. Lexical entries can probably be accessed by several different indexing schemes, just as library books can be indexed by author, title, or topic. The lexical index most useful to a reader is orthographic (spelling), consisting of the patterns of letters that constitute the written word. Seeing the written form of a word may allow a reader to directly access its meaning representation in the lexicon. Of course, other indexing schemes for the lexicon are available, such as the one based on the sound of a word.

Direct Access

It is sometimes difficult to conceive of a way that direct access can work. It seems almost magical to be able to find one item in a large set without having to search for it. But the nature of such a process can be clarified by an analogy to a physical system that provides direct access.

Suppose that word meanings were analogous to tuning forks, so that a mental lexicon consisted of a large collection of tuning forks, each sensitive to a different pitch. Suppose further that the encoded representation of a word, the word-percept, was analogous to a tone of a particular pitch. Then the question of direct access could be stated as follows: How can a tone (word-percept) of a given pitch directly activate the corresponding tuning fork (word-concept)? In this case, the answer is straightforward: The tone will produce a vibration in the tuning fork sensitive to the tone's pitch. For example, a tone that has a pitch corresponding to 200 cycles per second (cps) will activate the 200-cps tuning fork, making it vibrate. This phenomenon is called *resonance*. The resonance provides a direct access of the correct tuning fork without any search of any kind through the other tuning forks. Resonance depends on physical oscillation. A more likely basis for direct access in the human mind is that one pattern of activation directly activates another pattern. More precisely, the pattern of activation that represents a word-percept may activate the representation of the corresponding word meaning.

The analogy can be carried a bit further. Suppose that the input to the collection of tuning forks consists not just of one tone but of two tones of two different pitches. The two different tones will combine to create a new pitch (corresponding to what is called the beat frequency). Then, not only will the two tuning forks corresponding to the two parent tones be activated, but the tuning fork corresponding to their offspring pitch will also be activated.

The importance of this analogy extends beyond illuminating direct access. It also illuminates direct access to a single representation that corresponds to the convergence of the several inputs. For example, the encodings of the words *unmarried* and *man* may converge on and activate the concept of a BACHELOR. The analogy can be made more general. There are many instances in language comprehension in which multiple sources of information together specify the appropriate interpretation of a word or phrase or sentence. The mechanism that directly accesses the appropriate interpretation may function analogously to the resonance mechanism. The process of activating an interpretation that is specified by several different knowledge sources (inputs) is called **multiple constraint satisfaction.** Multiple constraint satisfaction can be accomplished by the convergence of activation on a given concept from several sources, as occurs in the READER model.

Normal reading experience provides readers the opportunity to develop links that directly relate written word forms to entries in their mental lexicon, links that the access mechanism can use to activate concepts. For example, students who have been reading for an hour a day from fourth grade to the senior year of high school (200 words per minute, five days a week, nine months a year) will have read over 20,000,000 words. With experience, the encoding of the printed form of a word can produce access of the associated word meaning directly, not by search.

Word-frequency Effects

How quickly a reader can access a word's meaning depends on how frequently he has encountered that word in the past. Words that are used more frequently in the language are processed faster and more accurately than words that occur infrequently, an effect that is known as the **word-frequency effect.** Frequent words are easier to recognize during a very brief presentation (Howes & Solomon, 1951) and take less time to classify as words (Glanzer & Ehrenreich, 1979; Rubenstein, Garfield, & Millikan, 1970). It is clear that the time needed to read and understand a word is related to its normative frequency in the language. To be precise, we should say that this phenomenon refers to the frequencies of word meanings, not the frequencies of the printed string of letters. For example, an ambiguous word like *bill* should be accessed more rapidly when used in its more frequent usage (invoice) than in its less frequent usage (bird beak). But word meanings are hard to count, so out of expediency, most researchers use norms that have counted the frequency of printed words in a large and carefully selected sample of texts (e.g., Kucera & Francis, 1967).

The new results The precise quantitative relationship between a word's frequency and the time it takes to process that word provides an impc .nt clue to the nature of the lexical access process. This relationship was first obser d in our reading experiment (described in Chapter 2 on word perception anc encoding), in which readers' eye fixations were monitored as they read 15 short technical passages from *Newsweek* and *Time* magazines (Just & Carpenter, 1980). One reason that we attach importance to these results is that the task the subjects are performing is as close to normal reading as experimental technology permits. The subjects are not discriminating words from nonwords, nor pressing one of two buttons to indicate the result of their discrimination, as they are in a lexical decision task. They are simply reading a text while their eye fixations are unobtrusively being recorded. Moreover, the natural texts provide a large range of word frequencies and a large number of words (just short of 2,000 words in the 15 passages altogether). Thus, the data reflect the comprehension processes that occur in reading normal text.

The relation between word frequency and the mean gaze duration was derived as follows. First, the data were sorted by word length, separating out the two-letter words, the three-letter words, and so on. Second, within each word length, the words were divided into four groups according to their frequency, producing four frequency quartiles. Third, the mean gaze duration for each quartile was computed. These means are plotted in Figure 3.3 above the mean log frequency for that quartile, using the digit denoting the word length to plot the point. These mean gaze durations were obtained by averaging over nonzero gazes only; if a reader happened not to fixate on a word, then his data did not enter into the calculations for that word. Finally, the best-fitting straight lines through the four points for each word length were computed and plotted in Figure 3.3. Thus, each of the lines in the figure shows the mean gaze durations for words of a given length.

The lines slope downward from left to right, indicating that the gaze durations decrease as the word frequencies increase. This result is independent of word length and applies to all word lengths. For words of a single given length (say, five-letter words), readers spend less time on more frequent words. We have found the same effects of word frequency on gaze duration with other types of passages, such as long narratives from *Reader's Digest* and technical articles from *Scientific American*. (Some of these other results are reported in Chapter 14 on speed reading.)

The results show more than just the fact that gaze durations are shorter on more frequent words. The gaze durations decrease linearly with the logarithm of the normative frequency of the word. That is, small differences in frequency among infrequent words had comparable effects on gaze duration to large differences among frequent words. This relation narrows down the range of possible mechanisms that can be performing the lexical access.

Before describing the mechanism that can produce these results, two comments can be made about the generality of the finding. First, these results general-

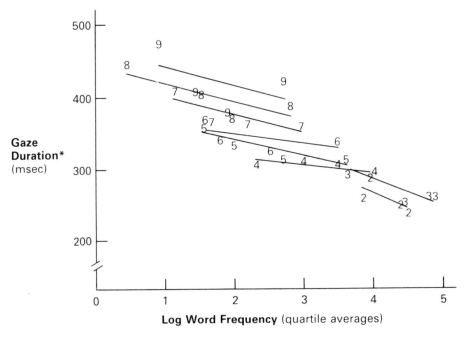

*Gaze duration averaged over fixated words only.

Figure 3.3   The average time a reader spends looking at a word (in milliseconds), as a function of the logarithm of the word's frequency. More frequent words (those with a larger log frequency) are looked at for less time than less frequent words. The eight lines represent words of different lengths—words that are two letters long, three letters long, up to nine letters long. Word frequency has an effect on words of each length. *Source:* Carpenter & Just, 1983, Figure 17.2, p. 288. Used with permission of Academic Press.

ize from our natural texts to experimentally controlled texts. When the frequency of certain target words in a text is systematically varied, keeping constant the word length and the preceding context, readers spend less time looking at the more frequent words (Rayner, 1983). Second, similar results are also found in a **lexical decision task,** a task which is frequently used to study lexical access. In that task, subjects are asked to decide as quickly as possible whether or not a given string of letters forms an English word. For example, they are to respond "yes" to *table*, because it is an English word, and "no" to *mafer*, because it is not. Their response times on "yes" trials serve as an indicator of the time taken to access the word meaning in the internal lexicon. In this task also, the response time decreases with the logarithm of the word's frequency (Gordon, 1985). The replication of our finding in a controlled laboratory task provides converging evidence.

The READER Model's Lexical Access Process

According to the READER model, the representation of each entry in the mental lexicon has a base activation level that is linearly related to the number of times the word has been previously encountered in the reader's lifetime. The base activation level can be thought of as an indicator of strength or availability.

The linear relation postulated between word frequency and activation level has some empirical basis in a study that asked readers to make subjective estimates of word frequencies. In that study, the ratings the subjects produced were linearly related to objective counts of word frequency (see Carroll, 1971; Tryk, 1968). Thus, the subjects' ratings reflected the existence of some internal information that is closely related to what we have called the base activation level.

READER's lexical access process activates the word meanings through direct access, using the written form of the word as an index. More precisely, the encoded perceptual representation of the word, the word-percept, reiteratively produces an increase in the activation level of the corresponding word meaning until that level reaches a fixed threshold. The activation increments occur repeatedly over successive cycles of processing. Consequently, the amount of time needed to accomplish the access depends on how many activation cycles it takes to bring the level to threshold, which, in turn, depends on the base activation level of the word meaning. Infrequently used word meanings with a lower base level of activation require more additional activation (i.e., more activation cycles) to reach a fixed threshold, so they should take more time to reach threshold.

What the model precisely proposes is that the amount by which the activation level is incremented on each cycle is proportional to the current activation level. The relevant production in READER can be stated informally as follows:

If a word-percept has been encoded and the activation level of no corresponding word meaning has reached threshold	→	*Then increase the activation level of the associated word meaning by a fixed proportion of its current level*

This production will fire for however many cycles it takes to bring the activation level of the word's meaning to threshold. The Appendix to this chapter explains how this model predicts that the number of activation cycles (and hence the amount of time) required to bring a word meaning to threshold will decrease linearly with the logarithm of a word meaning's base activation level (frequency).

When the activation level of a word meaning reaches the threshold, the word meaning is said to have been *accessed*. When access occurs in the course of reading, the accessed word meaning becomes the accepted interpretation of the word. A word meaning can be activated above its base level without its reaching threshold if a competing word meaning were to reach the threshold first. This may happen to the unfavored meaning of an ambiguous word.

The theoretical construct of an activation level is useful for characterizing a number of phenomena related to lexical access (Morton, 1969). First, it makes it easy to express how word meanings may have different initial strengths by having the base activation levels correspond to the frequency of previous encounters. Second, it is possible to represent how the availability of a word meaning can be modified temporarily by a local state of knowledge, such as the interpretation of a preceding word. Third, the activation level provides a locus at which different sources of evidence are integrated to converge on a single interpretation. Fourth, it is possible for a word meaning to be activated to a level that is intermediate between its base level and the threshold level, such that it can facilitate the access of a related word meaning without its being accessed itself. Finally, the time course of the change in activation level of a word meaning can be related to the time course of lexical access in human readers.

The discussions above apply to the process by which the encoding of a printed word activates its meaning. In addition to this access route, other processes could produce or contribute to lexical access. One alternative route is through the sound of a word. The printed word can activate the sound of the word, which, in turn, provides direct access to its meaning, a form of speech recoding that is discussed later in the chapter. Other alternative routes include the various levels of processing that operate on the current word, such as the syntactic level or the text level. If one of the other levels generates an expectation of a given word or word meaning, then the activation level of that word meaning will be raised. Similarly, the interpretation of the preceding words of the text can increase the activation level of a particular word meaning, prior to or in addition to the activation initiated by the encoding of the printed word.

Alternative models   Several alternative models of lexical access have been proposed, some of which are summarized by Henderson (1982). Many of these models attribute the frequency effect to a search of a lexicon in which the entries are ordered from most frequent to least frequent. For example, Glanzer and Ehrenreich (1979) propose that word meanings are found by searching through one or both of two lexicons: a small, "vest-pocket" lexicon of the most frequently used word meanings and a large lexicon containing all word meanings. Within both lexicons, meanings are arranged from most to least frequent. The search process finds a more frequent entry sooner because it is closer to the beginning of the set of entries.

Another well-known model of lexical access proposes a hybrid of search and direct access (Forster, 1976). This alternative model proposes that there is a single lexicon that can be accessed through several indexing systems: one based on orthographic (spelling) information, one on phonological (pronunciation) information, and one on syntactic and semantic information. Forster proposes that the indexing systems themselves are searched, but once the desired entry is found in one of the indexing systems, it provides direct access to the associated word meaning in the lexicon proper.

The reason we prefer the direct access model of lexical access is its compatibility with our general theory of comprehension, as well as with the observed properties of gaze durations in reading.

Lexical Decomposition

We have discussed lexical access of a word meaning, but we have also pointed out that word meanings have components, which can be construed as features. Lexical access consists of activating to threshold the top-level node of a word meaning. For example, on reading the word *father*, the top-level node of the corresponding concept would be activated to threshold. Does this access entail that some or all of the meaning components of the word are also activated? For example, does the feature [*+male*] become activated every time we read the word *father*? In this section, we consider when and if the features of the concept are also activated.

Accessing the component features of a word is called **lexical decomposition.** The evidence on whether readers access component features of words has been mixed. In the section below, we first describe the evidence for decomposition and then the evidence against. Finally, we offer a resolution to apparent conflicts in the literature, concluding that decomposition occurs on some occasions; we will describe the factors that govern whether it occurs.

Words whose components are obvious from their orthography A reader becomes most aware of decomposition when he consciously decomposes novel words that are made up of familiar stems and affixes (prefixes or suffixes) to guess at the new word's meaning. For example, most verbs that are preceded by *re* (including *redraw, reconnect,* and *restaple*) are interpreted as a repetition of the action denoted by the verb stem. A skilled reader can guess at the meaning of a new word, such as *resurvey,* by decomposing it and accessing the meaning of the individual components.

Even familiar affixed words (such as *hopeless*) may be decomposed into the constituent **morphemes,** minimal meaningful units (in this case, *hope + less*). One experiment used a lexical decision task to examine whether a word primes its components and vice versa (Stanners, Neiser, & Painton, 1979). It is known that in a lexical decision task, seeing a word (like *walk*) on one trial makes a reader faster to respond when the same word is presented on a later trial. The explanation of this priming effect is that the first presentation of the word activates (primes) the word meaning, and some residual activation increment from the earlier trial facilitates the access when the word is repeated on a later trial. The priming studies show that an inflected word (like *walking*) primes its stem (*walk*) as much as word repetition does. Stems that are presented in the context of other words (like *gress* in *regress*) prime related words (like *progress*) somewhat less. Similarly, there is some facilitation from stems presented alone (*comfort* primes *discomfort, trieve* primes *retrieve*). The fact that components of words prime the parent word to some extent suggests that prefixed words have both a unitary and decomposed representation, both of which can be activated during lexical access.

Some degree of lexical decomposition was also found in a second study that used a lexical decision task (Taft & Forster, 1975). It has been suggested that to access a word, the prefixes are stripped off and the word is accessed by the stem. For example, *rejuvenate* would be accessed by stripping off the *re* and accessing this component and *juvenate* separately:

> *rejuvenate* means: *re + juvenate*

This would be an economical way to store word meanings, since each stem and affix would have to be stored only once. If this hypothesis about storage is correct, then it should be hard to classify a stem such as *juvenate* as a nonword, since it would occur in the lexicon and thus could be lexically accessed. By contrast, some words that superficially look similar to *rejuvenate* cannot be decomposed:

> *repertoire* does not mean: *re + pertoire*

The *re* does not constitute a separate unit of meaning, and *pertoire* is not a true stem but a pseudo stem. Since *pertoire* is not represented in the lexicon, it should be easy to classify as a nonword. As predicted, Taft and Forster (1975) found that stems like *juvenate* took longer to classify as nonwords than pseudo stems like *pertoire*. Furthermore, the subjects in the experiment incorrectly indicated that stems like *juvenate* were words more often than they did pseudo stems like *pertoire* (17 percent errors versus 4 percent errors, respectively). If an inappropriate prefix was added, like *de*, it was still harder to judge the resulting nonword as such if the stem was a true stem. It took almost 100 milliseconds longer to classify stimuli like *dejuvenate* than stimuli like *depertoire*, and the errors were also asymmetrical (19 percent versus 3 percent). In sum, there is some evidence that the stems of words may be used in lexical access.

It initially seems economical to strip off affixes and access words by their stems. But this economy would have to be purchased at the expense of indexing the meanings of some words through relatively meaningless stems. For example, are words like *admit* and *remit* accessed by stripping off the prefix from the stem *mit*? Taft and Forster (1975) circumvented this potential problem by proposing that the economical storage of such stems occurs only in the orthographic index to the lexicon. The index merely points to the node in the semantic network that contains the word meaning. It is only in this index to the lexicon that *remit* and *admit* would share a stem. The lexicon proper is presumed to have separate entries for *admit*, *remit*, *submit*, and similar words.

Compound words   Compound words are another class of words whose components are obvious in their orthography and for which there is evidence of decomposition. To explore decomposition of familar compound words, Taft and Forster (1976) contrasted three possible models:

1. compound words are indexed as whole words;
2. compound words are indexed by their initial constituent (*day* for *daydream*); and
3. compound words are indexed by their final constituent (*dream* for *daydream*).

To test these possible models, Taft and Forster ran a lexical decision experiment that focused on compound nonwords whose initial or final constituent was a real word. As in the previous experiment, it should be hard to classify a string as a nonword if the constituent by which it was accessed occurred in the lexicon. If the initial constituent is used to index the lexicon, it should take longer to classify a nonword that begins with a real word than one that begins with a nonword. So it should take longer to classify *footmilge* than *trowbreak* because *foot* is an entry in the lexicon (according to model 2), and *trow* is not. The response times for various types of compound nonwords (shown in Table 3.2) indicate that the first constituent is particularly important for accessing a compound word in the lexicon. However, the second morpheme has at least some importance, since errors were slightly higher when both morphemes were words (e.g., *dustworth*). Although the task of deciding whether a string of letters is a nonword is not a part of normal comprehension, the results are suggestive of a possible indexing mechanism to the lexicon.

An experiment on reading in Chinese (discussed in Chapter 10) provides additional support for the idea that constituent morphemes of a word are accessed during reading. Chinese words are made of one, two, or three characters, each of which is a morpheme, much like English compounds (such as *taxbreak* or *smoke-*

Table 3.2 Response times to judge four types of compound nonwords

Compound	Response Time (milliseconds)	Description of the Two Components
dustworth	758	word-word
footmilge	765	word-nonword
trowbreak	682	nonword-word
mowdflisk	677	nonword-nonword

Source: Adapted from Taft & Forster, 1976, Table 1, p. 609.

stack) are made of multiple morphemes. If the Chinese internal lexicon is accessed by the component characters, then the gaze duration should be affected principally by the characters' frequency of occurrence. If the lexicon is accessed through the compound, then the gaze duration should be affected principally by the frequency of the compound. The interesting result was that the gaze duration was best predicted by the frequency of the compound, suggesting that word meanings often are accessed as a whole rather than by their individual constituents. But an important additional result was that the gaze duration was also (although to a smaller degree) influenced by the frequency of the component characters, suggesting that some lexical decomposition was also occurring.

Words whose components are not obvious from their orthography   When a reader sees the word *father,* does he access a feature, such as [+ *male*], or does he access only the top-level node of the concept? The answer appears to be that in normal reading, readers tend to access only the top-level node, without accessing all of the subsumed meaning components. That is, on reading a sentence like *Jack was having difficulty with his schoolwork, so he asked his father for help,* the "maleness" of *father* is not particularly salient, so this feature is probably not accessed (not activated to threshold). Consistent with this view, experiments that measure the amount of time needed to read a word have found that it takes no more time to read a word that has a large set of features than one that has a small set (Kintsch, 1974). Of course, a context can focus on a particular feature of a word, such as the following sentence's focus on the maleness of *father: Lucy urgently needed to talk with Ralph, who was in the men's shower room, so she asked her father to fetch him.* In this case, the feature [+ *male*] is probably accessed.

One important component of meaning that is sometimes not obvious from a word's orthography is a negation. Many English words, like *seldom* and *forget,* contain a negation that is not apparent in the spelling. Some comprehension tasks require that the negation be processed. In one such task, readers were asked to verify, as true or false, sentences like:

> *If John forgot to let the dog out, then the dog is out.*

The word-meaning components that are activated when *forgot* is read in this task must include not only the top-level node but also the component indicating the negation of *remembered.* The time needed to process a sentence with *forgot* is longer than the time to process *remembered* and resembles the time needed to process *didn't remember* (Just & Clark, 1973). This result suggests that readers are accessing the negation that *forgot* contains. Similarly, many other words in which the orthography gives no cue to the negation (such as *seldom* and *few*) produce access of that component if the task requires it (Just & Carpenter, 1971).

Another class of meaning components that may be accessed are some of the case roles typically associated with action verbs, such as the agent, object, instrument, and recipient of the action. For example, *gave* is associated with an agent, a recipient, and an object, as in *Kim gave the teaspoon to Mathilda*. It may be that reading an action verb activates the case roles that are typical of that verb. For example, comprehension of the verb *gave* may activate the case roles of agent, recipient, and object. The activation of these meaning components of action verbs may play an important role in the semantic analysis of a clause, which we describe in Chapter 6.

One reading study explicitly examined the activation of the case-role components of verbs that were strongly associated with a particular instrument, as the verb *sweep* is associated with the instrument *broom* (Just & Carpenter, 1978). Readers were given texts that contained a verb with a strong entailment (e.g., *sweep* strongly entails a broom) or a weak entailment (e.g., *clean* weakly entails a broom). One sentence in a short text mentioned one verb or the other, and the next sentence mentioned the instrument. The amount of time spent on reading this next sentence—and in particular, the gaze duration on the instrument (say, *broom*)—was reliably shorter if the preceding sentence contained the verb with the strong instrument entailment (*sweep*, in this case). The likely explanation for this result is that a verb like *sweep* has a component that refers to a likely instrument (*broom*), and that instrument has its activation level raised above its base level, although probably not to threshold, when *sweep* is encountered in the text. Then, when the word *broom* is encountered in the next sentence, it takes less time for its activation level to be brought to threshold by the encoding of the printed word. This account of the result implies that the instrument component of *sweep* is partially activated when *sweep* is encountered, suggesting that decomposition can be partial, rather than all-or-none.

Partial decomposition fits very comfortably into the activation formalism in READER that is used for lexical access. There is reason to believe that some components of meaning are more prominent than others. When a word meaning is activated, its more prominent features may receive subthreshold activation, while its less prominent features may receive little or no activation.

Context and decomposition   Context not only affects the interpretation of words with two or more distinct meanings but also can influence the interpretation of words that are not ambiguous. For example, the context makes different aspects of *piano* or *container* salient in the sentences below:

> *The piano was tuned.*
> *The piano was lifted.*
>
> *The container held the apples.*
> *The container held the cola.*

The context can determine which features are most activated in a given sentence. For example, the most salient feature of a *piano* is that it produces music. But the sentence context with the verb *lifted* causes a normally less important feature

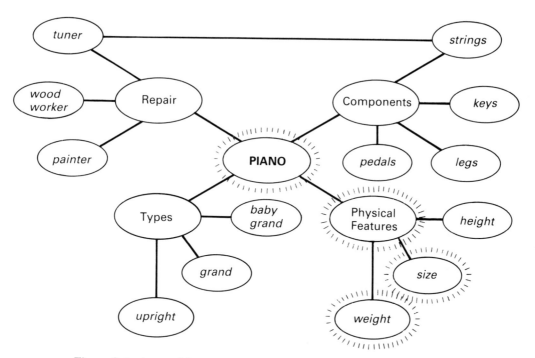

Figure 3.4 A part of the network linked to the concept PIANO, showing the possible activation of related concepts when the text says *The piano was lifted.*

(that it is a large, heavy physical object) to be more activated (see Figure 3.4). In the *container* sentences, the context would favor the interpretation of *container* as a basket in the instance of apples but as a bottle in the instance of cola. These examples indicate the flexibility with which meaning components of a word can be accessed, depending on the context (Anderson & Ortony, 1975; Barclay, Bransford, Franks, McCarrell, & Nitsch, 1974). In sum, the nature of the task, the context, and the word itself determine whether and how much a word's meaning is decomposed.

Individual and developmental differences Children and poor readers take longer to access the meanings of words than do skilled readers (Jackson & McClelland, 1979; Perfetti & Lesgold, 1977). Some theorists believe that the lexical access process is a major source of individual differences in reading comprehension performance. If readers take a long time to access word meanings, then other processes will be allotted less time, and storage limitations may cause the loss of some information from other levels before it can be used. There is fairly convincing evidence that slowness in lexical access is a contributing factor to poor reading comprehension, but the size of the contribution is currently unclear. This issue will be treated in more depth in Chapter 15 on individual differences in reading ability.

Lexical Ambiguity

A *bum bum* is a lousy hobo; a *fast fast* is a quick diet. Obviously, some words have more than one meaning and the appropriate interpretation must be selected, or at least guessed at. A word can have several unrelated meanings (such as the word *bank* meaning either "river's edge" or "financial institution"), which is called *homonymy*. Or it can have related meanings (such as the word *hand* meaning "body part" or "clock part"), which is called *polysemy*.

Accessing Ambiguous Words

While many words have multiple meanings, the reader is seldom aware of the ambiguity, as in the two following sentences:

> *The entire audience rose.*
> *John saw several spiders, roaches, and bugs.*

Although readers aren't conscious of alternative meanings, these sentences contain ambiguous words. *Rose* can mean "flower" instead of "stood," but the syntactic context requires a verb, not a noun. *Bug* can mean "wiretap device" instead of "insect," but the semantic context in the second sentence primes the "insect" interpretation. The findings we will describe below suggest that the multiple meanings of an ambiguous word are initially activated, but only one meaning reaches threshold. Moreover, only that one meaning remains activated after a few hundred milliseconds.

Two experiments used similar methodologies to determine whether the unselected meaning of an ambiguous word is activated during text comprehension (Swinney, 1979; Tanenhaus, Leiman, & Seidenberg, 1979). In these studies, the text comprehension happened to be listening comprehension, but the process of interest is likely to be the same in reading comprehension. While subjects were listening to the text, they occasionally had to process a visually presented, isolated word. Most of the visually presented words were unrelated to the listening text. However, the key experimental results hinge on the processing of a few visually presented words that *were* related to the text. In fact, these related words were close associates of one of the meanings of an ambiguous word in the listening text, and they were visually presented *at the same time* the ambiguous word occurred in the text. The logic behind the experiment is that the processing of the visual word (e.g., *stood*) should be faster if a related meaning of a word from the text (e.g., *rose*) has just been activated. This type of facilitation can be used to determine if a related word meaning has been activated.

In one of the experiments, the subjects were required to pronounce the visually presented word. If the text contained an ambiguous word (*rose*) in a syntactic context that indicated the appropriate interpretation (e.g., *They all rose*), the speed of pronouncing a simultaneous visual probe word related to either meaning (*stood* or *flower*) was faster than in a control condition (Tanenhaus, Leiman, & Seidenberg, 1979). Presumably, both meanings of the ambiguous word had been activated to a degree sufficient to facilitate the reading of the related probe words.

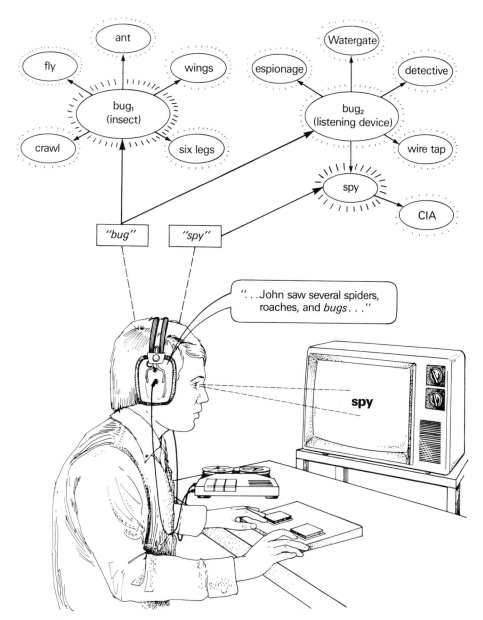

Figure 3.5 The unintended meaning of an ambiguous word *bug* temporarily raises the activation level of related concepts like SPY, making the lexical access of the simultaneously presented word *spy* faster.

In another experiment, the subjects listened to a sentence and simultaneously decided whether a visually presented string of letters was a word; that is, they made a lexical decision about the visually presented string (see Figure 3.5). When the text contained an ambiguous word (*bug*) preceded by a disambiguating context (. . . *John saw several spiders, roaches, and bugs*. . .), the speed of a simultaneous lexical decision related to either meaning (*insect* or *spy*) was faster than in a control condition (Swinney, 1979).

In both studies, the facilitation of the inappropriate meaning (*spy*) was obtained only if the visually presented word occurred within a few hundred milliseconds of the occurrence of the ambiguous auditory word. If the interval between the auditory ambiguous word and the visual probe word was longer than a few hundred milliseconds, the probe related to the inappropriate interpretation (*spy*) was no faster than the control, while the probe related to the appropriate interpretation (*insect*) continued to be facilitated.

These results indicate that both meanings of an ambiguous word are temporarily activated when an ambiguous word is encountered. However, the unselected meaning is deactivated shortly thereafter, and the only interpretation of the sentence that is pursued any further is the one indicated by the selected meaning of the ambiguous word. It is extremely likely that ambiguities at other levels of comprehension besides the lexical level are also handled in this way. That is, multiple interpretations are briefly activated when ambiguities first arise, but the available information is used to select one interpretation above others, and the unselected ones are discarded.

It has been asked whether all the meanings of a word are accessed (multiple access) followed by selection of one meaning that is consistent with the preceding context, or whether the context can cause only one meaning to be accessed (selective access) (Seidenberg, Tanenhaus, Leiman, & Bienkowski, 1982). Researchers who ask this question adopt the view that word meanings must be in one of two states, *dormant* or *accessed*. We propose a third state, in which the meanings of a word have their activation levels raised temporarily and, while in that state, can facilitate the processing of related meanings. However, the activation level of only one of the meanings will reach threshold first and become accessed. Many of the studies cited above show that meanings besides the one favored by the context temporarily enter a different state, such that they can facilitate the processing of words related to the unfavored meaning (Seidenberg, Tanenhaus, Leiman, & Bienkowski, 1982; Swinney, 1979; Tanenhaus, Leiman, & Seidenberg, 1979). Moreover, the degree to which the unselected meanings are activated depends on the nature and strength of the preceding context (Carpenter & Daneman, 1981; Seidenberg, Tanenhaus, Leiman, & Bienkowski, 1982).

The temporary activation of unfavored meanings appears to last a very short time—at most, a few hundred milliseconds (Seidenberg, Tanenhaus, Leiman, & Bienkowski, 1982; Swinney, 1979; Tanenhaus, Leiman, & Seidenberg, 1979). Moreover, readers usually seem to be unaware of the multiple meanings of a word if the preceding context clearly favors one meaning. The activation level of the accessed (selected) meaning remains at threshold at least until it has been integrated with the representation of the sentence.

In the READER model, the activation levels of unfavored meanings are reduced to their base levels before the next word is read. This way of dealing with lexical ambiguity avoids the memory-load problem and computational explosion that would result if a reader kept track of several possible meanings, semantic roles, and referents for each ambiguous word and computed the final interpretation at the end of a clause or sentence. Getting rid of the unselected interpretations this quickly allows a limited capacity processor to operate on a large semantic network without being bombarded by irrelevant associations. This minimizes the chances that the reader will be conceptually driven in many directions at the same time.

The cost of rapidly deactivating the rejected interpretations of a word is fairly low because the word meaning that is selected is usually the correct one. The selection process is effective because it takes a large amount of relevant information into account. First, many levels of analysis (including lexical, semantic, syntactic, and discourse) can contribute to the selection process. Second, the relative frequencies of different word meanings (based on past experience in the language and indexed by the base activation levels) create a bias in favor of more frequent interpretations. The first and second factors can collaborate to choose an interpretation. A third reason that the cost of choosing just one interpretation is low is that the reader can recover from errors—that is, choosing the wrong interpretation. It would be devastating if there were no way to modify an incorrect interpretation at some later point. However, there are error-recovery heuristics that seem fairly efficient, although the precise mechanisms are only now being explored (Carpenter & Daneman, 1981).

Influence of Context and Frequency on Disambiguation

The outcome of the lexical access process is dependent on both the frequency of a word meaning and on the preceding context. One of our eye-fixation studies examined how these factors determine which meaning is chosen as the interpretation of an ambiguous word (Carpenter & Daneman, 1981). We developed "garden-path" passages, using ambiguous words such as *sewer, tears,* and *wind,* and had 20 college students read them aloud while we monitored their eye fixations. One such passage was the following:

> *The young man turned his back on the rock concert stage and looked across the resort lake. Tomorrow was the annual, one-day fishing contest, and fishermen would invade the place. Some of the best bass guitarists in the country would come to this spot. The usual routine of the fishing resort would be disrupted by the festivities.*

If asked to read this passage aloud, most people initially pronounce the word *bass* in the third line of the text to rhyme with *lass;* that is, they interpret *bass* to mean "fish," the meaning primed by the earlier references to fishing. The "fish" interpretation turns out to be inconsistent with the subsequent disambiguating word, *guitarists,* but detection and repair of the inconsistency is not our focus here. Instead, we will decribe how the context and relative frequency of a meaning interact to produce the access of one meaning of an ambiguous word.

If a word has more than one meaning, then more than one candidate interpretation may receive at least some activation. How soon a given interpretation of a word reaches threshold depends in part on the relative frequency (and hence the base activation level) of each meaning. The meaning whose activation level is the first to reach threshold becomes the accepted interpretation. The effect of relative frequency can be very large if one meaning is very common and the other, very uncommon, as in the following sentences:

> *There is also one sewer near our house who makes beautiful suits.*
> *John asked, "Does are in the park, aren't they?"*

In both examples, one meaning is extremely infrequent compared to the other. "Tailor" is an infrequent interpretation of *sewer* and "deer" is an infrequent interpretation of *does*. Readers tend to produce the more frequent interpretation initially. However, these common meanings just happen to be incorrect in these sentences.

The other major determinant of which meaning will be selected is the prior context, which includes information from the preceding portions of text and previous knowledge about the topic. For example, the context in the sample paragraph above includes references to fishermen and a fishing resort. These references help to activate the FISH concept to some degree before the word *bass* is fixated.

While readers generally chose the meaning that was consistent with the preceding context, the relative frequency of the two meanings also had an influence. It was possible to tell which interpretation readers chose because they were reading aloud, and the two interpretations had different pronunciations. In paragraphs that primed the very infrequent meaning of a word like *sewer*, readers chose that infrequent meaning only 5 percent of the time, in spite of the priming context. By contrast, in paragraphs that primed the moderate or high frequency meaning of a word, readers chose that frequent meaning 80 percent of the time. The fact that the very infrequent meanings are seldom chosen reflects the strong bias that readers have towards common meanings; even context effects cannot entirely overcome this bias. This result suggests that the amount of influence that the context has on the selection of a given meaning depends on the relative frequency of that meaning. If the two meanings have similar frequencies, both meanings may be activated to a high but still subthreshold level, with context selecting the more appropriate one by augmenting its activation level (Swinney, 1979). But the disadvantage of a meaning with a very low relative frequency may be so great that it cannot be overcome by a preceding context unless that context is extremely constraining.

The amount of time readers take to encode, access, and integrate the ambiguous word is less if the accessed meaning has a high frequency and matches the preceding context. The gaze durations on the ambiguous word were reliably shorter in such cases. When the influences of context and relative frequency converge on the same interpretation, they bring one interpretation to threshold faster than when the two influences compete.

Puns A *pun* is a form of verbal humor (sometimes unappreciated) in which readers and listeners make more than one interpretation of an ambiguous word. Speakers of an intentional pun often must give their listeners a special cue—they wink or pause or say the sentence with emphasis or unusual intonation—because accepting two interpretations is not a normal comprehension strategy.

Puns are probably noticed less often in reading. To make a pun work, many factors have to contribute. The supposedly unintended meaning of the word must have some minimum relative frequency, and the context evoking the unintended meaning must be very strong. Several examples below come from a study that manipulated the strength of the context that primed the intended or unintended meaning (Reder, 1983):

1. *The smoker, who replaced his tobacco pouch, lit his pipe.*
2. *The smoker, who observed birds, lit his pipe.*
3. *The groom, who replaced his tobacco pouch, lit his pipe.*
4. *The groom, who took the message, lit his pipe.*
5. *The plumber, who repaired the sewer, lit his pipe.*

In all cases, the final verb phrase completely determined the appropriate interpretation of the ambiguous word at the end of the sentence, like *pipe*. This appropriate interpretation could be primed by both the initial noun phrase in the sentence and the relative clause (as in example 1), or by only the noun phrase (example 2), only the relative clause (example 3), or neither (example 4). Example 5 is the punniest. Both the noun phrase and the relative clause prime the inappropriate interpretation of *pipe*, maximizing the probability that the pun will be noticed. In general, sentences in which all the evidence points in the same direction (example 1) were comprehended fastest. The results are entirely consistent with the READER lexical access model that predicts that integration of convergent information from several sources will speed access.

Writers whose major goal is to communicate information with maximum efficiency try to avoid puns and avoid using the same word in two different senses in the same text. For example, in a text on syntactic processes, it would be unfortunate to describe how *subjects process subjects*, where the initial *subjects* refers to readers and the second *subjects* refers to a linguistic category. Good technical writers generally minimize lexical ambiguity.

Heuristics for Disambiguating Words

It is possible to construct a list of heuristics to help choose the appropriate sense of an ambiguous word. Hayes (1977) provided such a list used by a computer program that understands English, and it is plausible that some of these heuristics are also used by human readers.

1. Choose the most common sense of a word.

This heuristic is used by human readers, as we know from the *sewer* study described above. If subjects are asked to pronounce a word that has two different pronunciations for its two senses, then their pronunciation is usually of the more frequent sense. It is likely that the proportion of subjects that choose a given pronunciation is monotonically related to the relative frequency of the sense of that pronunciation. Even if an ambiguous word has only one pronunciation, it is still likely that the most frequent sense is favored. For example, *man* is more likely to mean "adult human male" than "checker piece."

2. Use information about the arguments a verb takes to select the appropriate sense of a noun.

For example, some verbs, such as *hit* and *burn*, require physical objects as recipients of the action. Thus, the word *ball* in *John hit the ball* means "spherical toy" rather than "formal dance."

3. Consider a word sense that is most closely associated with the other word senses in the surrounding context.

For example, *John went to withdraw some money from the bank* suggests that *bank* means "financial institution" rather than "river's edge," and this suggestion comes partially from the association with *money.*

4. Use knowledge of superset-subset and whole-part relations to choose the sense of a word.

Although the word *hand* has many senses, in the context of a clock, it tends to refer to a particular part of the timepiece. The interpretation of names for body parts is often clarified by considering the whole-part relation in which they participate.

5. Use knowledge of the referential situation to rule out certain senses of a word.

For example, suppose Bill is at work and a letter he had received the day before is at home. In this situation, *The letter touched Bill* cannot mean that there was physical contact between the letter and Bill.

Children's processing of lexical ambiguity   Children are less aware of ambiguity, at least as judged by their ability to talk about it. In one study, six-year-old children were asked why homonyms were related (Asch & Nerlove, 1960). For example, they were asked why *ring* was used as the name for a piece of jewelry and also for the sound of a telephone. Most children denied that there was any relation between the words; only one child proposed that the similarity was in the shared name. This lack of awareness of ambiguity at the conscious level may have a counterpart in children's processing of ambiguity—namely, that they may be unable to recover from interpretation errors caused by lexical ambiguity. When second-grade children read garden-path sentences containing ambiguous words, they seemed unaware of and untroubled by the inconsistency of their interpretation (Daneman & Carpenter, 1983a). Their obliviousness to ambiguity may explain why they don't cope with difficulties that can be corrected only by dealing with the ambiguity.

Context Effects

It is easier to understand a word in context than in isolation. Although this effect has been produced countless times in experimental tasks, it has not been simple to produce in normal reading, nor is it obvious what mechanism would be responsible. But it is important not to lump all context effects together. There are different kinds of contexts (sentences, words, and letters) that can influence the processing of various units of text (sentences, words, and letters) at various levels (word encoding, lexical access, and syntactic analysis).

In this section, we will focus on the context effect in which one or more context words influence the lexical access of a word that follows. But the context may have effects on other processes—the encoding of the word or its semantic, syntactic, referential, or text-level analysis. Many experimental demonstrations of context effects fail to localize which process or processes are the site of the facilitation.

Properties of Context Effects

Several paradigms have found that context can speed the processing of a word. Some of the important characteristics concerning the speed and scope of context effects have been explored with a task that involves listening rather than reading. This task, the **phoneme-monitoring task,** developed by Foss (1970) and his colleagues, allows context effects on a critical word to be monitored. Subjects listen to a sentence while monitoring for a word that begins with a given phoneme (say, /p/); they press a response button as soon they hear the phoneme. The response latency to the phoneme has been shown to be longer when the processing load due to comprehending the sentence is heavier, presumably because of competition between the comprehension processes and the phoneme-monitoring processes.

To study the effects of context, one can examine the monitoring latency for a phoneme that occurs just after a word that was preceded by a facilitating or neutral context. For example, Blank and Foss (1978) wanted to measure the relative difficulty of processing the word *eye,* depending on whether it had been preceded by a neutral or semantically related context:

Neutral: *The drunk scratched his aching eye probably without even knowing it.*

Related: *The drunk winked his bloodshot eye probably without even knowing it.*

Since *eye* should be easier to process when preceded by a related context, the /p/ in *probably* should be processed faster in the Related context, as the results of the study showed. So a related context consisting of a sentence fragment does appear to facilitate the processing of a given word during listening comprehension.

An important characteristic of the context effect is that the facilitation is due to more than just the occurrence of related words. The words must be arranged in the appropriate configuration. Consider a scrambled version of the related sentence:

Winked his the drunk bloodshot eye probably it without knowing even.

This version did not facilitate processing the target word, even though the related context still preceded the target (Foss, 1982). So the mere presence of associated words is not sufficient for facilitating the access of *eye* in this task. Some higher-order organizational principle besides simple association must govern this type of facilitation.

Several qualifications must be made before conclusions from phoneme-monitoring studies can be generalized to normal reading. First, the phoneme-monitoring latency on the word following the critical word is a fairly indirect indicator of processing ease. Second, the effect may not be due to the facilitation of lexical access but to the facilitation of some other process. And third, the time parameters underlying listening processes may not be identical to those in reading comprehension. Nevertheless, because these studies focus on temporal aspects of context effects in the comprehension of continuous prose, we will refer to them, with caution, when they provide relevant information.

Time Course of Context Effects

How far does the effect of context extend? In studies using the phoneme-monitoring task, it has been found that the contextual facilitation produced by a given word extends considerably beyond the next few words of the text (Foss, 1982). In the following example, the experiment examined whether the processing of the critical word *fish*—and hence the detection of the target phoneme /k/ in *caught*—was facilitated by a related word that had occurred far back in the text.

Near: *The entire group examined the* [RELATED:gills/NEUTRAL:spots] *of the fish caught...*

Far: *The entire group examined the* [RELATED:gills/NEUTRAL:spots] *with amazement. Everyone agreed that this was unlike any other fish caught...*

The experiment systematically varied the distance between the related context word and the critical word. In the Near condition, an average of 1.5 words intervened between the related word (*gills*) and the critical word (*fish*), while in the Far condition, an average of 12 words intervened. To provide a control condition against which to assess the degree of facilitation (speed-up in responding to the /k/ in *caught*) in the RELATED conditions, the experiment contained a NEUTRAL condition in which an unrelated word (*spots*) replaced the related context word. The result obtained in this study was that the facilitation was similar regardless of whether the critical word was Near or Far from the related context. This result suggests that as a person listens to a passage, the concepts related to the topic have their activation levels raised and remain raised as long as the local topic doesn't change. In this view, the contextual facilitation provided by the topic may last as long as the topic remains the same.

A lexical decision experiment supports the conclusion that once a text introduces a particular topic, the lexical access of topically related words is facilitated (Sharkey & Mitchell, 1985). In this study, the subjects read a brief story and immediately afterward performed a lexical decision task. For example, one of the stories concerned a child's birthday party:

> *The children's birthday party was going quite well. They all sat around the table prepared to sing.*

The reading of the passage was followed by the presentation of a string of letters that formed either a word related to the topic (e.g., *candles*), an unrelated word (e.g., *rabbits*), or a nonword (e.g., *banfers*). The response time was faster (by 34 milliseconds, in this case) to a topically related word like *candles* than to an unrelated word like *rabbits*. The explanation of the result is that a text about a child's birthday party activates the reader's knowledge of this familiar event. (Chapter 8 on extended texts describes this type of knowledge of familiar events as a particular kind of schema, called a *script*.) The activated knowledge includes some of the related concepts like CANDLES. The activation of the CANDLES concept above its base level then facilitates the lexical access. This account is similar to the one given for the Carpenter and Daneman (1981) experiment, described earlier in this chapter, in which a text about a fishing resort facilitated the "fish" interpretation of the ambiguous word *bass*.

The Sharkey and Mitchell (1985) study also showed that the facilitative effect of a familiar topic persisted as long as no new topic clearly displaced it. In the example above, the facilitation for accessing *candles* was still obtained even if the first two sentences of the text were followed by two neutral sentences that followed coherently but did not pertain to birthday parties. The facilitation disappeared only if the first two sentences were followed by three others that clearly established a new topic. Thus, it appears that lexical access may be facilitated for the words related to a familiar topic as long as the text does not introduce another topic.

Can one word affect the processing of the next? In a phoneme-monitoring task, a predictive adjective like *juvenile* can facilitate the processing of the very next word, such as *delinquent* (Foss & Ross, 1983). Consider the following sentence:

> *In a moment of helplessness, the* [   ] *delinquent contemplated suicide.*

The time to respond to the target phoneme (the /k/ in *contemplated*) was decreased when *delinquent* was preceded by *juvenile*, relative to a condition in which there was no adjective at all and relative to a condition in which the adjective was fairly neutral (*hostile*). This result shows that under some circumstances, the context effect in listening comprehension is fast enough (i.e., the activation is directed to the critical word soon enough) to affect the very next word.

The evidence concerning the time course of context effects in reading is mixed. One study that explicitly looked for context effects on adjacent words found only weak evidence. The reading task involved predictable adjective-noun phrases like *buttered popcorn* in the context of a description of a movie theater, compared to *adequate popcorn*. Once *buttered* is fixated and understood, can the concept corresponding to *popcorn* be activated soon enough to facilitate the processing of the very next word, namely, *popcorn*? McConkie and Zola (1981) reported that the duration of eye fixations on the noun in such adjective-noun phrases was only slightly shorter (14 milliseconds) when it was preceded by a highly predictive adjective, and the effect was only marginally reliable. So it is not clear whether the activation that begins to emanate during the processing of a given word in a passage can have its effect soon enough to provide a facilitative effect for the very next word of the passage.

The process most likely responsible for the facilitation effect in both the phoneme-monitoring task and the eye-fixation study is lexical access. However, neither experiment completely eliminates the possibility that the effect is partially or entirely due to other processes, such as those that do the word encoding or the semantic or syntactic analysis.

When does context influence reading? There are two main cases in which a preceding context pays a particularly large role in lexical access. One case occurs when the reader cannot rely on the text, perhaps because it is physically degraded. For instance, if part of a written text becomes somewhat illegible, a reader would be particularly likely to use the surrounding context to interpret that part. In fact, experimental studies show that context effects on the reading of a word are larger (more facilitating) if the text is somewhat degraded (Stanovich & West, 1979). Similarly, readers who are poor at encoding might have a somewhat "degraded" representation of the words, and they, too, show greater facilitation effects of context (Perfetti, Goldman, & Hogaboam, 1979). So context might contribute most to comprehension when the text is of poor physical quality, when the reading conditions (e.g., illumination) are poor, or when the reader's encoding skill is poor.

Two Types of Activation

Some time ago, Posner and Snyder (1975) suggested that there might be two types of activation: one that is fast and automatic and another that is slow and deliberate. We will describe some of the characteristics of each type and consider the possible role each plays in reading.

Automatic activation   Much of the research on automatic activation of concepts has used variants of the lexical decision task. For example, on each trial, subjects can be simultaneously presented with two letter strings to classify instead of one. On those trials in which both strings are words, response times are faster if the two words are related to each other. For instance, subjects are faster (by 30 to 100 milliseconds) to determine that both *doctor* and *nurse* are words than to determine that both *butter* and *nurse* are words (Meyer & Schvaneveldt, 1971). The usual explanation of this result is that the lexical access triggered by the word *doctor* activates not only the concept DOCTOR but also some related concepts, like STETHOSCOPE, MEDICINE, and NURSE. This activation of the related concepts temporarily raises their activation level above its base level, so when the word *nurse* follows, it will take less time than usual for the activation level to reach threshold because of its head start.

Several other properties of automatic activation also have been proposed or confirmed. Automatic activation appears to occur rapidly, such that the activation level of the related concept (like NURSE) is raised within 100 milliseconds of accessing the first concept (DOCTOR). Furthermore, automatic activation is presumed to have no inhibitory effects on the access of unrelated concepts. Thus, the processing of *doctor* does not inhibit the subsequent access of an unrelated word like *bread*. Finally, automatic activation is supposed to be unaffected by a subject's intentions or strategies. The word *doctor* will activate the concept of NURSE regardless of what the subject is trying to do.

Conscious prediction   The second type of activation occurs when a person deliberately tries to predict what word will come next in a sentence. Many of the experiments that examine this type of activation present a sentence, minus its final word, for a few seconds or for as long as the subject wants to look at it; then a final word is presented. In this situation, the subject has ample time to consciously predict the final word, and there is facilitation when the subject's guess matches the presented word. Some experiments measure the time a reader then takes to pronounce the presented word, while other experiments measure the time a reader takes to make a lexical decision about the presented word or nonword. For example, a subject might be presented with: *The detective patiently investigated the. . .* Then, after a few seconds, the word *murder* might be presented, with the subject either pronouncing it or deciding whether it is an English word. The processing of the final word is usually faster than in a control condition in which there is no sentence context or in which the sentence context is neutral (Stanovich & West, 1981). Also, the processing time (making a lexical decision) is shorter if the final word is very predictable, e.g., *She winked her* ------ *eye* (Fischler & Bloom, 1979). These studies do demonstrate context effects, but the tasks are different from reading.

Several other characteristics have been attributed to the deliberate activation process that requires attention. The deliberate activation process is slow and effortful, requiring several hundred milliseconds to activate predicted concepts. In the experiments in which a sentence context facilitates the processing of the final word in a sentence, the sentence context is presented far in advance of the test word, providing considerably more time than would be required for a rapid reading of the sentence. Second, the deliberate activation process inhibits the processing of an unpredicted word. If the sentence context *The detective patiently investigated the...* were followed by the word *cloud,* the time to pronounce *cloud* would be increased, compared to a control condition. Finally, the deliberate activation process is presumed to be under the subject's strategic control.

Much of the research on how sentence context affects the processing of the final word in the sentence has focused on the inhibitory context effects—taking longer on an unexpected word than on a neutral word. These experiments indicate that a context sentence slows down the processing of the entire set of words that could not reasonably complete the sentence and that the process that causes the inhibition has properties of both the automatic and attentional mechanisms, blurring the distinction between them (Fischler & Bloom, 1979). So although the distinction between automatic and attentional context effects (as described by Posner and Snyder, 1975) is intuitively appealing and has received extensive empirical support in lexical decision tasks (Neely, 1977), it is premature to assume that these mechanisms operate precisely the same way in reading as they do in a lexical decision task.

Two activation mechanisms in reading   We can speculate about the functioning of the two types of activation mechanisms in reading. The fast automatic activation could occur in all reading situations. One would expect the automatic activation mechanism to be fast enough for one word in a text to facilitate the very next one, and there is some tentative data described earlier in the chapter to suggest that this does occur. The phoneme-monitoring results, also cited earlier, indicate that one word can facilitate the very next word in listening comprehension.

The automatic activation might be initiated not just by the individual words of a text but also by the knowledge of the text topic and knowledge of the world. Thus, this automatic activation could account for the facilitated access of a word that is related to the text topic, as described previously in the chapter. This process involves no prediction, just prior association among concepts in the reader's knowledge of the language, knowledge of the world, and knowledge of the preceding portions of the text. The automatically directed activation would temporarily raise the activation level of the affected concepts, thereby making it easier for them to reach the threshold level with the help of some additional source of information, like the encoding of a printed word.

The conscious attentional mechanism might come into play only under strategic control. Certain texts invite mental elaboration, or extensive drawing of inferences, or explicit predictions. For example, a detailed description of a physical object (such as a house) might invite the reader to embellish his representation of it, mentally filling in the parts that weren't explicitly described. Certain genres of mystery stories invite the reader to guess the perpetrator of a crime explicitly. And some texts are more predictable than others, so the usefulness of deliberately generating predictions might vary from one to the next. There may also be individual differences among readers in their inclination to engage in such prediction. Moreover, the same reader may have different goals at different times, which would govern the amounts or types of prediction.

Finally, the two types of activation might play different roles in reading. Automatic activation seems to be an inherent part of reading, part of the collaborative processing of information from different sources. By contrast, deliberate prediction is a reading strategy that permits the reader to explore the implications of a text beyond the literal bounds of the words and sentences it contains. Moreover, a reader can use the accuracy of his predictions as a gauge of his understanding of the text. If many of the predictions are incorrect, it could be a sign that the reader does not have a good grasp of the text or that the text is a perverse one. What the two types of activation have in common is their provision of a mechanism for finding relations among concepts in a knowledge network.

Activation of related words and concepts as one reads along can be distinguished from proposals made in the 1960s and 1970s that suggested readers used their knowledge of the context to actually predict what word would occur next in the text (Goodman, 1967; Hochberg, 1970; Neisser, 1967; Smith, 1971). According to some of these theories, reading consisted of prediction making followed by an eye fixation to some upcoming word to confirm or disconfirm the prediction. Roughly speaking, these theories proposed that a reader could figure out what a text was saying, predict what it would say next, and fixate a word here or there to keep the predictions on track. This form of reading is called *top-down* because the comprehension is guided primarily by higher-level conceptual processes rather than lower-level processes that encode the words of the text.

It is clear that extreme forms of top-down theories are not correct. Readers show no evidence of making explicit guesses about upcoming words (Stanovich & West, 1983). In fact, readers are not accurate when asked to explicitly guess the next content word in a text that is written at an appropriate level of difficulty. In addition, explicit guesses take considerable time to formulate, and the time factor makes it unlikely that such guesses are routinely made during reading.

In the READER model, the topic and the linguistic context can activate related concepts. However, READER differs in two important ways from the top-down theories described above. First, the activation level of related words and concepts is seldom increased all the way to the threshold level solely on the basis of context. Second, in the READER model, the activated concepts need not be lexical concepts or words; rather, the context may activate more abstract concepts, such as an entire schema. Then, if the reader encodes specific words and phrases that are compatible with the partially activated concepts, the lexical access of the facilitated concept will reach threshold faster.

Speech Codes in Silent Reading

T. G. R. Bower, a Scottish psychologist, once wrote an article arguing that reading does not require a speech code (1970). In a commentary on the article, Roger Brown (1970) remarked, "As I read these sentences they came to me in Bower's familiar Scots accent and that seemed quite a thing for the eye alone to have accomplished" (1970, p. 178).

Brown's experience is not unusual. Many readers report hearing an inner voice while reading. In addition, some readers occasionally move their lips while reading a particularly difficult passage. And even adults sometimes sound out new words, just as they did when they were first learning to read. All of these phenomena, as well as a number of research results, indicate that processes related to the sounds of words do operate (at least on some occasions) during silent reading.

We will refer to the representation of the sounds of words generated during silent reading as the **speech code,** although it is also called the *phonological code.* The process of converting a visually based representation into a speech code will be called **speech recoding.** The speech code contains the information necessary to judge whether or not two words rhyme. There are several different aspects of the sounds of words that could be represented by the speech code. It is not important for our purposes to distinguish among them; however, we will briefly mention some of the alternatives. The code could be based on how speech is spoken or, alternatively, on how it is perceived. In addition, the code could be based on a surface representation of the speech sounds (so that *know* and *no* would have identical representations), or it could be based on a representation at a deeper level than just the sounds, one related to the meaning (so that the representation of *know* would indicate its relation to the word *knowledge* and it would be unlike the representation for *no*).

Understanding the role of the speech code in silent reading is important for several reasons. First, it would explain why readers experience the inner voice. Second, the speech code may play a role in the comprehension of even skilled readers. Third, the speech code may help a reader (particularly an unskilled or beginning reader) recognize an unfamiliar word by accessing its meaning through its sound. More generally, if print were first recoded into the same representation as speech, then listening comprehension processes could operate in reading. This is a tempting way to think about beginning reading, since children know spoken language before they know how to read. So using a speech code could be a step in learning how to read.

Two ways to generate the speech code   One way to generate a speech code is directly from the print, using spelling-to-sound rules. For example, the letters for *sat* could be converted into the corresponding phonemes, until the speech code for the entire word is generated (Coltheart, 1978). It is this pathway that is used to sound out unfamiliar words, and the speech code could then be used to access a word's meaning. Thus, the code is generated independently of lexical access and probably before lexical access, so we will call it a **prelexical** speech code. Such codes may be particularly important for beginning readers and unskilled readers, but we will argue that they are seldom activated to threshold during skilled reading. In the

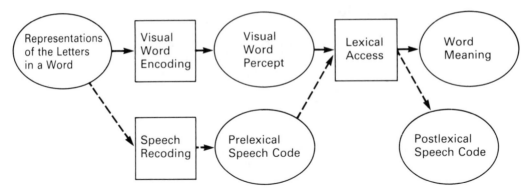

Figure 3.6 How the two kinds of speech codes are related to the lexical access process. The rectangles depict processes and the ovals depict representations. The processes and representations in the upper part of the chart, linked by solid lines, indicate the normal flow of processing. The processes and representations related to speech recoding, shown in the lower part of the chart and linked by dashed lines, indicate the two pathways along which speech codes can be generated.

flowchart in Figure 3.6, the pathway to lexical access that is mediated by the prelexical speech code is shown with dashed arrows.

A second way a speech code is generated is as a result of lexical access. The pronunciation of a word is linked to its lexical entry in the mental lexicon, along with information about a word's semantic features, its relations to other concepts, its syntactic properties, and so on. During lexical access, when various components of the lexical entry for a word are activated, the speech code is sometimes also activated to threshold. A speech code that is generated in this way, as a byproduct of lexical access, will be called a **postlexical** speech code. Figure 3.6 illustrates only the lexical input to the postlexical speech code, but other inputs are also likely. A postlexical speech code may help the reader remember more of the text's wording; thus, it could be particularly useful if the reader needed to interrelate information from different parts of a text.

Prelexical Speech Codes

Sounding out words is an instance of generating a prelexical speech code. Many children sound out unfamiliar words, either aloud or silently, when they are learning to read. And most skilled readers also occasionally sound out unfamiliar words while reading. Some experimental tasks may also foster prelexical speech codes, even with fluent readers (Meyer, Schvaneveldt, & Ruddy, 1974). But are prelexical speech codes routinely generated during skilled silent reading?

Our general conclusion is that even skilled readers activate prelexical speech codes to some degree, concurrently with the direct, visually based lexical access described earlier in the chapter. According to this view, the prelexical speech code is an alternate, concurrent pathway to lexical access (see Jorm & Share, 1983; McCusker, Hillinger, & Bias, 1981). However, it is a slower and less reliable pathway, so the visually based lexical access usually occurs long before the speech-based access. Consequently, the prelexical speech code seldom has an opportunity to manifest itself. But the prelexical code may often be at least partially activated, and in some circumstances, the use of the code is apparent.

The mechanisms within the READER model make it very easy to describe the activation of a prelexical speech code. Chapter 2 on word encoding describes how the letters of a word initiate the activation of the corresponding visual word-percept, and this chapter has described how the word-percept initiates the activation of the word's meaning, producing lexical access. When the letters of the word initiate the visually-based lexical access, they simultaneously initiate the activation of the prelexical speech code. The prelexical speech code, like the visual word-percept, initiates the activation of the word's meaning. Thus, there are two concurrent attempts at lexical access, one visually based and one speech based. However, the visually-based lexical access usually reaches threshold long before the slow and unreliable speech-based pathway can effect a lexical access. So the speech-based prelexical code is usually abandoned after having its activation level raised above its base level but before reaching the threshold activation level. This account is consistent with the finding that readers can access the meaning of a familiar word using the visual route with little evidence of speech recoding (Banks, Oka, & Shugarman, 1981; McCusker, Hillinger, & Bias, 1981). The account is also consistent with several studies that cause the prelexical code to emerge under certain circumstances (Coltheart, 1978; Doctor & Coltheart, 1980), as described below.

One reason that the prelexical speech code is unreliable and slow is that the English spelling-to-sound relations needed to generate the speech code are so complex. There is no simple algorithm to translate letters or letter groups accurately into sounds. Anyone who has listened to a child try to sound out a word, letter by letter, is aware that the process can be slow and error prone. One source of difficulty is that the more frequently used words in English are the very ones that often have irregular spelling-to-sound correspondences. Very frequently used words are often pronounced differently than slightly less common words; compare *have, come,* and *give* to the similarly spelled counterparts *gave, dome,* and *hive.* Even greater complexities arise in describing the pronunciation of letters in words that have multiple syllables and multiple morphemes. The pronunciation can vary, depending on several linguistic factors, such as the part of speech (as in the difference between *to refuse* and *the refuse*) or the syllable boundary (as in the difference between the *th* in *fathead* and *father*) (Venezky, 1970). Generating an accurate speech code from the sounds of the individual letters of a word is not a simple matter; this process will be discussed in Chapter 10 on orthography.

A more plausible way to generate a prelexical speech code is not to restrict the code to individual letters and their sounds but instead to allow groups of letters to activate their speech-based counterparts, as well. Several levels of speech codes could be activated by a printed word: codes associated with individual letters and letter pairs, with consonant clusters, with syllables, and with morphemes. A word like *hive* would activate speech codes associated with the individual letters *h*, the long *i*, and *v;* in addition, it would activate speech codes associated with the subword unit *ive*. A second assumption is that not all speech codes would receive equal activation. Those codes that are most often associated with a pattern would receive the strongest activation. Consequently, because of practice, even exception words would activate the correct pronunciation to threshold ahead of any of the incorrect pronunciations, even though the incorrect pronunciations would be activated to some degree (Glushko, 1979). A multiunit activation process makes the prelexical speech code a more plausible route, but it does so at the expense of moving in the direction of a visually based code. In order to activate the speech code for a unit as large as a syllable, a reader must have directly stored its sound. If the units of the prelexical speech code start to resemble lexical units, then the prelexical code becomes a lexical code.

Prelexical speech codes are particularly important for beginning readers. These readers are sometimes explicitly taught to sound out words by recoding letters and letter groups into sounds. Even if they are not explicitly taught, early readers induce the sounds of particular letters. More generally, it is the beginning reader's processes that seem to be most appropriately described as speech recoding. Particularly in instructional programs that stress symbol-sound correspondences, children can be seen actively segmenting words into units, retrieving their pronunciations, blending the sounds, and then recognizing the meaning of the spoken word.

The speech-recoding process provides a fallback routine for learning new words and checking the accuracy of the visual word-recognition process (Jorm & Share, 1983). In addition, the speech-recoding process itself may help readers develop the direct link between a printed word and its meaning by repeatedly providing the indirect, speech-mediated link. The direct links develop rapidly; even at the very beginning of reading instruction, children can access word meanings directly through the visually based pathway, at least for highly familiar, concrete words (Barron & Baron, 1977). So the prelexical speech codes become superfluous in reading acquisition as the sight of the printed word becomes more familiar.

In most skilled reading, the visually based pathway to meaning dominates over the prelexical speech code, since skilled readers are familiar with most of the words they are reading. But correspondingly, the prelexical route would play a role if a text contained many words whose visual form was unfamiliar. Other tasks that favor the prelexical speech code are those that focus on the sounds of words or require searching for spelling errors (Banks, Oka, & Shugarman, 1981). Thus, the degree to which a reader relies on the visually based pathway versus the prelexical speech code for lexical access varies with the task and the relative speed and accuracy of the two pathways (Jorm & Share, 1983).

At first, it may seem implausible that two different codes—visually and speech based—are being generated simultaneously. However, there is evidence that the two types of codes may also be generated even when people are listening to spoken language, increasing the plausibility of multiple concurrent codes. When listeners were given a target (like *tie*) and asked to judge whether it rhymed with another auditorily presented word, they were faster to respond if the test word was spelled similarly (like *pie*) than if it was spelled differently (like *rye*) (Seidenberg & Tanenhaus, 1979). Both the target and the list of test words were presented auditorily, and the task itself, rhyming, is an intrinsically auditory task. The word's written form was irrelevant to the judgment. However, readers seem to activate a visual code automatically, and if it differs from the target, it can slow down the speed of the rhyming decision. Thus, listeners may generate visual codes while listening, just as readers can generate speech codes while reading.

In sum, prelexical speech codes may be activated to some degree during reading. As readers become increasingly fluent, it is likely that the lexical access is accomplished through the visual word-percept and that the prelexical speech code doesn't reach threshold. The prelexical speech code is more important for beginning readers as a way to lexically access unfamiliar words.

Postlexical Speech Codes

There seems little doubt that some of the inner speech of a skilled reader is generated after lexical access. Like Roger Brown's experience of hearing Scottish inner speech, the skilled reader's inner speech has the appropriate stress and intonation patterns. But there is usually no way to know the appropriate stress and intonation without first interpreting a sentence at several levels, such as finding out what the words mean (lexical access) and how they are syntactically and semantically related to each other. The inclusion of appropriate stress and intonation in the inner voice suggests that the speech code is often generated after several other comprehension processes have done their work and that the speech code uses the information developed by these other processes (Banks, Oka, & Shugarman, 1981). This type of inner speech could not have been generated directly from the visual representation.

It is generally thought that the postlexical speech code helps the reader retain information in working memory. Reading makes heavy demands on working memory. The reader must keep track of the current word while understanding the phrase in which it is involved; she must also keep track of the phrase while analyzing the clause and integrating the current phrase and clause with preceding portions of the text. While the syntactic and semantic organization of the information reduces some of the burden, working-memory demands can still be large. The speech code may provide an additional level of representation—along with the visual word-percepts and word meanings—that can help the reader retain the exact wording until reaching the end of the current sentence and while processing the next.

There are three hypotheses about the way that a postlexical speech code might help retain information in working memory. One hypothesis suggests that the names of the words help readers retain the serial order of words in a text (Baddeley, 1979). Consequently, such a code could facilitate syntactic processing (Slowiaczek & Clifton, 1980) or verbatim memory in general. A second memory hypothesis states that the speech code supplements memory because its representation of prosodic features—such as stress, intonation, and pauses—may be a supplemental code for the outcome of the syntactic and semantic interpretation (Jorm & Share, 1983). Finally, the third hypothesis proposes that the speech code may be longer lasting than the visually based code (i.e., the visual word-percept) or that short-term memory is particularly suited to retaining speech codes. For example, in a short-term memory task that requires readers to recall a series of unrelated words, readers use a speech-based code to store the words, even if the list is presented in a written form. Their recall errors are speech-based confusions (such as confusing *poem* for *dome*), rather than visually based or meaning-based confusions (Conrad, 1964). Speech-based codes seem to be the preferred way of retaining verbal information for a short time in working memory, and this preference may apply to reading, as well. Finally, the speech code could play all of these roles in silent reading.

Detecting Speech Recoding

It is often difficult to tell whether or not a speech code is being generated by a reader. In this section, we describe several methods of detecting the presence of speech codes and indicate under what circumstances speech codes are more likely to be generated. However, the studies cited below generally do not distinguish between prelexical and postlexical speech codes.

Difficult reading tasks elicit more speech-related activity than easy reading tasks, even for good readers. Readers go as far as moving their lips if the text is very difficult. Less obvious speech activity can be detected by measuring the electrical activity in the speech muscles, even if the reader doesn't make any audible sounds. This technique, which is called *electromyography* or *EMG,* can detect only overt muscle activity, rather than more subtle motor commands that may be constructed but never executed. So if there is no muscular activity in the area of the larynx, one cannot conclude that there is no speech recoding. Among university freshmen, poor readers show more EMG activity during silent reading than good readers, and readers at all ability levels show more EMG activity when the text is difficult or blurred than when it is easy or clear (Edfelt, 1960). Thus, almost all readers subvocalize if the reading task is sufficiently difficult. However, Edfelt's study of university freshmen did not indicate whether the speech code was pre- or postlexical, nor what role the speech code played. Moreover, it isn't even clear that the subvocalization improved comprehension. Some readers manage to read faster and with better comprehension after they have been taught not to subvocalize (Ninness, 1979).

More subtle techniques are needed to detect the presence of speech codes that are generated without overt muscle involvement. Two major types of tasks have been used. The first type is the time-honored technique of interfering with a particular process, such as speech recoding, and determining whether the interference hampers reading. The typical means of interference is a simultaneous speaking task, like counting, or repeating the same word over and over, or listening to and repeating a list of spoken words as quickly as possible (a task called *shadowing*). If these speaking tasks interfere with reading, it suggests that speaking competes for the speech codes and mechanisms that are normally used in reading.

Numerous studies have examined the effects of a simultaneous speaking task on reading, and while the results do not all converge, a reasonable summary is that speaking interferes with demanding reading tasks. For example, readers can remember the general sense of a sentence almost as well when they are simultaneously counting as when they are not counting, but they have difficulty keeping track of the literal wording of the text while counting (Levy, 1977, 1978). Simultaneous speaking interferes less with reading single sentences than with reading a long text that requires integrating several sentences (Slowiaczek & Clifton, 1980). Shadowing interferes relatively little with judging whether two words are synonymous (like *mourn* and *grieve*), but it interferes much more with judging whether an entire sentence (like *Pizzas have been eating Jerry*) is nonsensical (Kleiman, 1975).

If we stopped at this point, the conclusion would be that difficult reading tasks are more likely to involve speech codes, and speaking interferes with their generation and use. However, an alternative interpretation is that some speaking tasks are simply too demanding to be done concurrently with a difficult reading task (Baddeley & Lewis, 1981). Easy speaking tasks interfere less with reading than do more demanding speaking tasks. Easy speaking tasks include repeating the same word or saying a well-learned sequence of words (such as the numbers from 1 to 10); a more demanding task is shadowing an unpredictable sequence of words. Thus, interference results from both the competition for general cognitive resources and the competition for speech-related resources. These two sources of interference make it difficult to sort out how much of the decrement in reading performance is attributable to just the competition for speech-related resources.

A second technique used to detect the presence of speech codes determines whether a word's pronunciation influences the speed or accuracy of processing the written word. For example, beginning readers and slightly more skilled ones make more errors when deciding that a phrase like *tie the not* is nonsense, because it sounds like an acceptable phrase, than when deciding about a control phrase like *tie the soup* (Doctor & Coltheart, 1980). Even skilled readers take longer to decide that a letter string like *brane* (which sounds acceptable) is not a real word than they take to decide about a string like *brone* (which does not sound like a word) (Rubenstein, Lewis, & Rubenstein, 1971). But readers are flexible, and if the task includes a high proportion of such nonsense words as *nale, kane,* and *loard,* readers will tend to avoid errors by relying less on the sound of the string (Davelaar, Coltheart, Besner, & Jonasson, 1978).

If a reader has just decided one word (like *bribe*) is a word, he is faster to classify an immediately following word that rhymes with the first one (e.g., *tribe*) (Meyer, Schvaneveldt, & Ruddy, 1974). There is no such facilitation if the two consecutive words only look alike but do not sound alike (e.g., *couch* and *touch*). In fact, it takes longer than otherwise expected to classify *touch*. These results suggest that a speech code is being used and, moreover, that the speech code generated in the processing of one word remains activated and can influence the processing of a later word.

Judging a single word isn't much of a reading task. The presence of speech codes is more convincingly demonstrated when people must read sentences or a more lengthy text. Such studies have found that readers take more time to silently read sentences that contain many words with similar pronunciations and spellings (Baddeley & Hitch, 1974; Treiman, Freyd, & Baron, 1983). For example, they take longer to read sentences like the first of the following two:

Peter packed a peck of pickled peppers.
Peter sacked a bunch of wilted lettuce.

These studies suggest that speech codes are being activated even by skilled readers.

Although speech codes are frequently involved in reading, they are not necessary. Profoundly deaf children, who presumably lack such speed codes, do learn to read. On the other hand, their reading skills typically lag behind those of their hearing peers. Surveys place the reading of deaf 15-year-olds at about the third-grade level and that of deaf high school graduates at the fourth-grade level in both the United States and Great Britain (Conrad, 1977). Thus, speech codes may play a role in attaining reading skill. But beyond this speculation, the lessons to be drawn from the dysfluency of deaf readers are not clear. Deaf children who are taught language orally have much less experience with language than hearing children; consequently, they have less experience processing sentences and texts and learning the linguistic conventions at every level. Therefore, these individuals are at a disadvantage with respect to many linguistic processes, not just speech recoding. Deaf children who are born to congenitally deaf parents and learn sign language at an early age do not have general linguistic deficits. On the other hand, sign language is structurally quite different from English, so for them, reading English is something akin to reading a foreign language. Reading skill in the deaf indicates that speech recoding is not an essential component of reading, but it does not tell us about the possible roles of speech codes among those readers who do hear.

Summary

To understand the printed words of a text, a reader must access their meanings in his mental lexicon. Even though subjectively, the process seems instantaneous, it takes some time for the access to occur, with more time taken for less frequent words. The preceding context can facilitate lexical access, making it faster or, in the case of an ambiguous word, helping to select the correct interpretation.

The lexical access mechanism in the READER model operates on a semantic network, a node-link structure with activation levels associated with the nodes. Individual nodes or constellations of nodes can represent a concept. The encoded representation of a printed word (the word-percept) has direct access to the corresponding concept in the semantic network through direct links that are built up over hundreds or thousands of encounters with a word. Lexical access occurs when a word-percept triggers a production that repeatedly raises the activation level of the corresponding concept above its base activation until it reaches a fixed threshold. Because concepts corresponding to infrequent words have lower base activation levels, they take longer to reach threshold and hence take longer to understand.

When an ambiguous word is read, all of its meanings are temporarily activated to some degree. The accepted interpretation will be the meaning that reaches threshold first; the time taken to reach threshold depends on the meaning's base level of activation and the degree to which it is activated by the preceding context.

Speech-based codes for the text can be generated either before or after lexical access; thus, these two types of speech codes play different roles in reading. A prelexical code provides a reader with an alternative pathway to the lexicon. A postlexical code provides an additional form of storage in reading tasks that impose heavy demands on working memory.

Suggested Readings

Henderson's book (1982) provides a broad and deep consideration of lexical access, describing the effects of many variables and discussing a number of alternative models of the process. His book deals primarily with performance in experimental tasks in which people process isolated words rather than reading a text.

One of the first proposals for a semantic network was Quillian's article (1968), while Anderson (1983) presents a contemporary version. Morton's (1969) paper is the grandfather of most activation-based theories. Key articles exploring lexical access include Allport (1979), Becker (1979), Coltheart (1978), Fischler and Bloom (1979), Forster (1976), Gordon (1985), Jorm and Share (1983), Meyer and Schvaneveldt (1971), Swinney (1979), and Taft (1979). An interesting topic in lexical access that we did not discuss in this chapter concerns the mental lexicon of bilinguals. Macnamara (1967) deals with the question of one versus two lexicons for bilinguals, as does Nas (1983).

Appendix

The fact that the gaze time is linearly related to the logarithm of the word's frequency can be explained by assuming that the activation level increases during each iteration by an amount that is proportional to the current activation level. If the base activation level is b, then, after one cycle, the activation will be the product of the proportionality constant, w, and b.

> Initial level of activation: b
> After one cycle: $b + bw$
> After two cycles: $b + bw + (w(b + bw)) = b(1 + w)^2$
> After N cycles: $b(1 + w)^N$

The number of cycles (and hence the amount of time) necessary to raise a word meaning's activation level to threshold will increase logarithmically as the base activation level decreases, in keeping with the empirical result. This result can be derived as follows.

At the fixed activation threshold level Y,

$$Y = b(1 + w)^N$$

Rearranging terms algebraically, we get:

$$(1 + w)^N = Y/b$$

Now take logarithms of both sides of the equation: The logarithm (to base $1 + w$) of $(1 + w)^N$ is N; the logarithm of the quotient on the right-hand side is the difference of the logarithms; and the logarithm of a constant, Y, is another constant, a.

$$N = a - \log b$$

Thus, N, the number of cycles needed to reach threshold, is a linear decreasing function of the logarithm of b, the base activation level of the word.

There is an alternative mechanism that can account for the effect that the lexical access time is logarithmically related to the frequency of a word. In the alternative account, the base activation level of each word would be logarithmically related to the word's frequency, and the activation level would be increased by a fixed amount per cycle, rather than a proportional amount. Then the number of cycles needed to reach threshold in this alternate model would also be a linear decreasing function of the word's frequency.

There is a finding, reported earlier in this chapter, that slightly favors the first account of the word frequency over this alternative account. The finding is that subjective estimates of frequency, which probably reflect base activation levels, are more linearly than logarithmically related to objective frequency counts.

4

Vocabulary Acquisition

In this chapter we describe how readers acquire the meanings of words—such as *amnesty, graving,* and *centrifugal*—that make up their mental lexicons. Acquiring a reasonably large vocabulary can obviously contribute to becoming a skilled reader. In addition, there is another, more subtle connection between vocabulary acquisition and reading: The meanings of many words are acquired and modified through reading. Reading may contribute more to vocabulary acquisition than does the intentional memorization of word meanings.

Vocabulary acquisition is interesting from a variety of theoretical perspectives. First, the growth of a reader's vocabulary is a striking phenomenon; readers acquire the meanings of a tremendous number of words. By the time he is in college, the average student is estimated to have a vocabulary of approximately 40,000 to 50,000 words. Once it is appreciated that vocabulary continues to grow and develop beyond the early preschool years, it also becomes apparent that it is important to understand the mechanisms responsible for that vocabulary development.

A second reason for exploring vocabulary acquisition is the close relation between linguistic knowledge and world knowledge. In theory, it is possible to distinguish between the two. For example, ignorance of a word can be distinguished from ignorance of the concept that it signifies. A nonphysicist who tries to read a technical physics article will not know the terms, but the larger problem will be not knowing the underlying concepts. While a specific lack of word knowledge can be distinguished theoretically from a lack of conceptual knowledge, in practice, the development of vocabulary usually goes hand-in-hand with the development of conceptual knowledge. Readers often master new words when simultaneously acquiring new concepts or refining their understanding of the concepts associated with familiar words. The close relation between conceptual knowledge and vocabulary was recognized by earlier researchers. As Seashore and Eckerson pointed out, "It might even be said that words, or the concepts for which they stand, are the coin of the realm of knowledge. These units of knowledge may be accurately defined, classified, and their numbers counted so that they give an inventory of the raw materials among our intellectual resources" (1940, p. 14). While our present focus is on the acquisition of word meanings, the acquisition process is related to general conceptual development.

In this chapter, we will be concerned with the acquisition of words that are unfamiliar in both their spoken and written forms. Thus, we will not discuss how young children in the early primary grades learn to visually recognize words whose meanings they already know; the acquisition of visual encoding skill will be discussed in Chapter 11 on beginning reading.

Overview   In the first section, **Vocabulary Size,** we will consider estimates of the size of readers' vocabularies at various ages. We will also describe an analysis of the number of different words that are used in printed school material. This analysis suggests that children encounter a large number of different words in school, maybe as many as are in a large, unabridged dictionary.

In the second section, **Processes in Contextual Analysis,** we will describe the processes involved in inferring a word's meaning from the context in which it occurs. We will also describe the properties of the context that may help the reader to infer a word's meaning. Finally, we will evaluate some instructional programs that teach vocabulary.

In the third section, **Processes in Structural Analysis,** we will describe how certain complex words, such as *gynecocracy,* can be decomposed into structural components, such as *gyneco* and *cracy,* and how the meanings of these components can be synthesized to infer the meaning of the complex word ("the political ascendance of women"). Also in this section, we will consider the properties of various word parts that make word meanings easy or difficult to acquire.

Vocabulary Size

Before discussing how many words a reader knows, we should be clear about which kind of vocabulary is being measured. It is possible to distinguish between four kinds of vocabularies: reading, listening, speaking, and writing. **Reading vocabulary**—the words readers recognize in written form—is the primary concern of this chapter. Reading vocabulary can be distinguished from *listening vocabulary,* the words people recognize in spoken form. The distinction is particularly important for young children who have not yet mastered visual encoding. But once encoding is mastered, readers can sound out a word they have never seen before and test whether they know its meaning in the spoken form. Consequently, the reading and listening vocabularies are very similar in the case of older children and adults (Seashore & Eckerson, 1940).

Reading and listening vocabularies are both *receptive* and can be distinguished from *productive* vocabularies, the words that are produced in speaking and writing. People produce many fewer words in their speech or writing than the number they can recognize while reading. In part, the smaller sizes of productive vocabularies may result because people write or speak about fewer topics than they read or hear about. In any case, estimates of the sizes of either speaking or writing vocabularies are markedly smaller than estimates of the size of a reading vocabulary. Even such famous writers as Milton or Shakespeare are credited with relatively small productive vocabularies (8,000 words and 15,000 words, respectively) when the computations are based on their writing (Marsh [1872], in Seashore & Eckerson, 1940). The reading vocabularies of adults are usually much larger than this.

Studies of Vocabulary Size

The size of readers' vocabularies and the rate with which the vocabularies are acquired indicate the magnitude of the learning process and indirectly suggest that the acquisition process involves more than rote memorization. Consequently, in this section, we will first examine estimates of the sizes of readers' vocabularies at various ages and then consider their implications for the nature and role of vocabulary-acquisition processes.

Methods for estimating vocabulary The size of a reader's vocabulary is typically estimated by testing the reader on a sample of words selected from a dictionary or word list and then extrapolating the estimate to the entire population of words. For example, if a student can define half of a randomly chosen sample of 200 words from a dictionary of 100,000 words, a researcher would estimate that the student knew about half the words in the dictionary, or 50,000 words.

This procedure, although a reasonable starting point, is also a source of discrepancy among the vocabulary estimates from different studies (Lorge & Chall, 1963). Studies that use smaller dictionaries yield smaller estimates, because the number of words in the dictionary or word list puts an upper limit on the size of the estimate. The subtle source of discrepancy among studies is that the words in a dictionary do not constitute a random sample of the words in a language. Dictionaries are more likely to include more important and frequent words, and the entries for such words are likely to be larger than entries for less important and less frequent words. Because of the nature of dictionaries and the nature of language, the particular procedure used to select the words in a study can bias the estimate of vocabulary size.

Another source of discrepancy among studies is the type of test that is used to determine if the reader knows the word. Some studies simply ask the reader if he recognizes the word; other studies require picking a synonym; still more stringent tests ask for a definition or example sentence using the word. These methods produce similar estimates for frequent words (Seashore & Eckerson, 1940), but they produce different estimates for less frequent words (Marshalek, 1981).

Studies also differ in their definition of what constitutes a distinct word. For instance, if a reader knows the meaning of *judge,* should it be assumed that he also knows the meaning of *judgment, judgmatic, judicial, judiciousness, judicable,* or *adjudicate?* The decision of which related words to credit to the reader has drastically influenced the estimates of vocabulary size (Lorge & Chall, 1963; Nagy & Anderson, 1984).

For all of these reasons, vocabulary estimates have varied by as much as a factor of ten (see Figure 4.1). Estimates of the vocabulary size of first-graders have varied from 2,500 words (M. E. Smith, 1926) to 26,000 (Shibles, 1959). Estimates for col-

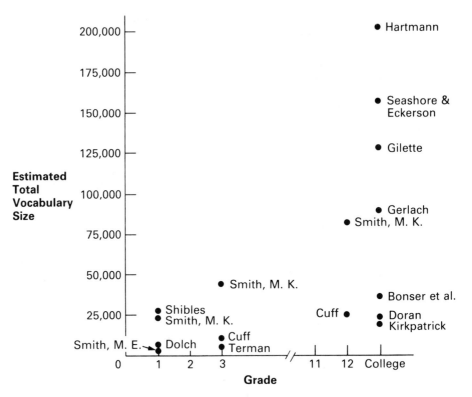

Figure 4.1 Estimates of the sizes of students' receptive vocabularies have varied tremendously among different studies. This figure illustrates some of the smallest and largest estimates for children in early primary grades and for students in high school and college. The wide divergence in estimates is due to differences in the way the test was constructed, as well as differences in the decision as to which related words constitute distinct words. *Source:* The original studies can be found by tracing the author citation in the summary provided by Lorge and Chall (1963) and by Seashore and Eckerson (1940).

lege students have varied from 19,000 (Kirkpatrick, 1891) to 200,000 (Hartmann, 1946). The most likely estimates are between these extremes—about 5,000 words for first-graders to about 50,000 for college students (Lorge & Chall, 1963; Miller, 1951).

Estimates of vocabulary size are interesting because they indicate the very rapid growth of vocabulary throughout the school years. The rate of vocabulary growth needed over time to produce these levels is approximately 3,000 words a year. A similar estimate can be derived from a study that measured the vocabulary sizes of over 900 school children between the first and twelfth grades (M. K. Smith, 1941). This study estimated that children acquire the meanings of about 2,700 words a year and that the rate of increase is fairly constant, as shown in Figure 4.2.

Although these studies provide estimates of the average vocabulary size at various ages, it is important to point out that the studies have simultaneously documented very large individual differences. In M. K. Smith's (1941) study, twelfth-

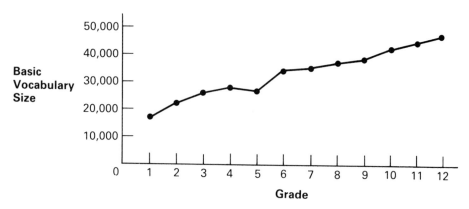

Figure 4.2 A study of the size of children's vocabularies indicates a substantial increase across grades. The study assessed children's knowledge of basic English words and found an average increase of about 2,700 words each year. *Source:* Adapted from M. K. Smith, 1941, Figure 1, p. 327.

graders at the top of the distribution had an estimated vocabulary over four times the size of their classmates at the bottom of the distribution; what's more, the best third-graders had vocabulary scores similar to those obtained by the worst twelfth-graders. Similarly, Seashore and Eckerson (1940) found the vocabulary size for the top 10 percent of college students to be approximately twice the size of the bottom 10 percent. Thus, while the vocabularies of readers tend to increase with age and education, there is enormous variability in the rate and eventual level of vocabulary development.

Implications for vocabulary acquisition Although these estimates are only approximations, the large increase in vocabulary size with age and schooling has two implications. First, it indicates that vocabulary acquisition is an ongoing process throughout the school years. Vocabulary acquisition by toddlers has always been considered a remarkable learning process; the young child goes from a vocabulary of zero words to several thousands of words in the space of only a few years. The current data demonstrate that vocabulary acquisition does not stop with the four-year-old who has acquired a basic speaking vocabulary. The acquisition of approximately 2,700 new words a year during grade school and high school would average out to be seven new words a day. The second implication of these data is also related to the magnitude of the increase; it suggests that rote memorization is an unlikely route for acquiring all of these word meanings. It is much more likely that a considerable proportion of the vocabulary is acquired by inferring word meanings during reading and listening (Nagy & Anderson, 1984).

The Vocabularies in Printed Material

Students may have large vocabularies, but analyses of the words in school materials indicate that they are likely to encounter many words they do not know. Children between grades three and nine may encounter about as many different words in school materials as occur in a large unabridged dictionary (Nagy & Anderson, 1984). This conclusion came from an analysis of the words from over a thousand pieces of published school materials, including books, kits, magazines, and encyclopedias. Nagy and Anderson found that there were about 100,000 proper names (such as *Chicago* and *Jefferson*) and another 200,000 different words, which could be grouped into 88,000 distinct word families. Exactly what constituted a distinct word family was decided by judging whether or not two words (such as *understand* and *misunderstand*) were sufficiently related to guess one word's meaning from the other; if the words were judged as being sufficiently related (as in the case of *understand* and *misunderstand*), the words were classified as belonging to the same word family. This analysis suggested that by tenth grade, a child might encounter approximately 300,000 different words: 100,000 proper names and about 200,000 other words grouped into 88,000 distinct word families. This analysis provides an important insight into the sheer size of the vocabulary encountered in grade school and the importance of vocabulary acquisition.

Word frequency   Although a reader may encounter thousands of words, the frequency with which each word type occurs in a text varies enormously. A relatively small number of word types occurs very frequently. For example, in a large sample of English texts, the eight function words—*the, of, and, to, a, in, that,* and *is*—account for almost a quarter of the words (Kucera & Francis, 1967). By contrast, most word types occur relatively infrequently. If the frequency with which each word occurs is tabulated and the words are ranked from most frequent to least frequent, there is a particular mathematical relation between the frequencies and ranks of the words. As shown in Figure 4.3, the logarithm of the word's frequency is linearly related to the logarithm of its rank, a relation that is known as **Zipf's law,** after the linguist George Zipf. Precisely what psychological processes give rise to this lawful relationship is not known. Nevertheless, the relationship provides a way to estimate how often readers will encounter various words in a large sample of text. In the current context, the importance of the relationship is that a very small number of words will be encountered extremely frequently, but most words will be encountered infrequently.

Zipf's law has been found to characterize the distribution of words in samples of texts from very different sources, such as James Joyce's *Ulysses,* as well as books written in other languages (Ijiri & Simon, 1977). The distribution of word frequencies in school materials is also consistent with this relation. For example, Nagy and Anderson (1984) found that a relatively small number of words (about 3,000) occurred more than ten times per million words; only about 10,000 words occurred more than once per million words. However, just because some words occur infrequently, it does not follow that their meaning is unimportant or that they need not be learned. Nagy and Anderson point out that some infrequent words—such as *amnesty, contemporary, rote,* and *stenographer*—are words that adults would judge as worth knowing. Even more rarely used words—such as *deform, template, inflate, sacrament,* and *flippant*—would be judged as reasonably belonging in a high school student's vocabulary.

These studies indicate that readers encounter a large number of different words in school material. The estimates would presumably be even larger for

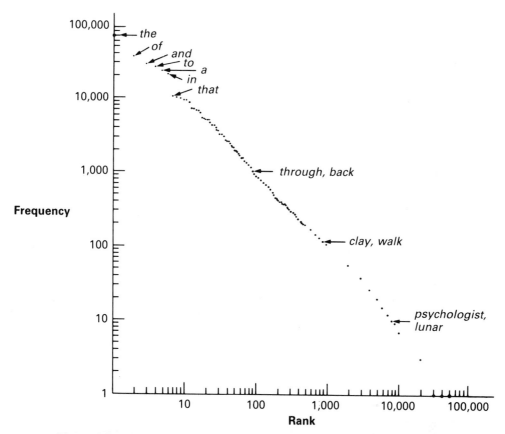

Figure 4.3 If the frequencies of each word type in a large sample of texts are tabulated and the words are ranked from most frequent to least frequent, it turns out that the logarithm of their frequency is linearly related to the logarithm of their rank, a relation known as *Zipf's law*. What this relation implies is that the most frequent words occur extremely frequently, while most words occur infrequently. For example, the seven most frequent words in English are *the, of, and, to, a, in,* and *that;* these seven words alone account for almost a quarter of the individual words in the sample. *Source:* Adapted from Kucera & Francis, 1967, Graph B–I, p. 358.

material from high school, college, or other adult sources. These estimates, then, indicate the need for vocabulary acquisition during school years.

The studies in this section have focused on the number of words that readers know; but it is also apparent that the amount of knowledge associated with individual words also develops with age and educational experience. This development is often more apparent for words that occur with only medium or low frequency, rather than for words that occur with high frequency (Marshalek, 1981). A reader may initially know only some general feature of the word's meaning but come to acquire a much more detailed representation of its meaning with repeated exposure to the word in a variety of contexts. The processes involved in acquiring the word's meaning from context will be examined in more detail in the next section.

Processes in Contextual Analysis

Readers often encounter unknown words, and they can devote various degrees of effort to inferring their meanings. The process of inferring a word's meaning from the context is called **contextual analysis.** As an example of contextual analysis, consider the following sentence, which contains some infrequently used words:

> *After the graving was complete, the workmen repainted the ship to prepare it for the christening.*

Consider what a typical reader, such as a high school girl, might infer about the words *graving* and *christening,* as used in this sentence. When the reader encounters the word *graving,* she can infer that it is a noun and refers to an action that can be finished (as indicated by *after* and *was complete*); by the end of the sentence, she can infer that *graving* may be related to repair work (as indicated by *workmen, repainted,* and *prepare*) and that it is probably done on a ship. Although she has not come up with the complete meaning of *graving,* the reader's inferences at this point would be reasonably consistent with the definition: "the act of cleaning a ship's bottom." The word *christening* presents a somewhat different problem. If she has not encountered *christening* in the nautical sense before, the reader must infer that since a ship is to be christened, the term cannot possibly refer to the baptism of a child. Consequently, she must modify her representation of its meaning to permit its use in a nautical context.

To make sense of these words, the reader must infer part of their meaning from the context. The inferences are based on the syntactic, semantic, and referential processes that constitute comprehension, and the processes use the cues in the text, as well as the reader's general knowledge. For example, when our hypothetical reader infers that the word *graving* must be a noun, she is using syntactic cues such as the word's position following *the.* When she infers that *graving* is related to repair work, she is using a variety of semantic cues from the rest of the sentence, as well as her more general construal of the situation that is being described. In this way, the process of inferring the meaning of an unknown word utilizes some of the same syntactic, semantic, and referential processes that constitute comprehension when the words are known.

Thus far, we have described vocabulary acquisition as if each word's meaning were either known or unknown. But many word meanings are only partially known, so that vocabulary acquisition is sometimes a matter of degree. The reader must build on and modify the retrieved meaning of a partially known word, a process that is similar to inferring some of the properties of a totally unknown word.

Also, many words have slightly different meanings in different contexts, so that part of vocabulary learning is acquiring the subtle distinctions that are associated with particular contexts. For example, consider the subtle distinction between the words *beneath* and *under.* Although these terms are synonymous when used to described spatial positions, they are not always interchangeable. For example, *under* has another meaning that is something like "during the time of," as in *It was under the McKinley administration that the largest monopolies developed.* In this context, the word *beneath* cannot be substituted. Similarly, *beneath* can be used in some contexts in which *under* cannot be substituted, as in *He considered it beneath him to sweep the floor.* Vocabulary acquisition consists of learning both the common meanings of words and the more subtle meanings associated with particular contexts.

Inferences during Reading

How are word meanings learned during reading? A number of researchers have made the point that vocabulary acquisition is a form of concept learning (Anderson & Kulhavy, 1972; Carroll, 1964; O'Rourke, 1974). The various components of the word's meaning include its part of speech, the superordinate category to which the concept belongs, and its typical and distinguishing features.

It is likely that in many cases, these components of word meanings are gradually acquired and refined without conscious effort on the part of the reader. But the process of inferring word meanings can also be conscious and effortful. The degree of attention a reader devotes to inferring the meaning of an unknown word may depend, in part, upon the word's perceived importance in the passage. If a word in a given text is deemed to be of no importance at all, it might be entirely ignored. Alternatively, if a word is important and the reader is processing the text carefully, she may devote considerable effort to inferring its meaning. Several cues could signal the word's likely importance. For example, words in topic positions and words that frequently recur in a text may be considered important. The next section describes a study in which readers were explicitly instructed to infer the meaning of an unknown word.

A study of the inference process   One interesting study required readers to guess the meaning of an unfamiliar word (in fact, an artificial word) encountered in a sentence (van Daalen-Kapteijns & Elshout-Mohr, 1981). The unknown word referred to a new elaboration of a familiar concept. For example, a new word *bogat* might elaborate the familiar concept of GARAGE by denoting garages that are built entirely underground. The unknown word occurred in each of five successive sentences that the subject read. The first sentence provided a strong cue to the identity of the familiar concept, and the subsequent sentences provided cues to the features that distinguished the new concept from the familiar one. The subject's task was to state the inferred meaning of the unknown word after reading each sentence.

The task can be illustrated with a set of sentences that were given for one of the unknown words, in this case, *kolper.* Consider what *kolper* might mean after reading each of the following sentences.

1. *When you're used to an expansive view, it is quite depressing if you must live in a room with one or two* kolpers *fronting a courtyard.*
2. *He virtually always studied in the library, because at home he had to work by artificial light all day because of those* kolpers.
3. *During a heat wave a lot of people suddenly want to have* kolpers, *so then the sales of sun-blinds reaches a peak.*
4. *I was afraid the room might have* kolpers, *but when I went and saw the room, it turned out that plenty of sunlight came into it.*

5. *In these houses you're stuck with* kolpers *all summer, but fortunately, it isn't true once the leaves have fallen.**

After the first sentence, most readers guessed that *kolper* was a kind of window. Presumably, this was inferred from the various cues in the first sentence—namely, that *kolpers* are in rooms; they front on courtyards; there can be one or two of them; and the more indirect inference that *kolpers* are somehow related to views.

After this point, good readers and average readers (classified on the basis of a verbal comprehension test) made different inferences about the meaning of the unknown word. Good readers were more able to modify those individual features of the superordinate concept that were incompatible with subsequent sentences. For example, the concept of WINDOW has a criterial feature (it is an opening in a building or vehicle) and a number of characteristic features: windows usually admit light, they usually have panes of glass, and they can often be opened and closed. Some of these characteristic features had to be modified to correspond to the meaning of *kolper*. Skilled readers were able to consider the characteristic features separately and modify or delete them, depending on successive sentences. For example, after sentence 2 in the *kolper* example, the good readers realized that window wasn't exactly the right meaning. A typical response was:

"Kolper is a kind of window all right. It is part of a room and it has to do with the incoming light. Maybe the glass is different for a kolper. It might be ground glass or something like that."

This response illustrates how a good reader could take the superordinate concept of WINDOW and separately consider how its characteristic features, such as "made of glass," might have to be modified to apply to *kolper*.

Consider another protocol in which a good reader makes his reasoning about the concept very explicit. He had just read sentence 5:

5. *In these houses you're stuck with* kolpers *all summer, but fortunately, it isn't true once the leaves have fallen.*

He then said:

"I think a kolper is a window. Obviously, a window doesn't vanish in winter. What does vanish is the shading effect of the tree. So, apparently a kolper is only a kolper if there is something shading it."

Good readers were able to use the context to infer how the individual features of WINDOW would have to be modified or transformed to apply to *kolper*.

In contrast to the good readers, average readers tended to generate unitary definitions and found it hard to consider or modify individual features of that definition separately. The average readers were more likely to reject the entire superordinate concept, rather than retain the correct features and discard or modify the inappropriate features. When asked to give their hypotheses, these average readers

---

*A *kolper* is "a window that transmits little light because there is something in front of it."

were more likely to restate the sentence intact, rather than make an inference. For example, a typical response by an average reader to sentence 5, the sentence about being stuck with kolpers in the summer, was, "Kolpers are found only in summer." Such a response illustrates the average readers' difficulty in inferring the word's meaning from the context. Good readers are more skillful than average readers in making these inferences.

It is only fair to point out that this study differs in several ways from normal reading. First, the inferences a reader normally makes about an unknown word's meaning are likely to be less conscious and probably less complete than the guesses that were generated in this experimental task. Readers in a normal task are probably more likely to hope that the text will be sufficiently clear without inferring the meanings of the unknown words. Moreover, in normal reading, the reader may be less concerned with attaining a consistent interpretation of a word across very different contexts that are separated in time and place. By contrast, in this task, the different components of meaning had to be synthesized across sentences that immediately followed each other. In spite of the likely differences between this task and normal reading, the data provide a useful illustration of the kinds of inferences readers can generate from the context about the meaning of an unknown word.

Not only are good readers more skillful in inferring the meanings of unknown words, they also usually have larger vocabularies than poor readers (Davis, 1944, 1968; Sternberg & Powell, 1983; Tuinman & Brady, 1974). One possible explanation that fits in with the current analysis is that good comprehension and vocabulary acquisition are related. The mechanisms used to comprehend the text when the vocabulary is known can also be used to infer the meanings of unknown words. The same lexical, syntactic, semantic, referential, and inferential processes help readers comprehend known words and learn unknown ones. Correspondingly, readers who excel (for whatever reason) in comprehending text with known words will excel in acquiring the meanings of unknown words, as well.

In addition to this explanation of the correlation between reading skill and vocabulary size, it is also possible that readers who know more words may do better in comprehension tests precisely because they are less likely to encounter words that they don't know. The relation between comprehension skill and vocabulary size will be examined further in Chapter 15 on individual differences.

Developmental trends in inferring meaning   Children between the ages of 8 and 13 gradually improve in their ability to acquire word meanings from text. Werner and Kaplan (1952) studied vocabulary acquisition in 125 children from 8 to 13 years old, using the *kolper* paradigm. One difference between the paradigm used with children and the previously described *kolper* study with adults is that the artificial words that children were given did have a familiar synonym (such as *stick, hole, gather,* and *hope*).

Not unexpectedly, older children were more likely to infer the correct meaning of an unknown word than younger children; the final reports of correct meanings increased from 7 percent for the youngest to 43 percent for the oldest children. But more striking than this overall measure of performance were the types of errors children made and the problems that they had with the task. First, we will describe a problem that was unique to the children, and then we will describe the problem that was similar to that of the average adult reader.

For the children between 8 and 10 years of age, the most common error arose because of their tendency to think that the unknown word's meaning included some of the sentence that contained the unknown word. Werner and Kaplan suggested that children had difficulty isolating the word's meaning from its context. For example, consider the unknown word *corplum* (which meant "stick") in the following sentence:

A corplum *may be used to close off an open place.*

The child might hypothesize that *corplum* meant "door." But then, when he read the next sentence, he would not simply substitute the hypothesis "door" into the slot for *corplum;* instead, he would substitute a phrase or clause, something like "a door closes off places." So the child's hypothesis for the next sentence would include parts of the preceding sentence. In some cases, the child could not separate the unknown word's meaning from the whole sentence. For example, one sentence containing the artificial word *bordicks* (which meant "faults") was the following:

People talk about the bordicks *of others and don't like to talk about their own.*

One child concluded from this sentence that *bordicks* meant "people talk about others and don't talk about themselves." Moreover, the child fit this whole interpretation into the slot for *bordicks* when reading the next sentence. Difficulty in isolating the word meaning from the sentence meaning was a common problem for the 8- to 10-year-old children, and it was also a problem for about a third of the 11- to 13-year-old children. Thus, children did not treat a word's meaning as a distinct, stable lexical unit; they often combined its meaning with aspects of the context.

In addition to this unique problem, the children, like the average adult readers in the *kolper* experiment, had difficulty analyzing the meaning of a word into its features. One way they avoided the problem was to generate a different solution for the unknown word's meaning based on each sentence and then finally aggregate all the solutions. Sometimes the child tried to connect the unrelated solutions with a causal or situational link, but sometimes the child provided no connection. For example, one set of sentences involved the unknown word *contavishes* (which meant "holes"). One sentence led a child to guess that *contavishes* meant "be dry":

Before the house is finished the walls must have contavishes.

Another sentence led the same child to guess that *contavish* meant "poison." To produce a single meaning, the child then added together the two disparate interpretations and suggested that *contavish* meant "dry and poison."

A more mature strategy was to develop larger conceptual categories that captured the specific solutions. In some cases, the superordinate category represented the intersection of features; in other cases, a superordinate category included the specific solutions.

The main problem in inferring word meanings from context appears to be a problem of decomposition. First, a reader must be able to separate the meaning of the unknown word from its context. Only children appear to have difficulty with this aspect of decomposition. Second, a reader must be able to use the context to separate the different components of the word meaning from each other and to reason about them individually. Both children and adults often have difficulty with this aspect of decomposition.

Contextual Cues and Vocabulary Acquisition

The text can provide cues about different aspects of an unknown word's meaning (Deighton, 1959; O'Rourke, 1974; Sternberg & Powell, 1983). Certain kinds of syntactic information (particularly word class) can usually be inferred from the sentence structure, but the inferrable semantic properties depend on the content of the text. The most informative semantic cues are explicit definitions, synonyms, and restatements, each of which can reduce the difficulty of inferring the meaning of an unknown word to a minor problem. Similarly, an example can be extremely helpful, particularly if it supplements the definition. More commonly, however, the text specifies only part of the unknown word's meaning, such as providing a cue to the referent's physical or functional properties, the word's semantic associates, evaluative comments, and so forth.

For a context to be helpful, the reader must recognize the connection between the unfamiliar word and the cue or definition. Deighton gives the following example of a context that fails to signal the connection:

> *We were flying at 22,000 feet. Mike called for echelon starboard. Our Hurricanes moved into single-file, each plane to the right of the plane in front.* (1959, p. 5)

If the readers are not airplane buffs, they might not guess that the definition of *echelon starboard* occurs in the third sentence; consequently, they would be unlikely to infer that an *echelon* is "a steplike formation" and *starboard* refers to the "right side." Even though the term *echelon starboard* was explained, the connection between the term and definition may not have been explicit enough.

The relation between the unknown word and the contextual cue related to its meaning may be signalled in several ways. For instance, a connecting word or phrase may tie together the unfamiliar word and the explanatory context. In the *echelon starboard* example, the relation could have been signalled by a connective like *therefore* at the beginning of the third sentence: *Therefore, our Hurricanes moved into single-file, each plane to the right of the plane in front*.

Another way to signal the relation between an unknown word and the contextual information is to use parallel structures. If two clauses or sentences have a similar structure, but the first contains an unknown word, then the second clause may contain a paraphrase (or a contrast), as in:

> *Dialogue gives sparkle and life, but it can be over done.*
> *Do not employ it for trivialities;*
> *do not let it become mere patter.*

The parallel structure of the last two clauses signals a semantic relation between *trivialities* and *mere patter*.

A third device that can be used to cue the relation of the unknown word to the text is the repetition of key words. The key word may be modified by the unknown word in one context and familiar words in another context. Repetition of key words, parallelism, and explicit markings of the contextual information are ways that the text can signal a cue to the meaning of an infrequent word.

A number of global properties of the text can influence the likelihood that a reader will successfully infer the meaning of an unknown word. Sternberg and Powell (1983) suggested the following determinants:

1. the number of times the unknown word occurs;
2. the importance of the unknown word;
3. how many unknown words occur; and
4. the variability of the contexts in which the unknown word appears.

Some of these factors, like the importance and number of unknown words, may influence how much attention the reader pays to a particular word. Another factor, the variability of the contexts, probably influences the likelihood that a reader can infer most of the features of the concept. These determinants apply not just to learning word meanings but to all concepts, whether linguistic, perceptual, or conceptual. Vocabulary acquisition reflects both language-specific processes and general learning mechanisms.

Instructional Programs

The studies described in the first section of this chapter showed that readers encounter many more words than they can hope to learn through memorization. Consequently, it is important that vocabulary programs also teach students how to learn word meanings from reading. In this section, we consider two kinds of instructional programs—those that teach students how to infer word meaning from context and those that provide direct instruction of word meanings.

Teaching contextual analysis   Successful vocabulary-training programs teach readers to make plausible inferences about a word's meaning as they encounter the new word in a variety of contexts (Mezynski, 1983). We will describe one such program that was based on the relation between comprehension processes and vocabulary acquisition (Beck, McKeown, & Omanson, 1984; Beck, Perfetti, & McKeown, 1982).

Each week, fourth-grade children were given vocabulary exercises on eight to ten new words that were semantically related to each other. For example, one set of words referred to mental states (such as *baffle, console,* and *inspire*); another group referred to moods (such as *jovial, indignant,* and *enthusiastic*). The rationale for teaching related words was to encourage children to interrelate them, as well as learn their individual meanings. The vocabulary exercises required elaborating the word meanings and integrating them into various contexts. In one of the exercises, the students were required to associate a new word with one of its typical consequences, examples, or actions. Another exercise compared and contrasted components of the words' meanings; for example, the sentence *Would you* berate *someone who* inspired *you?* contrasts the negative component of *berate* with the positive component of *inspired*. In a third type of exercise, the children were asked to create a scenario that fit a particular description, such as, *When would you* baffle *your mother by being* enthusiastic?

The study compared students who received such vocabulary instruction to those who were in a more traditional program that concentrated on teaching the dictionary definitions of words. Children who received the enriched instruction did much better on vocabulary tests than those who did not. One impressive result was that these enriched program students were more successful in reasoning with the vocabulary words in new contexts. For example, one test required children to make inferences about a vocabulary word presented in a new context that did not strongly cue its meaning. An example is the word *commended* in this sentence:

> When father heard that Lisa had ripped up the letter from Steve, father commended *her for it.*

The test question asked, "What do you think father thought of Steve?"

To answer such a question requires considerable skill in making inferences about why people are *commended* and what it means in this particular scene. Children who received the enriched vocabulary instruction performed much better than those who had only memorized definitions. The second impressive result of these studies was that the contextual analysis skills of the children in the enriched program generalized from the set of words on which they had been instructed to a new set of words. For both studied vocabulary items and new items, children in the enriched program outperformed children in the traditional vocabulary program.

The experimental program had many other facets besides these exercises, so the exercises may not have been the sole cause of the improved performance. But the results are certainly suggestive and consistent with the research on how good readers infer the meanings of unknown words.

Other features of vocabulary programs Learning a process such as contextual analysis may require considerable practice (Deighton, 1959; Johnson & Pearson, 1978). In addition, a process can sometimes be learned by watching someone else execute it. Practice and observation may help the reader learn which aspects of the text should be attended, as well as which processes need to be executed. However, because reading processes are largely covert, they cannot be learned through any simple observation process. Instead, the teacher may make some parts of the process overt by talking about what to notice and what to think about. Thus, it is also helpful if the teacher at least initially instructs the child on what cues are salient in the context.

Many kinds of exercises could provide opportunities for practicing contextual analysis. One such procedure is simply to ask students to guess the meaning of an unknown word from the context and to explain their answer. Another variant is the *cloze procedure;* the student reads a text in which some of the words are replaced by dashes and the student must guess the missing words. In all of these exercises, readers are given experience in using context to infer word meanings.

Another key aspect of an effective vocabulary program is motivating the students (Petty, Herold, & Stoll, 1968). Teachers who design vocabulary programs acknowledge the importance of motivation by describing how their technique engages the students' interest. Deighton expressed the role of motivation in vocabulary acquisition by noting, "What is needed for all learning is interest. A sense of excitement about words, a sense of wonder, and a feeling of pleasure—these are the essential ingredients in vocabulary development" (1959, p. 59). Although

Deighton's point is well taken, the importance of motivation is given little or no attention in the research literature on vocabulary learning.

While researchers and teachers assume that contextual analysis is a good method for learning words, a survey of instructional practices for The National Council of Teachers of English found that the method itself is usually not explicitly taught (Petty, Herold, & Stoll, 1968). Instructional practices tend to focus on securing the general meaning of a text, rather than inferring individual word meanings. Thus, teachers may be content to check whether the reader has acquired the gist of the passage, but not whether the reader has inferred the meaning of particular words in the passage or has learned how to use the context to infer their meanings.

Even in the early school years, when vocabulary instruction is part of a child's directed reading activities, vocabulary learning may receive little attention (Beck, McKeown, McCaslin, & Burkes, 1979). Most reading programs suggest that the child be familiarized with the unknown words before reading the selection that contains them. However, reading programs may contain few or no exercises to ensure familiarization. One reason for the lack of emphasis on vocabulary is that programs assume that the child learns word meanings primarily from reading. But in an analysis of two typical reading programs, Beck and her colleagues pointed out three problems with relying entirely on the text. First, the text often does not provide sufficient cues to word meanings. Second, the unknown word may be encountered only once or sometimes twice, so the reader has little practice or experience with it. And third, the child may not know how to use the text to infer word meaning. After the first and second grades, the practice of not explicitly teaching contextual analysis may have even more severe consequences because children read their selections independently. Then it is left entirely to the individual reader to decide how and when to infer the meanings of unknown words.

Direct vocabulary training   This type of program contrasts with contextual analysis because its goal is to teach the meanings of words directly. Such a program can be used in conjunction with contextual analysis and can be a useful way to learn words. We will review some of the research on direct vocabulary instruction in terms of the underlying processes and ways to increase their effectiveness.

Perhaps the most common technique for learning words is simply memorizing their dictionary definitions (Petty, Herold, & Stoll, 1968). Unfortunately, the **dictionary method** is also one of the least effective methods for learning vocabulary. Memorizing a definition does not require much active processing by the reader. Moreover, the definition, even if supplemented by a sample sentence containing the unknown word, may not provide a sufficient variety of contexts. Consequently, the rote memorization of definitions tends to result in poorer performance than other more active learning procedures. For example, Gipe (1978) found the dictionary method was much less effective for third-graders and fifth-graders than a method that required them to infer word meanings from a passage and generate other sentences using the target words.

In addition, dictionary paraphrases are not always sufficient for conveying a word's meaning, particularly the more subtle aspects of meaning. Miller and Gildea (1985) cited examples of the problems children encounter when trying to use words based on their dictionary definitions. The children were told to look up words—

such as *stimulate, chaste,* and *erode*—and use each in a sentence. The following sentences that the children produced illustrate a problem with the method:

> *The mother* stimulated *the chocolate cake.*
> *Milk is* chaste.
> *Our family* erodes *often.*

These bizarre sentences resulted from the way children used the dictionary definitions to generate sentences. They found a dictionary definition for the target word, such as the definition "eat out" for *erode.* They generated a sentence for the definition, *Our family* eats out *often,* and then substituted the target word, resulting in *Our family* erodes *often.* If the dictionary definition is substituted for the target word, the likely origin of the bizarre sentences is clear:

> *The mother* stirred up *the chocolate cake.*
> *Milk is* pure.
> *Our family* eats out *often.*

The dictionary is a good reference tool, but it is not always sufficient for teaching word meanings.

A dictionary approach might be enhanced if, in addition to the word's semantic meaning, more emphasis were placed on the objects, actions, or relations to which the word refers—in other words, the referent of the word. Focusing on referents is not always a part of current vocabulary programs beyond the first few grade levels, at least not as described in educational textbooks. For example, in a textbook on teaching reading conjointly with content, Herber (1970) describes a method for teaching technical vocabulary. The method gives very little consideration to referential meaning. Instead, the focus is on teaching new words in terms of other already known words. For example, a *spectrum* is defined as "the range of electromagnetic energies."

Besides using dictionary definitions, Herber's approach involves morphological and phonological analyses (such as stripping away affixes) to discover possible relations between new words and already known words. This approach focuses on semantics, on language. The complementary approach, which focuses on reference, suggests using field trips and slides in conjunction with teaching vocabulary in a given content area (e.g., Carillo, 1976; Ransom, 1978). Experience with the referents of new words enhances vocabulary learning. And the use of examples that focus on a particular referent is probably one of the most effective vehicles for teaching words to children and adults.

Recent evidence suggests that very young children may initially acquire word meanings in terms of prototypes (or typical referents). For example, Carey (1978) has shown that a young child's representation of *tall* is initially in terms of specific examples, such as a *tall man* or a *tall building.* Later, the child abstracts the more general semantic features (Anglin, 1970; Keil & Carroll, 1980). These studies of the acquisition of word concepts illustrate the importance of examples. The studies further suggest that the use of examples may be a natural learning tool that is likely to be useful even for older children and adults.

A number of people have suggested that a vocabulary program can also be made more effective if it stresses the relations among semantically related words (O'Rourke, 1974). For example, in the grade school vocabulary program by Beck and her colleagues (Beck, Perfetti, & McKeown, 1982), which we discussed earlier, the vocabulary words that were taught in a single lesson formed a cluster of semantically related words. O'Rourke (1974) claimed that elementary and secondary students do not easily make fine discriminations among semantically related words, such as noting the different nuances among synonyms (the difference between *insensitive* and *callous*). He suggested that students be given practice making progressively finer distinctions so that they learn both the main components of a word's meaning and the finer distinctions among words. O'Rourke suggested the study of synonyms and antonyms could help students learn meaning components.

Processes in Structural Analysis

Some words, like *gynecocracy,* contain parts that can be used to infer the word's meaning. Decomposing an unknown word into its structural components and inferring its meaning from them is called **structural analysis.** As an example of this process, consider how one might infer the meaning of the word *precautiousness* in this sentence:

> *The founder's* precautiousness *eventually thwarted his heirs' attempt to declare bankruptcy.*

A high school student may never have seen the word *precautiousness.* But she may recognize the component *precautious* and guess from it that the unknown word means something related to *precaution.* Moreover, the suffix *ness* signals that *precautiousness* is an abstract noun. Consequently, she might guess that *precau-*

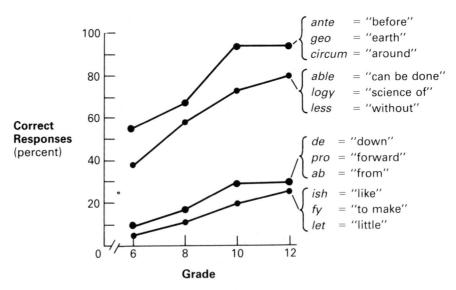

Figure 4.4 Students' ability to match affixes to their meanings can be traced across various grade levels. The graph shows the affixes that elicited the best performance (such as *ante* and *less*) and those that elicited the worst performance (such as *de* and *ish*). *Source:* Based on data from O'Rourke, 1974.

tiousness means something like "a tendency to take precautions." Such a conjecture would fit in with the meaning of the rest of the sentence, namely, that precautiousness prevented a bad thing. Her guess would be close to the dictionary definition of *precautiousness:* "the tendency to take actions to protect against possible failure."

Some college readers are not aware of the general strategy of decomposing a word into its parts to guess its meaning; even fewer high school students report knowing this strategy (Sternberg & Powell, 1983). Moreover, many students do not know the meanings of even some common affixes. This was found in a study of children between the sixth and twelfth grades who were asked to match affixes with their definitions (O'Rourke, 1974). Figure 4.4 shows some of the affixes that were most often correctly matched with their meanings and some that were least often correctly matched. The results suggested that grade school and high school students do not master many common affixes, presumably because they are not taught their meanings directly and do not infer the meanings on their own.

O'Rourke (1974) also reported a large study that successfully taught eighth-grade students structural analysis using a variety of affixes. The instruction resulted in large gains in their ability to infer word meanings and also to form novel words, such as the following:

> *audict:* "likes to hear records"
> *autocraft:* "self-steering boat"
> *linograph:* "written line"
> *solarscope:* "sun viewer"

Producing new words is a stringent test of the ability to decompose words, more stringent than is necessary for interpreting unknown words during reading. Consequently, it is good evidence of the students' mastery of this skill.

O'Rourke stressed two aspects of his program that make excellent pedagogical sense. First, he tried to teach the meanings of morphemes by using words that were already in the students' vocabularies. For example, if the student already knew the meaning of the word *democracy,* this could be the basis of teaching her the meaning of *cracy.* Then this morpheme could be pointed out in new words, such as *gynecocracy* or *theocracy.* The second feature O'Rourke stressed was the importance of wisely selecting the affixes to be taught in a vocabulary program. He suggested two important criteria: (1) that the affixes be consistent in meaning and (2) that they occur somewhat frequently (see also Deighton, 1959). These criteria are sensible, since the goal of such a program is to achieve the largest possible gains in vocabulary size.

When an unknown word has multiple parts, the reader may have some options in deciding how to analyze the word. It is not necessary or desirable to decompose a word into the smallest units; for example, *readjustable* need not be decomposed into *re-adjust-able* if the reader is already familiar with *adjustable.* A better strategy is to minimize the number of parts to be considered. If there is an obvious main component in the word, its meaning should be accessed first and used as the base for the remaining synthesis. Durkin (1976) suggested that children be taught to incorporate the meanings of suffixes, progressing from innermost suffix to outermost, and finally, to incorporate the meanings of prefixes. There is no theoretical reason to think that it is preferable to incorporate the meanings of suffixes before the prefixes or vice versa. In a few cases, the two orders may lead to different conjectures about a word's meaning. For example, *unlockable* could be analyzed as *unlock-able*—that is, "can be unlocked"—or it could be analyzed as *unlockable*—that is, "cannot be locked." But *unlockable* is a genuinely ambiguous word. Usually, the two orders would converge on the same inferred meaning.

Compound words   Structural analysis entails a slightly different procedure for one class of complex words that are called **compound words.** Compound words are formed by a combination of two independent words that can be from a variety of word classes, including the following:

1. noun-noun form: *pancake*
2. verb-noun form: *crybaby*
3. adjective-noun form: *strongman*
4. adjective-adjective form: *highborn*
5. noun-verb form: *spoonfeed*

The syntactic category of the resulting compound depends somewhat on the word class of its individual parts. Usually, if the two parts are from the same word class, the compound is also in that class. If the two parts are from different word classes, the word class of the second part usually dominates that of the first.

Noun-noun compounds are particularly frequent in English, and they are often used to create new words. To guess the meaning of a novel compound, the second noun should be interpreted as the head noun and the first, as its modifier. For example, a *placekicker* is "a kicker," not "a place." However, the exact relation between the two components cannot be unambiguously inferred from the word alone. For example, a *jelloshell* could be "a shell made of jello," "a shell for holding jello," or "a shell that has some of the properties of jello." But in any case, it is some kind of "shell." Theoretically, compound words can be concatenated endlessly, as in *salesman, insurance salesman,* and *life insurance salesman.*

English has orderly rules for interpreting such complex strings of nouns: The innermost noun (such as *salesman*) is to be interpreted as the head; this is then to be modified by the next innermost noun *(insurance)* to form a unit *(insurance salesman)*; this unit is then to be modified by the next noun *(life).* But in fact, most people do not follow this linguistic analysis when interpreting a novel compound. Even college students have difficulty interpreting a novel compound word of two parts if one of the parts is itself unusual and complex (Gleitman & Gleitman, 1970). For example, when asked to interpret a novel compound such as *house-door dog,* college students are likely to rearrange its parts into a more familiar configuration, perhaps corresponding to *dog-house door.* When interpreting complex novel compounds, adults rely much more on the plausibility and familiarity of the unit than on other cues, such as the order of the words in the string.

How READER Analyzes Unknown Words

READER analyzes unknown words using mechanisms that correspond to structural analysis and contextual analysis. First, READER determines whether or not the word is unknown by determining whether or not there is a meaning associated with a particular word-percept. If there is none, READER structurally analyzes the word by stripping off frequent affixes (both prefixes and suffixes) to identify the main word. Thus, READER can easily analyze unknown words that differ from a known word only by the presence of some familiar affix, such as a plural or past-tense marker.

READER also does contextual analysis by making inferences about the syntactic properties of the unknown word from the syntactic expectations that occur during reading. For example, if an unknown word occurred immediately after the word *the*, READER would expect it to be a member of a noun phrase; consequently, READER would conjecture that it was either an adjective or a noun. By the end of the noun phrase, READER could infer more precisely the syntactic properties of the word. READER can also make inferences about semantic properties and the possible referent of the word. In other words, for READER, the acquisition of new word meanings occurs as a consequence of reading.

Determinants of Structural Analysis

Words, like people, come in all shapes and sizes, with different ethnic backgrounds. In this section, we describe some of the properties of words that determine whether a reader is likely to subject it to structural analysis. In other words, we will consider why a word like *sports* is more likely to be stored and lexically accessed as a single psychological unit of meaning than a word like *neuroscience*, which is likely to be structurally analyzed into two units of meaning. The discussion will consider how the various determinants of structural analysis affect a psychological process that enables structural analysis.

Terminology   Before the discussion can become substantive, we need to provide some basic terminology and a taxonomy, which has been borrowed from the field of linguistics (see Table 4.1). The smallest unit of meaning or grammatical function is the **morpheme**. A morpheme has a relatively stable form and cannot be divided into smaller parts. For example, the word *widening* has three morphemes: *wide, en,* and *ing. En* is a morpheme that changes adjectives, such as *wide*, into verbs, such as *widen*. The morpheme *ing* indicates that the verb *widening* is in the present progressive tense.

There are two kinds of morphemes. Those morphemes that can stand alone, such as *wide, street,* and *survey,* are called *free morphemes.* Morphemes that cannot

Table 4.1 Linguistic terms for various kinds of morphemes

Term	Definition	Examples
Morpheme	The smallest unit of meaning or grammar	*tree, ing, pre*
Free morpheme	A morpheme that can stand by itself	*wide, walk, of*
Bound morpheme	A morpheme that can only occur with others	*logy, ing*
Inflectional morpheme	A bound morpheme that signals grammatical information	*ing, s, ed*
Derivational morpheme	A bound morpheme that changes the word class or meaning	*re, uni, able*

stand along (such as the *ing* in *widening*) but are always combined with other morphemes are called *bound morphemes*. In a word composed of both free and bound morphemes, such as *widening*, the main free morpheme is sometimes called the *root* or *stem*.

Bound morphemes include two kinds of affixes: inflectional morphemes and derivational morphemes. **Inflectional morphemes,** such as the past-tense marker *ed*, provide grammatical information about the stem without changing its word class or meaning. English inflectional morphemes are composed of a small class of eight suffixes (Bissantz & Johnson, 1985). Four of them (*s, ed, ing, en*) modify verbs (such as *walk, walks, walked, walking, eaten*); two of them (*s, 's*) modify nouns (such as *boy, boys, boy's*); and two others (*er, est*) modify adjectives (such as *slow, slower, slowest*).

Derivational morphemes are bound morphemes that can be used to create (or derive) new words by either changing the word class (such as changing the adjective *wide* to the verb *widen*) or by changing the meaning (such as changing *psychology* to *psychologist*). The derivational morphemes are a heterogeneous assortment, which includes both suffixes (such as *ly* and *ment* in *slowly* and *government*) and prefixes (such as *mis* and *uni* in *misinterpret* and *unicycle*).

The distinction between inflectional and derivational morphemes is primarily linguistic. Nevertheless, some distinctions between the two categories are related to psychological processes in vocabulary acquisition and lexical storage. For example, most times, if a reader knows the meaning of a given word, then he can structurally analyze and correctly infer the meaning of a new word that differs only by an inflectional morpheme. If he knows the meaning of the root form of a verb, such as *mystify*, he will be able to infer the meaning of *mystified*. In general, children learn the common inflectional morphemes from oral language, without formal instruction, and can use them to understand and create new word forms that they haven't previously encountered (Berko, 1958). Some but certainly not all derivational morphemes are as familiar and easy to use in structural analysis as inflectional morphemes. The sections below discuss those psychological considerations that determine when inflected and derived morphemes are processed similarly and differently. These considerations are based on a general analysis of what is known about concept learning as it relates to structural analysis.

The role of frequency   People are more likely to learn concepts they encounter frequently. This generalization applies to the meanings of bound and free morphemes. In particular, people are more likely to learn the meaning of a morpheme that occurs in many different word types, providing they know these words. For example, *un* (meaning "not") occurs with many adjectives and participles, as in *unable, unlucky, unlisted,* and *unhappy*. Morphemes that occur with many different words are often productive; that is, they can be used to create and interpret new words. For example, one can easily interpret new words created with *un*, such as *uncompiled, unpeppered,* or *unscooped*. By contrast, the prefix *apo* occurs in only a few words, including *apocalyptic, apogee,* and *apoplexy*. Consequently, the meaning of a prefix like *apo* is much less likely to be learned than that of a prefix like *un*. Thus, an unknown word that contains frequent component morphemes is likely to be structurally analyzed during reading.

The meaning of a derived word cannot always correctly be inferred from the meanings of its components. For example, *understand* does not mean "stand under," and *department* does not mean "the act of departing." It is interesting to note that such unpredictability of a derived word's meaning from its structural constituents is much more common among frequent words than among infrequent words (Nagy & Anderson, 1984). Thus, a reader's structural analysis of a new word he encounters is more likely to be correct if the word is an infrequent one. This is fortunate, because it is precisely an infrequent word that a fluent reader is likely not to know.

The phenomenon of the meanings of infrequent derived words being more rule governed is one example of a trend that is detectable at many levels of language, namely, that infrequent forms are often more regular than frequent forms. At the level of symbol-sound correspondences, less frequent words tend to be more regular, whereas the more frequent words have more exceptions to the common symbol-sound relation. For example, the less frequent words *cave, pave, rave,* and *save* make use of a regular pronunciation rule, while the frequent word *have* is an exception. At the syntactic level, less frequent verbs—such as *paint, type,* and *kick*—have a regular past tense (*painted, typed,* and *kicked*). Frequent verbs—such as *go, run, be,* and *have*—have irregular past-tense forms (*went, ran, was,* and *had*). It is difficult to say why the general phenomenon arises. Perhaps it is because more frequently used forms are more subject to adaptational change in a language community.

Another perspective is that the phenomenon is compatible with an acquisition mechanism that requires repeated practice for learning to occur. The acquisition mechanism must learn the general rules that apply to many items, as well as some item-specific information. There is no problem in obtaining sufficient repeated practice of general rules; the rule is instantiated repeatedly with different items. But in order for item-specific information to be learned, the item must occur relatively frequently. Hence, exceptional items would be much more likely to be acquired if they were frequent.

Syntactic factors An unknown word whose constituent morphemes signal a syntactic feature is more likely to be structurally analyzed than one whose morphemes do not. Inflectional morphemes are major carriers of the syntactic information in a sentence. Thus, a reader who is processing the syntax of a sentence is more likely to attend to the inflectional morphemes in any unknown words. One of the reasons that a reader can make syntactic sense of a sentence like *The pites gillomed after they moofed* is that the inflections on *pites, gillomed,* and *moofed* provide syntactic cues about their stems.

Some derivational morphemes also provide syntactic information, particularly word-class information. For example, word class is part of what is signalled by the following commonly used suffixes: *ly, y, able, al, ment,* and *ness* (as in *scathingly, splintery, imponderable, transcultural, preferment,* and *pompousness*). If a reader encounters an unknown word containing one of these morphemes, he is likely to use his knowledge of the morpheme's syntactic cue to structurally analyze the new word.

Reference As a reader progresses through a text, he is constantly trying to relate the words, phrases, and clauses he encounters to the objects and events to which they refer. A morpheme that consistently refers to the same type of concept is more likely to be learned and used in structurally analyzing a new word than one that does not make such reference. For example, the *ism* in *pantheism, anarchism, structuralism,* and *Freudianism* refers to "a doctrine or set of beliefs and practices." The consistency of the referential meaning, albeit abstract, of a morpheme like *ism* makes its meaning easier to learn. Faced with a newly invented *ism,* such as *Spencerism,* a reader can make some inferences about the type of entity it refers to.

By contrast, the referential meaning of some morphemes depends greatly on the other morphemes with which they combine, making their meanings harder to infer. This is particularly true of a type of structure called a *combining form,* such as *anthropo* and *centri.* These are bound morphemes, typically of Latin or Greek origin, that often combine with each other to form words, such as *anthropocentric* or *centrifugal.* Sometimes the referents of words with a shared combining form are very different. For example, the referents of *automobile, autograph,* and *autodidact* are "a car," "a signature," and "a self-educated person." The fact that the referents of the words in which *auto* occurs are so different makes it less likely that a reader will be able to infer the meaning of the morpheme *auto.* Such morphemes are not likely to be learned or used in structurally analyzing novel words that contain them.

Linguistic innovation over time In this chapter, we have discussed how word meanings are acquired by individual readers. But vocabulary acquisition can be seen at a societal level, as well as an individual level. A language group can acquire words, as well as modify the meanings of other words. The way in which new words come into existence or the way established words change meaning reflects a point that was made at the beginning of the chapter—namely, that linguistic knowledge is closely linked to world knowledge.

Sometimes the process of vocabulary change in a language community is relatively gradual and can only be detected by analyzing language use over a long period of time. For example, a linguist might examine texts to determine when a particular set of words began to be used in the society or what a word meant a hundred years ago compared to today. Such analyses often highlight the close relation between language use and political, economic, and cultural forces. Lexical innovation can sometimes be traced to political events, such as wars and colonization, that caused two cultural groups to interact more than they had before. For example, many now-familiar English words, including *bucket, pork, beauty, judgment, cardinal, penance,* and *attorney,* were borrowed from the French between 1250 and 1450 because the political circumstances of the times forced interaction between the English and their Norman-French neighbors.

Currently, linguistic innovation is a very common phenomenon. In part, it is driven by the rapid development of new technologies. For example, *radar* and *television* were coined not too long ago to name new technological inventions, just as the terms *chip* and *microcomputer* have been coined in more recent years. Also, many slang terms are simply newly invented words or new applications of old words to denote different concepts. As concepts become important in a culture, the society develops terms to refer to them. We pointed out at the beginning of the chapter that earlier researchers stressed how words can be considered the coins of the realm of knowledge for individual readers. This brief consideration of lexical innovation in a language community suggests a generalization of the point: The growth and development of vocabulary in a language community also reflects the repertoire of important concepts in that community.

Summary

Quite clearly, a close relation exists between reading comprehension and vocabulary acquisition. Reading comprehension involves a variety of syntactic, semantic, and referential processes; these same processes can be used to infer the possible features of an unknown word's meaning, the process of contextual analysis. These processes are evident when skilled readers are asked to guess explicitly the meanings of unknown words. Such readers manipulate the semantic information in the text to consider the features separately and infer how they apply in the particular context.

Since vocabulary acquisition and reading comprehension are so closely tied, some instructional programs teach vocabulary skills in a way that builds on that relation. For example, one important aspect of an enriched vocabulary program that was taught to fourth-graders (Beck, McKeown, & Omanson, 1984) was the variety of exercises used to provide children with experience in manipulating information in a text to make inferences about the meanings of words.

In addition to contextual analysis, vocabulary programs often provide direct instruction about word meanings. While the dictionary definition is the most common method of instruction, rote memorization is not a particularly effective method of acquiring vocabulary. The dictionary method can be made more effective by supplementing it with more active learning exercises (including those that present the vocabulary items in a variety of contexts), by acquiring words in semantically related clusters, by using examples, and by providing experience with the words' referents.

Finally, the structure of some complex words contains structural cues to their meaning. Derivational and inflectional morphemes can sometimes be identified in an unknown word and their meanings synthesized to infer part of the unknown word's meaning, a process referred to as structural analysis. Structural analysis of an unknown word is most likely if the components are frequent, if one morpheme signals grammatical information such as word class, and if the components have consistent referential meanings.

Suggested Readings

Numerous studies have measured and estimated the vocabulary sizes of readers of various ages. McCarthy (1954) and Dale and Razik (1963) can be consulted for bibliographies of these studies. The research of Nagy and Anderson (1984) and of Sternberg and Powell (1983) provide a more interesting and up-to-date examination of the relation between vocabulary acquisition and reading processes. Similarly, the research by Beck and her colleagues (Beck, McKeown, & Omanson, 1984; Beck, Perfetti, & McKeown, 1982) on vocabulary training in primary school can be consulted for more details about how vocabulary training can be successfully taught, as well as the problems that characterize many traditional vocabulary learning programs.

Children begin inferring the meanings of words in the first year of life, and the way they acquire words is a research topic with a large research literature of its own. Some of the recent research in this area can be found in Macnamara (1982) and some of the readings in the edited volume by Wanner and Gleitman (1982).

Finally, the suggested readings in Chapter 3 on the nature of words and their meanings are directly relevant to understanding how readers acquire vocabulary. It would be useful to consult those readings, too.

5

Syntactic Structures and Syntactic Processing

The most general meaning of the word *syntax* is "systematic arrangement." When applied to language, *syntax* refers to the systematic arrangement of grammatical constituents like words, phrases, and clauses. But why does human language have to have syntax? Why can't we communicate our ideas to other people without using syntax?

What forces us to use syntax is that we think in terms of nonlinear constellations of ideas, but we communicate by using linear channels of communication. Both spoken and written communication consist of a one-word-at-a-time sequence. It is syntax that provides us with a code to communicate a configuration of concepts in a sequence of words. As a person reads a sentence, his syntactic analysis attempts to recover the underlying interrelations of concepts from the sequence of words.

Syntactic analysis—or as it is sometimes called, syntactic parsing—segments sentences into grammatical constituents and determines how those constituents are related to each other. Grade school grammar teaches students the names for grammatical constituents such as clauses, noun phrases, verb phrases, prepositional phrases, adjectives, nouns, and verbs. An example of a relation between two grammatical constituents is a noun phrase (e.g., *a basket*) being modified by a prepositional phrase (e.g., *of peaches*) or a relative clause (e.g., *that he admired*) being embedded in a main clause. An example of what a syntactic analysis might accomplish is the determination that a sequence of words constitutes a noun phrase and that the phrase is the subject of the verb. As a reader encounters each successive word of a text, he attempts to relate it to the existing representation of the grammatical constituents and their interrelations.

Overview   There are five major sections in this chapter. In the first section, **The Purpose of Syntactic Analysis,** we will discuss the role that syntactic analysis plays in language comprehension. We will illustrate this role by describing how patients with Broca's aphasia, a selectively syntactic dysfunction, have difficulty in comprehending sentences whose meaning is critically dependent on correct syntactic analysis.

129

In the second section, **Cues to Syntactic Analysis,** we will describe a number of cues that provide a reader with important information about the syntax of a sentence. These cues include word order, word class, function words, affixes, word meanings, and punctuation. We will also illustrate how multiple cues converge on a single syntactic interpretation that simultaneously satisfies a number of constraints.

In the third section, **The Process in Syntactic Analysis,** we will describe some of the major operating characteristics of the syntactic processes. We will also describe how syntactic analysis uses the strategy of immediate interpretation. The characteristics of syntactic analysis are particularly revealed in the processing of syntactically ambiguous sentences, particularly sentences that lead a reader down a "garden path" and leave it to the error-recovery processes to find the correct path.

In the fourth section, we will describe **Two Models of Syntactic Analysis:** an Augmented Transition Network (ATN) and READER. The two models are compared and contrasted with each other and evaluated in terms of how similar they are to human performance.

In the fifth and final section, we will examine the relation between **Syntactic Analysis and Working Memory.** We will describe several syntactic comprehension strategies that effectively minimize the load placed on working memory. Sentences whose syntactic complexity overloads the limitations of working memory are difficult or impossible to understand. The syntactic information that is collected in working memory during comprehension tends to be forgotten at syntactic boundaries, particularly sentence boundaries.

The Purpose of Syntactic Analysis

Syntax allows a sequence of words to coalesce, forming higher-order constituents (phrases and clauses) that can bear a variety of grammatical relations to each other. The syntactic organization provides part of the temporary structure to organize the words until the underlying concepts are understood.

Configuring Concepts from a Sequence of Words

An analogy between the syntax of language and the syntax of video (television) transmission can help explain how a configurational object can be coded as a sequence of elements. One meaningful unit of video is a single screenful, which might depict something like a policeman sitting in a car. In our analogy, a single screenful of video roughly corresponds to single sentence. Like a human speaker or writer, a television broadcaster cannot send out an entire screenful simultaneously, so the screenful must be decomposed into constituents and transmitted one constituent at a time. As we know from looking closely at a television screen, the constituents of a single screenful are several hundred horizontal lines of video information. The horizontal lines must be broadcast one at a time, and the receiving television set must be able to put them back together appropriately to form the entire screenful. The syntactic rule used by the broadcaster and the receiving television set to reassemble the lines is that the first of these lines is displayed at the top of the screen, the next one, just below that, and so on, until the screen is gradually filled from top to bottom. To help the television set in its syntactic analysis of the electrical signal, the broadcaster inserts a segmentation cue (somewhat analogous to a comma) at the end of each horizontal line. Similarly, another segmentation cue is inserted at the end of each screenful (analogous to a period). The electronic conventions that relate the sequential signals to the spatial layout might be called the syntax of video.

The major difference between the syntax of video and the syntax of language is that the video syntax is trivially simple and identical for all screenful, regardless of the content. Each of the hundreds of thousands of screenful processed by a television set during an evening's entertainment is identical in its syntactic structure. By contrast, the syntactic structure in language varies from sentence to sentence. Some sentences are in the active voice, while others are passive, and some contain embedded clauses, prepositional phrases, gerundial phrases, and the like. A reader proceeding through a book must process tens of thousands of sentences, very few of which share the same syntactic structure. A reader must do a syntactic analysis of each new sentence he encounters to determine which syntactic rules to apply to interpret that particular sentence.

The focus of the analogy between video and sentences is that both a text and a television broadcast signal communicate a complex nonsequential structure, either a constellation of concepts, in the case of a sentence, or a spatial constellation of physical objects, in the case of a video screenful. Moreover, they both do so by squeezing the information into a communication channel that can deal only with a linear sequence of symbols; the arrangement of that sequence must be decoded by the receiver in order to recover the original configuration.

Configural information in a tree structure   Syntactic analysis deals with the grammatical structures and relations within a sentence. As an illustration, consider what these two structurally similar sentences have in common, despite obvious differences in meaning:

> *The delighted teacher uncorked the champagne.*
> *The rancorous teetotaler smashed the bottle.*

Both sentences have a subject-verb-object structure. The subjects and objects are noun phrases that consist of the determiner *the,* an adjective, and a noun. The verbs are in the past tense and the active voice.

These constituents and their interrelations can be expressed in a **tree structure** such as Figure 5.1. This diagram highlights two important features of a sentence's syntactic structure. First, the sentence is segmented into groups of words, such as the ones labeled *noun phrase* and *verb phrase.* Second, these constituents are interrelated, usually in a hierarchical structure. For example, the noun phrase can be further divided into smaller constituents such as a determiner (like *the*), an adjective, a noun, and so on. The tree structure portrays the constituents and the relations that the reader represents, although the mental representation is not in the form of an image or a tree but in a symbolic structure that contains approximately the same information.

Syntactic analysis can be distinguished somewhat from *semantic analysis* (which we will discuss in the next chapter). Semantic analysis is primarily con-

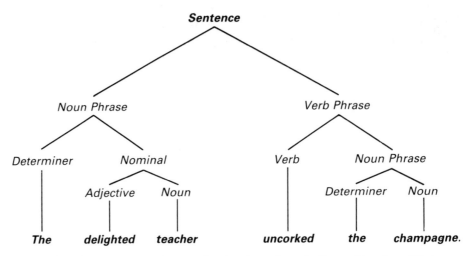

Figure 5.1   A tree-structure diagram showing the main syntactic constituents and their relations for the sentence *The delighted teacher uncorked the champagne.*

cerned with the content of a sentence, determining what action or state is being described, who the participants in the event are, and so on. Syntactic analysis distinguishes between sentences that a semantic analysis would treat as equivalent, such as the following:

> *The hero defeated the villain.*
> *The villain was defeated by the hero.*

In both cases, the *hero* is the winner. However, the syntactic analysis takes note of the fact that the sentences differ as to which person is designated as the subject of the sentence, the hero or the villain. Syntactic analysis is intended to discover the grammatical relations among constituents, rather than analyze the sentence's meaning. However, syntactic analysis contributes to semantic analysis.

A Syntactic Dysfunction: Broca's Aphasia

Because we have all been doing syntactic analysis without much awareness of it since early childhood, we tend to take the ability for granted and fail to appreciate the intricacy of the processes. One way to make the role of syntactic analysis more apparent is to consider a group of people who lose some of their ability to do syntactic analysis, often as a result of a stroke or accident that causes some brain damage. People with the syndrome called **Broca's aphasia** have problems in both speaking and understanding due to a specific impairment of their ability to syntactically analyze language. The most obvious symptom of Broca's aphasia is that the patient's speech is rather slow and lacks many of the inflections (word affixes like an *s* signaling pluralization) and function words (like *the, by, of, to*) that provide syntactic information. Because the symptoms are so obvious in speech, much of the clinical analysis of this aphasia has focused on speech production, particularly on the omission of function words. Nevertheless, since our interest in this book is on comprehension rather than production, we will describe how Broca's aphasia affects syntactic analysis during comprehension. Both the comprehension and production deficits are described in detail by Berndt and Caramazza (1980).

We start with a methodological point, namely, how difficult it is to evaluate syntactic analysis separately from other levels of processing. If a person with Broca's aphasia has normal world knowledge and normal lexical knowledge but an impaired ability to do syntactic analysis, he should still be able to make sense of a sentence like *The girl ate the apple;* his knowledge of the words *girl, ate,* and *apple* is sufficient to generate an excellent guess of what the sentence is about. Although people with Broca's aphasia might not have completely normal lexical processes, they comprehend normal conversation sufficiently well to make even trained clinicians think that this syndrome leaves comprehension unimpaired. To make the syntactic disability evident, experimental tasks must meticulously eliminate non-syntactic cues that can help a patient understand a sentence. The most common type of task requires patients to read or listen to a sentence that is carefully constructed to contain precisely the syntactic cues that are of interest. Then the patient must choose which of several pictures corresponds to the referent of the sentence. The distractor pictures correspond to sentences that are syntactically confusable with the test sentence.

This technique has been used to study the difficulty that Broca's aphasics have with word-order information. Word-order information (as well as other cues) is used to indicate the grammatical role of a word in English. Sometimes the cue may be as subtle as the position of the article *the:*

> *They fed her dog* the *biscuits.*
> *They fed her* the *dog biscuits.*

The difference in the position of the word *the* produces two different segmentations of the two noun phrases that follow the verb. In the first sentence, the two noun phrases are *her dog* and *the biscuits;* in the second case, they are *her* and *the dog biscuits.* Thus, the difference in the position of the word *the* results in very different interpretations.

Various sentences of this type were presented to Broca's aphasics (Heilman & Scholes, 1976). Each sentence was accompanied by four different pictures, and the patients were asked to choose the picture that depicted the referent of the sentence. The four alternatives consisted of one picture that depicted the correct answer, one that depicted the other syntactic structure, and two alternatives that contained incorrect referents for some of the content words. For example, the four pictures for the first sentence above might be: (a) someone feeding biscuits to a dog; (b) someone feeding dog biscuits to a girl; (c) someone feeding biscuits to a cat; and (d) someone feeding a piece of meat to a dog (as shown in Figure 5.2). The error made by Broca's aphasics on almost half the trials was to pick the syntactically incorrect depiction (e.g., Figure 5.2b in conjunction with the first sentence above). By contrast, they seldom chose incorrect depictions of individual words (Figures 5.2c and 5.2d). The Broca's aphasics have difficulty processing the serial position of an article that cues the syntactic structure, but they are capable of understanding the individual words in a sentence.

Test Sentence: *They fed her dog the biscuits.*

Figure 5.2   People with Broca's aphasia have difficulty deciding whether the correct interpretation of the test sentence is picture (a) or picture (b) because the choice depends on the syntactic cue of word order. By contrast, they are able to reject pictures (c) and (d) as having interpretations that differ from the test sentence.

Another study also found that Broca's aphasics have difficulty interpreting function words, which is consistent with the fact that function words are often omitted from their speech. This study examined their comprehension of the article *the* when it is used to specify a particular referent (Goodenough, Zurif, & Weintraub, 1977). An example of such a sentence would be:

Please point to the *white one.*

The phrase *the white one* would unambiguously refer to one object in a context that included a white square, a black circle, and a black square (see Figure 5.3). Aphasic subjects were asked to comply with requests such as this. They were also given these sentences in situations in which the article *the* was inappropriate because the referent of *the white one* was not unique—for example, a context that included a white circle, a white square, and a black square. When presented with an inappropriately used *the*, Broca's aphasics, unlike control subjects, seemed not to notice the inappropriateness. They did not hesitate between the two white objects they could select. This result indicates that their processing of the definite article is impaired in some circumstances.

Both word order and function words are crucial for interpreting sentences with embedded clauses. Broca's aphasics have problems with such sentences if

Test Sentence: *Please point to the white one.*

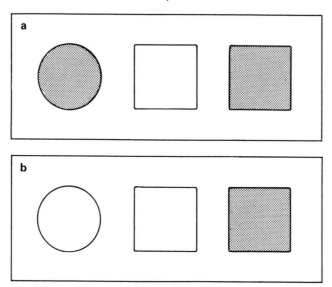

Figure 5.3 All subjects correctly responded to the test sentence when presented with the objects in picture (a). People with Broca's aphasia also responded to picture (b) without hesitation, while control subjects paused when presented with picture (b). People with Broca's aphasia seemed unbothered by the inappropriate use of the phrase *the white one* in conjunction with picture (b).

there are no semantic cues to aid their analysis. The following are examples of sentences with embedded clauses that differ only in the strength and type of semantic cues:

> *The bicycle that the boy is holding is broken.*
> *The dog that the man is biting is black.*
> *The man that the woman is hugging is happy.*

The first sentence is easy to understand because the nouns have semantic properties that help establish which noun goes with which verb. Bicycles cannot hold anything and boys usually are not described as broken, so the pairing must be between *bicycle* and *broken* and between *boy* and *holding*. Because of the semantic cues, patients with Broca's aphasia have relatively little difficulty with this type of sentence. By contrast, in the second sentence, the semantic cues are misleading, since dogs usually bite men, not the other way around. If the aphasic patient relies on this semantic relation, rather than on the syntactic structure, he will misinterpret the second sentence. The interpretation of the third sentence also relies on syntactic information, since either noun is semantically compatible with either of the two verbs. Broca's aphasics have considerable difficulty with both the second and third types of sentences. The aphasics' performance in a sentence-picture matching task (choosing the picture that best corresponds to the sentence) is at chance level (Caramazza & Zurif, 1976). Because the aphasics understand these sentences only if the semantic cues determine the relations, the study suggests that their disability is selectively syntactic in nature.

This brief consideration of Broca's aphasia highlights the types of information that this impaired syntactic analysis cannot correctly deal with—namely, word-order information and function words. In this way, Broca's aphasia helps us see what syntactic analysis does for normal readers by illustrating what reading might be like with impaired syntactic analysis. While comprehension can still proceed when syntactic analysis is impaired, the comprehension relies on nonsyntactic cues and, in the absence of such cues, produces comprehension errors. The selective impairment of syntactic analysis also justifies treating syntactic analysis as an identifiable level of language comprehension, distinct from other levels. But it is important to keep in mind that the separability observed in a language pathology does not indicate how syntactic analysis is interwoven with other processes in normal comprehension.

Cues to Syntactic Analysis

Before describing how syntactic analysis operates, we will describe what syntactic analysis operates on. Syntactic analysis relies on cues in the text to indicate how to group the words of a sentence into syntactic constituents and to indicate syntactic interrelations among the constituents. We have already described how people with Broca's aphasia have difficulty in using two types of cues, word-order information and information from the function word *the*. In this section, we consider a more complete set of six types of cues, listed below, not necessarily in order of importance:

- Word order
- Word class
- Function words
- Affixes
- Word meanings
- Punctuation

This set of cues shares some important properties. In most normal sentences a reader encounters, the available cues tend to converge on a given interpretation, rather than conflict. For example, we do not encounter sentences like *Claudius left the.*, where the period (a punctuation mark) indicates that a sentence has ended, while *the* (a function word) indicates to the contrary that the remainder of a noun phrase is yet to come.

Generally speaking, each type of cue constrains the range of possible syntactic interpretations, but a single cue is often not sufficient to specify an interpretation uniquely. For example, the meaning of the word *hammer* tells us that it is probably a noun or a verb, but this information about word class doesn't tell us which one of these alternatives is intended. However, when provided with additional information from another cue (like an *ed* affix on *hammer*), we can tell that it is the verb form. Similarly, several other types of cues can simultaneously impose **multiple constraints** that can usually be satisfied by a unique interpretation. The moral to remember is that the different types of cues tend to provide converging information that the syntactic analysis integrates to produce the correct interpretation. However, a single cue can sometimes be weak or even misleading, so it is the conjoint constraint imposed by all the available cues that leads to the correct interpretation. Keeping the simultaneous convergence of cues in mind, we proceed now with the discussion of individual types of cues.

Word Order

English and many other languages rely on word order to indicate the syntactic role of a word. Consider the differences among the following sentences:

> *The sheep train the dogs.*
> *The dogs train the sheep.*
> *The train dogs the sheep.*
> *The sheep dogs the train.*

Although all four of these sentences are composed of the very same words, they differ in the serial order of the words. This difference produces very different meanings. In these sentences, we use the word-order cue to interpret the sequence of a noun, simple active verb, and another noun as having the syntactic structure of a subject, followed by a verb, followed by a direct object. In this example, the word order is the major determinant of the assignments of words to syntactic roles.

Consider a slightly more complex sentence:

> *The minister gave the bride the groom.*

It is the order of the two noun phrases after the verb that tells us that *the bride* is the indirect object and that *the groom* is the direct object.

English is inflexible about some aspects of word order and flexible about others. An example of an inflexibility is that if *the* occurs, it must be the very first word of a noun phrase. We cannot refer to a *red car* by saying *red the car* or *red car the*. In contrast to these strict word-order constraints on *the* and some other articles, English often does not have strong constraints on the serial position of adverbs. For example, in the sentence below, the adverb *slowly* can appear in any of the five places marked by an (X), without causing much difference in the ultimate interpretation of the sentence:

(X) *the infantry* (X) *was* (X) *approaching* (X) *from the east* (X).

Regardless of which location *slowly* occupies, the syntactic analysis must associate it with the verb *approaching*. Another modifier, *only,* could also appear in most of these locations, but the syntactic analysis must associate it with different constituents, depending on the location of *only;* this produces somewhat different interpretations in different locations.

In general, word order is an extremely informative cue to the syntactic analysis of English text. The order of words tends to indicate what syntactic role a given word is playing. And the order of larger constituents like clauses and phrases tends to indicate how these constituents are syntactically related to other constituents.

Word Class

Grade school students learn that words can be classified into categories called **word classes,** such as nouns, verbs, adjectives, adverbs, prepositions, and the like. Some of these categories are defined in terms of what they refer to, such as the definition of a *noun* as "a word that refers to a person, place, or thing." Other categories, like prepositions, are harder to define.

Regardless of whether a reader can formally categorize each word she encounters, she has implicit knowledge about word classes and the association between word classes and syntactic roles. This association between word class and syntactic role is a useful cue to syntactic analysis. For example, the reader knows that the word *happy* is an adjective, which tells her that *happy* can enter into one of two main types of syntactic structures. It can either be part of a noun phrase, in which it is modifying the head noun (e.g., *a very happy milkman*), or it can be a predicate adjective (e.g., *The clergyman was happy*). Thus, encountering a simple adjective like *happy* provides the reader with some information that is useful for syntactic analysis. Similarly, determiners (such as *the, a*) and quantifiers (such as *many, several*) signal the beginning of a noun phrase, such as *the boy* and *many boys*. Knowledge of word class is used during syntactic analysis to infer a word's syntactic role, as well as the syntactic roles of some of its neighbors.

Many words can belong to several word classes. In particular, many words are capable of serving both as nouns and as verbs. Consider *pencil, hammer,* and *knife,* which are most often nouns but can also be verbs, whereas *hit, dance,* and *kiss* are most often verbs but can also be nouns. Similarly, *before* and *after* can be either prepositions or conjunctions:

Conjunction: *She danced* before *she left.*
Preposition: *She danced* before *the group.*

Moreover, nouns can be used as adjectives when they act as classifiers modifying another noun, as the noun *lawn* does in the phrase *lawn sprinkler.* Similarly, verbs can be used as nouns when they act as gerunds referring to an action, as *skiing* does in the sentence *I like skiing.*

Word-class information can sometimes evoke a syntactic interpretation that later turns out to be incorrect, as in the well-known garden-path sentence:

> *The old train the young.*

The fact that *old* is usually an adjective and *train* is often a noun leads the reader to think that *the old train* is a noun phrase, which, in this case, it is not.

In spite of the fact that word-class information is generally not sufficient to enable a complete syntactic analysis of a sentence, it nevertheless provides a useful constraint that can combine with other types of cues, like word order, to specify a syntactic interpretation.

Function Words

Word classes can be divided into two general categories: content words (including nouns, verbs, adjectives, and adverbs) and function words (including prepositions, conjunctions, determiners, and quantifiers). Function words are particularly informative for syntactic analysis. For that reason, we will discuss them here, separately from the discussion above of other word-class information. As their name suggests, function words (like *the, and, of*) tend to communicate the syntactic or semantic *function* of a constituent, rather than its content.

A function word generally indicates that a new syntactic constituent is beginning (Kimball, 1973). For example, determiners (*a, the*) signal the beginning of a noun phrase, conjunctions (*whereas, when*) often signal the beginning of a clause, and prepositions (*under, over*) usually signal the beginning of a prepositional phrase. Of course, many types of constituents (like clauses and noun phrases) don't necessarily begin with function words. Thus, function words are sufficient but not necessary cues to the segmentation aspect of syntactic analysis.

Function words not only signal that a new constituent is beginning, but, as in the examples above, they often indicate what type the constituent is. However, the function word's information about the nature of a constituent is less reliable than its information about segmentation. This is because some function words can be used in more than one sense, and each sense is associated with a different constituent. For example, the word *that* can:

1. begin a noun phrase (that *yellow windmill*);
2. begin a clause (*He squandered the money* that *she earned*); or
3. be the predicate of a clause (*I like* that).

The word *that* does indicate that a new constituent is beginning, but it doesn't reliably indicate what kind of constituent it is.

Sometimes the presence of a function word is optional; a writer can choose to insert it or not. For example, inclusion of the word *that* in the following pair of sentences is optional:

> *Mary acknowledged the speaker erred.*
> *Mary acknowledged* that *the speaker erred.*

Several phoneme-monitoring experiments have examined whether the presence of the optional *that* makes comprehension easier and so decreases the time listeners take to detect a target phoneme. The results of the studies are equivocal. Some studies found listeners were faster (Hakes, 1972) and some did not (Hakes, Evans, & Brannon, 1976). The facilitation provided by the function word may depend on whether there are sufficient other cues to permit a correct interpretation. It may also depend on whether the experiment is sensitive enough to detect a reader's momentary difficulty.

The presence of the optional *that,* as well as *whom,* is demonstrably beneficial to the comprehension of an unusual syntactic structure called a *double center-embedding of clauses.* Consider the difference between the following pair of such sentences:

> *The dog the accountant the infant liked bought barked.*
> *The dog that the accountant whom the infant liked bought barked.*

The second version, with the optional function words *that* and *whom,* is generally processed more quickly and accurately than the first version, which does not use such function words (Fodor & Garrett, 1967; Hakes & Cairns, 1970; Hakes & Foss, 1970).

Affixes

A word's syntactic role may be cued by an affix. Consider how the affix *ed,* a past-tense marker, eliminates the ambiguity of the familiar garden-path sentence:

> *The old train the young.*
> *The old trained the young.*

The *ed* affix indicates that *train* is being used as a verb rather than a noun, allowing the syntactic analysis to produce the appropriate interpretation of *The old trained.* Other affixes also indicate word class, thereby contributing information useful to the syntactic analysis. For example *ly* indicates adverbs (*slowly*), *ive* indicates adjectives (*comparative*), and other affixes indicate nouns, such as *tion* (*discretion*), *ness* (*madness*), and *ment* (*amusement*). Some affixes, like *er,* can indicate either a noun (*baker, writer*) or an adjective (*nicer, taller*).

Like many of the other cues, affixes are occasionally misleading. For instance, despite its *er* ending, *deter* is neither a noun nor an adjective. But most often, when used in combination with other cues, affixes are helpful to syntactic analysis.

The reason that Lewis Carroll's nonsensical language Jabberwocky can be given a syntactic interpretation is that it contains many cues to syntactic analysis, as in *"the slithy toves did gyre and gimble in the wabe."* This "clause" provides information in the form of word order, affixes indicating word class, and function words that are consistent with English syntax. Not only can we process the syntax of Jabberwocky sentences (which follow the same syntactic rules as English sentences), but the syntactic comprehension helps us remember the nonsense words in Jabberwocky. For example, consider these two sentences:

> *The murty dimbers fiped the tixing beves.*
> *Murt dimber fipe tix beve.*

Memory for the first, Jabberwocky-type sentence is better than memory for the corresponding second sentence, which lacks affixes and articles (Epstein, 1961). Thus, the syntactic structure developed from these cues helps us store more information in memory.

Although readers seldom need to comprehend Jabberwocky or store a sequence of nonsense words, they do often encounter novel words and novel combinations of old words whose meaning and syntactic role they must guess at with the help of minimal cues. Consider the following sentence:

> *He found the shirt vellicative.*

Most English speakers do not need the *Oxford English Dictionary* to tell them that *vellicative* is an adjective rather than an adverb. That fact can be inferred from the suffix (*ive*) even if the reader is unfamiliar with the word, which means "irritating." Affixes resemble function words in that they indicate the syntactic roles of content words. However, function words are free standing, while affixes are bound to content words.

Word Meaning

A word's meaning is an extremely powerful cue to its syntactic role in a sentence. Given nothing more than the meaning of a word, like *mustard,* we know that it can enter into a limited number of syntactic constructions. We know, for example, that *mustard* must be part of a noun phrase, that it cannot be the subject of a verb that requires an animate subject (i.e., we won't encounter *The mustard thought that...*), and so on. If we encounter a sentence like *Diana saw the hamburger with mustard,* we know to associate the prepositional phrase *with mustard* with *the hamburger* and not with *Diana saw.* By contrast, if Diana had seen *the hamburger with binoculars,* by virtue of our differential knowledge of the meanings of *mustard* and *binoculars,* we would associate the prepositional phrase with *Diana saw* and not with *the hamburger.* In general, the knowledge of individual words provides another constraint to help the syntactic analysis converge on an interpretation, although Jabberwocky demonstrates that word knowledge, like most of the other cues, is not an essential cue.

When the syntactic analysis is extremely difficult to perform (as in sentences with doubly center-embedded clauses), readers can comprehend a sentence more accurately if the word meanings provide an additional cue as to which noun goes with which verb. Of the following two sentences with center-embeddings, the first is easier to paraphrase:

> *The cow the farmer the dog bit milked mooed.*
> *The dog the cat the boy chased liked died.*

The first sentence is easier because a reader can guess how the *cow, farmer,* and *dog* should be associated with *biting, milking,* and *mooing,* just on the basis of the word meanings (Stolz, 1967). It is harder to match the *dog, cat,* and *boy* of the second sentence with *chasing, liking,* and *dying,* because each of the three nouns can be associated with each of the three verbs. The meanings of the individual words provide cues that are used in analyzing the syntactic relations among them.

Punctuation

Punctuation is a very strong cue to syntactic analysis, unambiguously indicating sentence boundaries and, with a slightly lower certainty, indicating clause boundaries. A comma or period at the end of a clause tells the reader to wrap up any loose ends in the syntactic analysis of the clause. Furthermore, it tells him to start a new constituent when he progresses to the word following the clause boundary. Periods and commas are such mundane parts of texts that we sometimes fail to recognize their importance in the normal syntactic analysis a reader performs. Besides providing cues to segmentation, some punctuation marks—like question marks, exclamation marks, and quotation marks—also provide cues to the syntactic and semantic roles of constituents. As Chapter 10 on orthography briefly describes, written languages differ in what punctuation they use. Some written languages, like classical Chinese, contain no punctuation to speak of.

Very few studies have examined how punctuation cues are used in reading comprehension. We know from common experience that a poorly punctuated text is difficult to comprehend because we have trouble segmenting the text into syntactic constituents. One of the very few studies of punctuation showed that even when the indentations that mark paragraph boundaries are missing, readers can tell where the paragraph boundaries should be (Koen, Becker, & Young, 1969). This result shows that like most other cues used in language comprehension, paragraph indentation is an informative but not a necessary cue.

Syntactic Cues across Languages

Languages vary in the cues they use to signal various syntactic properties of a constituent. For example, some languages rely heavily on inflections to indicate whether a noun phrase is the agent of the verb, the object of the verb, or a possessor. In Latin, a phrase such as *little friend* would have different endings depending on its role: *parvus amicus* in *The little friend waved; parvum amicum* in *David liked the little friend;* and *parvi amici* in *This is the house of the little friend.* Similarly, German uses different endings, as well as determiners, to distinguish among some of the roles played by the noun phrases: *Der kleine freund* in *The little friend waved; den kleinen freund* in *David liked the little friend;* and *des kleinen freundes* in *This is the house of the little friend.* By contrast, an English noun phrase, such as *the little friend,* is the same regardless of whether it is the agent, the object, or the possessor. English signals the noun's role through other cues, such as word order and prepositions. However, English does signal some of these distinctions in the pronoun system, by using different forms (for example, *he, him, his; I, me, mine;* and *we, us, our*).

In addition to nouns and their modifiers, verbs also can be inflected to convey syntactic and semantic information. For example, English sometimes uses variation in the endings and auxiliaries of verbs to indicate the number, tense, mood, and voice associated with the verb. Latin verb endings generally indicate the person (first, second, or third) and the number associated with the verb. For example, present-tense verbs, such as *amare* ("to love"), have different forms, depending upon the features of the subject, such as *amamus* ("we love"), *amatis* ("you love"), and *amant* ("they love"). Thus, the Latin verb form is more informative than the English verb form for a reader who is trying to determine which one of several candidates is the subject of the verb.

Different languages rely on various cues to different extents. For example, Chinese lacks the inflected determiners that German uses and the word endings or prepositions that English uses to cue certain semantic roles. In Chinese, the very same word often may be a noun, adjective, or verb. But Chinese relies heavily on

Test Sentence: *Him kicked the girl.*

a

b

Figure 5.4 Most native English speakers think that the meaning of the test sentence *Him kicked the girl* corresponds to picture (a). By contrast, most native German speakers choose picture (b), because in the German language, the case inflection (as in *him* versus *he* in English) is an important cue to grammatical role. Interestingly, native German speakers who also speak English choose picture (b) both when the test sentence is in English and when it is in German.

word order; it has even more word-order restrictions than English. On the other hand, German tends to be more flexible about the order in which constituents occur and relies more on inflectional endings to cue their syntactic roles.

Readers assign more weight to cues that are generally more informative in their language. The weights that a reader develops to combine the syntactic cues in his native language are subsequently used for interpreting the cues in a second language (McDonald, 1984; MacWhinney, Bates, & Kliegl, 1984). For example, English relies a great deal on word order and relatively less on case inflections, such as the use of *he* versus *him,* to indicate a subject or an object. If these two types of cues are pitted against each other in an ungrammatical sentence and the reader is asked to guess at the intended interpretation, an English reader will rely more on word order than case to decide which is the subject and which is the object (see Figure 5.4):

> *Him kicked the girl.*
> *The girl kicked he.*

A native English reader is likely to choose *him* as the subject in the first case and *the girl* in the second, consistent with the word-order cues. By contrast, because German relies more on case inflections, a German reader deciding about comparable German sentences is likely to choose *the girl* as the subject of the first sentence and *he* as the subject of the second, consistent with the case inflections. A German-English bilingual who has considerable experience in English interprets these strange English sentences differently than someone who only speaks English. German-English bilinguals rely more on case inflections. These studies make two points: (1) the weights associated with different syntactic cues differ from language to language and (2) the weights a reader acquires in his first language are carried over to the processing of other languages.

The Processes in Syntactic Analysis

Procedural Knowledge

The syntactic cues described in the preceding section were stated in forms such as "Cue X conveys syntactic information Y," as in "A determiner indicates the beginning of a noun phrase." Our discussion of what the cues indicate can be restated in terms of actions to be taken when a given cue is encountered. The actions are the mental symbolic processes that construct the syntactic representation of a sentence. For example, the following list illustrates the actions associated with some of the cues that we previously discussed (adapted from Clark & Clark, 1977):

Cue	Action
quantifier (*few, all, seven*)	Start a new noun phrase
preposition (*into, behind, of*)	Start a prepositional phrase
subordinate conjunction (*because, when*)	Start a subordinate clause
coordinate conjunction (*and, or*)	Start a new constituent of the same type as the one just completed

The knowledge of what information is conveyed by a cue can be expressed as **procedural knowledge,** a representation of the appropriate mental actions to be taken under a given set of circumstances. Similarly, other levels of comprehension besides syntactic analysis can be represented as procedural knowledge. The contrast is sometimes made between *procedural knowledge* on one hand (such as our procedural knowledge of how to syntactically analyze a noun phrase) and *declarative knowledge* on the other hand (such as our knowledge that Ottawa is the capital of Canada).

The procedural representation of syntactic analysis bears some similarity to the representation of other highly practiced skills, like riding a bicycle. Many college students who know how to ride bikes are unaware of the fact that a critical rule for keeping one's balance is to steer in the direction in which the bike is falling. Nor are they aware of the formal analysis of the physical forces that underlie this rule. Yet they do steer in the appropriate direction when the situation arises. Thus, these cyclists possess the relevant procedural knowledge and use it appropriately, but they cannot express it as declarative knowledge.

The procedural knowledge used in performing syntactic analysis (and in the other levels of comprehension, as well) shares many of these properties. Readers perform the appropriate comprehension processes with little awareness of what cues triggered a particular process. In fact, they have little awareness of anything but the final interpretation of the sentence.

Although the processes in syntactic analysis seldom reach a reader's awareness, it may be worthwhile to mention that some other levels of comprehension are open to awareness during certain stages of the acquisition of reading. Some subskills that are explicitly trained during the early years of schooling, such as the sounding out and blending of the component sounds of a word, are open to awareness while the skill is being taught but become automatic as the child becomes a fluent reader. Syntactic analysis does not need to be trained, nor are listeners or readers generally aware of the processes involved.

Importance of Multiple Cues

As we described in the section on the cues to syntactic analysis, it is imperative that the analysis take multiple cues into account. A single cue type can be weak, absent, or even misleading on occasion; only by attending to multiple cues can syntactic analysis be robust. Syntactic analysis must be able to integrate evidence from the various cues if more than one cue type has evidence to contribute. All models of syntactic analysis agree on the multiplicity of cues and the multiple constraints imposed by different cues. Some models do not allow the syntactic analysis to be influenced by nonsyntactic cues like word meanings or knowledge of the situation to which a sentence refers. Other models, like READER, permit relevant influence from any quarter. Models also differ in the mechanism that chooses or converges on a syntactic interpretation that satisfies the multiple constraints.

Immediacy of Syntactic Interpretation

When a reader starts a sentence, she doesn't know how it will end. But this does not stop her from processing the syntax as she encounters each successive word. A reader interprets a word and decides on its syntactic role before knowing what will follow. This strategy is part of the **immediacy** of interpretation that we have proposed is the default comprehension strategy. It stands in contrast to a wait-and-see strategy, in which the interpretation is postponed, pending the analysis of the words that follow.

The immediacy of syntactic analysis is demonstrated by garden-path sentences, which contain an ambiguity that the reader is enticed to resolve in a way that is ultimately inconsistent with the remainder of the sentence. For example:

The conductor stood before the audience left the concert hall.

Readers tend to interpret *before* as a locative preposition that specifies where *the conductor stood*. It isn't until the reader encounters the word *left* that she realizes this word is inconsistent with the interpretation she has already given the sentence. If syntactic decisions were postponed while the reader waited to see what was coming later in the sentence, she would never be led down such a garden path. The fact that readers are led down such paths demonstrates that the syntactic interpretations are being made immediately as readers encounter each word of a text.

Another source of evidence for the immediacy of syntactic interpretation is that the inconsistency produced by a garden-path sentence is often discovered on the first word that reveals the inconsistency (the word *left* in the example above), not at the end of the sentence. This result also indicates that each word's syntactic status is being evaluated when the word is encountered. Partly for this reason, a linguistic description of the completed structure of a sentence (such as a tree structure) sheds relatively little light on the process by which a reader produces the representation as she is reading.

We have previously contrasted the immediacy strategy with a wait-and-see strategy. The two reasons that wait-and-see strategies of syntactic analysis are still being proposed as psychological models is that (1) the data regarding the processing of garden-path sentences are fairly recent and (2) wait-and-see strategies can work quite well in computer programs that process language. It also seems plausible that people could avoid many garden-path effects if they didn't decide on a word's syntactic role until they knew the next word (Kimball, 1973; Marcus, 1980). For example, a reader would not be led down a garden path in *The old train the young* if the interpretation of *train* was postponed until *the* was encountered. But our eye-fixation data convincingly indicate that readers do not look ahead before making an interpretation (Just & Carpenter, 1980). On the contrary, if the sentence contains a plausible garden path, then readers will follow it and pause for an extra amount of time on the first word that indicates the alternate, correct interpretation. There is no empirical evidence for a wait-and-see strategy, whereas there is considerable evidence for immediacy.

Processing Syntactic Ambiguity

What do readers do when they encounter a syntactic ambiguity? A sentence such as *Time flies like an arrow* has several possible syntactic analyses, including:

Time passes as quickly as an arrow does.
I order you to time those flies as you would time an arrow.
Those little creatures called "time flies" are very fond of arrows.

Do readers compute all possible interpretations and, if not, at which point and on what basis do they choose one interpretation?

Although the evidence is preliminary, it suggests that readers deal with syntactic ambiguity as follows. They compute the multiple interpretations of a syntactic ambiguity when they first encounter it, but on the basis of the preceding context and relative frequency of occurrence, they choose the more likely syntactic interpretation and discard the alternatives. However, they mark that point in their representation of the sentence as a choice point. In most cases, readers will have made the correct decision because the writer does not try to mislead readers by using an infrequent or inappropriate structure.

This characterization has found support from a study (Frazier & Rayner, 1982) that recorded the eye fixations of readers as they processed sentences such as the following:

> *Since Jay always jogs a mile seems like a short distance to him.*

Like many other psycholinguistic experiments, this one presented sentences that are unusual—in this case, lacking a comma at the end of the subordinate clause (after *jogs*). Nevertheless, the readers' manner of dealing with unusual circumstances can be revealing about the processes they are using. In the absence of a comma, when most readers come to *a mile,* they assume that this noun phrase is part of the first clause, rather than the beginning of a second clause, which it eventually turns out to be. This is a reflection of the general preference to attach incoming lexical items to the clause or phrase currently being analyzed, rather than start a new constituent (Kimball, 1973). Readers slow down as soon as they discover they have made an incorrect syntactic decision—in this case, on the word *seems.* The pause on *seems* indicates that this word is inconsistent with the syntactic interpretation that the reader had previously given to the word *mile.* Although *mile* was syntactically ambiguous, it had been given a plausible syntactic interpretation before the next word, *seems,* was processed.

Recovering from misinterpretations   A reader who has incorrectly interpreted an earlier word or phrase can often recover the correct interpretation after encountering the disambiguation. Eye-fixation studies indicate that readers sometimes recover from the initial misinterpretation by returning to the choice point (that is, by refixating the word at which the ambiguity occurred and the choice between interpretations was made). They then reread most of the sentence from that point on, using the alternative interpretation (Carpenter & Daneman, 1981).

The probability of correctly reinterpreting a garden-path sentence appears to depend on at least three factors. One factor is the distance of the initially misinterpreted word or phrase from the word or phrase that disambiguates it. Given working-memory constraints, one would expect that it would be easier for readers to reinterpret a sentence if the cue comes sooner rather than later. Distance is not just determined by the number of intervening words but also by the presence of intervening clauses. In fact, readers are less likely to reinterpret a word if a sentence boundary intervenes between the incorrectly interpreted word and the subsequent disambiguation (Daneman & Carpenter, 1983b).

A second factor that influences the probability of recovering from a syntactic error is the relative frequency with which the two competing interpretations occur.

This factor may explain why people seldom spontaneously figure out their interpretation error in the following sentence:

> *The horse raced past the barn fell.*

The most frequent meaning of the verb *raced* with an *ed* ending in this position is the active voice interpretation. The alternative (and ultimately correct) interpretation is that *raced* is in the passive voice and is part of a reduced relative clause that is lacking a relative pronoun. In full, the alternative interpretation would be:

> *The horse (that was) raced past the barn fell.*

However, it is difficult to recover the correct interpretation of the reduced relative clause, in part, because the construction occurs infrequently. An infrequent alternative interpretation, if it is infrequent enough, effectively does not exist. Thus, error recovery from a syntactic garden path is easiest if the two alternative structures occur with equal frequency in the language and more difficult if the ultimately correct interpretation occurs very infrequently.

A third factor that influences recovery is whether semantic cues (as well as syntactic cues) are present to indicate which word or words were interpreted incorrectly. For example, such cues will make it easier to recover the correct interpretation of the following reduced relative construction:

> *The horse raced by the jockey past the barn fell.*

The phrase *by the jockey* provides both a semantic and syntactic cue that would enable the reader to reclassify *raced* as a passive verb in a relative clause. Just as multiple levels of analysis contribute to the initial interpretation given to a word, so do they also help in the disambiguation and recovery of an alternative interpretation.

Linguistic Theories of Syntax

It is worthwhile to note that the theory of how human beings do syntactic analysis has provoked controversy since the early 1960s. Linguists have been attempting to construct a formal, axiomatic system—a sort of algebra of sentences—that accounts for the structure of grammatical sentences and disallows ungrammatical ones. Most language researchers agree that this is an interesting and worthwhile endeavor. Certainly, there are many regularities within each language and universalities that span all languages, which could be accounted for within such a formal system.

The major issue for psychologists has been the relevance or irrelevance of the formal linguistic theory to a theory of human syntactic analysis. Does the algebraic specification of the syntactic structure of a sentence have much to say about the psychological processes a reader uses to understand that sentence? Countless computer-simulation models have shown that it is possible to specify a processing model that can understand the content of language and effectively make use of syntactic information, all without incorporating a formal linguistic theory of syntax. Our view in this book is that the psychological processes in human reading comprehension can similarly be specified without deciding the relevance of formal linguistic theories of syntax. Although the psychological relevance of formal grammars may be in doubt, there is no question that linguistic theories have provided essential notational and terminological tools. The interested reader can consult Berwick and Weinberg (1983) for a contemporary view of the issue and for citations of many previous articles on this topic.

Two Models of Syntactic Analysis

In this section, we discuss two computer models of syntactic analysis. The first model, called an **augmented transition network (ATN),** emerged from the field of artificial intelligence (Thorne, Bratley, & Dewar, 1968; Woods, 1973) and has been suggested as a model of human processing (Kaplan, 1973; Wanner & Maratsos, 1978). We will describe how a simplified ATN might work. The second model is the part of READER that does syntactic analysis. We present these two models to illustrate those properties of each approach that give us insights into human comprehension.

Augmented Transition Network (ATN)

The ATN's representation of the grammatical rules of language is in the form of a network that consists of nodes, along with arcs that link the nodes. Figure 5.5 shows two simplified networks, one for a sentence and one for a noun phrase.

The ATN's syntactic analysis of a sentence consists of tracing a path through the network that corresponds to the syntactic structure of the sentence. To trace a path through the network, the processor must move from node to node by traversing the arcs. The arcs have conditions associated with them, such that a given arc can be traversed only if the word (or constituent) being processed satisfies the arc's conditions. A condition corresponds to a cue or a combination of cues that indicates a particular syntactic status (like a determiner indicating a noun phrase). The arcs are pointers to other nodes that represent another syntactic status. Because an ATN-based syntactic analysis can be instantiated in many ways, we will focus on the type of ATN described by Wanner and Maratsos (1978), which was motivated by psychological considerations. This ATN deals exclusively with the syntactic level and is not embedded in a more general model that includes semantic and referential processes. Figure 5.6 describes how this ATN would analyze the following sentence:

> *The clever plumber repaired the broken pipe.*

The networks depicted in Figure 5.5 are highly simplified. For example, the noun-phrase network is too simple to analyze many acceptable noun phrases, such as *tall, dark, and handsome stranger* (because of the conjunction). Similarly, the sentence network is too simple to analyze many acceptable sentences, such as sentences with both direct and indirect objects (e.g., *Santa gave the girl candy*). But there is no theoretical limitation to expanding ATNs to accommodate these possibilities.

Several properties of an ATN resemble human syntactic analysis. The most obvious point of resemblance is its sequential one-word-at-a-time attack on the input sentence. Second, the representation of the syntactic rules is fairly modular, so

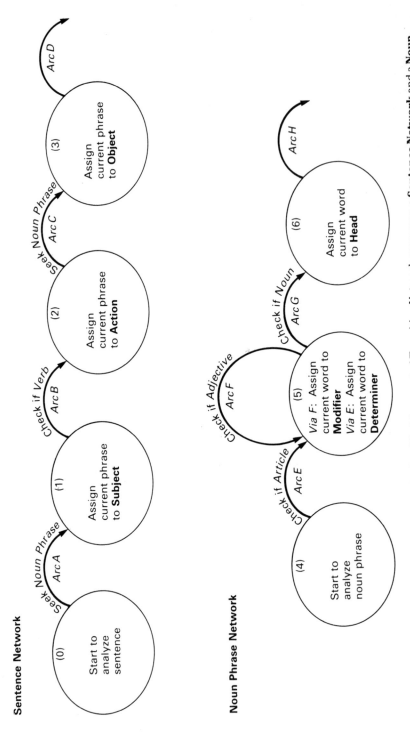

Sentence Network

Noun Phrase Network

Figure 5.5 A diagram of two components of a simplified Augmented Transition Network grammar, a **Sentence Network** and a **Noun Phrase Network.** The networks are traversed by considering each successive word of a sentence to determine if it fulfills the condition associated with the relevant arc. Figure 5.6 shows how the components are used to analyze a simple sentence. *Source:* Adapted from Wanner & Maratsos, 1978, Figure 3.1, p. 124. In M. J. Halle, J. Bresnan, and G. A. Miller (Eds.), *Linguistic theory and psychological reality.* Cambridge, MA: The MIT Press. Copyright © 1978 by The MIT Press. Used with permission.

Test Sentence: *The clever plumber repaired the broken pipe.*

1. Begin at State 0. To cross *Arc A*, the sentence must begin with a noun phrase. Call up the **Noun Phrase Network.**

2. To cross *Arc E* from State 4 to 5, you need an article. Check if the first word is an article (*the, a, an*).

   The satisfies. Assign *the* to the syntactic role of **Determiner.** Go to State 5.

3. To cross *Arc F* or *G*, you need an adjective or a noun. Check if the next word, *clever,* is an adjective.

   Clever satisfies. Assign *clever* to the syntactic role of **Modifier.** Remain at State 5.

4. To cross *Arc F* or *G*, you need an adjective or a noun. Check if the next word, *plumber,* is an adjective.

   It is not. Check if it is a noun.

   Plumber satisfies. Assign *plumber* to the syntactic role of **Head.** Go to State 6.

5. Cross *Arc H.* Associate the words with their functional labels. Send the results back to State 0 of the **Sentence Network.**

6. The noun phrase has been found, so cross *Arc A* from State 0 to 1. Assign the noun phrase the syntactic role of **Subject.**

7. To cross *Arc B*, you need a verb. Check if the next word, *repaired,* is a verb.

   Repaired satisfies. Assign *repaired* the syntactic role of **Action.** Go to State 2.

8. To cross *Arc C*, you need a noun phrase. Call up the **Noun Phrase Network.**

9–12. Process *the broken pipe* analogously to *the clever plumber.*

13. The noun phrase has been found, so cross *Arc C* from State 2 to 3. Assign the noun phrase the syntactic role of **Object.**

14. Cross *Arc D.* Associate the phrases with their functional labels. Send the results to the network, if any, that called up the **Sentence Network.**

Figure 5.6   The steps in analyzing a simple sentence using the Augmented Transition Network diagrammed in Figure 5.5.

every noun phrase is analyzed with the same noun-phrase network, regardless of whether it is a part of the subject of the sentence's main clause or the object in a subordinate clause or part of another noun phrase. The modularity permits the same procedural knowledge to be used in different circumstances.

Before describing the shortcomings of the Wanner-Maratsos ATN, we reiterate the distinction between the general approach of an ATN as opposed to a specific implementation. This is similar to describing shortcomings of the general concept of *democracy*, as opposed to the shortcomings of democracy as it is practiced in a particular country. Having made this distinction, we must also point out that it is sometimes difficult to tell whether a shortcoming is specific to a particular implementation or is inherent in the general concept. Winograd (1983) presents a detailed discussion of the general concept of an ATN.

One shortcoming of an ATN concerns the way temporary ambiguities are handled. This situation arises when the conditions of more than one arc are satisfied but just one arc may be selected to be transversed. The reason the ATN has difficulty in making the correct choice is that it relies on only syntactic information, rather than the full range of information that is available from the sentence. The ATN deals with this situation by making its best guess among the alternative arcs and continuing the analysis of the sentence until an inconsistency is later detected. If the choice later turns out to be incorrect, the processor backs up, reconsidering all the choices it had previously made. It starts its reconsideration at the point at which the interpretation error is first detected and works backward through the sentence until reaching the word at which the wrong choice was made. Thus, a wrong choice made early in a sentence but detected late in a sentence would take very long to undo.

Another difference between an ATN and human processing is that an ATN is inflexible and brittle; it has a tendency to break down easily when meeting resistance. Any syntactic aspect of a sentence that is not fully consistent with its network will cause the parsing process to fail. This rigidity has several facets. As soon as an ATN encounters a grammatical error (such as the determiner *the* followed by the verb *went*), it would be unable to progress any further, since none of the conditions for leaving the current node would be satisfied. But when human readers encounter such an error (as they sometimes do), they continue doing the syntactic analysis through the remainder of the sentence and usually succeed in understanding the sentence by using nonsyntactic information.

Another facet of the brittleness of an ATN is its inability to deal with novelty, such as a new word or an innovative use of an old word. The reason for the breakdown in these cases is that an ATN has no ability to perceive or give credit for a partial match between the input and its stored patterns of possible conditions. Another disparity between an ATN and human processing is that the Wanner-Maratsos ATN engages in a certain amount of nonimmediacy. Even though an ATN must process a sentence one word at a time to decide which arcs to traverse while progressing from node to node, this particular ATN does not construct the syntactic representation of a constituent like a noun phrase until it reaches the end of the constituent. Eye-fixation data disconfirm this account of the processing; we found that no extra time was spent on the last word of a noun phrase (Thibadeau, Just, & Carpenter, 1982). The data indicate that human readers do not behave like this ATN in this respect.

The reason that human readers do not postpone all of the syntactic work until the end of the noun phrase is that they use semantic and referential information to interpret a noun phrase syntactically as they are reading it, so that the syntactic analysis is distributed along the length of the phrase. For example, one of the texts in our eye-fixation studies was about red fire ants. The noun phrase *red fire ants* was repeated several times in the text. After the subjects had read this phrase one or two times, upon subsequent encounters, they spent inordinately little time on the word *ants*. This is probably because they were anticipating that the phrase refers to *red fire ants;* having guessed the referent of the phrase, there was not much point in belaboring the syntactic analysis. Thus, other levels of processing, such as the referential and semantic levels, can short-circuit the syntactic analysis, making it especially brief at the end of a familiar noun phrase, rather than especially lengthy, as the ATN account would have it.

The *fire ants* example illustrates the greatest weakness of this ATN, namely, that it has not been embedded in a full model of human language comprehension, coordinating the syntactic analysis with other levels. The ATN's insensitivity to semantics and other levels of analysis is part of the reason for its brittleness and less-than-full immediacy. Thus, the ATNs constructed to date have been inadequate models of the human process.

The READER Model's Syntactic Analysis

READER's syntactic analysis skills reside in a collection of productions (condition-action pairs). The analysis produces a symbolic structure indicating the major syntactic constituents in a sentence and relating them to each other. READER's analysis searches for surface syntactic relations, such as subject, verb, object, prepositional phrase, relative clause, and so on. The resulting information is similar to what is depicted in a tree structure.

READER's productions are the repository of all of its procedural knowledge. It is easy to see how a production contains the procedural knowledge of what action to take when a given cue to syntactic analysis is encountered. The production for recognizing a noun phrase that starts with a determiner illustrates the point:

> *If you see a determiner (*a, the*)* → *Start a new noun phrase*
> *Expect the phrase to end with a noun*
> *Expect the noun may be preceded by*
> *modifiers*

Many of READER's condition-action productions for doing syntactic analysis relate specific cues to their associated actions, such as the list of associated cues and actions we described previously.

The *condition* side of one of these productions encodes the enabling conditions or cues for a syntactic inference. The conditions correspond to the tests on an arc of an ATN. The *action* side of one of these productions inserts symbols into working memory (or modifies their activation level) that indicate some syntactic assignment or expectation. Some of the actions of the productions correspond to the ATN's traversal of an arc, while other actions correspond to the ATN's labeling of constituents and building the sentence representation.

READER represents the syntactic information it extracts (as well as all other types of information) by means of propositions that have an attribute-value structure. All propositions are constructed using only two fundamental relations, **:HAS** and **:IS.** The :HAS relation indicates that two symbols are joined by a dependency, such that the significance of one symbol is elaborated by the other. For example, to represent the syntactic relation between the subject and verb of a simple clause like *Birds fly,* the dependency (in its expanded form) would be expressed as:

WORD-1 :IS *birds*
WORD-2 :IS *fly*
WORD-2 :IS VERB-1
WORD-2 :HAS SUBJECT-1
SUBJECT-1 :IS WORD-1

Other syntactic predicates besides SUBJECT and VERB include OBJECT and HEAD (of prepositional phrase). The second fundamental relation, :IS, denotes equivalence between two symbols, like the equivalence relations between WORD-1 and *birds* in the example above. These equivalences are not a part of the dependency structure per se but reflect the use of different symbols to stand for the same concept. A search through :IS relations makes it possible to establish a correspondence between symbols created by different processes, such as the correspondence between the grammatical subject of a clause (a syntactic symbol) and the agent of the action (a semantic symbol).

READER contains a collection of productions that analyze the words of a sentence into grammatical constituents and their interrelations, using the representational scheme described above. The syntactic productions comprise a bank of procedural knowledge that can recognize phrases, clauses, and sentences of various types, arrayed in various configurations. Of READER's 225 productions, about 30 of them deal with syntactic analysis and another 15 check grammatical agreement and other forms of consistency. This classification is somewhat arbitrary because some productions are multifaceted. This very rough approximation indicates that 20 percent of the productions are related to syntactic analysis. In order for READER to comprehend texts other than the *Flywheels* passage, many productions of various types would have to be added, but perhaps the proportion of syntax-related productions would not change by an enormous amount. In other words, the procedural knowledge of how to analyze syntax seems to comprise a sizeable but not overwhelming proportion of the comprehension apparatus.

It is difficult to assess the generality of READER's syntactic ability in comparison to that of an ATN. READER's syntactic ability sometimes depends on collaboration with other sources of knowledge (as the next section describes), some of which is specific to the *Flywheels* passage. By contrast, a syntactic ATN does syntactic analysis on its own. In this sense, at least, a syntactic ATN is more complete. However, there is every reason to believe that human syntactic analysis is opportunistic in the same sense as READER, grabbing at any kind of information that assists in the interpretation of a sentence. READER's interreliance among processes echoes the heuristic nature of human comprehension, rather than an algorithmic determinacy.

Collaboration between syntactic and semantic analysis   One distinguishing feature of READER's syntactic parser is its nonreliance on any single aspect of the analysis. READER allows the syntactic analysis to collaborate with other levels of processing, which have access to each others' partial and final products in working memory at all times. Any number of productions of any type can fire at one time, as long as their conditions are satisfied. Thus, several types of computations may co-occur. For example, having encoded *hammer* and accessed the concept, the model can concurrently compute that it is used as a noun, that it is the grammatical subject of the clause, that it is an instrument, and that it refers to a previously mentioned "hammer." Generally, each level of READER's processing (such as syntactic analysis) requires several cycles to accomplish its function, so the concurrence between the various levels of processing spans several cycles.

READER uses a simple mechanism to produce collaboration among processes. Each production increments the activation level of the interpretation it thinks is the correct one, and the interpretation whose activation level reaches a standard threshold first becomes the accepted interpretation. Collaboration occurs when two or more processes converge on establishing a given interpretation by jointly incrementing its activation level to the standard threshold, when neither process alone may have effectively done so. For example, syntactic and semantic productions can collaborate on establishing the nature of a noun phrase. The same mechanism (conjoint incrementation of an activation level) also integrates information from different sources within the syntactic level, as occurs when several different syntactic cues converge on the same interpretation.

Even though the potential for mutual influence between the syntactic analysis and other levels always exists, any level can function in absence of others, although its functioning in isolation would be more susceptible to failure. READER can derive syntactic representations for semantically empty sentences like *The morsified miftab beprated the sork.* Some goodly proportion of normal sentences can be syntactically analyzed on purely syntactic grounds, so the interlevel influence need not occur for every sentence. However, for those sentences in which there is a need for collaborative input from another level, READER's syntactic analysis is not as brittle as a syntax-only parser.

Comparison of READER with an ATN   READER's syntactic analysis retains some of the attractive features of an ATN but embeds the syntactic analysis within a larger system in which other levels of processing can collaborate with the syntactic analysis. READER retains the one-word-at-a-time attack of the ATN. READER also makes use of sequential constraints in English, using knowledge about what classes of words (and larger constituents) can follow each other and permitting recursive embedding of constituents within constituents. Furthermore, READER retains the modularity of processing a constituent so that the same productions process a noun phrase, regardless of whether it is the subject or object of a sentence.

READER expresses the ATN's network in terms of expectations. For example, the READER production presented above encodes some of the same information contained in the ATN's noun-phrase network. The production encodes that if a determiner is encountered, there is an expectation that, ultimately, a head noun will be encountered, possibly preceded by any number of modifiers. As the words of the noun phrase are processed, the expectations become satisfied, somewhat like an ATN traversing the arcs of its network.

READER differs from an ATN in several important respects. One difference is that READER's syntactic analysis operates in collaboration with other levels, so that many different kinds of information can converge to select a sentence interpretation that is likely to be correct. ATNs operate exclusively at the syntactic level.

A related difference is that an ATN cannot easily do things in parallel, while READER can. READER uses its parallel processing in two ways that give it an advantage over an ATN. First, if several syntactic interpretations are possible for a given word in a sentence, several different productions in READER, corresponding to these different interpretations, can fire in parallel. Second, READER does the syntactic analysis in parallel with other levels, such that the other levels can assist the syntactic, and vice versa. The advantage of parallel processing applies only to READER and not to strictly serial production systems that are constrained to firing just one production at a time. A serial production system that dealt only with syntax would, in fact, be fairly similar to an ATN.

Syntactic Analysis and Working Memory

Syntactic processes help structure information so it can be held in working memory until the succeeding parts of the sentence are processed and while other nonsyntactic processes are executed. If a series of words is unstructured, readers have difficulty recalling even a small number of the words that they have read at a normal rate. Consider the following:

> *provide, transient, rich, processes, structures, information, by, linked, networks, parallel*

When given a list of unrelated words, a typical reader is able to recall no more than six or seven words in order. Of course, a reader can recall sentences that are much longer than seven words because a sentence has an internal structure that helps circumvent this memory limitation. Part of the sentence's internal structure is syntactic. The same words can be recalled if they form a syntactically acceptable string:

> *Transient structures, linked by parallel processes, provide rich information networks.*

The groups of hierarchically related constituents that make up a sentence's syntactic structure minimize the burden on working memory. It has long been known that people can recall more elements of a sequence if the elements can be combined into psychological units called *chunks* (Miller, 1956). For example, it is hard to recall accurately a list of eight unrelated digits: 4–8–9–1–9–3–8–1. But the same digits are easily recalled if they form two chunks: 1983–1984. Syntactic structure provides some of the analogous chunking framework for a sequence of words in a sentence.

In addition to providing some of the structure that minimizes storage requirements, syntactic analysis interacts with working memory in three specific ways:

1. Some parsing strategies reflect working-memory constraints.
2. Syntactic structures that tax working memory are difficult or impossible to comprehend.
3. Memory for the exact wording of sentences decays at sentence boundaries.

We will consider each of these topics separately in the following sections.

Parsing Strategies and Working-memory Constraints

Several parsing strategies that people normally use to analyze syntax help to accommodate a long sequence of words within a limited working memory. One strategy is to give a syntactically ambiguous constituent (i.e., one that has more than one possible syntactic analysis) the interpretation that is less taxing to working memory. For example, clauses and phrases that have the potential of modifying several preceding constituents are often interpreted as modifying the immediately preceding constituent (Kimball, 1973). Consider these sentences:

> *The woman that was attractive liked the project.*
> *The woman liked the project that was attractive.*

The phrase *that was attractive* is interpreted as modifying the immediately preceding constituent: *the woman* in the first sentence and *the project* in the second. This strategy of associating a modifying clause with an immediately preceding constituent generally produces the interpretation intended by the text. It also turns out that this strategy minimizes burdens on working memory. If a reader had to attach the modification to a structure that had occurred much earlier, he would have to retain that earlier structure for a longer time or retrieve it before representing the attachment. Thus, the structure of language and the processing strategies that operate on it in part reflect constraints imposed by capacity limitations of working memory.

There is an analogous memory-saving strategy for interpreting ambiguous conjunctions and prepositions. The conjunctions *and* and *or* tend to be interpreted as conjoining low-level constituents (such as objects), rather than as conjoining two clauses. For example:

> *Mary dropped the cup and the saucer accidentally landed on the rug.*

Readers have a tendency to initially interpret *and* as conjoining two low-level constituents—in this case, *the cup and the saucer*. This strategy initially assigns *the saucer* to the role of object of the verb *dropped,* rather than to the role of subject of a new clause (as it turns out to be). The sentence produces a garden-path effect because its ultimate structure is incompatible with the reader's initial interpretation of *and*. An analogous strategy initially interprets *before* as a preposition that modifies an existing constituent, rather than as a conjunction that begins a new clause (e.g., *He stood before the judge of the superior court entered the room*).

Readers' syntactic strategies are biased towards creating as few constituents as possible and at as low a level in the syntactic hierarchy as possible. There is a preference for modifying an existing constituent, rather than creating an entirely new clause. These biases favor simpler structures that impose a smaller burden on working memory.

Memory Load and Syntactic Difficulties

Syntactic analysis is seldom the main source of comprehension difficulty in reading a normal text. However, there are some syntactic structures that are awkward and a few that are almost impossible to comprehend. In some cases, the syntactic difficulties arise because the structure strains working-memory capacity.

Separated constituents Sentences with separations between syntactically related constituents are sometimes awkward or difficult to correctly analyze, for two related reasons (Kimball, 1973). First, the structure may violate the heuristic rule that a constituent is generally associated with the one immediately preceding it, assuming that the association is semantically and syntactically acceptable. Second, such a structure may impose a greater burden on working memory, requiring that the earlier constituent be retained and later correctly associated with a more recent constituent. As an example, consider the awkwardness of the following sentence:

> *Mary predicted she will win the race yesterday.*

This sentence is awkward because *yesterday* cannot modify the adjacent clause *she will win the race. Yesterday* must modify *Mary predicted,* but this clause is separated from *yesterday* by the intervening clause *she will win the race.*

Syntactic analysis is also noticeably difficult with other constructions in which syntactically related constituents are separated. One example is a construction in which particles (prepositions whose meanings combine with other constituents) are separated from the associated constituents, as in the following bizarre but grammatical sentence:

What have you brought the book I don't want to be read to out of up for?

The sentence is awkward in part because there is a string of prepositions at the end that must be paired with constituents that occur earlier in the sentence. The pairings are:

> *what-for*
> *brought-up*
> *read-to*
> *out-of*

Correct pairing requires that the reader keep track of the order in which constituents were presented. When the two members of a syntactic duo are separated by many other constituents, this can tax working memory.

Center-embedded clauses   One of the few structures that is genuinely difficult for adults to syntactically analyze is a sentence with center-embedded clauses, such as the following:

The salesman that the doctor met departed.

Subjects who listen to sentences with a single center-embedded clause make paraphrasing errors about 15 percent of the time (Larkin & Burns, 1977). Paraphrasing errors rise to 58 percent (almost random pairing of nouns and verbs) if the sentence has a double center-embedding, as in:

The salesman that the doctor that the nurse despised met departed.

A number of studies have identified two main sources of difficulty with these structures. First, the constituents of the outer clause (*the salesman* and *departed*) are interrupted by the embedded clause (*the doctor met*), so the reader must keep track of the initial noun phrase while he processes the embedded clause. The second factor is that *salesman* plays two different grammatical roles in the two clauses. *Salesman* must be treated as the subject of the main clause, and then the main clause is interrupted and left unfinished while the embedded clause is processed. And in the embedded clause, *salesman* must be treated as the grammatical object. Associating a single concept with two different syntactic roles simultaneously seems to be a source of difficulty (Bever, 1970). The sentence is easier to comprehend if its structure is changed so that *salesman* plays the same role—grammatical subject—in both clauses:

The salesman that was met by the doctor departed.

Storing, retrieving, and appropriately assigning the nouns and verbs to the correct syntactic roles taxes working memory. To illustrate some of the computations that are involved, consider how nouns and verbs are paired in the paraphrase of this singly embedded structure:

> *The salesman that the doctor met departed.*
> NOUN-1   NOUN-2 VERB-2 VERB-1

Clause	Noun–Verb Pairing
The salesman departed	NOUN-1–VERB-1
The doctor met (the salesman)	NOUN-2–VERB-2–(NOUN-1)

The paraphrase links the first noun with the last verb and the middle noun with the middle verb. In the case of a doubly embedded structure, the sequence of content words is NOUN-1 NOUN-2 NOUN-3 VERB-3 VERB-2 VERB-1. The paraphrases link NOUN-1–VERB-1, NOUN-2–VERB-2, and NOUN-3–VERB-3.

Part of the difficulty in figuring out how to pair up the nouns and verbs in these sentences is not specific to language comprehension or syntactic analysis. It is a general difficulty in storing a sequence of items and then unpacking them in a particular order. One experiment demonstrated that other kinds of materials, such as digits and letters, that must be paired this way are also very difficult to recall (Larkin & Burns, 1977). In one condition of the experiment, subjects listened to a sequence of digits and letters, such as *9–4–6–H–T–N,* and recalled them in an order that resembled the structure of sentences with embedded clauses, *9–N, 4–T, 6–H,* pairing the first digit and last letter, the second digit and second letter, and the last digit and first letter. In another condition, subjects listened to nouns and verbs, such as *nurse doctor parents watched worried stopped,* and tried to recall them appropriately paired: *nurse stopped, doctor worried, parents watched.* The experiment also varied whether the subject was given two pairs, three pairs, four pairs, or even five pairs. Recall of digits and letters and nouns and verbs was compared to recall of the paraphrases of sentences with embedded clauses.

Figure 5.7 shows that as the number of presented pairs increases, performance drops drastically. The recall for digit and letter pairs is somewhat better than the recall for noun and verb pairs, perhaps because digits are generally recalled better in working-memory tasks. But the general trend for digit and letter pairs is remarkably similar to the trend for sentences with embedded clauses. Moreover, performance with the nouns and verbs is indistinguishable from the performance with complete sentences, suggesting that working-memory constraints are a major limiting factor in retaining and re-pairing the constituents in such sentences.

Several studies help localize the point in the sentence where the processing difficulty arises with center-embedded clauses. One study (Forster & Ryder, 1971) compared sentences with single-center embeddings to sentences of the same length without embeddings:

> *The lawyer she wants is busy elsewhere.*
> *The wealthy child attended a private school.*

The sentences were shown one word at a time and very rapidly, 62.5 milliseconds a word, which is about a quarter of the time a normal reader would take. (This method of presentation is called *RSVP,* for *Rapid Serial Visual Presentation*). Recall was better for one-clause sentences than for the two-clause sentences that contained an embedded clause. But only the words in the embedded clause itself were more poorly recalled; the words of the main clause were recalled as well as the words of a one-clause sentence. It appears that the difficulty of determining the

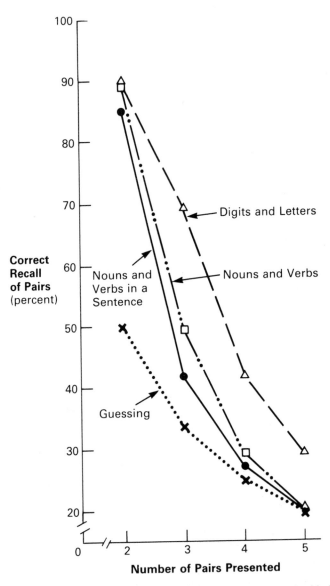

Figure 5.7 The percentage of correct recall of center-embedded items decreases rapidly as the number of presented pairs increases until subjects are close to guessing. This is true whether the items are nouns and verbs in a sentence, nouns and verbs without a sentence context, or digit and letter pairs. *Source:* Adapted from Larkin & Burns, 1977.

syntactic structure of the embedded clause prevented subjects from perceiving or storing the words of the embedded clause as well as they otherwise would have. Of course, RSVP reading is not normal reading, but the results are consistent with those from more normal tasks.

Another pair of studies localized the difficulty in parsing center-embedded sentences by comparing the processing time on each word for two types of structures (Ford, 1983; Holmes & O'Regan, 1981). The noun phrase that was modified by the embedded clause was either the object of the embedded clause or the subject of the embedded clause. These are referred to as *object-relative* and *subject-relative* constructions, respectively, as in the following examples:

Object-relative: *The paper that the senator* attacked admitted the *error.*
Subject-relative: *The paper that* attacked *the senator* admitted the *error.*

In both structures, the embedded clause intervenes between the subject and verb of the main clause. However, the noun phrase modified by the embedded clause plays different syntactic roles in the embedded relative clauses. The results showed that the sentence with the object-relative center-embedding took longer to process, as we will describe more precisely below. Moreover, the extra processing time required for the object-relative construction is expended during the reading of the two verbs. The difficulty is probably attributable to the pairing up of the verbs and subjects.

The first task that localized the difficulty was a combination of the lexical decision task and a word-by-word reading task. Subjects read the text word by word and on the presentation of each successive word judged whether it was a word or nonword (Ford, 1983). The data that were used to examine the hypothesis came from sentences that contained only real words. The decision times for the words in the two types of sentences were compared. The greater difficulty of the object-relative sentences was localized to the three words highlighted in the examples above: the relative clause verb, the main clause verb, and the determiner of the object of the main clause. Note that the subject-verb pair of the outer clause is the same in both cases (*paper-admitted*). But the process of putting this pair together is more difficult if *paper* has served as a grammatical object of the embedded clause in the meantime. The sheer memory load of retaining the first noun is not the problem. We know this for two reasons. First, the word-by-word processing times increase only at the end of the embedded clause. And second, retention of the first noun is necessary in both object-relative and subject-relative structures, so that retention can't be the distinguishing problem either. Thus, all the evidence points to the pairing process as the site of the difficulty.

Holmes and O'Regan (1981) used an eye-fixation study to pinpoint the difficulty of object relative structures. Their results confirmed that readers paused in the region containing the information about the pairings. They showed that object-relative constructions produced longer reading times and more regressive fixations starting at locations corresponding to *admitted* and *the*. Interestingly, their experiment happened to be done in French, showing that the problem of object-relative constructions is not specific to English.

Forgetting in Working Memory

People tend to forget the exact wording of a preceding sentence, whereas they can remember the words in the clause they are currently processing (Jarvella, 1971). Jarvella's experiment examined how verbatim (exact wording) memory decays after a sentence boundary is encountered. The experiment contrasted two types of texts in which a target clause (*after he had returned to Manhattan*) was either part of the second-to-last sentence (Condition A) or part of the last sentence (Condition B).

Condition A: *Taylor did not reach a decision until* after he had returned to Manhattan. *He explained the offer to his wife.*

Condition B: *With this possibility, Taylor left the capital.* After he had returned to Manhattan, *he explained the offer to his wife.*

The objective of the experiment was to determine how the presence of a sentence boundary between *Manhattan* and *He* in Condition A affected the recall of the *Manhattan* clause. The subjects listened to texts in preparation for later comprehension questions. They were interrupted at various times and asked to recall as much of the preceding text as they could. In some cases, the interruption occurred at the end of a sentence following the target clause, for example, after *wife* in Conditions A and B. In one method of scoring the recall, subjects were given credit for

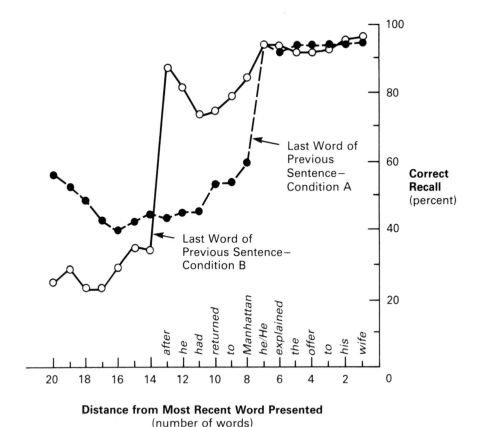

Distance from Most Recent Word Presented
(number of words)

Figure 5.8   The presence of a sentence boundary produces a sharp decrease in the percentage of words that are correctly recalled from the preceding clause. *Source:* Adapted from Jarvella, 1971, Figure 1, p. 411. Used with permission of Academic Press and the author.

any word they recalled, regardless of whether the words were recalled in the correct order. As Figure 5.8 shows, the percentage of words recalled from the last-processed clause (*he explained the offer to his wife,* words 0–7) was similar in Conditions A and B; since that clause had been processed so recently, the percentage was quite high in both conditions. However, the most important data concern the recall of the target clause (*after he had returned to Manhattan*) that preceded the last-processed clause. Recall of this clause was much poorer when the clause was part of the preceding sentence (Condition A) than when it was part of the last sentence (Condition B). Moreover, the drop-off in recall performance occurred right at the sentence boundary, rather than decreasing gradually with the distance from the end of the sentence.

In addition to this result in a free-recall task, Jarvella found a very similar pattern in a prompted-recall task that minimized the memory burdens imposed by the act of recall. The prompted-recall task presented subjects with a single word from the text and asked the subjects to recall the next word. In sum, both experimental tasks found that people tend to forget the exact wording of a preceding sentence, whereas they do retain the words of the clause they are currently processing.

There is also evidence of a drop-off in memory for the words from an earlier clause, even if it is part of the current sentence. In Condition B of Jarvella's experiment, the recall was slightly lower for the words of the first clause of the last sentence than for the second clause.

A seldom-cited aspect of Jarvella's study helps clarify which aspect of exact wording information from previous clauses or sentences is forgotten. What drops off sharply is not just the memory of the words but the memory of the word order. To measure the recall of word order, Jarvella used a second scoring method, giving credit for recall of a word only if all the subsequent words were recalled in the correct order. This second scoring method showed that word-order information from a previous clause drops off very sharply at the clause boundary. By contrast, the first, looser scoring method described above showed that memory for the words themselves does not drop off quite as much at clause boundaries. Figure 5.9 shows the two scoring methods for Condition B. This result indicates that people have very poor memory for the exact order of words in the preceding clause. Word order is a very important cue to syntactic analysis, and it may be that once the syntactic analysis has been done, the word-order information is no longer retained.

Further evidence of forgetting at a clause boundary comes from an experiment in which subjects decided whether or not a test word had been included in a two-clause sentence that they had just heard (Caplan, 1972). On the trials in which the test word had been a part of the sentence, the word came from either the first or the second clause. Two different groups of subjects saw a particular word (*oil,* in the following example) that either belonged to the first clause, which was always a subordinate clause, or to the second, main clause:

Now that artists are working in oil, *prints are rare.*
Now that artists are working fewer hours, oil *prints are rare.*

The subjects were slower (by about 60 milliseconds) to respond to a word like *oil* when it appeared in the first clause than when it appeared in the second. This shows that clause boundaries (the boundaries of major syntactic constituents) affect

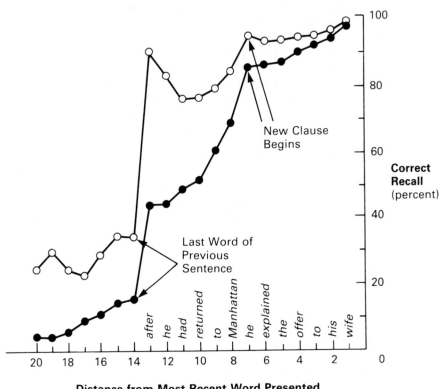

Figure 5.9   A comparison of the results for Condition B using a stricter and a looser method for scoring recall. The difference between the two methods suggests that the presence of a clause boundary produces a sharp decrease in memory for the order of the words in a previous clause. *Source:* Adapted from Jarvella, 1971, Figure 1, p. 411. Used with permisssion of Academic Press and the author.

the way readers organize information in working memory. The degree to which exact wording information from a previous clause is forgotten depends, to some extent, on what syntactic role that clause plays in the entire sentence—whether it is the main clause or a subordinate clause, for instance (Townsend & Bever, 1978).

The exact wording of a preceding sentence or clause might be forgotten for several reasons. One possibility is that after the syntactic analysis at the end of a clause has been performed, there may generally be little further need for retaining the exact wording information; thus, it may be deactivated. Another related possibility is that the syntactic computations that occur at the end of a major syntactic constituent are so demanding of working memory that the exact wording information is displaced by competing computations. The idea that computations may be particularly demanding at a syntactic boundary is consistent with some data from eye-fixation studies. Several studies have found that readers spent extra time on the last word of a difficult sentence and sometimes on the last word of a nonfinal clause (Just & Carpenter, 1980). This extra time may be attributed to "wrap-up" processing, tying up loose ends that have been unresolved until the end of the sentence. Some of these loose ends are probably syntactic. The demands of the wrap-up computations at sentence boundaries may cause the reader to forget the exact wording information.

While memory for the exact wording of a sentence decays fairly rapidly, memory for the meaning of a sentence usually persists much longer (Sachs, 1967). However, people do recall the exact wording of a text if it is very important, as it is, for example, in poetry. Exact wording also tends to be remembered if it has emotional import, such as an insult or a challenge (Keenan, MacWhinney, & Mayhew, 1977). Also, there are individual differences among people in the degree to which they are trained to focus on the exact words. Learning exact wording is stressed in some educational systems (such as the Latvian system mentioned by Hunt & Love, 1972) and in cultures that train the memorization of religious texts. People learning in that sort of educational environment may pay more attention to the exact wording of a text; as a result, they will have developed better mnemonics and heuristics for remembering the exact words.

Summary

One of the themes of this chapter is that syntax helps a reader decode a linear string of words into a more complex, interrelated structure. The syntactic organization helps to hold the words of a sentence together in working memory in their appropriate groupings while the meaning of the sentence is being processed.

Syntactic analysis uses several classes of cues in determining the interrelation, including word order, affixes, punctuation, word class, and word meanings. Often, any single cue is insufficient to determine a syntactic interpretation, but several cues together provide multiple constraints that aid in determining how various parts of the sentence are syntactically interrelated.

Like other levels of comprehension, syntactic analysis uses the strategy of immediate interpretation. For example, in processing words or phrases that are syntactically ambiguous, readers appear to choose a syntactic interpretation immediately, eliminating the need to store two developing representations simultaneously.

Another theme of the chapter, exemplified by the description of the READER model, is that a thorough understanding of a sentence often requires collaboration among several different levels of comprehension.

Several aspects of syntactic processing are reflections of the constraints imposed by working-memory capacity. First, some parsing strategies tend to minimize the limitations imposed by the capacity of working memory. Second, sentences with lengthy interruptions between syntactically related constituents are often difficult to comprehend. Third, memory for the exact words of a clause or sentence decays very rapidly at a sentence boundary, when most syntactic and semantic constraints are ended.

Suggested Readings

Winograd's book (1983) provides a thorough consideration of the computational issues in the processing of syntax. And the textbook by Fodor, Bever, and Garrett (1974) deals with the psychology of language, with a strong emphasis on syntax. Two interesting collections of articles dealing with the processing of syntax are the volumes edited by Cooper and Walker (1979) and by Dowty, Karttunen, and Zwicky (1985).

The article by Stabler (1983) and the rejoinders to it give some indication of the controversy regarding the implications of linguistic theories for psychology. Berwick and Weinberg (1983) provide an integrative discussion of the relation between linguistic theories and human processing. Wanner and Maratsos (1978) provide a good discussion of ATNs. Kimball (1973) and Clark and Clark (1977) describe some possible heuristics used in syntactic analysis. The paper on Broca's aphasia by Berndt and Caramazza (1980) is an elegant example of the way that an analysis of a pathology can tell us about normal psychological functioning.

6

Semantic Analysis

Suppose you hear or read the following sentence:

John gave the book to Peter in the library.

You probably understand this sentence to mean that in some past time, there occurred an action of giving, in which some person named John handed over a book to someone named Peter and that the action took place in a library. Even though the understanding seems to occur without any effort on your part, there are nevertheless sophisticated cognitive processes that analyze the semantic relations among the participants and circumstances of the action or state described by such sentences.

Our use of the word *semantics* is narrower than in some other psychological writings. Some researchers use *semantics* to refer to almost every aspect of meaning that is not syntactic, including general knowledge of the world or knowledge of the referent of a sentence. We, too, will deal with these other types of information (in Chapters 7 and 8) but not under the rubric of *semantics*. We use *semantic analysis* to refer to the process of recognizing the roles of people and objects that are part of the action or state described by a clause.

It may be worthwhile to consider how the semantic representation of part of the sample sentence *John gave the book to Peter in the library* differs from the referential and syntactic representations. The referential representation symbolizes the objects and actions to which the clause refers. For example, the *referential* representation of *the book* symbolizes a particular physical object. If the reader knows the context—say, that John had agreed to part with his copy of a handbook of organic chemistry—then the referential representation of *the book* symbolizes that particular handbook, as illustrated in Figure 6.1. In addition, this figure shows that the referential representation of *the book* is the same when it occurs in a second sample sentence, *The book was given to Peter. . . .* The *semantic* representation of *the book,* by contrast, encodes the fact that *the book* is the object of the giving. In fact, *the book* is the object of the giving in both sample sentences. Finally, the *syntactic* representation of *John gave the book. . .* symbolizes the structural or gram-

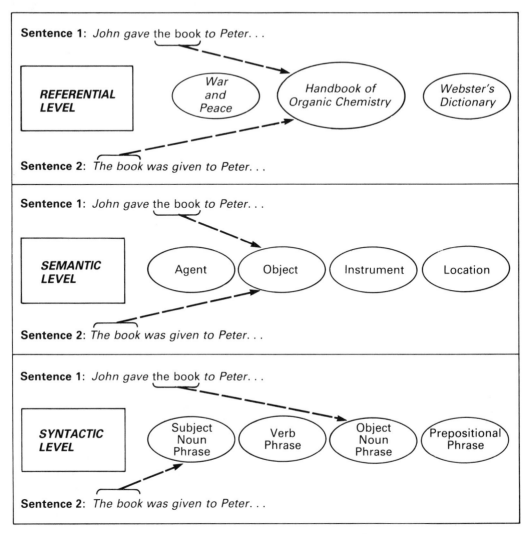

Figure 6.1 A contrast of the three different levels of representation of the phrase *the book* as it occurs in two sample sentence fragments: (1) *John gave the book to Peter. . .* and (2) *The book was given to Peter. . .* The three levels of representation—the referential, semantic, and syntactic—are depicted by the node pointed to by the dashed line in each of the three panels.

matical relations among the elements of a clause, indicating that *John* is the subject of the verb, that *the book* is the object noun phrase, and so on. In the syntactic representation of the second sample sentence, *The book was given to Peter. . .*, *the book* is represented differently, because in this case, it is the subject noun phrase.

Semantic analysis refers to the psychological processes by which a reader understands the conceptual relations among the elements of a clause and constructs a mental representation of those relations. Semantic analysis is concerned with three kinds of information:

1. the roles played by various participants in a state or action (in this case, who is the giver, who is the recipient, and what is given);
2. the state or action (in this case, the giving); and
3. the surrounding circumstances (when and where did all of this happen).

This chapter describes the information that is used in semantic analysis, the kind of representation that is produced, and the mechanism that performs the analysis.

Overview   In the first section of the chapter, **An Introduction to Semantic Analysis,** we will briefly illustrate the representation that is generated by semantic analysis and discuss its role in comprehension. The next several sections are organized around the three kinds of information processed by semantic analysis concerning participants, actions, and circumstances.

In the second section, **The Roles of Participants,** we will discuss both a linguistic approach and a computer-modeling approach to the analysis of the semantic roles played by various participants in an action. We will also discuss some of the linguistic cues that can indicate what the participant roles might be.

In the third section, **The Semantic Analysis of Actions and States,** we will discuss the parts of a clause (typically, verbs and adjectives) that describe actions and states. We will describe how verbs might be internally represented by the reader and how the representation might be used in the course of semantically analyzing a clause.

In the fourth section, **The Semantic Analysis of Circumstances,** we will describe some of the types of information included in the category of circumstances, such as the time and place in which an action occurred. To illustrate the analysis of circumstances, we will describe the representation and processing of negative sentences.

In the fifth section, **Propositional Representation,** we will describe how semantic information may be represented in a propositional format, and we will evaluate some of the data supporting this type of representation.

In the final section, **How Semantic and Syntactic Analyses Work Together,** we will consider the relation between these two levels of analysis. The main discussion concerns whether the two processes operate autonomously or interactively.

An Introduction to Semantic Analysis

Semantic Representation

To start, we present a slightly more precise semantic representation for the following sentence:

Yesterday, John inadvertently gave the old book to Peter in the library.

The proposed representation, adapted from van Dijk and Kintsch (1983), provides a concrete example of the output of semantic analysis. The structure and components of the semantic representation of this sentence will be explained in more detail later in the chapter. In the representation below, the three kinds of information—concerning the action, participants' roles, and circumstances—are indicated by the headings PREDICATE, ARGUMENTS, and CIRCUMSTANCES, respectively. The letters *a, b,* and *c* are variables that stand for the words to which they are linked by an equal sign:

> PREDICATE: *give (a,b,c)*
> > Modifier: *inadvertently*
>
> ARGUMENTS:
> > Agent: *John = a*
> > Object: *book = b*
> > > Modifier: *old (b)*
> > Goal: *Peter = c*
>
> CIRCUMSTANCES:
> > Time: *yesterday*
> > Place: *in the library*

This form of representation separates the three categories of semantic information and indicates the kinds of information that often occurs in each category.

The information about the **predicate,** an action or state, tends to come from verbs, but other parts of speech can also provide this type of information. Actions or states are easiest to identify when the action is simple and concrete, such as the *giving* in *John gave the book to Peter,* but not so straightforward in more complex sentences like *The arbitrariness of the decision was not apparent.*

The information about the **arguments** or participants in the action comes primarily from noun phrases. The participants can be animate or inanimate, physical or abstract objects. In a simple sentence like *John gave the book to Peter,* it is easy to tell that the participating objects are *John, the book,* and *Peter.*

Finally, the third kind of information, regarding the **circumstances,** includes the time, place, and world in which the action or state occurs. The circumstance information can come from a large number of possible sources, the most likely of which is the preceding context. But information about circumstances can also come from adverbs like *yesterday,* from prepositional phrases like *in the library,* and from verbs like *dreamed* (e.g., *John dreamed that yesterday, he gave the book to Peter in the library*).

The order in which the three kinds of information are comprehended depends largely on the sentence. If the participants are described first and the action, last, then the corresponding semantic representation is probably constructed in that order (e.g., *It was the cat who the dog chased*). If the circumstance information is being imported from the previous context, then it does not have to be constructed anew at all. If the sentence does introduce circumstance information, it can often do so at any point in the sentence. So the semantic analysis of who is doing what to whom and under what circumstances occurs as the relevant information is encountered in the text.

Processes in Semantic Analysis

Throughout this chapter, semantic analysis is construed as a process of filling in the slots of a **schema.** For each clause a reader encounters, he evokes a schema consisting of a frame with labeled but unfilled slots. The semantic information from the sentence is inserted into these slots.

The psychological issues in semantic analysis concern the reader's choice of a schema (how does he know which schema to use for a given clause?) and his ability to match up the information in the clause with the appropriate slots in the schema. The schema for the semantic analysis of a clause would consist of three sets of slots, one for each of the three categories of semantic information, namely, the action or state, the participants, and the circumstances. Sometimes, a slot of one sentence's schema is filled by the semantic representation of an entire other clause. For example, the object of the hitting in *John hit what I was holding* is the thing referred to by the embedded clause *what I was holding*. Different clauses use slightly different schemata (different subsets of all the possible semantic roles); the choice of schema is determined by the nature of the action or the state to which the clause refers. The verb (or the part of the clause that describes the action or state) is generally important in selecting the schema.

For skilled readers, semantic analysis is typically rapid and effortless. It is also an essential component of comprehension. A large part of what is informally called *understanding* consists of semantic analysis. Unfortunately, there are few experimental results that indicate exactly how readers determine the semantic roles and relations in a text. Instead, many of the insights concerning semantic analysis have come from the disciplines of linguistics and computer science. Linguistics has provided analyses that indicate what the semantic content of a clause might be; consequently, it provides some information about the end product of semantic analysis. And computer-simulation models of semantic analysis serve as examples of mechanisms that are sufficient for performing the analysis and might possibly resemble the processes that human readers use.

The Roles of Participants

The Linguistic Analysis of Cases

The linguistic approach most relevant to human comprehension of semantic content is the analysis of the constituents of a clause into semantic **case roles**. According to this approach, which is most commonly associated with Fillmore (1968), the semantic content of a clause can be analyzed into a set of case relations among the clause elements. According to Fillmore's approach, each clause is like an act of a play, and each conceptual element in the clause can be thought of as an actor playing a role. What's more, just as plays have heroines, villains, and foils, clauses have agents (animate objects that instigate an action), instruments (inanimate objects causally involved in performing the action), and objects of actions. So the sentence below might be analyzed into cases as follows:

Harold stirred the soup with the ladle.

Agent: *Harold*
Instrument: *ladle*
Object: *soup*

The same case analysis would be given to a syntactically different sentence:

The ladle was what Harold stirred the soup with.

Agent: *Harold*
Instrument: *ladle*
Object: *soup*

Fillmore suggested that there might be approximately half a dozen to a dozen different cases, but the number and nature of cases vary slightly from theory to theory. In addition to the three cases already mentioned, some other possible cases include the following (compiled by Winston, 1977):

Co-agent: *Sheldon painted the table* with his brother.
Beneficiary: *Alice went on an errand* for her mother.
Time: *George left* yesterday.
Location: *David painted the sundial* in the garden.
Origin and **Destination** of change in position:
    Olga moved the ashtray from the table to the cabinet.

One property of language that is congenial to case-role analysis is the use of explicit markings on words (such as word inflections) to indicate their case role. For example, in English, we use the word *he* for the agent of an action but *him* for a person affected by the action. And in Latin, the ending of the word *boy* changes with its case role, as seen in each of the following sentences:

Agent: *The* boy (puer) *likes Mary.*
Object: *Mary hit the* boy (puerum).
Recipient: *Mary gave the* boy (puero) *a book.*

The fact that morphological variation in some languages revolves around semantic case roles suggests that case roles might be an inherent organizational factor in all languages.

The relevance of the linguistic analysis of case roles to psychology is that comprehenders and speakers of sentences are probably organizing the semantic information in terms of cases. While doing a semantic analysis of a sentence, a reader may be producing a representational structure that resembles a linguist's characterization of the case relations in that sentence. The case-role analysis is particularly apt for clauses that describe physical actions.

The linguistic analysis of case roles is incomplete as a model of human semantic analysis in several ways. Most importantly, the linguistic analysis indicates nothing about the process that a reader might be using to perform the semantic analysis. For example, what cues does a reader use to determine whether a word denotes the agent or object of the action? How does he determine the possible and necessary case roles in a given sentence? The linguistic analysis does not provide answers to such psychological questions nor was it intended to.

The second way in which case-role analysis is inadequate as a psychological model is that much more semantic information than case roles is processed in a sentence. For example, case-role analysis is weak in its handling of states (as opposed to actions); verb-related properties (like mood, tense, and aspect); modification by adverbs, adjectives, and prepositional phrases; and the relations among the different clauses of a sentence.

A third inadequacy of case-role analysis as a psychological model is its disproportionate reliance on the verb. In a case analysis, the verb plays an important role, since it determines which of the cases are permissible in that clause and which are mandatory. For example, a verb like *sent* has case slots for at least three main participants: the sender, the recipient, and the object being sent. By contrast, a verb like *loved* has slots for only two main participants: the agent and the object of the loving. To analyze an isolated sentence into case roles, a linguist is totally dependent on knowing the verb. But a reader who is familiar with the context of an extended passage sometimes knows what roles various participants play before seeing the verb of a particular sentence.

Computer Models of Semantic Analysis

A computer program that performs a semantic analysis of English or any other language provides a model of a mechanism at work. Thus, we can observe not only its products but also how it operates. One such computer program developed by Schank (1975) and his co-workers analyzes semantic relations among the elements of a clause. The analysis is done by assigning each element to one of several roles in a schema. The schema has slots for an action, an agent, an object, an instrument, and so on. In addition, the action has subslots specifying a possible source and destination of the action. For example, *John gave the book to Mary* is analyzed as follows:

> **Agent:** *John*
> **Object:** *book*
> **Action:** transferred possession *(gave)*
> > **Direction to:** *Mary*
> > **Direction from:** *John*

This representation would also be produced for *The book was given to Mary by John.*

The computer program assigns sentence elements to semantic roles by using information from a lexicon that contains word meanings. The program relies particularly on the meanings of verbs. The lexical entry for each verb indicates which semantic roles are permissible or mandatory for that verb; it also indicates any special dependencies among the semantic roles. For example, one family of verbs describes the transfer of an entity from one location to another, as in *John loaned the book to Mary,* indicating transfer of the book from John's to Mary's possession. Other verbs—like *traded, sent, delivered, bequeathed, sold, donated,* and *relinquished*—also describe this same basic semantic relation. Some of these verbs describe additional semantic relations, too, such as the transfer of money entailed by *sold.* The lexical representation of each of these verbs would include a slot for the source and destination of the transfer of possession. More generally, every verb in the lexicon would be associated with a set of slots, such that the semantic elements of the clause could be assigned to the slots.

Cues to the Analysis of Participant Roles

Human readers and computer programs can use several different kinds of cues to help them assign participants to slots. The following discussion lists a number of cues to semantic analysis that a computer program might use (adapted from Winston, 1977).

1. The cue that is especially useful in English is the *syntax of the clause*—and in particular, the serial order of the constituents of a clause. For example, in the sentence *Gordon struck Jessica,* the main cue used to assign *Jessica* to the object-of-action role is the serial position of the word *Jessica.* The assignment of roles would be reversed if the serial order were changed, as in *Jessica struck Gordon.* In a slightly more complicated sentence, like *The postman gave the woman the dog,* the serial order of the noun phrases *the postman, the woman,* and *the dog* is the major cue indicating who is giving what to whom.

The heuristic rules for using the serial-order information must take other kinds of syntactic information into account, as well, such as the voice of the verb (active or passive) and the meaning of various particles and prepositions. For example, if only one noun phrase not preceded by a preposition follows a verb (as in *Albert shook* [some noun phrase]), it is likely to belong in the object-of-action slot, provided that the verb is transitive and in the active voice and that the noun phrase does not refer to a duration (such as *the whole day*). Other rules might ascertain whether the referent of the noun phrase is capable of undergoing the action described by the verb (unlike *He drank the wood*). These other rules could also contribute to the assignment of the semantic roles.

2. Another highly informative cue to semantic analysis is *the meaning and syntactic form of the verb.* Knowing what kinds of roles are typically associated with a given verb tells the reader what schema he should be using—that is, what the precise number and configuration of slots should be. Verbs can be classified in terms of how many direct participants can be involved in the action. An example of a one-slot verb is *to die,* as in *Harvey died.* An example of a two-slot verb is *to kill,* as in *Charles killed Harvey.* An example of a sentence with a three-slot verb is *Karl sent Jeff to Matthew.*

Knowledge of verbs and the actions they denote enables a reader to evoke the appropriate schema for a given clause. Moreover, the syntactic information is particularly helpful in indicating which participant belongs in which slot. For example, the verb *sent* has the same three slots regardless of whether it is in the active or passive voice *(Jeff was sent by Karl to Matthew).* The voice of the verb together with other syntactic information helps assign participants to semantic roles.

3. *The particles that accompany verbs* and constitute part of their meaning also help in selecting the appropriate schema. For example, the verb *put* combines with several particles to describe several different actions, such as:

a. *Wayne* put *the picture with the hammer.*
b. *Wayne* put up *the picture with the hammer.*
c. *Wayne* put up with *the picture with the hammer.*

Even though the three sentences above differ only in their verb particles, this difference produces a different semantic analysis of the phrase *with the hammer* in each case. In sentence (a), *with the hammer* provides locative information, indicating that the picture was placed next to the hammer. In sentence (b), the same phrase indicates that the hammer was the instrument used in the act of *putting up* the picture. In sentence (c), the verb *put* and the particles *up with* combine to mean "tolerated." In this case, the phrase *with the hammer* modifies *picture,* indicating that the *picture* contained a *hammer.* These sentences illustrate how pivotal the verb particle can be in the assignment of semantic roles.

4. Although the English language seldom inflects words to indicate semantic roles, *pronoun inflections* are sometimes helpful in this regard. For example, consider these two sentences:

> *Harry and Frank were building a boat.*
> *Harry accidently hit him/himself with a hammer.*

The choice of pronoun, *him* or *himself,* indicates whether Harry or Frank should be assigned to the object-of-action slot.

5. The *prepositions* that precede a noun phrase often indicate the semantic role of the object that the phrase describes. For example, if a noun phrase is preceded by a preposition like *above,* then there are only a few possible case roles to which the noun phrase can be assigned.

6. Although each type of semantic cue discussed above is informative, a reader must often use his *knowledge of the referent* of the noun phrase to choose among the possible case-role assignments for a participant. In the sentences below, only the noun phrase itself determines whether it should be assigned to the slot for an instrument (sentence [a]), a coagent (sentence [b]), a modifier of another participant (sentence [c]), or a modifier of the action (sentence [d]).

a. *Jake ate the sausage* with a fork.
b. *Jake ate the sausage* with a friend.
c. *Jake ate the sausage* with the dark skin.
d. *Jake ate the sausage* with enthusiasm.

The Use of Knowledge

Why is a sentence like *Jake ate the sausage with relish* ambiguous, while *Jake ate the ice cream with relish* is not? The answer is simple: A reader knows that relish is not normally eaten with ice cream and would probably not taste good with ice cream. This information is not specific to language use. A reader uses general knowledge about the tastes of foods to assign *with relish* in the sentence about ice cream to a modifier-of-action slot, describing the manner in which Jake ate the ice cream. However, since relish is sometimes eaten with sausages, *with relish* in the sausage sentence could mean *relish* was a condiment, or again, *with relish* could describe the manner in which the sausage was eaten. This pair of sentences illustrates that the semantic analysis depends on world knowledge, as well as knowledge of the context.

The role of knowledge can also be illustrated by considering verbs such as *get, have,* and *take,* each of which can have a number of different interpretations that differ in the semantic analysis they require. Even a syntactically simple sentence like *Paul took* [some noun phrase] can require different types of semantic analysis, depending on the nature of the noun phrase. If the noun phrase at the end of the sentence is *a beating,* then the semantic analysis should indicate that the action is *beating,* that the agent is unspecified in this sentence, and that the object of the action of *beating* is *Paul.* But if the noun phrase is *some medicine,* then the agent would be Paul, and the action would be ingestion. Similarly, if *John took* were followed by noun phrases like *a taxi, a job, a firm stand, the good advice,* or *a wife,* there would be a slightly different semantic analysis in each case. These examples illustrate that the ultimate semantic analysis is a product of several elements of a clause, as well as knowledge of the referents.

The semantic analysis processes that use these cues must operate according to several principles. First, most semantic-role assignments have multiple cues, so information from several cues generally must be combined, and their information value must be weighed in proportion to the reliability of the cue. Second, semantic analysis is performed as each word of a clause is encountered by the reader, so the order in which the cues are encountered will be a major determinant of the semantic analysis process. Third, many extrasentential information sources—such as the reader's knowledge of actions and objects in the world and her knowledge of the preceding text—will be brought to bear on the semantic analysis process.

Making Inferences about Semantic Roles

Under certain circumstances, readers may mentally fill in the slots of important semantic roles, even if the information is not explicitly provided by the sentence. For instance, consider the instrument implicit in this sentence:

Alice pounded in the nail until the board was safely secured.

This sentence invites the inference that the instrument was a HAMMER. When readers try to recall a sentence like the one above, they tend to recall having read something about a HAMMER, even if none was explicitly mentioned. However, the recall of an unmentioned instrument doesn't indicate whether the reader made the case-filling inference initially, while reading the sentence, or later, during recall (Corbett & Dosher, 1978).

A newer type of experiment (McKoon & Ratcliff, 1981) indicates that readers do infer probable instruments during reading if the instrument has been mentioned previously in the context. This experiment measured whether the representation of the implied instrument became activated while the sentence was being read. Readers were given short paragraphs in which the first sentence explicitly mentioned a target object, like a HAMMER, thus making it salient. In the experimental condition, the last sentence described an action, like pounding nails, that invited the inference that the target object was the instrument. In the control condition, the last sentence described an action, like gluing boards, that was unrelated to the target object.

Experimental condition:
Bobby got a saw, hammer, screwdriver, and square from his toolbox. . . . [Three more sentences about Bobby working]. . .
Then Bobby pounded the boards together with nails.

Control condition:
Bobby got a saw, hammer, screwdriver, and square from his toolbox. . . . [Three more sentences about Bobby working]. . .
Then Bobby stuck the boards together with glue.

Immediately after reading the last sentence, subjects were presented with a test word and they judged whether or not it had occurred in the paragraph. In the trials of interest, the test word was from the first sentence (say, *hammer* or *screwdriver*), so the correct response was "yes." In the experimental condition, where HAMMER had been the implied instrument in the last sentence, subjects were faster (by 68 milliseconds) to respond that *hammer* had previously occurred. Presumably, the concept HAMMER had been reactivated during the reading of the last sentence of the experimental condition, and this made it easier to verify that it had occurred. The same technique showed that a less probable instrument (in this case, MALLET) was not inferred during the reading of the last sentence of the experimental paragraph, even if it had been mentioned in the opening sentence. So this study indicates that readers do activate probable instruments of actions, at least in cases in which the probable instrument has been mentioned previously.

Inferences about participants are almost certainly made if they are necessary for text coherence. Consider how a reader would integrate the word *broom* in sentence (1b) below:

1a. *The maid diligently* cleaned *the floor until it was spotless.*
1b. *The broom had been worn down by her excessive zeal.*

Most readers infer that the *broom* mentioned in sentence (1b) refers to the unspecified instrument of the action in the first sentence. A study that monitored readers' eye fixations as they read such inference-inviting sentences indicated that the inference is often drawn when the reader first sets his eyes on the word *broom* (Just & Carpenter, 1978). The paragraphs the subjects read contained a critical pair of sentences, like the pair above. The first sentence of the pair described an action without implying any particular instrument, while the second sentence began with a noun that could plausibly have been the instrument of that action. In another condition, the first sentence used a verb that *did* imply that particular instrument:

2a. *The maid diligently* swept *the floor until it was spotless.*
2b. *The broom had been worn down by her excessive zeal.*

Even though the second sentences of the couplets, (1b) and (2b), are identical in the two conditions, (2b) took about 500 milliseconds less time to read because it is easier to relate the word *broom* to the (2a) preceding context than to the (1a) context. This facilitation probably occurs because accessing the verb *swept* in sentence (2a) raises the activation level of a probable instrument of the action, a *broom*, as depicted in Figure 6.2. By contrast, accessing the verb *cleaned* in sentence (1a) is much less likely to do so. The extra 500 milliseconds on sentence (1b) tended to be expended in two main places, indicating the points at which the inference was being computed: (1) on the word *broom* itself and (2) on the end of the sentence containing *broom*. This result indicates that one of the ways readers try to make a text coherent is by determining if a newly introduced entity (in this example, the *broom*) can be assigned to one of the semantic roles that was left unspecified by the

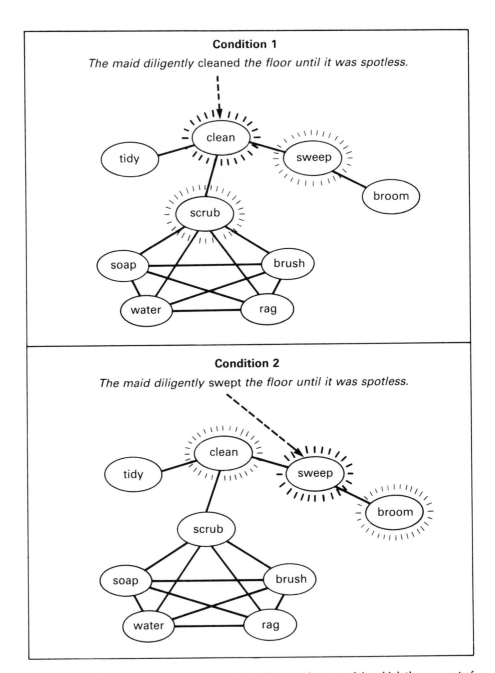

Figure 6.2 This figure represents a hypothetical semantic network in which the concept of CLEAN is not directly associated with BROOM, whereas SWEEP is directly linked to BROOM. Reading the word *swept* raises the activation level of BROOM, hence, making it easier to comprehend a subsequent sentence that suddenly introduces the concept of a BROOM.

previous sentences. The attempt to make that assignment is made either when the mention of the new object is first encountered or at the end of the clause that contains the mention.

The Semantic Analysis of Actions and States

The Semantic Analysis of Actions

The action of a clause is usually indicated by the verb. The verb not only provides information about the nature of the action, but it usually indicates the likely number and kind of participants that are associated with the action. For example, a prototypical action verb such as *hit* not only denotes the concept HIT, but the verb is also typically associated with an agent, the hitter, and an object of the action, the thing that was hit.

While a verb like *hit* is prototypical of action verbs, verbs differ in systematic ways that have implications for semantic analysis. For example, verbs can be intransitive, reflexive, causative, and so on (Lyons, 1968). *Transitive* verbs are verbs such as *hit,* for which the object of the action is usually explicitly specified in the clause; by contrast, for an *intransitive* verb, such as *brood* or *speak,* either there is no object of the action or it is not explicitly specified. Thus, the property of verb transitivity has direct implications for the semantic analysis of the clause.

Another example of a verb property that has implications for semantic analysis is *reflexivity.* If a verb is reflexive, two of the participant slots, the agent and either the object or the recipient of the action, are occupied by the same individual. In the sentence *Roger washed before supper,* the implicit object of the action is *Roger,* which is also the agent of the action. Sometimes, reflexive pronouns are used to indicate the reflexivity, as in the following example:

> *Roger and his young son came to visit us. Roger washed* (him/himself) *before supper.*

The distinction between the reflexive *himself* and the nonreflexive *him* provides the critical cue to indicate who belongs in the slot for the object of the washing.

Similar complexities arise with verbs called *causatives,* like *move, begin,* and *close.* These verbs have the interesting property that the grammatical subject of the clause can be either the agent of the action or the object of the action:

> *The farmer* moved *the rock.*
> *The rock* moved.

Even though these two sentences are superficially very different, they have a similar semantic representation, indicating that the action was an action of motion and that the object of the action was the *rock.* The first sentence additionally specifies the agent of the action, that is, the *farmer.* The analysis of the surface-level syntax of the second sentence might indicate that *rock* is the subject of the verb *moved,* while the semantic analysis must indicate that the *rock* is not the agent of the motion but the object of the action. These examples illustrate that semantic analysis depends on knowledge about various objects and actions and the kinds of relations into which they can enter.

Representation of verbs   Computer modelers of semantic analysis vary in their approach to representing the meaning of a verb. At one extreme, Schank (1972) has argued that verbs should be represented in terms of elementary semantic units, called **semantic primitives.** For example, the verb *to give* is represented, in part, by a semantic primitive called *ATRANS*, which entails the transfer of possession of something from one entity to another. ATRANS is a predicate with slots for the original possessor, the new possessor, and the thing that is transferred between them. ATRANS is used to represent not only *give* but also *take, buy, sell, loan,* and *borrow,* all of which have some common components having to do with transfer of possession. Of course, these verbs are not identical. In addition to transfer of possession, these verbs each denote other points, such as *buy*'s denotation of some money ATRANSing in the opposite direction to the object being transferred. *MTRANS* is another primitive action, which entails a mental transfer of information between or within people, as in *tell* or *remember*. Other primitives include PROPEL, MOVE, SPEAK, GRASP, INGEST, and EXPEL. Schank's general claim is that all action verbs can be represented in terms of 11 primitive actions. The claim derives some support from the computer simulations of Schank and his students that used this approach and had considerable success in performing a variety of language-understanding tasks, such as translating English sentences into another language.

The main alternative to representing action verbs in terms of semantic primitives is to represent them just like any other lexical item, with a top-level node corresponding to the main predicate and as many lower-level nodes, appropriately interconnected, as necessary. It is important to note that regardless of whether the representation of a verb is based on semantic primitives or on a conventional lexical network of meaning components, it must ultimately provide the reader with exactly the same information, but the information might be arranged and accessed somewhat differently.

One can evaluate the circumstances under which each type of verb representation is most useful (Rieger, 1979). Rieger suggests that representing verbs in terms of high-level predicates is more useful for relating the verbs to still higher-level structures, such as clause schemata or story schemata. By contrast, representing verbs in terms of elementary semantic units is more useful for relating the verbs to other structures of a similar level, such as nouns and other verbs. Unsurprisingly, Schank's advocacy of semantic primitives was strongest when his work focused on the semantic analysis of clauses, which involves the relations among verbs and nouns and so forth. As Schank's work moved to story comprehension and his need to relate verbs to higher-level structures like plans and motives increased, his appreciation of high-level predicates also increased (Schank, Lebowitz, & Birnbaum, 1980).

A likely resolution of the two approaches to verb representation is the one we proposed for the lexical decomposition of nouns. In Chapter 3, we suggested that the lexical representation of a noun like *father* contains a top-level node that represents the concept of FATHER, as well as lower-level nodes that represent individual components of meaning, such as the feature of maleness. Lexical access may always entail activation of the top-level node to threshold, while the lower-level nodes might be activated to threshold only if the context warrants it. This account of the representation and access of the meanings of nouns seems equally apt for verbs. The representation of a verb must surely contain all the detailed knowledge a reader possesses about the meaning of the verb, but not all of the information need be accessed every time the verb is encountered.

Some verbs can be grouped into families that have similar top-level nodes but can be distinguished from each other by their lower-level components of meaning. One family of verbs that concerns the transfer of physical objects, including verbs such as *give* and *take,* has already been described. Another family of verbs deals with acts of judging, like *accuse, criticize, scold,* and *blame.* Fillmore (1971) analyzed this family, trying to describe their meaning components. To take a sample sentence like *George accused Murray,* the agent of the verb *accuse* assigns responsibility for some negatively evaluated deed to the object of the verb. By contrast, in a sentence like *George criticized Murray,* the verb *criticized* presupposes Murray's responsibility for the situation and evaluates the performance of the deed as negative. Similar types of analyses have been applied to other families of verbs, such as verbs of motion: *jump, climb, run, withdraw,* and so on (Miller & Johnson-Laird, 1976).

During the semantic analysis of a sentence, a reader uses the verb meaning to determine what kind of action is being described and what types of participants that action usually entails. In addition, the representation of the verb contains all the subtleties of the verb's meaning that the reader knows. When the context warrants it, the relevant lower-level components of the verb meaning are activated and used to determine the roles of the participants in the action.

The relative importance of the verb   One aspect of the Schank and Fillmore approaches that seems incongruent with human semantic analysis is their disproportionately heavy reliance on the verb. In both these approaches, the verb is a major determinant of the configuration of roles to which the various participants are assigned. In contrast, it is likely that human readers and listeners use other sources of information to begin to tentatively assign a semantic role to each participant of the state or action as soon as that participant is referred to by the clause. In most clauses, at least one participant is referred to before the verb occurs, implying that readers are probably establishing the configuration of semantic roles even before they encounter the verb of the clause. The semantic analysis can begin to operate before the verb is encountered because there are a number of other types of information that indicate semantic roles, such as general world knowledge and the preceding context. In the absence of such world knowledge or contextual information, the mechanism in Schank's computer model that performs the semantic analysis must rely more heavily on the verb.

If languages had evolved to suit a processing mechanism that heavily relied on the verb to perform the semantic analysis, then we would expect most languages to place the verb at the beginning of a clause, as in *Hit John the ball;* thus, a reader or listener would know the semantic structure of the clause right at the beginning. But contrary to this expectation, only about 21 percent of the world's known languages usually place the verb at the beginning of the sentence (Ultan, 1969, cited in Clark & Clark, 1977). Thus, readers of languages such as Japanese or German, in which verbs sometimes occur at the ends of clauses, probably have a very good idea of the clause's semantic structure before they reach the verb. Comprehension is probably not impeded when the verb lies at the end of a clause.

The Semantic Analysis of States

The analysis of clauses that simply describe states or properties differs from the analysis of clauses that describe actions. Consider what the semantic analysis would be for a very simple sentence, like *Martha is tall.* The representation must indicate a predication or modification, associating Martha with tallness, perhaps as the single proposition (*Martha* :IS *tall*). The slot-and-frame approach of assigning clause constituents to semantic roles can still be used to analyze *Martha is tall,* but none of the important slots are being used. The semantic representations of clauses that describe states typically make use of only a degenerate form of the schema for semantic roles. In technical expository passages, many clauses describe states rather than actions. The semantic representation of these clauses consists of complex predications, complex in the sense that objects are reiteratively and recursively modified, resulting in many embedded propositions.

State descriptions can communicate several types of information, including the following:

1. the existence of an object: *There once was a wicked old woman.*
2. a property of an object: *The sky is gray; Flywheels are one of the oldest mechanical devices.*
3. spatial and temporal relations among objects: *The blue triangle is above the square; The warning signal preceded the explosion.*
4. logical relations, such as class inclusion: *Democracy is a form of government.*

In expository texts, state descriptions often occur as part of a larger description of a relation between a state and an action or between two states. For example, *Mother will be happy if Gabriel hits a home run* describes a conditional relation between a future state and the hypothetical occurrence of a given action—namely, Gabriel's hitting a home run. Similarly, *The alarm is activated when the light is on* describes the relation between two states. In these particular cases, each state is described by a clause, and the state-action or state-state relation is communicated by the clause conjunctions.

It is tempting but incorrect to assume that adjectives always describe states and that verbs always describe actions. Both adjectives and verbs can refer to an action (in which case they are called **dynamic**) or to a state (in which case they are called **stative**) (Lakoff, 1970). *Hit* is a typical dynamic verb, while *know* is a typical stative verb. A clause whose verb is *to know, see, hear,* or *believe* describes a mental state. Similarly, adjectives can be stative (*tall*) or dynamic (*noisy*). Stative verbs and adjectives have distinguishing syntactic properties. For example, a stative adjective cannot occur in a syntactic structure that already denotes transience, as in the unacceptable structure *John is being tall.* On the other hand, a dynamic adjective can occur in such a structure: *John is being noisy.* Similarly, stative verbs cannot occur in imperative constructions, as in the unacceptable *I order you to hear the noise.* On the other hand, dynamic verbs can occur in imperatives: *I order you to listen for the noise* (Lakoff, 1970). As a reader encounters verbs and adjectives, he must determine whether they describe an action or state on the basis of their meaning, rather than their form class.

State descriptions and interstate relations can easily be encompassed in the representational scheme described later in the chapter in the section on **Proposi-**

tional Representation. However, state descriptions do not form as regular a taxonomy as do action descriptions. The frame and slots of an action schema capture the regularity of relationships among the participants in an action. By contrast, the representation of state descriptions results in a heterogeneous network of relations among states. There is no fixed arrangement of default slots. The relationships among elements of a state are less orderly than the relationships among the participants in an action.

The Semantic Analysis of Circumstances

Of the three components of semantic analysis—actions/states, participant roles, and circumstances—circumstances is the most difficult component to systematize. There are too few basic categories of circumstances and too many miscellaneous instances. If the analysis of circumstances is construed as a schema-filling process, then the problem is that existing theories don't provide an orderly set of slots to be filled in the circumstance category. The prototypical circumstance slots are for the time and place of the action or state; prototypical slot fillers include words and phrases like *yesterday* and *in the garden.*

Beyond such simple issues, the analysis of circumstances has to deal with possible worlds (*John dreamed that he hit the ball*) and complex contingencies (*John ought to have hit the ball with the bat if. . .*). In addition, a clause can be overlaid with a communicative function such as interrogation (*Did John hit the ball with the bat?*) or command (*Hit the ball with the bat!*). Some of these points are part of the linguistic analysis of tense (pertaining to the time of the action or state), mood (declarative, imperative, interrogative), and aspect (pertaining to the temporal contour of the action, such as whether it is completed, habitual, or momentary, as in *John was reading the book* versus *John read the book*).

The semantic analysis of circumstances is relatively unstructured for several reasons. First, as mentioned above, the circumstance categories form a miscellany rather than a regular taxonomy. Second, many of the circumstance categories, such as tense and aspect, interact with each other. Third, circumstance information is often derived from the reader's knowledge of the referential context, which is difficult to encompass within a theory of reading comprehension. Fourth, circumstance information is not closely associated with any particular syntactic category. For example, the information about the point in time or the distribution over time of the action or state can come from a verb (*Jonathan* will read *the article*), from an adverb (*Marcus lectures* weekly), from a prepositional phrase (*Jeffrey makes his debut* in a week), or from an adjective embedded in a prepositional phrase (*Larry hit the ball on a* previous *day*). Similarly, the information about the mood of an action can come from an auxiliary modal verb (*would*) or from an adverb (*possibly*).

The Processing of Negation

Research on circumstance information has included study of the processing of **negation.** While most sentences have a direct correspondence with some referential situation, a negative sentence has an indirect correspondence, namely, that the sentence negates a correspondence between some of its own components and the referent. A reader can compare the referential representation derived from a sentence with another representation of the referent to decide whether or not a sentence is true. The time required to make the comparison is longer if the statement contains a negation (Carpenter & Just, 1975). For example, a reader can judge the truth of sentences like *Your shirt is blue* or *Seven isn't an odd number* by comparing the representation of the referent that is derived from the sentence to the representation that is derived independently. In the first example, she would derive an independent representation of a shirt's color by looking at it and encoding the color; in the second example, she would retrieve previous knowledge about the parity of the number seven.

The presence of the negation has its major effect when the representations from the two sources are compared. The presence of a negation reverses the truth value that would have been computed if the negation had been absent. Research has established that if a person reads a sentence (like *The shirt isn't blue*) and then looks at the object (a *red shirt*) to determine whether the sentence is true or false, her decision time is greater (by about 400 milliseconds) for a negative sentence than for a corresponding affirmative sentence (like *The shirt is red*). (See Carpenter & Just, 1975, for a review of findings and theories.)

Negation is just one of many semantic operators that can indicate that the circumstances described by a clause are different from the main domain of discourse. For example, a description of a dream world creates referents that are separate from referents in the real physical world. Thus, objects cannot be imported from one world into another (e.g., *When George told Harry about the delicious meal he had dreamed about, Harry hungrily ate it*). The circumstance information must indicate the nature of the possible world in which the state or action occurs so that correspondences among objects within worlds and between worlds can be computed correctly. Negation and other kinds of semantic operators create separate worlds that must be considered in the semantic analysis.

This brief account of the processing of negation illustrates that the semantic analysis of circumstances is often more complex than just inserting information into prearranged slots. Negation in a sentence imposes a much larger processing cost beyond the extra time it takes to encode and lexically access a word like *not*. Similarly, other types of circumstance information have extended implications for semantic analysis.

Propositional Representation

As a reader semantically analyzes a text, he produces a representation of the meaning he extracts. His representation may consist of **propositions,** which are units of meaning that describe a state or action. The propositional representation of a simple sentence like *Albert is tall* may be (*Albert* :IS *tall*), where :IS denotes simple predication. The elements of the propositions are not words but concepts that sometimes correspond to words. Each proposition has a predicate (like *:IS* in the example above) and some arguments. In addition, propositions can be embedded so that one entire proposition can be an argument of another proposition.

To specify the output of the semantic analysis process, it is necessary to specify both the *content* and the *format* of the resulting semantic representation. The content consists of the analysis into semantic roles (like those described throughout this chapter) and the format of the representation is propositional.

It is not difficult to see how a propositional representation could express semantic roles. The propositions would have the names of the semantic roles as predicates and the slot fillers as arguments. For eample, *John killed the snake with a knife on the veranda* might be represented as:

> (**Action** :IS *kill*)
> (**Agent** :IS *John*)
> (**Instrument** :IS *knife*)
> (**Object** :IS *snake*)
> (**Location** :IS *veranda*)

Many other formally equivalent propositional representations are also possible. The propositional representation expresses the meaning at an abstract level that is not bound to particular sentences or words. Consequently, all of the sentences that differ only in syntax or lexical items but express the same underlying semantic relations would have the same propositional representation of semantic content. For example, consider these three sentences:

> *Alfred executed the attorney.*
> *The lawyer was put to death by Alfred.*
> *The one who killed the legal counsel was Alfred.*

Each sentence would have the same semantic representation.

The use of propositional representations to represent the content of a text is widespread, thanks largely to their development and application by Kintsch and his colleagues (Kintsch, 1974, 1977; Kintsch & van Dijk, 1978). The propositional representation is a formalism that has been used to indicate the semantic content of a text and the semantic content of a reader's recall of a text.

An example of the propositional representation of semantic roles was given in the opening of this chapter. It was the illustration of the semantic representation of *Yesterday, John inadvertently gave the old book to Peter in the library:*

> PREDICATE: *give (a, b, c)*
>   Modifier: *inadvertently*
>
> ARGUMENTS:
>   Agent: *John = a*
>   Object: *book = b*
>   Modifier: *old (b)*
>   Goal: *Peter = c*
>
> CIRCUMSTANCES:
>   Time: *yesterday*
>   Place: *in the library*

For convenience, Kintsch often deletes the explicit labeling of the semantic roles in the representation; instead, he denotes them by the serial order of the propositional elements. For example, *John gave the book to Peter* would be represented as *(gave, John, book, Peter)*. In this abbreviated notation, the propositions have one predicate (the first item on the list) and one or more arguments. The particular role played by a given argument is usually indicated by its serial order in the list of arguments. An entire text can be represented by an ordered set of propositions that are interrelated by shared arguments and by propositions that are embedded in each other.

The kind of semantic representation that Kintsch works with has two important limitations. First, the proposed representation is produced by an experimenter, using a mixture of algorithmic rules and intuitions. It is difficult to specify the representation rules unequivocally; sentences that can be represented in more than one way always crop up. So there is some arbitrariness in specifying the representation. The second related limitation is that Kintsch has not specified the processes a reader might use to generate such a representation.

Nevertheless, this type of analysis provides the best available characterization of the semantic content of a text and of the recall produced by a reader. Also, it constitutes a significant advance beyond previous, less formal characterizations.

Empirical Evidence for Propositional Representations

The amount of time it takes to read a text of a given length increases with the number of propositions it contains (Kintsch & Keenan, 1973). Presumably, if more meaning units (propositions) must be extracted, then semantic analysis takes longer to perform; consequently, it takes longer to read the text. For example, it took longer to read the first sentence than the second:

1. *Cleopatra's downfall lay in her foolish trust in the fickle political figures of the Roman world.*
2. *Romulus, the legendary founder of Rome, took the women of the Sabine by force.*

Kintsch's analysis attributes eight propositions to the Cleopatra sentence and four to the Romulus sentence. The conclusions from this experiment should be viewed with caution because all other factors (besides number of underlying propositions) are difficult to control. In this particular study, the passages with more propositions are also syntactically more complex, so it is possible that the syntactic analysis also contributed to the longer reading times.

Another way that the semantic content affects reading is that texts that introduce many new arguments (word concepts) take longer to read than texts with fewer arguments, assuming that the total number of words and propositions in the two texts is the same (Kintsch, Kozminsky, Streby, McKoon, & Keenan, 1975). For example, the following passage contained few arguments:

The Greeks loved beautiful art. When the Romans conquered the Greeks, they copied them and, thus, learned to create beautiful art.

By contrast, the following passage was of similar length but contained more arguments:

The Babylonians built a beautiful garden on a hill. They planted lovely flowers, constructed fountains, and designed a pavilion for the queen's pleasure.

The second passage took about 10 percent longer to read. Reading about many new concepts takes longer than reading about a few concepts that reoccur repeatedly (Manelis & Yekovich, 1976). The reason may be that in the paragraphs with few arguments, the same concepts are repeatedly reactivated, perhaps before their activation level has completely decayed from the previous mention. Thus, on each mention after the first, they may take less time to reach threshold. Argument repetition not only reduces reading time but also produces better recall. These studies show that subtle variations in the semantic content of a passage affect the duration of the reading process.

Other research has shown that the organization of propositional arguments within a sentence affects not only the reading time but also how those arguments will be organized in the reader's mind (Ratcliff & McKoon, 1978). Arguments that belong to the same proposition are more closely associated with each other in the reader's memory than arguments from different propositions from the same sentence. For example, in the following sentence, there are two main underlying propositions, corresponding to the two clauses:

Geese crossed the horizon as the wind shuffled the clouds.

This experiment measured how long it took subjects to decide whether a probe word (*horizon*) had been included in one of several sentences they had previously read. The results focused on priming effects of one probe trial on the next trial. If on two successive trials the probed words belong to the same proposition (*horizon* and *geese*) and if arguments from the same proposition are closely associated in the reader's memory, then the first trial (which probes *horizon*) should raise the activation level of the other argument from the same proposition (*geese*), hence producing a shorter response time on the next trial. The results showed that words from the same proposition primed each other more (by 20 milliseconds) than words from different propositions. The word *horizon* primed *geese* more than it primed *wind*.

This result indicates that the meaning of a sentence is stored in clusters that correspond roughly to propositions, such that arguments within each proposition are more closely linked to each other than to the arguments of the other propositions. However, it is important to note that in this experiment, propositions and clauses covary, so some of the organizational influence attributed to propositions (semantic units) might actually be attributable to clauses (syntactic units).

How Semantic and Syntactic Analyses Work Together

Of the various strata of comprehension processes, semantic and syntactic analyses seem particularly close to each other, in that they operate on similar sizes of units (primarily phrases and clauses) and employ similar kinds of information about each word. Psychologists have often argued about the degree of autonomy between these two levels of processing. They questioned whether the syntactic analysis process, which operates on the grammatical form of the sentence, was influenced by the semantic content of the sentence.

The issue of **syntactic autonomy** arose for several reasons. The initial questioning did not come from psychology but stemmed from a concern in the discipline of linguistics. During the early development of linguistic theories of syntax, (approximately 1958–1967), some linguists assumed that the rules that govern the syntactic well-formedness of sentences could be described without consideration of semantics. This assumption later became a major focus of controversy within linguistics, and its resolution is still debated. It is important to recall that the linguistic autonomy assumption concerns the autonomy of the axiomatization of syntactic rules, not the autonomy of psychological processes. Nevertheless, many psychological studies of comprehension have adopted and adapted the linguistic issue, attempting to determine empirically whether semantic and syntactic analyses operate autonomously of each other. These attempts have continued up to the present, using increasingly sophisticated methodologies and theoretical approaches, a few of which will be described in this section.

A second reason for psychological interest in the issue of autonomy is its potential influence on theory and future research directions (Cairns, 1984). If syntactic analysis were performed by an autonomous process, then it would be fruitful for researchers in various subareas, such as language development, to search for a separate syntactic development or to contrast the development of syntactic analysis abilities with other abilities. Similarly, research on language pathologies might search for dysfunctions in a separate syntactic process. For example, Broca's aphasia seems largely to be a dysfunction of syntax processes, as described in Chapter 5.

Another motivation for the autonomy assumption (also advanced by Cairns) is that the more constrained theory—namely, the one that assumes autonomy—is more desirable on general philosophical grounds. Cairns argues that new empirical findings in a developing science lead to the relaxation of constraints on a theory but not to the imposition of constraints. She suggests that experiments that are intended to confirm an interactive (nonautonomous) theory are unlikely to produce data suggestive of autonomy among subprocesses. She argues that if researchers proceed the other way—starting with an assumption of autonomy and doing experiments that falsify the assumption—then they can legitimately reject the autonomy assumption and accept an interactive theory.

On the other side of the argument, there are a number of reasons to assume that semantic and syntactic analyses are not autonomous. One reason is that computer programs that attempt to parse text on purely syntactic grounds generally perform inadequately, in contrast to those that parse on the basis of both semantic and syntactic grounds. The syntactic information is often insufficient to indicate the syntactic structure of a sentence. This result leads many psychologists to assume that like the successful computer programs, human beings also do their syntactic analysis in close conjunction with other analyses. A related point is that people can understand sentences that are syntactically incorrect using their knowledge of the world and their knowledge of semantics to determine meaning. Similarly, computer programs that understand text on the basis of a semantic analysis can cope with syntactic ill-formedness. Thus, normal comprehension can occur in cases where syntactic analysis fails because syntactic analysis operates in conjunction with other analyses.

One computer model, called HEARSAY, has been particularly influential as an example of collaboration among levels of processing. The HEARSAY model (Reddy, 1980) is able to understand spoken utterances by concurrently analyzing them at several levels (including the semantic, syntactic, and phonological levels) and combining the outputs of these various levels. Each level writes its interpretation of the utterance in a central workspace that is available to all other levels. After all the levels have written their interpretation of the utterance in the workspace, then a weighted consensus is taken, reflecting the modal interpretation. The frameworks of several theories of comprehension, such as those proposed by Marslen-Wilson and Tyler (1980), Rumelhart (1977b), and Thibadeau, Just, and Carpenter (1982), can all be traced back to the HEARSAY model, which first demonstrated the attractiveness of a language-understanding system whose many levels collaborate to reach a final interpretation.

What Constitutes Autonomy?

The largest difficulty in interpreting experiments on the autonomy of semantic and syntactic analyses is that *autonomy* and *semantic analysis* are often poorly defined. The extreme and almost certainly incorrect form of the autonomy position is that an entire clause is subjected first to syntactic analysis and then later to a semantic analysis. This is incorrect because semantic and syntactic analyses are applied to each word of text as soon as it is encountered either by a reader (Just & Carpenter, 1984) or a listener (Marslen-Wilson & Tyler, 1980). Then the remaining processing question must concern the autonomy of semantic and syntactic analyses as they are applied to each word. One could ask about the temporal relations between the two processes (when does each begin and end, relative to the other?) and about the functional relations (do they influence each other? and if so, at which point and in what way?). It is possible that each process is completely autonomous of the other and that after both processes have completed their work on a word, a third, higher-level process coordinates and, if necessary, modifies their output. Or at the other extreme, it may be that the two processes operate concurrently and have the potential to influence each other continuously during their operation.

The issue of processing autonomy, as defined above, seems empirically undecidable given the current state of methodology, and furthermore, the question seems moot in the context of a model of human comprehension. It is difficult enough to know where to draw the line between semantic and syntactic analysis, let alone determine whether there is autonomy between the processes. The experimental evidence suggests that there is mutual influence between semantic and syntactic analysis, but it is currently indeterminable whether this influence is direct or through a third process.

Experimental Studies of Syntactic Autonomy

To determine empirically whether two processes like semantic and syntactic analyses operate autonomously of each other is not a simple matter. The evidence accrued to date does not overwhelmingly favor either side of the autonomy issue. Since this issue first arose in the early 1960s, many experiments have demonstrated that in a situation requiring subjects to process a string of words in some way, syntactic well-formedness and semantic sensibility have additive effects on performance. That is, if an independent variable associated with syntactic analysis affects performance by X units (say, milliseconds) and an independent variable associated with semantic analysis affects performance by Y units, then the two variables operating together should produce an effect of $X + Y$ units. If the effects are additive, the reasoning goes, then they are probably influencing different stages of processing, so they do not functionally interact. But the relation between additivity of effects and functional interaction is a slippery one. The only statement that can be made confidently is that nonadditivity implies functional interaction. However, additivity does not necessarily imply the absence of functional interaction, because it is possible, in principle, to have two effects influence the same process (to interact functionally) and still produce additive effects.

One example of a study that demonstrated additivity of syntactic and semantic effects was that done by Forster and Ryder (1971). In this study, readers saw sentences one word at a time, with each word being presented for 62.5 milliseconds. The syntax of the sentences was manipulated by having either one clause per sentence (*The wealthy child attended a private school*) or two clauses, with one clause embedded in the other (*The lawyer she wants is busy elsewhere*). In addition, the semantics of the sentences was varied. The semantic content of each sentence was either normal, bizarre (*The clever fly made some tiny drugs*), or anomalous (*The accidents were asked a muddy equation*). The objective of the study was to determine whether there was any interaction between the syntactic and semantic analyses by comparing the conjoint effect of the syntactic and semantic manipulations to their individual effects.

The interesting result was that semantic complexity and syntactic complexity additively decreased the recall. The semantic effect was that immediate recall was best for normal sentences, poorer for bizarre sentences, and poorest for anomalous sentences. On top of this effect, recall was better for one-clause sentences than for two-clause sentences. It should be noted that although the two effects were additive, the semantic effect was much larger than the syntactic effect. The additive effects of the semantic and syntactic variables observed in the Forster and Ryder study are a very weak indication of autonomy of the semantic and syntactic analyses.

A more convincing way to demonstrate such autonomy is to show that the semantic interpretation of a constituent such as a phrase or clause does not influence the syntactic interpretation of that same constituent. Unfortunately, those few experiments that have succeeded in providing such a demonstration are subject to alternative, more plausible explanations. For example, a recent study claimed to show that syntactic analysis is impervious to nonsyntactic information (Rayner, Carlson, & Frazier, 1983). The study monitored readers' eye fixations as they read garden-path sentences like this one:

> *The florist sent the flowers was very pleased.*

Such sentences contain a syntactic structure called a *reduced relative clause* (*sent the flowers*), which has been reduced from a conventional passive clause (*who was sent the flowers*). When a person has read as far as the word *flowers,* the syntactic interpretation she is most likely to make is that of a simple active sentence, in which *florist* is the agent of the sending, rather than the indirect object. Most English sentences that start this way do turn out to be simple active structures. But in this case, when the reader encounters the word *was*, she is probably surprised at the inconsistency between *was* and her current syntactic interpretation of the sentence, so she reinterprets the sentence in a way that is consistent—namely, with *sent* as the passive verb in a reduced relative clause.

To determine whether semantic factors influenced the syntactic interpretation, the experiment included another set of sentences in which the person or thing mentioned at the beginning of the sentence was more likely to be the recipient or object of the action, rather than the agent. For example, the following sentence corresponded to the sentence above:

> *The performer sent the flowers was very pleased.*

Presumably, performers are more likely to have flowers sent to them than to send flowers to others. The study examined whether this real-world knowledge about performers would induce readers to assign different semantic roles to nouns like *performer,* and whether this semantic assignment would affect the syntactic analysis. Specifically, would readers be more likely to assign the reduced relative clause structure to the *performer* sentence than to the *florist* sentence?

The experimenters determined how surprised the readers were when they saw the word *was* by measuring how long they paused and how much they subsequently slowed down their reading. The finding was that readers paused an equal amount on the word *was,* regardless of whether the earlier word had been *florist* or *performer.* This means that the possible difference in semantic analysis for the two sentences did not affect the syntactic interpretation, suggesting that at least for these types of sentences, syntactic analysis was not influenced by semantic analysis.

The conclusions of this experiment must be considered with some reservation, because the manipulation was a relatively weak one. Although it may be true that performers are more likely to receive than to send flowers, it is perfectly sensible to assume that a sentence beginning with *The performer sent the flowers. . .* is in the active voice. Even if the semantic and syntactic analyses were capable of influencing each other, this kind of sentence does not seem to warrant overruling the strong syntactic evidence by the weak semantic consideration. The manipulation in the experiment could have been made stronger if the object mentioned at the beginning of the sentence was totally implausible as an agent, such as *The dog paid the compliment was well trained* or *The infant read the story was uninterested.*

Despite these questionable conclusions, this study does illustrate a powerful methodology that can reveal the characteristics of the semantic and syntactic analyses as they are being executed. This study also illustrates how difficult it is to separate two closely related processes in an experiment. Many other studies have attempted to investigate the autonomy of syntactic and semantic analysis (see Forster, 1979), but none are convincing.

Semantic and Syntactic Effects on Memory

Semantic and syntactic analyses both make contributions to understanding a sentence, but in the long-term view, syntax serves as a code for communication, while semantics is the organization of content. It is therefore not surprising that people tend to remember the semantics of a sentence better than the syntax, especially if some time has elapsed since they processed the sentence.

An often-quoted finding in sentence-memory research is that a short time after hearing a sentence, listeners have difficulty distinguishing between the original sentence and a close paraphrase of it (Sachs, 1967). A *paraphrase* is a different sentence with a very similar semantic representation. In the Sachs experiment, subjects listened to passages that contained sentences like this one:

He sent a letter about it to Galileo, the great Italian scientist.

Sometime later, the listeners were presented with a test sentence and asked to judge whether it was identical to the original or changed somehow. Some of the test sentences preserved the underlying meaning but not the syntactic structure:

A letter was sent about it to Galileo, the great Italian scientist.

And other test sentences changed the meaning, as well as the syntactic structure:

Galileo, the great Italian scientist, sent him a letter about it.

Still other test sentences were identical to the original.

The finding was that if the listeners were tested immediately after having heard the original sentence, they were extremely likely to detect any difference whatsoever between the original and the test sentence. This result indicates that the listeners had a representation of both the syntactic and the semantic structure immediately after having heard the sentence. But if the presentation of the passage continued for a while before the test sentence was presented, then listeners had difficulty distinguishing identical sentences from those that merely preserved the meaning. If the presentation of the text continued for as little as half a minute, listeners' accuracy at detecting a syntactic change diminished considerably to almost chance level. The conclusion is that if enough time elapses after understanding a sentence, a listener will have much better memory for the semantic content than the syntax.

Another study came to a similar conclusion by timing how long subjects took to decide whether a test sentence agreed with or contradicted a previously read sentence (Anderson, 1974). The original sentence was either in the active voice (*The car struck the post*) or the passive voice (*The post was struck by the car*); the test sentence was also either active or passive. If the test was immediate, then subjects were faster to respond when the original sentence and the test sentence were in the same voice. This implies that their representation of the original sentence contained some syntactic information about the voice. However, if the test was delayed for a few minutes, then the response time was the same, regardless of whether the test sentence and the original sentence matched in voice. The syntactic information about voice had been forgotten in those intervening minutes. The general conclusion from these studies is that people generally don't retain the precise syntactic form of what they read. Instead, they store some of the semantic and referential representation.

The READER Model's Semantic Analysis

READER's semantic analysis operates according to a number of principles described throughout the chapter. READER analyzes each clause into the action or state, participants, and circumstances. And READER constructs the type of semantic representation that was previously described. The slots pertaining to the action or state, the participants, and the circumstances are filled in with the information from the clause as it is being read.

READER uses high-level predicates to represent actions and states. For example, a high-level predicate called CONTAIN is used to represent not only the verb *contain* but also any other relation that denotes containment, such as certain senses of *hold* and *have.* The semantic representation of *The engine has a flywheel* would indicate that the CONTAIN predicate entails both a container and a containee. It would also indicate the identities of these two objects, as follows:

(CONTAIN :HAS CONTAINER)
(CONTAINER :IS *engine*)
(CONTAIN :HAS CONTAINEE)
(CONTAINEE :IS *flywheel*)

The :HAS relation indicates the existence of a participant, whereas the :IS relation indicates the identity of a participant.

The CONTAIN predicate has stored with it several different types of information. First, it has the information that CONTAIN denotes a state involving a physical relation between physical objects. Also, it stores a collection of slots for its typical participants and circumstances. And the slots contain information about some of the typical participants, such as the CONTAINER, which is typically a solid object, and so on.

The high-level semantic predicates make certain relations very accessible. For example, the CONTAIN predicate symbolizes the containment relation in all three of the following excerpts:

. . . *every internal combustion engine contains a flywheel.*
. . . *the more energy can be stored in it.*
. . . *when the wheel is confined in a small space.*

The single CONTAIN predicate highlights the commonalities of *contains, stored,* and *confined,* at the cost of making the distinctions less accessible. The commonality makes it straightforward to relate the clause-level information to the schema for the entire expository paragraph, as described in Chapter 8.

READER's semantic analysis operates concurrently with other levels of processing, such as the syntactic, referential, and text-schema levels. Information from all levels is continuously accessible to others, creating the potential for mutual influence. The concurrent process that is probably most likely to influence semantic analysis is syntactic analysis, and the semantic analysis itself sometimes directly uses syntactic information. While the potential for a great deal of interaction exists, it does not always occur. Some semantic analysis can be done in the absence of syntactic information. READER can produce a semantic representation for a syntactically ill-formed structure (e.g., *ate pudding boy spoon*), albeit the likelihood of failure is much greater in such cases than for normal sentences. Researchers have focused on instances in which interaction between semantic and syntactic analysis occurs because it is such a theoretically important phenomenon, but its frequency of occurrence should not be overestimated.

Summary

Semantic analysis consists of determining the conceptual relations among the elements of a clause, without regard to their grammatical roles. Loosely speaking, it can be thought of as figuring out who is doing what to whom. Thus, the semantic analysis would be the same whether a sentence says that *Benjamin ate the peaches last night* or *The peaches were eaten by Benjamin last night*. Semantic analysis can be construed as a slot-filling process, in which the slots belong to a schema for simple actions or states. The three main categories of slots concern information about the action or state (*eating*), the participants' roles such as agent (*Benjamin*) and object (*peaches*), and the circumstances (*last night*).

In most linguistic approaches, verbs play a central role in semantic analysis; verbs not only specify the nature of the action or state, but they also constrain the number and configuration of slots to be specified. For example, the verb *eat* is typically associated with both an agent and an object, although either may be unspecified.

Readers aren't as dependent on verbs as are linguists. Readers can determine the semantic roles with the aid of additional information, such as that provided by the preceding linguistic context or inferences based on their general knowledge of the world. In fact, readers appear to make plausible inferences about the semantic roles of various participants as they are encountered during reading, rather than wait until they reach the verb to do semantic analysis.

The semantic roles (such as *agent, object,* and *instrument*) constitute a relatively small, informative taxonomy of participants associated with actions. By contrast, the analysis into participant roles is less orderly when applied to clauses that describe states. Often the semantic analysis of a descriptive text, such as a typical passage in a history textbook or magazine article, consists of a heterogeneous and interrelated set of properties and relations.

The question of whether syntactic and semantic analyses are autonomous of each other or if they are interactive cannot be answered definitely by existing research. Our general assumption is that the different component processes of comprehension do have the potential to interact with each other continuously. However, the READER model's operation suggests that the potential for interaction is exploited occasionally rather than continuously.

Suggested Readings

One of the most influential analyses of case structure is Fillmore's (1968) article. Another important paper on this topic, from a computational perspective, is Schank's (1972) article. The analysis of text into propositions is described in Kintsch's (1974) book, and the approach has been elaborated in the more recent book by van Dijk and Kintsch (1983). Cairns (1984) and Fodor (1983) provide interesting discussions of the autonomy of syntax from semantics. Leech (1969) provides a conventional linguistic analysis of semantic relations.

7

Understanding the Referent of a Text

As a reader progresses through a text, he constructs a representation of the objects and situations the text refers to. For instance, a text can refer to the current, real world, as a newspaper does; to a previous real world, as a historical text does; or to an imaginary world, as a fairy tale or a science-fiction story does. We will call the reader's representation of the world the text refers to the **referential representation.** Another name that is sometimes used for this representation (in particular, by van Dijk and Kintsch [1983]) is the *situation model* because it symbolizes the situation described by the text. The referential representation is often the most important level of analysis because the main function of many texts is to provide information about referents.

The referential representation can be distinguished from the syntactic and semantic representations, described in Chapters 5 and 6, respectively. For example, a sentence such as *He flew to Cairo* has only one syntactic representation and only one semantic representation. But as illustrated in Figure 7.1, it can have one of several different referential representations, depending on the context.

Overview In this chapter, we will describe the psychological processes used in constructing the referential representation of a text. In the first section, **The Content of the Referential Representation,** we will consider what kind of information about a referent is represented, particularly in the case of general and specific concepts, perceptible objects, linear orderings, mathematical concepts, and concepts defined by adjective-noun combinations.

In the second section, **Constructing the Referential Representation,** we will describe some processes used in finding or constructing a referential representation of an object referred to in the text. We will describe what occurs when a pronoun triggers a search for an existing referential representation of a previously mentioned object. The section also describes the two main types of cues used in constructing or elaborating a referential representation: (1) language-based cues in the text and (2) knowledge-based cues that evoke the reader's relevant knowledge of the world. The section ends with an illustration of these processes in operation in the READER model.

195

In the third section, **The Role of the Referential Representation,** we will consider the importance of this level of representation to text coherence, to text comprehension, and to text memory. We will also describe the dire consequences of the absence of referential processing, resulting in what we call *shallow comprehension.*

Finally, we will end the chapter with a brief discussion of **Philosophical Approaches to Reference.** In this section, we will consider several issues that have been difficult to handle within philosophical approaches to comprehension but present little difficulty for a cognitive approach.

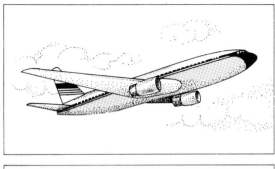

Figure 7.1   A reader will represent the referent of a sentence like *He flew to Cairo* quite differently, depending on what kind of world the text is referring to: the contemporary world, a historical world, or a fictional world.

The Content of the Referential Representation

The referential representation is constructed by representing the objects that the text refers to, the properties attributed to the objects by the text, and parts of the reader's previous knowledge of the described situation. Some portions of a text, called **referring expressions,** name a corresponding object in the text world; that is, they have a **referent.** Proper names, like *Susan, Pope John Paul,* and *Amsterdam,* are prime examples of referring expressions. The referential representation of one of these referring expressions—like *Pope John Paul* in the sentence *Pope John Paul visited the town*—is the reader's representation of Pope John Paul.

Many people have the experience of imagining a situation as it is described by a text. For example, while reading a novel, a reader may imagine what the characters and scenes look like. If the reader subsequently sees a film production of the novel, he may be surprised that the characters as portrayed by the actors look very different from the referents he constructed while reading the book. These phenomenological experiences are not limited to information about the visual qualities but also include other types of perceptual information, such as the olfactory representation that might be evoked by the description of a flower. The referential representation may also include functional properties, such as information about how or why events occurred or how objects work.

The referential representation need not be an image, but it must contain information about objects and actions and not about words. The referential representation seems to contain information about physical properties, which can be represented symbolically, in terms of propositions. These propositions, in turn, can give rise to the phenomenological experiences that are so familiar to readers.

Mapping between Text and Referents

The referential representation symbolizes some set of objects and actions that occur in the world the text refers to. However, the correspondence between the text itself and the referential representation is not straightforward for two reasons. First, not every word of a text refers to something; some parts of a text provide nonreferential information. Second, much of the content of the referential representation is based on the reader's knowledge, rather than on the content of the text. Nevertheless, we can start to examine the correspondence between some units of text—like words, phrases, and clauses—and the referential representation.

The parts of a text that are central to the construction of the referential representation are referring expressions, which can vary in size. At the extreme, a reader can construct a referential representation of a single word, like *eggplant.* The reader would construct a more elaborated referential representation if the referring expression were a noun phrase containing adjectives that provided additional specification (*the diced, purple eggplant*). She could also construct a referential representation of an entire event described by a clause (*The large eggplant fell onto the tile floor*). The referential representation of this clause would include an event involving an action and two objects.

The referential representation of an entire text might consist of the integrated collection of clause-level referential representations. The integration sometimes requires more than a simple conjunction of representations. The clauses of a text describe events that bear a particular relation to each other, such as temporal sequence or causality. These relations can integrate the representations of individual clauses in the referential representation. Thus, language units of all sizes, from a single word to an entire text, can be represented in the referential representation.

Not only is there great variability in the size of the linguistic unit that can be referentially represented, but there is also great variability in the size of the referential representation that corresponds to a single referring expression. This point can be illustrated by examining the range of possible referents for the pronoun *it*. A pronoun is often used to refer back to a previously established referent; such backward reference is called **anaphora** and any expression that refers to an established referent is called **anaphoric**. An anaphoric pronoun can refer back to referents of various sizes. For example, consider the following sequence of sentences, in which the referential representations of the pronoun *It* vary in how much information they encompass:

1. *Walter lit the match.*
2. It *ignited Mary's hair.*
3. It *produced second-degree burns.*
4. It *was the last straw leading to their divorce.*

The *It* in sentence 2 has a simple referent, the ignited match. The *It* in sentence 3 refers to the burning of Mary's hair. And the *It* in sentence 4 refers to the entire event described in sentences 1 through 3. As these sentences illustrate, anaphora allows reference to anything: objects, events, states, or processes. And the referring words can be any grammatical unit, such as a noun phrase, a verb phrase, or a clause.

Just as a *pro-noun* is **coreferential** with a noun phrase, sharing the same concept in the referential representation, so is a *pro-verb* coreferential with a verb. For example, in the sentence *Henry coughed and Rick did, too,* the pro-verb *did* points to the same action as *coughed,* indicating that both men performed the same action. Anaphoric reference by a pro-verb is called *verb-phrase ellipsis*. Pro-verbs, along with the other examples of anaphora, illustrate how a text can indicate elaborations of both objects and actions in the referential representation.

Some parts of a text, like function words, serve as guideposts to the construction of the referential representation. For example, sometimes the definite article *the* signals the fact that a noun phrase is referring to an already established referent (e.g., *Kate has a new car. The car is very useful.*). The fact signalled by *The*—namely, that it is Kate's new car that is useful, rather than cars in general—will be included in the referential representation. Many other function words, such as *of* and *a*, similarly help specify how a referential representation is to be constructed.

Quantifiers (e.g., *some*) also specify how to represent a referent. Unlike simple adjectives, like *red,* which indicate a modification of a concept in the referential representation, a quantifier specifies a partition of some set. For example, *some dogs* indicates a partition of the set of all dogs. To interpret a quantifier correctly, a reader must determine the quantifier's **scope,** or the set to which the partition applies. Determining a quantifier's scope can sometimes be complex. For example, if a single proposition contains more than one quantifier, then the relation between their two scopes must be computed (e.g., *All men love some vegetables*). Because of the interaction between the scopes of the two quantifiers, this sentence can mean either that there is a subset of vegetables that every man loves or that every man loves at least one vegetable. This particular ambiguity does not arise if there is only one quantifier (*Martin loves some vegetables*).

Several interesting studies have determined how certain types of quantifiers affect the referential representation when there is no ambiguity in their scope (Borges & Sawyers, 1974). The experiment required subjects to pick up some subset of marbles from a larger set, as specified by a quantifier (e.g., *Remove some of the marbles* or *Remove many of the marbles*). The total number of marbles in the set varied from trial to trial. The number of marbles that the subject removed indicated his referential representation of the quantified phrase. The results showed that *some of the marbles* refers to approximately 30 percent of a set of marbles, while *many of the marbles* refers to approximately 80 percent. The quantifiers tended to correspond to a fixed proportion of the set over a range of set sizes from approximately 10 to 100 marbles. Thus, the referential representation of *Some of the marbles are blue* symbolizes the entire set of marbles under discussion and associates blueness with about 30 percent of them.

The Specificity of the Referential Representation

The referential representation of a noun that refers to a particular concrete object, such as *the Golden Gate Bridge,* is simply the reader's representation of that object. However, it is more difficult to specify the referential representation of a noun that refers to a class of objects, such as *history professors*. A term that refers to a particular object is called a *singular term* while one that refers to a class is called a *general term.* It is possible for the same word to occur twice in a text, once as a general term and once as a singular term, in which case the two words do not have the same referent or the same referential representation (e.g., *Peter likes cauliflower. In fact, I saw him eating cauliflower last night*). In languages like French, the two occurrences of the word *cauliflower* would be preceded by different articles that indicate the difference between the two kinds of reference. In English, the action a verb describes can sometimes indicate whether the direct object is a general or singular term. For example, *John needed a dog* does not refer to a particular dog, but *John kicked a dog* does.

The referential representation of a general term (such as *a dog* or *a mountain*) is often a particular instance of the term (e.g., a collielike dog or Mount Everest). In this way, the referential representation particularizes or narrows the scope of reference. The phenomenon of particularization in the referential representation has been studied by examining a reader's memory for what he previously read. The studies show that if a text indicates how a term should be particularized in the referential representation, then readers store the particular instance, rather than a more general concept that the text actually referred to. For example, suppose a subject reads this sentence:

Alice poured the cola back into the container.

A likely instantiation of *container* might be a bottle. If one then asks the subject to recall the sentence with the help of a cue, then the word *bottle,* which corresponds to the instantiation suggested by the sentence, is a more effective recall cue than the originally presented word *container* (Anderson & Ortony, 1975; Anderson et al., 1976). This result suggests that when reading about the *cola* and the *container,* the readers represented a bottle in their referential representation of the sentence. Subsequently, the word *bottle* helped them recall the sentence. At the semantic level, they must have represented the meaning of *container,* as well, but that is not the concept that is most useful as a retrieval cue.

In the absence of constraining context (as *cola* constrains container), readers may instantiate references to categories in terms of their prototypes (see Anderson & McGaw, 1973; Rosch, 1975). For example, after subjects have read a sentence like *The bird landed on the porch,* a prototypical bird, *robin,* is a better cue to recall than an atypical bird, like *turkey.* Within each category, some members are prototypical, and it is likely that prototypicality strongly influences the choice of instantiation when the context is neutral. However, appropriateness to the context is the most important factor in determining the referential representation. For example, the mention of a bird in the context of cooking a meal would probably evoke an instantiation of a turkey or chicken, rather than a robin. And that is what the study showed. After subjects have read a sentence like *The bird roasted on the grill, turkey* is a better cue to recall than *robin* (Anderson et al., 1976).

Some recent studies that measured comprehension time confirmed many of the conclusions about referential instantiation that had previously been drawn from studies of prompted recall. Roth and Shoben (1983) examined the time it took to establish the coreference between a word in one sentence that named an exemplar of a category (like *robin*) and a word in the preceding sentence that named the category (*bird*). For example, they measured the time it took a subject to read the second of two sentences in a sequence like this:

> *Dorothy thought about the bird.*
> *She was very fond of the robin.*

The reading time for the second sentence was compared to another case, in which *robin,* a prototypical bird, was replaced by *turkey,* an atypical bird:

> *Dorothy thought about the bird.*
> *She was very fond of the turkey.*

In the absence of context that constrains the interpretation of the category name, it takes less time to establish the coreference if the exemplar in the second sentence is prototypical of the category. Specifically, it takes less time to establish coreference between *bird* and *robin* in the first pair of sentences than between *bird* and *turkey* in the second pair.

The results change when the context constrains the interpretation of the category. For example, the first sentence can be changed as follows to constrain the interpretation of *bird*:

> *Dorothy roasted the bird for the Thanksgiving dinner.*
> *She looked forward to eating the turkey (or robin).*

In this case, it takes less time to establish the coreference between the category name (*bird*) and a contextually appropriate exemplar (*turkey*) than between the category name (*bird*) and a normally prototypical exemplar (*robin*). These studies suggest that readers use the context and their knowledge of category members to select a likely referent to represent a general concept.

Perceptual Information in the Referential Representation

The referential representation probably contains information about the perceptible properties of the particularized instantiation. For example, the referential representation of *dog* may include a representation of a particular dog, including its perceptible properties. The perceptible characteristics are not represented as completely as when a dog is actually being perceived; they are more like the memory of a physical stimulus. Moreover, the particular perceptible qualities that are instantiated are strongly influenced by the context (Halff, Ortony, & Anderson, 1976). Even a word with a seemingly unchangeable referent, like *red,* produces a different instantiation in different contexts. Readers select a different referent (in this case, a color chip) to represent the word *red* depending on the noun it modifies, such as *fire, hair,* or *leaf.*

Referential Representations of Dynamic Physical Systems

Suppose that a text describes two meshing gears, side by side. If the gear on the left is described as rotating clockwise, in which direction must the gear on the right be rotating? Many people answer this question by forming a referential representation of the two gears, then imagining the left one rotating clockwise, then imagining the interaction between the meshing teeth of the two gears, and then inferring that the right-hand gear must be rotating counterclockwise. This type of referential representation, in which the dynamics of a physical or functional interaction are symbolized, is sometimes called a **mental model** (Gentner & Stevens, 1983).

Is there any value to introducing the term *mental model?* If the referent were a static physical object, like a chair, then it would not be particularly helpful to talk about a mental model of a chair. Rather, it would be simpler to call it the referential representation of a chair. The term *mental model* is useful in its connotations of the dynamic properties of objects and the dynamics of their spatial and functional interactions. However, a mental model should not be imbued with any reasoning apparatus or representational format that is unique or different from any other referential representation (Rips, in press). Within a mental model, normal reasoning operates in the confluence of general world knowledge and domain-specific knowledge. This reasoning can be as simple as representing the description from a text or as complex as extrapolating the actions of new devices. In fact, a number of prominent engineers and scientists have reported that their discoveries developed from their reasoning based on such mental models (Krueger, 1976).

Linear Orderings among Referents

Psychologists have studied the referential representation of objects that are ordered along some dimension of magnitude, such as height or area. For example, consider the following description:

> *Although the four craftsmen were brothers, they varied enormously in height.*
> *The electrician was the very tallest, and the plumber was shorter than him.*
> *The plumber was taller than the carpenter, who, in turn, was taller than the*
> *painter.*

What a reader knows about the relative heights of the four men after reading such a passage is based primarily on the referential representation she has con-

Tallness

Figure 7.2   Readers are faster to answer a question about two objects that are farther apart in the referential representation of a linear ordering than about objects that are closer, even if the latter information was explicitly stated in the text. For example, readers take less time to answer *Who is taller, the electrician or the painter?* than to answer *Who is taller, the plumber or the carpenter?* The pattern of response times suggest that readers consult a referential representation to answer such questions, rather than a representation of the information explicitly stated in the text.

structed, rather than on the semantic or syntactic representations of the individual sentences. Her referential representation symbolizes the linear ordering of the objects. Figure 7.2 shows a depiction of the linear ordering. (It is not intended to be a depiction of the referential representation.) Readers can rapidly answer questions about the relative magnitudes of objects that are farther apart in the ordering (like the relative heights of the electrician and the painter), but they take longer to answer questions about two adjacent objects (like the plumber and the carpenter) (Potts, 1972). This result is somewhat surprising because the information about the latter pair—the plumber and the carpenter—is explicitly provided in the first clause of the last sentence of the text, while the information about the more separated pair—the electrician and the painter—can be inferred from the sentences only by applying transitivity rules. This result implies that subjects are not using the representations of the individual sentences to answer the questions. Rather, they seem to be using a referential representation that integrates the linear-order information from all the sentences. The organization of the information in the referential representation makes the extreme items more accessible than the items in the middle of the ordering. This result illustrates the distinction between the referential representation and the semantic and syntactic representations of the text.

Referential Representations of Mathematical Concepts

While the nature of the referential representation is intuitively obvious in the case of descriptive prose, it is less obvious in the case of a text that is more abstract, such as a logical argument or a mathematical proof. Some mathematicians and logicians delight in thinking only of the syntax and semantics of various propositions, avoiding the thought of a referent. In fact, mathematical proofs are usually evaluated purely in terms of their semantics and syntax, without consideration of any objects that might correspond to a mathematical expression. During the reading of a text referring to abstract mathematical concepts, perhaps no referential representation is constructed, or perhaps individuals vary in whether or not they construct a referential representation.

An example of a mathematical concept that is familiar to students of calculus and that *can* have a referential interpretation is an *integral*. The common referential interpretation of an integral is that it is the area under the curve described by a function. Many other mathematical concepts do not have such readily available referents. Whether or not a mathematical function has a referent, it can always be treated purely as an abstract function with certain syntactic rules of combining symbols and interpretive rules for evaluating the function. Some branches of mathematics, like algebra, are referentially impoverished, while others, like geometry, are referentially rich. It is conventional in Euclidean and analytic geometry to use diagrams of the referent to explain new concepts, perhaps because geometry is the branch of mathematics most obviously related to perceptions of our physical world.

The comprehension and memory of a mathematical text might be enhanced by the presence of a referential representation of the mathematical concepts that are discussed. For example, Nobel laureate physicist Richard Feynman (1985) informally described how he follows a mathematical theorem by constructing a referential representation and evaluating the validity of the theorem with respect to that representation:

> When I'm trying to understand...I keep making up examples. For instance, the mathematicians would come in with a...theorem. As they're telling me the conditions of the theorem, I construct something that fits all the conditions. You know, you have a set (one ball)—disjoint (two balls). Then the balls turn colors, grow hairs, or whatever, in my head as they put more conditions on. Finally, they state the theorem, which is some...thing about the ball which isn't true for my hairy green ball thing, so I say "False!" (Feynman, 1985, p. 70)

Combining Words to Describe Referents

Objects are often described by a phrase that specifies the properties of a referent. A clear case is provided by the adjective-noun combination in a noun phrase, such as *blue carpet*. Some adjective-noun pairs co-occur so frequently (*log cabin, paper doll, revolving door*) that they conjointly describe an object that is probably mentally represented as a single concept even though it is described by two words. By contrast, many adjective-noun combinations are relatively novel, so that the specified object must be mentally constructed when the phrase is read (*exhausted aardvark, baroque basket, heavy pen*).

The time course of representing an adjective-noun combination has been studied by examining how quickly subjects could decide whether a noun phrase in an oral sentence matched an object in an accompanying picture (Potter & Faulconer, 1979). The nouns in the noun phrases were presented in one of two ways: (1) preceded by an adjective (*burning house*) or (2) alone, without an adjective (*house*). What was manipulated was the depiction of the object in the picture. In some cases, the depiction contained the named object and the modification described by the adjective (a picture of a house on fire); in other cases, the depiction contained only the unmodified object, as shown in Figure 7.3. In still other cases, the picture depicted an object not mentioned in the sentence, so that the task of discriminating mentioned versus unmentioned objects had some validity. The picture appeared on a screen while the sentence was being presented, and the subjects' task was to decide as rapidly as possible whether or not the depicted object had been named in the sentence.

In the trials of primary interest, the picture was presented immediately after the mention of the noun. Thus, the subjects' responses were based on the content of the referential representation at the time the noun was heard. When the noun was modified (*burning house*), subjects were faster to respond to a picture of a burning house than to a picture of a typical house, although their instructions were to attend only to the noun. This result indicates that when the subjects were presented with the adjective-noun combination, they represented the referent in a way that included the adjective's meaning. Moreover, this representation was available immediately after the noun occurred.

In a post hoc analysis of the data, the authors (Potter & Faulconer, 1979) separated the results of familiar adjective-noun combinations (e.g., *roasted turkey*) from novel adjective-noun combinations (e.g., *broken screwdriver*). They found that the advantage of pictures depicting the combination occurred primarily for familiar combinations. In other words, one can conclude that on hearing *roasted turkey,* the

Figure 7.3 If readers are presented with a drawing such as (a) or (b), they are faster to decide that the object in drawing (b) had been named in the sentence *It was already getting late when the man first saw the* burning house *ahead of him*. The difference in reaction times suggests that readers integrate the adjective and noun in their referential representation of the phrase *burning house*. *Source:* Adapted from Potter & Faulconer, 1979, Figure 1, p. 511.

listener constructs a representation of a roasted turkey, not just of a turkey. However, for an unfamiliar combination (e.g., *broken screwdriver*), the representation of the object does not appear to contain the modification described by the adjective, at least not immediately upon reading the noun. This conclusion pertains to the representation that exists at the time the noun is heard.

Another part of the study suggested that the representation of the unfamiliar combination is elaborated as the processing of the rest of the sentence progresses. If the test picture was presented at the end of the sentence, the effect of familiarity of the combination was negligible; by that time, the subjects had integrated the adjective and the noun in their representation of the referent, regardless of the initial familiarity of the combination.

The process that constructs the referential representation of the adjective-noun combination might operate as follows: If the concept denoted by the adjective-noun pair is very familiar (e.g., *roasted turkey*), then it would have a high base activation level. Consequently, it would take relatively little time before the concept's activation level reached the threshold level after receiving activation increments from the adjective and the noun. In fact, the representation of the familiar combination might reach threshold sooner than either the noun or the adjective concept alone, and the combination would become the accepted interpretation. Establishing the correspondence between the sentence and the picture would then take less time if the picture showed the adjective-noun combination than if it showed only the object named by the noun. In the case of a novel or infrequent adjective-noun combination, like *broken screwdriver,* the underlying concept would either have no pre-existing corresponding memory node or a memory node with a relatively low base activation level. If there is no pre-existing node, then the concept denoted by the noun would be activated and linked to the activated representation of the property denoted by the adjective. In either case, it would take a relatively large increment of activation (and hence time) before the representation of a novel combination reached the threshold level. So the process of constructing the referential representation of adjective-noun combinations may be explained in terms of a mechanism in which activation converges from different sources.

Constructing the Referential Representation

As a reader goes through a text, he progressively constructs his referential representation, guided primarily by the referring expressions in the text. Depending on whether the referring expression refers to an entity that is already included in the referential representation or to a new entity, he will either modify an existing part of the referential representation or construct a new part. In both cases, he will have to determine how any new information from the sentence is to be related to the existing information in his referential representation.

A common way for a text to unfold is by presenting new information that is grounded in what the text has already established. Thus, successive clauses and sentences tend to refer repeatedly to certain objects or persons that are central to the content and then present some elaboration or relational information about them. The processes that construct the referential representation must recognize the instances of coreference and distinguish them from references to new entities. The determination of coreference is made with the help of (1) language-based cues provided by the text, such as word meanings, syntax, and text structure, and (2) knowledge-based cues, which evoke the reader's knowledge of the content domain. In the following section, we illustrate the use of these two kinds of cues by describing how a reader establishes a referential representation for an anaphoric pronoun. And in later sections, we describe the use of language-based and knowledge-based cues in more detail.

Pronominal Reference

Personal pronouns play a pointing role because they point to a component of the reader's referential representation. Sometimes the pointing is completely unambiguous, as when there is only one possible antecedent for a pronoun (*Karl sleeps soundly but he wakes up on time*) or when the gender of the pronoun eliminates any ambiguity (*Karl and Mary both sleep soundly but only she wakes up on time*). A pronoun can provide linguistic cues to the identity of its referent by indicating the referent's gender (*he* or *she*), number (*he* or *they*), or case role (*he* or *him*). But on some occasions, these particular cues are insufficient to identify a referent uniquely. Then other more subtle cues, both language based and knowledge based, help to identify the referent. The search for the referent of a pronoun must satisfy the multiple constraints provided by language-based and knowledge-based cues. The cues can be stated as a set of heuristic rules for finding an antecedent of a personal pronoun. The list below presents some of the heuristics that have been studied in a number of psychological experiments:

1. Look for a referent of the *same gender and number* that has been a recent topic of the discourse (Corbett & Chang, 1983). This is a language-based cue.

   Melvin and Susie *left when* she *became sleepy.*

2. If there are two alternative candidate antecedents in a previous clause, favor the one that plays the *same grammatical role* (e.g., grammatical subject or object) in its clause as the pronoun does in its clause (Sheldon, 1974). This is a language-based cue.

   Floyd *saw Bert and then* he *drove away.*

3. If there are two alternative candidate antecedents in a previous clause, favor the one that was *more thematically prominent,* that is, the one that was the focus of its clause (Carpenter & Just, 1977b). This is a language-based cue.

   It was Gus *who met Earl;* he *wanted to discuss politics.*

4. If there are two alternative candidate antecedents in some previous clauses, favor the antecedent in the *most recent clause* (Daneman & Carpenter, 1980). This is a language-based cue.

   Dorothea ate pie; Ethel *ate cake. Later* she *had coffee.*

5. If the pronoun refers to the cause of a known action, favor the antecedent that is typically attributed with *causing that type of action* (Garvey & Caramazza, 1974). This is a knowledge-based cue.

   Clint *confessed to Archie because* he *wanted forgiveness.*

6. Use general knowledge about the candidate antecedents in the referential situation to determine which is the *more likely assignee* (Hirst & Brill, 1980). This is a very general knowledge-based cue.

   The Pope and the rabbi *met for lunch;* he *was accompanied by* his *wife.*

Determining the referent of a pronoun   Most of the research done on the assignment of pronominal reference has focused on discovering the cues that are used, rather than on the computations that use the cues to find the prior representation of the referent. Nevertheless, a few experiments have revealed some interesting performance characteristics associated with the processes themselves:

1. Computations are often executed when a reader first encounters a personal pronoun, rather than later in the sentence. Eye-fixation studies indicate that the computation of the coreference, as indicated by a pause in the eye fixations, occurs while the pronoun is being fixated (Carpenter & Just, 1977b; Ehrlich & Rayner, 1983; Just & Carpenter, 1978).

2. The duration of the computation (as indicated by the duration of the pause on the pronoun) is longer if the antecedent occurred much earlier than if it occurred only recently (Ehrlich & Rayner, 1983).

3. If it is not possible to assign a pronoun to a referent at the time the pronoun is read, then there is sometimes another attempt to assign the pronoun at the end of the sentence, as indicated by a longer pause on the final word of the sentence (Carpenter & Just, 1977b; Just & Carpenter, 1978).

4. During the search for the antecedent of a pronoun, nonantecedents of the appropriate gender are activated to some degree (Corbett & Chang, 1983). For example, the presence of the pronoun *he* in the second clause of *Scott stole the basketball from Warren and he sank a jumpshot* produces an increase in the activation level not only of the antecedent, *Scott,* but also of the nonantecedent, *Warren.*

These performance characteristics suggest the following model of the process that searches for the referent of a pronoun. The model is similar to the one proposed by Corbett (1984). The search for the referent of a pronoun is initiated as soon as the pronoun is encountered in the text. The search operates by using the various heuristic cues discussed above to activate the potential antecedents. That is, activation is directed from each cue source to all the elements of the referential representation that satisfy the constraint imposed by the cue. The amount of activation each candidate receives is a function of three factors: (1) the number of cues that support its candidacy; (2) the relative importance of each of the cues (e.g., a gender cue has more weight than a recency cue); and (3) the strength of the supporting evidence accompanying the cue in the current context.

The candidate whose activation level is the first to reach the threshold is chosen as the pronoun's antecedent in the referential representation. If no candidate's activation level reaches threshold by the time some deadline has expired, then the referential assignment is postponed until the end of the clause or sentence, when the search is reinitiated with the benefit of any additional cues encountered in the latter part of the sentence.

This process finds a referent that satisfies the multiple constraints imposed by language-based and knowledge-based cues. Although this model has been developed for pronominal assignment, a similar type of search for existing referential representations might also be used when the anaphoric reference is not pronominal. Any time that a referring expression initiates a search for a previously constructed referential representation, the same kind of mechanism may be used. This activation-based mechanism (of the type used by the READER model) permits multiple constraints to be satisfied; it is also a very general mechanism that may underlie a number of other processes, such as the selection of the appropriate meaning of an ambiguous word during lexical access.

Language-based Cues

The types of linguistic information provided by pronouns (gender, number, and case) are among the clearest examples of cues provided by the text about the referent of an expression. But pronouns are not the only source of information about coreference. Another cue to coreference occurs when the same expression is used twice to refer to the same referent. For example, consider the following pair of sentences:

> *Meredyth enjoyed her outing to the movie yesterday.*
> *The movie was about an opera star.*

The same object is referred to twice with the expression *movie*. During the reading of the first sentence, the referent of *movie* is initially represented; and during the reading of the second sentence, that same representation is elaborated. However, repetition of an expression does not always signal coreference, as the following pair of sentences illustrates:

> *Meredyth enjoyed her outing to the movie yesterday.*
> *The movie to be shown next week is a futuristic musical comedy.*

Conversely, the same object can be referred to by different expressions, as in the following sentences:

> *Meredyth enjoyed her outing to the movie yesterday.*
> *The film was about an opera star.*

In this case, *movie* and *film* are synonymous. When synonymous words are used to refer to the same object in the two sentences of a pair, the time needed to read the second sentence is about the same as when the same word is used twice (Yekovich & Walker, 1978). Thus, the occurrence of two synonymous noun phrases is as effective a cue to coreference as the repetition of the same noun phrase.

Another language-based cue to coreference involves the use of the definite article *the* instead of the indefinite *a* at the beginning of a noun phrase. *The* sometimes indicates that the referent of the phrase has already been mentioned or is easily inferred, whereas the indefinite article *a* indicates fairly strongly that a new referent is being introduced. For example, consider the definite and indefinite articles in the following sentences:

> *Elmer has* a *pet goat.*
> The *goat is very helpful around the house.*

Both of these sentences refer to the same goat. The noun phrase *the goat* in the second sentence clearly refers to Elmer's goat, which was introduced in the first sentence. By contrast, consider the following pair of sentences:

> *Elmer has* a *pet goat.*
> A *goat is very helpful around the house.*

In this case, the first sentence refers to a specific goat, Elmer's pet, whereas the second sentence refers to a generic goat.

The presence of the definite article preceding a repeated noun phrase encourages the inference that the same object is being referred to. In effect, this increases the probability that the successive sentences of a text will be integrated into a coherent sequence, thus improving the reader's subsequent recall (deVilliers, 1974).

The indication of coreference or new reference can be made more explicit, for example, by using the adjectives *same* and *different:*

> *Sheila was in love with a jockey, and Marcia was in love with* the same/a different *one.*

The same communicates coreference in two ways: with the meaning of the word *same* and with the presence of the definite article. The phrase *a different* indicates two separate referents both with the meaning of *different* and with the presence of the indefinite article.

Focus and coreference   The search for the referent of an expression is influenced by the thematic structure of the text. Those elements of a sentence that are more thematically central than others are called the **focused** elements. While various linguistic analyses deal with focus and thematic centrality in different ways (e.g., Halliday & Hasan, 1976), perhaps the most intuitively appealing analysis has been proposed by Chafe (1972). He compared the unfolding of a text to the staging of a play. At any given time, only a subset of all the actors are on stage, with only one or two of them engaged in the current dialogue, perhaps having their centrality accentuated by a spotlight. Similarly, a text refers to a number of entities, but not all of them are equally focused at any given time. Most paragraphs have a central theme or focus, and each sentence can have a focus of its own, as well. The portion of the sentence that is focused can be thought of as having a special marker, called the *discourse pointer,* that indicates its focused status (Carpenter & Just, 1977a).

An element of the referential representation that has recently been focused has a privileged status in the search for a referent for a new expression. For example, when readers encounter a pronoun for which they must find a previously mentioned referent, they favor a referent that was recently focused (Carpenter & Just, 1977b). This result was found in a study in which college students read brief stories containing ambiguous pronouns. The following sequence of two sentences is an excerpt from one of the stories:

> *The one who mocked the guard was the arsonist. He had been at the prison for only one week.*

The pronoun *He* in the second sentence does not uniquely specify its referent; nevertheless, readers had a strong preference to make *He* coreferential with the focused character in the preceding sentence. In this particular example, the first sentence focuses on the *arsonist;* thus, most subjects inferred that *He* referred to the *arsonist.* In another condition of the experiment in which the first sentence focused on the *guard,* the readers assumed that *He* referred to the *guard.* Thus, the thematic structure of a sentence, focusing on one referent or another, provides a language-based cue that readers use in computing subsequent coreference. The focus is not at the syntactic, semantic, or lexical levels, nor is it on a phrase or a noun or even on a linguistic object. Rather, the entity that is focused is a particular element in the referential representation.

Several different gradations of focus can be distinguished:

1. At the highest level of focus are those objects that are both recently mentioned and also marked by the discourse pointer. Thus, *the arsonist* is focused in the sentence *The one who mocked the guard was the arsonist.*

2a. At an intermediate level of focus are those objects that are recently mentioned but without the benefit of the discourse pointer, such as *the guard* in the sentence above.
2b. Also at an intermediate level of focus are those objects that were once marked by the discourse pointer but have since been displaced by other objects. *The arsonist* would have this status after a succeeding sentence focused on a different object.
3. At the lowest level of focus are those objects that are referred to implicitly, as well as those that plausibly might belong in the situation that is being described. For example, the word *arsonist* implies the possibility of a fire.

Notice that at all levels, the analysis of focus pertains to the status of elements in the referential representation. The greater the focus on an element, the easier it is to refer to it anaphorically. For example, consider this sentence:

> *The one who swept up the sawdust was the bartender.*

The word *bartender*, by virtue of its focal status, is an easy target for pronominal reference (Carpenter & Just, 1977b). If the next sentence began with *He*, it would be easy to infer that *He* refers to the *bartender*. If instead the next sentence began with *It*, the reference could be to the *sawdust* or the act of sweeping, both of which were mentioned in the first sentence but not marked with the discourse pointer as being

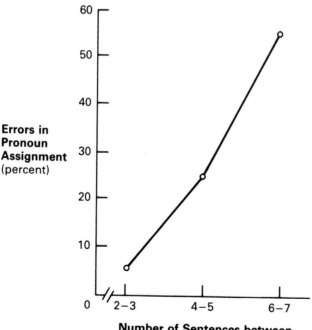

Figure 7.4 Readers make more errors in choosing the referent of a pronoun as the number of sentences intervening between the referent noun and the referring pronoun increases. *Source:* Adapted from Daneman & Carpenter, 1980, Figure 1, p. 456.

thematically central. But *It* could not refer to the broom that the bartender proba-bly used, because no broom has been explicitly mentioned, and pronouns normally cannot refer to objects whose existence has only been implied and not explicitly mentioned. Sentences in which a pronoun refers to an implied object sound awk-ward, as in the sentence *Joseph dreams nightly but seldom remembers them.* As these examples illustrate, anaphora depends on the focal status of an element in the referential representation.

The more recently the antecedent of a pronoun has been mentioned, the easier it is to assign the pronoun to its referent. One study systematically varied the distance in a text between the occurrence of a person's name and a following pro-noun that referred to that person (Daneman & Carpenter, 1980). After reading the passage, the subjects were given comprehension questions that probed their as-signment of the pronoun. If a few sentences had intervened between the occur-rence of the name and the pronoun, readers almost always assigned the pronoun to its referent correctly. But as the distance was increased (up to seven sentences), readers made many more mistakes in assigning the pronoun to a referent, as shown in Figure 7.4. Even if the assignment to the correct antecedent is made, the time a reader takes to make the assignment increases with the distance since the last men-tion, as shown in Figure 7.5 (Carpenter & Just, 1977a, 1977b; Clark & Sengul, 1979; Ehrlich & Rayner, 1983). Thus, a previously focused object becomes progressively less available for anaphoric reference as an increasing amount of new text is read.

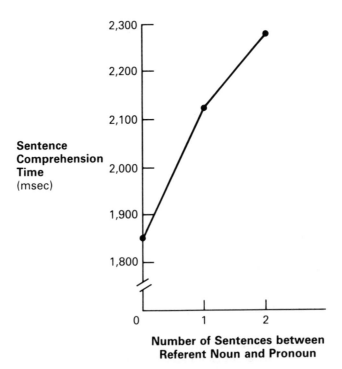

Figure 7.5   The time to retrieve the referent of a pronoun increases as the number of sen-tences intervening between the referent noun and the referring pronoun increases. *Source:* Adapted from Clark & Sengul, 1979, Table 1, p. 38.

In summary, thematic focus is a language-based cue contributing to the activation-directing process that searches for the referent of an expression. The strength of the cue—that is, the amount of activation it contributes—partially depends on the level of focus and the recency of mention.

Knowledge-based Cues

The construction of the referential representation is aided by the reader's previous knowledge of the content area. As we will describe in more detail in Chapter 8 on comprehension of extended texts, the main theory of the organization and use of such knowledge was developed in the course of explaining the comprehension of narrative texts that describe familiar events, such as going to a restaurant (Schank & Abelson, 1977). The knowledge that represents a familiar event is a particular kind of schema called a **script**. A script has slots for the components of the event, such as the component actions, the main participants in the actions, their goals, the typical position of each action in the entire sequence, and so forth. Slots can have default values, so that actions (such as ordering the meal) or participants (such as who took the order) that are not explicitly mentioned can be inferred, if necessary. Thus, a reader's going-to-a-restaurant script provides him with an outline of the objects and actions to expect. The script can make it easier for the reader to represent and relate the objects and actions in the referential representation when they are mentioned or implied by the text. The script knowledge seems indispensable to a computer simulation's understanding of simple stereotyped stories, such as newspaper articles reporting traffic accidents.

Scriptlike knowledge is probably also indispensable for a human reader's construction of the referential representation. Readers use their knowledge of stereotyped occurrences such as restaurant visits, baseball games, and courtrooms in constructing the representation. For example, when a text describing a restaurant meal first refers to a menu, the reader can make sense of what a menu is doing in that scene: how it is being used, who brought it, and the like. Atypical components of an occurrence can also be understood, but they require a rationale that can be provided by the text or inferred by the reader.

A script not only makes it easier to represent the presence of some element in the referential representation but also makes it possible to elaborate the representation of the element beyond the information provided by the text. The typical default values of the slot fillers in the restaurant script would permit a reader to elaborate his referential representation of the menu if this elaboration became necessary or desirable. For instance, knowing what kind of restaurant it was (e.g., a seafood restaurant) would permit a reader to infer some of the contents of the menu, without the text providing that information.

There is no doubt that readers use previous knowledge that is based on either their own experience with objects and events in the real world or on their indirect experience with a world described by a text or another person. When reading a text about familiar events, readers use these knowledge structures to augment and organize the information in the text.

Knowledge about objects and actions A broad definition of coreference does not require that two expressions share the very same referent; rather, it permits a whole-part relation between their two referents. For example, examine this pair of sentences:

Theodore purchased a used textbook.
The pages were stained.

A reader must infer that *The pages* refers to a component part of the previously established referent of *textbook*.

Another common type of coreference that is possible without identical referents occurs when two expressions refer to an object, once in terms of its category membership and once in terms of its own name (see Sanford & Garrod, 1981). Consider this sequence of sentences:

Franklin handed a fruit to his sister.
The apple was the largest he had seen that year.

The reader infers that *apple* and *fruit* refer to the same object. Therefore, he would integrate the information associated with *apple* with the previously read information about *fruit*.

Just as expressions can corefer to objects and their parts, as well as categories and their exemplars, they can also corefer to actions and their components, such as the instrument or agent or object of an action. As we described in Chapter 6 on semantic processes, there is evidence that as soon as the reader encounters a reference to an instrument (such as *broom*) of a previously described action (such as *sweep*), he makes the connection between the instrument and the action (Carpenter & Just, 1977b).

Knowledge about actions also helps a reader select a referent if an expression does not uniquely specify one of several participants in an action. For example:

John saw Henry fall down some stairs.
He ran for a doctor.

General knowledge of falling and doctors tells a reader that *John* is the one most likely to be running for the doctor (Hirst & Brill, 1980). Virtually any kind of knowledge can enter into this process. For example, script knowledge of a restaurant scene indicates how to interpret the pronoun in the following sentences:

The waiter spilled some water on the patron.
He quickly went to get some napkins.

A reader would probably infer that the *He* refers to the *waiter,* partly because his restaurant script indicates that waiters are much more likely to fetch napkins than are patrons.

Knowledge of causal relations   Some determinations of referential assignment depend on the knowledge of causal relations among actions. Consider how easily a reader can infer the referent of *he* in the following sentence:

Clint confessed to Archie because he wanted forgiveness.

He refers to *Clint*. But what psychological computation determines this? There are two inputs to this computation. The most obvious cue is that *he* is the wanter of forgiveness. A reader can infer that the wanter of forgiveness is likely to be the one who confessed, so *he* probably refers to *Clint*. This cue to the computation is unavailable until *after* the reader has read two words beyond the pronoun. Does that mean that during the reading of the pronoun itself, a reader has no idea who the pronoun refers to? The answer is that the reader *does* have some information about the pronominal assignment, thanks to information provided by the second cue.

The second and less obvious cue to the pronominal assignment—namely, the verb *confess* and the conjunction *because*—indicates that the antecedent is probably *Clint*. This cue is available at the time the pronoun is read. *Confess* describes an action whose instigation or cause is typically attributed to the agent of the confessing—in this case, *Clint* (Garvey & Caramazza, 1974). Garvey and Caramazza investigated the causal attribution associated with verbs by asking subjects to complete sentences like the following:

> *Martha scolded Annette because she...*

A possible completion is *had been misbehaving*. For some verbs, like *scold* and *confess,* there is strong agreement among subjects about the attribution of the causality. The action of scolding is generally thought to be caused by something the recipient of the scolding (*Annette*) has done. By contrast, confessing is generally brought about by the person who does the confessing. This type of knowledge about actions is useful not only in assigning pronouns to referents (which we focus on here) but also in determining causal relations among the events described in a text.

The READER Model's Referential Processing

In this section, we briefly describe how the READER simulation model constructs a referential representation by explaining how it processes the following excerpt:

> *Flywheels are one of the oldest mechanical devices known to man. Every internal-combustion engine contains a small flywheel that converts the jerky motion of the pistons into the smooth flow of energy that powers the drive shaft.*

READER's referential representation is centered around referring expressions. As READER encounters each noun phrase, it first tries to determine whether the representation of the referent has already been established, due to a previous mention of the object in a preceding portion of the text. If the representation of the referent already exists, then any new information about the referent contained in the current sentence is appended to the previous representation. If no previous representation of the referent exists, a new representation is created.

When READER encounters the word *flywheels* in the very first word of the text, no representation of its referent exists, so READER constructs one and calls it *FLYWHEEL1*. If READER had any relevant previous knowledge about flywheels, the information would be activated and associated with FLYWHEEL1. Moreover, when the remainder of the sentence provides more information about this object, the information is added to the FLYWHEEL1 referential representation. Thus, at the end of the first sentence, READER's representation of *flywheels* indicates that it is an ancient, man-made device; also, the reference is to the generic category of flywheels, rather than to a specific instance.

When the word *flywheel* occurs again in the second sentence, READER does not immediately assume that its referent is FLYWHEEL1. One knowledge-based cue that leads READER to reject FLYWHEEL1 as the referent is that internal-combustion engines are modern, while the generic flywheel is ancient. Another cue, this one language based, is the presence of the indefinite article *a* that modifies *flywheel*. Indefinite articles usually signal the introduction of a new referent. READER thus infers that the second sentence refers to a particular example of a generic flywheel, namely, the kind found in internal-combustion engines. READER constructs a new referential representation of *a small flywheel*, a previously unmentioned referent, calling it *FLYWHEEL2*. There are several other occurrences of the word *flywheel* later in the passage, some of which are coreferential with FLYWHEEL1 or FLYWHEEL2 and some of which have a different referent.

The READER model, like a human reader, must determine the referent in each case and represent it appropriately. READER searches for the referent of an expression by directing activation to potential antecedents in the existing referential representation. The sources of the activation are the various kinds of language-based and knowledge-based cues described previously. If any existing part of the referential representation satisfies the constraints imposed by the cues, then that part is accepted as the referential representation of the current expression. If more than one potential antecedent satisfies the constraints, then the one that received the most activation is selected.

Besides representing the referents of noun phrases, READER also elaborates existing referential representations when additional information about the referent is obtained. For example, the first sentence provides the additional information that *flywheels* are ancient and that they are mechanical devices. READER also represents relations among referents (the containment of a *flywheel* by an *internal-combustion engine*) and the participation of referents in actions and events (*a flywheel converts the jerky motion of pistons into a smooth flow of energy*). By the end of the passage, READER has a representation of all the objects, modifications, relations, and actions described by the text. Although the text is the immediate source of this representation, what is represented are entities described by the text, rather than the text itself.

The Role of the Referential Representation

The referential level of processing is especially important in reading, for several reasons. First, what a reader tends to remember best and for the longest period of time about a text is the referential representation. A reader generally remembers the situation that was described, rather than the text that described it. Sometimes it is said that after a while, a reader can recall the gist of a text but less so the particular words or expressions the text used. *Gist* tends not to be defined formally, although a dictionary definition indicates that it refers to "the substance of a matter." In essence, then, memory for gist is memory for the referential representation.

One experiment that illustrates this point presented subjects with pairs of sentences that together described a particular situation (Bransford, Barclay, & Franks, 1972). For example, one of the pairs read:

The frog sat on a log. The fish swam under the log.

Many subjects later erroneously thought that they had read a sentence that said *The fish swam under the frog*. The latter sentence can, of course, be inferred from the first two. The reason why subjects thought they had read this sentence is that it accurately describes the referential situation they had mentally represented. Memory for a text seems to be based to a very large extent on the referential representation.

A second reason the referential level is important in reading is that repeated reference across the sentences of a text provides coherence. Repeated reference to the same objects or persons or actions provides links across a sequence of sentences, such that the referential representation of the sequence is integrated. The linear ordering we presented previously (*The electrician was taller than the plumber; the plumber was taller than the carpenter; the carpenter was taller than the painter*) is an example of a sequence of sentences that results in an integrated referential representation.

One example of a literary device that relies on repeated reference for integration is *dovetailing*. Sentences are dovetailed if the object mentioned at the end of one sentence is referred to again at the beginning of the next sentence:

> *The animal trainer began to fear the elderly male lion. The lion had begun to show signs of insubordination on a disturbingly frequent basis.*

The *lion* referred to by both sentences above is the object that links them.

The critical integrative role of repeated reference is acknowledged within the model of text representation and memory proposed by Kintsch and van Dijk (1978), in which repeated reference is the main mechanism for relating the sentences of a text to each other. Kintsch and van Dijk propose that propositions that refer to the same referent are linked to each other in the representation. In sum, the referential representation provides much of the integrative glue that binds the various sentences of a text together.

A third reason the referential level is important concerns the acquisition of language by children (Macnamara, 1972). Learning the names of familiar objects is a very early and probably fundamental aspect of how a child learns his first language. Parents repeatedly point to objects and name them for the benefit of the child. Such parental instruction in language seems to focus on the referential level. The first objects to which children learn to refer are perceptually salient, including such objects as caretakers, foods, toys, and clothes. There is a strong perceptual basis to a child's acquisition of his early vocabulary. And the aspect of language that is probably acquired first is referential meaning, rather than syntax or semantics.

A related reliance on referential meaning is evident when adults try to learn a miniature artificial language that has been constructed to study aspects of language learning. Such languages may be composed of about 20 verbal symbols (words) and a set of syntactic rules for combining these symbols into sentences. An example of a sentence might be *Gava neso bifu naki*. In such studies, there is an initial learning phase, during which subjects attempt to induce the underlying syntactic rules of the language by examining a set of about 50 to 200 sentences of the artificial language. An example of a syntactic rule might be that "if *bifu* occurs, it must be preceded by *neso* or *yowu*." Another example might be that "if *Gava* occurs, it must be the first word in the sentence." After the subjects have examined a sufficient number of sentences, their knowledge of the syntactic rules is tested by having them judge the syntactic correctness of test sentences or by having them produce their own sentences.

The subjects' ability to acquire the rules of an artificial language is greatly enhanced if each sentence is accompanied by a drawing of its referent (Moeser & Bregman, 1972). For example, *Gava* might refer to a square, and *neso* might refer to redness, so the drawing accompanying any sentence that contained these terms would contain a red square. Moreover, there was a suggestion that the subjects used the referential meaning of the terms (such as the correspondence between *Gava* and a square shape) to infer the syntactic rules. In fact, subjects could not acquire some of the more complex syntactic rules unless the sentences in the learning phase were accompanied by their referents. Other factors might also play a role in the acquisition of syntax, such as the markers affixed to the words that indicate the syntactic function (much as the *ing* ending in English indicates a certain verb form) (Green, 1979; Mori & Moeser, 1983). But it is clear that referential meaning plays an important role in the acquisition of vocabulary and syntax of an artificial language. This conclusion probably generalizes to a child's acquisition of a first language, too.

Shallow Comprehension

The referential level of processing may lie at the heart of an interesting kind of reading in which a reader goes through some of the motions of reading, understands all of the words and sentences, but fails to grasp the gist of a text. Of course, there can be many reasons why a reader fails to comprehend; we will focus here on one particular kind of failure in which comprehension at the referential level is absent or disrupted. We will call this phenomenon **shallow comprehension.** Even though no experiments to date have specifically examined shallow comprehension, a number of findings appear to be related to the phenomenon.

1. If a reader doesn't know what the referent of a passage is, she feels as though she doesn't understand the passage and has difficulty remembering it.

In one well-known demonstration (Bransford & Johnson, 1973), readers were asked to understand and recall paragraphs like this one:

> *The procedure is actually quite simple. First you arrange things into different groups. Of course, one pile may be sufficient depending on how much there is to do. If you have to go somewhere else, due to lack of facilities that is the next step, otherwise you are pretty well set. It is important not to overdo things. That is, it is better to do few things at once than too many.* (1973, p. 400)

This paragraph is linguistically simple; it contains no difficult words or constructions, nor does it refer to complex concepts. It is relatively easy to do the lexical access, as well as the syntactic and semantic analyses. Then why is it so difficult to make sense of this paragraph? The problem is that a reader has little idea of what the referent is. Even though a reader knows the meanings of words like *things*, *groups*, and *pile*, she does not know what they refer to in this context.

In another condition, a different group of subjects was presented the same paragraph, but this time the paragraph was preceded by the title "Washing Clothes." In this second condition, the subjects rated the same paragraph as more comprehensible and they recalled it better. The title evokes the relevant knowledge contained in the washing-clothes or doing-laundry script, which, in turn, provides information about the referents of specific noun phrases (like *things, pile,* and *facilities*) and verbs (like *arrange* and *do*). This information allows the reader to construct a referential representation of all the mentioned objects and actions, making the paragraph comprehensible. Reading this passage without knowledge of the referents produces a very shallow level of comprehension.

In a similar study, Dooling and Lachman (1971) constructed biographies that were highly metaphorical. The metaphors were almost uninterpretable in the sense that referents could not be determined although each individual sentence made sense. Consider this excerpt:

> *Our hero bravely defied all scornful laughter that tried to prevent his scheme. "Your eyes deceive," he had said, "An egg not a table correctly typifies this planet." Now three sturdy sisters sought proof, forging along sometimes through calm vastness. . . .* (1971, p. 217)

Many of the subjects who were presented with this passage failed to realize that it refers to Christopher Columbus and his voyage to America. Without this realization, they could not construct a referential representation of the text. Their poor recall of the passage reflected this lack of understanding. Thus, ignorance of the referent produces shallow comprehension.

2. A reader's failure to detect a factual inconsistency in a text can indicate incomplete processing at the referential level.

Such failures seem frequent among adult readers and perhaps even more so among children. Children often fail to detect relatively obvious inconsistencies, even between successive sentences. For example, in one study (Markman, 1977), the text presented the following sentences about ocean fish:

> *There is absolutely no light at the bottom of the ocean. Some fish that live at the bottom of the ocean know their food by its color.*

An examination of a complete referential representation of these two sentences would reveal the inconsistency between the absence of light and perceiving color. Of course, if readers are told that a text will sometimes contain inconsistencies, and it is part of their task to detect those errors, then their detection rate is much higher. But in normal reading, many such inconsistencies slip by a reader, suggesting that shallow comprehension may have occurred.

3. Deep referential processing may lie at the heart of the mnemonic power of mental imagery.

A well-known finding in the field of memory (Bobrow & Bower, 1969; Bower, 1970) is that formation of a mental image that depicts two interacting items creates a strong mental bond between those items. For example, an arbitrary pair of nouns, like *apple* and *streetcar,* was remembered much better as an associated pair when readers were asked to form a mental image of the two objects interacting (such as a streetcar driving through a tunnel in a gigantic apple) (Bower, 1970).

However, another strategy produces an equally large mnemonic effect: namely, constructing a sentence that includes the two words, such as *The apple was crushed by the streetcar* (Bobrow & Bower, 1969). A single reference-based explanation can account for both mnemonic effects. In both cases, it is likely that constructing a referential representation in addition to a semantic representation improved memory performance. Intentionally forming a mental image of the referent during reading probably forces the formation of the referential representation and avoids the possibility of shallow comprehension.

4. Shallow comprehension may occur if a reader's attention is shared between reading and some other thought process, like daydreaming.

Although shared attention during reading has never been scientifically studied, it is common for people to finish reading a passage and become aware of having daydreamed while reading. They generally remember almost nothing about the passage. At the same time, they report a feeling of having read the words and sentences and, at some level, having processed the text. The following is a speculative account of what processes may occur when a person daydreams during reading.

Our hypothesis is that most levels of skilled reading (e.g., word encoding, lexical access, syntactic and semantic analysis) continue to operate normally during shallow comprehension but that the referential level of processing does not function properly. The hypothesis about the normal operation of processes like word encoding and lexical access could be tested by measuring the gaze durations on a paragraph during which a reader subsequently reported having daydreamed. If the word-encoding and lexical access processes continued to operate normally even when the reader daydreamed, then, as in normal reading, the gaze durations on each word of the passage should be governed by the length and the frequency of the words.

A detailed test of the comprehension of a passage that was read while daydreaming could reveal what, if anything, a reader learns during shallow comprehension. The comprehension deficits might include a general failure to establish representations of new referents, as well as a failure to establish anaphoric reference. The absence of a referential representation would explain the anecdotal reports of the failure to recall any of the gist of a passage immediately after having read it. Such results would confirm that the shallow comprehension that occurs in reading with shared attention is produced by disengagement of the referential level of processing.

This list of phenomena suggests that something like shallow comprehension occurs in several different circumstances. The sparse data that are currently available are consistent with our hypothesis that shallow comprehension consists of normal comprehension minus the referential level of processing. Certainly, this interesting topic invites further empirical investigation.

Philosophical Approaches to Reference

Reference has always played a central role in philosophers' attempts to define meaning. Reference, or at least truth value, is considered the fundamental relation in the philosophy of language. A proposition is true if it corresponds to the state of some particular world. When philosophical approaches to reference are extended to the psychology of language, the results are often unsatisfactory. This section describes some of the problems in applying philosophical approaches to a psychological theory.

According to a naive and ultimately unsatisfactory referential theory of meaning, the meaning of an expression is the entity, class of entities, event, or class of events that the expression names, refers to, denotes, designates, or stands for (Katz, 1972). So, according to this naive theory, the meaning of *Abraham Lincoln* is the man so named, the meaning of *women* is "the class of adult female human beings," and the meaning of *the assassination of Lincoln* refers to the events at Ford's Theater.

Philosophers correctly point out that this theory of meaning fails to satisfy certain formal criteria, such as failing to account for synonymy. If *synonymy* were defined strictly in terms of reference, then two expressions would have the same meaning as long as they had the same referent. This definition of synonymy is unsatisfactory because the relation defined by reference is just a transient correspondence between a linguistic expression and a state of some particular world. For example, if synonymy were based purely on reference, then two expressions like *chocolate cake* and *my dessert last night* might be synonymous. But even though they have the same referent, they do not have the same meaning. They cannot be used interchangeably, and they cannot always be equated to each other. By contrast, a more conventional approach to meaning would equate two expressions that share more than a referent, such as the expressions *opthalmologist* and *physician who specializes in diseases of the eye*, which are almost interchangeable. These examples illustrate that there is more to meaning than just reference. This is certainly true in the discipline of philosophy, and it is equally true of a psychological theory of comprehension.

Many of the reference-related issues that are problematic for philosophical analysis provide no obstacle for a theory of comprehension. It is very important to note that a theory of comprehension need not specify the referent of an expression; it need only specify the *representation* of the referent. A mental representation can vary from individual to individual, from one linguistic context to another, and from situation to situation. For example, the referent of *container* in the sentence *George put the apples/acid into the container* can differ depending on the linguistic context (*apples* versus *acid*) or on whether the reader is a layman or a chemist. The referential representation of a given expression is highly context sensitive. The reason people can still understand each other in spite of the context-sensitivity of referential meaning is that they share a great deal of common knowledge about the world. On the other hand, when two people who happen to speak the same language come from very different environments, they don't have a completely shared knowledge of referents. As a result, their communication will probably not be smooth.

Different Representations of the Same Entity

Even if two expressions have the same referent, they need not have the same referential representation. Frege (1960) pointed out that the star known as the "morning star" is the same heavenly body known as the "evening star," namely, the planet Venus. The fact that both expressions have the same referent is of no relevance to explaining comprehension. If a person knows that they are a single star, he might have a single referential representation of the two; if not, he would have two different representations. This is not very different from having two referential representations of Shirley Temple, one as a child movie star and one as an adult U.S. delegate to the United Nations. A reader might also have separate representations of Dr. Jekyll and Mr. Hyde because they are so different, even though they refer to the same object. However, a reader does not form a new referential representation of a person every time the person changes his clothes. A reader is likely to have as many different referential representations of a given object as he has functionally distinct impressions of it.

Representing Novel, Nonexistent, and Abstract Concepts

Readers can form referential representations of objects that don't exist in the real world or that they have never seen or experienced. A verbal description can indicate how to construct a referential representation of a new concept out of familiar components. For example, by combining the representations of *pinkness* and an *elephant,* a reader can construct a representation of a *pink elephant.* A unicorn poses no greater problem. Besides verbal descriptions, graphic depictions can provide information to be included in a referential representation. A reader can form a referential representation of real or imaginary objects, including an atom or a troll, without ever having seen one. Also, she can refer to and represent objects in the past and future, such as Louis XIV of France or her unborn great-grandchildren, without worrying about problems of existence. The reader represents the world to which the text refers, which may or may not correspond to the real world. A related issue is raised by the referential representation of abstract concepts, like *virtue* and *honesty. Honesty,* like *dog,* is a general term, and the referential representation may well be a prototypical instantiation. In a sentence like *The shop owner had faith in the honesty of the cashier, honesty* might be instantiated as "resisting the urge to take money from a cash register." However, *honesty* being attributed to a student might be instantiated as "resisting the urge to cheat on an examination." In sum, the referential representation of an abstract concept might be a specific instantiation of that concept. However, as pointed out previously, there is more to the meaning of a concept than just its referential representation.

Indeterminacy of Reference

A reader can never be absolutely certain what a text is referring to. Quine (1960) discusses the indeterminacy that is evident when translating from an unknown language. Suppose you were isolated with a person whose language was totally unknown to you. If, all of a sudden, a white rabbit jumped across a fence and your companion said the word *Gavagai,* you could not be certain what he was referring to. Your first guess may be that *Gavagai* means "rabbit," but it could also mean "small white mammal" or "furry-tailed creature" or "fence jumper" or even "rare event on a humid day." The indeterminacy can never be entirely removed, even if one systematically varied the scene and asked the informant whether or not *Gavagai* still applied.

Quine (1974) relates an interesting anecdote about the *Indri,* a lemur of Madagascar, which apparently owes its name to such an indeterminacy. The French naturalist who gave this animal the name *Indri* probably did so when his

Malagasy informant pointed to the animal and said, "Indri." But in fact, the meaning of the word *Indri* in the Malagasy language turns out to be "there it goes." It was a natural error to assume that the informant's utterance was the animal's name.

In normal reading, the problem of referential indeterminacy is much less severe because a reader usually knows almost all of the word meanings and has many sources of information to help determine the referent. Still, sometimes a reader is uncertain about what an expression is referring to. In that case, the reader must make a guess, or reread the passage in the hope of acquiring additional information, or tolerate the uncertainty about the referent.

Summary

The central importance of the referential representation is that it often contains the main information that the text tries to communicate to the reader. This centrality is manifested in several ways. Thoroughly understanding a text entails a complete and detailed referential representation, and remembering a text well entails good retrieval of the referential representation after some delay. Moreover, the referential representation is a site for integrating the information from the individual sentences of a text.

Previous knowledge of the world plays a large role in the construction of the referential representation, particularly filling in the gaps left by the text and indicating the relations among the parts of the referential representation. Understanding the referential level of a text is similar to understanding the referential situation that the text describes. For example, understanding a text about a chess game requires many of the same processes as understanding that same chess game while watching it. Understanding at the referential level is not a peculiarly linguistic process but a general cognitive process. Nevertheless, it is central and essential to normal reading comprehension.

Suggested Readings

The topic of reference has not been addressed as such within experimental psychology. However, Macnamara's book (1982) and article (1972) deal with the role of reference in language acquisition. Quine's book (1960) is a classic study of reference within the discipline of philosophy. Some of the demonstrations of Bransford and Johnson (1973) and Bransford, Barclay, and Franks (1972) make it clear how important reference is in text comprehension and memory. Rips' article (in press) considers what kinds of content can sensibly be attributed to the referential representation. And Corbett's article (1984) reports some interesting findings on pronominal assignment and summarizes previous results.

8

Understanding an Extended Text

What distinguishes a text, whether it is a children's story or an editorial, from a collection of unrelated sentences is the cohesion of the underlying ideas. To understand a text, a reader must not only make sense of each sentence in itself, but he must also determine its relation to the preceding portions of the text. He must determine the relations among the events, objects, and facts that are described by the text and construct a representation that integrates the information. The processes that contribute to representing such relations will be referred to as **text-level** processes.

Because the underlying relations among the events, objects, and facts that give a text its coherence can be unstated, the text-level processes may require the reader to make plausible inferences using his knowledge of the world and of the text's structure. This chapter describes the processes and the types of knowledge that are used in comprehending a text.

Overview The study of text comprehension has made it evident that a reader's previous knowledge plays an important role in understanding an extended text. Consequently, much of the chapter will describe the kinds of knowledge that are used in understanding a text, not just at the level of individual sentences but at the level of larger units, as well.

In the first section, **Knowledge about Story Structure,** we will describe two characterizations of story structure. One characterization is called a *story schema,* which is a frame-and-slots structure that can be used to represent what a reader knows about the story's structure. The second is a *story grammar,* a rulelike specification of the hierarchical relations among the categories of story information. Both characterizations can be related to the psychological processes at work when readers comprehend and recall a story.

The way a story is structured may be considered somewhat independently of its content. In the second section, **Considerations of Story Content,** we will evaluate the role of story content in comprehension. For stories, one of the most important aspects of the content is the causal chain that links individual events. The processes that initially construct a representation of these causal relations are central in determining how the story is understood and how it is subsequently recalled.

In the third section, **World Knowledge Used in Understanding Narratives,** we will specify some of the shared knowledge that underlies comprehension, including knowledge of human goals, tendencies, and traits. In another section, we will consider the knowledge of specific domains. For example, one such set of knowledge comes from the reader's familiarity with complex but everyday events, such as going to school, eating in a restaurant, or visiting a relative.

In the fourth section, **Integrating Different Types of Texts,** we will describe various kinds of texts—such as narratives, expositions, and descriptions—and consider the processes that are particularly important to the comprehension of each of these types of texts. Finally, we will end the chapter with a description of **The READER Model's Text-level Processing,** discussing in particular the way READER uses a schema to comprehend and recall an expository passage.

Knowledge about Story Structure

An Illustration of Text Integration

Text integration depends on several kinds of information sources and processes, including the following:

Factor 1: Knowledge of the structure of the text genre.
Factor 2: Knowledge about the referential situation.
Factor 3: Integrative cues in the text.
Factor 4: Constructing generalizations or abstractions.
Factor 5: Focusing on the causal or temporal chain of events in a narrative text.
Factor 6: Focusing on the described phenomena and their explanation in an expository text.
Factor 7: Focusing on the referential situation in a descriptive text.

The first three factors pertain to information sources, while the last four pertain to processes. Consider how these seven factors might operate in the comprehension of the following simple narrative:

1. *Charles was having dinner with Cynthia at the most elegant restaurant in town.*
2. *He was hoping to impress her with his knowledge of fine foods and wines.*
3. *When Charles reached for his wallet to pay the bill, he discovered it was not in any of his pockets.*
4. *He then looked for credit cards but found none of those either.*
5. *His search for a checkbook was equally futile.*
6. *As the beads of perspiration trickled to his brows, he was relieved to notice his Uncle Walter sitting at a distant table.*
7. *Charles discreetly asked Walter to lend him some money and avoided the embarrassment of being unable to pay for the meal.*

The opening sentence of this brief narrative presents the setting: a man and a woman having a meal at an elegant restaurant. A reader's knowledge of stories (factor 1) makes her familiar with openings that simply set the scene without describing any action (e.g., *Long ago, in a faraway land, there lived a very beautiful princess*). Knowledge about restaurants (factor 2) permits her to make a number of inferences about this particular setting, if the task requires them. For example, it is likely that Charles and Cynthia are adults, that they are dressed fairly formally, and that they are sitting alone at a table. Some of these inferences might be made as the first sentence is read if the reader is constructing a detailed referential representation.

The second sentence indicates Charles' goal and how the restaurant meal might help in attaining the goal. A reader's knowledge of story structure (factor 1) makes her familiar with characters having goals that they try to attain. Syntactic and semantic knowledge indicates that the *He* in sentence 2 refers to *Charles,* while the *she* refers to *Cynthia.* This knowledge can be used to elaborate the referential representation of these two people that was engendered by the first sentence.

The third sentence describes a complication. From her knowledge of restaurants (factor 2), the reader knows that after presentation of the bill, the diner pays the bill, often with money kept in a wallet. In an attempt to pay the bill, Charles reaches for his wallet but fails to find it. In the second reference to the wallet in this sentence, the pronoun *it* is used. To determine whether *it* refers to the wallet or the bill, the reader uses her knowledge of what occurs in a restaurant and where a man keeps a wallet. It is not a surprise that the story describes a complication (i.e., not finding the wallet) because almost all story plots contain a complication. For this reason, a reader expects the story to include some complication, and the information about the absence of the wallet fulfills that expectation (factor 1). Sentences 4 and 5 describe two failed attempts to resolve the complication. At this point, a reader might form the generalization that Charles tried to think of a number of ways to pay the bill, but none of his alternative plans could be put into effect (factor 4). This generalization is not directly presented in the text but may possibly be constructed in the minds of some or most readers. Sentence 6 describes a new character, Walter, which leads the reader to anticipate that this character might play some role in helping Charles to attain his current subgoal, namely, paying the bill. Sentence 7 describes the execution of the plan that attains this subgoal.

The causal chain of events in this story is clear. Every action can be explained in terms of an antecedent cause or a consequent state. For example, a reader will likely infer that the cause of Charles' perspiration was his nervousness over not being able to pay the bill, rather than the possibility that the weather was hot (factor 5). Similarly, a reader will likely infer that the reason Charles looked for credit cards was that he hoped to pay the bill with one of them. Sometimes the causal relation is made explicit by the text. For example, the text overtly states that Charles reached for his wallet in order to pay the bill (factor 3). The causal explanation provided by the text in this case is helpful but not essential, since it could be inferred even if the phrase *to pay the bill* had been absent from sentence 3.

The comprehension of this brief story illustrates some of the processes and knowledge a reader draws on in order to understand even a simple text. In the remainder of the chapter, we will describe the role played by each of the seven factors in more detail.

Story Schema

Our analysis of text-level processes will begin with a consideration of stories, particularly children's stories, in part, because previous researchers have focused on the structure and recall of children's stories. Stories are certainly an important genre; they have been used for entertaining and communicating cultural values in almost all societies. Their basic appeal suggests that they may fulfill a need to learn and be entertained through the experiences of fictional characters, rather than through abstract statements of the principles that the stories embody.

An important aspect of understanding a story consists of familiarity with the genre: knowing the components of a story, the purpose of each component, and the components' relations to each other (Mandler & Johnson, 1977; Rumelhart, 1975; Stein & Glenn, 1979). The modern analysis of story structures was largely motivated by Propp's analysis of Russian folk tales into 31 basic story components (1968, originally published in Russian in 1928). For example, one of Propp's story components involves a member of a family leaving home (e.g., *a prince goes on a long journey; parents leave for work; a merchant embarks on a foreign trip*). Table 8.1 gives other examples of the story components Propp found were frequently

Table 8.1 Examples of some of the 31 story components that frequently occur in Russian folk tales

1. A family member leaves home or dies.
   a. The prince goes on a journey.
   b. The children go out to gather berries.
2. An interdiction is addressed to the hero.
   a. "You dare not look into the closet!"
   b. "Take care of your little brother!"
3. A difficult task is proposed to the hero.
   a. The hero must eat a wagonload of bread.
   b. The hero must deliver life-giving water.
4. The villain attempts to deceive his victim in order to take possession of him or his belongings.
   a. A witch pretends to be a sweet old lady.
   b. A thief pretends to be a beggarwoman.
5. The villain causes harm or injures a family member.
   a. A dragon kidnaps the tsar's daughter.
   b. A clerk orders the magic duck to be killed.
6. The hero acquires the use of a magical agent.
   a. The hero obtains an eagle on which he flies home.
   b. The hero finds a magic ring that makes him invisible.
7. The hero is taken to an object he has been searching for.
   a. The hero is transported on a flying carpet to the dragon's cave.
   b. A fox leads the hero to the princess.
8. The hero and the villain compete.
   a. They fight in an open field.
   b. They stake an outcome on a game of chance.
9. The hero, unrecognized, arrives home or in another country.
   a. He arrives home but serves as an apprentice tailor.
   b. He arrives at the court of a king and serves as a groom.

Source: Adapted from Propp, 1968, pp. 26–65.

represented in Russian folk tales. Propp also enumerated the possible character roles in a tale, including the hero, villian, helper, and false hero, and discussed their distribution across story components. While specific characters and plots vary from folk tale to folk tale, Propp suggested that all Russian folk tales were built from the same components, with some variation occurring in the distribution of the components and characters from tale to tale.

The knowledge that members of a culture extract about the typical structure of stories can be called a **story schema.** The knowledge that Russian children possess about the components of folk tales is their schema for folk tales. Similarly, North American children might have schemata for the structure of stories like *Cinderella* or *Snow White.*

A story schema can be thought of as a mental framework that contains a labeled slot for each story component, such as a setting, complication, resolution, and the like (see Figure 8.1). As a person reads each component of a story, she fills in the schema slot for that component with the content of the story she is reading. For example, as a Russian girl reads about a resolution in a folk tale, she fills in the resolution slot in her schema with the particular resolution this story describes. Besides indicating what the various components of the story are, the story schema also indicates some of the typical temporal and causal relations among the components. For example, if a story schema contained a slot for a complication and a slot for a resolution, the schema would also indicate that the resolution temporally follows the occurrence of the problem and that the occurrence of the complication probably causes the resolution to be planned and executed by the protagonist.

Readers use the schema in comprehending and later recalling a story. During reading, the story schema provides a filing system for organizing the content of a story. If a story describes events out of sequence, then the inherent ordering among the schema slots helps the reader reconstruct the original sequence. To recall the

STORY

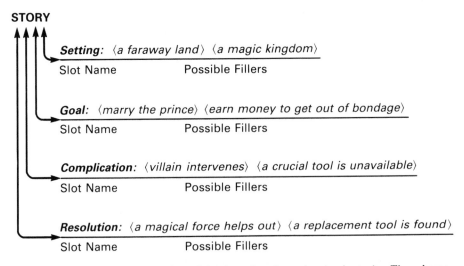

Figure 8.1 An illustration of a few of the slots of a schema for simple stories. The schema provides a framework within which to organize the information from a particular story.

story, a reader may recall the slot she associates with most stories and then try to retrieve the slot fillers that she had obtained from that particular story (Rumelhart, 1975).

Bartlett's experiment   Some fifty years ago, Bartlett (1932) reported that when people recall a story they have just heard, they tend to distort it in a way that makes it more compatible with their own story schema. This landmark examination of how people remember stories demonstrated several important characteristics of story recall. But recent findings suggest that the conventional explanation of Bartlett's results is not quite accurate. The story in the experiment that has received the most attention was the following North American folk tale (as presented in Bartlett, 1932, p. 65), which is clearly unusual by Western standards:

> *One night two young men from Egulac went down to the river to hunt seals, and while they were there it became foggy and calm. Then they heard war-cries, and they thought: "Maybe this is a war-party." They escaped to the shore, and hid behind a log. Now canoes came up, and they heard the noise of the paddles, and saw one canoe coming up to them. There were five men in the canoe, and they said:*
>
> *"What do you think? We wish to take you along. We are going up the river to make war on the people."*
>
> *One of the young men said: "I have no arrows."*
>
> *"Arrows are in the canoe," they said.*
>
> *"I will not go along. I might be killed. My relatives do not know where I have gone. But you," he said, turning to the other, "may go with them."*
>
> *So one of the young men went, but the other returned home.*
>
> *And the warriors went on up the river to a town on the other side of Kalama. The people came down to the water, and they began to fight, and many were killed. But presently the young man heard one of the warriors say: "Quick, let us go home: that Indian has been hit." Now he thought: "Oh, they are ghosts." He did not feel sick, but they said he had been shot.*
>
> *So the canoes went back to Egulac, and the young man went ashore to his house, and made a fire. And he told everybody and said: "Behold I accompanied the ghosts, and we went to fight. Many of our fellows were killed, and many of those who attacked us were killed. They said I was hit, and I did not feel sick."*
>
> *He told it all, and then he became quiet. When the sun rose he fell down. Something black came out of his mouth. His face became contorted. The people jumped up and cried.*
>
> *He was dead.*

After having read it twice, the subjects were asked to retell the story (following some delay interval). The most frequently cited finding is that the recall tended to distort the story in systematic ways. Subjects tended to omit certain parts of the original story, while fabricating other parts that had not occurred in the original story. These distortions were interpreted as indicating the mismatch between the subjects' story schema and the structure of this story.

Bartlett pointed out that many of his subjects noted the story's foreignness right away, commenting that it was "not an English tale." Bartlett's analysis focused on his subjects' treatment of the parts of the story that deviated the most from conventional English folk tales. He described the process of rationalization, in which readers tried to impose some organization on the apparently disconnected events. Often this was done by omitting events that did not seem to fit in or by providing connections that were not present in the text. Some excerpts of one subject's recall illustrate these unwitting connections:

> *"They . . . heard some canoes approaching them, and so hid. . . . "*
> *"One said he would not go as his relations did not know where he was."*
> *"He heard the Indians cry: 'Let us go home, as the man of Egulac is wounded.' "*
> *"The young man did not feel sick, . . .* but nevertheless *they proceeded home. . . . "* (Bartlett, 1932, p. 86)

By comparing the recalled versions to the original story, Bartlett found certain systematic distortions. The retold story lost the surprising and seemingly inconsequential elements of the original and tended to become a more orderly narrative. Moreover, explanations and relations that were implicit in the original were made explicit in the recalled version. To describe how the readers mentally reorganized the story, Bartlett adopted the terminology of **schema,** by which he meant a knowledge structure that contained the abstraction of past experience with a complex, serially organized concept. In this case, the schema referred to the knowledge about the serial organization of a narrative. Bartlett believed that the schema's structure contributed to the systematic distortions in the recalled story. This theoretical construct of the schema is one of Bartlett's main influences on recent research on stories.

Recent experiments have reexamined Bartlett's study, carefully controlling the texts and the instructions given to the subjects (Kintsch, 1977). The probability of distorting the story in a way that makes it fit a conventional schema was much lower if subjects were told to recall only what was in the story (although in their own words) and to refrain from embellishing and editorializing. So distortion towards the familiar schema may have partly resulted from the attempts to improve the story, rather than from an inability to retain the content of a story that has an unfamiliar structure. Nevertheless, Kintsch also found that the probability of distortion was much lower if the subjects read a story that fit the story schema for their culture. American subjects made fewer distortions when recalling a conventional fairy tale than when recalling an Apache Indian folk tale with an unfamiliar structure (four episodes with no obvious temporal or causal link among them). The most notable aspect of the recall of the Indian story was that subjects sometimes failed to recall an entire episode, presumably because for these non-Indian subjects the episodes were not linked by a story schema. Kintsch's study suggests that Bartlett's finding of distortion of a story such that it better fits the familiar story schema is a weaker phenomenon than previously suspected. But the notion that readers have and use a schema for a given text type remains valid.

Bartlett emphasized two additional points that are often overlooked. One concerned the role of affect in memory. He claimed that readers often first recalled a general attitude associated with a story and that their recall of the story tried to maintain consistency with this attitude. Contemporary research confirms this proposal. To demonstrate the effect of a reader's mood on reading, Bower, Gilligan, and Monteiro (1981) used posthypnotic suggestion to induce a happy or sad mood in readers as they read simulated interviews in which various happy and sad incidents from psychiatric patients' lives were described. The subjects had much better recall of the incidents that were congruent with their mood. Happy readers had better recall of happy events, while sad readers had better recall of sad events. Congruence between the mood of the reader and an event described in the text could affect comprehension by motivating the reader to make more elaborative inferences, to relate what he reads about to his own previous experiences, thus making the text representation more memorable, distinctive, and integrated with his own previous knowledge. Congruence could also raise his motivation to process the text as deeply as possible, perhaps to intensify his mood. The implication of this study is that a reader's affective state influences how he will comprehend a text, especially one that deals with affective states.

Bartlett's second point concerned the role of images. He suggested that such images help highlight items in a schema and provide individual instances. In current theories of reading comprehension, images are thought of as the reader's representation of the referential world, with less emphasis on the visual properties than the word *images* suggests and more emphasis on the physical and functional properties of the objects in the referential world. Chapter 7 on representing the referential world deals extensively with this matter. Thus, all three of Bartlett's contributions to story understanding regarding the roles of schemata, affect, and images have been revived by contemporary research but under slightly different guises.

For methodological reasons, Bartlett and many current investigators examined the recall behavior that occurs after the reading comprehension has been completed, rather than examine the comprehension processes that occur as a person reads a story. This chapter will report some of the most important memory findings that have implications for text comprehension and, where possible, describe experiments that examine the text comprehension processes as they are occurring. In particular, the chapter will later describe the on-line examination of the comprehension of expository texts.

Story Grammars

A slightly different characterization of the knowledge of story structures has been called a **story grammar.** Like a schema, a story grammar can be thought of as a framework with a number of slots that correspond to the various structural components of a story text (Mandler & Johnson, 1977; Rumelhart, 1975; Stein & Glenn, 1979). One slight difference between the approaches is that a story grammar denotes the hierarchical relations among the components (embeddings among the story-grammar categories) more directly than does a story schema.

Story grammars were developed in conscious imitation of syntactic grammars of sentences. Linguistic theories had been successful, to some degree, in developing a set of axiomatic rules that specified the possible syntactic structure of the grammatical sentences of a language. Story grammars attempted to specify the structural organization of simple stories in an analogous manner by trying to determine the structure of a story without regard to its content. This was analogous to the attempt in linguistics to specify the syntactic structure of a sentence without regard to its semantic content.

Story grammars specify a hierarchical structure, indicating the composition of a story in terms of constituents like settings and episodes, and further indicating the composition of episodes and settings in terms of other constituents, and so on. This is analogous to characterizing the syntactic structure of a sentence in terms of constituents like noun phrases and verb phrases, which, in turn, are composed of other constituents. Story grammars generate tree structures to characterize the structure of stories, similar to those generated by the linguistic analyses of sentences. Figure 8.2 shows an example of the type of tree structure that can be generated by a story grammar.

The attempt to emulate syntactic grammars of sentences was not entirely successful. Stories simply do not have as rigid a structure as sentences (Black & Wilensky, 1979). Nevertheless, the categories of information identified by story grammars do seem to play a role in how simple stories are read and understood.

According to the grammars for simple children's stories, the main structural components of a story are a *setting* and an *episode*. The setting introduces some of the characters and the context of the story. The episode often can be further decomposed into a number of other categories: *initiating event, internal response, attempt, consequence,* and *reaction.* The story-grammar structure can be illustrated with a simple story that was written to conform to the grammar:

Setting: *Once there was a woman who lived in a forest.*

Initiating event: *One day she was walking up a hill and she came upon the entrance to a lonely tiger's cave.*

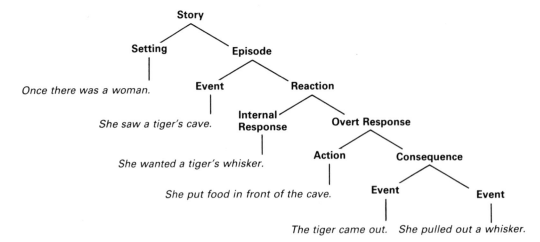

Figure 8.2   This tree structure depicts some of the structural components of a simple story. It also illustrates hierarchical relations among components, such as the fact that an *Episode* is composed of an *Event* and a *Reaction.*

Internal response: *She really wanted a tiger's whisker and decided to try to get one.*

Attempt: *She put a bowl of food in front of the opening of the cave and she sang soft music.*

Consequence: *The lonely tiger came out and listened to the music. The lady then pulled out one of the whiskers and ran down the hill very quickly.*

Reaction: *She knew her trick had worked and felt very happy.* (Nezworski, Stein, & Trabasso, 1982, Table 1, p. 197)

The *initiating event* starts the story and sets the goal. The *internal response* is optional, but it includes the protagonist's emotional response. The *attempt* is the action or series of actions toward attaining the goal. The *attempt* produces a *consequence,* which is either the attainment of the goal or a failure to attain the goal. This, in turn, causes the *reaction,* the internal response of the protagonist to the consequences.

A story grammar is a description of a reader's knowledge about the structure of simple stories. The story grammars that researchers have developed to date apply only to very simple stories and fables. Current story grammars show little potential of being generalized to narratives such as short stories or novels, whose structures are infinitely more varied and complex. Nevertheless, the story grammars have demonstrated that some stories have a relatively consistent structure, although they may differ in characters and content. More importantly, the characterization of story structure that was suggested by these story grammars does play a role in comprehension. The knowledge of story structure may be used in organizing information as it is read and then used again as part of a retrieval plan when the time comes to recall the information, as described in the following section.

The relation between story grammars and reading   One source of evidence that readers distinguish among the different categories of information in a story grammar is that readers spend more time reading a sentence that is higher in the story-grammar hierarchy. In one study, the same sentence was inserted into two stories, one in which the critical sentence was high in the story-grammar hierarchy and one in which it was low (Cirilo & Foss, 1980). An example of such a critical sentence was:

He could no longer talk at all.

The story in which this sentence was high in the hierarchy was about a king who was cursed by a witch such that he could not speak. The story in which the sentence was low in the hierarchy was about a soldier who found a king's ring and was momentarily rendered speechless by the shock of hearing how large the reward was for the return of the ring. Intuitively, it seems clear that *He could no longer talk at all* plays a much more important role in the witch's curse story than in the soldier's story. Consistent with this intuition, the experiment found that the reading time on this sentence was longer in the witch's curse story. The difference in reading time cannot be attributed to any inherent property of the critical sentence itself because the very same sentence was read in both cases. Thus, the role a sentence plays in a story affects the time taken to read it. Two mutually compatible explanations can account for the longer reading times on sentences that are higher in the story-grammar hierarchy.

The first explanation is that readers consider some categories of information they encounter in a story to be more important or interesting than others. When they come to an important category, they might slow down their reading to process the information more carefully. They may also make more inferences or elaborations. This explanation suggests that the reader's knowledge of story structures causes him to process different parts of the structure in different ways. This account requires an explanation of how a reader identifies each category as he encounters it. After all, authors don't use explicit headings like "goal" or "action." But adult readers can, if asked, segment a simple story into structural categories. What might the possible cues be? The cues might be key phrases or locations in the story. They might include shifts in the subject, the verb tense, or from a series of temporally linked events to a causally linked one. The process by which the different parts of a story are identified has not been specified in the case of stories, but it has been specified to some extent in the case of some short expository passages, which will be described later in the chapter.

A second explanation of why readers spend more time on sentences that are higher in the story-grammar hierarchy is that such sentences may take more time to integrate with the rest of the text. A sentence that plays a high-level role is more likely to introduce new information, rather than expand on previously introduced topics, and the construction of new referential representations probably takes extra time. Also, a sentence that is high in the hierarchy is likely to contain more causal and temporal links with preceding parts of the story, and it may take extra time to discover and represent these links. Thus, the relations between a sentence and the preceding portions of the text may require more processing if the sentence is high in the story-grammar hierarchy. This process would not require the reader to categorize the various parts of a story as he encounters them but simply to give them the treatment they naturally evoke. This process and the explicit recognition of categories described above probably both operate together, although there is no empirical evidence to distinguish them.

In addition to spending more time on sentences that have high-level roles in a story's structure, readers also spend more time on sentences that are at the boundary of an episode. In the reading of multiepisode stories with about six sentences per episode, readers spent more time reading those sentences at the beginnings and ends of episodes than those embedded in the middle (Haberlandt, Berian, & Sandson, 1980). This suggests that readers are segmenting a story into episodes as they read, and at the boundaries of episodes, they may be performing various comprehension bookkeeping tasks, such as identifying the protagonist, shifting perspective, formulating expectations, and forming generalizations. The structure of the story has a certain shape, and the reading time spent on various parts of the story reflects that shape.

Recall as a function of story-grammar categories   Story parts at high levels of the hierarchy defined by the story grammar are recalled better than those at low levels. This is called the **levels effect** (see Thorndyke, 1977). More specifically, major settings, initiating events, and consequences are recalled well, while minor settings, internal responses (emotional reactions and thoughts), and minor goals are only half as likely to be recalled. The recall of attempts and major goals is intermediate.

The fact that some categories of information are more likely to be recalled than others is a description of *how* readers behave but not an explanation of *why* they behave that way. The explanation of this behavior has three facets. One facet of the explanation is related to a comprehension process that was already described; even though the levels effect is a phenomenon that occurs at the time of recall, the effect may be produced, at least in part, by processes that occur at the time of comprehension. This conclusion is based on the finding that the best-recalled parts of a story are read more slowly. Thus, the memory results may be based on a comprehension mechanism. Another facet of the levels effect, which is described in the next section, is that story portions that come from the best-recalled categories tend to play a more central role in the causal structure of the story, and this causal role may influence recall. The third facet of the explanation, elaborated in the section on the READER model's text comprehension, is that those portions of a text that are more important to the reader's goals are read more carefully, and this selectivity in reading contributes to the levels effect in recall.

Considerations of Story Content

Causal Relations

Although readers undoubtedly process the structure of a story, the most salient aspect of a story seems to be its content. Stories amuse, entertain, or uplift not by virtue of their arrangement of story-grammar categories but because of their content. Unfortunately, story content is difficult to characterize, since stories can describe any sequence of events in real life or in a fictional world.

One way to circumvent the difficulty of having to characterize the boundless content of stories is to focus on the **causal relations** among the pieces of content. In this view, if a story consists of a description of two consecutive events, the content of each event needs to be characterized only insofar as it is necessary to explain the causal relation between the two events.

A narrative can be thought of as a description of a sequence of events and states; the reader's task is to understand what brought about each event or state. In this view, the reader must consider issues of physical causality, temporal co-occurrence, social norms for behaviors in a given set of circumstances, and the like. Thus, the events and states become linked to each other by means of causal relations, which provide a coherence among the parts of a story.

The characters in a narrative generally have some goal (such as discovering who killed the chambermaid or becoming a successful lawyer), and they take actions toward achieving that goal (Schank & Abelson, 1977; Wilensky, 1980). Typically, there are obstacles (complications) along the way to that goal. One type of obstacle is produced by other characters who have incompatible goals. For example, the detective in a mystery novel may have the goal of discovering the murderer, but the butler may have the incompatible goal of concealing the murderer, thus producing obstacles to the detective's success. Also, a single character can have two conflicting goals, such as being nonviolent and trying to protect his family. Thus, the source of an obstacle can be another character (an antagonist), conflicting goals in the same character, or environmental circumstances (e.g., a flood).

Much of a narrative consists of the description of the pursuit of a goal, fighting against the obstacles. Often, the actions described in a story can be given a causal interpretation if they can be seen as part of some character's plan to accomplish a goal. For example, if a murderous butler wipes fingerprints from a gun, a reader can infer that the cause of this action stems from his goal of concealing the murderer's identity.

Readers infer several other types of causal explanations for a character's actions based on their informal conceptions of causality. The following are examples of such informal causal reasoning about narratives:

1. Some actions are explained in terms of a character's local goals and plans. For instance, suppose a text describes a young man who desires a radio that he cannot afford to buy, and he takes on a new job without offering any explicit reason. The reader is likely to infer that the man took the new job in order to earn money to purchase the radio. That is, characters perform actions that are consistent with a plan to help reach a goal.

2. Some actions are habitually associated with certain vocations or life roles. For example, lawyers habitually address juries, fishermen repair nets, and train conductors collect tickets. When a reader encounters a description of a character performing a habitual action, the action is explained as being part of the character's routine behavior.

3. Some actions can be attributed to a character's personality traits. If a character described as a miser refuses his needy friend some money, the reader explains the miserly action in terms of the miserly trait. This type of explanation is often circular: The action defines the trait, and the trait explains the action. Nonetheless, people often reason this way, in spite of the circularity, as described below.

4. Some events are "acts of God," or "deus ex machina," and require no explanation. Lightning can strike, a flood can occur, a rich uncle can die and bequeath a large amount of money. The cause of such events usually does not need to be inferred, but the events themselves can constitute the cause or initiation of other events.

As a reader encounters each new event in a narrative, she reads or tries to infer the cause of the event, thereby producing the coherent causal or thematic framework that relates the events.

It takes time to infer the cause of an event, and the time taken increases with the size of the gap the inference must span. In one study, readers were presented with two-sentence paragraphs, in which the first sentence described a possible cause for the event described in the second sentence (Keenan, Baillet, & Brown, 1984). The type of event described in the first sentence ranged from a highly probable cause for the event in the second sentence to decreasingly probable but still plausible causes. Thus, one of the first sentences, 1a, 1b, 1c, or 1d (which range from most to least direct causes), was followed by sentence 2:

1a. *Joey's big brother punched him again and again.*
1b. *Racing down the hill, Joey fell off his bike.*
1c. *Joey's crazy mother became furiously angry with him.*
1d. *Joey went to a neighbor's house to play.*
2. *The next day, his body was covered with bruises.*

The reading time needed for sentence 2 increased as the causal inference between the two described events became less direct over the four levels of directness, as shown in Figure 8.3. The ease of drawing the causal inference influenced the reading time. Presumably, the search for a more distant causal connection takes longer.

Causal relatedness affects not only the reading time on a story part but also the recall. Those parts of the story most central to the causal chain of events are generally more likely to be recalled (Black & Bern, 1981; Trabasso, Secco, & van den Broek, 1984).

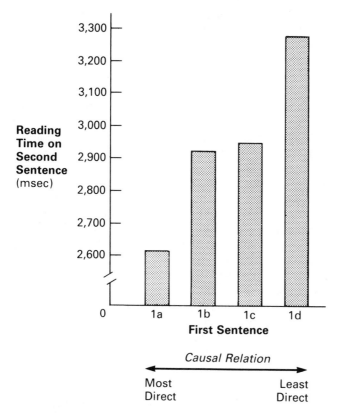

Figure 8.3   The time taken to read the second sentence of a related pair increases as its causal distance from the preceding sentence increases. *Source:* Adapted from Keenan, Baillet, & Brown, 1984, Table 2, p. 120.

Plot Units

A reader's understanding of story content goes beyond inferring the causes of events. He also has an understanding of plot development, based on **plot units** (Lehnert, 1981). A plot unit can be thought of as a particular configuration of goals, actions, and affective states. A frequent example of a plot unit is competition between two entities for a single goal, such as two students each trying to attain the top grade in a test, two football teams trying to beat each other in a game, or two companies trying to enlist the same client.

Although each of these examples of competition is clearly different, they all share some common properties. In each case, it is plausible that the competitors take actions to enhance their own performance, to hinder the performance of the competitor, to accept defeat gracefully or vengefully, and to be gracious or cruel in victory. Note that a plot unit like competition is not identified within a story grammar. It may simply be a part of a story-grammar category like a complication and would be treated by the story grammar no differently than any other complication, such as being disabled by disease or being thwarted by a villain. But readers do treat different complications differently. If asked to sort stories into separate piles or to write a story that is thematically similar to a template story, readers base their judgment or production of similarity on plot-unit similarity (Reiser, Black, & Lehnert, 1985).

It is likely that as a reader progresses through a story, he recognizes the unfolding of familiar plot units, such as competition, bargaining, threat, coercion, cooperation, and retaliation. Such a plot-unit analysis deals with slightly larger pieces of text than does a causal analysis of individual actions. Within each plot unit, the individual actions might be causally related to each other. Moreover, different plot units may be causally related to each other. For example, loss in a competition plot unit might result in a retaliation plot unit. The representation of the causal relations among the sequence of plot units in a story might provide the perceived coherence and organization for the understanding of a story.

Closely associated with plot units is the evaluative judgment about a story character and his motives. A character can enter a competition with noble motives, like two runners in a race, each trying to run as fast as possible. Alternatively, a competition may be entered on malicious grounds, to embarrass an opponent, to harm him, to seek revenge for a previous encounter. In general, plans and motives are evaluated in positive or negative terms, such as malicious or benevolent, noble or dishonorable, considerate or selfish. In simple stories, positive motives are associated with the hero, while negative motives are associated with the villain. It is striking how strongly young American children focus on determining who is the "good guy" and who is the "bad guy" as they attempt to understand a story. Adult readers also evaluate the motives of characters and make this evaluation part of their representation of the story.

Separating the Effects of Story Structure and Story Content

In a normal text, a confounding generally occurs between the content of a given part of a story and its role in the story grammar. The part of a story that describes a setting is generally quite different from the part that describes an internal response. So it is difficult to attribute the superior recall of major settings and consequences purely to their status in a story grammar. Several experimental methods have been used to separate the effects of content and structure on memory for the parts of a story. We will describe a number of relevant empirical results, pointing toward the conclusion that the major determinant of the recall of a given part of a story is its role in the causal structure of the story.

One way to assess the role of story structure is to present the different parts in a scrambled order, so that there is no coherence among the sentences. In this case, there is no story structure that can influence recall, so any remaining influences must be attributable to the content of individual sentences. In this condition, all the sentences are approximately equally recalled, indicating that the story structure is essential to producing the levels effect, and the content of the sentences alone does not produce the effect (Thorndyke, 1977).

Another way to assess the effect of story structure independently of content is to ask if the same information is recalled differently, depending on which story-grammar category it belongs to. One study examined this issue by inserting the same piece of information into one of five categories: setting, initiating event, internal response, consequence, or reaction (Nezworski, Stein, & Trabasso, 1982). For example, the "Tiger's Whisker" story was rewritten in several versions, with the critical information of why the woman wanted the tiger's whisker inserted into one of the five categories, as follows:

Setting: *There was a woman whose husband was very sickly and every day he took a medicine made with a tiger's whisker.*

Initiating event: *One day her husband became very sick and a doctor told her to make a medicine with a tiger's whisker for him.*

Internal response: *She knew that her husband was very sick and that he needed a medicine made with a tiger's whisker.*

Consequence: *She mixed the tiger's whisker with some other things to make a medicine which she gave to her sick husband.*

Reaction: *The woman knew that now she could make a medicine with the tiger's whisker for her husband who was very sick.* (Nezworski, Stein, & Trabasso, 1982, Table 2, p. 198)

Unlike previous studies that found some story-grammar categories were consistently recalled better than others, this experiment found similar recall of the critical information (by kindergarten and third-grade subjects), regardless of which category it had been a part of. This result indicates that in those studies that had previously found better recall of certain categories (like consequences), the superior recall may have been due to the content of the category (i.e., the type of fact that is usually a consequence). The result of this "Tiger's Whisker" experiment suggests that the story-grammar category that a sentence belongs to has only a minor effect on recall.

Contrary to the result of the "Tiger's Whisker" study, Cirilo and Foss (1980) found that the category to which a sentence belonged in a story did affect recall. In the study by Cirilo and Foss, described earlier, a critical sentence (like *He could no longer talk at all*) was either high or low in the story-grammar hierarchy of two different stories. The critical sentence was more likely to be recalled when it was at a high level in the story-grammar hierarchy.

A possible reconciliation of the two studies is that recall of a given piece of information in a story is determined primarily by how it is related to the main goal of the story—that is, by its role in the causal structure of the story events. The manipulation in the Cirilo and Foss study was to radically change the rest of the story, such that the critical sentence was strongly or weakly related to the main causal chain. The sentence was recalled much better when it was strongly related to the causal chain. In the "Tiger's Whisker" study, the story was similar in all conditions, so the causal chain remained unchanged, and the critical information was similarly related to the causal chain in all cases. Perhaps as a result, the critical information was equally likely to be recalled in all conditions. A more recent study (Omanson, 1982), to be described below, suggests that this explanation is fundamentally correct.

Causal centrality and story-grammar categories   Omanson's (1982) study manipulated the centrality of internal responses and reactions (two categories that generally tend to be poorly recalled) by varying their **centrality** to the goal structure of the story. A story event or state was classified as central if it fulfilled condition 1, as well as either condition 2 or condition 3.

1. A central event or state must describe a superordinate rather than a component entity (e.g., eating breakfast, rather than getting out cereal, pouring in milk, or eating cereal).
2. A central event or state may be part of the causal chain of events and states that lead from the beginning to the end of the story. Several kinds of roles in the causal chain are possible: An event or state can be brought about or enabled purposefully or unintentionally by a prior action. Alternatively, an event or state can disrupt a prior action or the goal of a prior action.
3. A central event or state may introduce a main character.

Omanson devised stories in which the internal responses and reactions were either central or noncentral according to these criteria. In this design, the centrality of an event or state is systematically varied while its story category is kept constant.

The results showed that central events or states were more likely to be recalled than noncentral events or states. This centrality effect occurred with the experimentally manipulated internal responses and reactions, as well as other parts of the story that were classified as central or noncentral. In addition, the usual levels effect was observed, such that major settings, initiating effects, and consequences were recalled better than other story-grammar categories. It was noteworthy that most but not all of the levels effect (i.e., the differential recall of the different story-grammar categories) was produced by the centrality effect. Although both effects occur, the levels effect is quite small (although reliable) when centrality is held constant by a statistical procedure (analysis of covariance).

The interrelation of story structure and story content   The empirical results from the studies we have described clarify the relative contributions of story content and story grammars to comprehension and memory. One clear conclusion is that the content of stories—particularly the causal relations among the events and states—is a powerful determinant of how stories are stored and recalled and probably how stories are comprehended in the first place. It appears that readers make sense of stories by reading or inferring the causal relations among a number of events and states. Information that is central to that causal chain is processed carefully and recalled well, while causally peripheral information is not. Thus, the causal reasoning and inference making that occurs in processing the content of stories is an inherent part of story comprehension.

The large impact of story content on performance and its ability to account for some of the levels effects has tempted some theorists to question whether story grammars or schemata should have any independent role in a theory of comprehension (Black & Wilensky, 1979). Nevertheless, there are several reasons to retain a role for story structure (some of which are discussed by van Dijk & Kintsch, 1983). First, experiments like Omanson's (1982) demonstrate an effect of story structure independent of causal centrality. A second reason to include a role for story structure is that the phenomena related to the cultural specificity of stories (Kintsch, 1977, discussed above) cannot be accounted for by a theory of story content. People from different cultures have different ideas of what constitutes a story, and these ideas are separable from the notions of causal relations among events (which might have some cultural specificity of their own).

A theory of reading comprehension should not have to choose between accounting for structure and accounting for content, any more than it should have to choose between the syntax and the semantics of a sentence. Stories, as well as other text genres, have both a content and a structure, with the knowledge of both of entering into the comprehension process. Future research should examine how the two kinds of knowledge are used collaboratively and determine the conditions under which one or the other type of knowledge plays a dominant role. Future research should also determine whether the conclusions suggested by the studies of simple stories will generalize to the comprehension of other types of texts, such as expositions or descriptions.

World Knowledge Used in Understanding Narratives

Much of the information that makes a text understandable is not included in the text at all but resides in the world knowledge shared by the author and most of the readers. For example, being able to infer the causal relation between fetching a ladder and painting a ceiling is dependent on the knowledge that ladders are devices used to raise a person vertically, bringing him within physical reach of otherwise unreachable objects. The crucial role of such knowledge became most apparent when computer programs that were supposed to understand text could not do so without such knowledge. Almost every text requires that the reader, human or otherwise, be able to draw on a rich store of shared knowledge about the world. Next, we will consider two particular types of knowledge used in story comprehension: knowledge of people and knowledge of specific content domains.

Knowledge of People

Readers use their knowledge about human needs, wants, motivations, attitudes, plans, and values to understand narratives. The characters in narratives are assumed to possess universal human qualities that constitute the basis for much of the integrative inference making. Even if the protagonists in a narrative are animals or countries or fictional entities, they are usually endowed with such human qualities (anthropomorphized) by the author and the reader.

Every reader has an implicit theory of human behavior and uses this theory to understand a narrative. One aspect of this implicit theory is that members of our culture believe that people have personality traits that are stable across situations (Mischel, 1968). The term *trait* can be broadly defined to include not only conventional traits, like honesty and patience, but also political attitudes and intelligence. For example, if a reader learns that George is honest about the money he handles in his job as a cashier, the reader may infer (sometimes incorrectly) that George is also honest about not cheating in an examination.

This assumption of trait consistency allows a reader to explain and predict the behavior of the characters in a narrative. If a character performs an action consistent with a trait, it can be explained in terms of the character's predisposition to perform such actions. If a larger boy punches a smaller boy, a reader can explain this by inferring that the larger boy is a bully and that he punched the smaller boy because bullies have a predisposition to abuse weaker people. The explanation is circular, but it seems to be a circularity that most readers are content with.

Besides having enduring traits, people also have transient affective states —such as anger, loneliness, depression, or jubilation—which can similarly be used as a basis for inferring why they behave in certain ways while they are in that state. People also have universal needs, such as the need for food and sleep; they enter into universal roles, such as parent and spouse; and they have universal interpersonal affects, such as love and hate.

Knowledge of Specific Content Domains

A second type of knowledge used in comprehending a narrative pertains to particular content domains, such as the knowledge of the events and objects involved in painting a room or attending a university lecture. As a simple illustration, consider these sentences:

> John had a splitting headache. He went up to the bathroom and looked in the cabinet.

Most readers would infer that John was looking for medication to cure his headache. Prior knowledge of headaches, pharmaceuticals, and bathroom cabinets provides the reader with enough information to make this inference. This type of prior knowledge consists of information about stereotyped events and objects, such as cars, lawyers, universities, and surgical operating rooms.

One of the most articulated theories of the role of previous knowledge of content has focused on the comprehension of narratives that describe very familiar occurrences, such as going to a restaurant. In this example, the knowledge might consist of what one does in a restaurant, such as sit down at a table, read the menu, order the meal, wait for the food, be served the food, eat the food, get the check, pay, and so on. The knowledge about familiar occurrences, sometimes referred to as a **script** (Schank & Abelson, 1977), can be thought of as a frame-and-slot schema, with slots for particular events. The slot for each event might specify the main characters involved, their goals, the typical position of this event in the entire sequence, and the like. Slots can have default values, so that events (such as paying for the meal) or parts of events (who received the payment) that are not explicitly mentioned can be inferred, if necessary. Thus, a reader's restaurant script prepares him to understand what particular sequence of events is likely to occur, what characters are likely to participate, what the various characters are likely to do, and what goals the various characters might have. Schank and his co-workers have developed a computer program that, with the aid of a script for routine events, understands stereotyped stories such as newspaper articles reporting car accidents.

We have used the word *schema* at several places in this book to refer to a frame-with-slots knowledge structure. In the paragraph above, we have used the word *script* as shorthand for "a schema for knowledge about routine occurrences" to maintain consistency with Schank's nomenclature. Now, we are in a position to contrast the roles of two kinds of schemata: a schema for knowledge about routine events (a script) and a schema for the story structure (containing slots like *complication* and *resolution*). The story schema indicates, for example, that when the protagonist encounters a complication, he is likely to devise a plan that will allow him to reach his goal nonetheless. By contrast, the script knowledge indicates what particular plan a protagonist is likely to devise in a given situation. For example, in a story about a knight in shining armor who is thwarted in his attempt to rescue a damsel in distress by a dragon, script knowledge might indicate that the protagonist knight is likely to slay the dragon with his sword, rather than choke the dragon to death with a garrotte.

A script can help a reader in two related ways. First, it can help him impose an organization on the information, providing him with a ready-made structure into which he can insert the new information he acquires from the text. If the information in the text is poorly or inappropriately organized for his purpose, his own script can provide a basis for reorganization. Second, if the text neglects to provide information that is necessary for text coherence, his script can provide a default value.

A series of studies compared how subjects who were either knowledgeable about baseball or knew very little about the game understood a description of a baseball game (Chiesi, Spilich, & Voss, 1979; Spilich, Vesonder, Chiesi, & Voss, 1979). Needless to say, the recall of the high-knowledge subjects was superior. The source of their superiority was that they were able to relate the various actions in the narrative to the goal structure of a baseball game and to each other. This result demonstrates how knowledge of a highly routinized sequence (organized as a script) greatly facilitates the acquisition and retention of a particular story.

The knowledge of content contained in a script can also explain why information introduced for the first time can be understandable, even if it has not been referred to previously. For example, sequence 1 makes sense, while sequence 2 does not:

1. *Harold sat down in the restaurant. The menu was illegible.*
2. *Harold sat down in the museum. The menu was illegible.*

Sequence 2 does not make sense because the reader's script for a museum visit does not specify a role for a menu. Even if the introduction of the object makes sense, the use of an appropriate script decreases the time required to integrate the new information. For example, readers take less time to read a sentence that mentions a lawyer for the first time if they know they are reading about a courtroom scene than if they don't (Sanford & Garrod, 1981, p. 112). The general point is that readers use their knowledge of content areas to understand text that deals with those areas.

Simply saying that readers use previous knowledge of routine occurrences leaves several questions unanswered. First, how does a reader choose the appropriate script when reading a given text? Presumably, just seeing the word *restaurant* is not sufficient to make a reader predict that the story is about going to a restaurant and ordering a meal (e.g., *Mabel remained on the tour bus as it passed the site where the restaurant had once stood*). And second, how does the reader coordinate different scripts? Suppose that the passage is about both restaurants and family reunions. How is the knowledge of family reunions coordinated with the knowledge of restaurants? Or suppose a story shifts from one script to another and then back again—say, from a courtroom to a restaurant and then back to the courtroom (Sharkey & Mitchell, 1985). Does the first script have to be reactivated for a second use, or does it remain in an activated state throughout the reading of the story?

The need for flexible and dynamic retrieval of relevant knowledge structures is apparent both in the study of human understanding and in computer understanding (Schank, 1979), but the precise mechanisms that perform this kind of retrieval are not well understood. A final question asks how information that is incongruent with a script is stored. There are often events described in a story that don't fit in with a script. If an ill-fitting event, such as a knight slaying a dragon with a garrotte, is important to the causal structure of a story, it is likely to be processed carefully and recalled well and stored as an addendum or correction to the script (Graesser, 1981). An ill-fitting event that is tangential to the causal structure is likely to be omitted in the recall.

While the necessity and ubiquity of knowledge in text comprehension is clear, a simple passage can demonstrate some of the knotty theoretical issues that remain to be resolved. This passage makes a reader aware of the repeated use of background knowledge:

> *John was on his way to school. He was terribly worried about the mathematics lesson. He thought he might not be able to control the class again today. He thought it was unfair of the instructor to make him supervise the class for a second time. After all, it was not a normal part of a janitor's duties.* (Adapted from Sanford & Garrod, 1981, p. 10)

The first two sentences make contact with the knowledge that schoolboys worry about classes on the way to school (evoked by the schoolboy script), inviting the inference that John is a schoolboy. This inference is rejected when the reader learns that John is trying to control the class, because this is inconsistent with what is known about schoolboys. Knowledge of what occurs in a classroom suggests that the person doing the controlling is an instructor. That inference, too, must be rejected when the next sentence indicates that John is under the authority of the instructor, so a reader might infer that John is a student or teaching assistant. The final sentence then causes this inference to be rejected, too, when it is stated that John is a janitor.

This passage illustrates that a reader continuously draws on his knowledge of the world as he reads a text and radically revises his interpretation if it is inconsistent with that knowledge. An empirical study of passages like this confirmed that a sentence requiring such a change in interpretation took longer to read by an extra 170 milliseconds (Sanford & Garrod, 1981, p. 115).

Although readers are usually not conscious of using knowledge as they read a narrative, the importance of such knowledge became apparent in artificial intelligence projects in which computer programs tried to understand stories. In order to understand even simple narratives, the programs had to be provided with such knowledge. Schank and Abelson (1977) have provided a possible outline of the knowledge structures that are used in understanding narratives.

Integrating Different Types of Texts

Although we have focused thus far on stories, stories are not necessarily the most frequently occurring type of text or the form most important to education. We will briefly describe some other discourse forms, with a focus on how the distinguishing features of the various forms might differentially affect comprehension processes.

Within the fields of rhetoric and literary theory, scholars have classified texts into various types, such as *narratives, descriptions,* and *expositions.* In addition to this classification, it is possible to classify texts in terms of their primary purpose, such as to inform, to entertain (e.g., amuse, frighten, or excite), to persuade, or to provide an aesthetic experience. Brewer (1980) used this organization of three text types and four purposes to classify different kinds of texts, such as biography, advertisement, science fiction, and editorial, as shown in Table 8.2. For example, one text that is a narrative and whose primary purpose is to persuade is a parable.

Table 8.2 Examples of descriptive, narrative, and expository texts, classified according to their main purpose

	Text Type		
Purpose	*Description*	*Narrative*	*Exposition*
Informative	Travelogue Art catalogue	Newspaper story History text Instructions	Scientific article Philosophy Abstract definition
Entertaining	Setting in a novel	Mystery novel Science fiction story Fairy tale Biography	
Persuasive	House advertisement	Social-purpose novel Parable Fable	Sermon Propaganda Editorial
Aesthetic	Poetic description	Classic novel Short story Drama	

Source: Adapted from Brewer, 1980, Table 9.1, p. 225.

While such taxonomies serve a useful organizational role, it is important to remember that texts are generally not homogeneous. Narratives and expositions almost always include some description, and expositions and narratives can include elements of one another. Texts that are purely descriptive are fairly rare. It is more common to find a few descriptive paragraphs embedded in an exposition or narrative. But one can still discern the dominant genre of a text.

Nonhomogeneity applies as much to text *purpose* as to text *type.* Many texts have combined purposes of informing, entertaining, persuading, and providing aesthetic pleasure, although a text usually has a dominant purpose. And a reader may have a different purpose than what the author intended. For example, a murderer might read an Agatha Christie novel in order to learn about homicidal techniques, rather than to be entertained by Miss Marple's problem solving. Moreover, the reader's goal may change from section to section of the text or on different readings of the same text.

Narratives

A **narrative** describes the occurrence of a number of events that are distributed over some time period and linked by causation or theme. This definition encompasses not only stories and novels but also instructions and histories (Brewer, 1980). Narrative texts can vary along many dimensions. The text can describe the events in the order in which they occurred or in some other order. For instance, flashback is a literary device used in describing events out of their order of occurrence. Generally, readers remember a text better if the order of description corresponds to the order of occurrence (Stein & Nezworski, 1978). Another way that narratives can vary is in the possible roles the narrator can play, from actively participating in the described events and presenting a strong point of view to being a neutral, nearly invisible observer.

The psychological process that seems highlighted in the comprehension of narratives is the filling in of gaps in the causal or thematic chain that relates the described events. Integrative, causal inferences are necessary to produce coherence in the representation of a narrative text.

Descriptions

Descriptions are texts that refer to a static situation in terms of its perceptible physical features. Descriptions often occur in a scene-setting paragraph within a novel, such as a description of the weather in a Thomas Hardy novel. The perceptual modality most often involved in a description is visual, but a combination of descriptions from any of the sensory modalities is possible. The vocabulary is largest for visual descriptions. For example, there are many fewer words available to describe smells than sights.

Descriptions of scenes provide information about spatial layout, the relative positions of the various objects in the scenes, which tells the reader which objects are above or behind each other, which are tallest, or which are thickest. Descriptions also provide information about shape, color, and texture. A descriptive text consists primarily of predications and modifications of objects, rather than descriptions of actions. The sequence in which the objects in a scene are described is usually organized along some physical dimension, such as proceeding from left to right along the horizontal dimension of space. Descriptions typically provide more detail about an object's physical properties than do other types of texts. The role and perspective of the narrator can vary, from being an integral part of the described situation and presenting an unusual perspective (e.g., an angry description of a vandalized room as seen from the floor by the victim of a beating) to being an inconspicuous, uninvasive narrator describing a pastoral scene.

The psychological processes that play a particularly important role in comprehending a description are those that construct the representation of the referential situation. As a reader encounters each new piece of the description, she must augment this representation by adding another object (e.g., *There was also a tree in the garden*), by adding a modification to an existing object (*The tree was a weeping willow*), or by specifying a relation among objects (*The tree was just to the left of the fountain*). Having some type of sequential organization to the description (e.g., left to right) probably helps the reader construct and maintain the representation.

A reader's prior knowledge plays a role in understanding a description by helping to organize the information, fill in gaps, and perhaps elaborate on details that are not specified by the text. A striking demonstration of the recruitment of previous knowledge during the comprehension of a description is illustrated by the following passage:

> *Imagine yourself walking into a room; it is the master bedroom of a quiet Victorian house, in a slum of Bombay, which has just had a fire and been rebuilt in modern style, except for the master bedroom which is only half remodeled having its decorative panelling intact but barely visible because of the thick smoke.* (Feldman, 1975, p. 93)

This passage plays tricks with the use of previous knowledge. During the reading of the description, a reader becomes conscious of frequent changes in construal of the scene. When the text says that the house is Victorian, a reader expects that it is in England or in an old city in the United States. If he had elaborated on the neighborhood of the house (the nature of the street, lawn, and adjoining houses), he would have to revise those elaborations as soon as he read that the house was in the slums of Bombay. And he must change his normal assumptions and elaborations as soon as he reads about the fire. But then, when he reads that the room has been remodeled, he must revert to the original nonfire elaborations, perhaps with some modernization of the room. This passage demonstrates that readers draw on prior knowledge while reading each successive portion of a descriptive text, using it to elaborate on the referential representation and to dismiss inappropriate elaborations.

One of the first computer programs that effectively understood language owed its success to its accurate representation of a static scene: a world of toy blocks that varied in size, color, shape, and position (Winograd, 1972). The program understood sentences like *Put the blue cube on top of the red cylinder*. It maintained and updated its representation of a configuration of toy blocks as it was presented with each new sentence. Toy blocks are relatively simple objects—with properties of size, color, and shape—and can have various spatial relations to each other (e.g., *to the right of, on top of*). Because the attributes of a scene consisting of toy blocks are limited, the program could understand almost anything that could be said about the blocks. The success of this computer program demonstrates the importance of the knowledge of a referent in order to understand a description.

Expositions

An **exposition** describes logically related events and objects in order to inform, explain, or persuade. The logical relations need not come from formal logic but are implicit rules of reasoning, of one kind or another. Expositions can and often do have a strong descriptive component, but the description is in the service of a higher-level objective, such as explanation or persuasion. Moreover, the description need not focus on physical features of objects but rather on functional features of objects and events. Even though description is not the main goal of an exposition, the descriptive aspect of an exposition often consumes more words than the logical aspect.

Expositions play an important part in communicating knowledge in formal education, in job-related reading, and in the printed news media. Textbooks are generally expository, as are scientific articles; they present facts or evidence in order to communicate them, to have the reader learn them, or to use them to further an argument. For this reason, expositions probably play a more important role than other types of texts in the normal day to day functioning of modern society. The psychological processes that play a particularly important role in the comprehension of expositions are those that extract the logical relations among the elements of a text and use them to construct a representation of the logical or hierarchical structure of the text.

Sometimes the different types of texts are divided by no more than a fine line. An exposition of how a sundial works is not very different from a description of a sundial. Still, intuitively, it seems that the explanation contained in an exposition is more than description. A *description* communicates what the sense organs perceive, while an *exposition* usually provides a deeper, conceptual analysis of the referent that goes beyond its perceptible physical properties. This extra something in an exposition often includes the functional or causal relations among the objects or events that are described. For example, in an exposition about a sundial, it seems essential to explain the correspondence between the position of the shadow and the time of day that is produced by the continual change in the sun's position and the resultant change in the position of the shadow. However, this correspondence could be omitted in a lyrical description of a sundial.

In the sections that follow, we will describe the processing of expository texts and compare it to the processing of narrative texts. However, such a comparison must be made with great caution, for several reasons. First, it is dangerous to generalize from the small samples of different types of expositions and narratives that have been examined by existing experiments. For example, many of the studies of the comprehension of narratives used simple children's stories as texts. The comprehension of other types of narratives that are more likely to be read by adults has not been examined as systematically. Similarly, the comprehension of only a few different types of expositions has been examined. Second, it is possible that expositions, whose purpose is primarily to inform, convey more new information than narratives. As a result, the comprehension of expositions may be less influenced than narratives by the readers' previous knowledge contained in scripts and schemata.

Several eye-fixation experiments have examined how the different parts of an expository passage are read (Carpenter & Just, 1981; Just & Carpenter, 1980; Thibadeau, Just, & Carpenter, 1982). The 15 texts that were used in the experiment were expository passages of about 140 words, and they described the workings of a man-made or natural mechanism, such as a flywheel or an insect's toxin. The structure of these passages conformed to a schema containing eight slots, such as the *PURPOSE* (of the mechanism) and its *PHYSICAL-PROPERTIES*. (These schema slots will be described in more detail in the account of READER's comprehension of the *Flywheels* text, which constitutes the next section of the chapter.)

The relevant empirical finding from the eye-fixation studies was that subjects read the information about more important schema slots at a slower rate than information about less important schema slots. They spent more time per word when reading about the purpose of a flywheel, for example, than when reading about its physical properties. This finding is similar to that of Cirilo and Foss (1980), who found that subjects took more time to read a particular sentence of a narrative when that sentence played a more important role in the story than when it played a less significant role. The importance of the schema slot affected not only the rate at which the information was read but also the probability that it would later be recalled. Information from the more important schema slots was more likely to be recalled, both in the case of expository texts (Just & Carpenter, 1980; Meyer, 1975) and in the case of narratives, where this result is the *levels effect* that was discussed earlier. The READER model will later account for the effect of the importance of a slot both on reading rate and recall.

Just as script knowledge about commonplace activities (such as going to a restaurant) helps a reader comprehend and recall a script-related narrative, knowledge of a content area (such as biology) helps a reader process an exposition dealing with that topic. During the reading of an exposition, readers spend less time processing those sentences that present a fact with which they are already familiar than they do processing sentences that introduce unfamiliar information (Johnson & Kieras, 1982). The effect of prior knowledge on the recall of specific facts varies interestingly with the nature of the task. If readers are unaware that their recall will be tested, then the prompted recall of those passage facts that they previously knew is better than the recall of unfamiliar facts. But if readers know that their recall will be tested, then they spend more time on the sentences that contain new facts; subsequently, they can recall the sentences with new facts just as well as the sentences with old facts (Johnson & Kieras, 1982). Thus, when readers are trying to memorize the content of a passage, they spend relatively more time reading unfamiliar facts and consequently succeed in equating their recall for previously familiar and unfamiliar facts.

Extracting the theme of an expository passage   An important part of reading an expository passage is extracting the main theme. Sometimes the theme is explicitly stated in a title or a topic sentence. But in many cases, a reader must formulate a statement of the theme as she reads the passage. This is an example of a process that constructs high-level generalizations or abstractions, referred to as a **macroprocess** by van Dijk and Kintsch (1983).

Some of the strategies for extracting the theme were analyzed in a study in which readers were asked to think aloud and guess the theme as they read a short technical passage (Kieras & Bovair, 1981). The passages consisted of descriptions of several instances that illustrated a single general theme. For example, the theme of one passage was the accuracy of clocks, and it explained how several different types of modern clocks functioned. The general strategy that readers used was to formulate a tentative statement of the theme after reading the initial sentence of the passage. Then, if they read any subsequent sentences of the passage that did not fit in sufficiently well with their notion of the theme, they revised their theme statement to accommodate the ill-fitting sentence.

In that experiment, the main clause of the opening sentence provided the basis for the theme statement in one of two ways. One possibility was that the clause contained general terms, in which case it became the tentative statement of the theme. An example of such a general statement is *Modern timekeeping devices are extremely accurate.* The second possibility was that the main clause did not contain general terms, in which case subjects tried to generalize the clause and use the generalization as the tentative theme. For example, if the initial sentence was *An inexpensive quartz crystal watch has one second accuracy for several weeks,* it might be generalized to produce the theme statement *Clocks can be very accurate.* If it was difficult to construct the generalization, readers reserved judgment about the theme until after reading the second sentence and applying the same strategy to it.

The tentative theme statement was rejected and replaced by a new one if subsequent sentences of the passage did not fit in. But the criterion for rejection differed for theme statements explicitly provided by the text and those constructed by the reader. If the current theme statement was explicitly provided by the passage, then the majority of the sentences had to not fit in before that tentative theme was rejected. The criterion for rejecting a theme statement was lower if the text didn't present the statement of the theme and the readers had to formulate it by constructing their own generalization. Encountering a single sentence in the passage that didn't fit in was sufficient ground for rejecting a tentative theme and constructing a new one. This result suggests that the initial sentence in a technical passage plays a particularly important role in the readers' formulation of the theme. Moreover, the sentence that states the main theme is read more slowly than other sentences (Just & Carpenter, 1980) and helps the reader organize the incoming information.

Cues and Processes in Text Integration

The coherence that distinguishes a text from a sequence of unrelated sentences is computed by a reader with the aid of a number of knowledge sources. Some of the processes and the associated knowledge have already been described, including knowledge of the text structure, the situation that is being referred to, and the logical and causal relations among the described events. In addition to this background knowledge, a reader can also use explicit cues provided by the text to guide his integrative processes. This section describes some of the explicit cues to the relations among the sentences of a text and some of the inference making that operates when the relations are left implicit.

Integrative cues in texts A text often contains explicit cues to indicate how some of the underlying ideas are related to each other. One important class of such cues consists of interclausal and intersentential connectives. For example, consider how the intersentential connective *consequently* helps the reader to relate the following pair of sentences:

> *It became very cloudy on that Sunday morning.* Consequently, *the picnic was cancelled.*

Consequently indicates that the event being referred to (in this case, the cancellation of the picnic) was caused by the previously described event or state (the cloudy Sunday morning). In cases in which the intersentential connective is not provided by the text, the reader must infer the relation among the sentences by drawing on his own knowledge of how such concepts may be related. Connectives can be classified in terms of the relations they denote. The list in Table 8.3 provides a representative set of relations denoted by various connectives.

In addition to connectives, a text can explicitly describe the relation among events or states, as in the following example:

> *There were several causes of the revolution:*
> 1. *The peasants were suffering from a food shortage.*
> 2. *The clergy were upset about their loss of power.*

Similarly, a text can provide titles or headings that indicate the interrelationships among the sentences. Also, a text can provide a high-level abstraction, like a sum-

Table 8.3 Commonly used connectives and the relation they indicate among text elements

Connective	Indicated Relation
also, again, another, finally, furthermore, likewise, moreover, similarly, too	Another item in the same series
afterwards, finally, later on, next, then	Another item in a time series
for instance, for example, specifically	An example or illustration of what has been said
accordingly, as a result, consequently, hence, then, therefore, thus, so	A consequence of what has been said
in other words, that is to say, to put it differently	A restatement of what has been said
all in all, altogether, finally, in conclusion, the point is	A concluding item or summary
but, however, on the other hand, on the contrary	A statement opposing what has been said
granted, of course, to be sure, undoubtedly	A concession to an opposing view
all the same, even though, nevertheless, nonetheless, still	The original line of argument is resuming after a concession

Source: Adapted from Brooks & Warren, 1970, pp. 37–38.

mary statement or the statement of a theme, that encompasses a number of sentences and relates them to each other. If such an abstraction is not provided by the text and the reader needs one, then he must construct it himself. The appropriate relation that links such states, actions, and concepts may be obvious in cases in which the general situation is very familiar. However, such relations may be difficult or impossible to infer when the topic is less familiar. In that case, connectives and an explicit description of the relations in the text may be essential to constructing an accurate and coherent representation of the information.

Making inferences   When a text does not explicitly indicate how the sentences or clauses of a text are related to each other, the reader must infer the relation. But inferences play a role in other processes besides the integration of different parts of a text. At the referential level, a reader might have to infer that two different expressions are referring to the same person, or at the schema level, she might have to infer how a fact in the text fits into a particular schema slot. A discussion of inferences could have been located in any one of a number of chapters of this book. We have placed the consideration of inferences in this chapter on text comprehension because the integration of the sentences of a text seems particularly dependent on inferences.

The ultimate content of an inference is no different than the content of any other knowledge, except that the confidence placed on its correctness may be lower. An element of plausibility or likelihood is involved in making inferences. Inferences are heuristic and probabilistic, as are many other comprehension processes. Inferences can pertain to any aspect of meaning—space, time, causality, logic, nature, artifice, concreteness, or abstractness. Inferences are based on the reader's knowledge of the world, of language, and of the text portions that have already been read. Anything that can be *thought* can also be *inferred* from text under the right circumstances, so to classify the content of inferences would amount to classifying thoughts. Nevertheless, a few properties of the process of making integrative inferences in text comprehension do merit special consideration.

Inferences can be classified into two main types. **Backward inferences** link the most recently read text to some portion of the text that came earlier (Clark, 1975). For example, consider this pair of sentences:

The radio suddenly started playing. The noise frightened the infant.

To integrate this couplet, a reader must infer that the noise mentioned in the second sentence refers to the sound implied by the first sentence. A backward inference must be made whenever the subject's reading goals require a complete integration of the text information but the text does not explicitly indicate how the new information is related to the old. The two endpoints of the gap spanned by a backward inference are provided by the text. Other names for backward inference include *bridging* inference, *integrative* inference, *connective* inference, and *linking* inference.

By contrast, **forward inferences** embellish the representation of the currently read text for reasons inherent to the current piece of text. For example, consider this sentence:

The two-year-old was eating the jelly sandwich.

A forward inference made in this case might be that the child's face was smeared with jelly. The purpose of such inferences may be aesthetic, to make the internal representation richer in detail, or they could be generated when a reader tries to anticipate what will come next in the text. Forward inferences are optional and less likely to occur than backward inferences, unless they are specifically encouraged by the task. Only one endpoint of a forward inference is provided by the text. Other names for forward inference include *predictive* inference, *extrapolative* inference, and *elaborative* inference.

Even though making forward inferences is not essential to comprehension, it may nevertheless be a useful study skill, particularly in reading expository texts. Generating the implications of a claim or argument requires a thorough understanding of the claim. Furthermore, comparing one's own forward inferences against the information provided in the subsequent portion of the text provides a test of whether the claim was correctly understood.

Because inferences have a probabilistic and sometimes optional nature, several issues concerning the inference-making process frequently arise. First, it is difficult to predict which of many possible inferences will be made in the reading of a given text. The determination of which inference will be made depends on the reader and the task. If a reader is comprehending at a shallow level or reading very quickly, then very few inferences will be drawn, perhaps not even the necessary ones. But if a reader is examining the minute detail of a logical argument or embellishing the representation of the text for his own aesthetic purposes, then a very large number of inferences may be made.

Another question that arises concerns the point in time at which an inference is made, which may depend on the inference type. A backward inference that is important to the text coherence might be made during the reading of the word or phrase that must be related to previous parts of the text. For example, if an inference is necessary to establish the referent of a particular word, the point in time at which the inference is made is usually during the reading of that word, as the immediacy strategy would dictate (Just & Carpenter, 1978). This conclusion is based on the result that the readers' eyes pause on the very word that triggers the inference. By contrast, some types of forward inference might be made long after the text has been read and the reader has had a chance to mull over the implications of the content.

Since inference making is such an integral part of comprehension, it is natural to ask whether there is any difference between the representation of information that was explicitly *stated* and information that was *inferred*. Generally, there is little difference in the case of a low-level, fairly direct inference. For example, consider these two sentences:

> *Norbert drove to work each day.*
> *Norbert drove his car to work each day.*

The first sentence invites the inference that a car was involved, while the second sentence explicitly states it. Because the involvement of a car should be activated to some degree after the reading of either sentence, the long-term representation might be similar, regardless of which sentence had been read (Corbett & Dosher, 1978).

The READER Model's Text-level Processing

In this section, we describe how the computer-simulation model, READER, comprehends a technical expository text, focusing on the processes that fill in the slots of a schema with the information from the text. READER'S text-level processes exemplify three characteristics that correspond to human comprehension of text. First, READER uses its previous knowledge of the text structure, contained in a schema for short technical passages, to organize the information in the passage as it reads along. Second, like human readers, READER spends different amounts of time on various parts of the passage, depending on that part's role in the schema. For example, in scientific passages, human readers and READER spend more time on the names and operating principles of the mechanisms being described and less time on who invented the mechanism and what physical motions it makes. Finally, READER uses the immediacy principle for text-level integration, as it does for all other levels of processing. As each successive portion of a text is processed, READER attempts to integrate it with the representation of the preceding text, just as human readers do (Carpenter & Daneman, 1981; Dee-Lucas, Just, Carpenter, & Daneman, 1982; Just & Carpenter, 1980).

An example of the kind of text that was used to analyze human reading was an expository text on mechanical devices. The passage, on the topic of *Flywheels,* was introduced in Chapter 1:

> *Flywheels are one of the oldest mechanical devices known to man. Every internal-combustion engine contains a small flywheel that converts the jerky motion of the pistons into the smooth flow of energy that powers the drive shaft. The greater the mass of a flywheel and the faster it spins, the more energy can be stored in it. But its maximum spinning speed is limited by the strength of the material it is made from. If it spins too fast for its mass, any flywheel will fly apart. One type of flywheel consists of round sandwiches of fiberglas and rubber providing the maximum possible storage of energy when the wheel is confined in a small space as in an automobile. Another type, the "superflywheel," consists of a series of rimless spokes. This flywheel stores the maximum energy when space is unlimited.*

Using the MECHANISM Schema

READER knows about the structure of only one type of text: namely, the type that explains the functioning of a mechanism. This knowledge resides in the *MECHANISM* schema, which specifies the kinds of information one might expect in a brief text about man-made devices and biological mechanisms as they are used by human or animal agents. The schema consists of slots for the various kinds of information encountered in such passages. For example, the schema has a slot for the *GOAL* (purpose) of the mechanism, and if given a passage about a mechanism like a pulley, READER would have a slot ready for information about the uses to which pulleys are put. The slots for the MECHANISM schema are shown in Figure 8.4, along with some examples of slot fillers. During comprehension, the schema slots are filled in with the information from the passage. Thus, the schema is used to or-

NAME: ⟨*The device is called a flywheel.*⟩

Slot Name   Example of Filler

GOALS: ⟨*The flywheel's goal is to store energy.*⟩

Slot Name   Example of Filler

PRINCIPLES: ⟨*Faster spinning stores up more energy.*⟩

Slot Name   Example of Filler

PHYSICAL-PROPERTIES: ⟨*One type of flywheel is made of fiberglas and rubber.*⟩

Slot Name   Example of Filler

PHYSICAL-MOVEMENTS: ⟨*Flywheels spin.*⟩

Slot Name   Example of Filler

MADE-BY: ⟨*Flywheels are made by humans.*⟩

Slot Name   Example of Filler

USED-BY: ⟨*Flywheels are used by humans.*⟩

Slot Name   Example of Filler

EXEMPLARS: ⟨*One exemplar of a flywheel is the car-engine flywheel.*⟩

Slot Name   Example of Filler

Figure 8.4 An illustration of READER's MECHANISM schema for a short scientific text with examples of actual slot fillers from the *Flywheels* passage.

ganize the information as it is being read; later, it is used to retrieve information or answer questions about the passage. The MECHANISM schema is sufficiently general to apply not only to the *Flywheels* passage but also to most of the 14 other test passages that were used in the experiment.

Schemata have the useful property that they can be embedded in each other. In the READER model's use of the MECHANISM schema during the reading of the *Flywheels* passage, a subschema is invoked during the reading about exemplars of particular flywheels, such as the superflywheel. The information about particular exemplars is fit into a MECHANISM subschema that is embedded in the *EXEMPLARS* slot of the main schema.

The slots of the schema have a default ordering that reflects their usual relative importance. The most important slots of READER's MECHANISM schema are

NAME, GOALS, and *PRINCIPLES,* while *MADE-BY* and *USED-BY* are marked as being less important. Importance is not a text property that emerges during reading (as topicality does). Instead, it reflects the relevance of various parts of the text to a reader's goals. The relative importance of different types of information changes with the reader's goals, as does the relative time spent reading them (Carpenter & Just, 1981). The task constraints can cause READER to modify its ordering of slots. For example, if READER were given the goal of determining the users of various mechanisms, it would attach the highest importance to the *USED-BY* slot. The relative importance of slots affects how carefully each slot filler is read, as described below.

The fact that READER knew only one schema allowed this model to finesse two problems that human readers have to face in choosing the appropriate schema. First, human readers must select the appropriate schema from the hundreds or perhaps thousands of schemata they might have previously stored. The selection by human readers is rapid and effective and is probably based on a variety of cues provided in the early parts of the text. Readers quickly recognize that a new text resembles other similar types that they have read previously. The recognition of a text type is probably no different than other forms of pattern recognition, such as the recognition of visual forms, faces, and other category memberships. The cues in the stimulus evoke the representations of previously stored categories. Knowing only one schema, READER is spared the problem of recognizing a text type and retrieving the appropriate schema.

The second problem finessed by the READER model is that unlike the subjects in Bartlett's (1932) experiment, READER never had to process a text that didn't fit into an existing schema. Human readers can cope with this situation in several ways. First, as Bartlett's results indicated, subjects sometimes use the best-fitting schema they have, producing some distortion in the way the story is recalled. Second, in the case of texts that are combinations of two or more familiar components, readers may construct a new schema by modifying or combining existing schemata as needed. For example, if a story describes a birthday party held at a baseball game, then readers might dynamically construct an appropriate schema by combining their schemata for birthday parties and baseball games. So the schemata that guide comprehension need not all be static structures that are used repeatedly but, in some cases, might be dynamically configured to fit a novel situation.

Filling schema slots   READER relates the clause and sentence-level representations to the text-level organization provided by the schema. The difficulty lies in determining into which slot a given piece of newly read information fits. This can be accomplished in several ways. The most important cue READER uses to relate the sentence-level representations to the appropriate schema slots is its knowledge of the meanings of the sentence-level predicates. The sentence-level representations are composed of predicates like CONTAIN, CAUSE, CONVERT, PURPOSE, and HAVE-AS-PART, and the schema-level slots to which they must be related are *NAME, GOALS, PRINCIPLES, PHYSICAL-PROPERTIES, PHYSICAL-MOVEMENTS, MADE-BY, USED-BY,* and *EXEMPLARS.* As part of its lexicon, READER knows enough about the meaning of the predicates to make some reasonable matches to the schema-level slots. For example, READER knows that CONTAIN and HAVE-

AS-PART specify physical properties. Consequently, information about the component parts of a flywheel represented by CONTAIN or HAVE-AS-PART would likely be inserted into the *PHYSICAL-PROPERTIES* slot. In this example, the processing is bottom up, from sentence-level predicate to schema slot. In other cases, the processing is more symmetrically collaborative between the levels. For example, in the sentence *The greater the mass of a flywheel, the faster it spins, the more energy can be stored in it,* the relation between mass and storage capacity must be inferred. Since mass is a physical property, spin is a behavior, and energy accumulation is a positive outcome associated with purpose (inferred from the second sentence), a causal link is inferred, relating physical properties and actions to the *GOALS* of the flywheel.

Sometimes, the text explicitly states how a given piece of information is related to the schema. Phrases like *X is called,* where *X* is the topic of the passage, explicitly cue the *NAME* slot. READER uses various heuristics to identify the topic of a passage, such as hypothesizing that the grammatical subject of the first or second sentence is also the topic of the passage.

Finally, the schema slots can be filled with default values for a given type of mechanism. For example, any mechanism that is a device can be assumed to be made by man, if the need for this information arises. And any mechanism that is part of a living thing can be assumed to be made by nature.

Thus, READER uses a number of methods to determine how a particular piece of information fits into the schema. Like READER's other knowledge structures, the inferences at the schema level have varying degrees of activation, reflecting the strength of the evidence for a particular proposition. In addition, various processes can collaborate, so there is often more than one source of evidence weighing in favor of inserting a piece of text information into a given schema slot. Some types of information that are perhaps unusual for this type of text may not fit into any schema slot and yet they may be congruent with the rest of the passage. In this case, the information will not be recalled, although it may possibly remain in working memory for a while.

The Time Course of READER's Text-level Comprehension

READER uses the immediacy principle for text-level comprehension, as it does for other levels of processing. As each successive word of a text is encountered, it is evaluated as a potential basis for action by the productions at all the levels of comprehension. Specifically, one group of productions is ready to fit the new information from a text into schema slots as each successive word of a sentence is encountered. However, the productions' conditions of application will not be satisfied until enough of the sentence has been processed to indicate how the new information fits into the schema. The point in the sentence at which the first schema-level production will be evoked depends on the sentence wording and structure. Sometimes an entire clause or sentence must be read in order to determine its relation to the schema. At other times, a particular word located at an arbitrary point in a sentence can trigger the schema-filling process.

This proposal is consistent with the results of several eye-fixation studies that examined the point in a sentence at which integrative processing is done. The two main processing loci are at the first word that provides sufficient information to indicate the appropriate schema slot and at the last word in the sentence (Carpenter & Just, 1977b; Dee-Lucas, Just, Carpenter, & Daneman, 1982; Just & Carpenter, 1978). Similarly, schema-level integration is done by READER as soon as possible, which sometimes turns out to be at the end of the sentence.

The time course of text integration is especially important to READER because it adjusts its reading rate to the importance of the information it encounters, just as human readers do. READER goes slower if it is processing information that it believes matches an important slot, and it continues at the slower reading rate for the rest of the sentence or until it determines a different slot filler has been encountered. Currently, READER deliberately slows down for the *NAME, PRINCIPLES,* and *GOALS* slots, on the assumption that this information is most important. The default goal in reading such short scientific passages is usually to determine what the mechanism is called (*NAME*), how it works (*PRINCIPLES*), and what it accomplishes (*GOALS*). Slowing down the reading rate improves READER's comprehension and recall of the more important parts of the passage, as described in more detail in Chapter 9 on the READER model. Briefly, slower reading rates provide enough time for a greater number of consistency-checking processes, such as processes that look for subject-verb agreement.

Recall and Forgetting

If human readers are asked to recall a short scientific passage immediately after having read it, their recall protocols are incomplete and sometimes inaccurate, but they do reflect the schema structure (Just & Carpenter, 1980). The recall protocol below from one of the subjects in the study illustrates how the schema is reflected:

> *The topic of this paragraph was flywheels and the basic function of a flywheel is to store energy. They come in various types, such as, well they can come in various types of materials, you can have rubber flywheels or plastic ones, etc. and they're also, well your engine in a car has a flywheel because it takes the jerky motion of a piston and converts into smooth energy if you will. Flywheels are one of the oldest form of energy producers known to man and they basically function by the wind turning them and that's about it.*

READER'S recall shows a fairly reasonable match to the human recall. The following protocol was produced by READER:

> *This paragraph was about a mechanism called a flywheel. The purpose of the flywheel is to store energy. The more the mass or speed of the flywheel the more energy stored. There are three types of flywheel. One is in automobile engines, another stores maximum energy in a small space, and the third stores maximum energy in unlimited space.*

READER's recall protocol is produced by outputting the contents of the various schema slots, in order of the slots' importance: the *NAME,* the flywheels' main *GOALS,* and some *PRINCIPLES* of operation. Similarly, the recall protocols of the human subjects include responses like "this passage was about flywheels," "flywheels store energy," or "if a flywheel spins too fast, it will break up." Physical properties tend not to be recalled in isolation but in the context of their relation to a

PRINCIPLE, if at all. There are no recalls like "flywheels spin, but that's all I can remember." Rather, there are recalls like "the faster a flywheel can spin, the better it is." The portions of the passage that constitute examples, physical properties, and motions not instrinsic to principles are less likely to be recalled.

The relative importance of each part of the text to the human readers can be inferred by observing how slowly that part is read and how likely it is to appear in the recall protocols. The information that fits in the more important schema slots is read more slowly and is recalled better (Just & Carpenter, 1980). This constitutes READER's explanation of the levels effect in the recall of an expository text and, by analogy, suggests a partial explanation of the familiar levels effect in story recall.

Neither the human readers' nor the READER model's recall is perfect. There are three main reasons for READER's imperfect recall. First, facts that READER comprehended but did not integrate into the MECHANISM schema are not recalled because the retrieval plan does not access them. Thus, READER knows more than it recalls, and this additional knowledge could potentially be accessed if READER were asked specific questions or asked to perform a recognition test. A second reason for READER's imperfect recall is imperfect comprehension. If an erroneous interpretation is accepted and integrated with the schema, then there will be an error of commission in the recall. This is especially likely at high reading speeds. Finally, READER may have imperfect recall because of some forgetting at the time of comprehension. For example, READER stores the exact wording it encounters only until it finishes processing the current sentence (see Jarvella, 1971). Thus, the exact wording is forgotten during comprehension, which might affect the final representation of the passage and hence the recall.

Summary

An important theme that emerges from this chapter is that knowledge plays a ubiquitous organizational role in the comprehension of text. The reader's previous knowledge is organized as a schema of interrelated slots into which new information can be classified. For example, knowledge of fairy tales tells a reader that a hero who faces an obstacle to his goal will search for ways to surmount it. Because of his previous knowledge, a reader will also know which goals are likely and the ways a particular hero will try to overcome an obstacle. For example, the weapon that the hero uses might be a lance, pitchfork, or pistol, depending on whether he is a knight, a farmer, or a cowboy. The schema can indicate how various pieces of information are related to each other and can provide default values for information that is not explicitly mentioned in the text. The comprehension of all types of texts involves inference making that uses previous knowledge of the text structure and content, conjointly with the information in the text, to produce coherence in the representation of the text.

Much of the research on text-level processes has centered around the comprehension of narratives, particularly well-structured, simple stories. An important aspect of the comprehension of such stories at the text level consists of generating causal explanations of the characters' actions in terms of their goals, plans, personalities, vocations, and the current circumstances. The ability to generate such a causal framework depends on knowledge and beliefs about the world, as well as knowledge about the structure of stories.

Simple stories often have similar structures that have been described by story grammars and story schemata. A reader's knowledge of these structures may be used during reading to help classify the components of a story and relate the various components to each other. Schemata may also play a role in recall, since they help organize the information into categories of varying importance; during recall, the schema can be used as a retrieval plan, favoring the content of important over unimportant slots and making it extremely unlikely that a reader will recall any unimportant information that does not fit into one of the schema slots. The main determinant of whether a particular part of a story will be recalled appears to be its role in the causal chain of events in the story.

A second theme of the chapter concerned the differences among text types. Narrative texts particularly engage the processes that compute causal relations; descriptions particularly engage the processes that construct the referential representation; and expositions particularly engage the processes that compute logical and hierarchical relations among the elements of a text. The comprehension of all types of texts may involve the same set of processes, but the relative involvement of a given process may vary across text types.

The READER model demonstrates how the collaboration of processes can construct a text-level representation of a well-structured expository text. READER relates the phrases and sentences it encounters to its MECHANISM schema, filling in the schema slots as it reads along. The schema helps READER organize the information during comprehension and later provides a retrieval plan during recall. Both of these uses of a schema also characterize human comprehension.

Suggested Readings

The comprehension of extended texts is a burgeoning research area, so many excellent articles and books address this topic. The book by van Dijk and Kintsch (1983) provides a comprehensive and integrative analysis of discourse comprehension. And their influential article (Kintsch & van Dijk, 1978) describes a small part of the entire theoretical structure. Two other books on prose comprehension and memory that consider a broad range of relevant issues are those by Graesser (1981) and Sanford and Garrod (1981).

Important articles on the role of schemata in the comprehension of stories include those by Mandler and Johnson (1977) and Rumelhart (1975, 1977a). The book by Schank and Abelson (1977) provides an artificial-intelligence perspective on the use of knowledge in text comprehension. And text grammars are discussed in books by van Dijk (1972) and de Beaugrande and Dressler (1981). The articles in Kieras and Just (1984) describe a number of contemporary methodologies for studying text comprehension, as well as summaries of the main conclusions obtained by each method. And Just and Carpenter (1977) contains a number of representative approaches to text comprehension.

9

A Computer Simulation of Reading: The READER Model

A theory of reading must not only explain how each component process operates but also how they all operate together. Throughout this book, the READER simulation model has provided a framework for describing the component processes in reading. Each of the preceding chapters described a particular component of reading in terms of the corresponding processing mechanism in the READER model. In this chapter, we focus not on the individual components of reading but on what these components have in common, how they are organized, and how they are coordinated with each other.

Because reading is just one of many forms of thought, a theory of reading must be embedded within a larger theory of thinking. The READER model is embedded within a larger information processing environment called **CAPS,** an acronym for **C**ollaborative, **A**ctivation-based **P**roduction **S**ystem. The CAPS environment provides an organization for not only the READER model but also models of several other types of thinking, such as spatial thinking and problem solving (see also Just & Carpenter, 1985; Just & Thibadeau, 1984; Thibadeau, Just, & Carpenter, 1982).

This chapter describes the READER simulation model and the CAPS environment, both of which were developed in collaboration with our colleague, Robert Thibadeau.

Overview In the first half of the chapter, **The READER Model,** we will summarize how the mechanisms at various levels of processing operate, how they represent information, and how they are coordinated. The first section ends with an evaluation of how well READER accounts for the empirical data and how it compares to other models of comprehension.

In the second half of the chapter, **The Psychological Basis of CAPS,** we will describe the general architecture of thinking within which the READER model was developed. We will describe the main mechanisms that characterize CAPS, such as activation and parallel processing; we will also describe the empirical findings that motivated the inclusion of these mechanisms in CAPS.

The READER Model

The Purpose of the Simulation

Most scientific models have a similar purpose: to provide an explanation of some phenomenon by constructing a model of it and demonstrating a correspondence between characteristics of the model and the phenomenon. In all cases, the correspondence is imperfect; the model may be incorrect in minor aspects or even in fundamental aspects. The correspondences indicate which parts of the model are probably correct and the noncorrespondences provide guideposts for future research. The fit of the READER model provides such information about the state of the theory of reading presented in this book.

The READER simulation also provides an integrative framework within which the many component processes of reading function together; thus, it demonstrates that the individual mechanisms that have been proposed for different processes are compatible with each other. Also, the fact that READER simulates important aspects of comprehension demonstrates that the proposed mechanisms are sufficient to accomplish the task of reading.

The unique purpose of the READER model is to simulate the time course of human reading, requiring more processing time at those points where people take more time. If the words of a text influence the duration of READER's computations similarly to the way they influence those of human readers, the similarity increases the plausibility of READER's mechanisms as psychological models.

The immediate goal of the READER model is to understand a short scientific passage, namely, the *Flywheels* passage that was presented in Chapter 8. In reading this passage, READER acquires the information necessary to answer questions about it or to summarize it. READER, of course, is more than a system to understand a single passage. The language-understanding mechanisms that READER uses are quite general; except for lacking lexical information and world knowledge, READER is sufficiently general to comprehend any other expository passage of this type. Moreover, we will show that the CAPS architecture is also general and provides a way to match characteristics of human performance with simulation models for a variety of complex processes besides language understanding.

Gaze-duration data and model development The READER model, unlike many other simulation models of language comprehension, was strongly motivated by a rich new source of empirical results, namely, the measurement of human gaze durations on each word of a text. People reading a text at the rate of 250 words per minute could spend an equal amount of time, 240 milliseconds, looking at each word of the text. But they don't. Instead, they spend systematically less time on some words than others, with gazes roughly ranging from 100 milliseconds to 1 second; and there are some words, mainly short function words, that are seldom directly fixated. As the preceding chapters have demonstrated, the gaze duration on a given word reflects the processing time expended on perceiving, understanding, and integrating that word.

The gaze duration on a word was found to be systematically related to the properties of the word, such as its length and frequency. This relation is mediated by the duration of the perception and comprehension processes of human readers.

The duration of the processes used by the model should be similarly related to these properties of words. Specifically, the human gaze duration increased linearly with the length of a word and decreased linearly with the logarithm of its normative frequency, and the two effects were additive. Also, the gaze duration increased on words or phrases that contained a misleading syntactic or semantic construction. Finally, the overall speed of reading became slower when the content of an important schema slot was encountered. These kinds of results from eye-fixation studies, as well as those from other types of experiments, impose constraints on how the computer simulation can function if it is to possess similar performance characteristics.

A more general constraint was that the model would have to understand the text; *understanding* in this case means extracting information from a text and being able to recall the passage approximately the way the human readers did. Alternative demonstrations of comprehension that humans or READER could provide include the ability to answer questions about the text or paraphrase it or be able to perform some other task as a result of having read the passage.

The Form of the Model

As we described in Chapter 1, READER is expressed as a production system model. A production system contains a set of condition-action rules that embody the procedural knowledge of what to do under various circumstances. Each production describes the symbol-manipulating action to be taken whenever a given condition arises in working memory. Working memory contains the set of knowledge elements that are currently in use.

On each processing cycle, all of the productions examine the current state of knowledge in the working memory to determine whether their enabling conditions are met. Then, all of the productions whose conditions are satisfied perform their actions; namely, they modify the current knowledge state. Then, a new cycle starts, and another set of productions is enabled, and they perform their actions, and so on. READER is an unconventional production system in that it allows *all* of the satisfied productions to fire on a cycle, producing concurrent streams of processing, as shown schematically in Figure 9.1.

As READER moves from state to state, performing its task, the sequence of processing is **self-scheduled.** The decision of what to do next is not predetermined, nor is it scheduled by a central executive. Rather, the decision is determined by the dynamically changing knowledge state in working memory. No detailed plan for performing a task needs to be constructed. Individual productions take the system from one state to the next. This somewhat resembles human mental and physical actions that are begun when only the main goal and the first step are evident but before many of the intermediate steps have been considered.

The measure of the simulation's processing effort is provided by the number of cycles of processing. A READER **cycle** is defined as a single iteration in which the working memory is scanned and all of the satisfied productions fire. All cycles are assumed to consume the same amount of time. The number of cycles spent on each word of a text provides the measure of processing time in the simulation that can be related to the human gaze duration.

READER continues the processing of a word of text until no further productions are satisfied—that is, until the processing has proceeded as far as it can. A production stops firing when its enabling conditions are no longer satisfied. This typically occurs when one of its conditions is the presence of an unsatisfied goal, and some action eventually satisfies that goal. When all of the productions have stopped

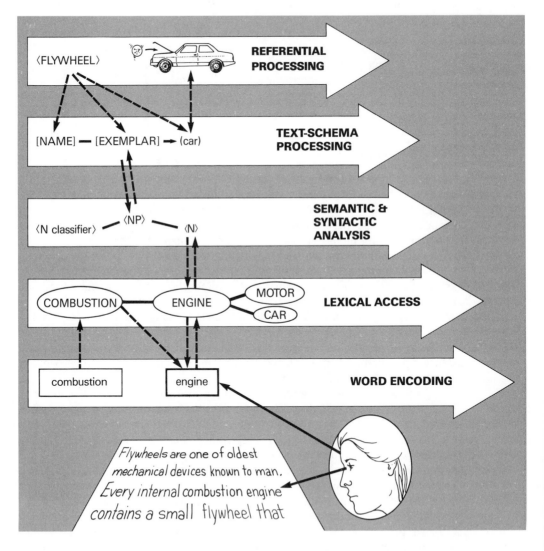

Figure 9.1   The major processing levels in the READER model that operate as the reader fixates the word *engine* in the text. *Source:* Adapted from Thibadeau, Just, & Carpenter, 1982, Figure 1, p. 169.

firing, the next word is encoded and another episode of processing begins. Not proceeding to the next word until the current word has been processed as far as possible corresponds to the eye-mind relation in human readers.

The Representation

The different types of knowledge that READER possesses or acquires are all expressed in the same representational format, namely, a propositional form. For example, all of READER's prior knowledge of word meanings and its rudimentary knowledge about their referents is represented propositionally. Each **proposition** is a triple consisting of a concept, a relation, and another concept. Together, the interrelated propositions constitute a semantic network of information.

The propositions contain one of the two fundamental relations, :IS and :HAS, which provide an attribute-value structure. As described in Chapter 5 on the nature of READER's representation, the relation **:IS** reflects the equivalence of two symbols that stand for the same entity. For example, in the representation of the clause *Flywheels are mechanical devices,* this relation can be used to denote the fact that the first word is *flywheels:* (**WORD-1** :IS *flywheels*).

The **:HAS** relation indicates that one symbol elaborates the significance of another. For example, in the same clause, the first word refers to a physical object; the representation of this referent is designated as *REFERENT-1;* the relation is expressed in a proposition using :HAS: (**WORD-1** :HAS REFERENT-1). As these examples illustrate, words and concepts are numbered as they are encountered. This is convenient for distinguishing among different instances of the same type of argument.

An important property of the dependency relations expressed with :HAS is that they can be extensively embedded, permitting arbitrarily large structures. For example, the representations of words, word meanings, and semantic and syntactic relations can all be embedded in the representation of a sentence. Table 9.1 presents only some of the propositions that represent the sentence *Flywheels are mechanical devices.* As the table illustrates, all of the propositions are constructed using :IS and :HAS as relations. However, the arguments in a proposition are often specific to a particular level of processing. For example, the argument *REFERENT* is specific to the referential level. Arguments such as *SUBJECT* and *OBJECT* are specific to the syntactic level. *CATEGORY-MEMBERSHIP* typifies a high-level semantic predicate that is used in semantic analysis to indicate that one entire conceptualization is an instance of another. Arguments such as *CONCEPT* originate at the lexical level. And although not represented in the table, arguments such as *WORD-PERCEPT* and *LETTER* express the perceptual representation of the printed word.

Each proposition has an associated level of activation that can be increased or decreased by the comprehension processes. The **activation level** indicates the extent to which the proposition has supporting evidence. For example, when READER encounters the word *cooking* in the clause *John likes cooking utensils,* a proposition would be constructed to express the hypothesis that *cooking* is part of a noun phrase. The next word, *utensils,* provides more evidence to support this hypothesis, resulting in an increase in the activation level of the proposition express-

Table 9.1 Some of the propositions that constitute the representation of the sentence: *Flywheels are mechanical devices*

Proposition	Processing Level
(WORD-1 :IS *flywheels*)	
(WORD-1 :HAS *CONCEPT-1*)	lexical
(*CONCEPT-1* :HAS REFERENT-1)	referential
(REFERENT-1 :IS FLYWHEEL-1)	
(WORD-2 :IS *are*)	
(WORD-2 :HAS *CONCEPT-2*)	lexical
(WORD-2 :HAS SUBJECT-2)	syntactic
(SUBJECT-2 :IS **WORD-1**)	
(*CONCEPT-2* :IS CATEGORY-MEMBERSHIP-1)	
(CATEGORY-MEMBERSHIP-1 :HAS SEMANTIC-SUBJECT-1)	semantic
(SEMANTIC-SUBJECT-1 :IS FLYWHEEL-1)	
(WORD-3 :IS *mechanical*)	
(WORD-3 :HAS ADJECTIVE'S-NOMINAL-3)	syntactic
(ADJECTIVE'S-NOMINAL-3 :IS **WORD-4**)	
(WORD-4 :IS *devices*)	
(WORD-4 :HAS *CONCEPT-4*)	lexical
(WORD-4 :IS OBJECT-2)	
(OBJECT-2 :HAS VERB-2)	syntactic
(VERB-2 :IS **WORD-2**)	
(WORD-4 :HAS REFERENT-4)	referential
(REFERENT-4 :IS DEVICES-1)	
(CATEGORY-MEMBERSHIP-1 :HAS SEMANTIC-OBJECT-1)	semantic
(SEMANTIC-OBJECT-1 :IS DEVICES-1)	

Source: Adapted from Thibadeau, Just, & Carpenter, 1982, Table 4, p. 173.

ing the hypothesis. When a proposition accumulates enough supporting evidence for its activation level to reach threshold, it thereby becomes part of the accepted interpretation of the text, and the propositions representing competing hypotheses are deactivated. Activation is typically directed from propositions that have exceeded the threshold to other propositions that have a subthreshold activation level.

READER's Processes

READER progresses through a sentence one word at a time, operating on several levels in parallel as soon as they are evoked. These include the lexical level, the semantic and syntactic levels, the referential level, and the text-schema level. The processing of each word proceeds as far as possible at all levels before moving on to the next word, thus instantiating the immediacy principle. In this section, we will briefly summarize the main mechanisms operating at each of the levels described in the preceding chapters.

Word encoding   READER encodes the constituents of a word sequentially, usually letter by letter, as described in Chapter 2 on word encoding. During encoding, READER checks for familiar prefix, suffix, and subword units that can be used to access the lexicon. The main result on word encoding that is addressed by the model is that the time a reader spends on a word increases with the number of letters in the word. A reader spends more time on five-letter words than on four-letter words, and so on. READER's word-encoding mechanism similarly spends more cycles on longer words.

Lexical access   READER uses an activation process to access the meaning associated with a word. The process, as described in Chapter 3, is initiated by the encoded word-percept, which directs activation to the associated word meaning. The base level of activation of the word meaning is a function of the word's frequency, so that more frequently used words require less additional activation to reach threshold. The major empirical result accounted for by READER is that readers spend less time on more frequent words. More precisely, the gaze duration decreases linearly with the logarithm of the word's frequency.

Semantic and syntactic analysis   The syntactic analysis and the semantic analysis operate collaboratively in READER, although the two types of processes can be distinguished by their goals. The syntactic analysis searches for grammatical relations such as grammatical subject, verb, object, and prepositional phrase; it also performs other syntactically oriented analyses, such as checking for the agreement between a noun and a verb or associating a relative clause with the constituent it modifies. The syntactic processes of READER and human readers were described in Chapter 5.

As described in Chapter 6, the semantic analysis uses similar types of information as the syntactic analysis; however, its goal is to associate various participants in an action or state with semantic roles, such as agent, instrument, location, object, recipient, and so on.

Both semantic and syntactic analyses contribute relatively little to the variance among gaze durations unless the sentence contains an infrequently used syntactic structure, such as the doubly center-embedded sentence *The boy the girl the man liked saw cried* or a misleading garden-path sentence like *Since Mary always jogs a mile seems a short distance.* In most cases, for both human readers and for READER, syntactic and semantic analyses occur concurrently with other processes that are longer or more variable in duration. In part, some of the concurrence occurs because READER can construct low-level syntactic and semantic expectations for a word based on earlier words. For example, if READER encounters a determiner such as *the* or *a,* it can expect to encounter a noun or adjective. When the noun or adjective is subsequently encountered, determining its syntactic class requires relatively little additional processing beyond what had been already developed based on the prior words.

Referential processes   READER constructs a referential representation of the world that is described in the passage. As described in Chapter 7, the referential representation is central in accounting for a variety of comprehension and memory phenomena. The noun phrases of a text typically have object referents, while the verbs tend to refer to actions or relations. Whenever READER encounters a noun phrase, it attempts to determine whether the corresponding referential representation already exists. If the noun phrase is coreferential with some part of the existing representation, READER relates the new information in the phrase or clause to the prior propositions about the referent. If the noun phrase is not coreferential, READER constructs a new referential representation of it. Thus, an important use of the referential level is to help interrelate information presented in different sentences of a text.

Schema-level processes   Like human readers, READER uses its knowledge of text structure to organize the information that it acquires. As described in Chapter 8 on text-level processing, READER has a text schema, called the *MECHANISM* schema, that represents its knowledge about technical passages that describe the functioning of a technological or biological mechanism. This schema, like others, is represented as a frame-and-slots structure. The slots designate the major kinds of information likely to be encountered, such as the device's *NAME,* its *GOAL,* the *PRINCIPLES* by which it operates, and *EXEMPLARS* of the mechanism. These slots are filled with appropriate information as it is encountered in the passage. If the text fails to provide information to fill in some slots that are needed for coherence, the schema contains default values for slot fillers, permitting READER to fill in gaps.

The amount of time that human readers and the READER model spend on different portions of a text depends on which schema slot is being filled. For example, readers spend extra time on more important types of information, like *NAMES* and *GOALS* and less time on *EXEMPLARS.* The schema can also be used as a retrieval plan to organize the sequence in which the stored information is recalled.

Forgetting in working memory   READER does not indefinitely store every piece of the representation it constructs. While there is no general decay function, several strategies and capacity limitations cause certain parts of the representation to be forgotten. An interpretation is forgotten (deactivated) if it loses the race to threshold to a competing interpretation. Also, the word-percepts that represent the exact wording are forgotten at the end of each sentence. This occurs in READER because the word-percept encodings of the next sentence reuse the numbered word-percept slots. In contrast to the forgetting of low-level information and subthreshold information, the high-level, suprathreshold information is not deactivated or overwritten, although interference from other information or retrieval failure may make it inaccessible.

The program   READER's procedural knowledge is contained in 225 productions, a few of which have been outlined in preceding chapters. Of these productions, about 20 are designed for handling word encoding and lexical access; 30, for surface syntactic analysis; 15, for agreement and other forms of consistency checking; 85, for semantic analysis; and 75, for text-schema processes. The referential-level productions are intermingled among the 160 productions for semantic and schema-level analysis. This description of the numbers of different types of productions is somewhat arbitrary because some productions are multifaceted. The CAPS/ READER model was written in the computer language MACLISP on a PDP-10 computer.

Evaluating the Model

A model like READER can be evaluated in several ways. Most obviously, the number of cycles that READER expends on each word of the passage can be compared to the amount of time a human reader spends looking at each word. A regression analysis on the mean gaze durations on each of the 140 words of the *Flywheels* passage, in which the independent variable is the number of READER processing cycles, accounts for 67 percent of the variance in the mean gaze durations. Much of this fit is attributable to the word-encoding and lexical access processes. In the absence of alternative models of this fine grain, it is difficult to evaluate the importance of this 67 percent. It does provide a benchmark against which other models can be compared, but it is not a very high benchmark. It is attainable by any model that accounts for word-length and word-frequency effects. READER does account for these effects, as well as accomplish the task for understanding, all in an internally consistent and plausible manner.

READER'S fit to the gaze-duration data can be improved. One very simple way to do so is to give READER the ability to sometimes encode a short function word (like *the, of,* and *and*) to the right of the current word without fixating it. Human readers do not directly fixate 60 percent of function words. Such skipping probably occurs when a fixation occurs close enough to the right-hand edge of a word to permit parafoveal encoding of an adjacent short word on the right.

The READER model can also be compared to the data generated by individual subjects. Currently, the model accounts for between 22 and 46 percent of the variance in the gaze durations of the individual human subjects. This percentage would be greatly increased if READER had the ability to process short function words without fixating them. Beyond this, to make the model fit individual readers better, it will be necessary to learn more about the individual readers' prior knowledge of the content area and their general reading skill. With these changes, the model would correspond much more closely to their individual data.

READER has several free parameters that can be tuned to bring the number of cycles and the gaze duration into closer correspondence. These parameters include the initial activation levels of propositions, the activation weights of productions (which are described later in this chapter), and various threshold levels. To the extent that these parameters might correspond to human characteristics that could be independently estimated, such a tuning exercise might be fruitful. However, since no such independent estimates are currently available, the tuning exercise would consist of a search of a large parameter space, with little psychological motivation.

Conventional questions about goodness-of-fit seem inappropriate because the model was constructed to fit the eye-fixation data, using plausible mechanisms sufficient to perform the task. An example of this is READER's lexical access mechanism, whose number of cycles to reach threshold is a logarithmic function of a word's frequency. Of course, the model fits the data in this regard. In other cases, a qualitative characteristic of the processing was inferred from the eye-fixation data using conventional statistical techniques; then that characteristic was made an inherent part of the model. For example, many results described throughout this book indicate that subjects use a strategy of immediate interpretation. As a result, the immediacy strategy was designed into the model, ensuring a good fit to this facet of the human performance.

Given this approach to designing a simulation, the issue to be evaluated is not so much the model's fit but rather the kind of model that emerges given the constraints imposed by the data. Chief among the characteristics that emerged are the **concurrence, immediacy,** and **collaboration** of the processes. The scope of the model, from perceptual to schema-level processes, is sufficiently broad to accommodate many properties of human reading. The specific mechanisms of word encoding, lexical access, syntactic, semantic, and referential analysis are compatible with a variety of detailed empirical results obtained in many different types of experiments. Moreover, the READER model provides a general framework that can continue to be filled in as more is learned about human reading.

A comparison of READER and other models   Another form of evaluation is to contrast READER with another psychological model of comprehension. The most prominent of such models is the one proposed by Kintsch and van Dijk (1978), although their model was intended to account for different phenomena and consequently has a very different focus. The Kintsch and van Dijk model describes the integration of successive clauses of a text, attempting to predict which propositions are more likely to be recalled. A major mechanism in the Kintsch and van Dijk model is the strategy of deciding what information to keep in working memory as the text is read: the most important points, the most recently mentioned points, or some combination thereof. Related to the information maintenance is the construction of high-level generalizations (macropropositions) that subsume some of the individual clauses of the text.

The model begins at the level of semantic analysis, with the assumption that the reader constructs a propositional representation of the semantic content of a text. The model proposes that only a limited amount of text (measured in terms of the number of underlying semantic-level propositions) is processed at a time because of the capacity limitations of working memory. Each cycle of processing consists of taking in some small number of new propositions from the text and attempting to connect them to previous propositions that are either currently in working memory or have already been shunted off to long-term memory. (Note that the Kintsch-van Dijk cycles are completely different than the READER cycles.) The connections among propositions are made on the basis of arguments that they share; if the currently processed proposition refers to the same concept as a proposition in working memory, a connection is made between the two propositions. After a group of new propositions has been processed in this way, all of the propositions in working memory are shunted off to long-term memory, with some probability of being retained there. Furthermore, a subset of all of the propositions in working memory is retained in working memory for the next cycle, while the remaining propositions are displaced from working memory.

The subset of propositions that is chosen to be held over in working memory for the next processing cycle includes those propositions that are more important and more recent. A proposition's importance is defined as its degree of interconnectedness with the preceding portion of the text. The recency factor is simply the recency of occurrence in the text. The Kintsch and van Dijk model predicts that the probability of recall of a proposition depends on the number of these processing cycles in working memory in which the proposition participates.

The model's prediction, in layman's terms, is that a clause that is related to many other clauses is likely to be recalled well. Also, new information is easier to integrate and recall if it is clearly related to information that the reader has recently encountered. In more formal terms, the model proposes a particular information-management strategy in working memory that produces this effect. In order to determine the model's predictions about which parts of a text are more likely to be recalled, the experimenter-theorist must construct a propositional representation of the semantic content of a text and determine by parameter-estimation techniques how many propositions can be held in working memory at one time. The predictions about the relative amount of recall of various portions of a text are generally accurate. This is because the degree of interconnectedness of a proposition is a good predictor of its recall.

The strength of the Kintsch and van Dijk model is its ability to predict the relative amount of recall of different parts of a text (such as the levels effect described in Chapter 8 on extended texts) using a principled evaluation of the text content. The approach somewhat resembles the prediction of story recall on the basis of an analysis of the causal structure of a story (Trabasso, Secco, & van den Broek, 1984). In addition, the Kintsch and van Dijk model has some interesting hypotheses about the management of clause-level information in working memory, on the assumption that not all of the information from a text can be represented in working memory and that strategic choices have to be made about what to keep in an activated state and what to relegate to long-term memory.

The shortcomings of the Kintsch and van Dijk model are not errors of commission but of incompleteness. The model deals well with only one or two levels of comprehension (semantic analysis and the text-schema level) and not with many others (word encoding, lexical access, syntactic analysis). A more recent version of the model (van Dijk & Kintsch, 1983) expands its scope in several directions. In particular, this new version pays more attention to the referential level. Another shortcoming of the original model is that the critical semantic analysis of the text into propositions is not completely specified, although there are guidelines for doing the analysis.

The Kintsch and van Dijk model is so different than READER that it does not make sense to ask which is better. Nevertheless, the consideration of another model illustrates the foci and strengths of the different approaches. The Kintsch and van Dijk model focuses on text integration, information management in working memory, and the determinants of recall. READER focuses on the time course of comprehension and the coordination of many levels of processing. Moreover, since READER is instantiated as a computer program, it concretely specifies how each of its component processes operates.

Comparison to other computer models So many computer programs have been written to understand language that it is not useful to single out one of them for comparison to READER. Almost all of the successful programs have some shared qualities that distinguish them from several failed attempts at computer translation in the 1960s (see Rich, 1983; Winograd, 1983). We will identify some of the criteria of success and comment on READER's grasp of some of the criterial qualities.

The successful programs seem to share three important characteristics. First, the programs have a rich background knowledge of the **referential situation**. One of the first successful programs understood sentences that referred to a world of toy blocks consisting of cubes, cylinders, spheres, and boxes (Winograd, 1972). The program was given previous knowledge about the referents, such as their shapes, colors, and possible physical positions (e.g., a sphere can be placed on top of a cube, but a cube cannot be placed on top of a sphere). A basic conceptual grasp of the topic seems to be a necessary precondition for language understanding by a computer program.

A second criterion of success is that the program *does not rely exclusively* on one level of linguistic analysis for determining the interpretation of a sentence. For example, programs that focus exclusively on the analysis of syntax run into difficulty whenever the syntax is complex, imperfect, or ambiguous. The successful programs often have recourse to more than one avenue to produce an interpretation; when one level of analysis (such as syntax) presents a difficulty, they can use another avenue, such as semantics.

The third characteristic of the successful language understanding programs is that they tend to have a richly **interconnected network** of word meanings. Semantic networks are used to interpret words in each other's contexts.

These three characteristics can be found in READER. Moreover, it is tempting to speculate that they are also important properties of human comprehension.

The Psychological Basis of CAPS

In this section, we will provide a rationale and a broad description of the CAPS framework and then relate several of the important mechanisms within CAPS to properties of human thinking.

Building a model of a mechanism sometimes requires that a model of the mechanism's environment be built, as well. For example, building a working model of a hydroelectric dam also requires the building of a model of the water channels, reservoir, and land mass around the dam. Similarly the operation of a model of a mental process, such as comprehension, must be examined within a model of its environmental terrain.

The environment of a comprehension model is the natural landscape of the mind, consisting of storage resources (such as working memory) and processing characteristics (such as parallelism) that constrain the comprehension process. A model of that environment, called *CAPS*, was designed in collaboration with our colleague Robert Thibadeau, who was its principal architect.

A production system was selected as the general architecture for the model for the following reasons (Newell & Simon, 1972):

1. Production systems have a working memory that can model human short-term memory.
2. Individual productions may correspond to basic processes in human thought.

3. The modularity of the procedural knowledge in a production system—each production constituting the smallest module—makes it easy to augment the corpus of procedural knowledge.
4. In both production systems and humans, behavior is determined by internal processes (acting on the working memory) as well as external stimuli (that cause new elements to be inserted in the working memory).
5. The use of production system models has generally been successful; those developed by Newell (1980) and his colleagues (McCracken, 1978) demonstrate that production systems are able to perform a complex, multilevel, knowledge-based task, such as understanding human speech.

In spite of the benefits of production systems as psychological models, current production systems are, at best, only first approximations of the human architecture. Many new kinds of production systems that are intended as psychological modeling tools are continually being developed (e.g., Anderson, 1983; Laird & Newell, 1983). Undoubtedly, the systems will require modification as research progresses.

The CAPS Architecture

CAPS shares the main features of other production systems. In addition, it has some innovative features. We will briefly summarize the main innovations and then return to a more detailed discussion of the CAPS features. The main innovations include:

1. The system's declarative knowledge base consists of propositional information in the form of concept-relation-concept triples, constituting a semantic network.
2. Every proposition has an associated numerical activation level. The condition elements of a production specify the minimum activation level of a proposition that satisfies the condition.
3. Activation can be directed by a production from one proposition to another. Each production has an *activation weight,* a multiplier indicating what proportion of the source proposition's activation level should be added to the destination proposition's activation level.
4. The conditions of all the productions are compared against the knowledge in working memory, and *all* of the productions whose conditions are satisfied perform their actions concurrently. Therefore, CAPS permits parallel processing.
5. The knowledge representations are fully accessible in working memory to all processes, so that different processes can collaborate by using each others' partial and final results. Low-level processes can influence high-level ones and vice versa.

Figure 9.2 schematically depicts the relation of the READER model to the CAPS environment. Some aspects of CAPS' innovations have also appeared in other contemporary production systems (Anderson, Kline, & Lewis, 1977; Langley & Neches, 1981; Newell, 1980; Rosenbloom, 1980).

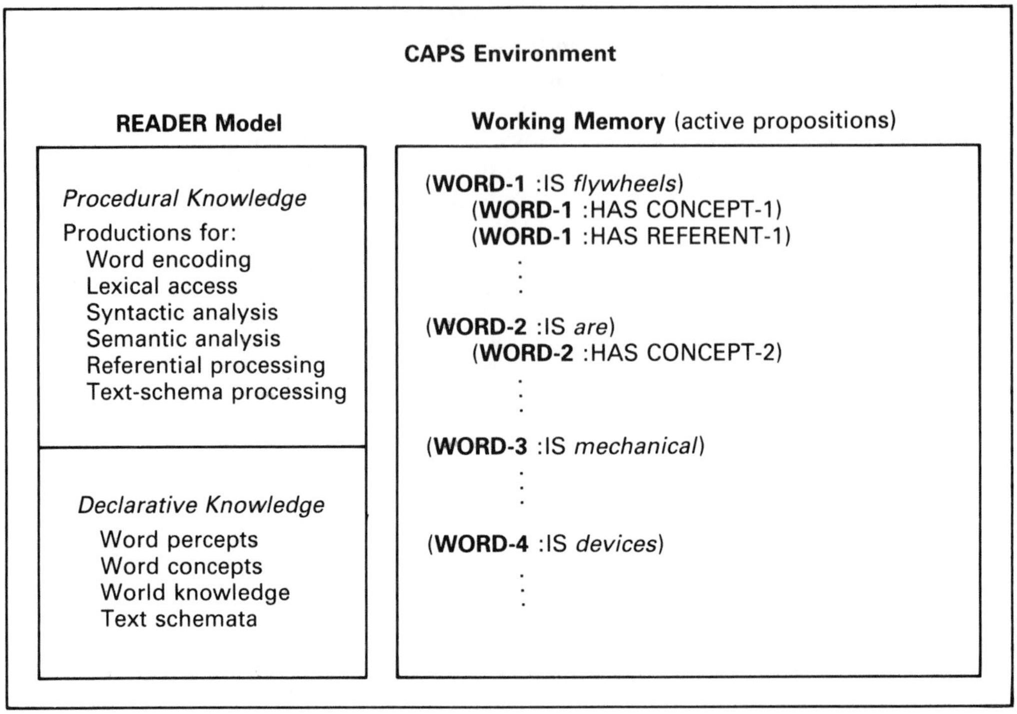

CAPS Environment

READER Model   **Working Memory** (active propositions)

Procedural Knowledge

Productions for:
  Word encoding
  Lexical access
  Syntactic analysis
  Semantic analysis
  Referential processing
  Text-schema processing

Declarative Knowledge

  Word percepts
  Word concepts
  World knowledge
  Text schemata

(**WORD-1** :IS *flywheels*)
   (**WORD-1** :HAS CONCEPT-1)
   (**WORD-1** :HAS REFERENT-1)
       :

(**WORD-2** :IS *are*)
   (**WORD-2** :HAS CONCEPT-2)
       :

(**WORD-3** :IS *mechanical*)
       :

(**WORD-4** :IS *devices*)
       :

Figure 9.2   The READER model operates within the CAPS processing environment, which includes long-term procedural knowledge in the form of productions, declarative knowledge, and the currently activated propositions that constitute working memory. In this illustration, the propositions depicted within working memory are part of the representation of *Flywheels are mechanical devices.*

Activation Levels of Knowledge Elements

In many approaches to the psychology of thinking, it has been useful to consider knowledge as having an activation level that corresponds roughly to a level of availability; moreover, the activation level can vary continuously from low to high levels. Activation levels can be used to explain how related concepts influence each other. For example, in Chapter 3, in the discussion of the mental lexicon, we described how activation has been used to explain how the presence of a word, such as *doctor,* raises the activation level of the underlying concept, DOCTOR, along with the activation levels of related concepts, such as NURSE, although to a lesser degree (Meyer & Schvaneveldt, 1971). The notion of one concept activating another can be traced to the connectionist theories of thought of the nineteenth century and earlier, and it is also found in more recent semantic network models proposed in psychology and artificial intelligence (Anderson, 1976; Collins & Loftus, 1975; Findler, 1979).

It is usually assumed that some time must elapse before the activation of one element affects the activation level of another (Posner & Snyder, 1975). Thus, the theoretical construct of activation can explain how the availability of a piece of knowledge may change over time because of the activation of related knowledge. In particular, this mechanism can account for some of the types of context effects described in Chapters 2 and 3; a prose context (a particular word or the general topic of the passage) can make semantically related concepts temporarily more available and consequently speed the processing of words that refer to those concepts.

Directed activation   The activation level of a proposition is increased as supporting evidence is accumulated, so that knowledge grows over time. What makes the activation level of an element increase is the output of various productions that direct activation from one proposition to another. For example, if the knowledge that the current word is *the* has a high activation level, then activation is directed to a proposition that the current constituent is part of a noun phrase and that some later word in this phrase will be a noun.

A major purpose of READER was to simulate the time course of many psychological processes. In particular, the model had to account for the finding that the same ostensible operation takes different amounts of time on different occasions. For example, the model had to account for the finding that the operation that accesses the meaning of a word takes longer in the case of the infrequent word *sable* than in the case of the more frequent word *table*. In a conventional production system and in most other computer programs, the same operation would simply retrieve the associated meaning in each case, making it difficult to explain why lexical access should take longer for *sable* than for *table*.

The solution proposed by the READER model is that knowledge is not just present or absent from working memory but can vary in activation level. Moreover, the activation level can rise as productions repeatedly fire over several cycles, each time incrementing the activation level of a proposition. In this scheme, the knowledge would grow over time. The duration of the growth process—that is, the number of iterations required by one or more productions to raise the activation of some proposition to threshold—can thus be related to the human processing time. The CAPS production system provides a means of modeling the time course of information integration.

The increase in a proposition's activation level over time is somewhat analogous to the accumulation of evidence in a court trial. A juror may have no initial bias at the beginning of a trial, but as pieces of evidence are introduced throughout the proceeding, he may gradually feel more confidence in one decision or another. The juror integrates different kinds of evidence concerning the motivation, opportunity, and alibi of the defendant. Similarly, the change in a proposition's activation level reflects the developing evidence for the proposition from one or more ongoing comprehension processes.

An example   The changes to the activation level of a proposition (including an increase or decrease of a level or the addition or deletion of an entire proposition) occur as part of the action of a production.

Table 9.2 The activity in working memory produced by the firings of two sample productions

Conditions and Actions of Two Sample Productions

Production Name	Condition(s)	Minimum Activation	Activation Weight	Action
Gamma:	(Proposition A)	<.5>	$\xrightarrow{.4}$	(Proposition B)
Delta:	(Proposition B)	<.8>	$\xrightarrow{.5}$	(Proposition C)

Initial Contents of Working Memory: (Proposition A) <1.0>

CYCLE 1

Gamma: (Proposition A) <1.0> $\xrightarrow{.4}$ (Proposition B) <.4>

Resulting Contents of Working Memory: (Proposition A) <1.0>
(Proposition B) <.4>

CYCLE 2

Gamma: (Proposition A) <1.0> $\xrightarrow{.4}$ (Proposition B) <.8>

Resulting Contents of Working Memory: (Proposition A) <1.0>
(Proposition B) <.8>

CYCLE 3

Gamma: (Proposition A) <1.0> $\xrightarrow{.4}$ (Proposition B) <1.2>

Delta: (Proposition B)   <.8> $\xrightarrow{.5}$ (Proposition C) <.4>

Resulting Contents of Working Memory: (Proposition A) <1.0>
(Proposition B) <1.2>
(Proposition C) <.4>

Consider a hypothetical production called *Gamma* that is shown at the top of Table 9.2. Gamma has as its condition that Proposition A must be present in working memory with an activation level of at least 0.5; its action is to increment the activation level of Proposition B. The size of the increment is obtained by multiplying the production's **activation weight** by the mean activation level of some or all of the conditions. Thus, if Proposition A is present in working memory with an activation level of at least 0.5, Production Gamma will multiply the activation level of Proposition A by the activation weight of 0.4 and add the result to the existing activation level of Proposition B. Table 9.2 also shows another sample production called *Delta;* when Proposition B is present in working memory with an activation level of at least 0.8, then Production Delta increments the activation level of Proposition C.

Table 9.2 shows the sequence of events that Gamma and Delta would produce if working memory initially contained nothing but Proposition A with an activation level of 1.0. On the first cycle, the initial contents of working memory satisfy the condition of Gamma. Gamma's action is to create Proposition B (because Proposition B is not already present in working memory) with an implicit activation level of zero, and then increment that level by 0.4, obtained by multiplying the activation level of Proposition A (1.0) by Gamma's activation weight (0.4). On the second cycle, the resulting contents of working memory again satisfy only Gamma, resulting in Proposition B's activation level being incremented to 0.8. On the third cycle, the presence of Proposition B with an activation level of 0.8 satisfies Delta's condition, while Proposition A again satisfies Gamma's condition, so both Delta and Gamma fire in the third cycle. Delta's action creates Proposition C at an activation level of 0.4, obtained by multiplying Proposition B's activation level (0.8) by Delta's activation weight (0.5). Gamma's action again increments the activation level of Proposition B. This example illustrates how the knowledge represented by Proposition B grows over several cycles as its activation level rises until it is high enough to trigger another production.

The activations in READER allow information to be integrated from different processes, such as the syntactic and lexical processes. For example, the syntactic contexts *the* and *they* alter the final interpretation given to a subsequent ambiguous word, *rose*—in *the rose,* it is interpreted as a noun; in *they rose,* it is interpreted as a verb. The preceding contexts establish differing expectations for which word class will follow at some later point: either a noun or a verb. The expectation in each case is expressed as a proposition with a relatively low activation level. The word *the* activates an expectation that a noun will follow at some point; when *rose* is encoded, both its noun and verb interpretations are activated to some degree. However, the prior activation of the noun expectation contributes to its interpretation as a noun. Thus, several sources of evidence can converge to activate one interpretation as opposed to another.

Activation can also be directed from a proposition back to itself. Self-activation of a mental representation is an old concept in psychological theories, from Hartley's notion of vibrating ideas (Boring, 1950) to Hebb's proposal of reverberating cell assemblies (Hebb, 1949); it has been used to explain the persistence of a mental representation when the external stimulus is no longer present. READER uses a self-activation production during lexical access. The encoding of a word-percept triggers the self-activation of the corresponding word meaning. The self-activation of a word meaning continues over several cycles until its activation level or the activation level of a competing word meaning reaches threshold.

Directed activation can be contrasted with *spreading* activation, a mechanism used in several other models to account for the activation of one concept by another (Anderson, 1976; Collins & Loftus, 1975). Directed activation in CAPS is propagated from a source proposition to other propositions, as specified by the productions. The productions establish the connectivity among propositions by relating a condition proposition to an action proposition. By contrast, spreading activation is propagated from a source to all of the other nodes to which it is directly linked in the network. Another contrast is that directed activation, like all other processes in the CAPS system, is manipulated by productions, making it qualitatively the same as other processes. By contrast, spreading activation is often treated as an autonomous, qualitatively different process, accomplished by a special mechanism that operates in the background of other thought processes.

Changes in reading rate   The processing rate of the entire system can be modified by altering the rate at which knowledge grows. This rate is altered by a special production, called **REWEIGHT,** that changes the activation weights associated with a group of productions. A decrement in activation weights will slow the overall processing rate because it will take longer for the knowledge developed by the affected productions to reach threshold. The REWEIGHT production is evoked when READER encounters what it considers to be an important or unimportant part of the text. Slowing down by decreasing the activation weights can be construed as being more careful about accepting evidence and hence reading more carefully.

The REWEIGHT production makes not only a quantitative change but also a qualitative change in comprehension by changing the relative rates of different sets of subprocesses. In particular, slowing down the reading rate with the REWEIGHT production makes the decrease in activation weights relatively greater for the main interpretive processes than for the processes that check for consistency among various parts of the interpretation. These consistency-checking processes are a form of quality control; for example, they include checking for subject-verb agreement, for unique fillers of single-argument predicates, and the like. The larger influence of the consistency-checking processes at slower reading rates increases the probability that incorrect interpretations of the text will be rejected. Thus, READER's slower reading of the important parts of the text not only emulates the human change in reading rate but also contributes to the type of superior comprehension and recall of the important parts that human readers exhibit.

Modeling the Time Course of Comprehension

The detailed timing information obtained in eye-fixation studies of reading provides some fairly precise estimates of the time course of the underlying comprehension processes. A computer-simulation model that is intended to exhibit a time course similar to that of human readers must provide a way to model processing time. The CAPS system provides this facility by allowing the behavior of a computer model to be segmented into a sequence of episodes (each episode corresponding to the processing of one word of text) and by providing a measure of the time expended on each episode. The measure is the number of CAPS/READER cycles spent on a given episode. Thus, the computer model's processing time on each word of a text can be compared to that of a human reader.

Three main factors can influence the number of CAPS cycles that READER spends on a word. First, the dependencies among productions set a lower bound on the number of cycles required to complete a given activity. For example, in Table 9.2, the condition of Production Delta is a proposition that is created by the action of Production Gamma. Delta cannot fire until Gamma has fired. One example of this kind of dependency in the READER model is that the processes that access the meaning of a word are often not evoked until the encoding of the printed word has been completed, simply because the encoding processes must first produce most of the information that evokes lexical access.

The parallel aspects of CAPS can also affect the time course of processing. Since the processing on a given word continues until all levels of analysis have been completed, the total number of cycles on a word will be determined by the longest process—that is, the one requiring the most cycles to reach completion. When no further productions from any level of processing are satisfied, the processing of a particular word terminates and the next word is read. Thus, the total number of cycles spent on a word is determined by the process that requires the most cycles. As the number of processes operating on a given word increases, the probability increases that one of them will be particularly long, involving many cycles. For example, if two words are processed identically except that one of them evokes the filling of a text schema slot while the other one does not, then the one initiating slot filling may require more cycles.

The third major factor affecting the number of cycles spent on a word is the rate at which knowledge grows. The number of cycles it will take for a proposition's activation level to reach threshold depends on the proposition's base activation level, the threshold level to be reached, and the production's activation weight.

Immediacy of Interpretation

A major constraint on the processing strategy was that the simulation had to use the strategy of immediate interpretation, trying to process each word as far as possible at all levels of processing before proceeding to the next word. **Immediacy of interpretation** follows rather directly from the CAPS production system architecture. Immediacy is instantiated by having each production fire as soon as its conditions are satisfied. There is no mandatory wait-and-see comprehension strategy. The productions fire as soon as they get the chance. If circumstances make waiting unavoidable, such that a word is uninterpretable without the benefit of the context that follows, then the system is capable of delaying the processing of that word. But it does so out of necessity, not out of design. Of course, it would be possible to construct a nonimmediate CAPS model, but a production system architecture particularly lends itself to immediacy of interpretation.

Functional Parallelism

In a complex but highly practiced task like reading, it is likely that there are concurrent processes, which is permitted in CAPS. Any number of productions can fire at one time, as long as their conditions are satisfied. In skilled reading, this means that several types of computations may co-occur. For example, having encoded *hammer* in a particular context and accessed the concept, the model can simultaneously compute its syntactic status as a noun, its semantic role as an instrument of the action, and its coreference with a previously mentioned hammer. Generally, each level of processing (such as syntactic analysis) requires several cycles to accomplish its function, so the concurrence between a few streams of processing spans several cycles. The functional parallelism applies not only between levels of processing but also within levels. For example, several facets of word encoding—related to visual features, letters, or syllables—could be concurrent.

Although the CAPS architecture allows concurrence among levels, it also permits sequentiality. One set of productions will follow another if the conditions in the later productions require that the earlier productions have completed their operation. Thus, there can be functional parallelism between some levels of processing and sequentiality between others.

Early information-processing models of reading were very bottom-up and sequential. Such models proposed that the level dealing with the lowest features (e.g., letters) operated first, while all other levels waited. Then the letter level would transmit its results to the next level, and that level would operate, while all higher ones would wait, and so on. The flow of information was exclusively from lower-level processes to higher-level processes, until the information was fed into the highest level. In this kind of bottom-up model, the information that was accumulated from the previous parts of the text (that is, the knowledge of the preceding context) or the reader's previous knowledge of the content could not influence the lower-level processes but could only combine with their outputs at the higher levels. Such strictly bottom-up models cannot account for the phenomenon of higher levels of processing influencing lower levels, such as the word-superiority effect described in Chapter 2 on word encoding. People are better at recognizing a letter when it is embedded in a word than when it is isolated. This effect shows that higher levels do not wait until lower levels have finished sending their information upwards; in fact, the higher level might send information downwards. This is called a top-down influence.

It is likely that similar top-down influences also exist between other levels of processing in reading (Levy, 1981). A suitable processing architecture must permit this form of interaction among levels, as the CAPS/READER model does. It is this type of interaction that permits a reader's domain knowledge or reading goals or knowledge of a preceding context to influence a low-level process.

Collaboration   One consequence of the parallel processing architecture is the potential for collaboration among processes. The word that is more commonly used to describe the mutual influence among processes is *interaction*, but that word fails to convey the mutual support denoted by **collaboration.** Some experiments pit one process against another to elucidate the nature of the interaction. But in normal reading, the processes tend to work with each other, not against each other. Information from different processes generally converges. What does sometimes occur in normal reading is that the information pertaining to one level of processing is weak, making it difficult to make a definitive interpretation of a unit of text based on just that one weak source of information alone. In these cases, collaborative interpretation means that reliance can shift to whatever process has strong information.

One way that the processes in READER collaborate to understand a portion of text is by activating their intermediate hypotheses or final results, making this potentially useful information immediately available to all the other processes. Another form of collaboration occurs when two or more processes converge on establishing a given piece of knowledge by jointly incrementing its activation level to threshold, when neither process alone could have effectively done so. Furthermore, two processes can collaborate not only bilaterally, supporting each other, but also by jointly supporting a third process.

Some recent language-understanding systems, such as the HEARSAY program (Reddy & Newell, 1974), have also explored some forms of concurrent processing but among relatively large modules, such as complete semantic and syntactic analysis of a phrase. After all of the modules in HEARSAY have completed their analysis on a phrase, they then collaborate on determining the phrase's interpretation.

By contrast, CAPS allows for collaboration among processes much more frequently. The potential for interprocess communication exists on every cycle, which, in the case of the READER model, occurs several times during the processing of each word. For example, in READER, the knowledge from one level of processing (such as the semantic analysis) can, in principle, influence another (such as the referential analysis) before the other has been completed. Similarly, McClelland and Rumelhart (1981) have proposed a parallel-processing model of word recognition with feedback between letter-processing levels and word-processing levels.

Although READER does have the potential for total concurrence and interaction, the informational constraints among processes impose some sequentiality. For example, the data suggest that word encoding generally precedes the other processes. Hence, there is orderliness in the type and extent of the interaction, and not all processes interact with all others.

Automaticity

The components of a skill are considered to be automatic if they meet several criteria:

1. They are evoked by a stimulus without conscious effort.
2. They require little processing capacity for execution.
3. They allow for functional parallelism.

The first criterion refers to the fact that automatic processes are evoked by a particular stimulus, without any conscious effort or decision (Posner & Snyder, 1975; Shiffrin & Schneider, 1977). In fact, it is difficult to consciously suppress an automatic process, a point that is illustrated by the Stroop task, which was described in Chapter 1. In this task, the subject names the color of the ink used to print a color term. Subjects take longer if the ink color mismatches the term than if it matches. For example, if red ink is used to write the word *blue,* subjects take a long time to say "red." Subjects cannot completely suppress the processes that automatically encode and access the printed word, even though accessing the word is detrimental to their performance. Similarly, it is very difficult to hear a simple sentence while suppressing the processes that automatically understand it.

The reading processes most likely to become automatic are the relatively low-level ones, such as letter and word encoding and lexical access. Consider, for example, word encoding, which may be conceptualized as a set of computations that operate on visual features, letters, syllables, and words. LaBerge and Samuels (1974) proposed that an important aspect of automaticity in word perception is the ability to execute these computations in parallel.

Processes become automatic if they are used extensively. In Chapter 11 on beginning reading, we will argue that the time spent practicing a task is an extremely important determinant of skilled performance, whether it is reading, typing, or proving mathematical theorems. The total amount of time spent on reading is one of the largest determinants of reading performance; in fact, in some large studies, the time spent on reading was the only schooling-related variable that correlated with reading achievement (Lerner, 1981).

Automaticity in CAPS   There are several ways in which some parts of a production system can become more automatic with practice. Automaticity can arise when several productions that are repeatedly used in a fixed sequence become compressed (compiled) into a single production. For example, if three productions repeatedly fire in the sequence A-then-B-then-C, then a single new production that subsumes all three of them can be constructed. Although READER does not have the capability of creating such new productions, other production system models do acquire automaticity with practice by constructing their own new compiled productions (Anderson, 1982).

Another way that automaticity can arise is by a shift from sequential to parallel execution of several productions. The shift can occur after repeated experience of an A-then-B sequence if the enabling condition of Production B is changed to allow B to fire when a partial rather than the final product of A is present in working memory. This is analogous to a painter starting to paint a house before the carpenter has completed constructing it. This form of automaticity could be acquired in a parallel system like CAPS, although READER's parallelism was built in.

The Generality of CAPS and READER

It is fitting to conclude a chapter about a theory of reading by noting that reading comprehension is just one of many types of intellectual feats humans perform. In addition to impressive linguistic abilities, people have other kinds of intellectual abilities, such as visual thinking, mathematical thinking, deductive and inductive reasoning, and analogical reasoning. In the widespread discussion of the diversity of mental processes (e.g., verbal-pictorial, analytic-Gestalt, left hemisphere-right hemisphere), there has been much emphasis on the distinctions between various families of processes and relatively little consideration of the commonalities. Within almost any processing system, it is possible to categorize the basic processes into families, all of which share some characteristic. For example, in a standard digital computer, one can distinguish between arithmetic operations and logical operations. But they work in concert within a common architecture, communicate with each other, and collaborate on performing tasks that require the participation of both kinds of operations.

While it is certainly important to categorize the types of operations available within the human processing system, it is equally important to consider the larger system that can embrace different types of processes. The READER simulation presented here, along with other CAPS models of nonlinguistic thinking, such as a model of mental rotation (Just & Carpenter, 1985), provides a demonstration that both linguistic and spatial processes of considerable complexity can be accommodated within a single processing environment. Syntactic analysis of a noun phrase and mental rotation of a complex three-dimensional object can both be expressed within a CAPS framework and still comfortably conform to human performance characteristics. Reading occurs in the context of many other types of thinking, and they are all performed by one mind.

Summary

Each of the levels of comprehension in the READER model operates as a well-defined set of procedures expressed as productions. The productions and the information from different levels are all of the same general form; consequently, processes at various levels (such as the syntactic, semantic, and referential) can interact. The products of both their partial and final computations are available to other levels of processing, and they have the potential of operating in parallel.

The READER model has four major strengths. First, the simulation provides a model of the individual mechanisms of word encoding, lexical access, semantic, syntactic, referential, and text-level processes. Second, the simulation provides an account of how the individual processes are coordinated. Third, the mechanisms of READER perform the task of comprehension well enough to extract the information from a text in a form that can be later recalled or used in other tasks, demonstrating the sufficiency of the model. The model also provides a good account of the gaze durations of human readers who are reading a technical passage; READER takes more cycles to process those parts of the text on which human readers spend more time. The fourth and perhaps the most important contribution of the READER model is its general architecture. The immediacy, parallelism, and collaboration of READER reflect the fundamental properties of skilled human reading.

READER operates within the CAPS framework of information processing. CAPS has several properties that are first approximations of the main features in the human processing system. The processes are expressed as productions; the productions may correspond to basic units of procedural knowledge. The productions operate on a declarative knowledge base in which information is expressed in a propositional format. Individual propositions can vary in their availability, which is reflected in their activation level. The action of a production is to create or delete propositions or to change the activation level of existing propositions. The design of CAPS lends itself to the immediacy, parallelism, collaboration, and automaticity of skilled intellectual performance such as reading.

Suggested Readings

More information about CAPS and the READER model is provided in the articles by Thibadeau, Just, and Carpenter (1982) and Just and Thibadeau (1984). Other relevant models of text comprehension include the framework described by Rumelhart (1977b), the description of the HEARSAY model (Reddy & Newell, 1974), and the theory outlined by van Dijk and Kintsch (1983). Another model that has some similarities to READER in architecture but is applied primarily to word encoding is described in two articles by McClelland and Rumelhart (1981; and Rumelhart & McClelland, 1982). A general discussion of the architecture of human cognition is provided by Anderson's book (1983).

Part Two

Variability in Reading

10

Orthography: Its Structure and Effects on Reading

Most adults have had some exposure to more than one writing system, either formally, while learning a foreign language, or informally, for example, from reading signs when visiting another country. Some writing systems look similar to English, and it may even be possible for an English reader to decipher some foreign words. For instance, a reader may be able to figure out some Spanish words in Mexico City or French words on the street signs of Montreal. But many writing systems appear strange and incredibly complex. Monolingual English readers cannot figure out the names of the foods written in Chinese on a menu or the evacuation instructions written in Eskimo on an Air Canada plane. One of the purposes of this chapter is to explore the ways in which such writing systems vary and how they affect the psychological processes in reading.

Some differences among writing systems are actually reflections of the differences in oral languages. For example, spoken English and spoken Italian differ in the syntactic structure of sentences and in the words or phrases that are used for similar concepts. Many, although not all, of these differences also exist in written English and Italian. The primary focus of this chapter is not on properties that are common to a spoken and written language. For that reason, the chapter will primarily focus on features that are more specific to the written languages, rather than on features that are common to the written and spoken language.

The major features of writing systems that will be explored are the graphic features of the characters and the rules for writing sounds and meanings. These features of a writing system influence reading processes, particularly the processes used to translate printed words into mental concepts. The relevant processes— word encoding and lexical access—were discussed with respect to English in Chapters 2 and 3. This chapter will examine how these processes may vary for readers of different writing systems.

Finally, the properties of a writing system can influence how children learn to read. Some of the major influences will be considered in this chapter; but a more detailed analysis of beginning reading in English will be presented in Chapter 11.

Overview The structure of a writing system is called its **orthography,** which refers to both the graphic features of the characters and the rules for writing sounds and meanings. In the first part of the chapter, **Properties of Orthographies,** we will discuss the ways in which different orthographies vary along both of these dimensions.

English has an alphabetic orthography, which means that the characters typically represent the spoken language at the level of basic sounds. For example, the letter *t* typically represents the sound /*t*/. However, it is also apparent that this generalization oversimplifies a very complex system of symbol-sound relations. In the second section, **A Description of English Orthography,** we will describe the characteristics of the English writing system, particularly the extent to which the relations between letters and sounds are regular.

After describing some of the properties of writing systems, we will turn to the question of how these properties influence fluent reading in a section called **Cross-linguistic Comparisons: Reading in Chinese and English.** This section compares the processes of fluent Chinese readers to those of fluent English readers to examine how the properties of the orthography influence word encoding, lexical access, and speech recoding.

In the fourth section, **The Effect of the Orthography on Learning to Read,** we will consider how the orthography influences reading acquisition. We will address three major issues: (1) the interpretation of data on the reading achievement of children from countries having different types of orthographies; (2) how the regularity of an orthography might influence the acquisition of reading skill; and (3) how teaching practices can be adapted to the properties of the orthography.

In a final section, **The Creation and Revision of Orthographies,** we will briefly explore how writing systems are developed for newly literate societies. Newly created writing systems are typically alphabetic. However, beyond that generalization, decisions about the design of a new writing system are based primarily on cultural concerns, rather than cognitive or educational concerns.

Properties of Orthographies

Writing systems vary along two major dimensions: (1) the graphic properties of the characters and (2) the level at which the writing expresses the spoken language. One way to appreciate both dimensions of difference is to examine how the same idea would be expressed in a variety of orthographies. Figure 10.1 presents the same sentence, *Everyone has the right to education,* in 16 languages (adapted from Gray, 1956). Even a brief inspection of the figure is sufficient to reveal the first dimension of difference, namely, variation among the characters used in different writing systems. The most familiar are the characters used in English and many modern European writing systems; in striking contrast to these familiar characters are the much less familiar characters used in the Middle Eastern, Oriental, and Indian writing systems.

The second major dimension of difference—the level at which the characters represent the spoken language—is not as easily inferred from Figure 10.1. In alphabetic orthographies, such as English, the characters typically represent basic sounds of the spoken language. But a written language can map onto the spoken language at other levels. In the Japanese sentence in Figure 10.1, some characters represent syllables (which are typically composed of a vowel and at least one con-

English	Everyone has the right to education
French	Toute personne a droit à l'éducation
Spanish	Toda persona tiene derecho a la educación
Icelandic	Hver maður á rétt til menntunar
Russian	Каждый человек имеет право на образование
Macedonian	Секој има право на школување
Greek	Πᾶν πρόσωπον ἔχει δι αίωμα ἐκπαιδεύσεως
Hebrew	כל אדם זכאי לחינוך
Arabic	لكل إنسان الحق في التربية
Japanese	何人も，教育を受みる権利を有する
Chinese	人人皆有受敎育之權
Thai	ทุกคนมีสิทธิในการศึกษา การศึกษาจะต้องให้เปล่าอย่างน้อยในขั้นปฐมศึกษาและการศึกษาชั้นหลักมูล
Tamil[1]	ஒவ்வொரு வருக்கும் படிப்பதற்கு உரிமையுண்டு
Telegu[2]	ప్రతి వ్యక్తికిని విద్యకు హక్కు-న్నది
Malayalam[2]	വിദ്യാഭ്യാസത്തിനു എ ല്ലാവക്കം അവകാശമുണ്ടു
Oriya[3]	ଶିକ୍ଷାଲଭ କରବାର ଅଧିକାର ପ୍ରତେ୍ୟକକର ଅଛି

[1]Southern India, Sri Lanka
[2]Southern India
[3]Northeastern India

Figure 10.1 The sentence *Everyone has the right to education* in 16 different languages. An inspection of these sentences reveals some of the large differences among various writing systems. *Source:* Adapted from W. S. Gray, *The teaching of reading and writing: An international study* (Chicago: Scott, 1956), pp. 24–25. © UNESCO 1958. Reproduced by permission of UNESCO.

sonantal phoneme). In the Chinese sentence in Figure 10.1, each character represents a morpheme, a relatively invariant unit of speech that has some associated meaning.

Differences among the Written Characters

One of the most striking differences among orthographies is the graphic symbols that are used to express the characters. There are many different alphabets. The most familiar to English readers is the Latin alphabet. But most adults are also familiar with at least some characters from the Cyrillic alphabet (used to write Russian) and the Greek alphabet (often used in mathematical notation).

The graphic features of alphabets differ in the visual discriminations they require of a reader. For instance, English readers must master distinctions among four relatively similar characters: *b, d, p,* and *q.* In Hebrew, the entire character set may be considered even more homogeneous, since it almost entirely lacks ascenders (*d, t, b*), descenders (*p, q, g*), and capital letter forms (Feitelson, 1973). Some orthographies require fine discriminations among letters because they use **diacritics,** small marks that are appended to the character to change its phonetic value. An example of a diacritic is the French *cedilla,* a hooklike mark at the bottom of the letter *c,* ç, which indicates it is to be pronounced as /*s*/. Hebrew uses diacritical marks to signal different vowels; consequently, an extremely minor graphic variation, such as the location of a single dot, may signal several different sounds.

The difficulty of the visual discrimination required by an alphabet can present problems for the beginning reader; children often find it difficult to remember which sound is signalled by *d* and *b,* for example. However, once the reader has mastered the orthography and learned to recognize words, this low-level factor has no general influence on reading speed. Reading speeds across many languages are very similar for fluent adult readers (Gray, 1956), suggesting that reading speed is generally uninfluenced by the specific properties of the character set.

Alphabets vary in the number of characters they contain. English has 26 characters (52 characters if all lower-case and upper-case characters are distinguished). The Indic family of scripts (used from the Middle East to Java) has up to 250 characters, although the set has been reduced and simplified to adapt it to mechanical reproduction (Grimes & Gordon, 1980). Arabic script has about 30 letter forms, but most have several variants, depending upon their position in a word (initial, medial, or final) or whether they stand alone (Ryan, 1980). The number of characters in an alphabet is more likely to influence early reading than skilled reading. Beginning reading programs in languages that have a large number of characters initially focus on a particular subset of characters that are usually either the most common or most discriminable. An example of such focus is the primary use of lower-case letters in beginning reading instruction in English.

The writing system is more than a collection of isolated characters. The nature of the system also depends on the distribution of characters—both the positions they can occupy and the characters with which they co-occur. Some orthographies use *digraphs,* pairs of letters that represent a single phoneme, such as *th* for /θ/ in *thigh.* Similarly, several languages contrast long and short vowels by the use of double and single letters.

Another property of orthographies is the direction of writing. English is written left to right; Hebrew is written right to left; and Chinese is typically written vertically, rather than horizontally. The existence of these different directions illustrates the general flexibility of skilled reading.

Another difference among orthographies is the units that are segmented by spaces. The spacing may be on the basis of subword, word, or supraword units. In

Chinese, morphemes rather than words are demarcated by spaces, comparable to writing *thoughtful* as *thought ful.* Many orthographies, like English, primarily segment words by spaces. However, the criterion of what constitutes a word may differ among writing systems. For example, in German, there is no space between a noun modifier and a head noun of a compound word; *life insurance salesman* would be written as a single unit, *lebensversicherungsvertreter.* Some orthographies, such as Thai, do not have spaces between morphemes or words, as can be seen in the Thai sentence in Figure 10.1, where allofthewordsinasentenceformasinglestring.

Orthographies also differ in the punctuation that is or is not used to signal various types of syntactic, semantic, or pragmatic information. The use of periods for sentence boundaries, commas for clauses and lists, question marks for interrogatives, and exclamation marks for emphasis is by no means universal. For example, classical Chinese lacked punctuation entirely. There are even differences in punctuation among languages that use the same alphabet. For example, in Spanish, question marks both precede and follow the question. Similarly, the rules for capitalization vary from orthography to orthography. In English, the words that are capitalized include proper names, the first words in sentences, and the pronoun *I.* By contrast, in German, the first-person pronoun is not capitalized. The second-person pronoun (corresponding to the singular and plural *you*) may be capitalized as a form of courtesy when directly addressing someone (as in a letter). Moreover, in German, not only are names capitalized, but so are all common nouns and even adjectives and verbs if they function as nounlike elements in a sentence. Thus, the particular types of information communicated by punctuation differs among writing systems.

The Relation of the Characters to Speech

A major distinction among orthographies is the level at which the characters represent the sounds and meanings of the spoken language. Three types of writing systems are typically distinguished:

1. alphabetic (e.g., English);
2. syllabic (e.g., Japanese); and
3. logographic (e.g., Chinese).

The system English readers are most familiar with is the **alphabetic** orthography, in which the characters primarily correspond to phonemes. A **phoneme** is a subword sound variation that makes a meaningful contrast in the language. For example, the initial sounds of *pit* and *bit* differ enough to distinguish these words, and so the sounds /b/ and /p/ are phonemes; these phonemes are usually graphically represented by the letters *b* and *p.* This description oversimplifies the alphabetic system, since a single letter may represent more than one phoneme, as happens with the *x* in *exempt.* Conversely, a group of letters can represent a single phoneme, as the *th* in *thin;* or a letter may be silent or change the pronunciation of another letter, as the *e* in *care.*

One difference among alphabetic orthographies is the regularity of the correspondence between the writing system and the sound characteristics of the language. On one end of the regularity continuum are orthographies such as English, Gaelic, and French, in which the sound-symbol correspondences are irregular because the same letter may represent different sounds. At the other end are orthographies such as Finnish and Serbo-Croatian, which have a regular sound-symbol correspondence. The description that has been suggested for these regular orthographies is that the person writes a word as it sounds. These orthographies have been called *shallow* because the regularity is at the phonological level, rather than the deeper, morphological level.

Gelb (1963) proposed another distinction among alphabetic orthographies based on the methods they use for indicating vowels. In the Latin alphabet, which includes English, vowels are indicated by separate characters, such as *a, e, i, o,* and *u.* In other alphabets, such as Indic and Ethiopic, vowels may be indicated by diacritics, the small marks that are appended to the character, or by internal modification of the character. In some orthographies, such as Hebrew, the diacritical marks are often omitted so that the vowels are not indicated. Some of these differences are apparent among the writing systems in Figure 10.1.

The second type of writing system is the **syllabic** orthography. Rather than express the sound system at the phonemic level, in a syllabic alphabet (or **syllabary**), each character roughly corresponds to a spoken syllable. The most commonly cited example is the Japanese kana system. In this system, one single character represents the spoken syllable "ga," a different character represents "ba," and so on. The vowels are not separately represented in the script the way English separates out the *a.* This practice is not as wasteful as it might initially seem to an English reader because the Japanese language has only five vowels and relatively few syllables.

The third type of writing system is the **logographic** orthography (or **logography**), in which each character corresponds to a morpheme, a unit that has some meaning. Chinese is the most commonly cited logographic system. For example, the Chinese logograph for *tricycle* is translated into three characters, roughly corresponding to "three-wheel vehicle." Each morpheme is represented by a single character. In a logographic orthography, the characters are not close representations of the speech sounds. One consequence is that the same writing system can be used throughout China, in spite of large differences in the spoken dialects and languages of various Chinese provinces.

Systems with mixtures of levels   Some writing systems, such as the Japanese, are a mixture of syllabic and logographic orthographies. The evolution of the current Japanese system illustrates how writing systems tend to develop. The Japanese initially adopted the Chinese logography between the third and ninth centuries A.D.; before that time, it is believed that the Japanese did not have any writing system. The Japanese initially used the Chinese logography, writing different words with different characters. However, with time, the Japanese began to adapt and simplify the Chinese logography to make it more compatible with the characteristics of the Japanese spoken language, which is very different from the Chinese spoken language. For example, the Japanese language has many grammatical inflections and word endings, while the Chinese spoken language has few. Consequently, the Japanese use a relatively small number of syllables with high frequency when marking grammatical information. The Japanese began representing these frequent inflections with specific characters borrowed from the Chinese logography, but eventually the Japanese simplified the characters and systematized them. Another difference between spoken Japanese and Chinese is that Japanese has a relatively small number of distinct syllables (approximately 70). Thus, it was feasible to represent each syllable with a distinct symbol. Eventually, simplified logographic symbols were used to represent each syllable, resulting in the **kana** syllabary. In fact, two separate kana syllabaries evolved, and each is currently used for different purposes. One system, called the *hiragana*, is used primarily to indicate grammatical inflections. The other kana syllabary, called the *katakana*, is used to write foreign loan words.

The current Japanese writing system also illustrates how some characteristics of a spoken language may be more or less amenable to a particular type of orthography. Because spoken Japanese has relatively few different syllables, it might appear to be a good candidate for a syllabic orthography. However, there is a mitigating complication of the language: namely, that spoken Japanese also has relatively few syllables per word. Consequently, it has a large number of homonyms, words that sound alike but have different meanings. If these words are written with the syllabary, they are ambiguous and additional syntactic and semantic information is required to resolve their correct interpretation. In part to minimize the confusions caused by such homonyms, the Japanese continued to use the Chinese logographic system, called **kanji,** for the major content words. Thus, the present Japanese writing system consists of a mixture of kanji logographic characters, which are used to write the content words, and kana syllabic characters, which are used to write inflections, foreign words, and sometimes content words whose kanji representation is unfamiliar.

This mixture is illustrated by the sentence in Figure 10.2, which roughly translates *A person named John split the tree for his mother.* Characters from the katakana syllabary are used to write the loan word *John.* Kanji logographic characters are used for most of the content words: *name, person, mother, tree,* and *split.* The remaining characters, which consist primarily of grammatical markers and inflections, are written with characters from the hiragana syllabary. Hiragana characters are also used to write the word *give,* a word that could have been written in kanji.

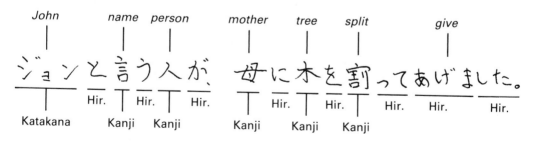

Hir. = Hiragana

Figure 10.2 A Japanese sentence, roughly translated as *A person named John split the tree for his mother,* which illustrates characters from the two kana syllabaries and the kanji logography. The word *John* is written with characters from the katakana syllabary, which is used to translate foreign loan words. The main content words are written in kanji logographic characters. The remaining characters, which consist primarily of syntactic markers and inflections, are written with characters from the hiragana syllabary.

Writing systems are frequently characterized as belonging to one of the three categories, alphabetic, syllabic, or logographic. But in fact, no writing system is entirely pure. Writing systems typically have mixtures of levels at which the characters map onto the spoken language. For example, English is not a purely alphabetic system. Many letters or groups of letters actually represent morphemes, so that the written form remains constant even if the spoken form is given a different pronunciation. For example, the plural ending of nouns is typically written as *s,* even though its pronunciation varies, as in *roses, desks,* and *dogs.* English even has a few logographic symbols; the most obvious are abbreviations, such as *Dr., X-mas,* and *$,* in which the written symbols have little or no relation to the pronunciation of the corresponding word. Thus, the characterization of a language as alphabetic, syllabic, or logographic can be an oversimplification.

Although the written words are related to the spoken words at some level, the written system can diverge from the spoken system both stylistically and in the rules of grammar. Written language tends to be more formal than spoken language. In English, the divergence between spoken and written language is most apparent if written language is compared to colloquial dialects. For example, the Pittsburgh spoken dialect includes double negatives (*I don't have no . . .*), deleted auxiliary verbs (*The car needs washed*), and different pronominal forms (*yuns* for the plural form of *you,* similar to the Southern *you-all*). None of these grammatical features will be found in written prose. At the same time, some constructions that occur only rarely in speech occur much more commonly in writing, as in the use of *whom* or rare sentence forms, as in the cleft and pseudocleft constructions: *It was John who wanted to leave.*

One reason for the divergence between speech and writing is that the speaker can use intonation, gesture, and the nonlinguistic context but the writer cannot. An extreme divergence between the spoken and written forms is called *diglossia.* Diglossia occurs in parts of Asia and the Middle East, for example, where the written language is classical Arabic and the spoken language is a different, modern form (Ryan, 1980).

Evolution of writing systems   Pictures and drawings by early man date back many tens of thousands of years, but a full writing system—that is, the use of conventional marks to denote linguistic elements—is no more than approximately 5,000 years old. The analysis of the evolution of writing systems suggests that sound-oriented orthographies evolved from more meaning-oriented orthographies. Logographic systems developed first; syllabaries typically evolved from logographies; and one alphabetic system—the precursor of perhaps all varieties of modern alphabetic systems—evolved from a syllabary.

Gelb (1963) suggested that the evolutionary steps reflected the intellectual difficulty of analyzing the communication into the constituents that make up the writing system. Analyzing a message into phrases and words, as in a logography, is not a difficult intellectual feat. By contrast, Gelb argued that dividing a message into syllables without regard to meaning, as in a syllabary, is a more difficult intellectual task. Finally, analyzing a message into its phonemes without concern for meaning, as in an alphabetic system, is extremely difficult because the phoneme is a more abstract level of sound than is the syllable. For example, it is impossible to pronounce a consonantal phoneme (such as /k/ or /t/) without the accompanying vowel that turns the unit into a syllable. The difficulty of analyzing speech into phonemes may explain why the alphabetic principle took such a long time to evolve.

Gelb also suggested that children show the same order of difficulty in comprehending the various units of speech: meaning is primary and the easiest, syllables are intermediate, and phonemes are the most difficult. This same developmental argument has been outlined by Rozin and Gleitman (1977), who further suggested that children who have difficulty learning alphabetic systems might more easily learn a logographic or syllabic orthography.

Perhaps as many as seven fully developed logographic systems evolved during the course of history, from 3000 B.C. to the present, including the Chinese logography. (There is some dispute, however, about how independently they evolved.) While logographic systems are often characterized as being word based, Gelb argues that a pure logographic system, with separate figures for each word, was never fully developed or used. And while logographic systems typically consist of symbols that represent word meanings, there is also some correspondence between the symbols and the sounds. The early systems typically had some characters that represented syllables, in addition to the purely logographic signs.

Some logographic systems eventually evolved into more purely syllabic systems. Gelb suggested that writing systems tended to evolve into new forms when one community adopted a writing system from another linguistic community, particularly if the borrowers had a different spoken language that would lead them to change the writing system to match the characteristics of this spoken form. One example of such evolution was described earlier—namely, the evolution of the Japanese kana system that resulted when the Japanese simplified and adapted the logography they originally borrowed from the Chinese.

Gelb argued that a syllabic system evolved into an alphabetic system only once, with the Greek orthography. One qualification is the possibility that the Korean *Hangul* alphabet was developed independently by Korean scholars in the middle ages; previously, Korea had only a syllabary. Even if the Hangul is an exception, all of the other alphabetic writing systems, past and present, appear to be traceable either directly or indirectly to the Greek.

The major contribution of the Greek civilization to the development of writing was to systematically use individual symbols for individual consonantal and vowel sounds. Others have argued that old Hebrew was an earlier alphabetic system but chose to indicate consonants and not mark vowel sounds, because vowels served primarily as grammatical markers (Venezky, 1980). However, Gelb argued that the use of specific symbols for vowels was only sporadically present in the earlier Semitic systems from which the Greek alphabet evolved. In any case, it appears that the major alphabetic orthographies then evolved from the Greek. New alphabetic writing systems that were designed from scratch borrowed the general idea of representing individual sounds from previously existing alphabets. Gelb argued that the alphabetic concept is extremely abstract and, for that reason, probably evolved only once.

The Relation of Written and Spoken Language

It may be useful to consider some of the theoretical positions linguists have offered concerning the relation between orthography and spoken language. The positions fall into two camps: the independence hypothesis and the transcription hypothesis.

The **independence hypothesis** asserts that the written and spoken systems are two independent manifestations of a more abstract system (Berry, 1977). In this view, both the written word *bite* and the spoken word "bite" correspond to the same linguistic concept. The relation between the two systems is indirect and mediated by this more general linguistic system. Some scholars find this position attractive because of the differences between spoken and written language in style and grammar. Like any communication medium, writing systems have developed some unique characteristics that have no analogue in spoken language. One example is the use of different kinds of type to convey visual effect; compare the contrasting effect of the modern, bold characters on a Coke can to the ornate, printed script on a college degree. Similarly, written language uses devices such as italics or quotation marks to signal emphasis or direct speech, which are conveyed through quite different means in spoken language.

Although spoken and written language diverge in some ways, the independence hypothesis has inherent difficulties (Tauli, 1977). In particular, there is no way to assess what the more abstract language system is, independent of written and spoken realizations. Also, the independence hypothesis underestimates the role that the representation of sound plays in orthography. All written language, even logographies, contain some representation of the sound system. Finally, written language is related to spoken language in the acquisition process. Children and adults learn to read after mastering a spoken language and they have difficulty learning to read a language that they do not comprehend in spoken form.

The opposite viewpoint, the **transcription hypothesis,** proposed that written language is a transcription of spoken language. The implicit process that the transcription hypothesis seeks to explicate is the process of pronunciation. The transcription hypothesis proposes that written language provides a transcript that can be used to generate its oral pronunciation. Of course, an extreme version of this hypothesis can be dismissed. No written language is a transcription of spoken language. This is most evident with logographies, in which there is only a slight relation between the spoken and written systems, or with irregular alphabetic orthographies, such as English.

A more reasonable viewpoint lies between these extremes. Written language should be conceptualized as a set of cues to a message. These cues are graphic, morphological, syntactic, semantic, and so on. No one level of cues need be complete, and ambiguity at one level may be compensated for at another level. For example, in Chapter 3 on lexical access, it was shown that ambiguous words like *bug* usually cause no interpretive difficulty because cues from the syntactic and semantic contexts are sufficient to make the intended meaning clear. An analogous point can be made about the orthography. The graphic symbols need not represent the sound system completely because the fluent reader can use other cues to recover meaning. This incompleteness is one reason why most people master English, in spite of its irregular symbol-sound correspondence. Similarly, Chinese readers learn to read Chinese, although it has even fewer sound cues.

This view of orthography as an incomplete set of cues can be further supported by considering orthographies that have purposely eliminated markings that represent some phonemic contrasts. Such elimination can result in more efficient reading performance for fluent readers. One such orthography is Hebrew, which can be written in two forms, with or without diacritical marks to indicate vowels. Hebrew is a highly inflected language and the vowels are grammatical markers. But the correct vowels can often be inferred from other cues to the word's meaning and its syntactic role in the sentence. Omitting the vowels causes relatively little difficulty for fluent readers; they take no more time to read a text that does not have the vowels marked than one that does. When reading aloud, an adult sometimes will make mistakes and correct himself, but this appears to be a minor problem in silent reading (Rabin, 1977). Thus, the vowels can be eliminated with relatively little effect on reading because there are other cues. Interestingly, the vowels generally are indicated in the texts intended for beginning readers. Beginning readers may need to have more redundancy among cues and be provided with certain types of cues, such as those at low levels that signal the sounds of words.

The Navaho orthography is another writing system that has been made more efficient by dropping the explicit representation of some contrasts. The Navaho orthography was developed relatively recently, in the 1940s, although earlier technical orthographies were used by linguists and scholars (Holm, 1980). The orthography originally represented several features of the intended vowel. The contrast between long- and short-duration vowels (like the difference between *a* in *can* and *cane*) was indicated by doubling letters. Another symbol (a cedilla) indicated whether the vowels were oral or nasal. Finally, Navaho has four variations in tone (high, low, rising, and falling), which were indicated with additional diacritical marks. The end effect was that written Navaho used a large number of diacritics. A simplification of the orthography in which the tone marks were omitted actually resulted in a 30 percent reduction in reading time and a reduction in errors by skilled adult readers (Holm, 1980). The text with tone markings was also unattractive to adult illiterates and made them less inclined to request reading instruction.

These analyses suggest that orthographies need not represent all of the contrasts in the language. Some contrasts are too infrequent to be of practical consequence. The added length or visual complexity caused by overtly marking them in the text may be detrimental if other levels provide enough cues so that the reader can infer the correct word. It is likely that few contrasts are absolutely essential, as long as enough other contrasts enable the reader to infer the missing information. An analogy can be made to computer systems that recognize speech. Such systems function well regardless of which subset of all of the possible features of the speech wave are coded, providing that the subset is large enough (Reddy, 1980). Similarly, human readers can read effectively based on a variety of cues that different orthographies provide.

A Description of English Orthography

A description of the English writing system must specify the sounds associated with individual letters and digraphs. Although English is characterized as an alphabetic orthography, there are so many apparent exceptions to particular symbol-sound relations that the system at first appears chaotic. Its irregularity has been assumed by many educators and would-be spelling reformers. For example, one reformer, playwright George Bernard Shaw, claimed that the English writing system was so arbitrary that it allowed the spoken word "fish" to be written as *ghoti*—using the *gh* from *tough,* the *o* in *women,* and the *ti* in *nation* (Haas, 1970). Shaw's claim is incorrect; there are positional constraints on English spelling that prevent "fish" from ever being written as *ghoti*. Nevertheless, the example illustrates an assumption that is implicitly or explicitly the basis of most objections to the way English words are written. The assumption is that a good orthography has a one-to-one relation between symbols and sounds; words should be pronounced as they are spelled and spelled as they are pronounced. Obviously, this description does not fit English. A less exotic example than *ghoti* will demonstrate that a single letter can have different pronunciations, as does the *a* in *fake, many, father, dad, call, sofa,* and *aisle*.

Although English does not have a one-to-one relation between symbols and sounds, the relation is not completely chaotic. The problem is to describe this relation in terms of the constraints represented in the English writing system. One such constraint is the position of a sound in a spoken word or a letter in a written word. The positional constraint explains the error in Shaw's claim that "fish" could be written as *ghoti*. The letter cluster *gh* is never pronounced as an /f/ sound when it occurs at the beginning of a word, nor would *ti* at the end of the word be pronounced as /sh/. Positional constraints do not account for all of the variation in the pronunciation or spelling of English words, but they exemplify one factor that reduces the apparent irregularity of symbol-sound correspondences.

A completely regular orthography would not be that difficult to devise (although it would not likely be accepted). In fact, the pronunciation of most English words could be represented by an alphabet having 25 symbols for consonantal phonemes and about 14 symbols for vowels and *dipthongs* (vowel sounds, like the *ow* in *how,* consisting of two parts, a vowel and a glide, in the same syllable). The alphabet in Table 10.1 illustrates such a writing system using characters from the International Phonetic Alphabet (IPA). (The IPA characters are part of a larger notational system that is used by linguists to transcribe the sounds produced in any language, not just English.) An inspection of Table 10.1 makes it clear that the traditional alphabet would be supplemented by several new symbols for vowel sounds, a few

Table 10.1   The International Phonetic Alphabet for pronouncing English words

Vowels		Consonants			
Character	*Example*	*Character*	*Example*	*Character*	*Example*
εi	fate	b	bat	p	pet
æ	apple	tʃ	chill	r	red
ə	ago	d	dog	s	sad
ɔ	paw	f	fill	ʃ	ship
i	meat	g	go	t	tap
ε	egg	h	hat	θ	thin
ɑi	die	dʒ	jar	ð	then
ɪ	pin	k	kit	v	van
o	toe	l	lamp	w	win
ɑ	father	m	man	ʌ	which
ɔi	boy	n	net	y	yell
u	due	ŋ	sing	z	zoo
ʊ	book			ʒ	vision
ʌ	dug				

new symbols for consonant sounds, and it would lose a few characters, *c, q,* and *x*.

The alphabet's application can be illustrated by using it to write the familiar opening of Lincoln's Gettysburg Address:

fɔrskɔr ænd sɛvɛn yirz əgo
auər faðərz brɔt fɔrɵ ɑn
ðIs kɑntInɛnt ə nu nɛiʃən, kənsivd
In lIbɛrti, ænd dɛdIkɛitɛd tu
ðə prapəzIʃən ðæt al mɛn ɑr
krɛitɛd ikwəl. . . .

This kind of alphabet permits a one-to-one relation between symbols and sounds, a characteristic that has been so important to spelling reformers, such as George Bernard Shaw. Clearly such an alphabet is initially difficult to read because the symbols are so unfamiliar. But even apart from the unfamiliarity of the characters, recent analyses of the writing system have called into question the assumption that regularity at the level of individual phonemes and characters would be a better way to represent words in the English language. These analyses will be described later in the chapter.

Reading Correspondences versus Spelling Correspondences

A writing system can be viewed from the perspective of either the reader or the speller. The two perspectives differ precisely because English does not have a one-to-one correspondence between letters and sounds. To make the difference more apparent, contrast the spoken interpretation of the written letter *k* with the written realizations of the /k/ sound. From the reader's perspective, the letter *k* is either pronounced /k/ or it is silent:

Pronunciation	Examples
/k/	*fake, keep*
silent	*knight, knock*

There is a one-to-two mapping of the letter *k* to pronunciations. By contrast, from the speller's perspective, the /k/ sound has many possible spellings. The most frequent spelling is *c*, as in *core*, which accounts for over 70 percent of the instances of the written realizations of the /k/ sound. But if the other spellings are included, even infrequent ones, the different spellings of /k/ are numerous:

Written Form	Example
c	*core*
k	*fake*
ck	*back*
qu	*bouquet*
kh	*khaki*
ch	*echo*

In many cases, the mapping between spelling and sound differs from the mapping between sound and spelling (Hanna, Hodges, & Hanna, 1971). The main concern of this chapter is the interpretation of printed words, the mapping from spelling to sound.

Historical Practices and Irregularity

Many words have irregular spellings because of historical accidents or changes in spoken English that occurred after spelling practices became fixed. Henderson (1982) has an interesting discussion of these historical developments. English spelling became somewhat fixed as a result of the efforts of fifteenth-century printers to standardize it. However, the pronunciation of words has changed and continues to do so, accounting for some of the lack of correspondence between symbols and sounds. For example, until the seventeenth century, *gh* had a unique gutteral pronunciation (as it continues to have in some words in the Scottish dialect). But after that time, *gh* was interpreted in one of two ways: (1) as an /f/ sound, as in *rough,* or (2) silently but influencing the preceding vowel, as in *light.* A similar divergence between spoken and written language describes the evolution of the silent *e.* The *e* at the ends of words such as *bite* represented an ending vowel sound that was pronounced until sometime between the fourteenth to sixteenth centuries, a time when there were other changes in the pronunciation of such words. After that time, the final *e* in such words was not pronounced and it only influenced pronunciation of the earlier vowel. These examples illustrate that some irregularities can be traced to the fact that the English writing system has changed much less than the English spoken language.

Further irregularities were introduced during the transition from Middle to Modern English by clerks who tried to use the orthography to reflect a word's morphological origin. In some cases, words were mistakenly attributed to particular derivations. For example, *scissors* mistakenly acquired a silent *c* because it was thought to derive from the Latin *scindere* ("to cut"), rather than *cisorium* ("a cutting instrument"). This movement became a major source of silent consonants, as in *thyme, crumb,* and *scent.* Another practice that developed during the late Middle English period was adding *e* after a final *v* or *u,* as in *love, glue, have, plague, glove,* and *continue.*

These historical practices may explain how certain words came to be spelled as they are today. However, the historical derivation of a word does not necessarily influence how it is learned or recognized because most readers do not know word origins. Whether the occurrence of the *c* in *scissors* or the *e* after *u* and *v* is seen as a pattern or an exception is largely a function of its frequency and consistency. An occurrence that is consistent and widespread throughout the orthography will not be considered irregular, irrespective of its historical origin.

How much regularity is there in English pronunciation? The answer depends on the definition of regularity. One approach, called the **analogy approach,** assesses regularity by determining if a group of similarly spelled words are pronounced similarly. By this criterion, *come* and *some* are irregular because their pronunciation differs from the similarly spelled words *dome, home, gnome, pome, Rome,* and *tome.* By this criterion, many frequent words—such as *have, give, great,* and *of*—are irregular because they are pronounced differently than similarly spelled words (Haas, 1970):

> *behave, shave, cave*—have
> *dive, hive, jive*—give
> *eat, treat, neat*—great
> *if, off*—of

Among the 1,000 most common words, approximately 16 percent are irregular; among the next 2,000 words, approximately 7 percent are irregular (Wijk, 1966). Using this criterion, very frequent words are less regular than slightly less frequent words. Because more frequent words occur several times on a typical page of text, 15 to 20 percent of the words on a typical page are irregular.

The analogy approach to regularity gives one insight into the relationship of frequency and regularity. However, this approach is ultimately unsatisfactory because it implicitly assumes that the basis for pronouncing words is an analogy to similarly spelled words at the letter level. But some apparent irregularity at the letter level turns out to be regular at the morphological level. Thus, regularity should be assessed with a model that describes the factors that influence pronunciation.

Venezky's Analysis of Symbol-Sound Correspondence

In this section, we present a linguistic analysis of the rules for pronouncing English words. There are several such analyses, including Chomsky and Halle (1968), Haas (1970), and Wijk (1966). Our discussion is based primarily on the work of Venezky (1970), which illustrates the nature of these approaches. In addition, Venezky's work is based on the 20,000 most common English words, a corpus large enough to be of general interest for a model of word pronunciation.

Terminology According to Venezky's analysis, the letters in a word can be divided into two main types: (1) spelling patterns and (2) markers. **Spelling patterns** are essentially the letters that are pronounced. In some cases, the spelling pattern is a single letter; in other cases, the spelling pattern consists of a vowel cluster (such as *oo, ui*) or a consonant cluster (such as *tch* in *kitchen* and *dg* in *pledge*). A **marker** is a letter that is usually not pronounced but whose occurrence either signals some feature of the pronunciation of other letters or preserves some morphological or graphic pattern. One of the most familiar markers is the silent *e*, which signals a change in the pronunciation of the preceding vowel, such as *mat/mate*. Another marker is the *u* following *g* in words like *plague*, which indicates that the *g* is pronounced /g/ rather than /j/, as in *pledge*. These pronunciation markers are dropped when another letter performs their function in a different environment. For example, the final *e* in words like *notice* signals that a preceding *c* should be pronounced as an /s/. The *e* is dropped if another letter performs its function, as with the *i* in *noticing*. By contrast, the *e* is not dropped if its function is not performed by another letter. The *e* is included before *able* in *noticeable*; if it were dropped and *able* directly followed *c*, as in *noticable*, it would incorrectly signal that the *c* would be pronounced /k/.

In addition to influencing pronunciation, markers can signal other features of the written language. Some markers signal something about a word's syntactic or semantic status. One example is the *e* at the end of some words that would otherwise end in *s*, which prevents the false appearance of being plural. If *moose, goose,* and *mouse* were written *moos, goos,* and *mous,* they would look like plural forms of *moo, goo,* and *mou.* Similarly, the extra *e* or consonant at the end of the short content words *bee, bye, toe,* and *inn* removes them from the class of two-letter words that consists almost exclusively of function words, such as *be, by, to,* and *in.* Thus, some markers help communicate syntactic information.

An example   Venezky compiled a list of the sounds given to consonant and vowel clusters according to their word position—beginning, middle, or final—and the conditions that predicted pronunciation. A sample of the entry for *c* gives the flavor of Venezky's analysis:

1. The pronunciations of *c*:
   a. usually pronounced /*k*/.
   b. pronounced /*s*/ before the spellings *i*, *y*, and *e*.
   c. silent in some cases, such as *victual* and *czar*.
   d. pronounced /*tʃ*/ in *cello* and *concerto*.
2. The positions in which *c* occurs:
   a. primarily in initial and medial position.
   b. in final position, occurs in the ending *ic* and in some words borrowed from other languages, such as *arc, havoc, sac*, and *zodiac*.

Given this approach, Venezky argued that the concept of regularity should be revised. **Regularity** usually means that the pronunciation of the spelling pattern is invariant. But only a few spelling patterns fit this restricted view of regularity; they include *j* as /*j*/, *q* as /*k*/, and *ck* as /*k*/. Venezky suggested that the concept of regularity be expanded beyond the narrow definition to include predictable variation. Spelling patterns should be considered as regular, even if their pronunciation varies, as long as the variation is predictable from the context. For example, *c* is not always pronounced the same way; it is pronounced /*k*/ in 74 percent of the occurrences and /*s*/ in 22 percent. However, the /*s*/ pronunciation can be predicted by the vowel that follows the /*c*/. Since the pronunciation of *c* is almost entirely predictable, it should be considered regular.

Factors in symbol-sound correspondence   The factors that determine the pronunciation of a spelling pattern are most straightforward for words that consist of a single syllable and a single morpheme. The pronunciation of a spelling pattern in such simple words often can be predicted on the basis of its markers and adjacent letters and on the position in which it occurs. For these words, English is often regular enough that the spelling patterns can be pronounced sequentially from left to right with some consideration of markers and adjacent letter contexts.

Another factor that governs pronunciation is the constraint on which sounds can follow each other in spoken English; these constraints are called *phonotactic* rules. For example, the initial *k* in *knight, know*, and *knife* is silent because the cluster /*kn*/ does not occur within a single morpheme in spoken English. When a consonant cluster used in the initial position of a morpheme contains an inadmissible sequence of sounds, the first consonant is not pronounced, as in *knee, gnat*, and *psychology*.

For more complex words—namely, those with more than one syllable and more than one morpheme—the symbol-sound correspondences are more complex. For such words, additional grammatical or phonological factors (such as word stress) can be important. An example of the effect of stress can be seen in the pronunciation of the letter *x* between two vowels, as in *exit* and *exist*. The pronunciation will be either /*ks*/ or /*gz*/, depending upon whether the main stress is placed on the vowel preceding the *x* (as in *exit*) or elsewhere (as in *exist*). Stress also plays a role in determining whether a vowel is reduced to a *ə* (schwa) sound, as in the pronunciation of the first *e* in *preparation* compared to *prepare.* The important point about stress is that the reader is not given any graphic cue in the word to decide which pronunciation is correct.

The grammatical factor of word class can influence stress and, consequently, change the pronunciation of particular letters. The effect of word class can be most easily illustrated with some multisyllabic words, such as *refuse* and *defect,* whose pronunciation changes depending on whether they are nouns or verbs. For example, in the verb phrase *to refuse,* the second syllable receives the primary stress; in the noun phrase *the refuse,* the first syllable receives the primary stress. The different stress assignments alter the pronunciation of the initial *e.*

Word class is correlated with other pronunciation differences. For example, the digraph *th* is pronounced differently in function words and content words. In function words (such as *the, that, this,* and *those*), the initial *th* is voiced (meaning that the vocal cords vibrate as the sound is produced); in content words (such as *thin, think,* and *thumb*), the initial *th* is unvoiced.

Pronunciation also sometimes depends upon syllable and morpheme boundaries. Such boundaries are important in deciding how to pronounce two letters (like *th, ph, dd, ea, ll*) that may constitute a single unit or two separate units. When the letters are on the boundary between two morphemes, as the *th* in *fathead,* they are treated as two units. When *th* occurs within a morpheme, as in *father,* the letters *th* are treated as a single unit. The identity of a morphological constituent may also influence whether or how a grapheme is pronounced within a morpheme. An example is the silent letter in a final consonant cluster, such as the *gm, gn,* and *mb* in *paradigm, sign,* and *bomb.* It is inadequate to simply suggest that certain letters are silent in word-final position, since these letters are also silent when followed by inflections, as in *paradigms, signs, signing, bombs,* and *bombing.* It is the identity of these morphemes that differentiates them from cases that have identical patterns but different pronunciations, such as *stigma* and *bamboo.*

These examples illustrate how a description of the relation between written words and their pronunciation requires information beyond the level of letters or letter clusters. English orthography has considerable regularity, but only if these other factors are considered.

Morphological representation Venezky proposed that written forms cannot be directly related to their pronunciations; there must be an intervening, intermediate linguistic representation that takes into account graphemic factors, grammatical factors, and phonological factors. He proposed that the intermediate level was a **morphophonemic** representation. The relation between the actual written word and the morphophonemic representation is complex. First, the written word maps onto a representation that has separate graphic units; for example, *signing* would be represented as *sign* and *ing.* These units would then be made to reflect factors such as the base morphological form, stress, and phonotactic constraints. According to Venezky, the resulting morphophonemic representation of a word is more directly related to its pronunciation than is the actual written form of the word.

Chomsky and Halle (1968; also Haas, 1970) offered a different analysis of English orthography but one that shares Venezky's proposal that English often violates phonological regularity to preserve morphological regularity. For example, the past-tense marker is written *ed,* even though it is sometimes pronounced as /t/ (*walked*), sometimes as /əd/ (*persuaded*), and sometimes as /d/ (*doomed*). Such variation is predictable because it is conditioned by the preceding sound. The reader who already knows how to speak English will always pronounce the past tense of *walk* with a /t/. Thus, by identifying *walked* as a combination of *walk* and a past-tense marker, the reader can generate its correct pronunciation. Chomsky and Halle (1968) argued that an abstract, morphological level is preserved in English orthography, at the expense of spelling-sound regularity. Chomsky and Halle's examples involve word families, such as:

history/historic	*symphony/symphonic*
courage/courageous	*outrage/outrageous*
telegraph/telegraphy	*photograph/photography*

In each pair, there is a root that appears in various derivational forms. In spite of the fact that the pronunciation of the root changes in the different derivational forms, its written form is constant. Moreover, a native speaker of English already knows the nature of the pronunciation change necessary to generate the root in a particular derivational form. For example, if an artificial word, like *dourage,* is pronounced, an adult can then produce its spoken adjectival form, *dourageous.* Since the adult knows how to alter the pronunciation of the base form to produce various derived forms, the orthography does not have to specify the particular sounds; such specification would be redundant information.

Chomsky and Halle postulated that this property optimizes English spelling. Fluent readers can more quickly retrieve the meaning of a derived word like *courageous* because of its consistent orthographic relation to the morphological representation than if a more regular spelling-sound correspondence were purchased at the expense of obscuring the morphological information. Moreover, Chomsky and Halle argue that this morphological representation is impervious to pronunciation differences among dialects.

Chomsky and Halle did not compute the relative frequency with which the morphological identity of a stem in various derivational forms is preserved or is not preserved (as in *beast/bestial, exclude/exclusion,* and *describe/description*). The characterization of English as preserving morphological information at the expense of letter-sound regularity would be more convincing if it were demonstrated that the morphological information is preserved most of the time.

Reading implications   These linguistic analyses of the relation between written words and their pronunciations have implications for some of the psychological processes in reading. First, because they reveal the complexity of symbol-sound relations, these analyses suggest that it would be difficult to accurately pronounce a complex word by translating individual letters into sounds, even taking into account possible markers and position effects. The concept of a symbol-to-sound translation route to word recognition was discussed in Chapter 3. The route, called **prelexical speech recoding,** was suggested as a supplementary route to visual recognition, one that might dominate if the printed word were unfamiliar. The reader might recode the written word into its spoken equivalent and then access the meaning of the oral form. Some initial proposals suggested that the translation process might be letter by letter. However, these linguistic analyses of English orthography make it clear that if prelexical speech recoding is to generate an accurate pronunciation, it must operate on abstract units that already require a fair degree of recognition skill, namely, the representations of morphemes.

The analyses also suggest that if other factors such as frequency and visual length are constant, the recognition of derived words that preserve the identity of the underlying morphemes (such as *exception/except*) should be faster than the recognition of derived words that do not (such as *description/describe*).

Venezky also pointed out that his conception of regularity might have implications for teaching word recognition in beginning reading. In particular, teaching practices should initially focus on words that contain not just spelling patterns whose pronunciations are invariant but also spelling patterns whose pronunciations are predictable, given markers and adjacent letters. Also, such words, particularly if they have only one syllable and one morpheme, are the most amenable to a process of symbol-to-sound translation. These are the words whose pronunciations can be transferred to other similarly spelled words. By contrast, other words that occur frequently but whose pronunciations are less predictable may have to be taught more rotely and in a way that discourages the child from generalizing their pronunciations.

One of the most concrete applications of these linguistic analyses has been in computer systems that are designed to read written text aloud. These systems have various uses; one of the most obvious uses is to provide spoken versions of arbitrary written material for the blind (see Allen, 1973, 1976). The details of these systems are beyond the scope of the present chapter. Nevertheless, such computer systems are interesting for three reasons. First, the systems actually produce spoken output; consequently, the intelligibility of the speech they generate is one measure of how adequately the system has addressed the problem of relating written language to speech. Second, because such systems must be able to read sentences and paragraphs, in addition to isolated words, their developers have had to consider how the sentence context influences the stress and pronunciation of individual words. The third and most important point, for the present purpose, is that to generate the pronunciation of individual words, these computer systems assume that written words are only indirectly related to speech. The systems instantiate the theory described above, namely, that the relation between the written word and its pronunciation is mediated by a morphologically based representation. Thus, the systems provide converging support for the general arguments made by Venezky and Chomsky and Halle.

Cross-linguistic Comparisons: Reading in Chinese and English

At a very general level, fluent reading appears similar across different languages and orthographies. Fluent readers recognize characters and morphemes, retrieve meanings, parse phrases, and construct and integrate propositional representations irrespective of the vast differences in character set, sound-symbol relatedness, and grammar. This general conclusion was supported by the research of Gray (1956), who compared the eye fixations and reading speed of groups of 78 adult readers of 14 different languages, including Arabic, English, Hebrew, Burmese, Chinese, Urdu, Navaho, and Yoruba. The readers were native speakers of their original language and had received all or most of their elementary education in that language, although they were currently living in the United States. (Most of the readers were university graduate students.)

Each reader was presented two texts that had been translated into his or her native language. One interesting aspect of the translations was the considerable variation in the number of words and lines of print among languages. For example, in English, each of the two experimental passages contained approximately 150 words and covered 13 lines of print. In Burmese, each took approximately 340 words and covered 16 lines; while in Navaho, each took approximately 44 words and covered 8 lines. These differences partially reflect variation in what is considered a separate word in different languages and also in the number of words needed to express the same concept in different languages. Nevertheless, the differences are also indicative of the large variation among the orthographies.

Gray's study exemplifies some of the difficulties inherent in cross-linguistic research. Orthographic differences are often accompanied by differences in the lexical, syntactic, and semantic structure of the language, which could introduce differences in the reading process. Moreover, such differences make it difficult to assure the comparability of the translations. In addition, there may be differences among the groups of readers themselves (independent of their reading performance), such as their exposure to print, their educational histories, and their decision of how carefully and quickly to read (see Brimer, 1973). So many such differences exist that differences among linguistic groups are often open to several interpretations.

Gray's conclusion was that orthography had little effect on the nature of the eye fixations of the readers. There was some slight variation in the average number of eye fixations and their average duration. For instance, the average number of fixations was 1.6 words/fixation for English, 2.5 words/fixation for Chinese, and 1.3 words/fixation for Hebrew. This variation may partially reflect the fact that the linguistic unit of a word varies from language to language. Gray himself ascribed these effects to accidental differences among the various groups of readers rather than to the orthography.

In a general sense, Gray's conclusion that fluent reading is roughly similar across languages and orthographies is correct. As he pointed out, all readers make a series of fixations and obtain meaning from the orthography. On the other hand, Gray eliminated any possibility of determining how orthographies influence fluent reading. By attending only to general characteristics of eye fixations (and even then, dismissing group differences), he could not possibly determine how specific reading processes (such as word encoding or lexical access) might be influenced by the orthographic structure of each language.

To analyze the effect of orthography, it is necessary to examine how the orthography influences specific reading processes. When doing such an analysis, it is reasonable to initially focus on the low-level processes, particularly word encoding, lexical access, and speech recoding. Given the nature and function of writing systems, these processes are the most likely to be influenced by the orthography. The following sections examine fluent reading in Chinese. Because Chinese writing is logographic, it contrasts strikingly with the English alphabetic system that has been the basis of much of the reading research discussed in this book. Consequently, it provides an opportunity for a more detailed analysis of the effects of orthography on reading processes. However, before analyzing individual reading processes, it is important to provide a more detailed description of the Chinese orthography.

Chinese Orthography: Logographic Types

This section describes the structure of Chinese orthography, drawing on discussions by Wang (1973, 1981) and Leong (1973). Chinese writing has several different types of logographs, some of which are illustrated in Figure 10.3. The most common, accounting for perhaps 90 percent of all Chinese dictionary characters, is the **phonetic compound**. Phonetic compounds have two parts, a **signific,** which hints at its pronunciation, and a **radical,** which hints at its meaning. The signific can be positioned in several different ways with respect to the radical: to its left, right, top, bottom, inside, or outside. The characters are graphically composed so that each takes up an approximately square area.

The signific is like a rhyming clue. Wang (1973) claims that the average Chinese can often correctly pronounce a character he has never seen before simply by making a shrewd guess based on this clue. However, another study found the success rate of guessing the sound of an unknown character to be less than 40 percent (Zhou, 1978, cited by Tzeng & Hung, 1981). The guessing rate probably depends upon the properties of the unknown word (such as the particular cues given and the word's meaning), as well as the presence of context.

The second component, the radical, hints at the semantic domain of the word. The radical also provides a basis for structuring arbitrary word lists, such as dictionaries, phone books, catalogs, and so on, similar to how the alphabet is used in English. To locate a Chinese word in a dictionary, the reader must look up its radical and then search according to the number of strokes used to draw the remainder of the character. The traditional number of radicals is 214, although Wang (1973) says that in a recent dictionary, some have been merged and the total has been reduced. Radicals vary considerably in frequency. Leong (1973) cites a study that showed that 17 radicals account for 50 percent of the 8,711 characters in a common Chinese dictionary.

Many people who do not read Chinese think of Chinese characters as pictures, but picturelike characters constitute only a small proportion of characters in a dictionary. Examples of these types of characters are also shown in Figure 10.3. One type, the **pictograph,** is somewhat related to the picture of the concrete object that is signified. A second type, the **ideograph,** is diagrammatically related to the abstract concept being portrayed (for example, the way arrows can be used to indicate *up* and *down*). There are also **compound ideographs;** one example is the formation of the word *grove,* which is symbolized by doubling the character used for *wood.* At the same time, the character for *wood* is the radical in the character for *tree.* There are other types of characters besides phonetic compounds, pictographs, and ideographs, but they constitute a very small proportion of the total number of characters. Phonetic compounds and pictographs are the most common and illustrate the main features of the Chinese writing system.

Evolution of pictographs As Figure 10.3 illustrates, the relation of a pictograph to its referent is quite abstract for someone who doesn't know how to read Chinese. For example, most people who cannot read Chinese would not guess that the pictographs in Figure 10.3 mean *person* and *wood.* However, if a Chinese reader explains their meanings, then it is possible to see a vague relation between the character and its referent.

Chinese Characters		Meaning	[Pronunciation]

A. *Phonetic Compounds*

Radical (person) → 传 ← Pronunciation hint [zhuān]   "biography"   [zhuān]

Radical (female) → 妈 ← Pronunciation hint [mǎ]   "mommy"   [mā]

Radical (wood) → 枯 ← Pronunciation hint [gu]   "withered"   [ku]

B. *Pictographs*

人   "person"   [ren]

木   "wood"   [mu]

C. *Ideographs*

林   "grove"   [lin]

森   "forest"   [song]

上   "up"   [shan]

下   "down"   [sha]

Figure 10.3 Examples of different types of Chinese logographs. The first type, *phonetic compounds,* are the most frequent type of character; they usually contain hints as to the character's meaning and pronunciation. *Pictographs* and *ideographs* are less common; also, such characters are only distantly related to their visual referents.

While many Chinese characters originated in a pictograph or iconic form, their current visual form no longer closely corresponds to the referent of the word. Figure 10.4, adapted from a book on Chinese calligraphy by Yee (1973), provides examples of how two characters have been written from the earliest times to the present. The form of the characters for *tiger* and *moon* were initially closely related to their referents but, with time, became stylized so that there is currently no relation between the character and its meaning, even for these concrete words.

Two forces contributed to the evolution of a character toward a more abstract form. First, changes were made in the way characters were formed, because different writing implements were used at different times and new artistic conventions and movements altered writing standards (Yee, 1973). Somewhat analogous changes in the English orthography include those initiated by the advent of the printing press and the standardization of English spelling. The influence of such forces can be seen on many Chinese characters as they evolved over the four thousand years of Chinese writing.

The second force that contributed to the evolution away from a close correspondence between character and meaning was that word meanings could be generalized to related concepts or more abstract concepts (Karlgren, 1929; Koriat & Levy, 1979). For example, a character that originally meant "accuracy in hitting a physical target" was generalized to mean "to succeed." The original character depicted a staff marking the center of a target and streamers showing the direction of the wind (Yee, 1973). The staff (without streamers) and the target persist in the current written character, although in a very stylized form as a line through the center of a rectangular figure. But even if a reader recognized the line as representing a staff and the rectangular figure as the target, the meaning "to succeed" has only a metaphorical relation to hitting a physical target. Thus, the characterization of the Chinese orthography as picturelike is a misleading simplification, even for the set of characters that are visually related to their referents.

An Experiment in Reading Chinese

To examine the fluent reading of Chinese texts, we conducted an experiment in our laboratory, in collaboration with Rosalind Wu (Just, Carpenter, & Wu, 1983). The study was the Chinese counterpart of the eye-fixation study that was described in

1800 B.C. 1700 B.C.   1600 to 250 B.C.   246 B.C. 200 B.C.   After A.D. 588

Figure 10.4   The historical changes in the written characters for *tiger* and *moon*, from ones that initially depicted their referents to the current abstract characters. *Source:* Adapted from C. Yee, *Chinese calligraphy*, 3rd ed., revised and enlarged (Cambridge, MA: Harvard University Press, 1973), p. 34, Figure 5. Reprinted by permission.

Chapters 1 and 2, in which American college students read short scientific texts. The English version of the experiment was particularly revealing about word encoding and lexical access processes that translate written symbols into mental concepts. The Chinese version of the experiment also focuses on word encoding and lexical access because these processes are the most likely to be influenced by the properties of a particular orthography.

The experiment examined the eye fixations of 13 native Chinese speakers as they read Chinese translations of the 15 scientific texts, such as the passages on flywheels and on pyramid construction. The readers had received their college undergraduate education in Hong Kong or the Republic of China. Their reading performance can sensibly be compared to the American undergraduate college students, in spite of the fact that the two groups of readers differed in several ways. (For ex-

---

a. Chinese Text

建築金字塔那不斷引人
好奇的问题，有人提議另
一個答案．五千年前，埃
及的工程師可能用一個叫
力臂的簡單的木造器具来
處理兩噸半至七噸重的金
字塔石塊。

---

b. Literal Translation

Build pyramid that not ending attract men curiosity of question, has man suggest another one unit answer. Five thousand years ago, E- gypt ('s) engineer expert can may use one unit called weight arm of simple of wood made device to handle 2 ton half to 7 ton weight of pyr- amid block.

---

c. English Equivalent

Another answer to the ever-intriguing question of pyramid construction has been suggested. Five thousand years ago, Egyptian engineers may have used a simple wooden device, called a weightarm, to handle the 2-½ to 7 ton pyramid blocks.

Figure 10.5   A sample from a Chinese text used to study the reading processes of Chinese readers. Part (a) is in Chinese, part (b) is a word-for-word translation, and part (c) presents the equivalent text in English.

ample, the Chinese students were bilingual and generally had more undergraduate or graduate education than the American students.)

The texts used in this study were translations of the scientific passages described in Chapter 2. The texts, initially excerpted from *Newsweek* and *Time* magazines, presented generally unfamiliar information on scientific or technological topics. The translations into Chinese were made by a native Chinese speaker who was also fluent in English. Every attempt was made to produce Chinese texts comparable in style and difficulty to the English versions, by translating the texts sentence by sentence and by using comparable vocabulary.

Figure 10.5 presents an excerpt of a Chinese text, its literal word-for-for translation, and its English equivalent. The literal version sounds stilted, in part, because Chinese has a very different syntactic structure than English. For example, it has few word endings, including inflections such as plural and past-tense markers, and it relies more on the word sequence to signal the syntactic structure. Chinese has function words and content words, but their distribution differs from that of English. For example, Chinese has an obligatory particle (translated here as *unit*) that follows demonstratives and numbers in noun phrases, resulting in a phrase such as *one unit answer*. Chinese uses the possessive particle and expresses it as a separate character, like the English *of*, rather than *'s*.

The average passage length was 181 characters, or 124 words, compared to an average of 132 words in the equivalent English passages. The Chinese passages were written from left to right, a format that was familiar to all of the readers. Each character and each punctuation mark occupied an approximately square area, with 11 characters per row and seven or fewer rows of characters on a screen.

Word encoding In English, fluent readers spend more time on longer words than on shorter words. The interpretation given to this finding in Chapter 2 was that encoding processes operate on letters or letter groups and that the letters or letter groups are processed one at a time. As a result, longer words take longer to encode. The word-length effect in Chinese cannot be identical because of the differences between the two orthographies. However, if the appropriate analysis is made, then an analogous although not identical length effect emerges in Chinese.

The first problem in evaluating a length effect on encoding in Chinese lies in choosing the unit of analysis. One unit is Chinese words, which almost always consist of either one, two, or three individual Chinese characters. The gaze duation on Chinese words increases with the number of characters in a word. While this effect is quite clear, the variation among one-, two-, and three-character words is not the only variation in the Chinese orthography that is likely to affect encoding.

Another approach is to examine the encoding of individual Chinese characters. Chinese characters vary in the number, type, and configuration of internal features they contain, such as lines and curves. One measure of the number of features is the number of strokes that make up a character. A single **stroke** is a line or curve that is completed before the pen leaves the paper. Some logographic characters are extremely simple, consisting of one or two strokes (like the character for *one*), and some are extremely complex and involve a number of components (as the character for *tiger*). The average number of strokes in the characters used in the current texts was eight, which is close to the average obtained for characters in other types of texts (Leong, 1973; Wang, 1981). The number of strokes is not a perfect indicator of the features in a Chinese character, since it ignores configural properties of the features. Nevertheless, the number of strokes provides a reasonable measure of the number of visual symbols that must be encoded in each character. Moreover, the encoding of the strokes of a character seems somewhat comparable to the encoding of letters of an English word.

The Chinese readers spent more time on the characters that contained more strokes. The average gaze duration increased reliably by 4.6 milliseconds for each additional stroke. Because the range of strokes varied from 1 to 24, from the simplest to the most complex characters, the effect of this variable had a range of 106 milliseconds. The encoding of Chinese characters appears to be sensitive to the number of constituents to be encoded; the constituents may be individual strokes or groups of strokes. This result is analogous to the readers of English texts spending more time on words that contained more letters.

A revealing comparison can be made between the effect of the number of letters in an English word versus the number of strokes in a Chinese character. In English, the number of letters in a word determines how physically long the word is. For this reason, the effect is called the *word-length effect*. Some theorists have tried to explain the word-length effect in English in terms of the physical size of the words, such that longer words are harder to perceive than shorter words in a single fixation. However, in the Chinese study, the effect of the number of strokes on encoding time cannot be explained in terms of the physical size of the words, because there is no such variation. In Chinese orthography, all of the characters take up approximately the same square area, though they vary in the number of strokes that they contain. Both the Chinese and English results can be explained in terms of an encoding mechanism that operates component by component. In English, the components that are encoded are individual letters or small group of letters; in Chinese, the components are individual strokes or small groups of strokes.

Lexical access   In English, the more frequent a word is, the less time a reader spends looking at it. This result was attributed to the activation process that underlies lexical access. The time needed to bring a word's activation level to threshold is logarithmically related to the base activation level of the word's meaning. The base activation level, in turn, depends on how frequently the reader has encountered the word in her lifetime.

Chinese words also vary in how frequently they have been seen by readers. To measure word frequency, another group of 10 Chinese readers who were not in the reading experiment rated how often they had seen each of the 472 words, presented in random order. Their responses were expressed in terms of whether they had seen the word several times a day, a week, a month, and so on. For English, such ratings by readers correlate quite well with objective counts of how frequently a word occurs (Tryk, 1968).

As in English, the logarithm of the word's frequency was related to how long the readers looked at the word. Chinese readers spent more time on infrequent words and less time on frequent words. The correlation between gaze duration and the logarithm of the word's frequency was 0.71. This result indicates that the same type of mechanism is used for lexical access in both Chinese and English. A word's meaning is accessed by a mechanism that activates a word's representation from its baseline activation level. The baseline level is higher if the reader has encountered the word more frequently in the past.

Words can be made of a single morpheme written as a single character or of two or three morphemes. Sometimes the same character occurs by itself and sometimes it is part of a longer word. This fact provides an opportunity to examine how the word context affects the processing of individual characters. The eye-fixation results suggest that the word context facilitates processing. Infrequently occurring characters that were parts of words were fixated for a significantly shorter time than infrequent characters that were words by themselves. This suggests that access to a character's meaning is faster in the context of other characters that combine with it to form a word. Once the meaning of a preceding character reaches threshold, it might raise the activation levels of other characters with which it often combines to form words. Then, if one of those characters is soon encountered, its access time will be shortened due to the activation it received from its associate.

Although lexical access in both English and Chinese refers to the activation of the meaning of a word, Chinese orthography makes it possible to examine the access of the individual characters (morphemes) that make up a word. The gaze durations were longer for less frequently occurring characters, suggesting that it takes longer to access the meaning of a less frequent character. Specifically, there was an increase of 18.4 milliseconds in gaze duration with a decrease of one logarithmic unit in the character's normative frequency. (This effect was independent of the stroke-count effect.) For example, *of,* one of the most frequently occurring characters, received a much shorter gaze than an infrequently occurring character, such as that for *fluoride*.

The analyses discussed thus far have concerned the access of the meanings of Chinese words and of the individual characters that make up the word. The data revealed that the time spent on a word is influenced by the word's frequency and that the time spent on a character is strongly influenced by the character's frequency. At this point, it is sensible to ask whether the lexical access of a Chinese word is anything more than the access of each of its component characters. This question was examined by determining whether the gaze duration on a word was more closely related to the word's frequency or to the sum of the frequencies of its component characters. The results showed that (1) the correlation between gaze duration on a word and the logarithm of the word's frequency was 0.71 and (2) the correlation between gaze duration and the logarithm of the sum of the frequencies of the individual morphemes (characters) that made up the word was less, only 0.50. Thus, the time course of lexical access is better predicted by the properties of the whole word than by the properties of the individual characters. At least some words are treated as a psychological unit. That is, the whole word is psychologically more than the sum of its morphemic components.

This study of Chinese reading shows that word encoding and lexical access are similar in Chinese and English, although the psychological mechanisms must operate on different types of orthographic units. In both orthographies, encoding time is affected by the number of graphic components to be encoded, letters in English and strokes in Chinese. In both languages, the lexical access time decreases linearly with the logarithm of the item's frequency. Moreover, the summaries of the texts that the readers produced were similar in the Chinese and English studies; both groups recalled more of the high-level, important information and fewer of the details or elaborations. Thus, even though the two orthographies are very different, they are processed by similar types of mechanisms and they ultimately result in similar representations of the text content.

The Effect of Orthographies on Speech Recoding

Speech recoding is a component process of reading that might differ for logographic orthographies and alphabetic orthographies. A reasonable hypothesis is that the likelihood of activating a speech code may depend upon how clearly the orthography reflects the speech characteristics of the language. In Chapter 3, the discussion of speech recoding distinguished between a **prelexical speech code,** which may be used as an alternative route for accessing the meaning of a written word, and a **postlexical speech code,** which may be activated as a consequence of accessing the meaning of a word. Most studies suggest that for fluent readers of English, a prelexical speech code is not essential for retrieving the meaning of a word. Speech codes, to the extent that they are activated in a reading task, are more likely to be postlexical; that is, they are a product of a later stage of comprehension (Kleiman, 1975).

Speech codes in alphabetic orthographies   One possible reason why speech codes may play a minor role in the fluent reading of English was highlighted by the linguistic analyses by Venezky and Chomsky and Halle, which were described earlier. Their analyses suggested that for complex English words, the relation between symbols and sounds is often expressed at the morphological level, rather than at a shallow, phonological level. If so, speech recoding might be less automatic and less frequent than it would be for an orthography with more symbol-sound regularity at the phonemic level.

This hypothesis has some indirect support from studies with Serbo-Croatian using lexical decision tasks, rather than normal reading (Lukatela, Popadic, Ognjenovic, & Turvey, 1980; Lukatela & Turvey, 1980). Serbo-Croatian has an extremely regular orthography. Moreover, it has two alphabets—a Latin one and a Cyrillic one—which both map onto the same phonemic, syntactic, and semantic structures. Both alphabets are very regular, conforming to the principle that "you write as you speak and read as it is written."

The two alphabets share some letters, which permits interesting studies of how letters activate speech-based codes. Although most of the characters in an alphabet are unique to that alphabet, some characters appear in both alphabets. Of these, some (*A, E, O, J, M,* and *T*) have the same pronunciation in both alphabets. A sentence with these letters would be pronounced in the same way whether it was written in Cyrillic or Latin. For example, the sentence *TO JE MOJA MAJKA* is meaningful and would be pronounced the same way in either alphabet. But other letters (*H, P, C, B*) are pronounced differently in each alphabet. Consequently, a sentence such as *CPHA CE BEPE* (written with these ambiguous letters) is only meaningful in one alphabet (in this case, Cyrillic). It is meaningless and pronounced differently when read according to the Latin alphabet.

In one set of studies, readers had to identify whether a letter string (in Cyrillic or Latin) represented a Serbo-Croatian word. Letter strings that would be pronounced differently in the two different alphabets took longer to accept as legitimate words and caused more errors than strings that would be pronounced the same in both alphabets. Thus, the existence of two different speech codes, one for each alphabet, slowed the decision. Such interference from the alternate alphabet was observed in tasks in which only one alphabet (such as the Latin) was necessary to successfully perform the task. Most important for the current purposes was the evidence that speech codes were activated in lexical decision tasks that usually do not show evidence of speech codes when English readers perform them with English words. While the comparison is indirect, these data suggest speech codes are more automatically activated if the orthography is more regular than English at the phonemic level.

Speech codes in logographic orthographies Speech codes appear to be activated in the fluent reading of Chinese under circumstances similar to the conditions that elicit speech codes in the fluent reading of English. This conclusion was drawn from the data of Chinese readers who were given a series of tasks analogous to those used with English readers (Tzeng & Hung, 1980). Readers were timed while they performed one of three tasks with Chinese characters. The first task, a phonological task, required subjects to judge whether two characters rhymed with each other; this task was expected to elicit a speech code. The second task, a graphic task, required subjects to judge whether two characters had the same radical; this task was not expected to elicit a speech code. The third task, a semantic task, required subjects to judge whether two characters were synonyms; the purpose of the experiment was to test whether the semantic judgment elicited speech codes. To determine whether speech codes were present, performance in these three tasks was compared to another condition in which the subjects made the same judgments while shadowing spoken Chinese digits. The shadowing task was expected to interfere with speech recoding; consequently, it should slow down a decision to the extent that the task elicits a speech code.

As expected, the shadowing task slowed the phonological judgment a great deal (320 milliseconds). By contrast, it slowed the graphic and semantic judgments much less (127 and 132 milliseconds, respectively). The fact that both the graphic and semantic tasks showed similar effects suggested that the role of speech codes was similar in these two tasks and that speech codes played a much smaller role in these tasks than in the phonological task. This pattern of results is very similar to the pattern obtained with English words and English readers. The suggestion is that meaning judgments of single words can be made without a speech code.

When the task required judging entire sentences, rather than single words, there was more evidence that speech codes were activated. In one such task, readers had to judge whether or not a sentence was grammatical and meaningful. A sentence written with words that sounded similar took longer to judge than a sentence with words that didn't sound similar (Tzeng, Hung, & Wang, 1977). Neither the studies with Chinese readers nor those with English readers established whether the speech codes are prelexical or postlexical. Nevertheless, the general conclusion from this work is that speech recoding can occur in reading Chinese logographs and it is likely to occur at the same stage as in English.

Although they are not as directly related to reading, memory studies also support this conclusion. In one recall study, after the words were initially presented, the subjects were given an intervening task requiring them to shadow words (Tzeng, Hung, & Wang, 1977). Even if the list was presented visually and the subject recalled it by writing out the characters, phonological similarity between the list and the shadowing task decreased the amount recalled. Such results suggest that Chinese readers, like their English counterparts, internally represent written characters in terms of their spoken names.

A similar conclusion can be drawn from memory studies showing that short-term memory for characters is significantly poorer if the written list contains homophones, characters whose pronounced names sound similar (Erickson, Mattingly, & Turvey, 1977). By contrast, there is no interference with a list composed of visually similar characters that do not have similar sounding names. Thus, speech codes are activated for readers of logographies in the same memory tasks that elicit speech codes with English readers.

The interesting but currently unverified hypothesis is that speech codes take less time to activate in a regular alphabetic orthography because the various units of encoding (letters, syllables, as well as whole words) are related in a consistent manner to phonological codes. At the other end of the continuum, logographic characters may activate speech sounds, but it may take longer and the process may be more easily suppressed. English may fall somewhere in the middle of the continuum. But this is only a conjecture. What does seem quite certain is that readers of logographies can and do use speech codes in reading tasks that are similar to those that elicit speech codes in readers of English.

The Effect of the Orthography on Learning to Read

Because learning to read requires breaking the orthographic code, the type of code may influence the learning process. In this section, we consider several possible differences among writing systems and their effects on reading acquisition. One contrast is between logographic and nonlogographic orthographies—namely, alphabetic and syllabic orthographies. The next two sections consider differences in the time children take to master different kinds of orthographies and differences in the rates of reading failure in countries with different types of orthographies. Another variation among alphabetic orthographies is the difference between regular and irregular writing systems and the influence of regularity on learning to read. Finally, we will make a general argument that instructional practices must be adapted to the properties of the orthography.

The Ease of Learning Logographic and Nonlogographic Orthographies

One important difference among the types of orthographies is that alphabetic and syllabic systems—nonlogographic systems—permit the reader to guess the pronunciation of an unknown word more than a logographic system does. A child who has learned to read the English words *tend* and *send* and knows the sounds of other consonants in initial position can make good guesses about the pronunciation of similar words such as *bend, lend,* and *mend.* Thus, the child does not have to ask a teacher or parent the pronunciation and may be able to access the meaning of a word she has never seen printed before by pronouncing it. Alphabetic and syllabic orthographies permit more transfer from spoken to written language than do logographic orthographies. Because of this lack of transfer, logographic systems, such as those used in China and Japan, require that children have many years of schooling to attain mastery.

This contrast is striking when one compares the relative time it takes for a Japanese child to master the Japanese syllabaries versus the Japanese logography. Young children usually learn one of the two syllabaries before they begin school, and they learn the second syllabary, the one used to write foreign words, in first grade. By contrast, the logographic system is introduced gradually and mastered slowly; approximately 50 characters are taught in the first grade, 100, in the second, a total of about 1,000 logographic characters by the end of elementary school, and another 1,000 by the end of high school, at which point the child has mastered the approximately 1,800 characters considered necessary for basic literacy. Undoubtedly, the syllabic systems are easier to master because they impose a smaller memory burden.

Does the logographic system have advantages that compensate for the lack of transfer from oral language? One hypothesis is that some logographic symbols may be more mnemonic, since some have iconic features that look like their referents. However, as was discussed in the section on the structure of the Chinese writing system, very few characters clearly resemble their physical referent. Thus, such mnemonic value—to the extent that it exists—is unlikely to compensate for the lack of transfer.

Because the memory burden required to learn logographic systems is so striking, one might wonder why Japanese and Chinese societies continue to use logographies, particularly since the Japanese already have developed easily learned syllabaries that are used for writing inflections and foreign words. China and Taiwan also have alphabetic systems that are used at the very earliest stage of reading instruction and which theoretically could be the basis of a complete alphabetic system. Part of the answer undoubtedly lies in cultural tradition; societies tend to identify with their own orthography. To part with an orthography that has been part of a culture for thousands of years would be extremely difficult. A second part of the answer is that mastering these logographies provides important benefits for readers. For both the Chinese and Japanese, the logography minimizes the confusion among a large number of words that are distinguished only by stress in spoken speech and could look identical if written in an alphabetic script. The logographic orthography also permits people with very different spoken dialects to read a common language.

Some researchers have approached the contrast between alphabetic and logographic orthographies from the opposite perspective. They have suggested that children may find it more difficult to master the principle underlying alphabetic orthographies, namely, the concept of using characters to represent individual phonemes (Kandel & Tsao, 1981; Makita, 1968; Rozin & Gleitman, 1977). According to this view, it may be easier for children to understand the principles underlying syllabic and logographic systems—that the characters represent syllables and morphemes—even if it takes more time for children to master the entire set of characters.

One fact that is taken as support for this view is that the alphabetic principle may have evolved only once in the history of writing and that the principle is quite abstract (Gelb, 1963; Rozin & Gleitman, 1977). But this fact, by itself, is not especially compelling evidence for the hypothesis. Children who are learning to read are not being asked to invent an orthography; they are being asked to learn an orthography. Just because the alphabetic principle was difficult to invent does not mean that it is difficult to learn.

Another piece of evidence that is interpreted as support for the hypothesis is that American children who have reading problems often have difficulty with oral language tasks that require isolating phonemes in spoken speech, whereas they have less difficulty isolating syllables or words (Wallach & Wallach, 1979). The data are interpreted as suggesting that the phoneme is a difficult unit to identify in spoken language, and so it is difficult to learn how it maps onto written symbols. Because syllables and words are more easily identified, children may find it easier to master an orthography that is based on syllables and words.

As further support for this hypothesis, one group of researchers attempted to demonstrate that children who were having extreme difficulty learning to read English could master a nonalphabetic orthography. They taught a group of poor readers English names for a small set of about 30 Chinese characters. After learning the associations, these children could subsequently decode English sentences that were written with the Chinese characters (Rozin, Poritsky, & Sotsky, 1971). Of course, learning the names of 30 characters is not the same as mastering an orthography. This demonstration does not prove that these children would master an logographic orthography with any greater facility than an alphabetic orthography. Nevertheless, the general hypothesis is one that many researchers have proposed; that is, some children find it particularly difficult to break the alphabetic code.

Another argument concerning the hypothesized difficulty of alphabetic systems is that estimates of severe reading problems are generally higher in the United States than in Japan or Taiwan (Kuo, 1978, cited by Kandel & Tsao, 1981; Makita, 1968). Some have interpreted these data as suggesting that the English alphabetic orthography is responsible for high rates of reading failure. The evidence for this argument is considered in more detail in the next section.

Reading Disability in the United States, Japan, and Taiwan

Several problems arise when assessing the rate of reading failure in different countries to evaluate the possible role of the writing system in reading failure. Societies differ in their view of the nature of reading. For example, one society might stress comprehension, another, word recognition. There may also be differences in what level of reading performance would be considered failure. Even if the problem of assessing reading performance can be solved, the relation between the orthography of various countries and their rates of reading failure is a correlation; consequently, it is unwise to assume that the orthography is the cause of the level of reading performance.

Many other social and educational factors could mediate reading difficulty. For instance, reading achievement might depend upon the importance of reading and literacy in a culture. In addition to differences in the major cultures, there might be differences in subpopulations. For example, reading failure is often associated with low socioeconomic groups (although the link here is also correlational). And quite certainly, the nature of minority groups and the extent and type of their cultural differences varies widely from country to country. Reading failure could be the result of many factors, including poor educational systems and cultural conflicts. Consequently, even if a correlation between the type of orthography and the percentage of reading problems were established, it is unwarranted to blame the orthography without further supporting evidence.

Evidence relating the rate of reading disability to the type of orthography is weak. The data showing low rates of reading disability in Japan and China are often flawed. One of the most commonly cited studies was based on a survey of Japanese teachers who were asked to identify the number of children in their classes who had severe reading problems (Makita, 1968). One obvious problem with this survey technique is that the criterion for judging who has a severe reading problem was never specified. While other researchers have also claimed a low incidence of reading disability in Japan and China, the details of the supporting studies are not generally available (see citations by Kandel & Tsao, 1981).

Some contrary data suggest that the incidence of reading problems in Japan and the United States might be similar for comparable groups of children (Stevenson et al., 1982). In this study, comparable reading tests were constructed in English, Japanese, and Chinese and used to test groups of fifth-graders from the United States, Japan, and Taiwan. The distributions of test scores were generally similar, at least for the English and Japanese groups; the Taiwanese children performed somewhat better.

The study will be described in more detail because in some ways, it is a model of careful cross-cultural research. In other ways, it highlights the difficulty of the cross-cultural approach. The conclusions depend entirely on assuming that the researchers were successful in constructing equivalent reading tests and selecting comparable groups of children.

The researchers tried to ensure that the three tests would be culturally fair and based on the educational practices of the respective countries. The main results came from two types of tests: (1) sight recognition of individual words and (2) text comprehension. The words chosen for the word-recognition test occurred with similar frequency in the most commonly used reading series in each country. Considerable care was also taken in constructing stories and grammatical structures for the reading comprehension test to ensure that they occurred with comparable frequency and were not stilted or unnatural in that language.

The subjects were approximately 450 children from Minneapolis (United States), 750 from Sendai (Japan), and 950 from Tapei (Taiwan). All three countries have universal schooling during the elementary years, and the three cities had comparable populations. Minneapolis was chosen because it is similar to Japan in having relatively few minority students. Eliminating cities with a large number of minorities may have made the U.S. sample more similar to the Japanese; however, the procedure also made the sample less representative of the U.S. school population.

The word-recognition test and the comprehension test scores were highly correlated within each sample; students who did well recognizing words also tended to do well on the comprehension test. But of most interest are the comparisons of word-recognition scores for the three countries. In general, the distribution of the scores for the Japanese and U.S. children overlapped completely, suggesting that there was no difference. However, fewer Taiwanese children received low scores. The Japanese-United States contrast, in particular, gives no support to the hypothesis that an alphabetic orthography is a large-scale source of reading problems.

This research does not exclude the possibility that some children could find an alphabetic orthography difficult, particularly since such children might constitute a very small proportion of the total number of children with reading problems. In fact, this possibility will be explored in Chapter 12 on dyslexia. In addition, as the researchers pointed out, nonalphabetic orthographies also have properties that might be problematic for their readers. For example, in the Chinese orthography, words are not demarcated by spaces, so word segmentation could be much more of problem in learning Chinese than in learning English.

Regularity among Alphabetic Orthographies

It has sometimes been hypothesized that among alphabetic orthographies, those with regular symbol-sound correspondences are easier to learn than those with irregular correspondences. (Notice that the focus here is on the acquisition process. The previously discussed arguments of Chomsky and Halle concerning the optimality of English orthography despite its irregularity pertained to people who already know how to read.) The regularity hypothesis is often not formally assessed; instead, researchers have offered their informal impression that beginning reading performance is better in countries such as Finland and Italy, where alphabetic orthographies are fairly regular, than in countries such as the United States, where orthographies are irregular (Kyostio, 1980). Even if the informal observations were confirmed by research results, the correlational data are vulnerable to the same interpretational problems as the cross-cultural comparisons of alphabetic versus logographic systems that were discussed in the preceding section, problems that prevent any firm conclusions about the effects of orthographies.

The i.t.a.   Another way to evaluate the effect of the regularity of an orthography is to examine the reading acquisition of beginning readers who are taught by means of a specially designed teaching alphabetic that is more regular than the natural orthographic system of the country. One such alphabet, devised in England by Sir James Pitman (1961; Downing, 1977), is the **initial teaching alphabet, or i.t.a.** The i.t.a. supplements the regular set of 26 characters with additional characters in order to provide closer symbol-sound correspondences than the traditional English orthography does. Table 10.2 shows the i.t.a. characters compared to the traditional English orthography. The sentence *I like to buy my pie at night* illustrates the problem that the i.t.a. attempts to solve. In the traditional orthography, the sound of the long *i* is signalled six different ways. In the i.t.a., the sound is represented the same way: *ie liek tω bie mie pie at niet*. In some ways, the i.t.a. is like the technical International Phonetic Alphabet that was shown in Table 10.1. In both systems, the mapping between the written characters and the spoken sounds is more consistent than in traditional English. The increase in regularity is accomplished primarily by introducing many new symbols for vowel sounds, as well as a few new symbols for consonant sounds.

The i.t.a. was devised to be an instructional tool. Its purpose was to serve as the initial alphabet for teaching children who would transfer to traditional English orthography after the initial stage of reading acquisition. Using the i.t.a., the opening line of the Gettysburg Address looks somewhat different than normal English (Downing, 1977):

> forscor and seven yɛɛrs agœ aur faჳhers braut forჳh on ჳhis continent a nu‍e næʃhon, consɛɛvd in liberty, and dedicæted ჳω ჳhe propœsiʃhon ჳhat aull men ar creæted ɛɛkwal.

This rendition in the i.t.a. looks somewhat foreign but perhaps not as alien as the International Phonetic Alphabet. The i.t.a. maintains some of the features of the traditional orthography. In fact, the i.t.a. is not a strictly regular orthography; compromises were made to make words written with the i.t.a. appear more similar to those written with the traditional orthography. For example, the consonants *c* and *k*, although associated with the same sound, are both used in the i.t.a. to increase the

Table 10.2 Characters in the initial teaching alphabet (i.t.a.)

Vowels			Consonants		
Character	*Example*	*Traditional Spelling*	*Character*	*Example*	*Traditional Spelling*
æ	fæt	fate	b	bat	bat
a	appl	apple	ჩh	ჩhill	chill
au	pau	paw	d	dog	dog
ɛɛ	mɛɛt	meat	f	fill	fill
e	egg	egg	g	gœ	go
i‍e	di‍e	die	h	hat	hat
i	pin	pin	j	jɑr	jar
œ	tœ	toe	k	kit	kit
ɑ	father	father	c	cat	cat
o	hot	hot	l	lamp	lamp
oi	boi	boy	m	man	man
u‍e	du‍e	due	n	net	net
ω	mωn	moon	ŋ	siŋ	sing
ω	bωk	book	p	pet	pet
u	dug	dug	r	red	red
ɑu	plɑu	plow	s	sad	sad
			ʃh	ʃhip	ship
			t	top	top
			ţh	ţhin	thin
			ჳh	ჳhen	then
			v	van	van
			w	win	win
			y	yell	yell
			z	zω	zoo
			ʂ	nœʂ	nose
			ʒ	viʒon	vision
			wh	when	when
			ɽ	biɽd	bird

visual similarity between the appearance of i.t.a. words and traditionally spelled words.

Evaluations of the i.t.a. have provided equivocal results. There is some agreement that slow children do begin to show some benefit at the end of three years, but the poorest 10 percent show negligible improvements (Downing, 1967, 1968). The effects are not generally large. Moreover, their interpretation is unclear because the introduction of the i.t.a. into an early reading program often results in many other simultaneous changes in the program. For example, teachers using the i.t.a. may stress symbol-sound relations more than teachers using the traditional alphabet. More generally, the regularity of an orthography is only one of several determinants of reading acquisition and probably not the most important one, at that (Venezky, 1978, 1980). Determining the symbol-sound relations is a necessary condition for reading success, but it is not a sufficient condition. Beyond the specific orthographic code, learning to read entails learning to execute and integrate a variety of comprehension processes and a high level of awareness of what reading is about. These other skills may also be used to help infer specific symbol-sound correspondences. Regardless of the phonemic regularity of the orthography, some children in all countries have difficulty learning to read. Irregularity probably constitutes something of a hurdle, but it is one that most children surmount.

Adaptive Teaching Practices

Cross-cultural research strongly suggests that teaching practices should reflect the characteristics of the orthography. Clearly, reading instruction should vary for the three different types of orthographies, alphabetic, syllabic, and logographic. Logographic orthographies must be taught primarily by nonphonic techniques; teachers of Chinese or Japanese must focus on different units of analysis (such as the radical) and provide different cues and mnemonics than those that are available to teachers of alphabetic orthographies, such as English.

A more subtle example of adaptive teaching practices within alphabetic languages comes from a case study of reading instruction in Hebrew (Feitelson, 1980). Early methods of teaching Hebrew, from 1920 to the early 1950s, were strongly influenced by the look-and-say method of teaching that was developed in English-speaking countries. These methods taught that word shape was an important cue to word recognition, so words with ascending letters, descending letters, and capital letters were introduced early and emphasized.

The Israeli school systems adopted this method and had generally good results, even though the Hebrew character set is much more homogenous than the English alphabet. (Word shape, which is not a good cue to word identity in English, is an even worse cue in Hebrew.) But reading problems began to occur in the 1950s, with the large-scale influx of Jewish immigrants from Arab countries who were illiterate or undereducated.

Interviews with the parents of good and poor readers revealed why the look-and-say method of instruction had managed to produce good readers over the preceding few decades, in spite of its apparent unsuitability to the Hebrew orthography. In brief, literate parents who discovered their child had difficulty in learning to read simply provided supplemental instruction at home. As a typical example,

Feitelson cites one couple who discovered that their child was having difficulty when he was home from school due to illness:

> "We thought our son read very well and we were delighted with his progress. But when he fell ill in the middle of the term we suddenly discovered that all he did was guess. So I [the father] explained the principle of the thing to him and by the time he returned to school a few days later he could really read." (Feitelson, 1973, p. 435)

By contrast, the parents who were new immigrants could not intervene in the schooling process because they were not literate in Hebrew. Since immigrant parents were not able to provide such supplemental instruction for their children, the rates of reading failure for immigrant students soared.

Further studies were done, comparing schools with high failure rates to other schools in middle-class, established neighborhoods. For the schools with high failure rates, it was found that entire classes tended to do well or poorly. Usually, the classes that did well were those in which the teacher did not adhere to the look-and-say method but rather spent considerable time in reading activities, including syllable drill. These teachers often achieved better results than those who had always been considered to be more resourceful and inspiring but had drilled their students less. Partly as a consequence of this research, teaching materials were changed so that by 1966, reading disability had virtually disappeared, according to Feitelson. Feitelson concluded that initial teaching methods had to be closely adapted to the writing system, particularly if the children were from disadvantaged backgrounds, since such children don't have other routes to learning.

The Creation and Revision of Orthographies

In addition to the effect on the cognitive and perceptual processes of readers, a writing system can have sociological consequences, as well. A shared orthography, like a shared dialect, can link one social group with another. And different orthographies can distinguish different social groups. Writing systems make the economic, religious, and literary activities of a group appear more or less accessible to another group, which may influence both their conception of their own society and that of another group. In support of this viewpoint, it has been found that sociological factors play a large role in the creation and adoption of new writing systems.

The widespread introduction of literacy to previously illiterate cultures in the past hundred years has revealed that whether a linguistic community adopts an orthography depends upon social and cultural factors more than linguistic, cognitive, or pedagogical factors (Fishman, 1977). A new writing system is typically introduced as part of some larger political change. It implies that a previously illiterate society will now have skills that accompany changes in the economic system, the educational system, the leisure and cultural institutions, and the distribution of power. By contrast, a revision in an established orthography (such as spelling reform) may not signal such revolutionary changes in society. The success or failure of orthographic reform is determined by a somewhat different set of factors, although these factors are also culturally tinged.

Many new orthographies are devised for a subgroup of a multilingual society in which the other subgroup(s) already has an orthography (Berry, 1977). In such cases, the prestige associated with the existing orthography often determines which of its properties will be accepted or rejected in the new orthography (Fishman, 1977). An example of this sociological influence is given in the case of a Mexican-Indian society that was familiar with Spanish orthography from billboards and road signs and wanted their orthography to graphically resemble Spanish, even though some of the properties of Spanish were not well suited to the Mexican-Indian's phonemic system. There are also some cases in which an orthography has been intentionally developed with distinctive graphic characteristics to emphasize and maintain cultural distance from another group.

One reason why cultural factors may be so important in the creation of new orthographies is that the new orthographies being created today are at least somewhat sound-based and usually alphabetic (Grimes & Gordon, 1980). Newly created orthographies are not logographic. Although the design decisions made in creating the alphabetic system may have cognitive and educational implications, the effects are presumably much smaller than the consequences of choosing an alphabetic system over a logographic one.

It has been more difficult to explain what governs the acceptance of a revision of an established orthography, as opposed to the acceptance of an entirely new one (Fishman, 1977). Why is it, for example, that Norway and Holland recently successfully revised their orthographies to simplify their spelling, whereas the numerous attempts to revise English orthography have been unaccepted? Similarly, why is it that after the revolution, the Chinese government announced that changing to an alphabetic system was a new goal of high educational priority but more recently returned to a policy favoring the traditional logography?

There are few satisfactory explanations of why orthographic reforms succeed in some countries and not in others. However, the case histories of both successful and unsuccessful movements document that the revision of orthographies is closely tied to social and political factors, rather than strictly educational or cognitive ones. The written language reflects the history and literature of a culture; thus, it is identified with the society and its goals. Another determinant is whether the orthographic reforms are championed by a political or cultural group that has political power or prestige with the group whose orthography is being altered. All of these cultural factors exert considerable influence on the extent and type of orthographic reform that can be implemented.

Summary

Undoubtedly, the most important psychological difference among orthographies is the level at which the written symbols relate to the spoken language, whether at the level of phonemes (alphabetic orthographies), syllables (syllabic orthographies), or morphemes (logographic orthographies). All writing systems reflect some aspects of the spoken language; however, no orthography, not even the most regular alphabetic orthography, is a direct transcription of speech.

While English is an alphabetic orthography, linguistic analyses show that the writing system sometimes preserves the graphic similarity between morphologically related words, such as *photograph* and *photography,* at the expense of symbol-sound regularity. In this example, the pronunciations of the o's differ between the words, but because *photograph* and *photography* are written similarly, their semantic relation is very apparent. Analysis of the symbol-sound relations in English shows that relatively simple factors can explain the pronunciation of single-syllable, single-morpheme words. However, for words composed of multiple syllables and multiple morphemes, the factors are much more complex and include the identity of the morpheme itself. These analyses suggest that a simple symbol-to-sound translation process would not be sufficient to pronounce complex words correctly.

The most interesting question for the present purposes is how the characteristics of the orthography influence fluent and early reading. Research suggests that many of the basic processes that operate in the fluent reading of an alphabetic orthography like English also operate in a very different orthography, namely, the Chinese logography. Word-encoding processes are affected by the complexity of the character; lexical access is influenced by word frequency. Finally, the availability and likelihood of retrieving speech codes during fluent reading may be influenced by the type of the orthography.

The review of cross-cultural research suggested that there is no strong evidence that the alphabetic orthography itself is a source of large-scale reading difficulties in U.S. schools. A more reasonable view is that it can be a difficulty but one that most children overcome with appropriate instruction. Nevertheless, it is also apparent that beginning reading instruction should be adapted to the characteristics of the orthography to help the child unlock the orthographic code.

Suggested Readings

Gelb (1963) provides an excellent account of the historical development of writing systems. We recommend Wang (1973) for a brief description of the Chinese orthography and papers in the volume edited by Kavanagh and Mattingly (1972) for descriptions of other writing systems.

Successful analyses of the English writing system are fairly recent. Venezky's (1970) analysis is readable and also one of the few to specify the body of words that was being analyzed (namely, the 20,000 most frequent words in English). For those who are ready to tackle more technical presentations, consult Klima (1972) and the seminal work of Chomsky and Halle (1968).

Hung and Tzeng (1981) review the literature on how orthographies influence fluent reading. A related clinical topic—how damage due to a stroke or brain injury affects the processing of different writing systems—is presented by Sasanuma (1975). Some researchers have used this data to argue that different orthographies are processed in different parts of the brain. But the article by Hung and Tzeng (1981) convincingly argues against drawing any strong conclusions.

The process of spelling a word, rather than reading it, is the topic of papers in the volume edited by Frith (1980). And Rozin and Gleitman (1977; Gleitman & Rozin, 1977) present an interesting discussion of the development of writing systems to support their conjecture that the late development of the alphabet in human history relates to the difficulty some children have in learning how to read an alphabetic system. Gray (1956) and the chapters in Downing (1973) describe how reading is taught in different countries.

11

Beginning Reading: Decoding Processes and Instruction

Although people learn to produce and understand spoken language without formal instruction, this is not the case in learning to read. Reading is a skill that is formally taught in schools as a matter of public policy. The important issues for psychology and education are the same as for any other skill: What are the component subskills, what are the prerequisite skills, which instructional techniques are most effective, and how is proficiency in the skill gained?

In this chapter, we focus on the kind of reading acquisition that a child of about five to seven years of age goes through in the early years of schooling. Our prototypical reading pupil—suppose it's a little girl—already has a fair amount of oral comprehension skill before she begins reading instruction, so we will not deal with general comprehension skills in this chapter. Instead, we will consider word-decoding skill, making sense of printed words.

In Chapters 2 and 3, we described how skilled readers encode and lexically access words, and we provided a theoretical account of the processes in the form of the READER simulation model. Now we turn to the issue of how these processes came to take the form they did. How do children come to encode a word as rapidly and automatically as an adult?

One immediate difference between adults and children appears in the terminology. The research literature on reading acquisition refers to word *decoding*, while research on adults reading refers to word *encoding*. We maintain this convention for continuity. The term **decoding** primarily focuses on the process of extracting information from the orthographic code. The term's focus is appropriate for early reading because written language is a code that beginning readers must crack. By contrast, the term **encoding** focuses on the process of transforming the information into mental symbols. In fact, both children and adults execute both processes, although skilled readers may perform both functions with a single process. However, for most children, decoding is the major skill to be acquired in early reading. The early reader's comprehension skills provide her with some degree of code-cracking ability but not enough to crack the orthographic code, which requires determining which word is denoted by a particular combination of written letters.

Overview   This chapter has four main sections. In the initial section, **Instructional Practices for Teaching Decoding,** we will contrast the two major instructional approaches, phonics and whole-word methods, which differ in the emphasis given to explicit phonics instruction. Currently, many teaching programs include aspects of both methods, although there are still distinctions between programs that have developed from one tradition or the other.

In the second section, we will examine **Processes in Beginning Word Decoding.** There are two main strategies in decoding: (1) direct visual recognition and (2) speech recoding (the use of a speech-based code to access a word's meaning). Fluent readers rely primarily on direct visual recognition. However, children make more use of speech recoding, which may help them acquire the visual representations that characterize skilled reading. In this section, we will also present a model of word decoding based on a study of the decoding skills of poor and average eight-year-old readers (Firth, 1972).

In the third section, **Acquiring Proficiency,** we will discuss how children make the transition from slow, laborious decoding in the first and second grade to the rapid, automatic process that characterizes fluent adult reading. Practice is a major determinant of reading fluency. With practice, words no longer need to be phonologically recoded and the attentional requirements decrease, allowing the reader to attend to other aspects of reading.

In the final section, we will discuss **Reading Readiness.** Reading readiness does not refer to a particular physical or mental age. Rather, it refers to a set of skills that children must acquire to benefit from a particular reading program.

Instructional Practices for Teaching Decoding

To learn to recognize a word, a child must analyze the graphic information in the printed word and build up an internal representation of it. This means learning the features, letters, and letter clusters that characterize a particular word and discriminate it from other words (Gibson, 1970). Also, the internal representation must be linked to the meaning of the word, so that eventually the encoded visual representation initiates lexical access. In this section, we will describe the importance of word recognition in early reading, the major approaches to teaching word recognition, and the variables that influence the success of early reading instruction.

The Importance of Word Decoding in Early Reading

Word decoding is an important component of early reading skill. This hypothesis is supported by several sources of evidence. First, moderately high correlations, between 0.50 and 0.80, have been reported for second- and third-grade children between their ability to recognize individual words presented in a list and their fluency in reading texts (Shankweiler & Liberman, 1972; Spache, 1963). High correlations have also been reported for nine-, ten-, and eleven-year-olds, comparing their scores on two reading tests (the Schonell test [1961] and the Neale test [1966]), which differ primarily in whether the words are presented in a list without any context or in short passages (Neale, 1966). The accuracy of word decoding without context is correlated with measures of reading skill in which the text is present. Such correlations are also consistent with the hypothesis that word-decoding skill is sometimes a bottleneck in attaining fluency, a hypothesis that will be examined in detail in Chapter 12 on dyslexia and in Chapter 15 on individual differences.

Not only the accuracy but also the speed of word decoding is important in early reading. The speed with which a child can pronounce words presented without a context correlates with more general measures of reading skill; consequently, pronunciation speed has been used as a measure of word-decoding skill (Lesgold, Resnick, & Hammond, 1985). Using this measure, one study of second-, third-, and fifth-graders found that for the youngest readers, reading comprehension scores were highly correlated with word-decoding skill (Curtis, 1980). By contrast, their reading comprehension scores were not correlated with their listening comprehension scores. However, the pattern of correlations changed as children progressed through school. For the fifth-graders, reading comprehension correlated more highly with listening comprehension than with word-decoding skill. The changing pattern of correlations suggests that in the early years, word-decoding skill is an important determinant of reading fluency. However, as decoding skill improves, individual differences in reading skill may be limited more by the comprehension processes that are common to reading and listening. Such a result also makes sense in the context of early reading instruction. It is only after children have sufficiently mastered decoding in the first two or three years of school that they begin to read materials that tax their comprehension and conceptual skills.

The emphasis on decoding is not meant to imply that comprehension processes are unimportant in reading acquisition or that they are never a source of individual differences among children. Clearly, decoding skill alone is insufficient for reading comprehension. For example, the reading skills of average third-grade children were studied as part of a larger project on word recognition that will be described in Chapter 12. In one experiment, the subjects read a difficult article from *Scientific American* out loud. These children had sufficient decoding skills to pronounce most of the words in this rather technical article; but unsurprisingly, they couldn't answer questions about what they had read, nor could they summarize it. They lacked the vocabulary, the world knowledge, and the linguistic sophistication that was necessary to understand the text they were saying aloud. Obviously, decoding skill is only one ingredient of reading.

Comprehension processes can aid word decoding. Goodman (1965) has been a major proponent of the position that children need to apply their general language comprehension skills to aid in decoding. To demonstrate this point, Goodman presented 100 first-, second-, and third-graders with a list of words, recorded the words they missed, and then presented the same words in a story. When the words occurred in a story, the children were able to pronounce many of the words they initially missed when they read them in the list. Of the 20 words (on average) that second-graders missed when reading the list, an average of only five words were missed every time they were encountered in the story. Although children were helped by the context, the exact facilitation of context cannot be inferred from this particular procedure, since the story came after the list and some words occurred many times in the story. Also, we simply do not know how easily the words could be guessed from the text. Nevertheless, Goodman's proposal that contextual information can be used in word decoding is very probably correct.

The decoding aspect of early reading instruction has two main goals. First, the child must learn to recognize certain words on sight, particularly high-frequency words such as *have, of,* and *though.* Second, the child must learn procedures for decoding new words. Initially, decoding new words may be slow and effortful. In the literature on early reading, these procedures are called *word attack,* a label that captures the often laborious character of early word decoding.

Instructional Methods

While several instructional methods are used to teach early reading, the two most dominant approaches are the **phonics method** and the **whole-word method,** which differ primarily in their relative emphasis on the use of symbol-sound correspondences to decode words.

In the pure whole-word method, children are supposed to learn to recognize words using cues from the previous part of the story, accompanying pictures, and the general shape of the whole word. One rationale for this approach is that the emphasis on entire words and high-level cues appears to be closer to the units that skilled readers use. However, part of the rationale is incorrect; as we argued in the section on word encoding in Chapter 2, skilled readers encode words in terms of letters, not shapes. A second rationale for the whole-word approach is that the child will be more motivated to read if the reading exercises are meaningful—that is, if words and stories are the major focus of the lessons, rather than meaningless letter clusters.

In the phonics method, children are explicitly taught symbol-sound correspondences and how to use them to decode words. The rationale is that a successful reader must learn these correspondences, and this method makes the induction task explicit, rather than leave it for children to infer on their own.

While the two methods historically were quite distinct, they are less distinct today. Current programs that originated in the whole-word tradition now incorporate varying amounts of explicit phonics instruction, and phonics programs recognize that some words must be taught as sight vocabulary. However, differences between the two systems still exist. In this section, we will describe the two approaches as they are reflected in the books and manuals used to teach early reading.

Most commercially produced reading series have several components: a set of graded reading books, students' workbooks with exercises, and teacher's manuals that include a variety of materials, such as suggestions for how to prepare the students for reading, points to bring out in the story, and exercises to follow reading. Surveys of early reading instruction show that at least in the early grades, teachers rely on published reading programs for much of the structure and content of their lessons. Consequently, an analysis of the materials in these programs provides one index of how children are taught.

Whole-word Programs and Phonics Programs

Examples of the main two types of reading programs illustrate their characteristics and make the contrasts more apparent. Figure 11.1 presents some sample stories and the accompanying vocabulary from a widely used basal reader that is prototypical of the whole-word tradition. This sample includes stories that a typical child would encounter at the beginning, middle, and end of first grade. As the excerpts il-

a. Beginning of First Grade

TIM

Come here, Tim.
We have to go.
Tim! Tim!
We have to go.

Mom, can you come here?
Can you come and help me?

b. Middle of First Grade

THE LITTLE ENGINE THAT COULD

Puff, puff, puff, puff.
The Little Train came up the track.
The Little Train was a happy train.
Puff, puff, puff, puff.
Up the mountain it came.

Vocabulary: could, stop, new, old, start, just, thought, had

Decodable vocabulary: had, puffing, pulled, started

c. End of First Grade

READING A MAP

A map is something that shows you
where things are.

If you can read a map, you can find
your way around a city or a town.

You can use a map to find
streets, parks, and mountains.

The map you see at the
top is a map of West Town.

What are the names of the streets?

Vocabulary: ponds, Uncle

Decodable vocabulary: map, Stone, Cliff, Space, West, quickest

Figure 11.1 Excerpts of lessons from a first-grade reading series that illustrate the whole-word approach. The stories appear with pictures and the child is encouraged to use the pictures and other contextual cues to identify and remember words. *Source:* (a) Harper & Row, 1980a, pp. 4, 5, 6; (b) Harper & Row, 1980b, p. 56; (c) Harper & Row, 1980c, p. 170.

lustrate, the vocabulary consists primarily of frequent words, which tend to be irregular in their pronunciation. But this series, like many other whole-word programs, also has a phonics component, in which children are taught symbol-sound relations. For example, the words listed under *decodable vocabulary* are used to reinforce phonics lessons. Nevertheless, the phonics component is not the primary method used to teach word decoding, nor is it the primary focus of the reading program.

In these programs, considerable stress is placed on using the context to guess words that are not recognized. As we mentioned earlier, one theorist whose views are consistent with the whole-word approach is Goodman (1969), who has argued that reading is a "psycholinguistic guessing game" in which children should use their knowledge of language to guide their decoding. We have already described his finding that children can sometimes recognize a word in context that they cannot decode when presented in a list (Goodman, 1965). Similar results were found in a longitudinal study (described in *Other determinants of reading success*) in which children's skill in decoding isolated words was compared to their skill in orally reading familiar stories accompanied by pictures (Calfee & Pointkowski, 1981). Some children who were in a very traditional whole-word program could read words in context even though they were quite poor in decoding isolated words. However, these children required considerable help from the instructor, even for familiar words. More generally, semantic and syntactic clues from the text cannot entirely replace the visual decoding of letters and words. Children in whole-word programs must learn to attend to both the context and the letter patterns that make up the words.

A somewhat different picture emerges from the phonics series. Figure 11.2 shows excerpts of stories and the corresponding vocabulary from a phonics-based series. Again, the stories were selected from materials for the beginning, middle, and end of first grade. With a phonics approach, the lessons center around particular symbol-sound correspondences and the words that illustrate these correspondences. Also, as part of the program, children are usually taught how to blend successive sounds into a word. Irregular words are taught as sight vocabulary. However, the major emphasis is on phonics.

Phonics programs generally acknowledge the importance of meaning in reading; the proponents of such programs typically argue that meaning and decoding are inextricably related and that decoding skills are necessary to prevent frustration in reading. But because phonics approaches emphasize symbol-sound correspondence, critics of the approach question whether the meaning side of reading receives too little attention. By and large, it appears that a phonics approach does not result in *word calling*—recognizing individual words without relating them to each other. Phonics programs also include stories to be read, so that reading comprehension, not just isolated symbol-sound correspondences, is an integral part of the program. Overall, children who learn through phonics-based programs do as well in text comprehension as those who are taught by a more whole-word approach.

Characterizing the differences between approaches Evaluating the differences between the two approaches requires an analysis of several reading programs, not just two. In a classic analysis of reading programs, Chall (1967)

a. Beginning of First Grade

> NAN, DAN, AND ANN
>
> Dan and Nan ran.
> Dan and Ann ran.

b. Middle of First Grade

> MARTIN
>
> Martin must not get up.
> It is hard for him to rest.
>
> Pat sends Martin a card.
> Pat did the art on the card.
> It has a red star on it.
>
> Grandma sent a card from the farm.
> Grandma's card has a gift in it.

> *Vocabulary: ar*—arm, art, car, cart, card, hard, harm, harp, far, farm, tar, tart,
>   darn, dart, part, start, star, scar, scarf, garden

c. End of First Grade

> A GRAND CELEBRATION
>
> Mr. Martinez was very excited when he came home
> from work. He picked up his wife and kissed her.
> Then he began to yell for everyone's attention.
>
> "What's the matter?" asked his wife.
> "Why are you yelling?" asked Ramon.
> "Papa, what is all the commotion?" asked Maria.
>
> "So many questions!" said Mr. Martinez
> with a big smile. "Quiet, everyone! I'll
> give you an explanation." He motioned for
> everyone to sit down.
>
> "I had a big surprise at work today," said
> Mr. Martinez. "They gave me a promotion. Now
> my position will be manager of the entire
> department store."

Figure 11.2 Excerpts of lessons from a first-grade reading series that exemplify the phonics approach. Symbol-sound relations are stressed and the vocabulary of the stories reflects the systematic selection of words to illustrate those relations. *Source:* (a) Walcutt & McCracken, 1981c, p. 7; (b) Walcutt & McCracken, 1981a, p. 7; and (c) Walcutt & McCracken, 1981b, pp. 79, 80, 81. (From *Lippincott Basic Reading A, B, C.* New York: Harper & Row.)

Figure 11.2   (cont.)

"They made a fine decision," said
Mrs. Martinez. "You have worked very hard.
You deserve a promotion."

Vocabulary: -*sion*—admission, expression, mission, permission, mansion,
decision, occasion, vision, television
-*tion*—action, nation, station, motion, lotion, education, deco-
ration, duration, vacation, explanation, invitation, celebration
addition, position, condition, definition, attention, question,
contradiction, commotion, promotion

showed several differences between early whole-word approaches and phonics
approaches in how they taught decoding, vocabulary, and comprehension. Beck
(1981) recently brought some of these observations up to date in an analysis of eight
popular reading series (listed in Table 11.1), half of which are modern-day descen-
dants of earlier whole-word approaches and half of which represent phonics
approaches.

Current whole-word methods incorporate considerable phonics instruction, in
part because of skepticism about the effectiveness of the pure whole-word approaches that predominated from the 1920s to 1950s. The difference between the
two methods is considerably less today than when Chall reviewed the programs.
Some researchers have suggested that there is no real difference between whole-
word and phonics programs outside of the sequence in which phonics concepts are
taught (see Venezky, 1978). Still others believe the differences continue to be significant (Beck, 1981). One reason for this difference of opinions is that reading programs within an approach vary considerably.

Beck concluded that phonics programs today have a number of features that
give primary emphasis to phonics instruction. For example, the phonics instruction
typically precedes the reading lesson, so the children can use the newly learned
symbol-sound correspondence to read new words in the story. Moreover, a high
proportion of the words in the story can be decoded using the phonics skills that the

Table 11.1   Beginning reading series analyzed by Beck (1981)

Emphasis on Phonics in Decoding

The Palo Alto Reading Program, Harcourt Brace Jovanovich
Distar I and II, SRA
Programmed Reading, Sullivan Associates, McGraw-Hill
The Merrill Linguistic Reading Program, Charles E. Merrill

Emphasis on Context in Decoding

Reading 720, Ginn
Houghton Mifflin Reading Series, Houghton Mifflin
The Bank Street Readers, Macmillan
The New Open Highways, Scott Foresman

child has learned up to that point. In the early stages, the stories may be stilted because they contain only those words that can be decoded using the phonics principles that have already been taught. However, the number of possible words expands rapidly because the phonics principles generalize to a large number of regular words.

Beck (1981) argued that whole-word programs still de-emphasize phonics and give primary stress to meaning and reading for enjoyment. For example, in the whole-word programs Beck analyzed, relatively few questions and directions in the teacher's manuals suggested that phonics be taught as a way to recognize words. Also, phonics generalizations could not be used to recognize new words in the story because phonics instruction usually followed the story. Throughout the first grade, a relatively small proportion of the words in a given lesson's story could be decoded using the phonics that had been taught up to that point. This was particularly true in the first third of first grade. Instead, stories used high-frequency words. In the reading programs she examined, Beck also found differences in the suggestions for teaching particular symbol-sound correspondences. In phonics programs, the teachers were told to produce the sounds explicitly when teaching symbol-sound correspondences. In several of the whole-word programs, teachers were told to avoid producing the sound in isolation from the word. The manuals in the whole-word programs emphasized the use of context to guess words and retain their meaning. To recognize unknown words, children were to use cues from the story, pictures, and their normal language patterns. To remember a word, the manuals suggested that children think of the meaning of the word while looking at the word, with little emphasis on the specific letters that make up the word.

Other reading programs combine features of the phonics and whole-word approaches or they use different techniques. One program that has properties of both approaches selects vocabulary words (such as *bat, fat, mat,* and *cat*) to illustrate systematic phonemic contrasts (Bloomfield & Barnhart, 1961). Bloomfield pointed out that the high-frequency words used in whole-word programs tend to have irregular symbol-sound correspondences, a point that was also clear from the orthographic analysis described in Chapter 10. The consequence for beginning readers is that such vocabulary items would complicate the child's task of inducing phonics principles. Bloomfield's answer was to stress whole words but carefully choose a simplified vocabulary to illustrate certain phonics principles. Current programs using this approach usually introduce analyses of single symbol-sound correspondences in addition to the controlled vocabulary, so that this method includes the critical property of a phonics program in addition to emphasizing whole words.

Other early reading programs may stress context and meaning but are distinguished from more traditional whole-word programs by other unique features. For example, one such program, called a *language experience* approach, begins with the sentence as a unit for reading and writing. The child may be asked to say a sentence and then be taught to read it; in the process, she is taught to recognize individual words. This method also de-emphasizes phonics and emphasizes context instead, based on the assumption that the units of instruction should be meaningful.

The distinction between phonics and whole-word approaches does not account for all of the variation among reading programs. In addition, programs vary in the *degree* to which symbol-sound relations are emphasized, in how systematically such contrasts are presented, and in whether the relations are to be induced from examples or stated initially and then illustrated with examples (Chall, 1967; Johnson & Pearson, 1978). Even though the classification scheme provides only a rough dichotomy among reading programs, one of the most persistent controversies in the instructional literature has been whether one approach is better than another or whether the differences are too small to matter.

Evaluating which method is better   Chall (1967) compared the phonics and whole-word methods by surveying studies on their relative effectiveness. Her conclusion was that the phonics method led to better early reading for children at all ability levels and particularly for slower children. Of course, when Chall evaluated the evidence in the 1960s, the difference between the two reading approaches was more pronounced than it is today. Some subsequent large-scale studies have also found the phonics method to be somewhat superior (cited by Beck, 1981), but other equally large-scale studies have found no consistent differences (Bond & Dykstra, 1967).

Overall, the general body of evidence favors systematic phonics instruction (Johnson & Baumann, 1984). It is obvious that most children learn to read using either method. Many children induce the symbol-sound correspondences, even if the correspondences are not explicitly taught. Beyond this general conclusion, two major questions remain: First, do children taught by the two methods reach comparable levels of mastery in similar amounts of time? And second, do children who are educationally at risk (for example, those who lack other basic skills or lack additional resources, such as help and encouragement from family members) learn better with one method than the other?

The answers to these seemingly clear-cut questions remain unclear for several reasons. One reason is that evaluation studies commonly ask teachers to classify their technique as exclusively one approach or the other. Such a dichotomous classification does not capture important features that may influence the nature of learning, such as whether a primarily whole-word method employs supplementary phonics instruction or whether a phonics method also stresses the use of context. An additional complication is that many aspects of instruction besides reading method contribute to successful learning: the time a child actually spends reading, the level of parental encouragement and help, and the child's motivation and cognitive skills. Finally, different approaches may be more effective with different children, an instance in which the child's abilities may interact with instructional technique.

Other determinants of reading success   Some of the factors that affect early reading were evident in a study that examined the decoding skills that children acquired during their first year of instruction (Calfee & Pointkówski, 1981). The study involved 60 children from 10 first-grade classrooms in four different elementary schools; the groups were selected so that they were roughly comparable in IQ and listening comprehension ability.

During the year, the researchers tested the children's decoding and oral-reading skills as they mastered the relevant material. At the beginning of the school year, all the students mastered early reading skills: identifying letters, identifying rhyming words, and matching letters to initial consonants in words. However, by November, significant differences appeared among the children. These differences persisted and increased such that by the end of the year, there were several distinct levels of decoding skill. The most successful children performed well at every decoding task: reading simple consonant-vowel-consonant words (such as *mop*), words with vowel contrasts (such as *tap, tape*), words with blends (such as *trap*) and digraphs (such as *read, show*), and polysyllabic words.

The least successful group consisted of 10 children who still had problems with the simplest words, such as *mop*. By May, these children had only progressed to the point of decoding the initial consonant and sometimes the final consonant of the simplest words, and then, only when given cues, such as first being shown a similar word and told its pronunciation. Some of these children could read words in a story by using cues from the context. However, their skill was severely limited, since they required a text that contained familiar words and needed the teacher to correct their guesses and offer encouragement. Nevertheless, one could imagine that given such support and encouragement, these children eventually might begin to pay more attention to the graphic information and induce the symbol-sound relations on their own.

Nine of the 10 children with the highest failure rate in decoding came from a school that used a basal series from the whole-word tradition; the teachers were described as having closely followed the manual, which stressed reading for meaning. However, the instructional method was not the major determinant of decoding skill, because the very same basal series was used by another school whose students did quite well. In the second school, the teachers supplemented the basal series with phonics exercises. There were also other important differences between the instructional methods. It turned out that the amount of time spent teaching in the first school was relatively low. The two teachers were described as "mild mannered and mechanical," and the children were often restless. By contrast, teachers in the more successful school were described as doing more teaching and using a firm and supportive teaching style. Thus, many factors determine successful learning, and many bright or average children (such as these) can learn to read with either method if other factors are supportive. Nonetheless, it is reasonable to conclude that the systematic phonics approach is the most successful in teaching word decoding to those children who do not acquire it on their own.

As this study graphically illustrates, the success of a beginning teaching program depends on the teacher's style and the time devoted to reading, in addition to the reading series that is used. Several attempts have been made to quantify these features of the teaching situation and relate them to the relative success of a program. In an interesting summary of such instructional analyses, Barr (1984) made the point that it is easier to list and rate components of a teaching situation than to provide a model of how they might interact. Overall, it has proven difficult to analyze the science and art of successful teaching, although this is certainly an area for further research.

Finally, future research should also examine the impact of home support and instruction on reading. The importance of the family in reading achievement became apparent in the Israeli study (Feitelson, 1973) described in Chapter 10 on orthography. That study found that the overall success of a given teaching method turned out to depend on whether parents monitored their child's progress and offered instruction if he had reading problems. Feitelson found that even though the standard, whole-word method was not well suited to teaching reading in Hebrew, the method had been used for years without large-scale problems. Its apparent success was due to parents providing supplementary instruction to their children. Consequently, problems did develop when there was an influx of immigrant parents who were unable to instruct their children in Hebrew. This study demonstrates that instruction by parents can be an important factor in children's reading success.

Correlational and Experimental Evidence

It is important to consider the limitations of correlational data because several studies in this chapter are based on correlational evidence. For example, in this chapter, we have described several studies that examined the correlation between a child's skill in pronouncing isolated words and in reading text; we have also described correlations between different teaching methods and the reading skills of children in the programs. Correlational studies are often a major source of evidence because they may be the only practical way to initially evaluate the potential effects of a complex, long-term instructional program. However, a correlation between two factors does not imply that one factor causes the outcome in the second factor. Other relations are possible; for example, the second factor could cause the outcome of the first or both factors could be determined by some third factor.

The pitfalls of interpreting correlational data as implying causality can be illustrated with a skill that has frequently been suggested to be an early reading skill—knowing the names of the letters of the alphabet. Several studies have found that children who know the names of many or all of the letters before they begin reading instruction tend to be better readers at the end of first grade. In fact, in the best-known large-scale evaluation of reading methods, knowledge of letter names was the best single predictor of reading success (Bond & Dykstra, 1967). However, this relation turned out to be only correlational; subsequent research found that knowing the names of letters did not cause better reading.

The correlation was deceptive because one can easily think of several reasons why knowing letter names might help a child learn to read. One might hypothesize that letter names would help the letter-recognition process, which is clearly important in reading. Alternatively, letter names could be an entry point to learning symbol-sound correspondences. Durrell (1980) found that kindergarten children were twice as accurate in identifying the initial sound of a word if it matched the phonemic value of the first letter (such as the /*be*/ in *beaver* and the /*ze*/ in *zebra*) than if it did not match (the /*b*/ in *ball* and /*z*/ in *zoo*). Children's guesses are usually based on the name of the first letter.

In spite of the positive correlation between knowing letter names and early reading, letter names are not part of the reading process itself. Teaching children letter names does not improve their reading performance (Venezky, 1978). Children can learn to recognize letters without learning their names. Moreover, in many cases, the name of a letter does not correspond to its most common sound. The names of these three letters—*h, w,* and *y*—are unrelated to their sounds; and the names of these seven others—*a, e, i, o, u, c,* and *g*—do not contain the sound that is most commonly taught in beginning reading. Finally, as was pointed out in

Chapter 10 on orthography, the relation of the letters to their sounds depends on many factors, including where the letter occurs in a word (Venezky, 1976).

The factor that explains the correlation between knowing letter names and early reading is still a matter of speculation. Perhaps children who learn letter names come from families that give more emphasis to reading-related activities. Perhaps these children are smarter or at least more interested in reading. In any case, this example illustrates the danger of interpreting a correlation as a causal relation. The same caution must be applied to interpreting other correlational data, including correlations between reading methods and reading achievement.

Processes in Beginning Word Decoding

In Chapters 2 and 3, we described how fluent readers encode words and access their meanings primarily on the basis of a visual representation of the constituent letters. Young children, even as early as second grade, can also recognize familiar words on the basis of a visual representation (Barron & Baron, 1977; Jorm & Share, 1983; Rader, 1975). However, young children may rely more often than adults do on prelexical speech recoding as a second, alternative route for recognizing a word. As described in Chapter 3 on **prelexical speech recoding,** the visual representations of letters and letter groups activate speech codes; these speech codes, in turn, activate the word's meaning. Speech recoding in skilled readers is usually an automatic, unconscious process. However, it can be overt and conscious, as when a reader sounds out a word by overtly retrieving the sounds associated with letters or letter groups, blends them, and pronounces the word. Both overt and covert speech recoding play an important role in the early years of reading instruction.

Speech Recoding in Early Reading

Speech recoding is important in early reading for two reasons. First, young readers encounter many words that are visually unfamiliar to them. Speech recoding can provide a back-up procedure for decoding these words. In Chapter 4 on vocabulary acquisition, we explained that in almost any large text, a few high-frequency word types (like *the, of, is*) occur many times and thus account for a large proportion of the word tokens. The other side of this coin is that many words occur very few times. This relation is true not only for the texts that adults read, but also for the reading materials found in grade schools and early reading programs. An analysis of a reading series used in the first two grades in Australia found that 50 percent of the words in the text occurred only once and about 70 percent occurred fewer than five times (Firth, 1972). Beginning readers may encounter many unfamiliar words.

The second reason for the importance of speech recoding is more speculative. It is possible that the speech-recoding process helps a child develop representations of multiletter units—letter clusters, syllables, and morphemes—that are needed to visually encode words. As described in Chapter 10 on orthography, the relation between symbols and sounds is regular at many levels—letters, letter clusters, or entire morphemes (like *tion*). Learning to recognize and pronounce a unit, such as *tion* or *ing,* may help a child acquire a visual representation of these units. Thus, speech recoding may contribute to the development of representations that are important to the visual encoding of words.

A Model of Beginning Decoding

One of the most interesting attempts to analyze word decoding in reading acquisition examined the word-recognition skills of average and poor eight-year-old readers who were of similar general intelligence (Firth, 1972). Firth found that the poor readers could recognize and pronounce very frequent words, but they had great difficulty with infrequent words or nonwords, like *pard*. By contrast, the average readers could pronounce frequent words, infrequent words, and nonwords.

Firth developed a model of the kinds of information that children need to pronounce new words, information about the sounds associated with words, syllables, and letters. He wrote a computer program that used this information to generate pronunciations for words and nonwords. Firth tested the program with the same words the children were given. He could make the program perform either at the level of the poor readers or the average readers. The program acted like a poor reader if it relied only on visual recognition for familiar words. And the program improved its performance to the level of the average reader if it additionally used more detailed knowledge of how syllables and letter patterns were pronounced to decode unfamiliar words and nonwords. Because the model paralleled the children's performance, it is worth examining exactly what information the model used in the two conditions.

When given a string of letters, the program's first strategy was analogous to visual recognition; it tried to retrieve the previously stored pronunciation of the word. The program had access to a dictionary that linked each frequent word to a phonetic transcription of its pronunciation. If one of these frequent words occurred in the test, the program automatically looked up the word and produced its pronunciation. However, this strategy only worked with frequent words, those that occurred five or more times in the first- and second-grade texts. There were about 800 such words, or 30 percent of all of the words in the texts. Using only this whole-word information, the program obtained a score equivalent to a reading age between six and seven years in two standardized tests, a level that was similar to the reading level of the eight-year-old poor readers. On the basis of this similarity, Firth conjectured that the poor readers were primarily relying on sight recognition of frequent words.

To improve its performance to the level of the average eight-year-old readers, the program required additional information, as well as procedures for decoding unfamiliar words. The additional information included a dictionary of syllable pronunciations, analogous to the dictionary of word pronunciations. Using the syllable dictionary, the program was sometimes able to recognize and pronounce an entire syllable. However, the syllable dictionary was not generally useful in this form because English has too many different syllables. In the reading material the students were given in first and second grade, there were about as many distinct syllables as there were distinct words. Consequently, recognizing individual syllables offered no savings over recognizing individual words. However, the information about the pronunciation of syllables was extremely useful when the syllables were analyzed into parts.

The main power of the program's decoding skills came from analyzing syllables into consonant and vowel clusters and giving them the pronunciation that was associated with similar patterns. The best way to explain the program is to describe how it determined the pronunciation of an unknown word such as *began*:

1. The word was decomposed into syllables: *be* + *gan*. (The program used a number of heuristics for identifying syllable boundaries that we will not describe.)
2. The pronunciation of *be* was found and retrieved from the syllable dictionary.
3. The second syllable, *gan*, was not in the syllable dictionary. The program then worked on the initial *ga* by consulting its stored pronunciation of other syllables that had the same initial consonant-vowel structure, such as *gal* and *gas*. The program then pronounced the *g* of *ga* as it was pronounced in these words, namely, /g/.
4. The program then analyzed *gan* into its vowel and final consonant, *an;* it consulted syllables that had the same vowel-consonant structure, such as *an, can, han;* and pronounced *an* similarly.
5. The pronunciations of *be* - *g* - *an* were blended and the final word was pronounced correctly.

Notice that the pronunciation assigned to the initial consonant depends upon the following vowel. The pronunciation of *g* could have been different if it had been followed by an *e* (as in *germ*). Similarly, the pronunciation of the vowel depends upon the following consonant in the syllable. This strategy removes some of the irregularity in English orthography by automatically taking into account the letter's position, the adjacent letters, and syllable boundaries. These three constraints will not generate the correct pronunciation for all English words, but they are sufficient to mimic the performance of average eight-year-old readers.

This description of the program has been in terms of single consonants and vowels. In fact, the program applied the same strategy to consonant clusters and vowel clusters. If presented a nonword like *troup*, the program would have segmented it into three units—*tr, ou,* and *p*—and operated on these clusters using the same strategy described for *gan*.

The program also had a heuristic for resolving conflicts if a particular pattern had two possible pronunciations: It would choose the pronunciation associated with the greatest number of syllable types. For example, the last three letters of the nonword *rive* have two possible pronunciations: (1) as in *give* and (2) as in *hive, dive, five, drive,* and *thrive*. The program would choose the latter pronunciation because it is used in more syllable types. Firth tested and rejected a pronunciation strategy that relied entirely on using an analogy to a single similar syllable because it caused too many conflicts when vowels had multiple pronunciations. By contrast, the conflicts were avoided if the program had a bias to use the most common pronunciation of the unit.

In addition to information about the pronunciation of words and syllables, the program also had information about the sounds associated with single letters. However, the program utilized individual letters only as a last resort. Larger units—words, syllables, and clusters—were preferred to single letters. Larger units require fewer retrieval steps and less blending, and they take more context into account; consequently, they are less prone to error.

In sum, the model made three important claims:

1. Poor eight-year-old readers visually decode frequent words.
2. Average eight-year-old readers can use their knowledge about symbol-sound relations to decode infrequent words or nonwords.
3. The symbol-sound relations are based on subsyllable patterns, like a vowel and consonant or consonant cluster.

Firth's work is one of the very few detailed models of how children decode words before they have acquired the kinds of complex representations of words that are available to skilled readers.

Evidence for the process Some instructional data provide evidence that supports parts of Firth's model. First, it does appear that vowel-consonant clusters are useful units for recognizing words. A number of researchers have found that children learn to recognize words faster if they are taught to attend to such units in recognizing and pronouncing the word. In one such technique, a word (such as *heat*) is visually presented and pronounced, then a consonant is substituted (such as in *m + eat*), followed by the pronunciation of the entire new word (*meat*) (Cunningham, 1975, 1977; Haddock, 1978). Children are taught to try to match words on the basis of visual patterns and then to substitute sounds. Some researchers have found that this technique is better than those that teach children to simply pronounce individual word parts or that stress only letters and sounds (Haddock, 1978).

On the other hand, the support for syllabification as a process in word decoding is mixed, and the issue remains a controversy in early reading instruction. In a series of studies (Cunningham, 1975, 1979; Cunningham, Cunningham, & Rystrom, 1981), children were taught a modified syllabification strategy. Fourth- and fifth-graders were taught a compare/contrast strategy, which involved comparing unknown two-syllable words to known one-syllable words (such as *problem—rob, them*). These children were subsequently better at pronouncing previously unpronounceable two-syllable words than a control group, although they were not better at syllabification per se.

Other studies have found mixed results. In some cases, syllabification instruction was useful (Biggins & Uhler, 1978); in other cases, it was not (Canney & Schreiner, 1977). Although there are many possible explanations for the mixed results, the most important consideration is that syllabification by itself is not a useful skill. Firth's model, when faced with an unfamiliar word, tried to recognize syllable-like units, retrieve similar syllablelike units, and substitute sounds. The syllable boundary was useful only to the extent that it helped to identify useful units. Similarly, just being able to find syllable boundaries may not be very useful in beginning reading.

Firth's model of decoding suggests roles for both the visual decoding process and the prelexical speech-recoding process in early reading. The pronunciation of very familiar words may be retrieved after the words are encoded and accessed on the basis of their visual patterns, a process that may be a slower version of the visual encoding processes used by fluent readers. At the same time, unfamiliar words may be recognized by constructing their pronunciations from subword units and using the constructed pronunciation to access the word's meaning through its auditory representation, the prelexical speech-recoding route.

The units used to analyze unfamiliar words may reflect the child's increasing acquisition of a larger and more extensive set of visual patterns. By second grade, a child may have learned a large set of syllables, consonant and vowel clusters, and many entire words. The units available for analyzing unfamiliar words may continue to develop with the child's reading skill. For example, there is evidence that even fifth-graders decode an unfamiliar word in terms of smaller units than those used by college students. Fifth-graders who were asked to pronounce a series of nonwords, like *zign* and *risten,* were more likely to use a left-to-right, syllabic pronunciation strategy, producing interpretations like *zig-n* and *ris-ten* (Marsh, Desberg, & Cooper, 1977). College readers were twice as likely to generate a pronunciation based on the entire word, something like an analogy to similar words, like *sign* and *listen.* Thus, as reading skill is acquired, students develop the internal representations of syllables, morphemes, and word percepts; the internal representations of these larger units allow the reader to analyze new words into a small number of large visual chunks and to use that representation when pronouncing the new word or accessing its meaning.

Speech Processes in Reading Acquisition

Even though a skilled reader relies primarily on visual representations for coding words, a child may not. At the very least, a child who is able to use speech recoding has some advantage over a child who must guess or rely on global cues such as word shape. There is evidence that a redundant, speech-related code can help a person who is learning to read. Adults learn an artificial writing system (made of artificial characters) faster if there is a systematic relation between the characters and English sounds than if there is no such relation (Brooks, 1977; Brooks & Miller, 1979).

The role of speech recoding as a back-up mechanism seems to be crucial in explaining the rapidity with which children learn to pronounce words, for example, when compared to the acquisition of the logographic orthographies in Japan or China. In this section, we will explore some of the individual speech processes in learning to read.

Phonemic segmentation   Reading acquisition appears to require the ability to segment an auditory word into phonemes, minimal units of sound that are associated with distinct meanings, such as the difference between /b/ and /p/ in *pit* and *bit.* Why is this auditory skill important in mastering what appears ultimately to be a visual process? A child who can segment an auditory word into its units can then match these units to letters and letter clusters and consequently induce the symbol-sound relations that are basic to English orthography.

Correlational studies have shown that children who lack phonemic segmentation skill tend to have poor reading achievement. For example, Firth (1972) found evidence in his own and others' research that poor readers had difficulty with tasks that depended on phonemic segmentation. One example of such a task is producing a word that rhymes with another; a second example is deleting a sound from a word, such as deleting the /s/ sound from *sand* to produce *and*. Poor readers do much worse at these tasks than do good readers. Although consistent with the idea that phonemic segmentation skill is important, these correlational studies are not conclusive.

Training studies provide much firmer support for the hypothesis that segmentation skills can facilitate reading acquisition. Several training methods have been developed to teach phonemic segmentation (Marsh & Mineo, 1977; Wallach & Wallach, 1979). For example, in one training method used with four- and five-year-old prereaders, the children listened to a sound and were asked to choose one of several alternative words that began or ended with that sound (Marsh & Mineo, 1977). In general, children who have been instructed in segmentation skills show better performance in reading tasks than those who receive no such instruction (see Golinkoff, 1978 for a review).

Learning to segment spoken words into phonemes does help early reading. However, the relation between phonemic segmentation and reading skill is a two-way street; learning to read also helps one to segment spoken words. This conclusion came from a study of the phonemic segmentation skills of illiterate and literate Portuguese adults (Morais, Cary, Alegria, & Bertelson, 1979). The illiterate adults did much more poorly than the literate adults on tasks that required phonemic segmentation, tasks such as deleting a sound from a spoken word and pronouncing the remainder. The poorer performance of illiterate adults cannot be attributed to other factors, such as uncooperativeness; they performed as well as the literate adults when the task involved syllables rather than phonemes. The conclusion from this research is that the awareness of the phoneme as a unit of sound may emerge partially as a consequence of acquiring reading skill. The relation between phonemic segmentation skill and reading is interactive; both skills may mutually develop and contribute to each other.

Phonemic discrimination   In order for a child to segment a spoken word into phonemes, she must be able to discriminate phonemes from each other. Phoneme discrimination is not a problem for most normal children (Dykstra, 1966). Before they learn to read, children already discriminate words that differ by a phoneme, such as *nail* and *mail* or *pin* and *pen*. Of course, if a child does have difficulty discriminating phonemes, it will presumably interfere with her acquisition of speech, as well as with reading.

Associating and retrieving sounds   Similarly, learning to associate single sounds with letters is not difficult for young children, even those in kindergarten. Children learn better if the symbol-sound correspondences are explicitly taught and interesting mnemonics are used, such as relating the sound of a letter to the sound produced by a graphically depicted object (like the sound of an *s* related to the hiss of a snake) (Venezky, Chapman, Seegal, Kaam, & Leslie, 1971, reported in Venezky, 1976).

Memorizing the association between a letter and an associated sound is also not difficult for very poor readers. Firth (1972) found that eight-year-old poor readers knew the typical sounds associated with individual letters. On the other hand, as the analysis of orthography in Chapter 10 made clear, the orthographic code of English is not particularly consistent at the level of individual letters. Consequently, to break the code, the child must learn to code larger units such as digraphs, consonant and vowel clusters, and morphemes. Thus, the English orthographic code is not mastered by merely memorizing 26 letter-sound associations.

Blending   If a child retrieves the sounds of several individual phonemes or syllables, these sounds must be combined into a continuous sound that constitutes a single word. **Blending** may be used in reading new or infrequent words that aren't immediately recognized. Blending is an overt strategy that is part of phonics instruction (Resnick & Beck, 1976). Some children spontaneously develop the ability to blend, as well as induce some minimal aspects of the phonics principles on which it draws (Whaley & Kirby, 1980). Of course, many children must be explicitly taught how to blend. Such instruction is particularly important if the child is to generalize symbol-sound correspondences to new words (Golinkoff, 1978).

Children who do better in blending tasks also tend to do better in reading tests. The correlations range between about 0.2 and 0.7 (Whaley & Kirby, 1980). Of course, successful blending is the end product of a large number of important subprocesses—segmenting the word, keeping track of the left-to-right order of letters, retrieving the associated sounds, and putting them together. So the correlation between a large subset of reading subskills and the entire set is not surprising. Moreover, the subskills in blending would probably improve with practice so that children who were good readers and read often would acquire blending skills.

Visual Processes in Reading Acquisition

Although speech processes play a role in early reading, word recognition is based on the acquisition of a large repertoire of representations of visual patterns. In this section, we will examine some of the components involved in this acquisition process.

Recognizing letters   Word decoding involves discriminating letters from each other and identifying letters and letter clusters. Discriminating two letters from each other—even similar ones like *m* and *n*—is not difficult for most beginning readers. Even four-year-old children who did not know the names of most of the letters could match capital letters to the correct target embedded among six alternatives (Gibson, Osser, Schiff, & Smith, 1963, reported in Gibson & Levin, 1975). While children make very few errors, the errors they do make tend to be confusions between letters with similar features, such as *M/W, N/M, Q/O, E/F, P/R,* and *K/X*.

Young readers and kindergarteners often confuse characters that differ in orientation, such as *b* and *d* or *p* and *q* (Calfee, Chapman, & Venezky, 1972). Children may initially confuse such letters because before they learn to read, left-right orientation is not an important cue that they need for discriminating among objects or drawings; for instance, a car is a car, no matter which way it is pointing. But children do learn to attend to this cue as they acquire reading skill, and they can generalize to other tasks involving printed symbols. For example, in a study that required young children to discriminate between letterlike squiggles that differed in orientation, the error rates decreased with age, from approximately 50 percent for four-year-olds to about 20 percent for six-year-olds (Gibson, Gibson, Pick, & Osser,

1962). Beginning readers learn to distinguish among visually confusable letters (like *b* and *d*) by learning their role in words (such as *dad, dab,* and *bad*) that have different meanings and pronunciations.

The confusions among these mirror-image letters are common for very young readers; however, beyond the ages of seven or eight, only children with severe reading problems continue to have major difficulty (Kaufman, 1980). As we will discuss in Chapter 12 on dyslexia, such children confuse these letters because they are not learning to read; the letter confusions are not the cause of the reading failure.

Encoding units larger than single letters Children initially pay primary attention to the letter at the beginning of a word; only later, as they become more proficient, do they attend to other aspects of the word, including its internal letters. There are several sources of evidence of a bias for attending to initial letters. One source is the study by Calfee and Pointkowski (1981), described earlier, which followed the development of the decoding skills of first-graders in different types of reading programs. When presented a simple word, like *fan,* many children could decode the first letter long before they could decode the last letter or middle vowel. Other studies have also found that nonreaders and beginning readers attend to the beginnings of words. For example, in tasks that required children to match words that looked similar, both nonreading kindergarteners and first-graders with five months of reading instruction showed strong biases to attend to the beginnings of words (Marchbanks & Levin, 1965; Rayner, 1976).

There are probably several reasons for this bias. The initial sound may be more salient when the word is pronounced. Or perhaps the initial letter is visually more discriminable than the internal letters. Also, the initial letter is stressed in beginning reading programs; in many early reading exercises, it is the only cue a child needs in order to choose the correct answer.

In addition to recognizing individual letters, children must attend to their sequential left-to-right order, distinguishing *pat* from *tap.* Children who have not yet begun to read are especially likely to make sequence errors in tasks that require them to match words (Calfee, Chapman, & Venezky, 1972). As with the confusions between mirror-image letters, the confusions between words with different sequences of letters decrease as children acquire reading skill. The acquisition of reading skill involves acquiring the internal representations of units larger than single letters, including digraphs (such as *th*), syllables, and entire words. These larger units provide a more economical code for a sequence of letters, since they incorporate order information as part of the identity of the unit.

Acquiring the internal representations of complex visual patterns such as words is a key aspect of expertise in many skills. As we mentioned in the opening chapter, the perceptual skills of a skilled reader in some ways resemble the perceptual skills of a chess master. A chess master develops a vocabulary of chess configurations that allows him to rapidly encode an arrangement of several chess pieces as a single chunk (Chase & Simon, 1973). The master's vocabulary of chess configurations makes him faster than the beginning player at encoding the layout of a chess board and more accurate in subsequently reproducing it. Like a chess master, a skilled reader has internal representations of tens of thousands of visual patterns. The patterns a reader knows are words and morphemes, each of which acts as a single chunk, providing an economical code to represent the identity and sequence of letters. However, if a skilled reader is shown a random sequence of letters, such as *TNCNEBA*, she will have difficulty encoding and remembering it. Consequently, she will perform much like the beginning reader, for whom most letter sequences are unfamiliar and must be coded letter by letter.

The process of acquiring the visual representations of words is an instance of perceptual learning. Both the nature of perceptual learning and the factors that influence it have been a topic of concern in psychology, education, and computer science (see, for example, Feigenbaum & Simon, 1963; Gibson, 1969, 1970; Gibson & Levin, 1975; LaBerge & Samuels, 1974; Winston, 1975). The acquisition of visual patterns is influenced by the frequency with which the words and letter groups are seen, by the distinctiveness of their visual features, and by the relation of words and morphemes to their meaning and pronunciation.

Acquiring Proficiency

Once the ability to decode words is established, reading performance starts to improve in several ways, becoming faster, less effortful, and more automatic. In this section, we will describe several aspects of this improvement, as well as the processing changes that underlie it.

Integrating Graphic and Linguistic Information

To become a fluent reader, a child must attend not only to the graphic information but also the linguistic context. Children do learn to use both types of information; even at the end of first grade, children's reading is faster and more accurate if both graphic and high-level linguistic information correspond to familiar patterns (Thompson, 1981). The children studied were 24 first-graders who had received a year of instruction that combined a meaning orientation (called a *language experience* approach) along with phonics instruction. The children were timed as they read aloud texts that were either normal or semantically anomalous and that were either in familiar lower-case typography, less familiar upper-case, or mixed typography, such as *jUMP iN tHE wATER*. The children were asked to read as quickly as possible and given one normal and one anomalous practice passage before their performance was measured. Substitutions, insertions, and omissions of words were counted as errors.

A normal text in lower case (the most familiar text and typography) began:

> *"Sit down Jack!*
> *"The boat will tip," said Father.*
> *Splash! Jack fell into the water.*

An anomalous text in mixed type (the most unfamiliar text and typography) began:

> *"sIT dOWN wATER!*
> *"fATHER wILL tIP," sAID tHE rOD.*
> *fATHER! jACK fELL iNTO tHE rOD.*

For normal text in familiar lower case, the reading time was 70 words per minute (wpm) and the error rate was 5.8 percent. If only the typography or only the linguistic pattern was unfamiliar, reading was slightly impaired. But if both were unfamiliar, reading speed decreased considerably (to 42 wpm) and the error rate doubled. These children used both the graphic patterns and language patterns; their reading was particularly impaired when both sources of information were degraded. In general, the child's interpretation of a word must depend on both graphic cues (the pattern of letters) and linguistic cues (the text and the child's knowledge of oral language).

The relative weight a young reader assigns to these different cues depends on the instructional program the child is in. The phonics approach initially stresses letter cues; however, since graphic information can be ambiguous at the level of individual letters, the text can be helpful in suggesting a likely meaning for an unrecognized word or in speeding the recognition of known words. A child can check whether his guess is plausible by comparing its meaning and syntactic appropriateness to the context. It has been repeatedly shown with adults that the time to recognize a word decreases if there is a language context. Several information sources together—in this case, both graphic and contextual information—can raise the activation level of a candidate word to threshold sooner than only one of those sources alone.

Children who are taught with a method that stresses graphic information do learn to attend to the linguistic context, as well. Their transition can be seen in the pattern of errors they make as they progress through a phonics program. The errors show initial sensitivity to letters and increasing sensitivity to grammaticality. This result came from a longitudinal study that followed children for three years through an individualized reading program with a phonics emphasis (Lesgold & Curtis, 1981). The study found that the oral-reading errors of commission were generally words that were graphically similar to the printed word; 62 percent shared at least half the letters, and this percentage remained constant. Presumably, this reflects the phonics emphasis of the program. By contrast, the contextual effects increased. After one-seventh of the program, 27 percent of the errors didn't make sense given the context; for example, a child may have incorrectly read a word as a verb where only a noun or adjective could be used. After two-thirds of the program, only 10 percent of the errors were contextually inappropriate. Moreover, the low- and medium-skill readers contributed the highest proportion of inappropriate errors; the high-skill readers made very few errors, presumably because they paid more attention to the linguistic context even in the early stages of the program.

The whole-word approach stresses the linguistic context from the beginning and gives less emphasis to symbol-sound correspondence. A child who has learned to decode using a whole-word method might be expected to differ in two major ways from the pattern we described above. First, she might initially give more weight to the syntactic and semantic context in guessing an unknown word. Second, she may attend less to graphic information, since she is not taught to explicitly segment the word into letters or letter clusters or to retrieve and blend the associated sounds. The whole-word methods typically do encourage children to attend to the word in some global way, presumably to its shape. A child who learns through the whole-word method must eventually give more weight to the letter patterns.

The errors children make in whole-word programs indicate their growing sensitivity to graphic information. In one study, children were found to go through three stages in decoding (Biemiller, 1970). First, they tended to make errors that were contextually acceptable but unrelated to the graphic display. In the next stage, they looked at the word but didn't respond. In the third stage, their errors were not only contextually acceptable but also showed sensitivity to the letters in the printed word. This has been interpreted as showing stages in the integration of context with increasing skill in attending to the graphic information. This sequence likely reflects the reading program's emphasis on context, which may have resulted in more meaning-preserving errors until children began to infer the symbol-sound correspondences. Thus, the pattern of errors that children make indicates the different emphases placed on information sources by reading programs and reflects the child's increasing attention to both sources of information.

Speed

Perhaps the clearest development that occurs during the first two years of reading acquisition is the increasing speed and facility with which children decode words. Initially, decoding is a slow, piecemeal process that often involves overt pronunciation. With practice, a child becomes faster and does less overt segmentation and blending. Eventually, the visual pattern of letters initiates the lexical access process.

The rapid gains in fluency that occur in early reading were documented in a longitudinal study referred to above that followed approximately 70 children in an individualized phonics curriculum over an approximately three-year period (Lesgold & Curtis, 1981). The children made large gains in various measures of reading skill, doubling their oral-reading speed, making fewer errors, and, overall, becoming faster and more accurate. But there were also large differences in the reading speeds among children who were eventually classified as good or poor readers at the end of the program. The good readers' advantage was apparent relatively early in the program and was maintained throughout. Early in the program, the good readers achieved rates of approximately 50 words per minute; by the end of the program, they read new material at twice that speed, approximately 100 words per minute. By contrast, early in the program, the poor readers read at a much slower rate, approximately 20 words per minute; by the program's end, they read new material at a rate of approximately 50 to 60 words per minute. Moreover, because children moved through the curriculum at a rate that depended on their mastery of each unit, the poor students took much more time than the good students to achieve their gains. Thus, even though children may show increases in reading speed and accuracy, there are large differences in the rates of improvement and in the eventual levels of skill that they attain.

In order to assess how the speed of word recognition contributed to eventual reading comprehension skill in this longitudinal study, the investigators measured the time each child took to pronounce isolated words at various times throughout the curriculum (Lesgold, Resnick, & Hammond, 1985). Early measures of word-decoding speed were correlated with a child's eventual scores in reading comprehension in fourth grade. Although statistically reliable, the correlations were small. The investigators hypothesized that word-decoding skill was correlated with reading skill because it was an indicator of the automaticity of the word-encoding process. Children who are more skilled in decoding do not have to devote as much attention to recognizing words; consequently, they may have more attentional capacity available for acquiring and executing high-level comprehension and conceptual processes needed to understand texts in the later years. Although such correlational results must be interpreted cautiously, these results are important because they show a relation between early decoding skill and eventual comprehension. This is one of very few longitudinal investigations of the role and development of word recognition in learning to read.

A parallel study by the same researchers followed another group of children in a more traditional, whole-word instructional program (Lesgold, Resnick, & Hammond, 1985). The second study also found that early word-decoding skill was correlated with eventual reading comprehension skill. However, the best measure of early word-decoding skill for this group included decoding accuracy (pronouncing the word correctly) in addition to a measure of decoding speed. These measures together were actually better predictors of fourth-grade reading comprehension than was a measure of first-grade reading comprehension.

Practice effects What underlies increases in processing speed? Common sense and several lines of evidence suggest that practice is necessary to attain proficiency in any skill, even beginning reading. On a microscale, it has been found that children are faster to pronounce words that they have seen frequently and slower to pronounce words they have seen less often (Beck, 1981). At a more macro level, the time devoted to a school subject is moderately but consistently correlated to achievement in that subject (Fredrick & Walberg, 1980). An observational study of 88 first-graders showed that the amount of time a student spent on decoding tasks correlated 0.44 with word-recognition performance; the same 0.44 correlation was found when pre-existing differences among students in reading readiness were controlled using statistical procedures (Samuels & Turnure, 1974).

Practice also produces increases in speed for an adult who is acquiring a skill. A survey of a variety of motor, perceptual, and cognitive skills found that the time a person required to perform a task decreased as a function of the frequency with which the task was performed (Newell & Rosenbloom, 1981). Examples of skills that have been studied include reading words that are printed with mirror-image characters, adding digits, rolling cigars, and proving geometry theorems. All of these skills are similar to reading in that they involve both perceptual and cognitive components; consequently, the process by which they are acquired is relevant to learning how to read.

Several hypotheses have been offered to explain the effect of practice on improving speed. One hypothesis is that practice causes people to change the kind of information they use to perform a task. For example, with practice, typists shift their basis for knowing about finger position from visual information to kinesthetic information. In the course of skill acquisition in reading, there may be an analogous shift in the basis for accessing a word's meaning from its sound to its visual pattern.

A related explanation of the practice effect in skill learning is that people begin to perform a task by using a variety of methods and submethods. But with practice, they gradually converge on the most effective method and stop using the slower, less accurate ones (Crossman, 1959).

Another hypothesis concerning the increase in speed with practice is that the component processes in a complex skill each become faster and more smoothly coordinated with each other. Component processes in reading (such as decoding, lexical access, syntactic analysis, and inference making) may all become faster and better coordinated with practice. In general, the more subprocesses involved in a skill and the more they interact, the more opportunity there will be for improvement (Welford, 1976). The large gains that occur during the first few years of reading instruction are most likely due to a combination of these factors.

One result of increasing skill in word decoding is that the process will require less attention and working-memory capacity. A number of experiments have demonstrated that with increasing practice, various tasks that initially consumed attention and capacity become much less demanding (Shiffrin & Schneider, 1977; Schneider & Shiffrin, 1977). As word decoding requires less capacity, the reader has more time and processing resources to devote to other high-level comprehension processes, such as syntactically and semantically analyzing sentences, making inferences about relations among sentences, determining the text's main points, and so on. While fluency in word decoding is not sufficient for good reading, it may be necessary to allow these other processes to be executed smoothly.

Coordinating Processes

The analysis of the skills in word decoding overwhelmingly suggests that no single subskill is intellectually difficult for the average six-year-old child. But such an analysis should not overlook the crucial importance of integrating and coordinating decoding with other linguistic and cognitive processes, such as syntactic and semantic processes.

Coordination of several subprocesses requires that various information sources be given appropriate weight. In particular, children must learn to give appropriate weight to graphic, syntactic, and semantic sources of information in generating an interpretation for a word. For example, the weight attached to the recognition of an entire word should be greater than the weight attached to the sound associated with one of its letters. The appropriate weights would gradually be arrived at if feedback about the correctness of an interpretation were used to modify the current weights. Also, teachers often prompt a child to pay explicit attention to particular cues, such as the story or the letters in the word, when the child is trying to guess a word. This kind of instruction might directly influence the weight children give to these sources.

A second coordination skill a reader must acquire is to allow various processes to operate in parallel. When a child is first learning to read, she must consciously organize the component processes into their appropriate sequence: first, process A; then, B; and so on. But the automaticity that comes with experience is partially due to increased parallelism among processes. Such parallelism is particularly obvious in the case of perceptual processes like word encoding. The parallelism may also apply to the coordination of perceptual and cognitive processes. As beginning readers gain fluency in decoding, they can initiate syntactic and semantic processes sooner. According to this interpretation, the increase in reading speed with practice arises from an increase in functional parallelism among processes as a child gains more experience in reading.

Both aspects of change in coordination with experience can be accounted for in terms of the mechanisms of the READER model that were described in Chapter 9. The convergence on an appropriate set of weights to be attached to various information sources can be explained in terms of the amount with which a given production can raise the activation level of a piece of information. A production that has a record of activating the interpretation that ultimately turns out to be correct will acquire a higher activation weight. The other facet of coordination, the increase in parallelism among processes, may come about by lowering the threshold for initiating the later of several processes. Rather than force a later process B to wait until the earlier process A has computed all the information it can, B could begin at the same time as A. Although READER is a model of skilled performance, it is easy to see how some of the aspects of the skill can be acquired with practice.

Eye Fixations in Beginning Reading

Several studies have examined the average number and duration of fixations as children acquire reading skills (Ballantine, 1951; Buswell, 1922; Taylor, 1965). In these studies, all of the measures of eye-fixation behavior reflect their increasing skill, as illustrated in Figure 11.3. The average number of both forward and regressive fixations decreases substantially with grade level. Also, the average duration of fixations is shorter for children who have had more reading experience; the average fixation duration decreases from first to third grade but changes relatively little after fourth grade. Of course, these data are averaged over large samples of text and readers. As we described in Chapter 2 on perceptual processes, both the number and average duration of individual fixations can vary, depending on the particular reading task.

A recent experiment provided a more detailed description of the differences in eye-fixation parameters of children who varied in reading fluency (Daneman & Carpenter, 1984). This study compared the eye fixations of a group of second- and third-graders who were not yet fluent readers to a group of third- and fourth-graders who were relatively fluent. The children read narratives written at the second-grade level that contained occasional ambiguities.

Like skilled readers, both the fluent and dysfluent readers spent more time looking at longer words, because longer words take more time to encode. The dysfluent readers spent an average of 50 extra milliseconds for each additional letter in a word, while the more fluent third- and fourth-graders spent 36 extra milliseconds for each letter. These results show that the fluent children's speed of word encoding starts to approach the speed of college students, who spend about 30 extra milliseconds for each additional letter while reading age-appropriate texts.

Both dysfluent and fluent readers spent more time on infrequent words, largely because infrequent words take longer to lexically access. The dysfluent readers spent an additional 49 milliseconds for each log-unit decrease in word frequency, whereas the fluent readers spent an additional 18 milliseconds. Both groups spent less time on content words that they had already seen in the passage, presumably because they were easier to encode or lexically access on subsequent encounters.

This analysis of eye-fixation behavior shows that the same variables that govern encoding and lexical access in adult reading operate similarly for young readers, although the processes are slower in children. The parameters of the fluent third- and fourth-graders are nevertheless within the range of those found for adults. It is easy to understand why children are slower than adults when they are

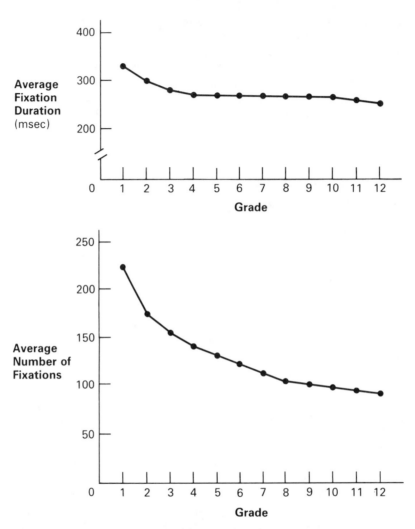

Figure 11.3   As children gain increasing reading skill, they make many fewer fixations than in the first two years of reading instruction. The average duration of a fixation also decreases, but it levels off around third or fourth grade and remains fairly constant thereafter. *Source:* Based on data from Taylor, 1965, Table 2, p. 193.

just starting to read. Beginning readers have not yet learned to recognize the letters of a word as a familiar pattern, so the rate at which they process individual letters is slower than that of fluent readers. Also, the beginning readers' familiarity with word meanings is lower, so the base activation levels are lower, and it takes longer to access meanings.

Thus, several processes contribute to a child's increasing speed and fluency. Part of the increasing skill depends on developing internal representations of the letters that make up words and morphemes. Words that initially take a half-second to recognize eventually take only half that time. A second component depends on learning to utilize different processes, such as relying less on overt sounding out processes. The implicit speech-recoding process plays a decreasing role as visual word patterns become more familiar. Finally, young readers learn to use and coordinate several information sources, appropriately weighing the evidence from each source.

Reading Readiness

Kindergarten and first-grade children vary as to how ready they are to enter the stream of formal instruction in reading. This common observation has given rise to the notion of **reading readiness,** a concept whose meaning has changed since it first arose in the 1920s. At that time, *reading readiness* denoted the idea of a critical mental or physical age at which children had the cognitive and motivational skills necessary to learn to read. It was generally accepted that a biological process was responsible for readiness. However, relatively little empirical support has been provided for this hypothesis, and the original studies that were thought to support it had serious problems (Coltheart, 1979). Several lines of evidence suggest that there is no single critical mental age that constitutes readiness. Rather, readiness should be viewed as mastery of a set of intellectual and motivational skills that children should have when they begin to read. Consequently, the psychological and instructional goal is to determine what the necessary skills are and how best to teach them to children who are not yet reading-ready when they enter first grade at the age of five or six.

Earlier and Current Conceptions of Readiness

Two studies were extremely influential in promoting the view that children couldn't learn to read before a specific mental or physical age. One study was interpreted as showing that children below the mental age of 6.5 years did not make satisfactory progress in learning to read (Morphett & Washburne, 1931). In this study, *satisfactory progress* was defined as being able to sight-read 37 words and complete 13 steps in a particular reading program after four months of instruction. This measure of satisfactory progress was responsible for the finding that a specific age, 6.5 years, was a prerequisite for learning to read. The flaw in this study was that children who did not reach the criterion were not credited with what they had learned, even if they could read some words and had completed some steps (Coltheart, 1979). This analysis made learning to read appear to be a discrete function of age. Obviously, the finding that 6.5 years was a critical age was a function of the arbitrary choice of tasks. If the criterion had been lower, then the age at which children attain the skill would have also been lower.

The second influential study investigated children's ability to use phonics to match one of four similar written words to a target word spoken by an experimenter (Dolch & Bloomster, 1937). This study found that children younger than the mental age of seven years performed randomly. Once again, the results were over-interpreted as implying that seven years was the minimum age at which phonics instruction could begin. However, Dolch and Bloomster did not test whether children could *learn* from phonics instruction, only if children could perform a particular task that required phonic skills. Moreover, the age at which a child can perform a task depends upon the task's difficulty. Thus, in summary, the two most influential studies fail to support the notion of a critical age for beginning reading.

Further evidence against the earlier view of readiness is the fact that reading instruction begins at different ages in different countries (Downing, 1973). For instance, in Great Britain, Hong Kong, Lebanon, Uruguay, and Israel, formal schooling and reading instruction begin at age five or before. In the United States, children begin formal reading instruction at age six in first grade, although some children receive instruction in kindergarten and even preschool. In the Scandinavian countries, formal reading instruction typically begins at age seven, perhaps reflecting the harsh winters and dispersed population, which made it difficult for young children to travel to school before the availability of buses and cars (Downing, 1973). Whatever the historical reason, Scandinavian countries place no premium on early reading. This variance in the age at which formal instruction begins is consistent with the hypothesis that there is no single physical or mental age at which children are absolutely ready for reading instruction.

More generally, the whole concept of readiness is now recognized to be a relative one. The intellectual and motivational prerequisites depend on the type of instruction, the conditions of instruction, and the materials to be mastered. This relative notion denies the existence of a single stage of reading readiness. *Reading readiness* is best conceptualized as the possession of specific cognitive and motivational skills that are related to the cognitive requirements of a particular reading program.

Motor skills and readiness   An alternative viewpoint is that reading readiness is a less differentiated state linked to general motor and perceptual development. This alternative view explains why some readiness programs focus on skills that are fairly remote from reading processes. A survey of practices in a stratified random sample of 15 school districts in New York state reported the use of language-based readiness programs. But in addition, over two-thirds reported nonlanguage activities, including awareness of body image, hand-eye coordination, two- and three-dimensional form perception, auditory awareness, and identifying patterns by touch, taste, and smell (Carducci-Bolchazy, 1977). Such skills may be of interest in their own right, but there is no evidence that they directly contribute to reading.

Perceptual tasks are not usually helpful in assessing readiness, unless they involve letters, words, or similar materials (Paradis, 1974). The same can be said about copying tasks that assess fine-motor skill. Although form-copying tasks often correlate with reading readiness scores (from 0.40 to 0.70), such correlations may result because the copying tasks use letters or similar geometric shapes. These correlations diminish if the copying task does not involve letters (Pryzwansky, 1972). In a study of approximately 550 children, half of whom were given fine-motor training for 15 minutes a day for 13 weeks, there was no improvement in readiness relative to a control group. The only group to show improvement had been explicitly taught to copy letters. Such data suggest that motor skills are neither necessary nor causally related to reading success.

Tests to Assess Readiness

Reading readiness is often assessed using one of a variety of commercially available tests that have been developed to assess which skills a child possesses. Figure 11.4 describes some of the types of items in a widely used test, the *Metropolitan Readiness Tests* (Nurss & McGauvran, 1976), to illustrate the range of information that is tapped by conventional readiness tests. Some of the items are related to visual discrimination, some require more direct reading skills (such as letter identification), some tap listening comprehension, and others tap mathematical knowledge (such as counting). The *Metropolitan* test is not unique in its variety.

Another commonly used test, *The Gates-MacGinitie Readiness Skills Test*, consists of several subtests that cover a variety of skills. Some subtests primarily tap auditory skills, such as discriminating among similarly pronounced words or blending sounds into words; some subtests involve reading skills, such as recognizing printed letters, discriminating among printed words, or completing letters; and some subtests tap listening comprehension skills, such as comprehending spoken sentences or following directions.

As these descriptions suggest, readiness tests often cover a wide constellation of skills. But the tests vary in the particular skills that are tested, the tasks used to test them, and the directness of the relation between the tasks and beginning reading processes themselves.

The typical way to assess the usefulness of a reading readiness test is to correlate the readiness score with reading performance at the end of first grade. If the correlations are reasonably high, then the tests are considered useful for assessing reading readiness. The typical correlations are around 0.5 to 0.6, depending on the test. However, predictive validity does not necessarily mean that the tests actually measure skills that are specific to reading. The tests may gauge some general learning ability or school readiness, since they do equally well in predicting first-grade mathematics achievement (Engin, 1974). The tests also correlate with IQ, which is understandable because some readiness tests were constructed as general measures of verbal aptitude (Nurss, 1979).

In other cases, it is clear that some readiness test items directly recruit reading skills. For example, the ability to recognize the letter that represents the initial sound of a word is a skill that a child acquires when learning to read. Thus, the predictive success of some tests may be attributed to the fact that some children have already learned something about reading; a test will reflect this and predict reading success. Thus, just because a test correlates with reading success does not mean it accurately measures readiness. A review of such tests suggests that they tap some skills that appear necessary for learning to read, some skills that result from learning to read, and some skills that are simply good general skills for beginning schooling.

A more recently developed test by Clay (1972), the *Concepts about Print Test*, has been specifically designed to assess what a child already knows about reading, without concern for her more general readiness. For example, the test assesses whether the child recognizes and distinguishes all of the upper- and lower-case letters and knows to scan from left to right. The results can be used directly to determine what reading skills the child has already acquired, which can be a useful diag-

Accompanying Picture

a. Speech and Listening Skills

Item Description

The child hears a word—in this case, "clock"—and must pick the picture that has a name beginning with the same sound.

The child must find the picture that corresponds to a simple spoken sentence—in this case, "The duck is beside the flower."

The child hears a sentence and must pick out an item that was mentioned in it. For example, the sentence in this case is, "It was raining and cold outside so David put on his coat, boots, and hat. Mark what David put on his feet."

b. Reading-related Skills

The child must pick the letter that matches the beginning sound of a word—in this case, "sock."

The child must look at the first pattern—in this case, "CA"—and find another pair of letters that is identical.

The child must look at the first pattern—in this case, "ba"—and find the same letters among the words.

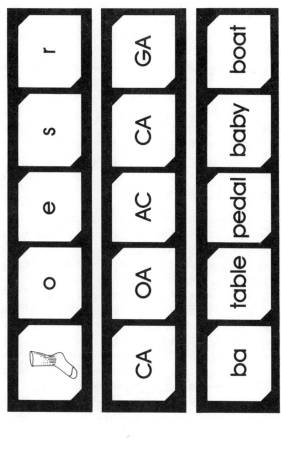

Figure 11.4 A description and pictures of items used to assess reading readiness of beginning first-graders. These items illustrate subtests of (a) speech and listening skills and (b) reading-related skills. *Source:* Nurss & McGauvran, 1976, pp. 15, 18, 20, 22, 24, 25. Reproduced by permission from the *Metropolitan Readiness Tests*. Copyright © 1976 by Harcourt Brace Jovanovich, Inc. All rights reserved.

nostic tool for a teacher. However, this test also does not address the issue of reading readiness.

One general objection to readiness tests is that they do not assess how *ready* the child is to learn but rather what the child has already learned. The distinction is clear if we consider a child who, for one reason or another, has not been exposed to reading and, as a result, has learned very little about it. The typical readiness test is not very useful in determining whether this child is ready to learn. To measure readiness to learn, a test might include some lesson or opportunity to learn reading-related skills and then assess how rapidly the child learns these kinds of skills from this kind of instruction. The test would have to take into account what the child already knew in order to measure learning, rather than previously acquired knowledge. Such a test would come much closer to assessing the concept of readiness as it has been defined here.

The Advantages or Disadvantages of Early Reading

A number of investigators have asked whether early readers ultimately become better or poorer at reading than children who learn to read somewhat later. The evidence is mixed as to whether there are any advantages or disadvantages in providing reading instruction for a very young child. But it is very difficult to assess the effects of early reading instruction. Some of the difficulties are illustrated by a study that examined the reading performance over a six-year period of children who received early instruction (Durkin, 1974–75). Durkin designed a two-year language arts program for preschool children in a small Midwestern town. The children who participated were voluntarily enrolled by their parents. Upon completing the program, the children then attended first grade. The plan of the study was to compare the performance of these children to those who had a standard kindergarten background that did not include reading or prereading instruction.

One of the initial complications occurred because parents whose children were enrolled in the regular kindergarten learned about the experimental program and sought to have some prereading training provided for their children. Hence, the comparison immediately changed; the new plan of the study was to compare children who had different degrees of prereading and reading instruction. Other difficulties arose when the first- and second-grade teachers failed to capitalize on the reading facility attained by some of the children in the experimental program. Durkin found that some teachers assigned children to reading textbooks that were calibrated by grade level, even though some children in the experimental program had already mastered that level. Durkin also observed that some teachers devoted less attention to children who had already acquired some reading skills and gave more attention to children with reading difficulties. All of these factors would decrease the chances of detecting any advantages that the early readers might have had. In spite of this, Durkin found significant advantages for the early readers in first and second grade, as well as smaller, nonsignificant advantages in third and fourth grade.

Other studies have also claimed advantages of early reading instruction, although the advantages tend not to persist (Gray & Klaus, 1970). But many of these studies have methodological difficulties that make any strong conclusions impossible. For example, a possible confounding in many studies is that children whose parents enroll them in an early reading program or children who learn to read on their own initiative may differ in many relevant ways from other children. Any advantages of early reading may actually be due to the selection procedures that may recruit unusually interested, motivated, or bright children.

Beyond this obvious difficulty, there is a larger issue to be addressed in this research. The analysis of early reading requires some framework that describes the possible source of the advantage, the measures that should reflect the advantage, and, consequently, its likely time course. Without such a framework, current studies lack a rationale for predicting the type of advantage that children might have or its likely duration. Of course, it is possible to generate some hypotheses about the possible consequences of early instruction. For example, one might hypothesize that early reading instruction is very motivating for children; if so, any difference between early and later readers might diminish if later programs were made equally motivating. Alternatively, one might hypothesize that the advantage of early reading is the one or two years of additional reading practice that the early reader has by beginning at age four or five. In that case, however, children who begin later but who have equivalent practice would be expected to read as well as the early readers. These hypotheses are only meant to illustrate the need to articulate a rationale for how and, consequently, how long, early readers might have an advantage.

Some researchers have attempted to demonstrate that there may be a disadvantage to early reading instruction; early readers may benefit less from instruction than they would one or two years later (Feitelson, Tehori, & Levinberg-Green, 1982). In a series of three small studies, the younger children in a class learned fewer decoding skills during an instructional period than their older classmates. For example, in one study, about 30 kindergarten children were given approximately 25 reading lessons by teachers who were unaware of the children's ages or the purpose of the experiment. The average difference between the ages of the younger and older groups was eight months. At the end of this instructional program, the older children far outperformed the younger ones on a variety of word-decoding tasks. The study did not determine how long the younger students' disadvantages persisted, nor did it suggest the cognitive or motivational skills that the younger children lacked. Nevertheless, Feitelson and her coauthors raise the point that early reading instruction might be disadvantageous for some children because their time might be better devoted to acquiring the comprehension and motivational skills that contribute to reading acquisition.

It is clear that there are cognitive and motivational differences among children who enter formal reading instruction. The research on early readers also makes clear the need to reconceptualize reading readiness in terms of the skills needed to learn from instruction, rather than in terms of a particular age.

Summary

Learning to break the orthographic code of English is an important aspect of early reading. In fact, it is one of the central skills taught in the first two grades. It is also one skill that some children find difficult to master. Decoding requires understanding how symbols relate to sounds, both at the letter level and above. Our review of the instructional programs suggested that systematic phonics instruction is the most successful in teaching word decoding to those children who do not acquire it on their own.

The model proposed by Firth illustrated the kinds of information children need for word decoding. According to Firth's results, both poor and average eight-year-old readers can visually recognize familiar words. However, poor readers cannot recognize unfamiliar words visually. To decode an unfamiliar word, a reader must be able to decompose it into smaller units, retrieve similar units and their associated sounds, and then synthesize the results. One or another of these skills is lacking in poor readers.

In addition to accuracy, two other equally important aspects of word decoding are its speed and automaticity. Fluent adult readers are not only accurate in recognizing words, they are also rapid. The rapidity of word recognition is important because it permits an entire set of processes that depend upon retrieving the meaning of a word to be executed sooner. In addition, for fluent readers, word recognition is effortless and requires little attention; consequently, more attentional resources can be devoted to other comprehension and conceptual processes, such as determining the meaning of a sentence and its role in the text.

The analysis of reading readiness suggests that earlier conceptions that defined readiness in terms of some biological stage were not well supported. Readiness is better conceptualized as a set of cognitive and motivational skills that are closely linked to the reading instruction the child will be given. Moreover, to assess readiness, it would be preferable to use a test that measured what the child can learn, rather than what the child has already learned.

Suggested Readings

Because early reading school programs vary, research on how children read should also consider what they are being taught. Beck's (1981) research has been a particularly interesting example of how learning is related to the instructional program in the areas of word recognition, vocabulary acquisition, and the use of knowledge. Other papers on early reading and its school context can be found in recent edited volumes (Anderson, Osborn, & Tierney, 1984; Pearson, Barr, Kamil, & Mosenthal, 1984; Resnick & Weaver, 1979; Waller & MacKinnon, 1981). These edited volumes can also be used as bibliographic indices to the literature on children's reading.

The nature of comprehension instruction in schools is described by Durkin (1978–79, 1984) and Tierney and Cunningham (1984). A quite different approach to comprehension is represented by the literary tradition that considers what children read, rather than how they read it. One interesting and large compendium of children's literature is by Sutherland, Monson, and Arbuthnot (1981).

Finally, classroom practices themselves have a large social component that interacts with cognitive processes. We recommend the chapters by Rosenshine and Stevens (1984) and by Otto, Wolf, and Eldridge (1984) for an overview and further references on this topic.

12

Dyslexia:
Characteristics and Causes

"I've always had problems reading. I remember second grade starting off I had problems. By third grade I started into a special class.

"To read a word I don't know, I try to do a real quick sounding out, and then try to read the rest of the sentence and try to get it by context. I see if maybe I've heard the word or if it sounds anything like that. If not, if I still can't get it, if I still can't find anything, I try to make something in my head that might justify it for the next time I come to it in the reading."

—a dyslexic college student

Dyslexics, like the student quoted above, have inordinate difficulty reading and learning to read. The difficulty is not only extreme but unexpected, too, because their ability to learn other school subjects, such as arithmetic, indicates that they are smart enough to learn to read.

The dyslexic's reading problems appear in the early school years and are increasingly evident beyond third grade, when other children of similar intelligence have mastered the rudiments of word encoding. Many dyslexics have difficulty mastering symbol-sound correspondences, especially the more complex ones that are dependent on the context.

Dyslexics often have other language-related problems. They have trouble in spelling, and their handwriting is sometimes poor, containing awkward, irregularly spaced letters, misaligned words, and incorrect punctuation, as shown in Figure 12.1. Some of these problems improve with schooling and age, although they are sometimes still evident in a highly educated adult dyslexic.

Overview In the first section, **Who is Dyslexic?** we will describe the major approaches to defining *dyslexia*, which reflect different hypotheses about its nature and cause. Moreover, these different approaches may lead to different groups of subjects being selected for study and, consequently, to conflicting results in the research literature.

361

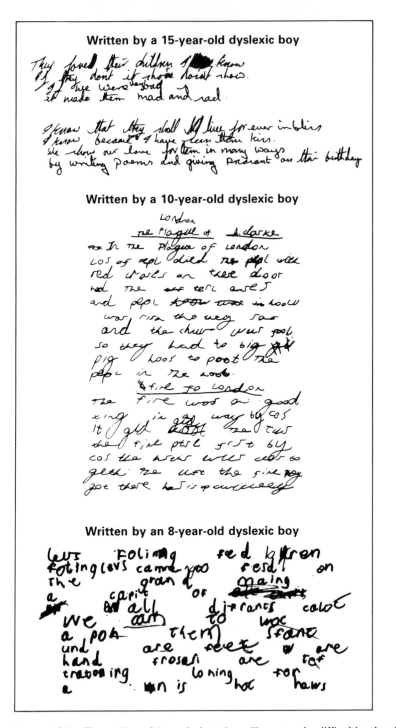

Figure 12.1 The writing of three dyslexic boys illustrates the difficulties they have in spelling, grammar, and handwriting. *Source:* Critchley, M., & Critchley, E. A. (1978). *Dyslexia defined.* London: William Heinemann Medical Books Ltd., pp. 48, 49, 64. Reproduced with permission of the authors and publishers from: William Heinemann Medical Books Ltd., 23 Bedford Square, London WC1B 3HH.

In the second section, **Reading Processes of Dyslexics,** we will report an experiment that examined in detail the reading and spelling of five adult dyslexics who were successful college students. We will argue that their reading problems can be localized to word encoding and that they have failed to master the symbol-sound relations that underlie English orthography.

In the third section, **Theories about the Underlying Deficit,** we will evaluate four theoretical proposals that attribute dyslexia to a deficit in a particular cognitive or perceptual process. Although the evidence is mixed, we conclude in favor of the proposal that the deficit is related to the retrieval of verbal codes.

In the fourth section, we will discuss **Correlated Characteristics of Dyslexia,** both characteristics that suggest a hereditary component to dyslexia and those that suggest environmental influences. The strong evidence of sex differences in the incidence of dyslexia suggests that a hereditary factor is involved in at least some types. In addition, survey studies suggest that environmental factors such as the socioeconomic background of the child and the nature of his schooling also play a role in dyslexia.

In the final section, **Acquired Dyslexia,** we will discuss studies of adults who lose some aspect of their ability to read as a result of physical damage to their brain caused by a stroke or head trauma. Recent studies of acquired dyslexics have revealed some of the neurological underpinnings of reading skill. We will compare the reading of such acquired dyslexics to that of dyslexics who fail to learn to read normally in the first place.

Who is Dyslexic?

The term **dyslexia** literally means "faulty reading." However, it is intended to designate a much more specific syndrome: reading that is markedly below what is expected, based on a person's intelligence. This discrepancy between reading performance and IQ distinguishes dyslexia from **poor reading,** in which a person's poor reading performance is consistent with other measures of general intellectual ability. Throughout this chapter, we will use the terms *dyslexics* and *poor readers* to contrast these two groups of people. In addition to this theoretical distinction, researchers have also implicitly defined dyslexia by deciding which readers to include in their experiments. In this section, we will consider how the selection criteria constitute an answer to the question Who is dyslexic? and, equally important, how the criteria have influenced the resulting theories of this disorder.

Definitions of Dyslexia

Two main approaches have been used in defining dyslexia: (1) the exclusionary approach and (2) the inclusionary approach.

The **exclusionary approach** classifies as dyslexic a person who has severe reading problems in spite of sufficient intelligence and for whom there is no other obvious noncognitive explanation for the problem (Critchley & Critchley, 1978). The term *exclusionary* refers to the exclusion of people who have characteristics that could contribute to poor reading: low IQ, poor schooling, hearing or visual problems, neurological damage, or emotional problems. The people selected by the exclusionary approach certainly constitute the most compelling cases of dyslexia—average or bright students, who for no fathomable reason, read atrociously.

Most researchers who use the exclusionary definition assume that dyslexia can also occur in people who do not fit the exclusionary criteria; that is, they assume that dyslexia can also occur in people who have a low IQ, poor school attendance, neurological problems, or emotional difficulties. The decision of who to study and who to exclude reflects a research strategy. It is an attempt to select for study a sample of children or adults who are more likely to have similar problems (Eisenberg, 1978). For example, some poor readers who attend school sporadically may be dyslexic; on the other hand, others of them might have been able to read normally if their schooling had been more regular. The requirement that schooling be normal is an attempt to exclude those poor readers who would have otherwise learned to read and thereby obtain data that are more systematic and amenable to a theoretical explanation.

Similarly, the lower bound on the IQ score is an attempt to select a more homogeneous sample. Critchley and Critchley (1978) pointed out that low levels of decoding skill can be achieved by children with an IQ as low as 60 (the average IQ is 100). But children who have IQs between 60 and 90 often have a host of learning-related difficulties. Consequently, it is difficult to identify among low-IQ children those who have a specific reading difficulty and those who have a more general intellectual impairment. By excluding from study those poor readers with IQs lower than 90, researchers try to select readers who all have problems that are specific to reading.

An undesirable outcome of the exclusionary approach is that it may produce a sample of people that is not representative of most dyslexics (Benton, 1978). Dyslexics may typically have one or more of these complicating characteristics. Thus, the exclusionary approach produces a more homogeneous sample of dyslexics, but it may be an atypical sample.

A different approach to dyslexia, the **inclusionary approach,** defines as dyslexic anyone who is reading markedly below their expected level, even if they display other characteristics such as low IQ, poor schooling, emotional difficulties, and so on. One proponent of the inclusionary approach, Rutter, advocates studying readers with these characteristics so that the contribution of these factors to severe reading problems can be evaluated empirically (Rutter, 1978). Rutter defines dyslexia as a severe reading impairment (which he calls *specific reading retardation*).

Rutter and his associates studied the incidence and correlates of severe reading problems in various large populations, such as the entire population of 10-year-olds on the Isle of Wight and a large sample from inner London (Rutter & Yule, 1973). Each subject's IQ score was used to calculate what level of reading attainment could be expected from him. A comparison between the expected level and the actual reading score was used to identify children who read far below expectation. This procedure allowed low-IQ children to be included in the sample. In fact, most of the children who would typically be excluded by the exclusionary approach were included in this approach. It was found that the incidence of specific severe reading problems was correlated with environmental factors, such as the quality of the schooling and family size, as well as personality factors, such as impul-

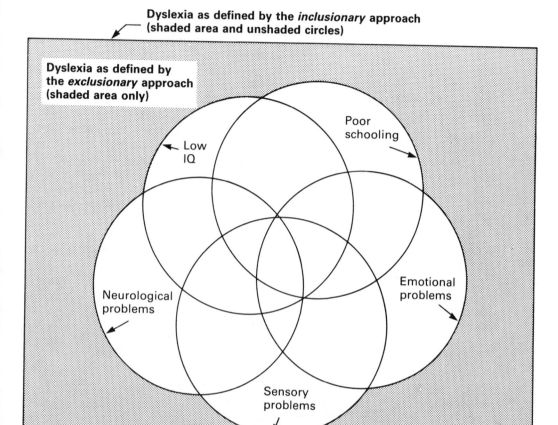

Figure 12.2   A Venn diagram illustrating the characteristics of dyslexic readers. The exclusionary approach selects readers with severe reading problems who do not have identifiable characteristics such as low IQ, poor schooling, visual or auditory problems, and so on. These would be represented by people who are not in any of the circles. The inclusionary approach selects readers with severe reading problems irrespective of the presence or absence of other concomitant problems such as poor schooling or a low IQ. Thus, this approach would select readers from either inside or outside of these circles. Clearly, the two approaches may select somewhat different samples of dyslexics.

siveness and restlessness. This research approach has significantly influenced Rutter's theory of dyslexia. He argued that dyslexia results from some basic problem that leaves the child at risk for reading difficulties. But whether the risk translates into dyslexia depends on these other environmental factors, such as the quality of schooling, the family characteristics, and the reader's personality characteristics.

Comparison of approaches   It is no surprise that the inclusionary approach is likely to lead to a model that proposes multiple causes or types of dyslexia. Because this research admits complex cases, it ends up with a complex theoretical account.

By contrast, the exclusionary approach simply excludes from study those readers with other problems. Children who fit the exclusionary definition of dyslexia would presumably constitute one subset of children identified through the inclusionary approach, as illustrated in Figure 12.2. The difference between these two approaches may explain some of the inconsistencies in the research literature on dyslexia. The results of studies that use one population may differ from those that use another.

Each approach is useful for different purposes. The inclusionary approach is useful for evaluating the influence of nonreading factors on dyslexia, for estimating the incidence of severe reading problems, and for formulating public policy, such as deciding who should receive remedial education. The exclusionary approach is useful for isolating dyslexia in a form that may be more amenable to cognitive research. After an adequate model has been formulated and the basic processes in dyslexia are understood, the exclusionary approach could be broadened to investigate how the other factors affect the basic processes. The exclusionary approach seems a necessary first step toward constructing a precise model of the psychological processes in dyslexia.

Other approaches   Unfortunately, the inclusionary and exclusionary approaches are not the only ways in which dyslexia has been defined. For example, some researchers believe that the term *dyslexic* should be applied only to readers who remain functionally illiterate in spite of remedial instruction. For these researchers, the phrase *remediation of dyslexia* is a contradiction in terms (Zigmond, 1978). This particular approach is undesirable because the definition of a condition should be kept conceptually distinct from its possible remediation. For example, one would not want to include as part of the definition of a disease the proviso that it be incurable.

Another common research approach is to label as dyslexic children who are reading two years or more below their grade level. The major problem with this approach is that there often is no attempt to determine if the child's difficulties are specific to reading. A sample selected by this approach could include a large proportion of poor readers who are generally intellectually slow and whose problems are not specific to reading. A second problem with this approach is that a fixed time span, such as a two-year deficit, is a proportionally larger deficit for younger children than for older children. Thus, if this criterion were used to select dyslexics of different ages, there could be systematic differences in the degree of their reading difficulty.

In summary, different operational definitions of dyslexia cause different groups of subjects to be selected for study. These differences may account for some of the conflicting results and theories that characterize the research literature in this area.

Different Types of Dyslexia

Regardless of whether dyslexia is defined by an inclusionary or exclusionary approach, it can be conceptualized as a single condition or as an umbrella term that covers several distinct reading problems (Applebee, 1971; Wiener & Cromer,

1967). Those investigators who conceptualize dyslexia as an umbrella term have recognized the need for a typology to categorize what they consider to be different types of dyslexia. While many typologies have been proposed, several focus on a distinction between a dysfunction in a *verbal* versus a *visual* aspect of reading (Boder, 1970, 1971; Ingram, Mason, & Blackburn, 1970; Mattis, 1978; Mattis, French, & Rapin, 1975; Myklebust & Johnson, 1962). Other typologies have been based on familial versus nonfamilial patterns of reading disability or on differences in various cognitive, perceptual, or motor behaviors.

Boder's typology We will describe one particular typology that is based on the distinction between the verbal and visual components of reading (Boder, 1971, 1973). Our purpose is to illustrate this approach to dyslexia and to raise several theoretical questions about this particular typology, as well as about the more general approach.

Boder's typology was developed with a population of 107 children, 92 boys and 15 girls, between 8 and 16 years in age, selected from approximately 350 children referred to a school neurology clinic. The selected children fit the exclusionary definition of dyslexia: They were two or more years behind in reading, with adequate IQ (90 or above), normal hearing and vision, good health, and without gross neurological or emotional problems. The children were classified on the basis of their reading skills (particularly their sight vocabulary) and their spelling skills (particularly their ability to spell words that were in their sight vocabulary and words that required overt word-attack skills for pronunciation). On the basis of reading and spelling patterns, the children were classified into three major groups and a remaining fourth group that consisted of children who were not classifiable:

Group	Nature of the Problem	Percentage of Children
1. Dysphonetic	Phonological analysis	63
2. Dyseidetic	Visual perception and visual memory	9
3. Mixed	Both phonological analysis and visual memory	21
4. Unclassifiable		6

The most common type (63 percent) of dyslexic was the **dysphonetic,** who had difficulty learning sound-symbol correspondences. Dysphonetic readers could identify some words, but their sight vocabularies were small. What was more striking, however, was their lack of word-attack skills to pronounce words that were not in their sight vocabulary and their nonphonetic spelling of words that they could not visually identify.

Another group (9 percent), the **dyseidetics,** had difficulty memorizing word forms or, at an earlier age, had difficulty recognizing letters. These children had extremely small sight vocabularies, presumably due to their inability to remember what words look like. They spelled unknown words phonetically and, more generally, they learned and used symbol-sound correspondences to pronounce some words. However, they used word-attack skills past the point at which normal readers recognized words visually.

The third group (21 percent), described as **mixed,** displayed both problems and, consequently, had worse reading and spelling problems than the other groups. Like the dyseidetic dyslexics, this group had small sight vocabularies. And like the dysphonetic dyslexics, they had difficulty learning symbol-sound correspondences and lacked word-attack skills. Boder said it was difficult to distinguish these children from dysphonetic dyslexics. Both groups were very poor spellers, but the mixed group's spelling was less phonetic. For example, a 10-year-old boy in the mixed group spelled *mother* as *methen* and *kitten* as *llk*. While Boder gave no data on the stability of these classifications, she said that some children in the mixed group learned phonics. As a result, their patterns changed, becoming dyseidetic. Boder also commented that the long-term prognosis for the children in the mixed group was poorer than that for the other two groups. Thus, perhaps the mixed group contained children who represented more extreme cases of the problems exemplified by the first two groups.

Evaluation of the typology   The idea of multiple types of dyslexia is intuitively appealing because reading requires so many component skills and resources that it is reasonable that one or another could be impaired, resulting in different types of disability. In spite of this intuitive appeal of dyslexia typologies, their premature use creates difficulties.

The central theoretical issue in evaluating a typology is whether the proposed differences among types of dyslexia reflect distinct disabilities or just quantitative variations of a single type of disability. Deciding between these two alternatives requires a clearly articulated model of the interrelations among reading skills. For example, to evaluate Boder's typology, one would need a clear theory of the relation between sight vocabulary and the mastery of symbol-sound relations at various levels. Boder's typology assumes that these are independent skills. However, as we proposed in Chapter 11 on beginning reading, the mastery of symbol-sound relations may contribute to the development of a sight vocabulary, thus calling the typology's assumption into question. This example illustrates that typologies are implicit forms of a theory, which must be made explicit in order to evaluate their assumptions.

A second issue in typology evaluation concerns the effect of instruction on the skills that are the basis of the classification. Could the different groups in a typology reflect different educational histories or reading strategies, rather than qualitatively different types of dyslexia (Vellutino, 1979)? This question is particularly important if the classification scheme is based on school subjects like spelling and reading, as Boder's is. For example, could Boder's dyseidetic group simply consist of children who had more phonics instruction than those in the dysphonetic group?

A third issue is the possibility that different types of dyslexia are manifestations of the same syndrome at different stages of development. Age differences, in general, merit careful attention. Older dyslexic children generally have larger sight vocabularies and are more familiar with orthographic regularities. Consequently, an older child will read differently than a younger child simply because of the skills he has acquired. The child's developmental level should be taken into account in any typology, but the importance of this factor is clearest in the typologies based on cognitive skills.

Finally, the empirical validity of the typologies has been questioned by researchers who fail to find the proposed distinct types of dyslexics (see Firth, 1972; Naidoo, 1972; Vellutino, 1979). Their failure to replicate might simply be attributed to the possibility that certain types of dyslexia are relatively rare, so that there may be a low likelihood of sampling such subjects. Alternatively, the populations used in various studies may differ systematically. For example, the kinds of dyslexics who are selected from clinical populations, such as those in Boder's study, may differ from dyslexics who are not referred to clinics. There may also be sampling differences between studies that use exclusionary and inclusionary approaches. On the other hand, instead of being due to differences in sampling, the failures to replicate could reflect the unreliability of the proposed classification.

It is unclear whether there are distinct types of dyslexia and whether such types are associated with different causes and eventual outcomes. Many of the theoretical questions raised about Boder's typology can also be raised about other proposed typologies. Thus, a reasonable position is to consider the various typologies as plausible hypotheses for which there is no strong evidence. Nevertheless, the general idea of different types of dyslexia will continue to remain intuitively appealing because reading is a complex cognitive process that seems likely to be vulnerable to more than one type of dysfunction.

Incidence of Dyslexia

A study of over five thousand British children between the ages of 9 and 11 found that 3 to 6 percent could be classified as dyslexic (Yule, Rutter, Berger, & Thompson, 1974). In this classification, the researchers used the correlation between reading skill and IQ to identify those children who were reading significantly below the expected level. The researchers did not eliminate from the dyslexic category those readers with poor schooling or environmental, sensory, or neurological problems. Thus, this 3 to 6 percent estimate of the incidence of dyslexia is higher than an exclusionary definition would produce. A much lower estimate of the incidence of dyslexia was obtained by surveying studies that used the exclusionary definition of dyslexia (Benton, 1975). According to that survey, the incidence of dyslexia is about 3 percent in boys and 0.5 percent in girls, based on the results of several studies in the United States and Britain. The higher incidence in boys is a point we will return to in the section **Correlated Characteristics of Dyslexia.**

Dyslexia is much rarer than milder forms of reading difficulty. The proportion of children with some reading difficulty (defined as having reading skills significantly below expectation for their chronological and mental age) is between 10 and 30 percent by various estimates (Benton, 1975).

The incidence of dyslexia is more than just the bottom of the distribution of reading ability. It might be expected that reading skill, like many cognitive skills and physical traits in a population, would follow a normal distribution. For example, along the distribution of heights, there are a small number of extremely tall people at the top of the distribution and a similar number of very short people at the bottom of the distribution; most people's height lies within one standard deviation of the population average. However, the distribution of reading skills differs from that for heights; there are more readers at the very bottom than one would expect in a normal distribution. In eight large-scale studies, the incidence of dyslexia (defined as reading at least 30 months below what would be predicted on the basis of age and IQ) was greater than if reading skill were simply normally distributed like a physical trait, such as height (Rutter & Yule, 1975). This finding suggests that dyslexia is a particular syndrome or set of syndromes and not just the bottom of a normal distribution of skill levels.

Reading Processes of Dyslexics

Comparing the reading of dyslexics to that of normal readers can provide powerful clues about the nature of dyslexia. To characterize normal readers, we have described studies that examined their eye fixations during reading, their level of comprehension, and other task performance (Just & Carpenter, 1980). To obtain a comparable characterization of dyslexic readers, the reading skills of five dyslexic college students were compared to those of normal college students in a series of experiments (Carpenter, Just, & McDonald, 1984). In this section of the chapter, we will describe our study of reading by dyslexic college students.

The dyslexics (four men and one woman) had been diagnosed in reading clinics and fit the exclusionary definition of dyslexia; in spite of being above average in IQ, they had marked difficulties in reading. There was no obvious educational, neurological, emotional, or physical explanation of their problems. The dyslexics were recruited through university-level reading clinics and informal contacts in the Pittsburgh area. In addition to the usual exclusionary criteria, we added the stipulation that their overall academic performance in college or university be at least passable. The control group consisted of nine normal college students.

In the main study, the dyslexics were asked to read a variety of articles, either aloud or silently, while their eye fixations were recorded. After they read a passage, they briefly summarized what they had read and then they answered a number of short-answer questions about the passage. The articles varied from 500 words to about 1,000 words in length. Some were on scientific and technical topics and had been excerpted from *Scientific American,* while others were nontechnical and had been excerpted from *Reader's Digest.*

In addition to the study of actual reading, a number of additional experimental tasks examined other cognitive skills. One such task was a spelling test. Other experiments tapped visual skills, such as visual matching and mental rotation. These other experiments will be described in later sections of the chapter.

Reading Errors and Eye Fixations

Oral reading   As soon as the dyslexics began reading aloud, it was apparent that they were not normal college readers. The dyslexics read much more slowly and with little intonation or expression. They made many more pronunciation errors. They also answered fewer comprehension questions correctly at the end of each passage, approximately 45 percent compared to approximately 60 percent for the normal readers. Moreover, the dyslexics read at 76 words per minute on average, which was half the speed of the normal college readers (154 words per minute). Thus, the dyslexics' problems were evident from a variety of measures.

(no response)
Toscanini called them the "best boys' choir in the world." They

> *sang*   *commadors . . . I don't know*
have sung to kings and commoners, capitalists and comrades. With the

> *young*
freshness of youth yet all the professionalism of mature musicians, they

> *hands*   *where it be where it be the inter . . .*
put their hearts and souls into every note, whether it be the interlacing

harmonics   *Gos . . . I don't know*   *they infarences of*
harmonies of a Gastoldi madrigal or the infectious three-quarter-time of

Scores
a Strauss waltz.

> *Through the performance, through the performer*
Though the performers are young—from 10 to 14—their choir is

> *18, 1498 where Hangsinvar . . .*
ancient. It was formed in 1498, when Hapsburg Emperor Maximillian I

> *the . . . I don't know*
collected a group of eight boys to sing in his chapel, the Hopburgkapelle,

> *Virginia's imprissit imperial*
in the heart of Vienna's imperial palace.

Figure 12.3 An excerpt illustrating the typical mispronunciations of a dyslexic who was reading aloud from a *Reader's Digest* article. The regular type is the text; the underlined words are those that were mispronounced or skipped; written in italics above the text are the dyslexic's mispronunciations or comments. The words that are not underlined were pronounced correctly.

A more detailed analysis of the dyslexics' oral reading gives a better indication of their reading problems. The problems seem to reside at the level of word encoding. For example, Figure 12.3 illustrates the mistakes made by one dyslexic, which were typical of the mistakes of all five readers. The figure contains an excerpt from a *Reader's Digest* article about the travels of the Vienna Boys' Choir. This part of the article had been preceded by several other paragraphs that described the illustrious history of the choir, so the reader had been presented with a rich context. In spite of his general familiarity with the topic, this dyslexic made several errors. The words that are underlined are ones that he mispronounced, skipped, or for which he substituted a different word; his mistakes are written above the text. For clarity, the correctly pronounced words have not been written above the text.

As the figure makes clear, this dyslexic had difficulties that were not experienced by other university students. His difficulties are even more striking given that this individual was very bright. He was a college senior, with a B grade-point average, majoring in engineering at a prominent university. Still, he not only made many errors, but he also could not pronounce some words that other university

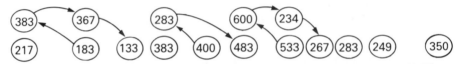

Toscanini called them the "best boys' choir in the world." They

have sung to kings and commoners, capitalists and comrades. With the

freshness of youth yet all the professionalism of mature musicians, they

put their hearts and souls into every note, whether it be the interlacing . . .

Figure 12.4 The sequence of gazes on the text while the dyslexic was reading aloud. The numbers in the circles are the duration of the gaze (in milliseconds). The gazes were forward through the text, unless an arrow indicates the direction to and back from a regressive gaze to earlier words. As the figure illustrates, the dyslexics had extremely large average gaze durations and made a large number of regressive fixations.

students recognized on sight. He had the most difficulty with proper names. For example, he read *Vienna's* as "Virginia's," *Gastoldi* as "Gos," and *Hapsburg* as "Hangisvar." Presumably, proper names are difficult to decode because they occur infrequently and some may be entirely unfamiliar.

Not only were the word-encoding problems evident in the dyslexics' mispronunciations, but they were also evident in the patterns of eye fixations. The dyslexics had large average gaze durations and, unlike normal readers, made many regressive eye fixations. To illustrate these characteristics, Figure 12.4 shows the sequence of gazes made by the dyslexic while he was orally reading the text shown in Figure 12.3. This reader fixated more words than a normal reader, the durations of the gazes were much longer than normal, and he spent a very long time on the words he pronounced incorrectly. For example, he spent over 10 seconds on the phrase *commoners, capitalists and comrades,* over 2.5 seconds on *young,* and over 4 seconds on the phrase *the Hopburgkapelle.*

These same features characterized the eye fixations of all five dyslexics. They all spent a long time on words the first time they looked at them, made many regressions to previously fixated words, and spent an inordinately long time on words that they ultimately mispronounced. On average, the dyslexics spent an average of 1,663 milliseconds fixating a content word that was mispronounced and 2,529 milliseconds on a proper name that was mispronounced. By contrast, a normal reader can orally read a six-word sentence in about 2,500 milliseconds. Although the dyslexics' difficulties were quite evident in the pattern of eye fixations, unusual eye fixations are not the cause of the reading problems; the numerous regressions and long fixations are a reflection of the dyslexics' problems in recognizing words and understanding the text.

The pronunciation errors of the five dyslexics were quantitatively and qualitatively different from those made by the normal college students reading the same texts. Overall, the dyslexics made five times as many oral-reading errors as the normal college students. A response was classified as an error if the reader skipped, substituted, or mispronounced a word. The dyslexics had the most difficulty with proper names (like *Gastoldi*). The most common error was to mispronounce a proper name or to misread one word as another visually similar one. The errors could frequently be localized to a particular part of a word, typically the middle or end. The dyslexics usually pronounced the first letter or first syllable correctly. This pattern was apparent in the errors in Figure 12.3. For example, *youth* was pronounced as "young" and *Budapest,* as "Bomaress." The dyslexic readers may have encoded only the beginnings and sometimes the endings of long words. By contrast, when the normal readers made errors, they produced a response that was much more similar to the correct word. Moreover, normal readers never gave up trying to pronounce a word, as dyslexics sometimes did.

In some ways, the dyslexics' oral reading resembled that of much younger readers. A group of 12 third-graders orally read the passages at a similar overall rate (60 words per minute) as the dyslexics (76 words per minute) and with as little inflection. As Figure 12.5 shows, the third-graders also made a similar number of oral-reading errors. The figure shows how both the third-graders and dyslexics made the most errors on proper names. Also, like the errors that dyslexics made, the third-graders' mispronunciations and substitutions were more similar to the first part of the actual word than to the other parts.

In spite of the similarity in overall word-encoding skill, there were important differences between the third-graders and dyslexics. The third-graders' problems were not due as much to a lack of decoding skill as to a lack of familiarity with the topics and words. The passages would have been difficult for the third-graders even if they had heard them rather than read them. Not suprisingly, the third-graders were unable to answer the comprehension questions. By contrast, although the dyslexics had difficulty encoding words, they possessed more general knowledge, which partially compensated for their poor word-encoding skills. Thus, even though the third-graders' reading rate and level of pronunciation errors were comparable to those of the dyslexics, the difficulties experienced by the two groups arose from very different sources.

Silent reading Our study also examined the silent reading of these dyslexic college students. Figure 12.6 shows a typical eye-fixation protocol, illustrating the dyslexics' slow, effortful reading. On average, the total gaze duration was around 460 milliseconds per word, that is, almost half a second per word. By contrast, nor-

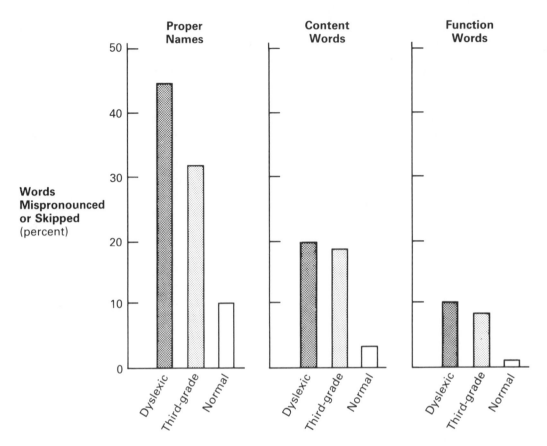

Figure 12.5   The percentage of words that were mispronounced or skipped during oral reading for three groups of readers: dyslexic college students, third-graders, and normal college students. The three panels show the percentages separately for three types of words: names (like *Strauss*), other content words (nouns, verbs, adjectives, and adverbs), and function words (such as prepositions, conjunctions, and determiners).

mal college readers in this experiment and in other research averaged about half that long on a word.

In both normal and dyslexic readers, long and less frequent words produced an increase in gaze duration. However, the increase was larger for the dyslexics than the normal readers. By contrast, dyslexics spent much less time at the ends of sentences than normal readers. Also, the way that dyslexics treated new words depended on whether they were part of an easy or difficult text. When reading an easy passage, most of the dyslexics gave up on a new word relatively quickly, perhaps because they believed the rest of the context would help them understand the gist of the passage. When reading a much more difficult, technical passage, most of the dyslexics spent a long time on new words, presumably because the context was less useful for inferring their meaning. Finally, the dyslexics' scores on the question-answering comprehension tests were about 20 percent lower than those of the normal college readers.

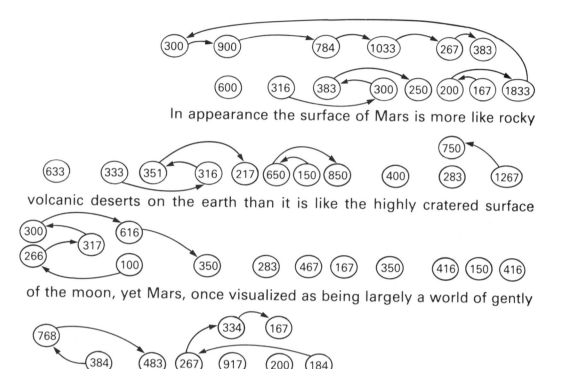

In appearance the surface of Mars is more like rocky

volcanic deserts on the earth than it is like the highly cratered surface

of the moon, yet Mars, once visualized as being largely a world of gently

rolling dunes, seems to possess little sand.

Figure 12.6 The sequence of gazes on the text while the dyslexic was reading silently. The numbers in the circles are the durations of gazes (in milliseconds). The arrows indicate regressions to earlier parts of the text. This reader read the first part of the sentence twice and then continued to make more and longer gazes than a normal reader.

Word encoding The data from these experiments on oral and silent reading, along with other studies we will describe, suggest that the dyslexics' problems are primarily at the level of word encoding. The dyslexics have not mastered the context-sensitive symbol-sound relations that characterize English orthography. While they could generate the most common sounds associated with English letters, they lacked the word-attack skills necessary to decode fairly unfamiliar words, such as *Budapest*. The dyslexics had great difficulty visually segmenting words into units corresponding to letter clusters, syllables, and morphemes and retrieving their sounds. Of course, these dyslexics do visually recognize words. They were able to visually encode and pronounce many words, particularly more familiar words. However, they required much more time than did normal readers and they made more errors. In sum, in spite of years of remediation, these dyslexics never became fluent at encoding words.

The dyslexics also obtained less information from the texts they read. They were significantly worse than the normal readers in answering comprehension questions. However, their comprehension deficit may be attributable to their poor

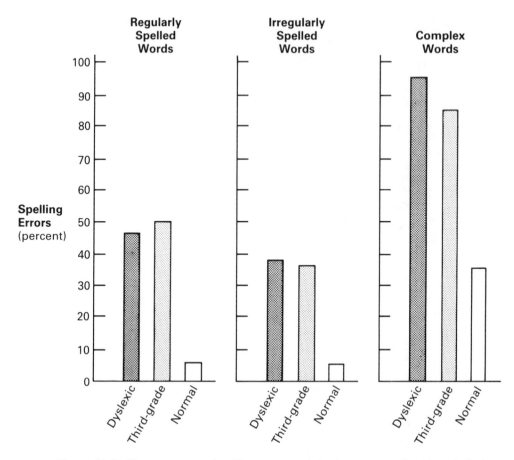

Figure 12.7   The percentage of spelling errors made by three groups of readers: dyslexic college students, third-graders, and normal college students. The three panels show the percentages separately for three types of words: regularly spelled words (like *counter*), irregularly spelled words (like *country*), and complex words with multiple morphemes and doubled consonants (such as *accommodation*). As the figure illustrates, dyslexics and third-graders made many more errors than normal college students for all three types of words.

word-encoding skill. The dyslexics were not poor at listening comprehension. Their deficits were relatively specific to reading.

Spelling   Because dyslexics have difficulty acquiring the relations between symbols and sounds that underlie English orthography, it is not surprising that they also have difficulty in spelling. It has been anecdotally observed that spelling skills often improve less than reading skills as a dyslexic progresses through school (Critchley & Critchley, 1978).

To examine the spelling skills of the five dyslexics, a 70-word spelling test was administered. The test included several categories of words expected to elicit different levels of performance: frequent words and infrequent words, words that varied in their orthographic regularity, words with doubled consonants and multiple morphemes, and homophones (words that sound alike but are spelled differently, like *sight, cite,* and *site*). Each word was pronounced and then given a sentence context that cued its meaning.

On this 70-word test, the normal college readers made an average of about seven errors; the best score was zero errors and the worst, 14 errors. By contrast, the dyslexics averaged 37 errors. The third-graders were similar to the dyslexics, averaging 38 spelling errors. Figure 12.7 presents the percentage of misspelled words for the normal college readers, the dyslexics, and the third-graders, for three categories of words that elicited some of the best and worst performance (regularly spelled, frequent words; irregularly spelled, frequent words; and complex words with double letters and multiple morphemes). Normal college students averaged about 5 percent errors for both regularly spelled, frequent words (such as *counter*) and for irregularly spelled, frequent words (such as *country*). By contrast, the dyslexics and third-graders made eight times as many errors (about 40 percent). The dyslexics performed much worse than the normal students, especially in spelling words that college students found the most difficult—words with multiple morphemes and double consonants (such as *accommodation*).

An important measure of the dyslexics' spelling skill is the phonetic acceptability of their error. A **phonetically acceptable** error is one that would sound like the target word if it were pronounced using a standard orthographic interpretation. For example, a phonetically acceptable error would be *yurned* for *yearned* or *kords* for *chords*. Phonetically acceptable errors were often generated by omitting a repeated consonant, incorrectly spelling an unstressed vowel, substituting a consonant or consonant cluster that can have the same phonemic value, or making some combination of these errors (as, for example, in spelling *cinimin* for *cinnamon*). Nonphonetic errors could differ in many ways from the target: They could omit phonemes or syllables or add extraneous ones; include letters that seldom or never take on the required phonemic value; or have no obvious resemblance to the target. Examples of the extreme nonphonetic spelling by one dyslexic included *outloul* for *pouch* and *orless* for *awkwardly*. More than half of the dyslexics' errors were phonetically unacceptable. The same was true of the third-graders. By contrast, only 15 percent of the normal students' spelling errors were phonetically unacceptable.

Most of the dyslexics' phonetically unacceptable spellings contained phonetically correct beginnings but erroneous word endings (*insules* for *insult*) or an additional or omitted middle or final phoneme (*scareces* for *scarce*). This pattern paralleled the pronunciation errors that dyslexics made in oral reading. They correctly pronounced the beginnings of words but made mistakes on the middles and ends. Both in spelling and reading, the dyslexics' errors occurred more often with less frequent words and words containing several morphemes.

The spelling results support the conclusions of the oral and silent reading studies that dyslexics have problems with tasks that require knowledge of symbol-sound relations. They are particularly slow in retrieving such information and they make significantly more errors than normal readers in both encoding words and in spelling words. In spite of the fact that these five dyslexics were all bright, successful college students, their mastery of symbol-sound relations was approximately at the level of third-graders.

These studies have focused on a small number of college-age dyslexics. In the next section, we will review studies that have analyzed younger dyslexics. These other studies also support the characterization of the dyslexics' problems as being at the level of word encoding.

Failure to Master Symbol-Sound Correspondences

A number of studies have found that dyslexics lag behind their classmates in mastering context-sensitive symbol-sound correspondences. This deficit was revealed in a study that compared 36 dyslexics to 18 normal readers of the same reading levels (Snowling, 1980). The two groups had similar IQs, although the normal readers were younger, with ages ranging from 6 to 11 years, than the dyslexics, who were from 9 to 15 years old. The children were presented with pronounceable nonsense words (like *snod/sond*) that they had to judge as being the same or different. In one experimental condition, a written word like *snod* was presented first and then a short time later, a spoken word like "sond" was presented. In another experimental condition, the first word was spoken and the second was written. Thus, both experimental conditions required some internal translation between written symbols and spoken sounds, although no overt pronunciation was required. By contrast, in two control conditions, subjects were required to compare two spoken nonsense words or two written nonsense words. Thus, neither control condition required symbol-sound translation.

Compared to normal readers, dyslexics had great difficulty in the conditions that required them to translate between written symbols and sounds. Their major deficit occurred when the first nonsense syllable was written and the second was spoken, presumably because they could not accurately or quickly translate the written symbols into their corresponding pronunciation. By contrast, the dyslexics had no more difficulty than the normal readers in the two control conditions that involved two spoken words or two written words. These data support the idea that dyslexics lack facility in translating from symbols to sounds.

Firth's computer simulation (1972), described in Chapter 11 on the acquisition of decoding skill, provides further support for the hypothesis that dyslexics have difficulty with symbol-sound correspondence. Firth studied average eight-year-old readers and very poor readers who read well below what was expected on the basis of their IQ. The poor readers had problems pronouncing single isolated words and also words embedded in a text, suggesting that some aspect of word encoding was responsible for their difficulty. The task that was the hardest for the poor readers required them to pronounce nonsense words. Nonsense words cannot be recognized on the basis of a visual code; rather, they require symbol-sound translation. Firth argued that to decode unfamiliar words, children had to decompose words into syllable-size units, retrieve the pronunciations of similar syllables, and decompose and synthesize parts of the syllable. Poor readers failed to master these symbol-sound relations.

The research described in this chapter suggests that dyslexics' reading problems are at the level of word encoding (Firth, 1972; Vellutino, 1979). Failure to master the symbol-sound relations makes it extremely difficult to pronounce an unfamiliar word and may also impede the acquisition of a sight vocabulary used to encode frequently encountered words. In sum, word encoding appears to be the locus of reading problems for many dyslexics, both young children and adults, such as the college students described earlier in this section.

Up to this point, we have described the dyslexics' problems as focused on word encoding and, moreover, as specific to reading. An alternative possibility is that word-encoding difficulties are one manifestation of a more general problem that might be apparent in nonreading tasks, as well. Next, we will evaluate several hypotheses that attribute the dyslexic's word-encoding problems to a more general deficit.

Theories about the Underlying Deficit

In this section, we will describe four proposals that differ in their characterization of a more general deficit that may cause the dyslexic's reading problems. They attribute dyslexia to:

1. verbal coding;
2. a general language problem;
3. problems in learning and memory; and
4. visual deficits.

None of these proposals has overwhelming and clearcut support. Some studies find supporting evidence, while others are inconclusive or negative. At this point, no firm conclusions can be drawn either about the likelihood that there is a general deficit underlying dyslexia or its specific nature. Nevertheless, some of these proposals are currently more plausible than others. For example, the first proposal, that there is a general problem related to verbal coding, is one that is currently receiving a great deal of investigation. By contrast, the fourth proposal, that dyslexia is due to visual problems, has been extensively investigated in the past without obtaining clear support.

Verbal Coding Deficits

The first proposal is that dyslexics have some deficiency either in identifying, coding, or retrieving verbal codes. The idea is that even though dyslexia manifests itself in reading, its origins can be traced to the verbal component of reading acquisition. The two versions of this proposal we will describe differ in their characterization of the particular locus of the problem.

Phonemic segmentation The ability to segment a spoken word into phonemes is needed in order to relate sounds to symbols and, consequently, to master English orthography. It is possible that severe reading problems result from difficulty in segmenting speech into phonemes. (See Gleitman & Rozin [1973] and Liberman & Shankweiler [1979] for related versions of this proposal.) As described in Chapter 11 on the acquisition of decoding skill, there is considerable evidence that poor readers often lack this skill. Such a lack would impair the acquisition of decoding skill, which depends, in part, on mapping symbols onto phonemes. Moreover, training in phonemic segmentation has been shown to improve early reading (Golinkoff, 1978). Because of such studies, it appears plausible that an inability to segment speech into phonemes may underlie reading problems and perhaps be responsible for dyslexia.

In spite of the supporting evidence, there are at least two reasons to be cautious in assigning phonemic segmentation a central role in dyslexia. First, many of the studies that have examined phonemic segmentation have not specifically studied children who have been diagnosed as dyslexic, as distinct from generally poor readers. Thus, while difficulty with phonemic segmentation may contribute to poor reading skill, it is not clear that it is a causal factor in the specific problem of the dyslexic. Second, phonemic segmentation skills develop with reading skill (Morais, Cary, Alegria, & Bertelson, 1979). Thus, even if the dyslexics were shown to lack this skill, their lack could be the result rather than the cause of not learning to read. While the data are suggestive, it has not yet been convincingly demonstrated that phonemic segmentation contributes to dyslexia.

Slow verbal retrieval   Rather than a deficit that is specific to phonemic codes, an alternative hypothesis is that dyslexics, like poor readers, are generally slow and errorful in retrieving and keeping track of many different types of verbal codes. The verbal codes are internal representations of linguistic units such as phonemes, syllables, morphemes, and words. These verbal codes are not dependent on articulation because dyslexics show deficits even when no overt pronunciation is required. Such retrieval difficulties would interfere with learning to encode words because the dyslexic would be slower and less accurate in retrieving the code that is used to initially learn to read. Moreover, difficulty in retrieving verbal codes could create a bottleneck that would effectively decrease working-memory capacity both in reading and in other demanding tasks that involve such codes. A version of this hypothesis was originally formulated to explain general poor reading (Hunt, 1978; Perfetti, 1983). However, in a more extreme form, it may generalize to dyslexia.

Consistent with this hypothesis, dyslexics often have deficits compared to normal readers when they must retrieve a verbal code, whether the code is a letter's name or the pronunciation of a word or digit. This point was examined in several experiments with the five dyslexic college students whose reading was described at the beginning of the chapter (Carpenter, Just, & McDonald, 1984). One task that required retrieving verbal codes was a letter-matching task devised by Posner (Posner, Boies, Eichelman, & Taylor, 1969; Posner & Mitchell, 1967). Subjects were timed while they decided if two visually presented letters (like *A-A, A-a,* or *A-e*) had the same letter name. If the two letters were physically identical, such as *A-A,* a subject could make the judgment on the basis of their visual identity. In this condition, both dyslexics and normal readers were relatively fast and their response times were indistinguishable. By contrast, when the letters were not physically identical, such as *A-a,* subjects could make the judgment only by retrieving verbal codes (the letter names). In this condition, dyslexics took much longer than normal readers. The additional time presumably reflects their difficulty in retrieving a verbal code.

Dyslexics also performed more poorly than normal readers in a task that required retrieving digit names, showing that their deficit is not specific to letters or words. One such task was a matching task in which subjects were required to compare two simultaneously presented strings of digits, such as 79413—79613, and judge if they were the same or different. Both dyslexics and normal readers reported that they recoded the first string into the digits' names and rehearsed the names while matching them sequentially against the digits in the second string. Dyslexics took much longer than normal readers and made significantly more errors in this task, even though the verbal labels to be retrieved were the digit names, not letter or word names. In sum, dyslexics did appear to have a specific difficulty whenever the task required retrieving a verbal code, even though no overt pronunciation was involved.

Another finding has suggested that dyslexics may also take longer to retrieve the names of depicted objects. Denckla and Rudel (1976) compared approximately 50 dyslexics with approximately 50 nondyslexic, learning-impaired children and 120 normal children. Across all ages (7 to 12) and four kinds of materials (colors, numbers, letters, and pictures of objects), the dyslexic children took longer to generate names than the nondyslexic children with learning disabilities, and both groups took longer than the normal readers. Denckla and Rudel argued that the dyslexics' slowness was not some general slowness in perceptual motor reaction time. Their argument was based on the indirect evidence that the dyslexics were generally faster than the learning-impaired children on timed tests, such as timed IQ tests. The results support the proposal that slowness in verbal retrieval is not specific to retrieving sounds associated with letters but is a general problem that exists for several types of verbal codes.

Most of the tasks that have revealed difficulties in the time to retrieve a verbal code have used a visual stimulus, whether a letter, digit, or picture of an object. Dyslexics may have a problem that is specific to the association between visual and verbal material. Alternatively, dyslexics may have a general problem in retrieving verbal codes in response to nonvisual stimuli, as well, such as auditory or tactile stimuli.

Slowness in retrieving verbal codes might put the dyslexic at a disadvantage in working-memory tasks that involve verbal codes (Jorm, 1983). Studies of dyslexics have found that their working-memory capacity is correlated with the time they take to retrieve verbal codes (Spring & Capps, 1974; Torgeson & Houck, 1980). For example, in one study, working-memory capacity was measured using a digit-span task in which the child's span was the number of digits he could repeat after a rapid presentation (Torgeson & Houck, 1980). The child's digit span was found to be correlated with his speed in naming individual digits, which was a measure of the child's speed in retrieving verbal codes. The correlation suggests that slow verbal retrieval reduced the child's ability to retain and rehearse the verbal labels and, consequently, resulted in poor memory performance. This deficit may not characterize all dyslexics because not all of the dyslexics in this study had small digit spans. Nevertheless, the study demonstrates that slowness in retrieving verbal codes is associated with poor performance in working memory.

General Language Deficit

Some investigators have proposed that dyslexia results from general language impairment at a level beyond the processes of segmenting phonemes or retrieving verbal codes (see Vellutino, 1979). One type of evidence for some general language impairment comes from studies that followed the reading progress of children whose oral language development was delayed (Rutter, 1978). Two years after starting school, one-third of the children who had earlier experienced articulatory problems or whose language acquisition had been delayed were significantly behind in reading and spelling. By contrast, only one of twenty children in the control condition was behind. Moreover, early language problems were more closely associated with later reading problems than were early visual or motor problems. In fact, children who had problems in visual perception or visuomotor coordination were no more likely than the control group to have later reading problems. These studies suggest a link between early language problems and eventual reading disability.

One difficulty with this approach is that it does not illuminate the nature of the child's earlier or later language problems. A delay in acquiring language could be due to many factors. Without some more detailed analysis of why these children were delayed in acquiring language, it is difficult to conjecture what its relation is to dyslexia.

Another type of evidence for a general language problem comes from experimental studies that assess the existence of comprehension deficits beyond those due to word encoding. One study compared older dyslexics to younger normal readers (Guthrie, 1973). The two groups were matched on IQ and on the ability to read single words. The children read through a passage that presented three alternative words at certain points, such as:

horses	had	blanket.
Both flowers *lifted their ears. They* were *heard the forest ranger's* kept.		
talk	some	voice.

The children were asked to circle the most appropriate alternative. The dyslexics made more errors than the normal readers, even though the two groups had been matched in the ability to read single words.

Such results are open to several interpretations. One interpretation is that dyslexics have a general language impairment at levels other than word encoding—for example, an impairment in syntactic or semantic processing, in referential processing, or the like. Alternatively, such comprehension difficulties could be a result of a history of encoding problems that impede the development of reading comprehension skills. Because dyslexics may devote more attention to word encoding and retrieval, they may not learn to properly interrelate clauses, identify the topic, or make appropriate inferences. Either explanation could account for the results of studies that demonstrate comprehension deficits in dyslexics.

A more fundamental problem with the proposal that dyslexics have a general language impairment is that at least some dyslexics do not have obvious problems in auditory language comprehension. Consequently, any proposal for a general language deficit must also explain why the deficiencies are more apparent in reading than in listening.

General Learning Deficits

A third proposal is that dyslexics have general learning deficits that are not specific to mastering symbol-sound correspondences. Characterizations of the possible learning deficit have varied considerably. Any theory must accommodate the specificity of the dyslexics' problem. That is, dyslexics are able to master a variety of complex tasks, both in the laboratory and in everyday life. The proposal of a general learning disability would have difficulty explaining how some dyslexics become engineers, scientists, and medical doctors, although they cannot fluently encode words.

One of the best-known proposals concerning a learning deficit was that dyslexics have problems in associating information from the visual and auditory modalities (Birch & Belmont, 1964). However, this proposal has not held up as a result of research showing that dyslexic children do not have difficulty learning to associate nonlinguistic sounds, such as coughs, with visual figures (Vellutino, Steger, Harding, & Phillips, 1975).

Generally, dyslexics do not show an inability to learn, although they do have problems if asked to learn to associate a word or nonsense word with a referent. For example, one study required learning an association between auditory and visual stimuli (Vellutino, Steger, Harding, & Phillips, 1975). The study tested 120 children, half of them dyslexics and half of them normal readers, between grades four and six. The dyslexics had no more problems than the normal readers in learning to associate familiar, simple sounds, like hums and coughs, with visual patterns. Thus, they did not display a general learning problem or even a problem associating visual information with nonspeech sounds. However, the dyslexics made twice as many errors as the normal children if they had to associate a spoken nonsense word like *pex* to a shape or to a scribblelike written form. Vellutino (1979) has convincingly argued that dyslexics are at a disadvantage if unfamiliar verbal codes are involved in the learning task but that they do not have a general learning problem.

Visual Deficits

The reading errors of dyslexics sometimes look like visual confusions. For instance, dyslexics often confuse reversible letters, such as *b* and *d* or *p* and *q*. And they sometimes confuse the order of letters in a word—such as *was/saw, clam/calm*, and *loin/lion*—and write letters in a mirror-image form, such as Ͱ for *N* (Kaufman, 1980). Such errors have led some investigators to suggest that dyslexia is caused by a visual disorder related to orientation (Bender, 1957; Hermann, 1959; Orton, 1925, 1937). The idea that dyslexia is essentially a visual disorder is a very commonly held opinion among the general population, as well. In spite of these widely held views, as we argued in Chapter 11 on beginning decoding, such letter confusions do not necessarily indicate that dyslexia is due to a visual deficit. In fact, letter confusions may be the result of poor word-encoding skills, rather than the cause of them (Vellutino, 1979). Young children who do not have reading problems often make such errors, although the frequency of the errors decreases as the child acquires reading skill.

One of the most influential theorists who argued for a visual basis of dyslexia was Orton (1925, 1937), who believed that orientation confusions between letters, particularly the mirror-image confusions, were the fundamental cause of dyslexia. Orton developed an explanation of letter reversals based on the asymmetries between the two halves of the brain. The general idea that brain asymmetries are somehow involved in reading problems is a persistent one, although the evidence concerning the nature of the involvement is mixed (Young & Ellis, 1981). But the hypothesis that a visual deficit underlies dyslexia can be evaluated independently of Orton's theory concerning its possible physiological basis.

The most direct evidence against the visual-deficit proposal is that dyslexics have no deficit in visual tasks that do not entail verbal mediation. Two reviews of the research literature on visual deficits found that in spite of some positive results, the weight of the research evidence was against the hypothesis of a visual deficit (Benton, 1962, 1975; Vellutino, 1979). Benton wrote:

> My conclusion is that deficiency in visual form perception is *not* an important correlate of developmental dyslexia. By this I mean that, while it may be a determinant of the language disability in some cases, it is not a significant factor in the majority of cases. (1962, p. 94)

In general, most dyslexics' reading difficulties are not due to deficiencies in binocular coordination, faulty scanning, or other oculomotor deficiencies (Rourke, 1978), nor are they due to a disability in registering visual information (Morrison & Manis, 1982). However, there continue to be clinical reports of children who show basic visual disorders (Boder, 1971; Mattis, 1978; Pirozzolo & Rayner, 1979). At most, visual disorders may account for the problems of a very small proportion of dyslexics.

Visual tasks with implicit verbal components   In this section, we will review the arguments that some so-called visual errors are the result, not the cause, of reading problems. Many apparently visual tasks permit or encourage verbal coding, which may be the source of error for the dyslexic. As an example, consider a typical visual matching task in which a child is shown a letter and asked to find an identical letter among a given set of distractor letters. Young children who have reading problems often have difficulty with this task (Calfee, 1977). However, Calfee pointed out that a child who attempts to perform the matching with a purely visual representation might have difficulty maintaining an accurate representation of the target throughout the time needed to make a sequence of comparisons to the distractors. Successful performance might depend upon retrieving, rehearsing, and comparing verbal codes for the letters—exactly the processes that would be difficult for a child with reading problems. Consequently, poor performance might appear to arise from visual processes but would actually arise from a lack of proficiency in verbal processes.

To support his analysis of the tasks, Calfee designed visual matching tasks that minimized the role of verbal coding. For example, in one version, only two figures were presented at one time to minimize the number of comparisons that were required. The figures were letterlike but not actually letters to minimize the likelihood that a verbal code would be retrieved. Under these conditions, kindergarteners and first-graders who were at risk for reading problems had no difficulty with the visual matching tasks.

The research with the five dyslexic college students whose reading performance was described in the first section of the chapter also indicates that they do not have difficulty with visual matching tasks (Carpenter, Just, & McDonald, 1984). When required to compare simple geometric shapes or more complex shapes (such as doors, faces, or small figures), the speed and accuracy of the five dyslexic readers was well within the range of the normal control group. In fact, in a variety of tests of visual processing, such as a test that required mentally rotating complex forms to decide if two figures were the same or different, the dyslexics performed as well or better than the normal college readers. The only visual tasks that elicited less than average performance were those that were typically performed using a verbal code, consistent with Calfee's data for very young children.

Other studies support the conclusion that many dyslexics have no difficulty with tasks that draw heavily on visual abilities, as long as the task does not evoke verbal coding. For example, dyslexic children have little difficulty with simple copying tasks that do not involve words. In two studies with children between 8 and 15 years of age, dyslexic and normal readers were equally accurate in copying a sequence of geometric figures (Vellutino, Steger, & Kandel, 1972; Vellutino, Smith, Steger, & Kaman, 1975). By contrast, the dyslexics did have problems in copying words. The dyslexics had even more difficulty pronouncing the words. Because dyslexics could copy words more accurately than they could pronounce them, Vellutino argued that perceptual difficulties are unlikely to be the root of their reading problem. Thus, there is little evidence of a visual deficit as the major problem in dyslexia.

In summary, we have reviewed a number of proposals that assume some nonreading process underlies the word-encoding problems of dyslexics. These are not the only proposals in the research literature, but they are the more frequently explored ones. At the present time, the research is equivocal and no one proposal is clearly supported. However, extensive evaluation suggests that visual deficits are unlikely to be the cause of most cases of dyslexia. The proposals of a general learning deficit or a general language deficit are not as easily rejected, partly because they have not been specified or tested as thoroughly as the proposal concerning visual deficits. But either proposal will eventually have to account for the fact that a dyslexic's problems are relatively specific to reading and do not generalize to other complex learning tasks. Finally, the proposal that dyslexics are slow in retrieving verbal codes has a great deal of supporting evidence. However, this proposal has not yet been subjected to the same level of scrutiny as the visual-deficit hypothesis, and research on all of these proposals is still ongoing.

Prognosis and Remediation

A variety of remedial reading programs have been developed to help dyslexics, as well as poor readers (Johnson, 1978; Naidoo, 1981). Programs that focus on language and reading are more successful than those that focus on visuomotor or visuoperceptual training (Benton, 1978; Guthrie, 1978; Jorm, 1983). However, the evaluation literature is very sketchy. Evaluations of remedial programs seldom include control groups to determine the relative effectiveness of the program or long-term follow-ups to determine whether the improvement is long lasting. Also, many studies do not distinguish dyslexics from poor readers.

The prognosis for dyslexic children is that they will make some progress in reading as they go through school, but typically, their final level of reading achievement is not very high. "If there is a typical course, it is one where reading ability slowly improves through the years of puberty and adolescence, the patient finally becoming a relatively slow reader and a very poor speller" (Benton, 1975, p. 7).

The prognosis for dyslexics may be worse than that for poor readers. One of the few longitudinal studies that assessed the reading attainment of dyslexic children contrasted about 80 dyslexic children with 80 poor readers (Rutter & Yule, 1975). Both groups were reading about 33 months below the level of normal readers, but the poor readers had lower IQs, by about one standard deviation, and so were reading closer to the level that was expected. After about five years, the dyslexic group, in spite of their higher IQs, had made significantly less improvement in reading and spelling than the poor readers. By contrast, dyslexics made relatively more progress in arithmetic (although both groups were performing below age level). Unfortunately, it is not known whether these children received remediation and, if so, how much or what kind. Nevertheless, this study suggests that the outlook for dyslexic children can be bleaker than that for poor readers.

Although the overall prognosis appears pessimistic, scattered studies have reported that some dyslexics improve their reading skills and can attain considerable academic and professional success. One particularly optimistic report came from Rawson's (1968) review of 20 dyslexic boys who had all attended the same private school and received remedial instruction. All but 35 percent were reading close to their grade level when they left school. Moreover, most worked as professionals, including medical doctors, lawyers, research scientists, and businessmen. Clearly, dyslexia does not necessarily prevent people from learning and practicing these demanding professions. However, occupations that require proficiency in the mechanical aspects of spelling and reading, such as proofreading and dictation transcription, are undoubtedly difficult for a dyslexic to pursue successfully.

The academic performance of the five dyslexic college students whose reading skills were described earlier in the chapter reinforces these conclusions (Carpenter, Just, & McDonald, 1984). The five students reported using a variety of coping strategies that had permitted them to not only survive but even excel in their academic careers. Understandably, reading was not their favored way of mastering school material, although they could and did struggle through textbooks, assignments, and exams. They reported paying close attention to lectures and sometimes arranged for friends and parents to read course materials to them. In only one case had the reading difficulty previously caused academic problems that reflected a mixture of both cognitive and motivational difficulties. The student had not been diagnosed as dyslexic until he was in high school. Until that time, he had considered his earlier academic problems to be due to a lack of intelligence or conscientiousness. Once he was identified as dyslexic, he no longer doubted his intellectual ability. Although his reading skills continued to be extremely poor, he became academically motivated and, at the time of the experiment, he was planning to enter graduate school in biology.

Although these reports demonstrate that some dyslexics manage to attain high academic and professional goals in spite of poor reading skills, their achievements should not be construed as an argument that dyslexia is not an enormous impediment. As Benton (1975) pointed out, dyslexic children from private schools who have the help and support of parents and specialists are certainly not representative of most children with severe reading problems.

Not only do dyslexics typically have school problems, but they can experience great frustration with everyday activities, including mundane tasks such as using a telephone book or street directory, looking up a word in a dictionary, or even reading highway signs for directions (Hermann, 1959). Similarly, dyslexics may sign documents without reading or understanding them, just to avoid frustration and embarrassment. And of course, writing and spelling, whether for personal or business reasons, continually cause error and humiliation for the dyslexic. One of the five dyslexic college students in our experiment reported relief at being able to prepare his written class assignments using a text-editing program that checked his spelling.

Correlated Characteristics of Dyslexia

What causes dyslexia? Is it an inherited trait? Is it due to poor schooling? Or is it caused by some combination of factors, such as a basic disposition that interacts with certain schooling techniques? In this section, we will discuss some hereditary and environmental factors that are correlated with the incidence of dyslexia.

Hereditary Factors

Some types of dyslexia may be biologically inherited, like baldness or color blindness. Baldness and color blindness happen to be hereditary traits that occur more often in males than females. Similarly, there may be a hereditary component to dyslexia.

Sex differences   Many different kinds of survey studies have found that boys more frequently have reading problems than girls do. For example, a large survey of over 2,500 children in Britain found that more boys than girls were markedly poor readers and that the difference was most marked for children with average or higher IQs (Lovell, Shapton, & Warren, 1964). Presumably, the average- and high-IQ group primarily reflected reading disability due to dyslexia, whereas the low-IQ group included more children who were poor readers due to general intellectual impairment. The data, presented in Figure 12.8, also show how the proportion of children with severe reading problems decreases with age, except for boys with average and high IQs. Several smaller studies of dyslexics that used exclusionary definitions also found a much higher proportion of male than female dyslexics (Benton, 1975). This higher incidence has been interpreted by some as evidence for a biological component in dyslexia, such that males are more susceptible to this disability (as they are to color blindness and baldness).

Other researchers have suggested that sex differences may be due to cultural factors that encourage language skills in girls, including the disproportionately high number of female reading teachers and the fact that girls more often than boys are encouraged to play reading and language games (Downing, 1973; Gibson & Levin, 1975). Such cultural factors may account for part of the difference in the incidence between boys and girls; however, it seems unlikely that they could account for the greater incidence of dyslexia in boys being even greater among high-IQ children than low-IQ children. This finding suggests some role of heredity in dyslexia.

Familial studies   If some cases of dyslexia are influenced by hereditary factors, the obvious question is whether dyslexia runs in the family. Overall, there is an impressive amount of evidence for some hereditary component in dyslexia (Benton, 1975). However, its exact nature is not clear. In particular, researchers who have

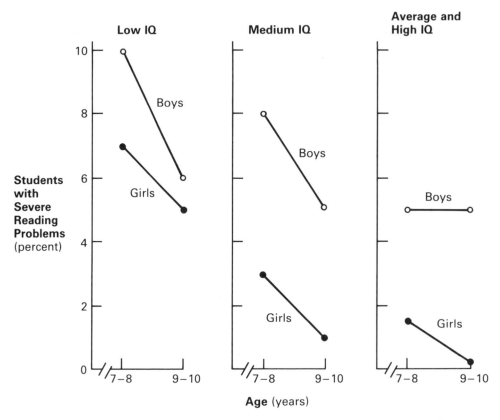

Figure 12.8 The percentage of boys and girls who have severe reading problems. The three panels show the percentages for children with low IQs (less than 90), medium IQs (between 90 and 99), and average to high IQs (greater than 99). While a higher proportion of boys than girls have reading problems in each group, the difference is largest for children with IQs above 99. The data also show that the proportion of children with specific reading problems tends to decrease with age, except for the average- and high-IQ boys. *Source:* Based on data from Lovell, Shapton, & Warren, 1964, p. 58.

tried to fit a particular genetic model to dyslexia—for example, by assuming that it is a male-linked recessive genetic trait—have not been particularly successful in acccounting for its patterns of incidence. Moreover, neither of the two major kinds of evidence for a hereditary factor is entirely conclusive nor is either likely to answer the question of the role of heredity.

One kind of study that is used to assess the role of heredity is the survey, which simply asks which other family members have reading problems. Families of dyslexics often report a higher incidence of reading problems than families of normal readers of comparable IQ and social status. However, this evidence has a potential bias, since parents of dyslexics might be more likely to report reading problems than parents of nondyslexics. In addition, the studies do not always differentiate dyslexia from generally poor reading. In fact, reading problems and language delay are reported by families of generally poor readers almost as often as by families of dyslexic readers (Rutter, 1978). Although not typically feasible, a more direct assessment of the reading skills of family members would be a better way to determine patterns of heritability.

Another type of heritability study compares the reading skills of twins. Usually, identical twins (who are genetically similar) show more similar reading performance than fraternal twins (who are genetically no more similar than siblings). At first glance, the results of these studies are striking, and many researchers and laymen treat them as very strong evidence for the hereditary foundation of dyslexia. However, the data are not conclusive because many twin studies have not distinguished general poor reading from dyslexia. To be convincing, the twin studies should show that the problems experienced by the twins are specific to reading and not due to correlations in their general intelligence. Verbal ability, and intellectual performance, in general, has some hereditary component. But there is relatively little evidence beyond this concerning a hereditary component that might be specific to dyslexia (Rutter & Yule, 1975).

Overall, studies that indicate a higher incidence of dyslexia among boys and survey studies support a role for heredity. However, the data are not entirely conclusive. More to the point, unlike color blindness, which is solely genetically determined, dyslexia is likely to have cognitive components that influence its manifestation and remediation. Thus, it is unlikely that dyslexia will ever conform to a purely hereditary model.

Minimal brain dysfunction   Another biologically based explanation of dyslexia is a diagnosis of **minimal brain dysfunction**. This term is sometimes applied when the reader shows no obvious evidence of brain damage, although there may be a subtle pattern of symptoms that suggests neural involvement. However, this approach generally does not provide a satisfactory explanation of dyslexia (Gibson & Levin, 1975). First, the pattern of symptoms is often so subtle that the diagnosis becomes circular. Reading or learning problems are taken as evidence of the minimal brain dysfunction, and the minimal brain dysfunction is the explanation of the reading or learning problems. Second, many dyslexics do not show signs of any neurological problems. By definition, minimal brain dysfunction cannot account for dyslexics identified using the exclusionary approach because this approach excludes children who have signs of neurological impairment. Finally, this approach has not been particularly illuminating, either in guiding remediation or in characterizing the nature and course of dyslexia.

Environmental Factors

Although there is evidence of a possible role of heredity in dyslexia, there is also strong evidence that environmental factors are associated with the incidence of dyslexia. These factors include the socioeconomic status of the family, family size, and the characteristics of the school.

Family characteristics   The fathers of dyslexic children are more likely than the fathers of normal readers to have jobs that are classified as manual and are less likely to have clerical or professional occupations (Rutter, Tizard, & Whitmore, 1970). Also, poor reading and dyslexia occur more frequently in families of low socioeconomic status (Rutter & Yule, 1975). One explanation is that children from low socioeconomic groups may tend to receive poor schooling or less individualized tutoring. On the other hand, almost all environmental factors can be given an alternative interpretation that would be consistent with a heritability explanation (Jorm, 1983). For example, suppose one hypothesized that dyslexia is a male-linked inherited trait. Then the fathers of dyslexics would be more likely to be dyslexic than would the fathers of normal readers, and this might explain their greater likelihood of having manual labor occupations rather than clerical or professional occupations.

Dyslexia correlates with other factors that suggest environmental characteristics can play an important role. For example, dyslexics tend to come from large families (Rutter, Tizard, & Whitmore, 1970). Children in large families might get less individual tutoring from their parents or others if they have severe reading problems. Of course, family size is also correlated with socioeconomic status, which introduces many more possible explanations for the relation between family size and reading disability. Nevertheless, family interactions could influence the incidence of dyslexia.

Other social factors   The incidence of dyslexia also depends on community characteristics. In the discussion of the inclusionary definition of dyslexia, we described a large correlational study by Rutter and associates that identified children who were reading markedly below what was expected on the basis of their IQs (Rutter & Yule, 1975). The study contrasted the incidence of dyslexia in both urban and rural areas of Britain and found that there was a much higher incidence (6 percent of the 10-year-olds) in inner-city London than on the Isle of Wight, a rural area (3.5 percent) (Rutter & Yule, 1975). Dyslexic children tended to come from large families whose fathers were employed in low-status jobs and from schools that had high levels of absenteeism and pupil turnover (Rutter, Yule, Quinton, Rowlands, Yule, & Berger, 1975). These factors also distinguished urban London from the largely rural Isle of Wight, since the London sample came from large families and schools with high teacher and pupil turnover. Based on data like these, Rutter argued that dyslexia is a multidetermined syndrome, a predisposition that is affected by environmental factors like schooling and family life.

Cross-cultural incidence of dyslexia   Similar descriptions of the reading and writing problems of dyslexics have been documented in many countries, including Britain (Critchley & Critchley, 1978), Denmark, Sweden, and Norway (Hermann, 1959). The presence of dyslexia across different societies, writing systems, and educational systems suggests that none of these factors is solely responsible for dyslexia. Nevertheless, differences in the frequency of dyslexia among different countries or societies could provide evidence of possible environmental influences on dyslexia.

Cross-cultural studies are of interest from a variety of perspectives concerning possible factors that contribute to dyslexia. For example, if phonemic segmentation were the bottleneck in dyslexia, then it would be of interest to analyze the incidence of dyslexia in countries whose orthographies are syllabic or logographic, rather than alphabetic, and do not require segmentation at the level of individual phonemes. Alternatively, it has been proposed that dyslexics have difficulty learning complex rules with numerous exceptions (Morrison & Manis, 1982). It would be of interest to test this proposal by analyzing the incidence of dyslexia in languages that have more regular alphabetic orthographies. Finally, if dyslexia were influenced by particular educational practices or social factors, then it would be of interest to analyze the incidence of dyslexia in countries and communities that differ with respect to these factors.

In spite of the desirability of such data, it has been difficult to assess the incidence of dyslexia across different countries. Moreover, as we argued in Chapter 10 on orthography, the collection and interpretation of such cross-cultural data on reading skill is fraught with problems, both in methodology and analysis. Thus far, cross-national comparisons have produced only suggestive speculations, not substantive evidence concerning the possible causes of either poor reading or dyslexia.

These studies of correlated characteristics support a role for both heredity and environmental factors in the incidence of dyslexia. But at present, the research is far from conclusive and does not specify what role each plays or how they interact in dyslexia.

Acquired Dyslexia

One day, in 1895, a 58-year-old language teacher suddenly found that he could no longer read. He was still able to write words, but he could not read what he had written. He also suffered blindness in the right side of his visual field (Hinshelwood, 1917, in Geschwind, 1962). His disability was one of the first documented cases of **acquired dyslexia,** the loss of reading skills due to stroke or head injury. It has also been called **alexia** and **word blindness**. By contrast, the type of dyslexia that we have been describing up to this point is called **developmental dyslexia;** it applies to children and adults who fail to learn to read normally in the first place. This section describes two main types of acquired dyslexia and contrasts them with developmental dyslexia.

It has been proposed that acquired and developmental dyslexia are based on similar neurological dysfunctions and that the sites of brain damage in adult acquired dyslexia correspond to sites of abnormal development in children who cannot learn to read well. We will argue that there is no strong evidence that the two syndromes are identical.

The Neural Basis of Language and Reading

The study of acquired dyslexia has the potential of revealing important properties of reading. When some neurological trauma physically damages portions of the brain that process language, the resulting patterns of disruption in reading provide cues as to the functional relations among the component processes. Moreover, an increasing number of behavioral studies on the reading processes of acquired dyslexics are being conducted in conjunction with the use of new diagnostic imaging techniques such as PET scans. These approaches are likely to relate dysfunctions to particular brain structures.

Although all psychological processes have a neural basis, the neural basis of language has been of special interest, for many reasons (Lenneberg, 1967). One of these reasons is that language processing is more lateralized than most other psychological processes. One cortical hemisphere does most of the language processing. In most right-handed people and at least half of all left-handed people, the majority of language processing and speech production occurs in the left cortical hemisphere. The evidence for this asymmetry between the hemispheres comes from many sources. Adult patients who have had their left hemisphere removed due to injury or illness usually have difficulty speaking, understanding, or remembering verbal information. About 95 percent of all speech disorders stemming from brain damage result from left-hemisphere damage (Geschwind, 1979). The left hemisphere can decode more words, perform more sophisticated syntactic analysis, and retain verbal information better than the right hemisphere. However, the right hemisphere does have certain language abilities. It recognizes some words and may process simple sentences describing actions or spatial and temporal relations (Zaidel, 1978).

Localization of language function   Within the left hemisphere, different regions are particularly involved with different aspects of language: meaning, syntax and morphology, and articulation. Some of these areas are indicated in Figure 12.9,

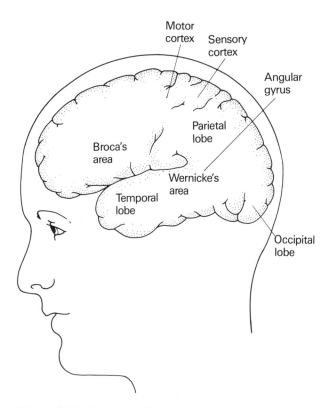

Figure 12.9   A sketch indicating some of the major areas in the left hemisphere. *Broca's area* is involved with syntactic processing. *Wernicke's area* is involved with semantic processing. Strokes in the area of the *angular gyrus* sometimes result in acquired dyslexia.

which shows a sketch of the left hemisphere from the left side. Most brain theories attempt to specify which brain structure performs which psychological process. In this spirit, we will describe the theories that associate brain locations with particular language-related information storage and computation. The theories are formulated by relating the specific symptoms of language pathology to the destruction of specific information processes or capacities at a particular site (Geschwind, 1979). This is called a *localist* approach. It is important to note that nonlocalist approaches focus on generalized dysfunctions. For example, Lenneberg (1967), who was not a localist, argued that some of the symptoms associated with acquired dyslexia could be interpreted as being due to general factors, such as disruption in the timing mechanisms in reading.

The three brain areas most commonly associated with language processing are Broca's area, Wernicke's area, and the angular gyrus. Many other areas (such as the areas that process visual information) are also involved in reading, but damage to these three areas is particularly associated with language pathologies. The localization of language function is relatively recent scientific knowledge. It was in the 1860s that Broca pointed out that speech disorders often resulted from damage to a particular region of the left hemisphere, an area now known as **Broca's area.** As we described in Chapter 5 on syntax, Broca's aphasics have difficulty with syntactic analysis. Their speech is slow, inarticulate, ungrammatical, and often lacks function words and syntactic markers, although it does make sense. Geschwind (1979) gave the following example of the speech of a person with Broca's aphasia who was asked about a dental appointment:

> "Yes . . . Monday . . . Dad and Dick . . . Wednesday nine o'clock . . . ten
> o'clock . . . doctors . . . and . . . teeth."

While such patients have difficulty speaking normally, they do not have problems with articulation since they can sing song lyrics.

Wernicke's area, named after the investigator who identified it in 1874, is more involved with semantic and referential processing (see Figure 12.9). Patients with Wernicke's aphasia have phonetically and grammatically reasonable speech, but the content is often nonsense. Geschwind cited the following speech sample of such a patient who was asked to explain a picture showing two boys stealing a cookie behind a woman's back:

> "Mother is away here working her work to get her better, but when she's
> looking the two boys looking in the other part. She's working another time."

Wernicke's area also plays a role in understanding speech and in reading.

A third area, the **angular gyrus,** may be a site in which the visual form of the word is associated with the corresponding auditory pattern (Geschwind, 1979). Lesions in the angular gyrus are often accompanied by reading problems. The angular gyrus may play a role in the communication that must occur in reading between the sites that process visual information (such as the occipital lobe) and the areas that process language.

The neurological basis of acquired dyslexia As every clinical researcher knows, it is extremely difficult to categorize patients with brain damage on the basis of their behavioral symptoms. The symptoms are often unstable, overlapping, and masked by other problems. Consequently, not all clinicians agree on the typology of acquired dyslexia. Nevertheless, we will focus on two main types (Benton, 1978):

1. **Pure alexia:** reading problems without writing problems or oral language problems; orally spelled words are recognized.
2. **Alexia with agraphia:** reading and writing problems and sometimes oral speech problems.

Pure alexia is striking and well understood. Alexia with agraphia is the form of acquired dyslexia that more closely resembles developmental dyslexia.

There are other types of acquired reading pathologies, as well. Some researchers have suggested a third type that entails more difficulty recognizing letters than words; in addition to having some of the symptoms above, patients of this third type cannot recognize orally spelled words. This syndrome, associated with lesions in the frontal lobe, is often accompanied by Broca's aphasia. A fourth type of reading pathology is characterized by general visual and spatial problems that interfere with reading and writing. Mattis (1978) suggested that the third and fourth types are parallel to other subtypes of developmental dyslexia, but we will not review the evidence here.

Pure Alexia

The classic symptoms of pure alexia or *word blindness* are very much like those of the 58-year-old language teacher described earlier, who suddenly discovered that he could not read even though he could still write. The symptoms are an inability to read words or letters (although letters can be identified if their contours are traced), the ability to write dictation without being able to subsequently read what was written, and blindness for visual information to the right of the fixation point. The original neuroanatomical explanation proposed for word blindness by Dejerine is still largely accepted today (Geschwind, 1962; Goodglass & Kaplan, 1972). Word blindness results when the visual-processing area is disassociated from the language-processing areas of the brain.

Pure alexia is usually associated with a lesion in the visual cortex of the left hemisphere, which processes information from the area to the right of the point of fixation. This explains why such patients are blind to visual information that is to the right of the fixation point. Pure alexia patients also have damage to the communication pathway in the corpus collosum that carries information from the right visual cortex to the left hemisphere. Thus, although the language area of the left hemisphere is undamaged, it is isolated from visual input from either the left or right hemisphere. Consequently, these patients can understand spoken language, but they cannot linguistically process visual information.

This syndrome provides further evidence of the important role of the left hemisphere in normal reading. However, it is unlike developmental dyslexia. Pure alexia is not only rare, but it is primarily a difficulty in the visual system and communication between the visual-processing areas and the language-processing systems. By contrast, in developmental dyslexia, the problem is more intimately tied to language processing.

Alexia with Agraphia

The second general class of acquired dyslexia is more similar to developmental dyslexia because it typically involves reading problems, as well as writing and spelling problems. Whether speech production and comprehension are normal varies considerably among these patients (Goodglass & Kaplan, 1972). The severity of the reading problems ranges from an inability to match letters or words across different type fonts, to the ability to recognize letters and sometimes short words, to slow reading with misperception of some words. Sometimes patients are unable to write individual letters from dictation, although they often can copy letters. In milder cases, they can write words but they make gross errors in spelling and lose track of the grammatical features of the word they are writing.

The brain site that is implicated in alexia with agraphia is the angular gyrus, the area that lies at the posterior margin (the rear edge) of the language area. The angular gyrus bridges the posterior regions of two main parts of the cortex, the temporal and parietal lobes. In addition, some patients with alexia with agraphia may have lesions in the parietal lobe, associated with nonlanguage problems such as difficulty in numerical calculation, finger identification, right-left discrimination, drawing, and some spatial construction tasks. Those who propose a parallel between developmental dyslexia and this form of acquired dyslexia have conjectured that developmental dyslexia is due to faulty development of the parietal area that meets the temporal and occipital areas. This area is a proposed site of convergence or association of information acquired through different sense modalities.

Word-encoding differences among acquired dyslexics Recent studies of acquired dyslexia have focused less on localizing the site of brain damage and more on analyzing the precise nature of the disruption in the reading processes. Behavioral experiments attempt to determine the functional organization of various language-related processes. The initial results from this new approach have suggested the category of alexia with agraphia itself contains at least two (and possibly more) distinguishable types of acquired dyslexia (Marshall & Newcombe, 1973). The two groups differ in the processes used to pronounce words: One group depends primarily on prelexical speech recoding, while the other group depends primarily on directly accessing the representation of the pronounced word using a visually based, word-level representation.

Patients in the first group pronounce words using a prelexical speech-recoding process; that is, they retrieve sounds associated with letters or a subword unit, such as letter clusters. Such patients have been referred to as **surface dyslexics** (see Patterson, Marshall, & Coltheart, 1985). The most convincing evidence of their deficit is that they tend to pronounce irregular words as though they were regular—for example, pronouncing *pint* as though it rhymed with *lint*. These readers do not appear to store and retrieve a lexically based representation of the word's pronunciation that would permit direct retrieval of irregular words.

Another group of patients has the opposite problem. They have difficulty recoding letters or letter clusters into sounds to check their pronunciation of an infrequent word or to generate the pronunciation of a nonword (Marshall & Newcombe, 1973). Such patients have been referred to as **phonemic dyslexics** (Patterson & Marcel, 1977). Phonemic dyslexics often make errors pronouncing nonwords, such as *dake* or *jub,* or infrequent words. A common interpretation is that these patients rely primarily on lexical-level codes, which are not accessible for nonwords or infrequent words (Saffran & Marin, 1977; Shallice & Warrington, 1975). Their pronunciation errors sometimes appear to result from visual confusions. For example, they may pronounce *chair* as "charm" or *origin* as "organ." These apparently visual errors do not result from peripheral visual impairments but are specific to reading.

The word-recognition processes of phonemic dyslexics appear not to be based on word shape or any global cue. At least one acquired dyslexic was reported to have no additional difficulty recognizing words that were presented in mIxEd CaSe or words that were vertically disarranged (Saffran & Marin, 1977). Also, these patients' pronunciation difficulties vary with the linguistic properties of the word. For example, several patients were reported to have more difficulty pronouncing words with abstract referents than words with concrete referents.

Other acquired dyslexics make meaning-related errors when pronouncing words. Such a dyslexic might say "pony" when reading *horse.* These patients also make derivational errors, for example, reading "twisted" for *twist* or "buy" for *bought.* Whether these derivational errors are due to visual, morphological, or semantic confusions, however, is difficult to decide. And whether these patients are distinguishably different from phonemic dyslexics is also unclear. These acquired dyslexic syndromes are also sometimes accompanied by various aphasic problems, that is, difficulties in producing or comprehending spoken speech.

Comparison between acquired and developmental dyslexia   Some of the acquired dyslexia syndromes are similar to developmental dyslexia. Like the phonemic dyslexics, children who are identified as developmentally dyslexic often have difficulty with the grapheme-to-phoneme translation that is required to pronounce unfamiliar words. This is one striking similarity between the acquired dyslexics and the most general characteristic of the developmental dyslexic. In addition, one might argue that there are similarities between the surface dyslexics' problems and the problems experienced by developmental dyslexics who remain slow in visually encoding words. In fact, it has been proposed that different acquired dyslexic syndromes may parallel different subtypes of developmental dyslexia (see Frith, 1985). Although the detailed investigations of these acquired dyslexics are still rather preliminary, the functional analyses of their problems do show intriguing parallels to the word-encoding problems of developmental dyslexics.

On the other hand, there is every reason to be cautious about such a parallel. There are differences among patients even within these groups. At this point, the typologies for acquired dyslexia are not entirely established or agreed upon. In addition, although studies have been done on acquired dyslexics and on developmental dyslexics, there are few direct comparisons. Moreover, a stroke does not selectively impair a single pathway without altering the rest of the system. Furthermore, these patients often learn to use compensating strategies for coping with their language deficits, and they may also be using these strategies in the experimental situations (Marcel & Patterson, 1978).

In addition to these practical difficulties, there are theoretical reasons to be skeptical about the parallel between developmental and acquired dyslexia. First, direct electrophysiological investigations of developmental dyslexics have not been consistent in identifying brain abnormalities (Benton, 1975; Jorm, 1983). Second, the structures necessary to *acquire* a skill like reading may not be the same as those involved in its *execution*. There are intriguing disassociations among related behaviors. For example, adult patients with brain damage often show disassociation between the same skill when it is the focus of conscious attention and when it is performed automatically under aroused conditions. Luria (1970) anecdotally cited the case of a patient who could not pronounce the word *no* when asked to do so; after many frustrating attempts he responded angrily, "No, doctor, I cannot say 'no' ."

Perhaps the most important reason to be cautious in drawing parallels is the neural differences between children and adults. One such difference is that a child's developing brain has more potential for one site to take over the functions of another damaged site. For example, right-handed adults who lose their left hemisphere almost always suffer severe language impairment, whereas young right-handed children who lose the left hemisphere can still acquire language and learn to read.

Only recently have researchers investigated the reading development of children who have known brain pathologies. The most significant study examined three children who had each had one of their hemispheres removed in infancy to control intractable epileptic seizures (Dennis, 1983). The child who had only a left hemisphere acquired a somewhat different constellation of reading skills than the two children who had only a right hemisphere. The child with only a left hemisphere attained a higher level of fluency and retained meaning better, not just of single words but of units larger than a sentence. At the word level, he was more familiar with the morphophonemic structure of English.

Dennis argued that the left hemisphere's advantage was not necessarily an enhanced capacity for relating sounds to signs but a better ability to master and manipulate the rules of English morphology. At the same time, the left-hemisphere child's reading was more disrupted when words were presented in isolation than in a sentence, suggesting that the left hemisphere also relied more on the syntactic and semantic context.

The two children who had only a right hemisphere also learned to read, but they relied more on visual processes to recognize words. They were not as proficient at decoding unfamiliar words and were generally deficient in inferring the morphophonemic structure of English.

Thus, research showed that the two hemispheres had different cognitive strengths. The left hemisphere plays a larger role in semantic and syntactic analysis, including English morphology. The right hemisphere is more visual or spatial; it can recognize words, but its linguistic skills are limited. Still, the children with only the right hemisphere did learn to read and understand. Thus, this study also illustrates the striking differences between children and adults. A child's brain is much more flexible and capable of reassigning the functions of damaged areas. By contrast, adults who lose their left hemisphere do not show ability to recuperate; they typically have severe and lasting language and reading problems.

The data on the neurophysiology of reading suggest caution in generalizing from acquired dyslexia in adults to developmental dyslexia. Nevertheless, the data on acquired dyslexia are informative. They support the theory of two different routes for recognizing words, the speech recoding route and the visual pathway. Moreover, this syndrome offers interesting insights into the role of particular brain structures in fluent reading.

Summary

Many dyslexics appear to have a relatively specific decoding problem. They do not master the context-sensitive rules of English orthography. They are generally less accurate than normal readers in recognizing words and certainly much slower. They are also notoriously poor spellers. Some people who were diagnosed as dyslexic at some point do eventually learn to read reasonably well. However, available evidence indicates that dyslexics are less likely to achieve reasonable reading skills than are poor readers.

The definition of *dyslexia* influences the resulting theory and estimates of its incidence in a population. Exclusionary approaches to dyslexia select out people who have no obvious explanation for their reading problem—for example, no abnormal schooling history or vision or auditory problems. This approach attempts to initially simplify the scientific investigation of dyslexia by selecting people for study who are more likely to have similar problems. But the approach may result in an atypical sample of dyslexics. By contrast, the inclusionary approach selects for study any children or adults who are reading below their expected potential, irrespective of environmental, sensory, or schooling complications. The argument for this approach is that such factors may contribute to the manifestation of dyslexia. Certainly, survey data suggest that various environmental factors, as well as hereditary factors, influence the incidence of dyslexia. But exactly what kind of role these factors may play has not yet been determined. Moreover, the answers are unlikely to come from the currently available survey techniques that are used to investigate their correlation with dyslexia.

Although the dyslexic's problems are primarily manifested in reading, there are several proposals that word-encoding difficulties are symptomatic of some processing difficulty that may have nonreading consequences, as well. Of the various proposals, perhaps the most widely held is that dyslexia results from visual deficits. However, extensive evaluations of various versions of this proposal do not support visual deficits as the basis of the problem for most dyslexics. Although less thoroughly investigated, the proposal that dyslexics have difficulty in retrieving verbal information is currently a more viable proposal. Several studies have documented that dyslexics have problems when required to retrieve the names of letters, words, or visually depicted objects. Other proposals have been made concerning the possibility of a more general language or learning deficit as the basis of dyslexia. These proposals are currently being refined and evaluated, and no single proposal has unequivocal support.

Finally, we discussed acquired dyslexia and the role of various brain structures in fluent reading. Only recently have investigators begun to examine the psychological processes used when acquired dyslexics pronounce words. These studies provide some converging support for particular processes in skilled reading. Moreover, particular types of acquired dyslexia show behavioral similarities to developmental dyslexia. However, at present, it is premature to assume that the same brain structures mediate acquired dyslexia and dyslexia in children and adults who fail to learn to read normally.

Suggested Readings

Critchley and Critchley's book (1978) provides an interesting description of the reading and spelling problems of dyslexia from a clinical viewpoint. A readable short book by Jorm (1983) gives a general overview of reading and spelling disabilities. The readings edited by Benton and Pearl (1978) provide an excellent sample of the different research approaches to dyslexia. In his monograph, Vellutino (1979) presents his evidence and case against the visual basis of dyslexia. Other recent papers on the topic are in Pavlidis and Miles (1981).

The renewed interest in neuropsychology is a potentially exciting field of work. Some introductory articles on dyslexia, aphasia, and other clinical syndromes can be found in the edited volume of Heilman and Valenstein (1985). A newly edited volume describing surface dyslexia is Patterson, Marshall, and Coltheart (1985).

13

Learning from Text

We read for much more than entertainment. Particularly in instructional settings, we read to acquire knowledge. This process begins in third and fourth grade, when *learning to read* is gradually supplanted by *reading to learn*. At the college level, much of the content a student must learn is mastered by reading and studying. In this chapter, we will explore how readers learn from text—that is, how they acquire new information to use at some later time.

There are both similarities and differences between reading a text and studying it. What the two activities share is the normal reading comprehension processes. But studying, unlike ordinary reading, includes a strategic acquisition of information from the text. Studying is not so much a matter of stuffing information into one's head but rather constructing a plan for how to get it out at a later time. A text that is understood at a deep level has succeeded in getting into the student's head. The difficulty lies in storing it in a form that is retrievable. This chapter examines what students can do and what texts can do to facilitate such learning.

Overview Learning from text usually implies some process in addition to just reading. In the first section, **The Relation between Learning and Reading,** we will consider how learning occurs during reading. We will begin by describing two learning mechanisms, namely, organization and rote association. Although both mechanisms operate during reading, organizational processes play a larger role. These organizational processes include using a schema to organize the content of a text and constructing a referential representation of the described situation. The operation of these mechanisms during reading is also affected by the text and the reader's goals.

In the second section, **Organizational Study Strategies,** we will examine several study strategies, such as outlining the main points of the text or simply rereading the text, and evaluate their relative effectiveness. In this section, we will also describe the role of mnemonic devices in studying. Unlike study strategies, mnemonic devices are not intended to deepen the reader's understanding of the content but merely to improve retention.

In the third section, **Instructional Programs on Learning from Text,** we will discuss the study strategies that are taught in study-skills programs, such as an early program called SQ3R (for *S*urvey, *Q*uestion, *R*ead, *R*ecite, and *R*eview). These programs teach students a number of activities aimed at improving their reading comprehension, as well as their postreading review and rehearsal of the material. More recent study-skills programs teach specific organizational techniques that are tailored to particular types of texts, such as scientific texts.

In the fourth section, **How the Text Can Improve Learning,** we will describe properties of the text that are intended to improve learning, such as summaries, examples, outlines, and advance questions. The section evaluates the effectiveness of various text properties and considers which psychological processes may be responsible for the differential effectiveness of various text aids.

The Relation between Learning and Reading

When a reader has finished going through a text, he typically has learned something new. The amount of learning that occurs during reading is influenced by several factors, such as the reader's previous knowledge, the nature of the text, and the reader's goals and strategies. These factors have been discussed as determinants of comprehension in Chapter 7 on referential processing and Chapter 8 on understanding a text. Because comprehension is a part of studying, these factors are also determinants of learning. The main additional constraint imposed in reading to learn is that a large amount of information be retained.

The intuition of many people is that reading and studying differ primarily with respect to intention: Studying involves the intention to learn, whereas simply reading does not. In spite of this common intuition, a surprising research finding is that the *intention* of learning does not directly contribute to learning. Memory studies have found that students who do not intend to learn acquire as much information as students who do intend to learn, *provided* that they process the information the same way (Hyde & Jenkins, 1973; Postman, 1964). For example, suppose that a group of subjects is instructed to intentionally learn a list of items by forming mental images of the items. The list will be learned equally well by a control group of subjects that forms mental images for some purpose other than learning, say, to evaluate the vividness of the image (Bower, 1972b). In practice, the role of intentionality is to recruit the appropriate processes to accomplish the learning, but it is the recruited processes and not the intentionality that do the job.

Students who are trying to learn from a text are often advised to process the material *actively*. *Active* processing refers to the need for conscious attention, rather than relying on automatic processes. The conscious attention is required for the high-level comprehension processes that use a schema to organize the information. Discovering connections and constructing an organization typically requires active processing.

Determinants of Learning

Theories of human learning have attempted to determine what psychological processes underlie the acquisition of information and what factors influence those processes. Even though the learning theories have been developed from the analysis of simplified material (such as lists of unrelated words), many of the conclusions can be generalized to the learning of information from a text.

Learning theories have identified **organizational processes** as a key determinant of learning. Many experiments have demonstrated that learning is greatly facilitated if either the text or the learner imposes an organization on the information to be acquired (see Dixon & Horton, 1968; Katona, 1940). For example, a long list of grocery items is remembered better if the items have been organized into categories, such as fruits, vegetables, meats, canned goods, and so on. Moreover, if adults are asked to learn poorly organized material, they often reorganize it themselves in the process of learning (Bower, 1972b). The major mechanism of such organizational learning is the process of relating the items to be learned to an organizational framework. In the terminology that has been used in this book, learning consists of inserting the new information into the slots of an appropriate schema.

An organizational structure influences the way information is acquired, remembered, and used (Katona, 1940). The benefits of an organizational structure are many. An organizational structure permits material to be learned in fewer learning trials, it produces better recognition or recall of the material after a long delay, and it increases the likelihood that the information will be applied appropriately in a new situation.

Recalling a text consists of reporting the contents of the schema slots. The nature of the recall depends in part on the fit between the information in the text and an existing schema, if one exists. The information from the text that is likely to be learned best is that which fits well into an existing schema slot, and the information most likely to be omitted in recall is that which does not fit into the schema. Recalling information is a constructive process in the sense that readers use the schema to construct a plausible account of what they have read. These constructive processes are evident when readers confuse information that they just learned with information in their prior schema (Bartlett, 1932; Bower, Black, & Turner, 1979; Cofer, 1977). Such confusions were a prominent feature of the way Bartlett's subjects recalled the story "War of the Ghosts," which was presented in Chapter 8 on text comprehension. The story had originally been derived from a North American Indian folktale and readers systematically distorted it during recall to make it more like a typical Western folktale.

A second important facet of learning, besides organization, is **rote association.** Some forms of learning consist primarily of establishing associations between concepts. The main mechanism underlying the learning of associations is thought to be simple rehearsal or repetition (see Hilgard & Bower, 1975; Horton & Turnage, 1976). For example, suppose that a reader was trying to learn that the word for *apple* in some exotic foreign language is *mksh*. She would have little choice but to repeatedly associate *mksh* with *apple*. Associative learning is most applicable to the acquisition of information that has no obvious organizational structure. It is a demonstrably less efficient form of learning than organizational learning.

The distinction between organizational and associative learning is not as sharp as the theories imply, because organizational processes manage to make their way into associative learning. Information that is being acquired by association can eventually be organized. In the example above, a learner may eventually notice that *mksh* contains some of the same consonant sounds as *Macintosh,* a particular kind of apple, and she may use this information to help her organize the components of the new word. In any case, both organizational and associative learning occur during reading, with organizational learning playing a much larger role.

The interweaving of the two learning mechanisms can be illustrated by the processes proposed by the Kintsch and van Dijk model (1978) of how text information is learned. That model, which was described in comparison to the READER model in Chapter 9, attempts to account for the likelihood that a particular unit of text, a proposition, will be recalled by a reader. The Kintsch and van Dijk model invokes the organizational mechanism when it focuses on the relatedness among propositions. According to the model, propositions are linked to each other if they have at least one shared argument. Propositions that share arguments with many other propositions are more central in the organization of the text and, as a result, are more likely to be kept in working memory for a greater number of processing cycles. And the model invokes the associative mechanism by relating the probability of recalling a proposition to the number of cycles (rehearsals) in which the proposition has participated. Thus, the organizational mechanism determines which propositions will be rehearsed, and the associative mechanism determines that rehearsal will lead to retention.

Learning during Reading

As a person reads, the reading comprehension processes described in previous chapters interpret the information in the text, and the organizational and associative learning mechanisms cause the interpreted information to be acquired. The comprehension and learning are intertwined, rather than separated. The interplay between comprehension and learning processes can be illustrated by an experiment that examined how readers learn about the properties of arteries and veins from a passage about blood circulation (Bransford, Stein, Shelton, & Owings, 1981). Suppose that the passage describes *arteries* as "thick and elastic" and explains that "they carry blood that is rich in oxygen from the heart." By contrast, *veins* are described as "thin, less elastic" and as "carrying blood that is rich in carbon dioxide back to the heart." If no other information about the blood vessels were given, then the two groups of properties might appear to be an arbitrary list. Any learning of these properties of blood vessels that occurred would be based primarily on association, rather than organization. To learn these facts well, a reader would probably have to review them several times.

Another way to learn these facts would be to relate the characteristics of blood vessels to their function with the help of a schema of the cardiovascular system. For instance, it would be easier to learn that arteries are thick if it were clear that they carry the blood that is pumped out by the heart; the thickness provides the strength to withstand changes in pressure associated with the heart's pushing the blood through in spurts. By contrast, the stress is not as great on the veins that return the blood to the heart, so there is no need for thickness; similarly, the arteries' elasticity is necessary for preventing the blood from flowing back towards the heart after a spurt caused by a heartbeat is completed. Rather than learn isolated properties of the different blood vessels by rote association, the reader can use a schema of the cardiovascular system to organize the individual facts. This schema could be provided by the text, or it might be something that the reader imposes based on her previous knowledge of physiology. Thus, the type of learning that occurs depends on the organization of the information.

Task and text effects   Reading for learning occurs in the context of some goal for how the learned information is to be used. For instance, students study in slighty different ways, depending on their goal. Their studying is more effective if they know how their knowledge will be tested (Brown, Bransford, Ferrara, & Campione, 1983). The task goals can influence what kind of information is attended and how it is organized. For example, Hyde and Jenkins (1973) examined the effects of different task goals on the learning of a list of words. Some tasks required only a superficial analysis (such as checking each item for the occurrence of the letters *e* or *g* or indicating a word's part of speech), while some tasks intuitively seemed to require more processing (such as rating a word's frequency or pleasantness). The nature of the task affected the ability to later remember the words. Several studies have demonstrated that what is learned depends on the learning task (see Craik & Lockhart, 1972; Craik & Tulving, 1975).

One task property that affects learning from text is the importance of the exact wording of the text. *Learning* a text most often refers to learning its gist, along with some supporting points. However, many texts contain specific terms that have to be learned verbatim. All disciplines require students to master the basic terminology in the field and their referents. For example, a medical student must learn the names of some prescription drugs; he will not be able to write prescriptions that are based on a paraphrase. And some texts, such as poems, song lyrics, and religious scripts, are occasionally learned word by word. While a schema may help in organizing the main points, it will seldom result in mastering the exact wording. Usually, this requires additional rote association.

Texts, as well as tasks, influence what is learned. Texts can include many different types of information that vary in complexity and abstractness: vocabulary, names, numbers, statements, definitions, relations, summaries, retrieval indices, as well as high-level abstractions. The type of material to be learned influences the learning process. Moreover, different texts tend to be associated with different task goals. Thus, the confluence of the text, the task, and the reading goals have a strong influence over what is learned during reading.

Organizational Study Strategies

The psychological processes involved in studying have been called *mathemagenic,* a word derived from Greek, meaning "giving rise to learning" (Rothkopf, 1970). The main ingredient of successful learning is developing an organization, based on the structure and content of the text itself, that the reader can use to relate the new information to what she already knows. This organizational scheme can be acquired through many study strategies, including rereading, outlining, and underlining. These strategies have a shared characteristic: Both in content and application, such strategies are closely related to comprehension processes. Of course, there are also some obvious differences between study strategies and reading comprehension. One difference is that study strategies are more conscious and explicit than comprehension processes. The explicitness may increase learning if the reader is more accurate or thorough in understanding the text. Also, study strategies require the reader to spend more time on the text than if she were just reading. This additional time may also improve learning. Finally, some study processes involve written outlines or graphlike representations of the content. The spatial layout of the summary information provides an alternative representation of the text, which may improve learning.

Learning the Information's Organization

Many strategies have been devised for learning the material in a text: taking notes, underlining important parts, making an outline, summarizing or paraphrasing, generating questions about the material, imagining the referent, recalling or reviewing the main points, or simply rereading a few times. Most people spontaneously use only the more conventional techniques of rereading and rehearsing. A survey of Navy trainees, instructors, and job incumbents indicated that their most frequently reported study strategy was rereading and rehearsing (Sticht, 1977). Similarly, most school students report that they study a text by reading and rereading, with some underlining and notetaking (Anderson, 1980). More demanding strategies are seldom used, according to these self-reports. Thus, in this section, we will consider the psychological processes involved in two common study strategies—rereading and outlining—and then discuss experiments that compare the effectiveness of various study strategies.

Rereading   Learning studies using lists of words show that sheer repetition of information produces less learning than organizational processes (Bower, 1972a). Of course, a list of words differs from a text in an important way: The text already has a structure that can be used to organize the information while studying. Consequently, reading a text several times can be more than rote repetition. Because rereading can provide an opportunity for the reader to master the material's organization, it can lead to considerable learning.

Successful students know that reading a textbook once is usually insufficient preparation for doing well on a test of the book's content. At the very least, a conscientious student will read a text twice before a test. The main reason that a single reading generally is not sufficient for learning is that the reader usually does not know the structure of the information in a textbook until after she has read it once. Thus, when she reads the text a second time, she can use the knowledge of the structure obtained on the first reading. This is why reading a text twice is so helpful.

The more times a text is studied, the better it is learned. However, the amount of improvement decreases in size with increasing repetitions; the increment in learning will be smaller after the fourth iteration than after the third, for example. The time for reading also tends to decrease over iterations (Rothkopf, 1968). The time a student spends studying a chapter for the fourth time will generally be less than the time spent studying it for the third time. Experiments on these effects are generally not precise enough to indicate whether the amount learned per unit study time remains the same over iterations.

Outlining   Several study aids improve learning because they involve organizing the information. An outline, for example, consists of a hierarchical structure that represents the different categories of information in the text. Outlining also requires arranging the categories into levels that parallel their relative importance and relating the categories to each other. Thus, making an outline involves considerable organization. Other study procedures, like writing down the main points or summarizing a text, also entail organizational processes to the extent that the reader must abstract the main points and their interrelation. Such strategies improve learning because they provide a framework around which a knowledge structure can be built (Bower, 1972a). The framework can subsequently be used to retrieve the information or relate different pieces of information to each other.

Although it is probably most helpful to know the outline in advance of reading the text, it is also helpful to know the outline soon after (within minutes of) reading the text, providing the text is relatively short (a few paragraphs or a short chapter) (Anderson, 1980). Also, if the students themselves generate the organizational information immediately after reading—for example, by generating questions about the text—their memory of what they have just read improves. Thus, learning can be improved not only by acquiring an outline before reading but also by acquiring an outline immediately after reading. Presumably, sufficient information is still retrievable after reading so that the information can be reviewed and reorganized with the benefit of the outline. However, an outline that is acquired as late as a day after reading a text will probably not improve the learning of the information from that reading.

Effectiveness of Study Strategies

Many experiments have examined the effectiveness of study strategies. At first glance, the results are surprising. The surprise is that study strategies do not always improve performance; and when they do improve performance, the improvement is often slight. After a little consideration, the results become more understandable. The difficulty lies in choosing a standard of comparison against which to evaluate the study strategies. What would one expect notetaking or underlining to be superior to? These study strategies do generally produce better learning than just reading the text once, but a single reading is not generally considered to be a form of study.

Study strategies are usually compared to each other and, in particular, to reading the text twice. Rereading gives a student the opportunity to form a schema of the main points during or after the first reading and then organize information and acquire more details on the second reading or selectively attend to the more difficult parts. A number of studies that compared the effectiveness of several different study strategies, such as notetaking and underlining, showed no difference in performance on immediate or delayed tests among the various strategies (Anderson, 1980). Furthermore, active, intentional strategies did not consistently produce better performance than rereading. It appears that many strategies encourage readers to master the content and organization of the material and consequently improve learning. Exactly which strategy is best may depend on the material being studied and on how well the strategy is executed. Unfortunately, most experiments fail to evaluate how well a given study strategy was executed. The effectiveness of a strategy like notetaking, for example, probably depends on the quality of the notes.

Mnemonic Devices

If a reader needs to learn names, dates, places, or other miscellaneous terms from a text, then the organizational strategies discussed so far are sometimes of no use. In such cases, an effective learning technique is to use mnemonic devices, such as rhymes, acronyms, or mental imagery. A mnemonic device is simply a memorization strategy. Mnemonics provide an organizational structure for storing and retrieving information that has little inherent organization of its own. A schema, by contrast, organizes the material to be remembered in terms of that material's inherent structure.

Verbal mnemonics　　Some verbal mnemonics are familiar to everyone, including **rhymes** that contain critical information, as in "In fourteen hundred and ninety-two, Columbus crossed the ocean blue." Another device is an **acrostic,** a sentence whose words begin with the same letter as the items to be learned. For example, *Richard of York gave battle in vain* helps to recall the colors of the visible spectrum: red, orange, yellow, green, blue, indigo, and violet. A third device is an **acronym,** a word or a pronounceable nonword consisting of the initial letters of the items to be remembered. For example, *CAPS* is an acronym for *C*ollaborative, *A*ctivation-based, *P*roduction *S*ystem. A text or a reader can facilitate learning by using such mnemonics to interrelate information.

Mental images　　A number of mnemonic devices involve forming a visual image. Forming mental images improves memory for isolated sentences (Bobrow & Bower, 1969), and this result generalizes to the learning of text information (Rasco, Tennyson, & Boutwell, 1975). The precise reason for the effectiveness of mental imagery in learning is not well understood. Possibly, forming the image assures that the referential level of processing of the text is fully executed. This level may play an important role in both comprehension and in providing a rich representation for later recall.

Because images, at some level, seem similar to illustrations, several studies have compared the facilitation in learning produced by imagery to that produced by illustrations (Schallert, 1980). Generally, these two manipulations each improve learning by similar amounts. When students use both, the learning still improves but only by the same amount as when either manipulation alone is used. The two manipulations may affect the same learning process, but circumstances may make one or the other strategy more effective in a particular situation. Both images and illustration may improve memory because they help the reader think about the referent to be remembered.

Some imagery techniques involve additional mnemonic structures that contribute to their effectiveness. One such technique is the **method of loci,** in which the items to be learned are imagined at successive locations in a familiar geographic site. For example, one might imagine each of 20 items at the entrance to each of 20 buildings on a university campus. To recall the items, one mentally walks around the campus and retrieves the imagined objects at each building. The knowledge of the campus layout is the organizational device; it has the property of already being familiar, and its structure can be used to organize the items and prompt their retrieval when it is time to recall them.

Another imagery-based mnemonic device is the **pegword system,** in which the student imagines an interaction between each of the items to be learned and a well-learned list of items embedded in a rhyme: *One is a bun, two is a shoe, three is a tree, four is a door,* and so on. The first item to be learned is imagined to be interacting with a bun, the second, with a shoe, and so on. To recall the items, the student uses the first 10 integers and the rhyming words with which they have been associated as retrieval cues. Even simpler than the pegword system is an interactive image that can interrelate a small number of items to be learned, like four items to be purchased in a grocery store. The items can be imagined as interacting with each other in a single image, such that the recall of any one item will be a retrieval cue for recalling the others.

The effectiveness of mnemonics   Any information from a text that has been understood has been represented, at least transiently, in the student's mind. The difficulty lies in storing it in a form that is retrievable. When the material consists of a list of items, mnemonic devices can provide the retrieval plan. Mnemonic devices usually provide retrieval cues for each of a number of items to be learned, sometimes by linking the successive items to each other, so that recall of one item will provide the retrieval cue for another. This cuing function is clear in the method of loci, in which the recall of one building on a campus can act as a retrieval cue for an adjacent building. Thus, the mnemonic device is an organizer that brings together items that were not previously linked. Moreover, some mnemonics—including acronyms, the pegword method, and the method of loci—require that the items be learned in an ordered list, such that not only the particular items but also their order is learned. Many laboratory studies have shown that students using mnemonic devices can recall much more information than control students who devise their own strategies or who are told to memorize by repeating the items (Bower, 1970, 1972b).

The mnemonic devices discussed in this section differ from the study strategies such as rereading and outlining that were reviewed in the previous section because the organizational schemes associated with the mnemonics are not elaborations of the content. Mnemonics are not intended to deepen the reader's understanding of the information.

Repetition   Although repetition and rehearsal are generally less effective than mnemonic or organizational strategies, they are sometimes a last resort when no other strategy is applicable. For example, repetition and rehearsal provide a way of acquiring initial familiarity with new terms or vocabulary items (Mandler, 1979). After the reader becomes familiar with the terms by using repetition, he may be able to evoke organizational or mnemonic techniques to interrelate the information with some of his other knowledge.

Monitoring Comprehension to Improve Learning

Study strategies can build on and interact with comprehension processes. Consider how a student may study the same text over repeated study-test iterations with the goal of recalling its gist. The reader acquires progressively more information and must continuously shift attention from what was just learned to the next most important points.

One experiment examined this progression in learning by asking college students to recall a folktale with the aid of selected portions of the text as retrieval cues (Brown, 1980; Brown & Smiley, 1978). Which portions did they select to be the retrieval cues? And how did the selection of portions change over study-test trials?

The tales were divided into approximately 60 idea units (each roughly the length of a clause or sentence), and each idea unit was categorized into one of four levels of importance. The students were permitted to select 12 of the 60 idea units to use as retrieval cues to help them recall the tale. The study revealed that the students learned the material in a sequence that went from the more important parts to the less important parts. In the early study trials, the students chose the most important idea units (Level 4) as retrieval cues. On subsequent trials, they chose Level 3 units as retrieval cues, and so on. Thus, as learning progressed, the focus of studying shifted correspondingly. Of course, to employ this study strategy requires that the student be able to choose which parts are the most important and which are the least important and switch their attention to new points after another set has been mastered.

Older children and adults can order information in terms of importance and can improve their learning by focusing on the appropriate level of information. This skill is useful in taking good notes or underlining. More generally, the ability to determine which information is important is helpful in efficiently apportioning study time. Children above seventh grade learn more efficiently than do younger children, in part, because they are better at identifying important parts of a text (Brown, 1980).

Comprehension processes can be monitored and directed by study strategies. This occurs when students allocate extra processing resources to parts of a text they think they cannot recall or do not understand. By explicitly attending to the problematic section, the reader may be able to construct an organization that was not initially apparent. In this way, comprehension and study strategies can interact. In the next section, we will consider three instructional programs that build on this link between reading and studying.

Instructional Programs on Learning from Text

Although many people learn to study without receiving any formal instruction, the ability to learn from text seems to be enhanced by instruction on how to study. Robinson (1970), who devised a popular study program, suggested that learning to study be compared to learning to swim. Either skill can be self-taught or formally taught, but Robinson argues that formally taught swimming is more efficient because it is based on scientific research on the reduction of body resistance in water and on obtaining the most powerful forward push with the least effort. He suggests that rapid increases in swimming speeds over the past years (indicated by new swimming records) are largely attributable to improved coaching techniques.

By analogy, formally taught study skills based on scientific knowledge about the process of learning should improve the effectiveness of studying. For that reason, this section describes three representative study programs: Directed Reading Activity, the SQ3R program, and the Dansereau program. All three programs emphasize strategies for organizing the information in the text and relating it to what the reader already knows about the topic.

Unfortunately, the effectiveness of a study strategy is more difficult to evaluate than a coaching technique in swimming. One major difficulty lies in finding an appropriate comparison group. Students who enroll in a study-skills program tend to have different abilities and motivations than students who don't enroll. Although statistical corrections for initial ability level can be made (using analysis of covariance, with initial ability level as the covariate), such corrections are imperfect. Another problem is that improvement in study effectiveness could be produced by the degree of individual attention that students in a program receive or the amount of time they devote, rather than by the specific skills they are taught. To control for these possibilities, the performance of the study-skills group could be compared to that of another group that receives a comparable amount of attention and practice of irrelevant skills. However, this "nontreatment" can actually depress performance because the students in the comparison group become frustrated and bored (Dansereau, 1983).

In spite of these difficulties, a general conclusion about the effectiveness of study-skills training can be drawn: Study-skills programs generally improve the ability to recall information from the text after a retention interval of about one week. Other types of performance, such as recall immediately after the study period or recognition memory for the information from the text, generally show little or no effect due to study-skills training.

Educators and psychologists first started to develop how-to-study programs in the 1920s, when psychological research was being applied to educational problems. So-called study-skills courses were developed for the college or high school level to teach effective strategies for learning from text. The strategies were aimed at improving the understanding, storage, and use of information from a text, usually one that is approximately of chapter length, rather than paragraph or book length.

Quite often, the study process is divided into a three-part sequence: prereading, reading, and postreading. *Prereading* involves skimming, browsing, and reading advance organizers (such as text headings). The purpose of prereading is to produce a general outline and some learning goals. The *reading* period consists of reading carefully, possibly trying to answer questions about the text or making brief written notes. *Postreading* consists of producing a representation (written or mental) of the text structure and content. The postreading period seems to be particularly significant in improving learning, and it is the main target of most study-skills programs. This focus assumes that either the original text or a sufficient representation of it (mental or written) remains available for enhancement in the postreading period.

Directed Reading Activity

Study-skills training has been incorporated into many reading programs in the upper-primary and lower-secondary grades. One example of such an instructional program, called **Directed Reading Activity,** consists of three main activities (see Herber, 1970):

1. building background knowledge by introducing new vocabulary, reviewing previous lessons, and drawing on students' experience; previewing material to determine its purpose and how it should be read;
2. silent reading and study to accomplish the established purposes; and
3. follow-up questioning and discussion to determine how the reader's understanding relates to the text's content and the purpose of the lesson.

Most primary school reading programs currently include something like Directed Reading Activity. However, the particular exercises vary in their effectiveness. An analysis of the prereading activities for grade school classrooms showed that some activities emphasized irrelevancies and did not focus on central concepts (Beck, Omanson, & McKeown, 1982). When the activities were made more relevant, the children's subsequent comprehension of the text improved. What characterizes many of these programs is that students are engaged in recommended study practices without explicit instruction about the nature of the practices. By contrast, study-skills courses directly instruct students on what each process should involve, as well as give them practice in execution. However, formal study-skills courses are generally restricted to high school and college students. We will discuss two such representative programs, the SQ3R program and the Dansereau program.

The SQ3R Program

Perhaps the best-known comprehensive study strategy that is explicitly taught is called **SQ3R.** This acronym comes from the first letter of each of the suggested study strategies—*S*urvey, *Q*uestion, *R*ead, *R*ecite, and *R*eview—which produces *SQRRR,* or *SQ3R* (Robinson, 1970). The first version of SQ3R appeared in the 1946 edition of Robinson's book, partially stimulated by the special need during World War II to train soldiers rapidly for specialized jobs. The five steps in SQ3R deserve to be described in somewhat more detail:

1. *Surveying* entails the acquisition of a general outline of the text, the main topics covered, and the organization of the topics across pages. It involves some skimming, reading headings, reading the summary paragraph, glancing at illustrations, and the like. This step should take about one or two minutes.
2. *Questions* are constructed by the student, based on the headings and topics discovered during the *Survey* step. The act of generating a question may in itself be beneficial to learning because it forces the student to be attentive and to think about what she knows about the topic.
3. *Reading* the text, in this case, means reading one section of the chapter at a time while trying to answer the question that was generated for that section. It may involve taking brief notes in outline form.
4. *Recitation* involves generating answers to the questions, possibly citing an example. The notes taken while reading may be used to facilitate recall.
5. *Review* refers to going over the main points with the help of the brief notes, citing major subpoints, and trying to memorize both the main points and subpoints.

A subsequently developed method called *PQ4R* by a different Robinson (Thomas & Robinson, 1972) differs from SQ3R in two major ways: (1) reading is expanded to include *reflection* (essentially, careful reading) and (2) the first step, *survey,* is called *preview*. Both programs try to explicitly describe the steps in learning from text.

Prior to the introduction of programs like SQ3R, studying was treated as a basic mental process, like perceiving, that required no special instruction. Students were supposed to learn a text by reading it repeatedly with deep understanding. SQ3R made it clear that systematic studying can be divided into component processes and that those processes can be taught. The promise of SQ3R was that students could study more effectively. Although it is likely that the promise is fulfilled (Robinson cites several studies that apparently demonstrate the effectiveness of SQ3R), it is often difficult to evaluate quantitatively, for reasons outlined above. The questions, recitation, and review are obviously aimed at improving the reader's understanding of the organization and content of the text. However, the SQ3R program is expressed at a very general level; it is up to the student to generate specific questions that are appropriate for the reading material.

The Dansereau Program

In the 1970s, some thirty years after the initial development of SQ3R, a new generation of study-skills programs evolved, differentiated by being more specific and making use of some developments of cognitive psychology. The best-known program was developed by Dansereau and his colleagues (Dansereau, 1978; Holley, Dansereau, McDonald, Garland, & Collins, 1979).

Programs such as Dansereau's are typically taught as part of a study-skills course, with about 20 to 40 hours of instruction. The texts that students study are between 2,500 and 10,000 words. The students are given about one hour to study the text, using the strategy that is being taught. Then, about five days later, they are given a number of different types of tests such as essay, multiple-choice, short-answer, or fill-in-the-blank. The strategy is intended primarily for improving long-

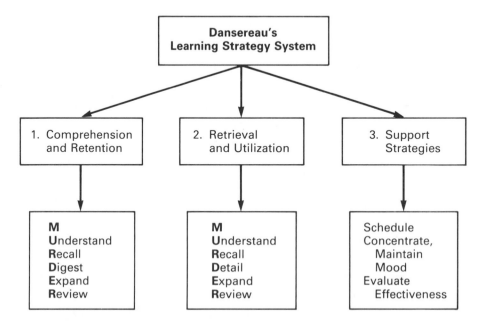

Figure 13.1 Three main types of strategies in Dansereau's study program. The first type is used in the initial comprehension and their names make up the acronym for first-degree MURDER. The second type is for retrieving and using the information; their names form the acronym for second-degree MURDER. The third type includes the support strategies to control and monitor study processes. *Source:* Adapted from Dansereau, 1983, Figure 1, p. 52.

term retention of information. If the test is given immediately after the end of the hour of study, the improvement due to the course is small or nonexistent.

The Dansereau program includes three types of strategies: primary strategies for improving the initial understanding; strategies for improving the use and retrieval of information; and support strategies to monitor when and how to study. The three groups of strategies are shown in Figure 13.1.

1. *Comprehension and retention.* This group of strategies is meant to be fairly independent of the reading goal and is intended to improve the level of understanding of the text. It includes a set of processes that make up the acronym *MURDER:*

- *M*
- *U*nderstand the material,
- *R*ecall the material,
- *D*igest the material through elaboration and organization,
- *E*xpand knowledge by making elaborative inferences, and
- *R*eview mistakes and inadequacies revealed by the test.

This group of strategies is called *first-degree MURDER* to distinguish it from the second group, which is tagged with the same acronym (although representing slightly different processes) and referred to as *second-degree MURDER.*

2. *Using the information.* The second-degree MURDER group of strategies is much like the first, except that the attempt to organize, store, and plan the retrieval of the information is adapted to the particular learning purpose at hand. The *D* in this set of strategies stands for *D*etailing the main ideas. These strategies are directed toward the particular kind of test that is anticipated. By contrast, first-degree MURDER is more goal-independent, aiming primarily at deep understanding.

3. *Support strategies.* This group of strategies has three components: planning and scheduling, concentration management, and monitoring the effectiveness of studying. To schedule their study time, students keep a diary and record their study schedule. The schedule is altered as the studying proves to be more or less effective than anticipated. Students are taught to induce a tension-free, relaxed mood during study and test taking and to maintain a relaxed mood overall. To manage their concentration, students are taught to deal with distractions consciously, to give themselves motivating sermons about studying, and to decrease any aversion to studying with the help of systematic desensitization and rational behavior therapy. Finally, students are supposed to use the feedback from tests to determine how effectively they have been studying and to modify their performance accordingly.

These control strategies are intended to govern the students' cognitive and affective states during studying and test taking. Like most intellectual activities, neither studying nor test taking occur in an affective vacuum. Affective states can certainly influence comprehension and learning.

The relation between Dansereau's program and SQ3R is that the first group of strategies, called first-degree MURDER, resembles SQ3R. However, as Dansereau points out, unlike SQ3R, his program teaches specific techniques for each part of the general strategy, rather than leave students to their own devices. For example, almost all study programs include a phase in which the student organizes information for later recall. In SQ3R, the student must decide how to do this for himself. In the Dansereau program, students are taught a specific technique for improving recall, the most notable of which is called *networking* (see discussion below). Alternative strategies for improving recall include writing out the main ideas in outline form, indicating their properties and interrelations, and forming mental images of the main ideas and their interrelations.

The networking strategy   This study strategy is a method of diagramming the main ideas of a text and their interrelations. The main concepts are written down, circled, and linked by labeled arrows that indicate their interrelations. The resulting diagram shows a network of concepts discussed in the text. Students are taught a set of six different types of links, with a description of the relation each link symbolizes and key words that often signal a particular relation in a text. The six relations are:

1. *part-of*—for example, a finger is part of a hand
   key words—*is a part of, segment of, portion of*
2. *type-of*—for example, a collie is a type of dog
   key words—*is a type of, example of*
3. *causal*—for example, rain causes wetness
   key words—*leads to, causes*
4. *analogy*—for example, a pet cat can behave like a child
   key words—*is similar to, is like, corresponds to*
5. *characteristic property*—for example, garbage is usually smelly
   key words—*has, is a feature of*
6. *indicator*—for example, swelling of cheeks indicates mumps
   key words—*indicates, supports, is proof of*

These relations certainly do not exhaust all of the types of relations that can exist among different types of information in a text. Nevertheless, it may be that the act of thinking about and classifying relations helps the student to process the text more carefully.

Figure 13.2 shows how these nodes and links can be used to construct a network representation of a text, in this case, a representation of part of the previous section on organizational study strategies. Linked to the major node is one characteristic and two examples, and these nodes lead to further elaborations. The network itself provides a spatial organization of the main points in a format that can be studied later or used for further analysis or elaboration.

Perhaps as important as the final product is the process of constructing the graphic network. To draw the network, the reader must abstract and note the main points and supporting details and spatially arrange them in a way that reflects their connectedness. The labels on the links require that the reader explicitly consider and classify the interrelations among concepts. These organizational processes encourage deep understanding and, consequently, better memory of the text.

It isn't clear exactly how readers execute the networking strategy or whether it plays exactly the role we have suggested. However, networking does improve memory. The strategy helps the reader extract and retain main ideas but does not appear to affect how the reader retains details (Holley, Dansereau, McDonald, Garland, & Collins, 1979). The Dansereau program, used in conjunction with networking, generally produces a larger precourse-postcourse improvement (larger by

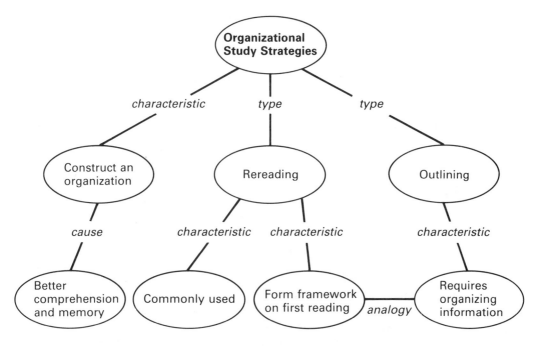

Figure 13.2 An example of a network diagram using material from the section on organizational study strategies. The network depicts the main points and indicates their interrelations with labeled lines.

30–40 percent) than does a no-treatment control condition. The effects tend to be larger for tests that require recall (such as essay tests) than for tests that require recognition (such as multiple-choice tests). The assessment of effectiveness is generally made at the end of the instructional program, and it is not known whether the study strategies continue to be used effectively for months or years after the course.

A given strategy may be taught in a number of different ways, and there is some indication that there is not much difference in the effectiveness of the various teaching methods (Dubin & Taveggia, 1968). Dansereau expresses a strong personal preference for teaching by modeling, that is, by demonstrating correct use of the strategy. This includes having students listen to an expert think aloud as he applies the strategy. The students are then asked to apply the strategy to a text, producing various written study aids, such as a network diagram of the passage content. Then, they are presented with optimal versions of the aids, with annotations indicating how various parts were derived, to which they can compare their own outputs. The students also work in pairs, taking turns at playing the roles of the instructor and the student applier of the strategy. Several characteristics of such instructional situations probably determine their effectiveness: the opportunity for observation and feedback, so that the student learns the correct skills; guided practice, so that the experience is not frustrating and there is some amount of positive success; and motivational support (such as playing both the instructor and students roles), so that the student perseveres.

Content-dependent Study Strategies

Instructional programs vary as to how much they are tailored to a particular kind of text. On one end of the continuum are highly tailored strategies, called **content-dependent strategies,** and at the other end are programs that are general enough to be applied to any text, or **content-independent strategies.** In using a content-independent program like MURDER, students have difficulty adapting the strategies to the particular types of texts they encounter (Dansereau, 1983). Content-dependent programs (like the one described below) are probably more effective for the texts to which they apply, but that range is narrow. This trade-off between generality across texts and effectiveness for a particular text is one that is familiar in the evaluation of most tools, such as a general purpose hammer versus an upholsterer's hammer. The preferred choice depends on the intended use of the tool. People who anticipate diverse uses would probably profit more from learning a general strategy, while people with a single, specialized use might benefit from learning a content-dependent strategy.

One way to make a study strategy content dependent is to teach students a text schema for a particular kind of text and then have them mentally fill in the schema slots as they read. Dansereau developed a schema for texts of about 2,000 words that describe a scientific theory. The schema resembles the MECHANISM Schema that READER uses to understand 150-word scientific and technical texts. The schema has six main slots: Description of the Theory, Inventor, Consequences, Evidence, Other Theories, and Miscellaneous Information. Within each slot are three or four subslots. For example, the Description slot has four subslots: Definition, Predictions, Observations, and Phenomena. The schema acts as an organizer and retrieval plan, as it does for READER. Students who were trained in the use of the schema performed significantly better than the control group on an essay test (Dansereau, 1983).

This content-dependent study strategy can be used in conjunction with a content-independent strategy. For example, students could be taught schemata for several different kinds of texts and still use the three groups of strategies, replacing second-degree MURDER with the strategy of filling in the schema slots of the appropriate schema.

In summary, study-skills programs make use of several time-tested learning mechanisms, such as organizing information and repeating it between practice sessions. These programs have made three major contributions to the scientific analysis of studying. First, they have demonstrated that study skills can be improved through instruction. Second, the programs have developed strategies of several different kinds, offering guidelines for which one to use in a given situation. The third and least explored contribution concerns the relation between study skills and affect. The demonstration that tension, distraction, and motivation can be dealt with strategically in a study situation is an important reminder of the interaction of cognition and affect.

How the Text Can Improve Learning

In the preceding sections, we focused on the processes that the reader brings to the learning task, such as comprehension processes to improve learning, along with specific study strategies. In this section, we will examine how learning is influenced by features of the text such as illustrations and examples. Because a text can have so many types of features, we have tried to organize the research according to which processes are most likely affected by a particular feature. The first section considers ways in which a text may present new information so that readers understand how it relates to what they already know. The second section considers text features that play a role in organizing information or selecting which information is important. However, this division represents only a best guess on our part. One of the major weaknesses of the research in this area is that seldom is any attention given to exactly what students do in response to a particular text feature.

Referential Processing: Examples

Examples can be powerful aids to understanding and remembering a text. Teachers quickly learn that examples are sometimes the most memorable part of their lectures. In technical domains, particularly, examples often are preferred to more general, abstract descriptions.

A dramatic demonstration of how examples can influence learning from a text was found in the context of a university course on the introduction to computing (Pepper, 1981). In response to student complaints about the text, the instructor decided to test whether students learned more from a text that they liked. He gave the students excerpts from two introductory textbooks. One text was described as the favorite of most of the instructors who taught the course; it had a crisp, precise presentation that was described as almost mathematical in its terseness. The second text was described as the underdog in the contest; it was clumsy and verbose because it initially had been written for a different programming language and was only superficially rewritten for the language the students were studying. The researcher was surprised to find that students greatly preferred the poorly written, verbose text. When asked about this preference, many students noted that it contained examples. However, students performed equally poorly on a test of the content of the two excerpts. Thus, the experiment suggested a negative answer to the initial question of whether students learn more from a text that they prefer. But the researcher also realized that the verbose text had poor examples, and he subsequently demonstrated that good examples improve learning.

In a follow-up experiment, the students learned more from a chapter that was specifically constructed to optimize their learning. The new chapter had numerous examples that highlighted the important points. In addition, the chapter had many illustrations and the prose was written in an informal style. It also had an outline, a brief introduction, a summary, and a page of definitions. The newly written chapter was 13 pages long and had 94 short examples. By contrast, the crisp, precise text (originally favored by most of the instructors) took only 6 pages to cover the material, compared to 13 pages; had 38 examples, compared to 94; and had no summary or page of definitions. Students' performance on a test was 50 percent better after reading the optimized text than the text that the instructors had favored. Morever, the optimized text was rated as 50 percent more readable. Of course, the optimized text had many more features to aid learning besides examples, but the examples seemed to be one of its more potent features.

An understanding of why examples are powerful learning aids must begin with an analysis of what examples are and how good examples differ from poor ones. What constitutes an example depends upon the abstractness of the principle that is being explained. If the topic is poetry, then some point may be illuminated by referring to Shakespeare's sonnets; if the topic is Shakespeare's sonnets, then the principle may be exemplified by one particular verse. The specificity of the example is relative to the principle being described.

One important property of a good example is that it contains the central characteristics of the construct or principle it is exemplifying. A *bear* is a good example of the concept of MAMMAL because a bear contains the typical features of a mammal. On the other hand, a *whale* is a bad example because, although it is a mammal, it is not a typical mammal.

Another example of a good example is Chomsky's (1957, p. 149) classic sentence:

Colorless green ideas sleep furiously.

This sentence was meant to demonstrate the separability of syntax and semantics. Each pair of words makes no sense semantically; nothing can be *colorless* and *green, ideas* aren't *green, ideas* don't *sleep,* and one cannot *sleep furiously.* On the other hand, the sentence is syntactically acceptable because each word belongs to the correct syntactic category given its order in the sentence and the inflectional endings. Thus, Chomsky's example is a good one because it focuses on the main point, with no room for misinterpretation.

Good examples can make a general point more understandable by highlighting the important features and by stripping away nonessential features. An example that contains irrelevant features may be misleading unless it is made clear that these features are irrelevant. A knowledgeable reader may be able to identify the important aspects of an example more easily than an unknowledgeable reader. For this reason, an example that is clear to an instructor may be totally bewildering to a person taking an introductory course in programming.

Good examples not only illustrate the principle to be learned; they illustrate it with concepts that are already familiar to the learner. A good example bridges the gap between what learner already knows and the concept or principle to be taught. The concept of bridging this gap is an intuitive one. But the general idea is that good examples are based on experiences or concepts that are already familiar to the reader and can be reconfigured to teach the novel, more abstract principle. This is one reason why good writers (and teachers) must be familiar with what their readers know.

Illustrations

Illustration is a generic term that includes photographs, realistic sketches, cartoons, maps, diagrams, flowcharts, and graphs. Their functions in texts are as diverse as their formats. In texts for beginning readers, illustrations are commonly used to aid the child in acquiring vocabulary and, more generally, to provide clues to the referent and to pique the child's interest. But in more advanced texts, illustrations can play a wider range of roles. The following section briefly considers the role of illustrations in technical expository texts; a subsequent section considers the role of illustrations in narratives.

Illustrations in technical texts Some of the various types of illustrations can be grouped according to three main functions:

1. Diagrams depicting *spatial information*
   Examples: Maps, blueprints, illustrations of objects
2. Diagrams depicting *functional information*
   Examples: Venn diagrams, electronic circuit diagrams
3. Graphs depicting *quantitative relations*
   Example: A graph of data

Illustrations depicting spatial information are useful for indicating an unfamiliar referent, its main physical components, and their spatial interrelations. For example, a biology text might present a diagram of a flower with labels pointing to the major components, such as the petals and stamen. The illustrations that accompany assembly instructions also tend to be used in this way. Moreover, such diagrams help the reader understand spatial relations that might be difficult to express in a prose description.

In addition to depicting spatial information, diagrams can also depict functional information. For example, a circuit diagram shows how various components are electronically interrelated, without concern for their physical locations within the electronic device. Functional diagrams often have local conventions for their interpretation that may differ from those depicting spatial information. For example, the convention for interpreting the functional information in a Venn diagram attaches no importance to the absolute size of a circle.

A third type of illustration is the graph, which can be used to depict quantitative information. Graphs may help the reader compare variables to detect general trends, as well as bring out other aspects of data that may be more difficult to discern from a tabular or prose format. Graphic design is governed by principles that are intended to enhance the effectiveness of various types of illustration (see Bertin, 1983; Tufte, 1983).

Several different factors determine how easily someone learns information from illustrations. One such factor may be the readability of the illustration, analogous to the readability of a text. A diagram may be cluttered and misleading, or it may effectively highlight the important components and their interrelation. The mere presence of an illustration can play a highlighting role by directing the reader's attention to an important topic.

Illustrations in narrative texts The most common illustrations that accompany narratives are realistic drawings or photographs, and the illustrations most frequently studied are those in children's reading. Consequently, the effect of only one type of illustration has been extensively studied: pictures of people, scenes, or actions. Such illustrations can increase learning, but to do so, they must contain information that is important without being redundant. Illustrations provide a concrete instantiation of some of the referents of the text and hence supply an enriched level of representation (at the referential level) that can be used in interpreting, organizing, and retrieving the information presented. For example, first-graders listening to stories remembered them better if they were accompanied by illustrations (Lesgold, DeGood, & Levin, 1977; Lesgold, Levin, Shimron, & Guttmann, 1975).

In the case of a schematic illustration, the picture is a metaphor for the referent (Schallert, 1980). Like pictures of people and scenes, schematic illustrations depict the spatial (or temporal) relations among objects. As Schallert points out, illustrations sometimes have the advantage of being more vivid and economical than words (by a factor of one thousand, if the proverb comparing their value is to be believed). Moreover, some types of information in an illustration, such as an awe-inspiring photograph taken from a satellite, cannot easily be expressed in words.

Exactly how much the illustration of a narrative aids the reader can be traced to the nonredundant information it provides. One study (Peeck, 1974) presented a story with or without illustrations to nine- and ten-year-olds. The test questions probed three types of information:

1. information that was presented only in the text;
2. information that was presented only in the illustrations; and
3. information that was presented both in the text and the illustrations.

The nine- and ten-year-old children who read the story *with* the illustrations remembered more of the story, and the extra information they picked up came largely from the illustrations. The illustrations did not improve how well the child learned information that was presented only in the text; the presence of illustrations did not motivate the reader to learn the text better. In this study, illustrations helped students learn additional information that was related to the story but was not contained in the text.

Other studies have suggested that illustrations providing supplementary information may be superior to additional text providing similar supplementary information (Rigney & Lutz, 1976). Perhaps an illustration generally provides richer referential information than a text. When a supplementary text explicitly attempts to provide referential information by appealing to physical analogies or by referring to familiar physical objects, then it can promote as much learning as supplementary illustrations (Royer & Cable, 1976). Thus, illustrations can increase the amount of knowledge that is learned from a text by providing important but nonredundant referential information. This conclusion particularly applies to children; adults may be more able to construct an adequate referential representation from the text alone.

Adjunct Questions

Text features such as questions, summaries, and headings help a reader select and organize information. These features are called *adjunct study aids* because they are provided by the text, rather than generated by the student.

The main type of adjunct study aid that has been researched is a question in the text that probes for some information contained therein. Such questions are called **adjunct questions.** For example, an adjunct question in a text on the French Revolution could ask, *What were the immediate noneconomic causes of the French Revolution?* The presence of adjunct questions can increase the amount of information that is learned. In studies evaluating their effectiveness, the texts are typically fairly long, consisting of a few thousand words, divided into segments of a few hundred words per page. The adjunct questions are generally presented between segments; therefore, they can probe for information contained in the immediately preceding segment or in the segment to come. To assess comprehension, a number of test questions are presented after the entire text has been read. These test questions can probe for the same information as an adjunct question (to determine what direct effects the adjunct question had) or they can probe for previously uninterrogated information (to test for indirect effects). In some studies, all the adjunct questions are presented at the end of the text, and the effect of the questions is measured on a test that is administered later, usually within one to seven days.

Considerable research has been directed at determining how the location of adjunct questions in the text influences learning. Summarizing the results of a number of studies, Anderson and Biddle (1975) concluded that if the adjunct questions *follow* the text, then performance improves not only on the information interrogated by the adjunct questions but also on uninterrogated text information. The improvement in performance is considerably larger for the interrogated information. However, many more points are uninterrogated, so even though the improvement on an individual uninterrogated point is lower, the cumulative effect of an adjunct question over all the potential uninterrogated points is larger than on the few interrogated points. If the adjunct questions *precede* the text, then students perform better on items pertaining to the interrogated information but do more poorly on text information that is not probed by the adjunct questions.

Adjunct questions may initiate different processes, depending on whether they precede or follow the text. When they precede the text, they perform a selective function, telling the reader what to look for, what to memorize, and what to ignore. By contrast, adjunct questions that follow a text provide a partial outline of the text, helping the student organize the information immediately after reading in a way that will increase further retention. Moreover, postreading questions can evoke deeper processing of the interrogated information by initiating a search through the newly stored information. Both of these properties of postreading adjunct questions cause improved retrievability and understanding of the text information (Rothkopf & Bisbicos, 1967). Further support for this interpretation comes from the finding that learning improves if the questions are close to the information that they interrogate, rather than distant. If the adjunct question is replaced by an equivalent statement that provides the answer to the question (in effect, a review statement), then the learning effect is smaller, probably because a statement does not require any retrieval or search (Bruning, 1968).

Adjunct questions interspersed throughout the text can induce a strategy of frequently monitoring one's comprehension, thus maximizing the organization of the information as it is being read and consolidating the specific answers to the questions. The adjunct questions can also have a generalized motivating effect, as well as evoke a mental review of the newly read information. If an adjunct question probes a particular sentence of the text, there is an increase in learning of not only the interrogated information but also the portion of the sentence that is not alluded to by the question. An adjunct question that follows a text can produce consolidation, organization, and review of recently read information.

The adjunct questions that follow the text can also vary in their abstractness; they can be high-level, conceptual questions or low-level, factual ones, perhaps requiring verbatim knowledge of a particular phrase in the text. Adjunct questions that require high-level abstraction (such as the application of a principle) produce more learning than factual questions (Watts & Anderson, 1971). High-level questions probably encourage deeper processing and more thorough organization, while low-level, factual questions may primarily play a selective role, indicating which information is important. Moreover, the content of the question can influence what is learned. For example, if postreading adjunct questions probe for numerical information, then numerical information will be learned better. This applies to both the numerical information probed by the adjunct questions and to other numerical information (Rothkopf & Bisbicos, 1967).

Adjunct questions vary in different ways, some of which have been evaluated by Anderson and Biddle's (1975) review of research in this area. Short-answer adjunct questions seem to produce somewhat more learning than multiple-choice adjunct questions. Subjects learn more when they are required to answer adjunct questions with a written or oral response than when they answer mentally. Providing feedback on the overt responses to adjunct questions increases the learning of the interrogated information even further, above the substantial learning effect produced by the adjunct questions themselves.

Adjunct questions have been of interest to educators because such questions promote not only the learning of specific facts but the learning of generalized concepts and principles, as well. The extra learning produced by adjunct questions extends beyond the information actually interrogated by the question to produce better knowledge of the text as a whole.

Another kind of adjunct aid is an **advance organizer**—an exposition or outline that is at a higher level of abstraction than a typical summary. Advance organizers were first investigated by Ausubel, who proposed that they provided a framework around which more detailed text information can be organized (Ausubel, 1960). Advance organizers do not consistently produce better performance than reading twice (Barnes & Clawson, 1975). Several explanations may account for their seeming ineffectiveness, including the possibility that such organizers are too abstract. Nonetheless, the failure of advance organizers to improve learning should not be interpreted as indicating that prior knowledge is not useful or unimportant. Too many other results have indicated that it is.

A related aid is a list of instructional objectives that tells students what they are expected to learn from the text. Instructional objectives sometimes improve learning of the information targeted by the objective and almost never improve learning of information unrelated to the objectives (see the review by Anderson, 1980; Rothkopf & Kaplan, 1972). Again, a difficulty in interpreting such data is the lack of analysis of how readers interpret and respond to the instructional objectives or the advance organizers. Do readers respond differently to material that is mentioned in the objective versus material that is not? What are the implicit instructional objectives that readers use in studying when none are provided? More detailed understanding of what occurs during reading and studying is necessary to understand the conditions under which these text features may improve comprehension.

Summaries

In one study, students who only read the summary of a chapter learned the main points better than those who read the entire 4,000- to 5,000-word chapter, even though the summary was only about 20 percent of the length of the chapter (Reder & Anderson, 1980). The mastery test required students to judge some statements as being either true or false, based on what was said in the text. The true statements were either restatements of the text or could be inferred by integrating over two parts of the text. Both the summary and the full text provided the information required to answer the questions. Students who had read only the summary were more accurate (by about 10 percent), both in a test immediately after studying and in another one a week later. When the subjects were tested on the same material 6 to 12 months later, performance was still slightly higher (though not reliably so) for the students who had studied only the summaries than for those who had studied the full text.

This experiment makes one wonder what benefit the other 80 percent of the chapter could have that would outweigh the poorer learning of the main points. The study used existing texts, and certainly not all texts are well written. Perhaps the details that authors considered colorful or explanatory were distracting as much as helpful. One must also keep in mind that the test measured only recognition memory. It may be that the details in the chapter (the 80 percent of the text that was not included in the summary) would help a student construct the kind of text representation that would be easier to recall.

Finally, summaries are certainly insufficient if the reader is to be given the full opportunity to analyze the issues for herself and determine whether the conclusions are in fact substantiated. Nevertheless, the experiment suggests that recognition knowledge of main points can be effectively acquired from substantial chapter summaries.

Text Embellishment

A text can be embellished by headings, underlinings, italic print, notations, and highlighting. These embellishments differ somewhat from the ones generated by the students themselves, because the author probably has a more accurate conception of the content and the relative importance of various parts of the text. Such text embellishments are clearly effective when they play a selective role—that is, when the text is long and the embellishments indicate which specific parts of the text are to be learned. It is unclear whether text embellishments produce more generalized, indirect effects on learning.

One study explicitly contrasted the performance of students who read texts that either did or did not contain embedded headings (Dansereau, Brooks, Spurlin, & Holley, 1982). Those students who read the text with headings performed significantly better than their counterparts in a test presented a few days after studying the text. The effect was very small on a test administered immediately after the studying. Instruction in the use of headings further improves performance, particularly on tests that require recall, like essay tests.

In addition to ancillary aids that affect learning, intrinsic text characteristics—including the topic's inherent interestingness and the text's readability—also influence learning (Klare, 1963). Many aspects of a text can enhance learning by prompting the student to process the text more thoroughly by organizing the information. An important property of the text, as opposed to organizational study strategies that are generated by the student, is that the author can use his expertise to organize the information and to relate it to other information. But to be helpful, the author must make the organization apparent to the reader and try to relate the new information to familiar experiences and concepts. If the author is successful, the text's features will not only improve how long the reader remembers the information but also make the comprehension process itself more effective.

Summary

Many study strategies can help readers understand the text's content and organization and relate it to what they already know, including rereading, outlining, and networking. These strategies are closely related to normal comprehension processes; they require elaborating on and making more explicit the kinds of informational structures that readers construct during comprehension. Surprisingly, the more active study strategies like notetaking and outlining are often no more effective than rereading a text, which may reflect the fact that rereading permits considerable organization.

Study strategies have been the focus of formal study-skills programs, such as SQ3R and the Dansereau program. Since the first study-skills programs, there has been an evolution toward teaching content-specific processes and organizations in conjunction with more general study processes. For example, a student in such a program may be taught a way to study scientific texts in addition to some general skills for setting up study goals and evaluating his performance.

Finally, text features such as examples, adjunct questions, and text embellishments work to improve learning. Such features may have two primary functions—helping to specify the referent of a portion of text and helping to organize and select information. Retrospective adjunct questions help readers review and consolidate information after they have finished reading.

Suggested Readings

Many programs are available to teach study skills. For those who want to explore a program that has both practical implications and some research support, Dansereau's (1978) work is recommended. Brown and her colleagues have examined learning and remembering in a way that both a student and researcher would find interesting (Brown, 1980; Brown, Bransford, Ferrara, & Campione, 1983). Finally, some of the traditional research on studying is described and evaluated in two chapters by Anderson (1980) and Anderson and Armbruster (1984).

Chapter 7 on referential processing and Chapter 8 on text structure are directly relevant to learning from text, as are the suggested readings at the ends of these chapters.

Some of the most fascinating research on mnemonic devices is that reported by Chase and Ericsson (1982) and G. Bower (1970). A more practical guide to mnemonics is the short paperback by Lorayne and Lucas (1974).

The question of how the text can improve learning is a very broad one. It can include legibility due to factors that influence perceptual processes, including type font and layout (see Spencer, 1968, for a summary). The choice of an effective format (prose, table, illustration) is discussed by Wright (1977).

14

Speed Reading

One type of skilled reading that has drawn the interest of educators, professionals, and students is speed reading, a form of rapid reading that is reputed to increase reading speed by a factor of three to ten without much, if any, loss in comprehension. Speed reading came to public attention when it was rumored that President Kennedy read through many newspapers each day at a very fast pace; he credited Evelyn Wood, an early proponent of speed reading, for her method of instruction. And Senator William Proxmire has argued that speed reading is an important resource in America's accomplishment of its national and international goals. In addition, countless numbers of conscientious people in the academic and business worlds have received speed-reading instruction. Since speed reading has such widespread appeal and potential pedagogical importance, it is useful to examine objectively the psychological processes that differentiate speed reading from normal reading, as well as the degree to which it lives up to its reputation.

Overview In this chapter, we will begin with a brief review of some of the existing research on the eye fixations and comprehension levels attained by speed readers in a section called **The Processes in Speed Reading.** The central point of this discussion is that readers can increase their reading speed by sacrificing the amount they understand from a text; faster speed usually implies lessened comprehension, a trade-off. Consequently, the evaluation of speed reading requires assessing just how much information the speed reader misses.

In the main part of the chapter, we will present a detailed report of an experimental investigation of speed reading, done in our laboratory in collaboration with Michael Masson (Just, Carpenter, & Masson, 1982); this section is called **A Study of the Eye Fixations and Comprehension of Speed Readers.** The experiments assessed how speed readers scan a text and what they understand about that text. The speed readers are compared to normal readers and to students who skim the text. The study argues that the speed readers' advantage comes not from better perceptual processes but from better conceptual-level processes.

Finally, in the third section we will describe another technique for rapid reading, **RSVP Reading—*Rapid Serial Visual Presentation*.** As the name suggests, the words of a text are presented at a rapid rate. We will compare this technique to speed reading, pointing out the primary differences.

The Processes in Speed Reading

To understand speed reading, we need to know about the processes that occur during speed reading and about the resulting information that the speed reader acquires. As in the study of other types of reading, eye-fixation studies are likely to be particularly informative about the processes in speed reading. Unfortunately, only a few scientific reports describe eye fixations during rapid reading, and these reports usually lack an accompanying test of the speed readers' comprehension, so we do not know what has been comprehended. Finally, these studies have focused on very high reading rates, 2,000 to 10,000 words per minute (wpm), which are too far beyond the rate of normal reading to be of general interest.

Three studies are fairly typical. McLaughlin (1969) described a self-taught speed reader, reading at 3,500 wpm, who generally read a page of 260 words in 14 fixations distributed "in a rough zig-zag down the page," sometimes moving "back up the page to make a flattened loop" (p. 502). Most of this reader's fixations were about 250 milliseconds long.

Thomas (1962) described a speed reader with a reading rate of 10,000 wpm, who made an average of six fixations per page, scanning vertically downwards on the left-hand page and upwards on the right. The reader made no fixations on the bottom third of a page and had a mean fixation duration of 320 milliseconds. These studies had no formal measure of comprehension, so it is unclear what information the reader obtained from these fixations.

Finally, Taylor (1962) studied a group of 41 graduates from a speed-reading course who had an average rate of about 2,200 wpm. These readers entirely skipped some lines of print and made more than one fixation on other lines, producing an average of one fixation per line. The finding common to all three of these studies is that rapid readers skipped large portions of the text and their eye fixations generally traced a path that is very unlike the left-to-right path of normal readers.

The Comprehension Level of Speed Readers

When someone asks, Do speed readers lose anything by reading rapidly? they are implicitly comparing the possible loss of comprehension of speed readers to the comprehension level of readers who have read the text at a normal rate. However, in a situation in which an already skilled reader like a college student is reading a text that imparts a fair amount of new information (like the first reading of a textbook chapter in an academic course), one would naturally expect some decrement in comprehension performance with increased speed, as occurs in most complex cognitive tasks. The general term for the relation between speed and accuracy is

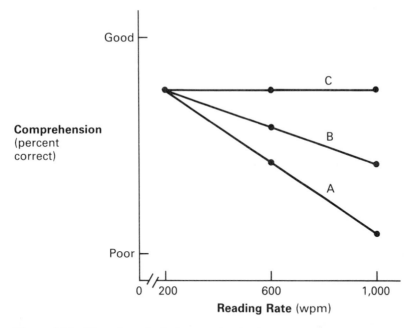

Figure 14.1 Three hypothetical curves showing how comprehension might be related to the speed of reading. In Curves A and B, comprehension level decreases with increases in reading rate, but at different rates. In Curve C, comprehension is consistently high, even if the reading rate is high; this is an unlikely relation, but some speed-reading courses claim that comprehension will not suffer at high reading rates.

trade-off, because people can trade away accuracy for more speed and vice versa, not only in reading, but in many other cognitive tasks. Figure 14.1 depicts some hypothetical curves relating reading speed to comprehension accuracy. Curve A depicts a typical speed-accuracy function for normal, untrained readers reading at both conventional speeds and high speeds, indicating the decrease in comprehension level as the reading speed increases (e.g., Juola, Ward, & McNamara, 1982). For convenience and simplicity, we will be primarily concerned with the middle range of the speed-accuracy function, as depicted in Figure 14.1, where comprehension is neither at the ceiling nor the floor levels, and the function is approximately linear.

The effects of training in speed reading can be assessed in terms of possible changes in speed-accuracy functions. The first possibility, a remote one, is that training in speed reading might allow a person to increase his reading speed without producing any decrease in comprehension. In that case, his speed-accuracy function would change from Curve A (before the training) to Curve C (after the training). Having a curve like C seems implausible, except under unusual circumstances, such as reading texts that contain little or no new information. A second, much more likely possibility is that speed reading produces a lower comprehension level than reading at conventional speeds; that is, the speed readers' speed-accuracy curves probably slope downward.

But it is important to ask how the comprehension of speed readers compares to that of the untrained rapid readers represented by Curve A. To put this question in terms of a trade-off, we can ask whether speed readers are able to increase their speed while making a smaller sacrifice of accuracy than untrained readers would have to make. In this case, the speed-accuracy function would change from Curve A (before the training) to Curve B (after the training). In the third and worst possible case, the training in speed reading would have no effect at all on a reader's speed-accuracy curve.

What Speed Readers Understand from a Text

Although the goal of speed reading is to gain information, curiously, researchers often overlook this purpose. Many studies of speed readers don't check what the speed reader learned, while others use poorly constructed tests, and still others fail to evaluate the speed readers' performance in comparison to the performance of an appropriate control group. For example, some studies use extremely easy tests to assess comprehension after speed reading. The problem is that the tests—usually multiple choice—were so easy that they yielded relatively high comprehension scores for subjects who never read the passages (Rauch, 1971). For example, Liddle (1965) showed that speed readers could read at three times the rate of normal readers and still obtain a comprehension score of 68 percent. However, Carver (1971) proceeded to demonstrate that comparable subjects who had never read the material scored 57 percent on the same test. Many existing studies do not systematically check what new information the speed readers learned.

Besides obtaining an overall estimate of how well a speed reader comprehends a text, more precise questions can be posed about the kind of comprehension produced by speed reading. In particular, one can ask whether certain types of information within a text are more amenable to speed reading than others; similarly, one can ask whether certain types of texts are more amenable than others. An early study (Dearborn, 1906) reported the case of a Harvard professor whose rapid reading skills produced rather poor comprehension of information that would be considered details but satisfactory comprehension of the main ideas or the gist of the passage. Similar findings have been reported from more recent studies of speed readers (Hansen, 1975). When normal readers and speed readers were given the same amount of time to read a passage, the speed readers naturally covered more of the material, and their recall indicated comprehension of the gist of the passage. The speed readers recalled more idea clusters than normal readers but recalled less detail about each idea.

Sometimes understanding the gist may be entirely sufficient for performing well in a task, in which case speed readers should have no disadvantage compared to normal readers. For example, one study required subjects to read a chapter of a social psychology textbook and then produce a written outline of the chapter (Barrus, Brown, & Inouye, 1978). Writing a satisfactory outline requires knowledge of the main points and their organization, but it does not require knowledge of details or subtleties. The study found that even though the speed readers (particularly proficient ones, in this case) read at a rate five and one-half times faster than the normal readers (1,800 wpm versus 320 wpm), they produced outlines that were judged to be as good as those of the normal readers.

It is likely that speed readers aim for a different type of comprehension than normal readers, a type that does not attend to details or to local coherence between ideas. In fact, if the local coherence is absent, speed readers do not even take notice. This was demonstrated quite dramatically when the graduates of a speed-reading course were asked to speed read a text in which, unbeknownst to them, every alternate line had come from one of two unrelated source passages (Ehrlich, 1963). They read the material three times, for an overall speed of 1,700 wpm, and reported that they had understood it to their satisfaction. They failed to notice that the material consisted of two unrelated texts. Ehrlich's study illustrates that speed readers have a different criterion for having understood a text, suggesting that their reading goals are different than those of normal readers.

It is plausible that speed reading is effective only if the reader has adequate background knowledge of the topic (Stevens & Oren, 1963). In that case, the reader has a pre-existing schema for the content and could proceed to fill in schema slots with information obtained from the text. Moreover, the reader might be familiar not only with the general content area but also with some of the specific content of the text. In studies of normal readers who have not had training, it is certainly the case that familiarity with a topic improves reading efficiency for topic-relevant texts (Dixon, 1951). Also, preliminary skimming of a passage to provide familiarity with the text structure and content produces faster reading of that passage without loss in comprehension (McClusky, 1934). If these results with normal readers generalize, one might expect topic familiarity to be an equally important determinant of the performance of speed readers. However, it has also been suggested that the special skills acquired in speed-reading courses can be effectively applied to texts on less familiar topics (McLaughlin, 1969; Wood, 1960). No substantial evidence has been provided for either viewpoint.

A Study of the Eye Fixations and Comprehension of Speed Readers

People often ask, Does speed reading really work? As we pointed out earlier, the answer depends upon what is meant by *work*. The following study found that the comprehension level of speed readers is below that of normal readers, yet for particular kinds of information, speed readers do better than untrained readers who are reading at the same rapid rate (Just, Carpenter, & Masson, 1982). Beyond these comprehension comparisons, a major goal of the study was to analyze the eye fixations of rapid readers and compare their pattern to those of normal readers.

The 11 speed readers who participated in the study had just graduated from a well-known commerical speed-reading course. Their eye fixations and comprehension levels were compared to 25 untrained readers from the same college population. Half of the untrained readers were asked to read normally (the normal group); the other half were asked to read quickly, using whatever strategies they felt comfortable with. These untrained readers will be referred to as **skimmers,** while the skimmers and speed readers will be collectively referred to with the general term **rapid readers,** to distinguish them from the **normal readers.**

In addition to this comparison of different groups, three of the speed readers were studied longitudinally, before and after they took the course. Before the course, they were comparable to the untrained normal readers when they were reading normally and comparable to the untrained skimmers when they were reading rapidly.

Training in Speed Reading

The speed reading instruction was given by Evelyn Wood Reading Dynamics, a large instructional corporation. The instruction focused on two aspects of reading: (1) making fewer fixations and (2) using previous knowledge to organize the information that is read. Both aspects were stressed during approximately fifty hours of practice at rapid reading. The training was distributed over seven weeks, with at least one hour of structured homework per day for six days a week, as well as a total of 17 hours of class time that included a fair amount of reading drill. Readers were given drills in which they read passages while being timed, and they were given progressively less and less time. In addition, their comprehension was sometimes tested to determine if they were learning the content of the text.

The hand as a pacer   To drive the reading to higher speeds, the readers were taught to use their hand as a pacer, moving it across the text at increasingly rapid speeds as training progressed. Several specific types of hand movements were taught and practiced. The most conventional was one in which the hand moved rapidly from left to right under each line of print, as if underlining it. This was also the only movement that was subsequently used by subjects in the experiment, who were permitted to choose their hand motions. The course included other hand motions that were less conventional because they did not maintain the left-to-right sequence of information inherent in the way a page is printed. For example, one motion zig-zagged back and forth on successive lines: left-to-right on one line, right-to-left on the next, and so on. A third technique made something of an *X* across two pages, going from the upper left to the lower right and then from the upper right to the lower left. With these techniques, the speed reader would sometimes take in words and phrases in an order that not only violated English syntax but was out of order in terms of the story's structure.

The instructor and the students were under the impression that the main purpose of the hand motions was to guide the eye to fixation locations. However, informal observation of the relation between the hand motions and the eye motions of the speed readers in the experiment revealed a different but still interesting relation. The hand motion of the speed reader seemed to act more like a metronome than a pointer. The hand and eye beat out similar rhythms, in terms of the amount of time devoted to each line of print, but there was no close relation between the location of the hand and the eyes' point of regard within a line of print. The hand motion seemed to serve a temporal pacesetter function rather than a locative function. This observation is informal because there was no way of automatically recording the hand motions in conjunction with the eye fixations.

The advantage of using the hand as a pacer rather than directly trying to pace the eyes is that people have experience at making their hands move rhythmically, but they seldom try to control the rate or rhythm of their eye movements.

Study skills   A second focus of the course was similar to that of other study-skills courses, as discussed in Chapter 13 on learning from text. The speed-reading course stressed the importance of using previous knowledge before, during, and after the high-speed reading. Before reading a text, readers were told to think explicitly about the text's organization and its likely content. For example, most college readers know how newspaper articles are organized; in other words, they have a text schema. The course stressed the use of text schemata (although they were not called by this name), explicitly teaching how to associate slot fillers with particular locations and cues in the text. The course dealt with the structure of different kinds of texts, such as textbooks, newspaper articles, and stories.

A similar approach stressed the importance of thinking about the likely content of the text. For example, even nonspecialists in an area like biology have some knowledge that can be recruited before reading an article in biology. Actively recruiting previous knowledge of structure and content was to be supplemented by *prereading*—skimming the table of contents, titles, headings, illustrations, and so on for indications about the organization and content of the text.

All of this knowledge was to be applied to the information obtained during the rapid reading itself. Moreover, the knowledge was to be used again immediately after the reading to recall the information from the text. The recall often took the form of structured outlines or diagrams that organized the major points and their interrelations. The process of recalling the text provided a chance to rehearse and organize the information. While some of the specific techniques differ, this aspect of speed-reading training is very similar to the prereading and postreading parts of the Dansereau study-skills course and the various SQ3R courses described in Chapter 13.

The training sometimes included rereading the same passages at high speeds, such that the sample of words that was fixated during the speed reading could be processed in terms of what the reader had previously learned about that very passage. This gave the readers practice in making sense of a text on the basis of a combination of what they already know about the topic (from their previous reading of that passage) and a sample of the words from the text. Gradually, the students learned to read rapidly, without having read the text previously, by using alternative sources of knowledge, such as their general knowledge of the world.

A minor focus of the course was on test-taking skills, such as how to take true-false and multiple-choice tests and how to write answers to various types of essay questions. Many of these skills are already part of the repertoire of test-wise college students, and they are also often taught in courses on general study skills.

Experimental Procedure

The subjects read two kinds of texts—(1) relatively easy texts that had been excerpted from *Reader's Digest* and concerned generally familiar topics and (2) texts that had been excerpted from *Scientific American* and were on more technical and less familiar topics. All of the texts were long, 1,500–2,000 words, to allow speed readers to attain their full speed. The analyses of comprehension and eye fixations focused on two passages: one from *Reader's Digest* and one from *Scientific American*. The *Reader's Digest* passage was a 2,004-word story that described the expeditions of John Colter, an early nineteenth-century explorer who traveled through the American West; it will be referred to as the **Colter** passage. The *Scientific American* passage was a 1,527-word excerpt describing what various space-exploration projects had revealed about the geological properties of the surface of Mars in relation to scientific theories about the planet's evolution; this text will be referred to as the **Mars** passage. Some of the passages were also used in the research on dyslexia, described in Chapter 12.

To assess the speed readers' ability to comprehend gist and details, 20 short-answer test questions were developed for each passage. Half probed for high-level information, corresponding to gist, and half probed for details. A sample question from the *Colter* passage is:

How did Colter hide from the Blackfeet who were chasing him?

This refers to an entire episode in which Colter was concealed under some driftwood in a river. An example of a detail question from the same story is:

How far behind Colter was the nearest brave when Colter first noticed him?

This refers to a single, briefly mentioned fact. The questions were such that readers could not have responded correctly without having read at least some of the text. Two points were awarded for a completely correct answer, one, for a partially correct answer, and zero, for an incorrect answer.

Before reading each passage, all the subjects were given a one-sentence abstract of the passage, which was to provide a bit of prereading knowledge of the kind that the speed readers had been accustomed to acquiring by glancing at a text before speed reading it. For instance, the following abstract was provided for the *Colter* passage:

The following passage is about the adventures of an American frontiersman named John Colter.

The text was presented on a video monitor, in conventional layout. Each screenful of text contained approximately 140 words. After reading a screen of text, the subject pressed a button and the next screen of text appeared. The reader's eye fixations were monitored remotely. The eye fixations were analyzed by determining the duration of the gaze on each word. After reading a passage, the reader gave an oral summary of about 100 words and then answered the 20 comprehension questions asked by the experimenter.

The speed readers were 11 graduates of the Reading Dynamics speed-reading course. The three speed readers who were studied longitudinally were among these 11. The skimmers and normal readers were 25 students from the same college population, who were totally untrained in speed reading. The reading rate of the skimmers was determined by first asking them to read rapidly, measuring their rate during the reading of the early practice passages, and asking them to adjust their rate if it was much slower or much faster than the reading rate of the speed readers. This permitted comparison of the scanning patterns and comprehension performance of the two groups of rapid readers, the trained speed readers and the untrained skimmers.

The three speed readers who were studied longitudinally read a total of 18 passages before the course (that is, before they were speed readers) and 14 passages after the course. Some of these passages were for practice, to allow the readers to acclimate themselves to the speed, the type of passage, and the comprehension test. The remaining speed readers, as well as the skimmers and the normal readers, were given a subset of these texts.

Overview of Results

Speed readers covered the material three times faster than normal readers, while the skimmers were two and one-half times faster. The reading rates and frequency of fixations were essentially identical for *Colter* and *Mars,* so we will present the means for both types of materials together. As Figure 14.2 shows, the normal readers read at a rate of about 240 wpm, the speed readers, at about 700 wpm, and the skimmers, at about 600 wpm. While the normal readers comprehended better than the two rapid-reading groups, it is clear that both groups of rapid readers had some understanding of the content. We will discuss the comprehension results in detail in a later section.

A small sample of the eye-fixation protocols (shown in Figure 14.3) on a *Colter* excerpt for a normal reader (the upper part), a speed reader (the middle part), and a skimmer (the lower part) illustrates several points. First, both of the rapid-reading groups fixated many fewer words of text than did the normal readers. Overall, the normal readers fixated 64 percent of the words, the speed readers, 33 percent, and the skimmers, 40 percent. Second, as shown in Figure 14.2, the normal readers spent more time on the words they did fixate than the speed readers and skimmers. The average gaze duration for normal readers was 330 milliseconds, for the speed readers, 233 milliseconds, and for the skimmers, 221 milliseconds. Third, the scan-

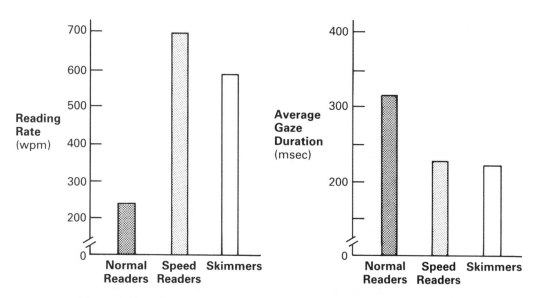

Figure 14.2   The normal readers naturally read more slowly than the speed readers or skimmers, as shown in the left-hand part of the figure. In part, the difference in reading rate occurred because normal readers spent more time on the words that they fixated, as shown in the right-hand part of the figure.

ning pattern of all three groups of readers was invariably left-to-right and top-to-bottom. These results suggest that rapid readers save time both by looking at fewer words and by spending less time on those words that they do fixate.

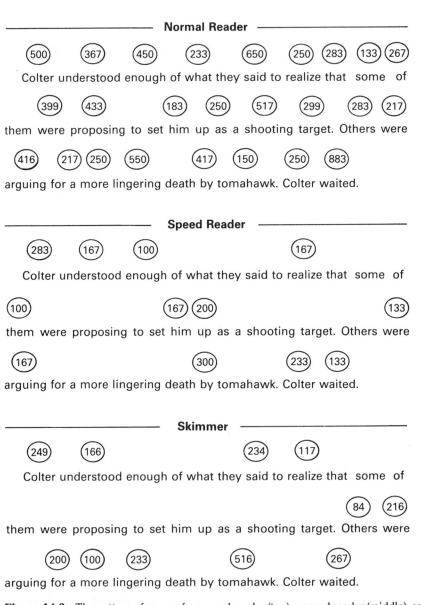

Figure 14.3 The pattern of gazes of a normal reader (top), a speed reader (middle), and a skimmer (bottom). Both the speed reader and the skimmer were much more likely than the normal reader to skip over several words in a row. They also spent less time on the words they fixated than did the normal reader. All the fixations shown in this figure are forward fixations, proceeding from left-to-right.

As the reading rate trebles from normal reading to speed reading, the pattern of eye fixations changes in several ways, as Figure 14.3 illustrates. The analyses below attempt to answer three main questions:

1. How do rapid readers select which words they will fixate?
2. What determines the amount of time readers spend on the fixated words?
3. Do rapid readers process the information from the words that they don't fixate?

Where Do Speed Readers Fixate?

Sampling algorithms   At the heart of rapid reading is the question of how speed readers increase their speed. Early studies, along with the one we are discussing, show that rapid readers are fast, in part, because they fixate a smaller proportion of the words than do normal readers.

While the numbers above indicate what proportion of words was fixated, they do not indicate how the fixated words were distributed in the text. For example, did speed readers fixate 33 percent of the words by looking at every third line of print or by looking at every third word in the text? To better understand the sampling pattern that the rapid readers used, we counted the number of times each reader skipped exactly one word, or exactly two words, and so on to determine the frequency of each skipping pattern. For example, if a reader were fixating every third word in the text, then she would always skip exactly two words. If she were reading every third line, she would usually skip about 20 words (about two lines' worth). Thus, the number of successively unfixated words was counted using the same kind of analysis described in Chapter 2 on perceptual processes; the resulting analysis gave the frequency with which readers skipped no words, exactly one word, exactly two, and so on between words that they did directly fixate.

Figure 14.4 shows the results for the three groups of readers. The result for the normal readers for these long passages was similar to the previously reported result for a different group of normal readers described in Chapter 2. When normal readers moved their eyes forward in the text from one word to some other word, most of the time (89 percent), they fixated the next word or skipped over only one word. In the *Colter* passage, for every 100 words of text, on average, the readers fixated adjacent words in 36 cases and skipped only one word between consecutively fixated words in 20 cases, skipped two words in 6 cases, 3 words in 1 case, and almost never skipped more than three words. Readers tended to have similar patterns of runs of unfixated words for the *Colter* passage and the *Mars* passage, as shown in the two parts of Figure 14.4. The similarity in the distribution reflects the fact that normal readers read these passages at very similar rates.

In contrast to normal readers, both speed readers and skimmers were less likely to fixate adjacent words and more likely to skip several words between consecutive fixations. Figure 14.4 indicates that for every 100 words of text, speed readers fixated adjacent words in only 10 cases and skimmers, in about 15 cases. By contrast, both rapid-reading groups were much more likely to skip several successive words, including four or more words.

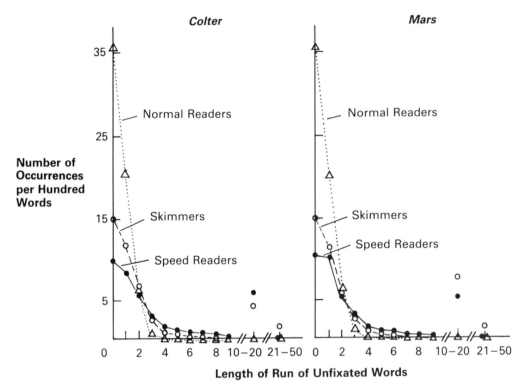

Figure 14.4   These curves show the proportion of times readers fixated adjacent words, or skipped over exactly one word between successively fixated words, or skipped over two words, and so on. Both the speed readers and skimmers were much more likely to skip over several successive words than the normal readers. The patterns are very similar for the *Colter* passage and the *Mars* passage.

Eye-fixation differences between speed readers and skimmers   The major difference in the scanning patterns of the speed readers and the skimmers was that the speed readers sampled the text somewhat more uniformly than the skimmers. Analysis of the lengths of unfixated runs showed that skimmers sometimes skipped over large portions of text (more than 20 words) while sampling other portions more densely.

Another measure that reflected the greater variability in the skimmers' sampling scheme was the variance in the proportion of words fixated in each sentence. The normal readers had the lowest variance in this measure (because they always fixated a high proportion of words in a sentence); the speed readers were intermediate; and the skimmers had significantly higher variance than the speed readers for both passages. Thus, both speed readers and skimmers skipped more words than normal readers, but the sampling scheme was somewhat more uniform for the speed readers.

It is tempting to speculate that speed readers learn to target their fixations on the most important words of a text. However, the eye-fixation data disconfirmed this speculation. To quantify the relation between a word's importance and its probability of being fixated, an independent group of subjects rated the importance of each of the 1,318 content words in the *Colter* passage (on a four-point scale). Then the correlation between the importance rating of a word and the proportion of readers in the group who fixated it was computed. This correlation was low for both skimmers and speed readers, but the speed readers' correlation was slightly lower than the skimmers', indicating no special eye-fixation targeting skill on the part of the speed readers.

Fixations on content versus function words   Normal readers fixated 77 percent of the **content words** (such as nouns, verbs, and adjectives) and about half as many **function words** (such as prepositions, conjunctions, and determiners). The higher frequency of fixation on content words is not simply due to the content words' tendency to be longer. Figure 14.5 shows that normal readers fixated three-letter content words (like *ice, ran*) significantly more often than three-letter function words (like *and, the*). If the reader fixates close to a short, frequent, and predictable word, such as these function words, he may on some occasions acquire information from that word without fixating it.

Speed readers and skimmers also fixated content words more often than function words, as shown in the left-hand part of Figure 14.5. However, the rapid readers' pattern can be explained by a tendency to fixate longer words. When only three-letter words were analyzed (as shown in the right-hand part of Figure 14.5), speed readers and skimmers did not fixate content words significantly more often than function words. Two related explanations can be offered for the rapid readers'

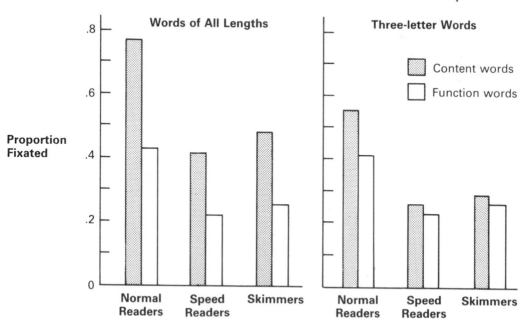

Figure 14.5   All three groups of readers were more likely to fixate content words (such as nouns and verbs) than function words (such as articles and prepositions), as shown in the left-hand part of the figure. However, as the right-hand part of the figure shows, only normal readers were more likely to fixate three-letter content words than three-letter function words.

lack of selectivity between content and function words, both of which are based on the fact that they are skipping so many of the words. First, skipping over words implies that the next word to be fixated is far away from the current point of regard. Since acuity drops off rapidly with distance from the fovea, the peripheral information from nonadjacent words is probably too degraded to permit a rapid discrimination between content and function words. The related explanation for the lack of selectivity is that the rapid readers' knowledge of only 33 percent of the words is too little to take advantage of syntactic dependencies among words. Although syntactic information can sometimes help predict something about the next word in a text when all the preceding words are known, it is almost impossible to predict anything about the third word from the current word, particularly if the reader only knows the current word and the word that occurred three words before. Thus, rapid readers have much less peripheral information and syntactic information than normal readers to help them decide which words to fixate.

Span of semantic processing   The span of semantic processing, the area of a page from which a reader encodes words while fixating on one given word, is fairly small. In Chapter 2, we argued that in normal reading, the reader encodes and accesses the meaning of only the directly fixated word and sometimes a few letters to the right. The few letters of a word to the right may be sufficient to recognize a short, frequent, linguistically constrained word, often a function word like *the, and, of,* or *an.* We also argued that the constraints on the span are both perceptual (namely, limitations of visual acuity) and conceptual, due to the large attentional demands of processing a text.

The perceptual and conceptual limitations on the size of the semantic span may be different in speed reading. Bold statements have been made about the spans of rapid readers, but no supporting data have been provided. Some claim that speed readers can apprehend many words on each fixation (McLaughlin, 1969), while others claim that speed readers can apprehend only one or two words (Taylor, 1962). No one has actually measured the span of rapid readers, but various sources of evidence suggest that the span is unlikely to be a major locus of difference between speed readers and normal readers. A study of fast readers who had developed their skill without formal training found that their span did not differ from that of slow readers, although faster readers did better at encoding the information that was presented (Jackson & McClelland, 1975). Another kind of negative evidence comes from studies that attempt to train readers to increase their spans; the attempts generally have not been successful and the comprehension assessments have been equivocal (see Brim, 1968; Sailor & Ball, 1975). The speed-reading study described in this chapter makes it possible to evaluate the question empirically: Do speed readers develop a larger span that permits them to encode more words while fixating a smaller proportion of them?

To assess the size of the span of the rapid readers, we determined whether they ever learned a fact they did not fixate during their reading of the text. Since the performance of the speed readers and skimmers was indistinguishable in this regard, the two rapid-reading groups were analyzed together. The analysis focused on a particular subset of the comprehension questions, namely, those questions that interrogated a one- or two-word fact that was not common knowledge and could not be inferred from other parts of the text. During their reading of the passage, the rapid readers could have directly looked at the one or two words that contained the answer, or they could have skipped over them. In the 175 cases in which a rapid reader looked directly at the one- or two-word answer or within three character spaces adjacent to it, the correct answer was given about 20 percent of the time. In the 30 cases that a rapid reader did not look at or within three letters of the answer, the correct answer was produced only *once* (the fact was 1976—the year of the Viking Lander touchdown on Mars). This result strongly suggests that the speed readers and the skimmers obtain little, if any, information from the 60 to 67 percent of the words of a text that they don't fixate. Like normal readers, trained readers and untrained skimmers have a relatively small span over which they process semantic information. Thus, the conjecture that training in speed reading increases the span in reading can be rejected.

Analyses of Gaze Duration

Not only did the rapid readers fixate fewer words, they spent about one-third less time, about 100 milliseconds less, than normal readers on the words they did fixate. This difference is evident in the mean gaze durations in Figure 14.2. The gaze durations in Figure 14.2 were obtained by averaging the time spent on each word over only those readers who fixated that word. The rapid readers, unlike normal readers, had few very long gazes. Over 15 percent of the gazes of normal readers were greater than 490 milliseconds, but for skimmers and speed readers, only 4 percent and 1 percent (respectively) of the gazes were that long. In addition, rapid readers had many more short gazes (less than 200 milliseconds) than did normal readers.

What determines how long readers spend on the words they fixate? An analysis of gaze durations indicated that rapid readers show many of the effects that normal readers show, but the sizes of the effects are usually much smaller. The presence of word-length and -frequency effects suggest that rapid readers, like normal readers, recognize words immediately as they encounter them, rather than use a wait-and-see strategy. Rapid readers' extra long pauses on novel words also provide evidence of immediacy.

Word-length and word-frequency effects　The gaze durations of all three groups of readers were influenced by the word's length and frequency. Figure 14.6 shows the length and frequency effects for the normal readers for the *Scientific American* passage. The graph is reminiscent of the one presented in Chapter 3 on lexical access, which was based on the reading of short technical passages. The *x*-axis represents the logarithm (base 10) of the word's frequency. The four points for each word length were obtained by dividing the words of that length into quartiles on the basis of frequency and then plotting the mean duration for each quartile against the mean frequency of the quartile (except for three-letter words, in which the word *the* constituted a tertile). Each line is the best-fit straight line for words of a particular length, from two to nine characters. The results here are very similar to those obtained in the reading of much shorter technical passages (Carpenter & Just, 1983; Just & Carpenter, 1980), indicating the reliability of the word-length and word-frequency effects on gaze durations.

Similar results were obtained for the *Reader's Digest* passage, with one interesting deviation; the duration on very infrequent six-letter words was exceptionally

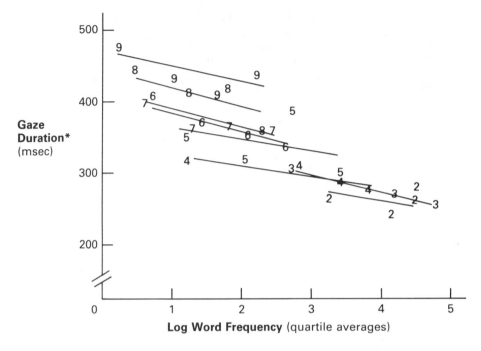

*Gaze duration averaged over fixated words only

Figure 14.6 Normal readers spent more time on longer words and on less frequent words. Less frequent words are those with a smaller log frequency. The eight lines correspond to different word lengths, from two letters to nine letters. Word frequency has a similar effect on words of each length, as the downward slope of all the lines indicates. These results are for the normal readers who were reading the *Mars* passage.

short. It turned out that the infrequent six-letter word was *Colter;* because readers encountered this topic word so often, they were able to recognize it unusually quickly.

How the READER Model Would Speed Read

The differences between the speed readers' and the normal readers' performance can easily be explained in terms of the mechanisms in READER. The patterns of results indicate fairly precisely which mechanisms change and in what ways. The first, most obvious change that would have to be made to READER is that it would have to sample every third word in the text and skip over the intervening two words.

A second important change in READER is indicated by a prominent clue in the data, namely, that the sizes of the word-length and word-frequency effects on gaze duration are smaller in speed reading. Although word length and word frequency reliably affected the gaze durations of all three groups of readers, the effects were considerably smaller in the case of the speed readers (as well as the skimmers). For example, although all three groups spent more time on longer words, the speed readers spent about 10 milliseconds less than the normal readers per each additional letter in the word. This result suggests that although the speed readers use the same mechanisms of word encoding and lexical access as normal readers, the time course of the growth of knowledge is different.

The READER model can account for the smaller effects of word length and word frequency in terms of increased activation weights for all the productions, using the REWEIGHT production to change them. Recall from Chapter 9 that activation weights are the fractional multipliers of the source proposition's activation level. Raising the activation weights would permit a production to increase a proposition's activation level at a faster rate, thus bringing it to threshold in fewer cycles. Moreover, as suggested in Chapter 9, faster reading may entail a relative decrease in the influence of the consistency-checking productions, which would be effected by a relatively smaller increment in their activation weights. Not checking for syntactic or semantic consistency makes a great deal of sense in speed reading when only one out of three words is being read.

The effect of larger activation weights on the lexical access mechanism would be that the activation level of a word meaning would reach threshold sooner (that is, after fewer cycles), while retaining the logarithmic relation to frequency. This is precisely the pattern obtained in the human data. Also, the decrease in the influence of the consistency-checking productions and the drastic reduction in the knowledge of preceding context (because only one-third as many of the preceding words would have been fixated) would make it more likely that a word would be given an incorrect interpretation. The speed readers' greater likelihood of selecting the wrong sense of a word could account in part for their poorer comprehension performance.

Similarly, if the word-encoding productions had higher activation weights, this might allow a word-percept to reach threshold when only some proportion of the letters of a word (say, 75 percent) had been encoded. This would diminish the size of the word-length effect correspondingly, as the data indicate.

A third modification to the READER model to simulate the speed readers is the imposition of a deadline—an upper limit on the number of cycles that could be spent on any fixated word, regardless of whether the processing had been completed. A time limit on each fixated word would explain why the speed readers never produced the extremely long gaze durations on difficult words commonly found among the normal readers.

These three changes to READER would have several side effects, which would be consistent with the results of the human speed readers. The low sampling density (one out of three words) would provide READER with much less information, and as a result, the representation of the text would be far less complete at all levels than in normal reading. In particular, the syntactic analysis would have a much diminished influence on choosing an interpretation because the sparse sampling of the text would provide impoverished syntactic information. Also, the lower amount of information would lead to errors of commission based on incorrect inferences and incorrect interpretations of individual words. Finally, READER's previous knowledge of the text content would have an increased influence on making an interpretation.

Thus, all the differences in performance between normal reading and speed reading can easily be accounted for in terms of simple modifications of READER's simulation of normal reading. Moreover, it seems plausible that these modifications correspond to the way that speed readers (and skimmers) change their normal reading processes when they read rapidly. This theoretical account of the differences between normal reading and speed reading illustrates the usefulness of the model in expressing variations in the way people read.

Changes in Reading Speed

All three groups read some parts of the text much faster than other parts. Figure 14.7 shows the reading rates per screen for the three groups. As shown in Figure 14.7, the fluctuations in reading rate across screens of text were large, especially

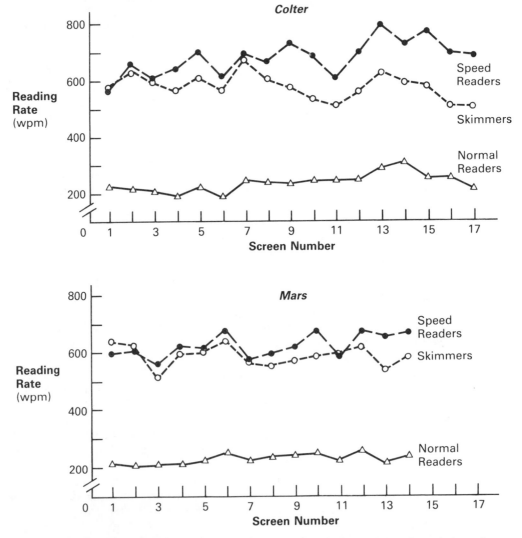

Figure 14.7 All three groups of readers tended to speed up and slow down their reading at similar places in the two passages. These two figures show the reading rates for successive sections of the two articles.

among speed readers, where the rate ranged from 564 to 786 wpm. The fact that the curves for the speed readers and skimmers were generally parallel to each other indicates that the two groups of rapid readers tended to slow down and speed up on the same screens of text. The normal readers did not change their reading rate quite as much, but the graph indicates that what changes they did make tended to follow the same pattern as for the rapid readers.

The rapid readers varied their reading rates across successive screens primarily by varying the proportion of words that they fixated, rather than varying the gaze duration. The reading rate for a screen was very highly correlated with the proportion of words fixated (a correlation of 0.9 for both the speed readers and the skimmers), whereas the reading rate was not as highly correlated with the mean gaze duration (a correlation of 0.6 for speed readers and 0.4 for skimmers). This suggests that rapid readers change their reading rate primarily by varying the proportion of words that they fixate.

What text properties produce modulations of reading rate?   To address this question, we can first describe two plausible hypotheses that *did not* account for fluctuation in reading:

1. Readers slow down for certain categories of information, as described by a story-grammar analysis of the text.
2. Readers slow down for the paragraphs that are rated as important by independent judges.

By contrast, a third hypothesis that was supported is that much of the variation in reading rates across the segments of a long passage is due to local variables that are idiosyncratic to the text. If readers happen to encounter an important phrase or difficult construction, they may sample the text more densely in that vicinity. This point is exemplified by a paragraph in the *Colter* passage that was read particularly slowly by the rapid readers, at less than 500 wpm. The paragraph contains a number of features that together make it difficult to read. The critical paragraph is presented below (beginning with "Colter answered ambiguously. . ."), along with the paragraph that preceded it.

> *Finally, the chief came over to him and asked if he was a fast runner. Colter guessed that they were considering letting him run for his life. Some chance, with 500 braves on his tail, and him running naked and barefoot through the cactus—but a chance.*
>
> *Colter answered ambiguously, in his limited Blackfoot: "The long knife is a poor runner and not swift.*
>
> [NEW SCREEN]
>
> *He is considered by the other long knives to be very swift, but he is not." A half-challenge.*

Several features contribute to the difficulty of the short paragraph that begins, "Colter answered ambiguously . . ." First, the paragraph begins with a response to a question, but the question and response are separated from each other by two sentences (containing 32 words) that describe Colter's thoughts. By the time the response is encountered, the representation of the question may no longer be in activated working memory, so it may be difficult to determine what the word *answered* is referring to. Second, Colter's utterance contains stilted phrases, referring to himself in the third person, using common words in unusual ways (e.g., *long knife*). Third, the paragraph ends with a enigmatic nonsentence (*A half-challenge*). Fourth, the utterance is interrupted by a screen boundary, much as a normal text is interrupted by page boundaries, that may have distracted the readers. The conclusion that the modulation of the reading rate over the passage is governed primarily by idiosyncratic properties applies equally to other paragraphs that were read slowly. The idiosyncracy can arise at any level of processing, such as the lexical level or the syntactic level.

The modulation in reading rate can be construed as a general type of context effect, such that a reader who encounters a difficult or important part of the text may sample the subsequent text more densely. This type of modulation can occur in the READER model if the processing of one part of the text can change the activation weights that are used in processing the text that follows.

The Comprehension Results

Normal reading led to much better comprehension than did speed reading or skimming. This was true both for the three readers who were studied before and after the course and for the cross-sectional comparison of the three groups of readers. The comprehension advantage varied across the two types of passages, the two types of questions (probing high-level or low-level information), and the two types of rapid reading; but the advantage of the normal readers was almost always present. The experiment showed that reading at a normal rate produces better comprehension than reading at a rapid rate, even if the readers have had training in speed reading. But it is important to keep in mind that the total reading time is considerably longer in the case of normal reading.

Figure 14.8 shows the question-answering accuracy for the normal group and the two rapid-reading groups; the top panels show the performance for the high-level questions and the lower panels, for the low-level questions. Two other comprehension results that were easily predictable are obvious in this figure. First, the readers' comprehension was better on the high-level questions that probed the gist than on the low-level questions that probed for details. Second, the comprehension performance was better on *Reader's Digest* passages than on *Scientific American* passages.

How did the speed readers perform compared to the skimmers, the untrained rapid readers? This comparison, involving the two rightmost columns in the four panels, reveals that the speed readers had an advantage, but only for one kind of information—the high-level, gist information for the easier *Reader's Digest* passage about Colter. The speed readers answered reliably more questions, in spite of an overall reading rate that was about 100 wpm *faster* than the skimmers. There was no other advantage, however; the speed readers performed similarly to the skimmers on questions about details and on the high-level questions about the technical, *Scientific American* passage about Mars.

A virtually identical pattern was found for the three readers who were studied longitudinally, before and after the speed-reading course. Their rapid reading without training before the course (that is, skimming) was compared to their speed-reading performance after the course. The only improvements occurred for the high-level questions for the easier, *Reader's Digest* texts.

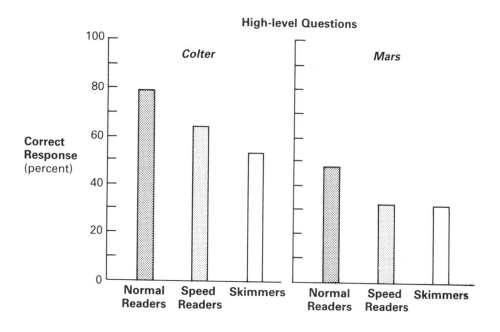

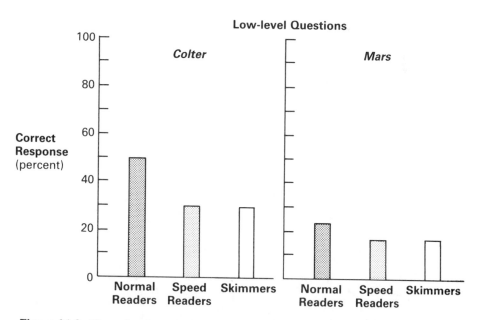

Figure 14.8   The only advantage of the speed readers in the comprehension test occurred on high-level questions that interrogate the gist of familiar, easy passages. The speed readers were able to answer more questions than the skimmers about the gist of the *Colter* passage. Speed readers had no advantage in answering questions about details or answering questions about the more difficult *Mars* passage. Neither group of rapid readers performed as well as the normal readers, showing that reading faster does lower comprehension.

This analysis, however, does not take into account the fact that the speed readers were reading faster than the skimmers. It is necessary to consider the trade-off between speed and accuracy for the speed readers and the skimmers. The interesting question concerns the effect of training on the nature of that trade-off.

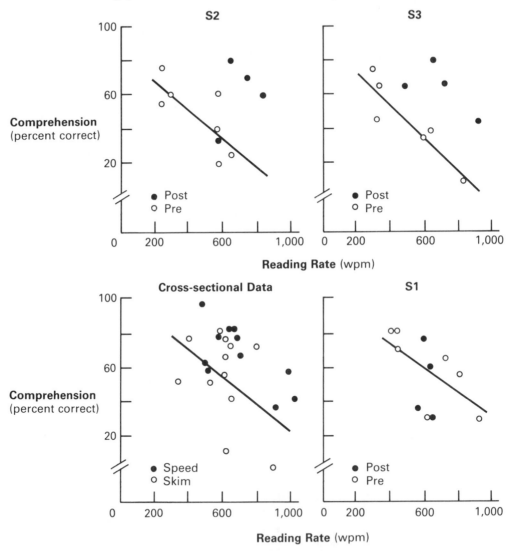

Figure 14.9   This figure shows the effect of training in speed-reading on the speed-accuracy trade-off, where *accuracy* refers to comprehension scores on the high-level questions on the *Colter* passage. The open circles and the downward-sloping lines that have been fit through them depict the speed-accuracy function obtained without any training, while the filled circles depict performance after training. The graphs for the three longitudinal subjects (S1, S2, S3) show the performance of the same people before and after training, while the bottom left-hand graph (cross-sectional data) compares the entire group of speed readers to the skimmers. To the extent that the filled circles lie above and to the right of the line, the data indicate that speed readers obtained higher comprehension scores than untrained skimmers reading at comparable rates.

When both speed and accuracy are considered, the speed readers' only significant advantage is with questions that probe for the high-level information from the easier, *Reader's Digest* text.

This advantage is shown in Figure 14.9, which depicts the speed-accuracy trade-off for the high-level information for the *Reader's Digest* passages. There are three panels for the three individual readers (S1, S2, and S3) who were studied before and after they took the course; the bottom-left panel contrasts the entire group of 11 speed readers with the skimmers. First consider S1, S2, and S3. The unfilled circles represent the speed-accuracy relation for the *Reader's Digest* passages that were read before the course. The downward slope of the best-fit straight lines indicates that comprehension generally deteriorates as reading speed increases. The filled points represent the speed-accuracy relation after the course. For two of the readers (S2 and S3), the filled points tend to fall above the line; this indicates that after the course, these readers were able to read rapidly without sacrificing as much comprehension as before the course. In terms of the hypothetical curves shown in Figure 14.1, these two readers have shifted from a curve like A to one like B. For S1, who even before the course read faster and had better comprehension than S2 and S3, there was no improvement, indicating no change in the speed-accuracy function. Thus, the training in speed reading improved the performance of two of the three longitudinal subjects.

A similar pattern of results emerged from the cross-sectional comparison of the speed readers (filled circles) and the skimmers (unfilled circles) for the high-level questions probing the *Colter* passage (bottom-left, Figure 14.9). The line is fit through the data for the skimmers; it shows the skimmers' speed-accuracy trade-off function. If there were no effect of speed-reading training, we would expect about half of the speed readers to lie above that function and half, below the function. As Figure 14.9 shows, nine of the eleven speed readers had better comprehension performance than the skimmers' speed-accuracy function would predict, indicating that the training produced an ability to read rapidly while decreasing the loss of comprehension. In this experimental design, the untrained skimmers represent the speed-accuracy function without any training, while the speed readers' function indicates the effect of training. In general, the speed readers' function shifted from curves like A in Figure 14.1 to curves like B. In both longitudinal and cross-sectional comparisons, the shift in speed-accuracy functions occurred only for the high-level questions probing the *Reader's Digest* passages.

Passage summaries   The three groups of readers summarized each passage after reading it, and there were no large differences in the performance of the three groups, in spite of the far greater reading time of the normal readers. The absence of major differences among the summaries produced by the three groups of readers should be contrasted with the question-answering performance described previously, which indicated that the normal readers consistently acquired more information from the passages than either group of rapid readers. The summaries are imprecise indicators of comprehension.

Conclusions about This Study

In summary, this study suggests that speed readers attain a new reading skill but one with limited applications. Relative to untrained rapid readers, speed readers had a comprehension advantage only on high-level information from texts on familiar topics. That is, the skill is not helpful in all texts or for all types of information. This evidence strongly implies that speed-reading skill is not at all perceptual but conceptual, instead. Acquiring speed-reading skill consists of learning to infer connections between those segments of the text that happen to have been sampled. It is only for the familiar material that readers have sufficiently detailed schemata to support the inference making. The speed readers, in effect, do more top-down processing (using previous knowledge to infer what is in the text) and less bottom-up processing (perceiving words and word sequences) than normal readers.

The eye-fixation behavior of normal readers, speed readers, and skimmers provides several insights about the processes that underlie rapid reading. While normal readers sample a text fairly densely (fixating about 80 percent of the content words), rapid readers fixate only about half as many words (30–40 percent) and for only two-thirds the duration (200–240 milliseconds) per fixated word. Content words are twice as likely to be fixated as function words, both by normal readers and rapid readers. However, in the case of rapid readers, this result is almost entirely due to the generally greater length of content words. Neither speed readers nor skimmers are very selective about fixating the most important words of a text. The span over which rapid readers extract word meaning is relatively narrow. Rapid readers cannot answer questions about a detail if they did not fixate directly on it or within three character spaces of it. Both rapid-reading groups modulate their reading rate over various portions (screens or paragraphs) of the text. Finally, the gaze durations of normal and rapid readers on a fixated word are proportional to the word's length and the logarithm of its normative frequency, although the parameters associated with these two effects for the rapid readers are considerably smaller than for normal readers.

The eye fixations indicate where the speed readers' advantage does *not* lie. The speed readers do not use an exotic scanning strategy, except that their scanning is more uniform, which may free some attentional resources. Nor does the speed readers' advantage reside in sampling more important words or in a wider perceptual span.

The speed readers' advantage is *primarily conceptual,* in putting together the information that is fortuitously sampled. It probably is best to look at speed reading as a means of realizing an already existing potential for inference making, rather than a radical transformation of the reading comprehension process. Admittedly, this study examined only a limited range of speed-reading skill (newly trained readers who took a seven-week course), and the conclusions might not generalize to expert speed readers who have had much more practice and might attain rates considerably faster than 600–700 wpm. It is also true, however, that many speed readers are probably of the same skill level as the subjects we have discussed.

The general notion of a speed-accuracy trade-off in reading is a good one for understanding some of the conflicts in the literature about the benefits of speed reading. In particular, this concept helps explain why some researchers have reported speed gains without losses in comprehension. Whether a reader can learn to read faster without loss of comprehension will depend upon the reader's initial location on the hypothetical speed-accuracy curve. If the text is easy, the reader should be able to read much faster without sacrificing comprehension. On the other hand, if the text is difficult, then increases in speed are likely to result in sacrifices in comprehension. Although the speed-accuracy function is a useful concept, it is also a simplification, because the accuracy of comprehension is not a single dimension. Comprehension consists of obtaining several different kinds of information which may vary in its susceptibility to variations in reading speed.

There is another salient aspect of speed reading that we have not formally assessed: how stressful and effortful it can be. Several of the speed readers volunteered that they found speed reading to be a very demanding technique. Presumably, some of this stress may be due to the acquisition of a new technique. However, even expert speed readers have informally commented that prolonged speed reading is effortful and difficult to maintain. There may be some costs to extended running of the mental engine at high speeds.

RSVP Reading—*Rapid Serial Visual Presentation*

An unconventional form of rapid reading, called *RSVP,* was developed by Forster (1970). In this technique, the text is presented one word at a time, each word appearing for the same duration at the same location on the screen. This presentation mode differs from normal reading in several ways. First, the duration of gaze on each word is not under the control of the reader. Second, there are no eye movements. Third, no words can be skipped. And fourth, the words that have already been seen cannot be looked at again.

In some ways, the RSVP paradigm resembles speeded listening comprehension. For instance, the pacing of an RSVP reader is not under the reader's control, just as the rate of listening is not under the listener's control. Also, subjects do not have to make selective fixations in listening or in RSVP. Moreover, since the text is not continuously available, there is no possibility of previewing, regressing, or rereading.

Clearly, RSVP does not mimic the way readers naturally speed up their reading processes. Our speed-reading experiment shows that the major part of the speed gain in rapid reading is attributable to a sparser sampling of the text, while only a minor part is attributable to shorter processing times on individual words. By contrast, in RSVP, all of the speed gain is provided by shorter processing times on each word; rather than make the sampling sparser than in normal reading, RSVP makes it maximal, presenting every single word of the text.

RSVP was previously used only as a laboratory tool to examine how perception and comprehension were affected if the time allotted to look at each word of a sentence were greatly reduced from the normal duration. Forster (1970) found that at the rate of 62 milliseconds per word, only about four words of a six-word sentence were detected, let alone integrated, into the representation of the sentence. Moreover, the probability of correctly reporting a given word was partially dependent on the complexity of the syntax of the sentence and on the lengths of the words that preceded and followed the word. Thus, there are clear limits to the amount of information that can be perceived, let alone integrated, in high-rate RSVP presentation.

A New Reading Technology?

RSVP presentation is currently being evaluated by some investigators as a form of rapid reading on video terminals (Juola, Ward, & McNamara, 1982). Normal eye movements during reading may involve some planning and execution time that is made unnecessary by the computerized text presentation of RSVP. Juola and associates proposed that by eliminating the need for eye movements, the exposure duration necessary to process a word under RSVP conditions might be less than the corresponding gaze duration. The evaluations generally indicate little difference in comprehension and memory performance produced by RSVP reading and comparably rapid normal reading (Juola, Ward, & McNamara, 1982; Potter, Kroll, & Harris, 1980). However, it is important to remember that the performance measures that have been used in these studies to evaluate comprehension have generally been fairly insensitive, testing only for overall comprehension or recall, rather than attempting to localize specific comprehension deficits that may be produced by RSVP reading.

In the study done by Potter, Kroll, and Harris (1980), readers recalled and understood a short RSVP text slightly less well than a conventional text. In the RSVP conditions, the text was presented at 250, 125, or 83 milliseconds per word. In the conventional reading, the text was presented for the same total duration as the corresponding RSVP condition, which turns out to be 33, 17, or 11 seconds per passage. The people who read the passages under conventional reading conditions (in normal format, but with a deadline) could recall slightly more (12 percent) of the content. Moreover, the conventional format produced somewhat fewer misinterpretations (better comprehension) of the content of the passage. In both types of reading, performance was generally better when the total processing time was longer, reflecting the familiar speed-accuracy trade-off that was described previously.

The evaluations of RSVP comprehension have searched for possible benefits of this reading technique and found few. However, they have not diligently searched for costs. It is likely that many of the words presented in RSVP may not be adequately comprehended if they are presented for considerably less than the mean gaze durations (about 230 milliseconds) observed for the rapid readers; a detailed comprehension test would likely detect the deficit (Just, Carpenter, & Woolley, 1982).

In evaluating a new reading technology such as RSVP, it would be wise to ask under what conditions it is effective, rather than attempt to establish a universal superiority or inferiority to normal reading. The effectiveness of RSVP reading very likely depends on the nature of the text, the reader, and the task. For example, if the text contained many infrequent words and concepts, extra processing time would be required for these selected words, which would be unavailable in RSVP reading. By contrast, a relatively easy text, like a narrative about commonplace events, might be tractable in RSVP, because high-level processes could use the reader's prior knowledge to fill in comprehension gaps.

The effectiveness of RSVP reading could also depend on an individual reader's memory capacity, such that readers with large capacities could store the RSVP words that are very demanding until the processing resources became available. It may be that the large individual differences in readers' memory capacity for the material they have just read are predictors of their RSVP comprehension ability (Daneman & Carpenter, 1980).

Finally, the effectiveness of RSVP reading surely depends on what kind of information the reader is trying to obtain from a text: the topic, the major theme, supporting arguments, or specific evidence and facts. For example, the results of the speed-reading experiment discussed earlier suggest that rapid reading is more detrimental to the comprehension of low-level details than to the comprehension of the gist. RSVP probably produces similar effects.

RSVP of the Future

Can speed reading be made more efficient by using a modified form of RSVP to enhance those processes basic to rapid reading, as revealed in the earlier experiment? First, only a sample of the words of the text would be presented (say, one out of every three words) in their original order of occurrence. Second, the sampling would be intelligent rather than random, using plentiful computer-processing capacity rather than scarce speed-readers' capacity. An example of an intelligent sampling algorithm might be one that selects the most informative words of a sentence, such as the least frequent content words and semantically critically function words, like negations and quantifiers. Third, the presentation duration of each of the presented words would be determined by the theoretical estimate of the processing time for the word, as specified by a model like READER.

This new paradigm might have all the advantages of standard RSVP (the computer obviating the need for motor control of eye movements) and most of the advantages of natural reading (exposure durations designed to match processing times). One disadvantage of this proposed paradigm relative to speed reading is that it does not allow for individual differences between readers with respect to the locations of extra long pauses. This speculative proposal illustrates the important role that the underlying cognitive processes play in designing and evaluating new reading technologies.

Summary

The contrast between the eye-fixation patterns of normal readers and those of speed readers and skimmers illuminates many of the processes that underlie rapid reading and indicates how it differs from normal reading. While normal readers sample a text fairly densely, rapid readers can read two and one-half to three times faster by fixating half as many words and spending only about two-thirds the time (200–240 milliseconds) on each fixated word. The gaze durations of normal and rapid readers on fixated words are proportional to the word's length and the logarithm of its normative frequency, although the parameters associated with these two effects are considerably smaller for the rapid readers than the normal readers.

The comprehension level of rapid readers was inferior to that of normal readers. However, training in speed reading did produce an advantage over untrained skimming, but the advantage was limited to easy texts on familiar topics and, even then, only to high-level information. The advantage may depend on rapidly inferring the relations among those fragments of the text that happened to be visually sampled; such inferences may only be available for the kinds of material for which a reader has a well-developed schema.

A new form of rapid reading, involving Rapid Serial Visual Presentation of the words of a text, enables people to read rapidly, but the comprehension consequences of the new paradigm have not yet been adequately evaluated. The RSVP paradigms that have been examined to date have not made full use of what is known about speed reading. The potential of RSVP as a reading technology of the future remains to be evaluated.

One theme of this book is that *reading* is a generic term because reading processes vary widely, depending on the text and situation. In some situations and for some texts, speed reading can be an extremely adaptive form of reading. The results in this chapter suggest that it will be useful for texts that conform to relatively familiar schemata and for situations that only require the gist, or situations in which the reader neither has the time nor desire to understand the text deeply. It would be ludicrous, for example, to use speed reading while studying a religious text or evaluating poetry. But speed reading can be seen as a useful, if limited tool that can permit a skilled reader to respond flexibly to different texts and reading tasks.

Suggested Readings

Several of the articles that were referred to in this chapter can be consulted for specific points, but we have no general readings to recommend. In fact, the sparse knowledge about the nature of speed reading was one of the motivations for doing the research that is reported in this chapter.

15

Individual Differences

There are enormous differences in how well different people read. The average adult reads at a rate of about 250 words per minute (wpm), although some adults read faster, at 300 wpm or more, and others read half as fast, at 150 wpm or less. Readers also differ in the amount of information they obtain from what they read. Good readers not only understand the literal facts in a passage, but they also make the appropriate inferences, note the organization of the material, and attend to the author's tone and approach. By contrast, less skilled readers may not even accurately comprehend or retain the main point.

Some children and adults remain painfully slow and inaccurate readers and never attain fluency, as described in Chapter 12 on dyslexia. But even apart from the extreme cases of dyslexia, individual differences in reading skill are persistent and pervasive and, if anything, become more pronounced with schooling. The differences among the reading achievement levels of twelfth-graders are much larger than the differences among first-graders (Goodlad, 1966).

This chapter is concerned with the range of individual differences that might be observed in a typical class. Most of the research that will be discussed does not deal with severely impaired readers, such as dyslexics. The purpose of the chapter is to account for differences in reading skill among individuals in terms of the processes and structures in reading that were described in Chapters 1 through 9. It is a fitting final chapter for the book because it revisits many of the important component processes in reading while considering their contribution to overall reading skill.

The individual differences among readers are not all caused by a single process, for several reasons. First, entire clusters of slow or errorful processes tend to be associated with poor reading, not just one. Second, the nature of the individual differences varies with the population of readers under discussion. For example, the processes that distinguish excellent college-age readers from average ones are not necessarily the same ones that distinguish excellent third-grade readers from poor ones. Thus, the chapter accounts for individual differences in terms of more than one process.

Overview   Each of the first three sections of this chapter focuses on one particular group of reading processes, evaluating their role in explaining the differences among readers. In the first section, we will examine the role of **Word Recognition.** In some poor readers, word recognition is slow and effortful, so much so that it may consume attentional resources that are needed for comprehension processes. This section examines how word recognition might constitute a processing bottleneck in some cases.

As readers become more practiced in the visual aspects of reading, the nonvisual aspects—namely, those processes that are common to reading and listening—account for much of the individual differences in reading skill. We will discuss this topic in the second section, **Language Comprehension Processes.** Correlational studies have found that beyond the early grades, good readers are likely to be good listeners and poor readers are likely to be poor listeners.

The correlation between listening and reading skills could also be due to their both using shared knowledge or shared attentional capacity. We will examine this account of individual differences in the third section, **Shared Resources.** In particular, we will examine how knowledge can play an important role in the ability of readers to draw inferences and organize the information in a text. Another source of individual differences may be *working-memory capacity,* a term that refers to the conjunction of computation and storage in short-term memory. Readers must not only retain words, phrases, and clauses but also compute their syntactic, semantic, and referential relations. It is the ability to simultaneously perform computations and store information that may distinguish skilled and unskilled readers.

In the fourth section, **Home and School Background,** we will briefly summarize the results of a large survey on the correlates of reading skill. The survey found that good readers tend to come from homes and schools that encourage reading practice and foster high aspirations.

Standardized reading tests play an important role in educational practice and an equally critical role in reading research. In the fifth section, called **Reading Tests,** we will describe two different kinds of tests, how they are constructed, and their limitations from the viewpoint of investigating the nature of individual differences in reading skill.

Word Recognition

Several researchers have proposed that word-recognition processes are an important determinant of reading skill (LaBerge & Samuels, 1974; Perfetti & Lesgold, 1977). As in previous chapters, we will use the term *word recognition* to refer collectively to word encoding and lexical access. In fluent readers, word recognition is fast and automatic and seldom a stumbling block. The rapid recognition of a word makes the information about the word's identity and meaning quickly available to high-level processes, such as syntactic, semantic, and referential analysis.

By contrast, consider the implications for reading if the word-recognition processes are slow and effortful. If word recognition is slow, then those high-level processes that await the output of word recognition will be delayed. In addition, if word recognition consumes the reader's attention, she might not have sufficient resources left to execute those high-level processes that could normally be executed in parallel with word recognition. Thus, a bottleneck in word recognition could not only cause slower reading but also result in qualitatively poorer comprehension. In this section, we will review the role played by the word-recognition processes, word encoding and lexical access, in accounting for individual differences in reading skill.

Word Encoding

The speed with which a reader can pronounce written words is correlated with his reading skill. Among both children and adults, poor readers take between one-quarter to one-half second more time than good readers to recognize and pronounce an isolated word or nonword (like *troom* or *rast*) (Frederiksen, 1978, 1981; Mason, 1978; Perfetti, Finger, & Hogaboam, 1978; Perfetti & Hogaboam, 1975). Because the poor readers' disadvantage extends to nonwords, which cannot be lexically accessed, the suggestion is that at least part of their difficulty lies in **word encoding,** rather than in lexical access.

The poor reader's word-encoding deficit may not be the same problem as the dyslexic's word-encoding deficit. As we described in Chapter 12 on dyslexia, several studies have found that dyslexics are slower in pronouncing not only words and nonwords but also the names of digits, colors, or objects. By contrast, at least some groups of poor readers take longer than good readers *only* when they have to pronounce a written word or nonword; they do not take longer to name colors, pictures, or digits (Perfetti, Finger, & Hogaboam, 1978).

In sum, a large number of studies have found that poor readers are slower at pronouncing words or nonwords than good readers. The word encoding of poor readers not only consumes extra time but also attentional resources that are needed to execute high-level comprehension processes.

Lexical Access

The second component of word recognition is **lexical access,** the process of accessing the representation of a word's meaning. This process may also contribute to some differences among readers. In a paper entitled "What does it mean to be high verbal," Hunt and his associates (Hunt, Lunneborg, & Lewis, 1975) examined a variety of processes to determine which ones differentiated college students who had high scores on a verbal ability test from those who had average scores (see also Hunt, 1978; Hunt, Frost, & Lunneborg, 1973). The process that differentiated high- and average-scoring students was the time they took to access a verbal code. Although the speed was measured in a nonreading task, the implication was that the retrieval of verbal information during lexical access (such as the access of a word's meaning or pronunciation) would show a similar pattern of differences between good and average readers.

The time a reader takes to retrieve a verbal code was estimated in the task of comparing letter names, as described in Chapter 12 on dyslexia. Subjects were timed while they compared two visually presented letters (like *A-A, A-a,* or *A-b.*) In one condition, they judged if the letters were physically identical. In another condition, they judged if the letters had the same name (Posner, Boies, Eichelman, & Taylor, 1969; Posner & Mitchell, 1967). To judge whether letters are physically

Table 15.1   The conditions and results for high- and average-verbal students

		Response Time (msec)	
Display	Condition	High-verbal	Average-verbal
A-A	Physical match	524	543
A-a	Name match	588	632
	Difference	64	89

Source: Data from Hunt, 1978, Table 3, p. 114.

identical (like *A-A*), the subject needs only to encode and compare two visual symbols. To match letters that are physically different but have the same name (like *A-a*), the subject must also retrieve their names. The difference in the time needed to make these two judgments provides an estimate of the time taken for name retrieval.

Table 15.1 shows the mean response times that Hunt (1978) obtained for the high-verbal and the average-verbal students. As the table shows, readers who performed well on a verbal ability test took less time to make a name judgment. The good readers also had a smaller difference between the name- and physical-match conditions, 64 milliseconds compared to 89 milliseconds. Hunt found that this parameter, the difference between the physical-match and name-match conditions, was correlated with the scores on the verbal ability test. The correlation has been replicated many times, and it tends to be around 0.30. Thus, good reading skill is associated with faster speed in retrieving the verbal code for a letter's name and presumably with retrieving other verbal codes, as well.

Because the size of the correlation is low, one can conclude that the speed of verbal access is not a very large determinant of verbal ability. On the other hand, it was somewhat surprising at the time the research was done that the speed of this relatively low-level process was at all important in accounting for differences among college readers.

In another study, the time to access verbal codes was correlated with reading speed (Jackson & McClelland, 1979). The study compared two groups of college readers—fast readers (with an average reading rate of about 350 wpm) and slow readers (with an average reading rate of about 200 wpm)—on a variety of simple tasks, including the name-match task, to obtain estimates of the speed of various psychological processes that might play a role in reading. Overall reading speed was correlated more highly with the time required for the name-match decision than with other processes. So faster readers are particularly fast in retrieving name codes. The advantage of faster readers does not extend to all speeded tasks; they had no advantage in nonreading tasks, such as judging whether two dot patterns were the same or different. In sum, faster and perhaps better readers probably encode words and access their names more quickly than slower readers.

The Use of Context

Several models of reading that were developed in the 1960s and 1970s hypothesized that readers use context to guess the upcoming words in a text (Goodman, 1967; Levin & Kaplan, 1970; Smith, 1971). The implication of these models was that the advantage of good readers lay in their use of context, rather than in perceptually based word-recognition skills. However, recent research has disproved the hypothesis and its implication. Good readers are better than poor readers at word recognition, both in and out of context (Stanovich, 1980; Stanovich & West, 1981). Moreover, context helps poor readers recognize a word more than it helps good readers.

Context has its effect when a high-level comprehension process—such as syntactic, semantic, or referential analysis—partially activates a concept or word-percept, as described in Chapters 2 and 3 on word encoding and lexical access. The high-level processes can co-occur with the low-level processes, word encoding and lexical access. Lexical access occurs when the activation level of a word meaning reaches threshold, regardless of whether the source of the activation is a high-level or low-level process. The type of process (high- or low-level) that is executed faster will have the greater influence on the time taken to recognize a word, because it will be more influential in activating the word meaning. For a poor reader, the encoding and lexical access processes are slow; consequently, the high-level processes can have a large influence on the speed of word recognition. By contrast, a good reader's encoding and lexical access processes are fast; consequently, high-level processes have little opportunity to influence the speed of word recognition.

If a good reader's encoding and lexical access processes are slowed down artificially—for example, by making the word difficult to perceive—then context also has a large influence on the good reader's word-recognition time (Stanovich & West, 1981; West & Stanovich, 1978). An elegant demonstration of this point was made in a study of good readers and poor readers from fourth grade (Perfetti & Roth, 1981; Roth, Perfetti, & Lesgold, 1979). To vary the speed of the word-encoding and lexical access processes, words were printed in one of three ways that made them more or less perceptible: (1) normal print; (2) moderately degraded print; and (3) highly degraded print. Word-recognition time was measured by the time a reader took to pronounce a word.

To determine how much context helped word recognition, the experimenters first measured how long readers took to pronounce printed words in the absence of context. When the words were presented without context, good readers were faster at pronouncing them than poor readers, as shown in Figure 15.1. Also, both good readers and poor readers were faster when the print was normal than when it was degraded.

The words were also presented in one of two types of contexts: (1) a more constraining context that made the target word very predictable or (2) a less constraining context that made the target word moderately predictable, as in the following examples:

More Constraining Context:

I had a sore neck when I went to bed last night. I laid down slowly and gently placed my head on the _____. (pillow)

Less Constraining Context:

Jack was making dinner and he went to pick some things in his garden. He picked an onion, some beans, and a _____. (pepper)

The amount by which the context facilitated pronunciation time depended on the base time taken to pronounce the word when it was presented without a con-

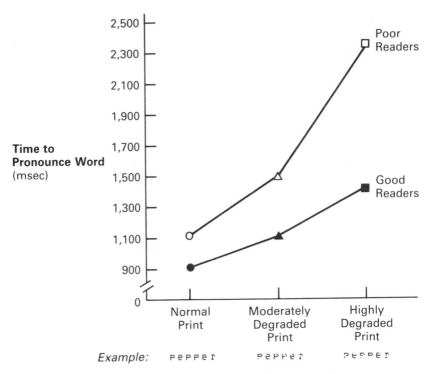

Figure 15.1 The time taken by good and poor fourth-grade readers to pronounce words that were presented in one of three print qualities: normal, moderately degraded, or highly degraded. These are the base pronunciation times for words presented without any context. *Source:* Adapted from Roth, Perfetti, & Lesgold, 1979, Figure 4, p. 8.

text. If the base pronunciation time was long, either because the print was degraded or because the subjects were poor readers, then context had a larger effect than if the base pronunciation time was short. The speed-up due to the context is shown in Figure 15.2 for the more constraining context and the less constraining context as a function of the base time to pronounce a word without context. The difference between the two lines is attributable to the result that a more constraining context facilitated pronunciation time more than a less constraining context. Thus, the size of the context effect depends upon the speed of the encoding and lexical access processes. The poor readers are helped more by the context only because they typically take longer than good readers to encode and access words. These results suggest that the contextual influences on the speed of word recognition are not a primary source of individual differences. Rather, such effects are due to differences in the speed of word encoding and lexical access.

Training in Word Recognition

Efficient word recognition is not sufficient for good reading. A number of training studies that improved the word-recognition speed of poor readers did not find

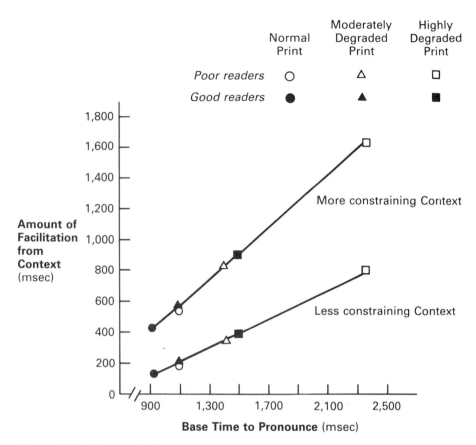

Figure 15.2 The speed-up in pronunciation caused by presenting the word after a two-sentence context. The *x*-axis shows the base time to pronounce the word without any context; the *y*-axis shows the amount of speed-up. The two lines correspond to the two kinds of context sentences, less constraining and more constraining. With either kind of sentence, context had a greater effect if the base pronunciation time was longer. For example, the good readers with moderately degraded print were helped by context as much as the poor readers with normal print. *Source:* Perfetti & Roth, 1981, Figure 11.8, p. 288. Used with permission of Lawrence Erlbaum Associates and the authors.

commensurate increases in their reading level (Fleisher, Jenkins, & Pany, 1979; Samuels, Dahl, & Archwamety, 1974). For example, one study with fourth- and fifth-grade readers gave poor readers training in recognizing individual words and phrases until their speed was comparable to that of good readers (Fleisher, Jenkins, & Pany, 1979). The poor readers' scores on a subsequent reading comprehension test were no higher after training than before. The results indicated that rapid word recognition is not sufficient for good comprehension.

The simplest interpretation of these negative results is that other kinds of training and additional practice are necessary to improve reading. Children who have had four or five years of reading instruction and are still having difficulty with word recognition may not have had sufficient practice in high-level comprehension processes, such as making inferences, abstracting the theme, organizing the information, and so on. Reading, after all, requires the coordination of a complex number of processes. It is not likely that efficient word recognition would be sufficient for these other processes to operate normally. Poor readers may need to practice these high-level processes after the word-recognition bottleneck has been removed.

These training studies also serve as reminders that the results linking word recognition and reading ability are primarily correlational. The assumption of a causal relation is speculative. Until more definitive training studies are done, the link between word-recognition skill and reading comprehension for nondyslexic poor readers remains a hypothesis supported by correlational evidence.

Word-level and Text-level Processes

Processes at the word and sentence level, not at the text level, are the ones primarily responsible for the differences between fast and slow readers. One study localized the level responsible for the differences among college readers by timing 24 fast college readers and 24 slow ones while they read several texts, one sentence at a time (Graesser, Hoffman, & Clark, 1980). To assess the influence of word- and sentence-level processes, the study examined how sentence reading times were affected by three properties:

1. the number of words in the sentence;
2. the number of propositions in the sentence; and
3. the proportion of syntactically unpredictable words in the sentence.

The results showed that each of the three properties was significantly correlated with the reading time for individual sentences. But more importantly, from the current perspective, these properties accounted for much of the difference between fast and slow readers. The slow readers were particularly slow for sentences containing more words, more propositions, and more syntactically unpredictable words. Thus, the slow college readers' disadvantage may primarily arise from word- and sentence-level processes.

To assess the influence of text-level processes, the researchers examined how sentence reading times were affected by the following three properties:

1. the rated "storiness" of the passage;
2. the familiarity of the passage topic; and
3. the number of new concepts introduced in that sentence.

The first two properties were rated by an independent group of readers. For example, they rated *Snow White* as being more storylike than a text on *Coal Utilization,* and they rated a text on *Emotions* as dealing with a more familiar topic than a text on *Armadillos.*

The results showed that these properties were correlated with sentence reading time. Moreover, they had a larger effect on sentence reading time than did the word- and sentence-level properties. However, these properties were not responsible for differences between the fast and slow readers. Both the fast and slow readers slowed down similarly for sentences that were in less storylike passages, that were on unfamiliar topics, or that contained many new concepts. In conclusion, text-level processes influenced reading time, but they were not a source of difference between the fast and the slow readers.

These results also illustrate the point that a process that does not distinguish between good readers and poor readers, like the text-level processes in this experiment, can still play an important role in reading comprehension.

The Relation between Speed and Comprehension

Reading skill must be assessed in terms of the products of comprehension, as well as its speed. As we argued in Chapter 14 on speed reading, comprehension accuracy and reading speed can sometimes be traded off against each other. Readers may read faster and sacrifice comprehension of details or read slower to integrate and evaluate the text more carefully. When speed and accuracy are viewed in this way, it becomes clear that different readers may adopt different criteria for trading off the two, resulting in an apparent difference in reading skill if only speed or only comprehension is evaluated. The relation between speed and comprehension could be assessed by simultaneously measuring both variables and then comparing the speed-accuracy functions of good readers and poor readers. Unfortunately, such data do not exist.

One study that was described earlier (Jackson & McClelland, 1979) suggested that speed and comprehension accuracy are empirically distinguishable. That study tried to determine which basic processes distinguished between fast and slow college readers. Their reading speed was correlated with their comprehension accuracy, as assessed by the ability to answer questions about the passage. Thus, the individual differences among these readers are not simply the result of some of them choosing to read faster and less accurately. The correlation between reading speed and comprehension accuracy indicates that the ones who were reading faster also tended to be comprehending more accurately. On the other hand, the processes that were correlated with reading speed were not correlated as highly with comprehension accuracy. For example, the speed of retrieving verbal codes correlated the best with reading speed, but it did not correlate with comprehension accuracy. By contrast, reading comprehension accuracy was correlated with listening comprehension accuracy. Thus, somewhat different processes may influence individual differences in reading speed and individual differences in comprehension accuracy. An account of individual differences that focuses only on reading speed deals with just one facet of the multidimensional differences among readers.

The multidimensionality of individual differences in reading makes it apparent that *reading skill* itself must be construed more carefully. Reading skill is typically operationalized as the score on a standardized reading test; that score is then used to categorize readers as *good* or *poor*. But there has been little analysis of what combination of processes and structures produce a given score on the test. The general assumption that researchers often make is that standardized reading tests provide reasonable measures of reading skill. This assumption needs to be evaluated in more detail. In particular, it is not known how different tests assess speed in comparison to accuracy; that is, it is not known which point on the speed-accuracy function they are assessing. For example, suppose that one standardized test significantly stressed reading speed. That test would tend to favor readers who, for whatever reason, were generally fast, and the resulting analysis of the individual differences would reflect that bias. In general, it is not clear to what extent the tests assess the multidimensional nature of reading. The properties of these tests will be examined in more detail in the final section of the chapter, **Reading Tests.**

Vocabulary

Skilled readers have larger vocabularies than poor readers, and they give better definitions of the words they know. The correlation between vocabulary knowledge and reading comprehension is both robust and well documented. In a classic, large-scale study of individual differences in reading, Davis (1968) found that knowledge of word meanings correlated about 0.55 with reading comprehension skill. In some studies, the correlation between vocabulary knowledge and reading comprehension is almost as high as the correlation between alternate reading comprehension tests (see Brady & Strater, 1974). The high correlation suggests that vocabulary tests tap the same sorts of processes that reading comprehension tests do.

One interpretation of the correlation is that the students who know more words read better because they know more of the words they encounter. However, numerous studies have found that vocabulary instruction does not automatically improve reading comprehension (Tuinman & Brady, 1974). In Chapter 4 on vocabulary acquisition, we argued that vocabulary programs improve reading ability only if they teach readers how to reason with words and sentences, in addition to teaching the meanings of specific words.

Vocabulary knowledge may reflect the relative success of past vocabulary acquisition, which consists, in part, of inferring word meanings from reading and listening. Consequently, vocabulary knowledge is partially a product of reading comprehension. The same types of syntactic, semantic, and referential processes that are used to understand a text containing known words also help a reader infer the meanings of unknown words. If these processes are functioning effectively, the reader will acquire a large vocabulary over his many years of reading. To the extent that these processes are functioning improperly, the reader will have an impoverished vocabulary and will also perform poorly on a comprehension test.

Chapter 4 on vocabulary acquisition cited data to support this interpretation of the relation between vocabulary and reading skill. Sternberg and Powell (1983), for example, found that the ability of high school students to infer the meanings of low-frequency nouns that occurred in paragraphs was correlated significantly with reading comprehension (0.65), as well as with other vocabulary test performance, and with IQ. Thus, vocabulary tests can be seen as a measure of vocabulary-acquisition skill and, in particular, as a measure of the reader's ability to learn from text. Research using think-aloud protocols documented individual differences among adults and developmental differences between children and adults in the general strategies they use in inferring the meanings of unknown words, particularly in their ability to analyze the meanings of words into components (van Daalen-Kapteijns & Elshout-Mohr, 1981; Werner & Kaplan, 1952). Thus, while readers obviously differ in the size and nature of their vocabularies, these differences may primarily be due to differences in reading skill.

A final factor that contributes to individual differences in vocabulary is simply exposure to language. Children and adults who seldom read or read about a small range of topics will have less opportunity to either learn new words or gain new comprehension skills. In sum, vocabulary knowledge is related to individual differences. However, it may be viewed more as a result of differences in reading skill than as the primary cause of such differences.

Language Comprehension Processes

In this section, we will explore the role played by comprehension processes beyond the level of word recognition. These include sentence-level and text-level processes. These processes may account for some of the individual differences in reading skill among readers who have learned to decode words.

The Relation between Listening and Reading Comprehension

Among adults, general language comprehension skills are a major source of differences among readers. One type of evidence for this thesis is that good readers tend to be good listeners and, conversely, poor readers tend to be poor listeners. The correlation between listening and reading skills suggests that the processes and structures that differ among readers are also used in listening comprehension.

One study that showed a close relation between reading and listening performance investigated the comprehension of approximately 100 Army recruits (Sticht, 1972). The recruits were divided into two groups—those who scored poorly and those who scored well—on a mental aptitude exam that tested vocabulary,

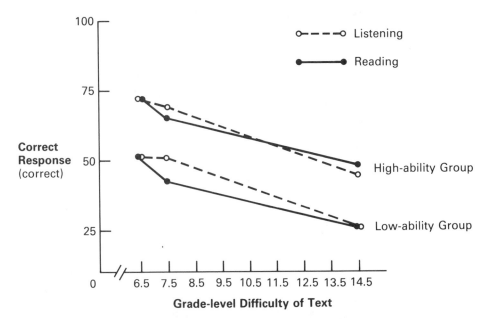

Figure 15.3 The scores on listening and reading tests for two groups of Army recruits (a high-ability group and a low-ability group). The similarity in the scores shows that among adults, poor readers are often poor listeners, as well. *Source:* Based on data from Sticht, 1972, Table 2, p. 288.

arithmetic, mechanical knowledge, and spatial skills. The recruits either read or listened to passages at three levels of difficulty: (1) relatively easy (suitable for the 6.5 grade level); (2) slightly harder (suitable for the 7.5 grade level); and (3) difficult (suitable for the 14.5 grade level). When the passages were presented in the reading condition, the reading time was limited to the time required to listen to the text. Because speaking rates (about 150 wpm) are much slower than most silent-reading rates (about 250 wpm), presenting the passages for the longer time should not have hampered reading. After reading or listening to a passage, the recruits had to answer factual questions about the passage.

What is perhaps most striking about Sticht's data (shown in Figure 15.3) is that the reading and listening scores were so similar. There was no evidence that the recruits were generally better listeners than readers. Sticht did not present the correlation between listening and reading performance for individuals, but the group averages suggest that similar processes govern reading and listening comprehension. Sticht concluded that "much of their reading difficulty may result from reduced ability to comprehend language rather than (or perhaps in addition to) lack of ability in decoding written symbols" (Sticht, 1972, p. 288). These results suggest that adult poor readers are poor language understanders.

The correlation between listening and reading comprehension increases with the amount of schooling, as shown in Figure 15.4. Among college students, good listeners are likely to be good readers. In the early school years, listening skill is less predictive of reading skill. Of course, the absolute size of the correlation depends upon many factors, such as the range of reading and listening skills in the sample

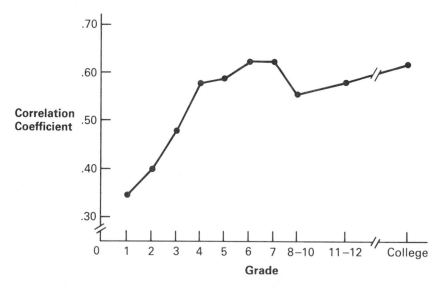

Figure 15.4 The correlation between listening and reading skills increases as children progress through school. After grade four and until college, the correlations are usually between 0.6 and 0.7. This suggests that once children have completed early reading instruction, their listening and reading skills are similar. *Source:* Sticht & James, 1984, Figure 10.3, p. 297. From *Handbook of Reading Research*, P. David Pearson, ed. Copyright © 1984 by Longman Inc. All rights reserved.

that is being tested. Nevertheless, the general trend is consistent with the idea that comprehension and conceptual processes, rather than the visual aspects of reading, account for much of the variation among readers in later school years.

Among college students, reading skill is correlated with listening skill more than with measures of simpler processes, such as the time to access name codes. Earlier, we described a study that compared a group of 12 fast college readers to 12 slow college readers on a battery of tests, including measures of lexical access, simple matching tasks, and listening comprehension (Jackson & McClelland, 1979). Reading comprehension accuracy correlated best with listening comprehension, suggesting that the same processes account for variation in both. Other researchers have also argued that when word-recognition abilities are similar, individual differences are attributable to language comprehension skills (Guthrie, 1973). Reading comprehension *is* language comprehension. Presumably, material that is conceptually or linguistically difficult to read would be difficult if it were presented orally. Of course, people do not usually speak the way they write or speak about the same topics that they write about. However, if the reading and listening material are comparable, and if the readers are adults who have had ample reading practice, their reading and listening skills are often similar.

High-level Comprehension Processes

Relatively few studies have examined exactly which high-level processes account for individual differences. Individual differences could arise from any combination of high-level processes, such as syntactic-, semantic-, referential-, and text-level processes. One could imagine, for example, that some individuals are faster or more accurate than others in computing the referent of a pronoun, the agreement between a subject and its verb, or the syntactic role of a particular type of clause. At the intersentential level, there could be differences in the speed, accuracy, and type of inferences that are drawn to interrelate sentences. At the text level, there could be differences in the readers' familiarity with the structural characteristics of particular types of texts (such as narratives, expositions, arguments), leading to differences in recognizing the categories of information or interrelating them in a particular text schema. All of these are plausible sources of individual differences.

In general, readers who are poor at one or another of these processes may be poor at others. The studies that suggest this conclusion are primarily correlational. We will explain their rationale and then their limitations. The relation among various comprehension processes has been examined using the tools of **psychometrics,** a research technique based on the analysis of the pattern of correlations among tests. In psychometrics, tests are constructed to tap a particular set of abilities. People who are good at some given ability should perform well on all tests that tap that ability. If performance on two tests is correlated, then the tests are said to tap a single **factor** (presumably, some shared processes and structures). Alternatively, if the performance on two tests is unrelated, then they presumably draw on different processes and structures.

In one of the most careful analyses of the component factors in reading comprehension, Davis (1944, 1968, 1972) identified approximately five factors. He constructed passages and multiple-choice items to tap several abilities that had been suggested as components of reading comprehension. Figure 15.5 gives some

---

Test type: Remembering word meanings

Guffaw means: A. make fun of   B. sneeze   C. cough   D. laugh

Test type: Reasoning about the content

The delight Tad had felt during his long hours in the glen faded as he drew near the cabin. The sun was nearly gone and Tad's father was at the woodpile. He was wearing the broadcloth suit that he wore to church and to town sometimes. Tad saw his father's hands close around a bundle of wood. He was doing Tad's work—and in his good clothes. Tad ran to him. "I'll get it, Pa."

When Tad saw his father, he felt: A. disappointed   B. impatient   C. angry D. guilty

---

Figure 15.5   Sample items to illustrate the major sources of individual differences found in Davis' study. *Source:* Davis, 1968, pp. 511–512.

sample items. Davis examined the test performance of about 1,000 twelfth-grade students on the different types of items. There was some correlation among all of the different items; readers who did well on one type tended to do well on the others. However, there was some evidence that five types of items were somewhat independent. He associated these items with five comprehension factors:

1. remembering word meanings;
2. reasoning with the content;
3. following the passage's structure;
4. recognizing the writer's purpose, attitude, tone, and mood; and
5. finding answers to questions asked explicitly or in paraphrase (Davis, 1972, pp. 654, 655).

Of these five factors, the first two—vocabulary knowledge and reasoning—were the most clearly identifiable.

Other studies have often failed to find such distinct factors. A common outcome is that performances on different types of questions are so highly intercorrelated that only one factor clearly emerges, and that factor is often labeled and interpreted as vocabulary knowledge (Thorndike, 1973). Ever since these data were presented, there has been considerable controversy over which factors, if any, are independent of the others (see also Carroll, 1972; Spearritt, 1972; Thurstone, 1946). The generally high intercorrelations suggest that people who are good at the processes that contribute to one factor tend to be good at other processes, as well. Why might this be true? The psychometric approach did not answer this question, but several plausible alternative explanations can be offered.

One of the least interesting explanations for the intercorrelation is that the tests were not constructed adequately. If the questions did not tap the ability they were supposed to, then the pattern of correlations will not necessarily reflect the factor labels, a criticism that has been leveled at some studies (see Davis' comments, 1972). But even if the tests are well constructed, the correlations among different types of items can still be given alternative interpretations. One possible interpretation is that these abilities are acquired under similar conditions; students who acquire one ability will tend to acquire the others concomitantly. Another possible reason for the intercorrelation is that the abilities are not psychologically independent because they are based on shared processes. It may be impossible, for example, to recognize the writer's purpose if the reader cannot syntactically analyze the individual sentences or cannot retrieve the appropriate schemata.

In summary, there is some evidence that readers who are good at one high-level aspect of comprehension tend to be good at others. However, the psychometric approach provides little insight into the specific processes readers use to read a passage or to answer questions about it, and the data are open to many interpretations.

Identifying the Theme of a Passage

For some poor readers, one high-level process, identifying the theme of a passage, has been indicated as the source of comprehension problems. Training these readers in the process has resulted in significant improvements in comprehension. A recent set of studies on this point is significant, both from the viewpoint of individual differences and from the viewpoint of an instructional technique for improving reading. The studies involved junior high school students who were very poor readers but who were not retarded and who were described as having mastered word recognition (Palincsar & Brown, 1984). What the students were taught was to formulate a question that would be answered by the most important point of a passage.

The training sessions themselves were an important part of the study. Table 15.2 presents the interaction between one of the students and the teacher. The table illustrates what the teacher was doing, as well as the large improvements made in the child's mastery over the two weeks.

As the table suggests, the sessions between the teacher and student were highly interactive, with the teacher gradually shaping and structuring the student's responses until the student could independently generate the question. At the end of several weeks, the readers were then tested on new and different material and then given a general reading comprehension test. As Figure 15.6 shows, the children who had training on comprehension processes showed very general and large improvements, particularly compared to other students who were not in the training group but were in regular classes or who received other types of training. Thus, learning how to organize and structure information was clearly a bottleneck. Once the students were taught this skill, their reading comprehension improved markedly.

In a series of such training programs, Palincsar and Brown documented that these techniques resulted in large and general reading improvement. All of the instructional programs had somewhat similar properties. In all cases, the cognitive aspects were intertwined with motivational ones, a characteristic that is probably true of most effective instructional techniques. Both the children and the teachers

Table 15.2 The acquisition of question asking by a seventh-grade student

Note: T = Teacher, S = Student

Day 1:

TEXT: The water moccasin, somewhat longer than the copperhead, is found in the southeastern states. It lives in swampy regions. It belongs, as do also the copperhead and the rattlesnakes, to a group of poisonous snakes called pit vipers. They have pits between their eyes and their nostrils which, because they are sensitive to heat, help the snakes tell when they are near a warm-blooded animal. Another name for the water moccasin is "cottonmouth." This name comes from the white lining of the snake's mouth.

1. S: What is found in the southeastern snakes, also the copperhead, rattlesnakes, vipers—they have. I'm not doing this right.
2. T: All right. Do you want to know about the pit vipers?
3. S: Yeah.
4. T: What would be a good question about the pit vipers that starts with the word "why?"
5. S: (No response)
6. T: How about, "Why are the snakes called pit vipers?"
7. S: Why do they want to know that they are called pit vipers?
8. T: Try it again.
9. S: Why do they, pit vipers in a pit?
10. T: How about, "Why do they call the snakes pit vipers?"
11. S: Why do they call the snakes pit vipers?
12. T: There you go! Good for you.

Day 4:

TEXT: Spinner's mate is much smaller than she, and his body is dull brown. He spends most of his time sitting at one side of her web.

13. S: (No question)
14. T: What's this paragraph about?
15. S: Spinner's mate. How do spinner's mate . . .
16. T: That's good. Keep going.
17. S: How do spinner's mate is smaller than . . . How am I going to say that?
18. T: Take your time with it. You want to ask a question about spinner's mate and what he does, beginning with the word "how."
19. S: How do they spend most of his time sitting?
20. T: You're very close. The question would be, "How does spinner's mate spend most of his time?" Now, you ask it.
21. S: How does spinner's mate spend most of his time?

Day 7:

TEXT: Perhaps you are wondering where the lava and other volcanic products come from. Deep within our earth there are pockets of molten rock called *magma*. Forced upward in part by gas pressure, this molten rock continually tries to reach the surface. Eventually—by means of cracks in the crustal rocks or some similar zone of weakness—the magma may break out of the ground. It then flows from the vent as lava, or spews skyward as dense clouds of lava particles.

22. S: How does the pressure from below push the mass of hot rock against the opening? Is that it?
23. T: Not quite. Start your question with, "What happens when?"
24. S: What happens when the pressure from below pushes the mass of hot rock against the opening?
25. T: Good for you! Good job.

Table 15.2 (continued)

Day 11:

TEXT: One of the most interesting of the insect-eating plants is the Venus's flytrap. This
plant lives in only one small area of the world—the coastal marshes of North and
South Carolina. The Venus's flytrap doesn't look unusual. Its habits, however, make
it truly a plant wonder.

26. S: What is the most interesting of the insect eating plants, and where do the plants live
at?
27. T: Two excellent questions! They are both clear and important questions. Ask us one at
a time now.

Day 15:

TEXT: Scientists also come to the South Pole to study the strange lights that glow overhead
during the Antarctic night. (It's a cold and lonely world for the few hardy people
who "winter over" the polar night.) These "southern lights" are caused by the Earth
acting like a magnet on electrical particles in the air. They are clues that may help us
understand the Earth's core and the upper edges of its blanket of air.

28. S: Why do scientists come to the south pole to study?
29. T: Excellent question! That is what this paragraph is all about.

Source: Palincsar & Brown, 1984, Table 4, pp. 138–139. Used with permission of Lawrence Erlbaum Associates and the authors.

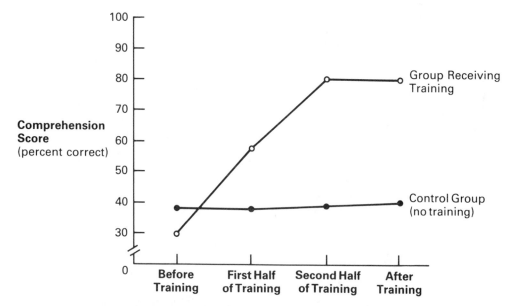

Figure 15.6 The comprehension scores of children who participated in the interactive
training on comprehension skills compared to children who were not specifically trained
(although they were in a conventional program). The training resulted in large and long-
lasting improvements in reading comprehension. *Source:* Adapted from Palincsar & Brown,
1984, Figure 1, p. 145. Used with permission of Lawrence Erlbaum Associates and the
authors.

found the programs stimulating. On a standardized reading test, these children improved from extremely poor comprehension levels to about the seventieth percentile.

This research is a striking demonstration of the existence and importance of individual differences in high-level comprehension processes. It shows how removing the bottleneck with an intensive training program can improve reading comprehension. At the same time, the procedures used to train the students demonstrate some of the features of successful remedial education.

Shared Resources

Individual differences in reading skill could be due not only to specific processes but also to resources that are shared by many processes. This section examines the role of two resources shared by several processes: knowledge and working-memory capacity.

Knowledge

Reading teachers have long appreciated the importance of background knowledge in reading. The effects of topic knowledge are large and easily demonstrated. In Chapter 13 on learning from text, we described how study-skills courses focus on background knowledge, teaching readers to use what they know about the topic to organize what they are reading. The same point was made about speed reading in Chapter 14. These are both instances in which reading improvement can be partially attributed to better use of background knowledge to organize the information that is acquired from reading.

As described in Chapter 8 on text comprehension, knowledge about a topic entails not only knowing facts but also knowing how those facts are related and organized. A baseball fan knows many facts about the game (such as the names of teams, managers, and players, batting and pitching records, and so on). But in addition, the expert knows how these facts are interrelated (such as strategies for deploying players or relations among players and managers). The interrelation of information plays an important role in reading. Such knowledge of baseball helped baseball experts to comprehend and recall a text about a baseball game by allowing them to draw the appropriate inferences when relations among facts in the passage were left implicit (Chiesi, Spilich, & Voss, 1979; Spilich, Vesonder, Chiesi, & Voss, 1979; Voss, Fincher-Kiefer, Greene, & Post, 1985). Specifically, they could relate the description of individual events (such as the occurrence of a line drive) to the goal structure of the game as they were reading.

Recent research with young children also supports this hypothesis. Second-grade children who either knew much or little about spiders were given a passage to read about spiders; they were then given comprehension questions that tested facts presented in the passage or facts that had to be inferred from the passage (Pearson, Hansen, & Gordon, 1979). The children were similar in IQ and overall reading ability, so any comprehension differences could be attributed to their knowledge about spiders. The spider experts scored better than those who knew little about spiders but only on questions that required making inferences, not on questions that probed for explicitly presented facts. The studies on content knowledge suggest that knowledgeable readers have an advantage in drawing inferences that are based on a schema for the topic.

In both the baseball and spider experiments, the tasks made clear which schema was relevant. But in reading, the relevant schema is not always so obvious. If the text is complex, the influence of topic knowledge may depend upon a prior decision concerning *which* schemata are relevant, a decision process that is largely unexplored. Most readers have had the experience of getting off the track by relating the information in a book to some idiosyncratic experience or to an inappropriate schema. These informal observations suggest that the ability to evoke the appropriate schema, as well as the knowledge in the schema itself, could be a source of individual differences in reading.

Background knowledge in early reading The importance of background knowledge has been recognized in reading instruction. As early as the 1930s, the instructional literature provided demonstrations that background knowledge improved reading comprehension (Smith, 1963). Consequently, teachers were encouraged to enhance their pupils' familiarity with a topic before reading instruction began. Current basal reading books continue this approach. For example, a teacher may try to elicit relevant personal experiences from the children or introduce activities to develop their knowledge of the topic.

The treatment of background knowledge in several basal programs has three shortcomings, according to an analysis by Beck and her colleagues:

1. The text selections often contained many tangential concepts that were likely to be very unfamiliar to the readers. For example, this problem might arise if a story is adapted from a Middle Eastern folktale or some other culturally distant source.
2. The instructional exercises sometimes led children too far afield. They were encouraged to think about concepts that were only marginally related to the text.
3. The exercises were often too sketchy to help in understanding the story; important relations were not explained; they were only mentioned or left implicit (Beck, McKeown, McCaslin, & Burkes, 1979).

Having identified these problems, the researchers then made two changes in a standard reading lesson. They rewrote the lesson to emphasize the relation of the background knowledge to the passage and they reduced the irrelevancies (Beck, Omanson, & McKeown, 1982). Third-grade children who were given the revised lesson recalled about 10 percent more of the text and correctly answered about 10 percent more of the comprehension questions than children given the standard, unrevised lesson. The revised lesson was particularly helpful to the average readers and less helpful to the superior readers (third-graders reading at the fifth-grade level). The ability to acquire and use new knowledge may be related to the child's current level of reading skill.

These studies demonstrate that knowledge influences reading comprehension. However, there are no data on the question that was posed at the beginning of the chapter: What role does knowledge play in accounting for individual differences in general reading skill? While there are no direct answers, it is likely that knowledge plays an increasingly important role as the conceptual difficulty of the material increases. It is at that point that readers may differ most strikingly in the availability of schemata to organize information, to interrelate it, and to draw the appropriate inferences.

Working-memory Capacity

Working-memory capacity is another possible resource that could account for individual differences in reading skill. The term **working memory** refers to a conception of short-term memory that includes both storage and computational functions. Most theories assume that short-term memory plays an important role in reading. However, measures of short-term memory span, such as the ability to recall a list of digits or unrelated words, are not significantly correlated with reading comprehension performance. A possible reason for the low correlation may be that span measures are primarily tests of passive storage capacity. For example, in a digit-span test, the subject must encode a string of digits and try to maintain some record of their order of occurrence. By contrast, working memory reflects a conception of short-term memory that includes computations. Moreover, the computational and storage functions may trade off against each other (Baddeley & Hitch, 1974). A computationally demanding task may leave less capacity for storing information, and vice versa. For example, a person will be able to retain fewer digits if she must also compute their running total. This conception of working memory can be applied to reading skill differences.

One study hypothesized that skilled readers have greater working-memory capacity in reading than less skilled readers (Daneman & Carpenter, 1980). The greater capacity for computing and storing information may arise from a variety of sources, rather than a single one. For the good reader, many processes may be both faster and more automatic, such as encoding, lexical access, and semantic and syntactic analysis. Working-memory capacity is a property of the processing system that is the aggregate of several factors that could contribute to individual differences in reading. A good reader may have a larger functional capacity of working memory than the poor reader, for a number of different reasons. A measure of working-memory capacity provides the aggregation that encompasses the multidimensionality of individual differences in reading.

This hypothesis was explored by constructing a test that required both the processing and storage functions of working memory to be used (Daneman & Carpenter, 1980). The test, called the **reading-span test,** required subjects to read a group of unrelated sentences and, at the end of the group, recall the final word of each sentence. For example, consider this group of two sentences:

When at last his eyes opened, there was no gleam of triumph, no shade of anger.

The taxi turned up Michigan Avenue where they had a clear view of the lake.

After reading these two sentences, the subject was to recall the words *anger* and *lake*. A reader was presented with groups containing two to seven sentences to determine the largest group size from which he could reliably recall all of the sentence-final words. The largest such group size was defined as his reading span. The rationale behind the test was that the comprehension processes used in reading the sentences would consume less of the working-memory resources of the better readers. This would leave the better readers with more capacity to store the sentence-final words.

The reading spans of college students, which ranged from 2 to 5.5, were highly correlated with their reading comprehension test scores, with these correlations lying between 0.5 and 0.6 in various experiments. The correlation with reading span was even higher when specific comprehension abilities were considered individually. For example, the ability to answer a factual question about a passage was correlated between 0.7 and 0.9 with reading span in various studies. The correlation between conventional digit-span or word-span tests and reading comprehension was considerably lower, as it usually is. Thus, the reading span, unlike indices of pure storage capacity, seems to measure something that is strongly associated with reading comprehension performance.

A separate experiment examined how a large working-memory capacity could facilitate particular facets of reading comprehension. Having a large working-memory capacity would permit a reader to store a greater number of recently processed propositions in an activated state. This would be an advantage whenever there was a need to relate a newly read proposition to another one earlier in the passage. In the experiment, college subjects read passages, such as the one in Figure 15.7; some of the passages contained a pronoun that had to be related to a referent that had been mentioned some number of sentences previously. In the experiment, the number of sentences that intervened between the mention of the referent and the pronoun varied from two to seven.

Readers with larger reading spans were better at assigning the pronoun to the referent mentioned several sentences previously in the text. Moreover, the maximal distance across which a reader correctly assigned the pronoun was closely re-

---

Sitting with Richie, Archie, Walter and the rest of my gang in the Grill yesterday, I began to feel uneasy. Robbie had put a dime in the juke box. It was blaring one of the latest "Rock and Roll" favorites. I was studying, in horror, the reactions of my friends to the music. I was especially perturbed by the expression on my best friend's face. Wayne looked intense and was pounding the table furiously to the beat. Now, I like most of the things other teenager boys like. I like girls with soft blonde hair, girls with dark curly hair, in fact all girls. I like milkshakes, football games and beach parties. I like denim jeans, fancy T-shirts and sneakers. It is not that I dislike rock music but I think it is supposed to be fun and not taken too seriously. And here he was, "all shook up" and serious over the crazy music.

1. Who was "all shook up" and serious over the music?
2. Where was the gang sitting?
3. Who put money in the juke box?

Figure 15.7 Readers with small reading spans had difficulty answering the questions that followed this passage. *Source:* Daneman & Carpenter, 1980, Table 1, p. 455. Used with permission of Academic Press.

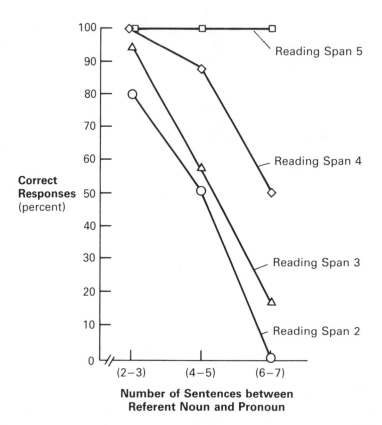

Figure 15.8 The ability of people with different spans to correctly associate a pronoun with its referent. Readers with large spans (span 5) always made the correct association. Readers with small spans began making errors when too many sentences intervened between the pronoun and the prior referent. *Source:* Daneman & Carpenter, 1980, Figure 1, p. 456. Used with permission of Academic Press.

lated to his reading span, as shown in Figure 15.8. These results suggest that a larger reading-span score indicates the ability to store and integrate a larger portion of text during reading comprehension. Relating a pronoun to its referent is one type of integration process used in constructing a referential representation of the text. As described in Chapter 7, the referential representation is particularly important to comprehension. Readers with larger reading spans were better able to keep track of information in this representation. More generally, the conglomeration of processes that produces the larger reading span also produces a larger working-memory capacity that facilitates reading comprehension.

Home and School Background

So far in this chapter, we have described the processes and structures that account for individual differences in reading skill. In addition, educational and family experiences can foster the development of reading skill. Home and school backgrounds have typically been evaluated with survey studies, such as the large-scale survey taken in 1970 by the International Association for the Evaluation of Educational Achievement (Purves, Harnisch, Quirk, & Bauer, 1981). The study tested students from several countries on a number of school subjects, including reading and literature. The students tested were 10-year-olds, 14-year-olds, and 17-year-olds (who were still in school). In addition, the study surveyed the students' home background, school environment, and reading-related habits (such as television watching or reading for pleasure).

The goal of the study was to discern some features of the home or school environment that seemed to promote good reading skills. No single characteristic uniquely differentiated good readers from poor ones. For example, fathers' occupations (an index of socioeconomic status) were highly related to reading skill. Fathers with prestigious or high-paying jobs tended to have children who were good readers. Not surprisingly, fathers' occupations were related to many other variables, such as the size of the family and the type of school, so no particular characteristic was uniquely related to reading achievement. Nevertheless, the pattern of characteristics for elementary students (10-year-olds) was summarized as follows:

> High scorers tend to be girls from small families whose fathers have relatively high status jobs and which leave the child alone. They tend to be advanced in grade and in more academically oriented schools, with fewer teachers' aides, newer principals, and a dormant PTA. They are eager for school, read a fair amount, watch less television than others, and do well in other subjects. (Purves, Harnisch, Quirk, & Bauer, 1981, p. 48)

Similar patterns emerged for the junior high and high school students:

> Better readers come from higher socio-cultural homes. They read, do their homework, have high aspirations, and like literature. Their schools have a high retention rate, are strictly evaluated, and have well-trained teachers. (Purves, Harnisch, Quirk, & Bauer, 1981, p. 48)

Thus, general language exposure, both at home and school, is important to good performance. Purves made a point of refuting earlier summaries of these data that had attributed achievement primarily to the home background, rather than the school. He argued that both the home and school had effects. "Opportunity to learn appears as a phenomenon occurring in home and in school; it may occur in rich and poor, but its hallmarks are the same" (Purves, Harnisch, Quirk, & Bauer, 1981, p. 77).

This survey focused on the importance of reading experience in developing good reading skills. On the other hand, the relation between reading skill and reading experience is not unidirectional. It seems equally likely that poor reading skills may incline a reader to avoid reading. Poor readers prefer to receive information such as directions or instructions in oral form, rather than in written form (Sticht, 1977). Thus, reading skills and reading habits interactively contribute to reading performance. Poor readers need some way to break this cycle. They must learn to read well enough to make reading enjoyable.

Reading Tests

The analysis of individual differences has been influenced to a large, if unacknowledged, extent by standardized reading comprehension tests. Such tests are used to categorize subjects as good readers or poor readers in research on individual differences. Thus, the score on a standardized reading comprehension test represents the construct of reading skill. Such tests are also of obvious educational importance to schools, students, and parents. Because of their role in both research and educational practice, we will describe how such tests are constructed and evaluate their strengths and weaknesses from the perspective of understanding individual differences.

Norm-referenced Approaches

The conventional way to evaluate a reader's performance on a reading comprehension test is to compare his score to a set of normative scores obtained by some large sample of students. This kind of standardized test is called **norm referenced.** Such tests indicate how well the test taker has performed relative to some sample population, but they provide little insight into the processes that resulted in the particular score.

An example of some items from a typical reading comprehension test illustrates some features of such tests. Figure 15.9 shows an example of a passage and questions taken from a nationwide test; the items were later released to the public by the National Assessment of Educational Progress (1973). The two items differ in the type of information they attempt to elicit. The first question tests whether the reader was able to glean the significant facts. The second question requires that the reader identify the tone or style of the passage.

Directions: Read the story and answer the question which follows it.

The wind whistled woefully as it wound its way through the nearly leafless trees. The pale yellow moon cast eerie shadows as it slipped in and out from behind the clouds like a blinking flashlight. Strange figures could be seen dashing and darting through the streets. Ghosts, goblins—what could they be? What do they want? Whom have they come to haunt? Beware . . .

Question type: Gleaning significant facts

What does the author compare the moon to?

1. Clouds.   2. A flashlight.   3. Ghosts.
4. Shadows.   5. The wind.   6. I don't know.

Question type: Critical reading

The mood or feeling of this story is

1. amusing.   2. frightening.   3. gay.
4. ridiculous.   5. sad.   6. I don't know.

Figure 15.9   Example of a passage and questions from a typical norm-referenced reading test. *Source:* National Assessment of Educational Progress, 1973, p. 83.

As this example suggests, test publishers try to include questions that tap a number of different types of information. In fact, different standardized reading comprehension tests tend to probe for the same categories of information. The descriptions of three widely used tests of reading comprehension (National Assessment of Educational Progress, 1973; unpublished guidelines for the *Scholastic Aptitude Test* from the Educational Testing Service; and the description of the *International Educational Achievement Tests* [Purves, Harnisch, Quirk, & Bauer, 1981]) converged on the following four categories:

1. understanding important facts;
2. abstracting the passage's main point;
3. making inferences that the author intended; and
4. analyzing the passage's organization.

Two of the three descriptions referred to two additional categories:

5. reading critically to evaluate the passage's logic; and
6. recognizing the passage's tone and style.

The particular categories of information to be probed are often developed in consultation with a panel of educators. Thus, the categories reflect consensual agreement about what readers should be able to do. This aspect of the test-construction process tends to result in tests that have **content validity;** that is, the test's content and format seem reasonably related to the construct that is purportedly being tested—namely, reading skill.

What do standardized tests measure? Performance on reading comprehension tests—or more generally, verbal ability tests—is correlated with high school and college grades. In fact, verbal ability tests are one of the best single predictors of academic success (Lavin, 1965, cited in Hunt, Lunneborg, & Lewis, 1975). A high correlation between test scores and subsequent academic or job performance is evidence of a test's **predictive validity.** But as many have pointed out, predictive validity does not ensure that the test measures the skill that it purports to measure. For example, the correlation could result from the fact that the test measures how successfully a student has absorbed academic information to that point, information that is also a cornerstone for future academic performance. Another possible explanation for the correlation is that the format of reading tests is very similar to that of conventional academic tests; in both cases, the student is required to answer substantive questions under speeded conditions. Thus, even though reading tests tend to be correlated with future grades, the correlation by itself does not provide firm evidence that the tests are good measures of reading skill.

Careful examinations of the content of reading comprehension tests have found serious flaws in at least some tests as instruments to measure reading skill. In some standardized tests, students can answer some of the questions without relying on the comprehension passage, using instead their world knowledge or inadvertent cues in other questions. As a result, students can perform at better than chance level even if they answer the questions without being presented the passage (Pyrczak, 1972; Tuinman, 1973–74). Another imperfection in some tests is that some of the incorrect response alternatives in the multiple-choice format are implausible answers. Unsurprisingly, the presence of implausible response alternatives helps children pick the correct response (Drum, Calfee, & Cook, 1981). Being able to select a response on the basis of its plausibility is not an important component of reading ability.

Generally speaking, standardized tests of reading comprehension are constructed relatively atheoretically. Test constructors are given guidelines about what types of information to probe (such as the six categories described previously), along with previous versions of the test that have been validated, and they are expected to construct new items of the same genre. There is no formal consideration of the processes required to understand the passage or to answer the questions. For example, the test constructor has no detailed model of how a reader analyzes the passage's organization, even though an item must be constructed to test this ability. New test items constructed in this fashion are then validated by determining if performance on the new items is correlated with performance on previously validated items. Items that do not meet this criterion during the development of the test are simply deleted from the final version. In addition, the predictive validity of the new version of the test, its correlation with other measures of academic performance, may be checked. Thus, the focus of the test development is on the statistical properties of the resulting test scores. Test development shows little concern for understanding the psychological processes that readers use in comprehending the test.

Criterion-referenced Approaches

Among the dissatisfactions with norm-referenced tests of reading comprehension is that they select reading passages and comprehension questions unsystematically. As an alternative, some educators and researchers have proposed that reading tests should be constructed with materials that are more objectively specified. This is a **criterion-referenced** approach (Glaser, 1963). The passage characteristics are usually specified in terms of the type of source from which it is taken (such as an insurance policy or instructions for installing a kitchen appliance), not in terms of its linguistic properties.

Although the criterion-referenced testing approach could be applied to many kinds of reading skill, in practice, it has been applied almost exclusively to assessing the kind of basic reading skills needed in day-to-day life, such as understanding the instructions on government forms, job applications, notices, or schedules. Criterion-referenced tests containing such materials are intended to assess **functional literacy.** Figure 15.10 illustrates the type of item used in a functional literacy test. If a reader can understand such materials, then he should have sufficient skills to read adequately in his day-to-day life.

One of the early functional literacy tests assessed reading skills in such tasks as completing the applications for Social Security benefits, a personal bank loan, public assistance, Medicaid, and a driver's license (Louis Harris & Associates, 1970). The study found that 8 percent of the representative sample of 1,685 people could not correctly answer over 80 percent of the questions. The implication was that 8 percent of the population were seriously handicapped by their inadequate skills. A more recent study by the National Assessment of Educational Progress (1975) classified about 13 percent of the 17-year-old high school students as being illiterate by the criterion that they answered less than 75 percent of the questions correctly.

Look at this poster about equal opportunity. The XYZ Company has 20 employees. It has a contract with the Federal government. Suppose a job applicant to this company believes he has been discriminated against because of his religion. Circle the address of the agency he should contact.

Title VII of the Civil Rights Act of 1964
Administered by

THE EQUAL EMPLOYMENT OPPORTUNITY COMMISSION

Prohibits discrimination because of RACE, COLOR, RELIGION, SEX or NATIONAL ORIGIN

By EMPLOYERS with 75 or more employees, by LABOR ORGANIZATIONS with a hiring hall of 75 or more members, by EMPLOYMENT AGENCIES, and by JOINT LABOR-MANAGEMENT COMMITTEES FOR APPRENTICESHIP OR TRAINING. After July 1, 1967, employers and labor organizations with 50 or more employees or members will be covered, after July 1, 1968, those with 25 or more will be covered.

ANY PERSON
who believes he or she has been discriminated against
SHOULD CONTACT

THE EQUAL EMPLOYMENT OPPORTUNITY COMMISSION
1800 G Street, N.W.
Washington, D. C. 20506

Executive Order Number 11246
Administered by

THE OFFICE OF FEDERAL CONTRACT COMPLIANCE

Prohibits discrimination because of RACE, COLOR, CREED or NATIONAL ORIGIN, and requires affirmative action to ensure equality of opportunity in all aspects of employment.

By all FEDERAL GOVERNMENT CONTRACTORS AND SUBCONTRACTORS, and by CONTRACTORS PERFORMING WORK UNDER A FEDERALLY ASSISTED CONSTRUCTION CONTRACT, regardless of the number of employees in either case.

ANY PERSON
who believes he or she has been discriminated against
SHOULD CONTACT

THE OFFICE OF FEDERAL CONTRACT COMPLIANCE
U.S. Department of Labor
Washington, D. C. 20210

Figure 15.10   An example of a functional literacy test item that is often answered incorrectly. *Source:* Item reproduced by permission of Educational Testing Service.

Fisher (1978, 1981) argued that these estimates of illiteracy rates were too high because of inappropriate treatment of the data. He pointed out that some of the questions were so unclear that even educated professionals often answered them incorrectly, suggesting that these questions be omitted from consideration. Fisher also suggested that some percentage of failures (1 percent) could be due to boredom or fatigue during the test administration. When Fisher reanalyzed the data with such considerations factored in, he found that the estimate of functional illiteracy among high school graduates was between 0.6 and 7 percent. These estimates are less discouraging than the 8 to 13 percent originally estimated, but they are still somewhat sobering, given the minimal criterion set by the functional literacy tests. More discouraging still is Fisher's point that high school graduates are not the ones with the greatest literacy problems. Rather, the ones with severe literacy problems are those who repeat grades and drop out of school prior to graduation (as many as 25 percent of the students who enter high school, by some estimates). This group consistently has lower achievement scores than students who stay in school.

Problems with the functional literacy approach The functional literacy criterion-referenced approach, like the norm-referenced approach, does not illuminate why readers obtain the scores they obtain. The test results do not indicate *why* readers make an error—whether it is due to lack of word-recognition skill, general comprehension skills, lack of topic knowledge, or problems in reasoning and memory. All of these components can play a role in a reading task, but the relative sizes of the contributions of each of these components to the problem of illiteracy is unknown. Identifying the comprehension components that are most responsible for low scores is important if functional literacy tests are to provide educational implications.

A second problem with functional literacy tests is that they contain passages and questions that are difficult to understand for reasons other than illiteracy. This problem is illustrated by the finding that some items on functional literacy tests are missed by a high proportion of people who are very good readers (Fisher, 1981). For example, the National Assessment of Educational Progress (1975) found three items on its functional literacy test that were missed by a large proportion of superior readers (a sample of high school graduates who scored above the ninety-fourth percentile on the *College Entrance Examination Board* reading test). One item was a replica of an automobile insurance policy; the second was an application for enrolling in a book club; and the third was a replica of a traffic ticket. Inclusion of such items in the test provides a faithful sample of the kinds of reading problems encountered in everyday life but does not help to evaluate the literacy of the person taking the test.

The criterion-referenced functional literacy approach and the norm-referenced approach do not illuminate what makes someone a good or poor reader. However, in their defense, it may be said that many of the tests do not have this goal. Their goal is related primarily to their predictive validity, that is, to be instruments for assessing achievement or aptitude (see Glaser & Bond, 1981). However, illuminating the nature of individual differences is one of the goals of a psychological and educational approach to comprehension.

The analysis of reading presented in this book suggests that tests can be constructed to meet the goal of providing diagnostic information about the source of reading difficulty. Verbal ability tests sometimes separately assess vocabulary knowledge and grammatical proficiency. However, the reading comprehension test could provide information about specific reading processes. First, a test could provide a separate measure of word-recognition skill to assess its speed and accuracy. Second, it could assess listening comprehension in comparison to reading comprehension, which would help distinguish people who have a specific reading difficulty, such as dyslexics, from those who have more general problems with language and reasoning. Third, the test could be more analytic in examining the reader's comprehension processes, such as the processes related to syntactic and semantic analysis and processes related to the text and referential level. An example of such a test is the one described in Chapter 5 on syntactic analysis that detected the syntactic dysfunction of Broca's aphasics. Fourth, the test could compare the reader's performance on passages on a familiar topic versus an unfamiliar topic, which would assess the individual's ability to apply her knowledge in making inferences and guiding comprehension. One of the benefits of a theory of reading is that it provides guidelines for assessing reading ability.

Summary

The existence of individual differences in reading skill has important implications for other aspects of education because reading is a major medium of acquiring knowledge and skills. A poor reader not only has difficulty in English literature; he will have difficulty in history, economics, and science, as well.

Current research underscores the importance of fluency in word recognition. Good readers tend to be faster than poor readers at word recognition. Context effects on word-recognition speed are not a major source of differences among readers. However, context effects are larger for poor readers than for good readers because poor readers take longer to encode and lexically access words using perceptual information. While good readers also have a better vocabulary than poor readers, vocabulary differences are probably a result of differences in reading comprehension, rather than a cause.

In addition to word recognition, there may be bottlenecks in high-level comprehension processes. As readers progress through school, their reading and listening skills tend to become highly correlated. This suggests that differences in reading skill may be attributed to processes and structures that are shared by listening and reading. One example of such a process is identifying the main theme of a passage. A training program that taught this skill resulted in dramatic improvements in the reading skills of poor readers, improvements that were both general and long lasting.

Two other sources of individual differences in reading skill are topic knowledge and working-memory capacity. Differences in the availability of a schema can profoundly influence a reader's ability to organize the information he has read or draw the appropriate inferences. Another source of individual differences is working-memory capacity, a term that stresses the computational aspects of reading, in addition to its storage role. A measure of working-memory capacity, the reading-span test, consistently correlates with reading ability. A measure of working-memory capacity may indicate the degree to which a reader has automated a number of comprehension processes required to understand text.

Finally, many of the theories of individual differences rely on standardized tests of reading comprehension to classify the level of a person's reading skill. These comprehension tests include two major types: norm-referenced and criterion-referenced tests. Neither type provides insights into the processes that account for differences among readers.

Suggested Readings

Hunt's question What does it mean to be high verbal? (1978; Hunt, Lunneborg, & Lewis, 1975) is partly responsible for sparking the current interest in individual differences in reading. A more detailed exploration of the role of word recognition in reading may be found in a monograph recently published by Perfetti (1985). A series of volumes edited by Sternberg (1982, 1984, 1985), *Advances in the Psychology of Human Intelligence,* and the papers in Resnick (1976) present a variety of approaches to individual differences in reading and other cognitive skills.

Cronbach (1957, 1975) issued a now-classic call for experimental and psychometric researchers to join forces in exploring individual differences. While the gap has narrowed, the two fields are still quite distinct. The *American Psychologist* devoted a special issue (1981, No. 10) to *Testing: Concepts, Policy, Practice, and Research* (Glaser & Bond, 1981). The articles provide an excellent overview of test construction, interpretation difficulties, and impacts on educational and public policy decisions, as well as the new links between the field of psychometric testing and cognitive research.

References

Allen, J. (1973). Reading machines for the blind: The technical problems and the methods adopted for their solution. *IEEE Transactions on Audio and Electroacoustics, 21,* 259–264.

Allen, J. (1976). Synthesis of speech from unrestricted text. *Proceedings of the IEEE, 64,* 433–442.

Allport, D. A. (1979). Word recognition in reading: A tutorial review. In P. A. Kolers, H. Bouma, & M. Wrolstad (Eds.), *Processing of visible language* (Vol. 1). New York: Plenum Press.

Alpern, M. (1962). Muscular mechanisms. In H. Davson (Ed.), *The Eye* (Vol. 3). New York: Academic Press.

Anderson, J. R. (1974). Verbatim and propositional representation of sentences in immediate and long-term memory. *Journal of Verbal Learning and Verbal Behavior, 13,* 149–162.

Anderson, J. R. (1976). *Language, memory, and thought.* Hillsdale, NJ: Erlbaum.

Anderson, J. R. (1982). Acquisition of cognitive skill. *Psychological Review, 89,* 369–406.

Anderson, J. R. (1983). *The architecture of cognition.* Cambridge, MA: Harvard University Press.

Anderson, J. R. (1985). *Cognitive psychology and its implications* (2nd ed.). New York: Freeman.

Anderson, J. R., Kline, P., & Lewis, C. (1977). A production system model of language processing. In M. A. Just & P. A. Carpenter (Eds.), *Cognitive processes in comprehension.* Hillsdale, NJ: Erlbaum.

Anderson, R. C., & Biddle, W. B. (1975). On asking people questions about what they are reading. In G. Bower (Ed.), *Psychology of learning and motivation* (Vol. 9). New York: Academic Press.

Anderson, R. C., & Kulhavy, R. W. (1972). Learning concepts from definitions. *American Educational Research Journal, 9,* 385–390.

Anderson, R. C., & McGaw, B. (1973). On the representation of the meanings of general terms. *Journal of Experimental Psychology, 101,* 301–306.

Anderson, R. C., & Ortony, A. (1975). On putting apples into bottles—A problem of polysemy. *Cognitive Psychology, 7,* 167–180.

Anderson, R. C., Osborn, J., & Tierney, R. J. (Eds.). (1984). *Learning to read in American schools: Basal readers and content texts.* Hillsdale, NJ: Erlbaum.

Anderson, R. C., Pichert, J. W., Goetz, E. T., Shallert, D. L., Stevens, K. W., & Trollip, S. R. (1976). Instantiation of general terms. *Journal of Verbal Learning and Verbal Behavior, 15,* 667–679.

Anderson, T. H. (1980). Study strategies and adjunct aids. In R. J. Spiro, B. C. Bruce, & W. F. Brewer (Eds.), *Theoretical issues in reading comprehension: Perspectives from cognitive psychology, linguistics, artificial intelligence, and education.* Hillsdale, NJ: Erlbaum.

Anderson, T. H., & Armbruster, B. B. (1984). Studying. In P. D. Pearson, R. Barr, M. L. Kamil, & P. Mosenthal (Eds.) *Handbook of reading research.* New York: Longman.

Anglin, J. M. (1970). *The growth of word meaning* (MIT Research Monograph No. 63). Cambridge, MA: The MIT Press.

Applebee, A. N. (1971). Research in reading retardation: Two critical problems. *Journal of Child Psychology and Psychiatry, 12,* 91–113.

Asch, S. E., & Nerlove, H. (1960). The development of double function terms in children. In B. Kaplan & S. Wapner (Eds.), *Perspectives in psychological theory.* New York: International Universities Press.

Ausubel, D. P. (1960). The use of advance organizers in the learning and retention of meaningful verbal material. *Journal of Educational Psychology, 51,* 266–274.

Baddeley, A. D. (1979). Working memory and reading. In P. A. Kolers, M. Wrolstad, & H. Bouma (Eds.), *Processing of visible language* (Vol. 1). New York: Plenum Press.

Baddeley, A. D., & Hitch, G. (1974). Working memory. In G. H. Bower (Ed.), *The psychology of learning and motivation* (Vol. 8). New York: Academic Press.

Baddeley, A. D., & Lewis, V. J. (1981). Inner active processes in reading: The inner voice, the inner ear and the inner eye. In A. M. Lesgold & C. A. Perfetti (Eds.), *Interactive processes in reading.* Hillsdale, NJ: Erlbaum.

Ballantine, F. A. (1951). Age changes in measures of eye-movements in silent reading. In *Studies in the psychology of reading* (Monographs in Education, No. 4). Ann Arbor: University of Michigan Press.

Banks, W. P., Oka, E., & Shugarman, S. (1981). Recoding of printed words to internal speech: Does recoding come before lexical access? In O. J. L. Tzeng & H. Singer (Eds.), *Perception of print: Reading research in experimental psychology.* Hillsdale, NJ: Erlbaum.

Barclay, J. R., Bransford, J. D., Franks, J. J., McCarrell, N. S., & Nitsch, K. (1974). Comprehension and semantic flexibility. *Journal of Verbal Learning and Verbal Behavior, 13,* 471–481.

Barnes, B. R., & Clawson, E. U. (1975). Do advance organizers facilitate learning? Recommendations for further research based on an analysis of 32 studies. *Review of Educational Research, 45,* 637–659.

Barr, R. (1984). Beginning reading instruction: From debate to reformation. In P. D. Pearson, R. Baar, M. L. Kamil, & P. Mosenthal (Eds.), *Handbook of reading research.* New York: Longman.

Barron, R., & Baron, J. (1977). How children get meaning from printed words. *Child Development, 48,* 587–594.

Barrus, K., Brown, B. L., & Inouye, D. (1978, November). *Rapid reading reconsidered.* Paper presented at the meeting of the Psychonomic Society, San Antonio, TX.

Bartlett, F. C. (1932). *Remembering.* Cambridge: The University Press.

Beck, I. L. (1981). Reading problems and instructional practices. In T. S. Waller & G. E. MacKinnon (Eds.), *Reading research: Advances in theory and practice* (Vol. 2). New York: Academic Press.

Beck, I. L., McKeown, M. G., McCaslin, E. S., & Burkes, A. M. (1979). *Instructional dimensions that may affect reading comprehension: Examples from two commercial reading programs* (LRDC Publication 1979/20). Pittsburgh: University of Pittsburgh, Learning Research and Development Center.

Beck, I. L., McKeown, M. G., & Omanson, R. C. (1984, April). The fertility of some types of vocabulary instruction. In R. Glaser (Chair), *What is the role of instruction in learning and using vocabulary?* Symposium conducted at the meeting of the American Educational Research Association, New Orleans, LA.

Beck, I. L., Omanson, R. C., & McKeown, M. G. (1982). An instructional redesign of reading lessons: Effects on comprehension. *Reading Research Quarterly, 17,* 462–481.

Beck, I. L., Perfetti, C. A., & McKeown, M. G. (1982). The effects of long-term vocabulary instruction on lexical access and reading comprehension. *Journal of Educational Psychology, 74,* 506–521.

Becker, C. A. (1979). Semantic context and word frequency effects in visual word recognition. *Journal of Experimental Psychology: Human Perception and Performance, 5,* 252–259.

Becker, C. A., & Killion, T. H. (1977). Interaction of visual and cognitive effects in word recognition. *Journal of Experimental Psychology: Human Perception and Performance, 3,* 389–401.

Becker, W., & Jurgens, R. (1979). An analysis of the saccadic system by means of double-step stimuli. *Vision Research, 19,* 967–983.

Bender, L. A. (1957). Specific reading disability as a maturational lag. *Bulletin of the Orton Society, 7,* 9–18.

Benton, A. L. (1962). Dyslexia in relation to form perception and directional sense. In J. Money (Ed.), *Reading disability: Progress and research needs in dyslexia.* Baltimore: Johns Hopkins Press.

Benton, A. L. (1975). Developmental dyslexia: Neurological aspects. In W. J. Friedlander

(Ed.), *Advances in neurology* (Vol. 7). New York: Raven Press.

Benton, A. L. (1978). Some conclusions about dyslexia. In A. Benton & D. Pearl (Eds.), *Dyslexia*. New York: Oxford University Press.

Benton, A. L., & Pearl, D. P. (Eds.). (1978). *Dyslexia: An appraisal of current knowledge.* New York: Oxford University Press.

Berko, J. (1958). The child's learning of English morphology. *Word, 14,* 150–177.

Berndt, R. S., & Caramazza, A. (1980). A redefinition of the syndrome of Broca's aphasia: Implications for neuropsychological model of language. *Applied Psycholinguistics, 1,* 225–278.

Berry, J. (1977). 'The making of alphabets' revisited. In J. Fishman (Ed.), *Advances in the creation and revision of writing systems.* The Hague, the Netherlands: Mouton.

Bertin, J. (1983). *Seminology of graphs* (W. J. Berg, Trans.). Madison: University of Wisconsin Press.

Berwick, R. C., & Weinberg, A. S. (1983). The role of grammars in models of language use. *Cognition, 13,* 1–61.

Bever, T. (1970). The cognitive basis for linguistic structures. In J. R. Hayes (Ed.), *Cognition and the development of language.* New York: Wiley.

Biemiller, A. J. (1970). The development of the use of graphic and contextual information as children learn to read. *Reading Research Quarterly, 6,* 76–96.

Biggins, C. M., & Uhler, S. (1978). Is there a "workable" word decoding system? *Reading Improvement, 15,* 47–55.

Birch, H. G., & Belmont, L. (1964). Auditory-visual integration in normal and retarded readers. *American Journal of Orthopsychiatry, 34,* 852–861.

Bissantz, A. S., & Johnson, K. A. (1985). *Language files* (3rd ed.). Reynoldsburg, OH: Advocate Publishing Group.

Black, J. B., & Bern, H. (1981). Causal coherence and memory for events in narratives. *Journal of Verbal Learning and Verbal Behavior, 20,* 276–275.

Black, J. B., & Wilensky, R. (1979). An evaluation of story grammars. *Cognitive Science, 3,* 213–230.

Blank, M. A., & Foss, D. J. (1978). Semantic facilitation and lexical access during sentence processing. *Memory & Cognition, 6,* 644–652.

Bloomfield, L., & Barnhart, C. L. (1961). *Let's read, a linguistic approach.* Detroit: Wayne State University Press.

Bobrow, S. A., & Bower, G. H. (1969). Comprehension and recall of sentences. *Journal of Experimental Psychology, 80,* 455–461.

Boder, E. (1970). Developmental dyslexia: A new diagnostic approach based on the identification of three subtypes. *Journal of School Health, 40,* 289–290.

Boder, E. (1971). Developmental dyslexia: Prevailing diagnostic concepts and a new diagnostic approach. In H. R. Myklebust (Ed.), *Progress in learning disabilities.* New York: Grune and Stratton.

Boder, E. (1973). Developmental dyslexia: A diagnostic approach based on three atypical reading-spelling patterns. *Developmental Medicine and Child Neurology, 15,* 663–687.

Bolinger, D. (1965). The automization of meaning. *Language, 41,* 555–573.

Bond, G. L., & Dykstra, R. (1967). The cooperative research program in first-grade reading instruction. *Reading Research Quarterly, 2,* 5–142.

Borges, M. A., & Sawyers, B. K. (1974). Common verbal quantifiers: Usage and interpretation. *Journal of Experimental Psychology, 102,* 335–338.

Boring, E. G. (1950). *A history of experimental psychology* (2nd ed). New York: Appleton-Century-Crofts.

Bouma, H. (1970). Interaction effects in parafoveal letter recognition. *Nature, 226,* 177–178.

Bouma, H., & deVoogd, A. H. (1974). On the control of eye saccades in reading. *Vision Research, 14,* 273–284.

Bower, G. H. (1970). Analysis of a mnemonic device. *American Scientist, 58,* 496–510.

Bower, G. H. (1972a). A selective review of organizational factors in memory. In E. Tulving & W. Donaldson (Eds.), *Organization and memory.* New York: Academic Press.

Bower, G. H. (1972b). Mental imagery and associative learning. In L. W. Gregg (Ed.), *Cognition in learning and memory.* New York: John Wiley & Sons.

Bower, G. H., Black, J. B., & Turner, T. J. (1979). Scripts in memory for text. *Cognitive Psychology, 11,* 177–220.

Bower, G. H., Gilligan, S. G., & Monteiro, K. P. (1981). Selectivity of learning caused by affective states. *Journal of Experimental Psy-*

chology: General, 110, 451–473.

Bower, T. G. R. (1970). Reading by eye. In H. Levin & J. P. Williams (Eds.), *Basic studies on reading.* New York: Basic Books.

Brady, M. E., & Strater, D. (1974, December). *A further exploration of how increases in knowledge of specific words are related to the comprehension of prose from which the words are drawn.* Paper presented at the annual meeting of the National Reading Conference, Kansas City, MO.

Bransford, J. D., Barclay, J. R., & Franks, J. J. (1972). Sentence memory: A constructive versus interpretive approach. *Cognitive Psychology, 3,* 193–209.

Bransford, J. D., & Johnson, M. K. (1973). Considerations of some problems of comprehension. In W. G. Chase (Ed.), *Visual information processing.* New York: Academic Press.

Bransford, J. D., Stein, B. S., Shelton, T. S., & Owings, R. A. (1981). Cognition and adaptation: The importance of learning to learn. In J. Harvey (Ed.), *Cognition, social behavior, and the environment.* Hillsdale, NJ: Erlbaum.

Brewer, W. F. (1980). Literary theory, rhetoric, and stylistics: Implications for psychology. In R. J. Spiro, B. C. Bruce, & W. F. Brewer (Eds.), *Theoretical issues in reading comprehension: Perspectives from cognitive psychology, linguistics, artificial intelligence, and education.* Hillsdale, NJ: Erlbaum.

Brim, B. J. (1968). Impact of a reading improvement program. *The Journal of Educational Research, 62,* 177–182.

Brimer, M. A. (1973). Methodological problems of research. In J. Downing (Ed.), *Comparative reading: Cross-national studies of behavior and processes in reading and writing.* New York: Macmillan.

Brooks, C., & Warren, R. P. (1970). *Modern rhetoric* (3rd ed.). New York: Harcourt, Brace, and World.

Brooks, L. (1977). Visual pattern in fluent word identification. In A. S. Reber & D. L. Scarborough (Eds.), *Toward a psychology of reading.* Hillsdale, NJ: Erlbaum.

Brooks, L., & Miller, A. (1979). A comparison of explicit and implicit knowledge of an alphabet. In P. A. Kolers, M. E. Wrolstad, & H. Bouma (Eds.), *Processing of visible language* (Vol. 1). New York: Plenum Press.

Brown, A. L. (1980). Metacognitive development and reading. In R. J. Spiro, B. C. Bruce, & W. F. Brewer (Eds.), *Theoretical issues in reading comprehension: Perspectives from cognitive psychology, linguistics, artificial intelligence, and education.* Hillsdale, NJ: Erlbaum.

Brown, A. L., Bransford, J. D., Ferrara, R. A., & Campione, J. C. (1983). Learning, remembering and understanding. In J. H. Flavell & E. M. Markman (Eds.), *Carmichael's manual of child psychology* (Vol. 3). New York: Wiley.

Brown, A. L., & Smiley, S. S. (1978). The development of strategies for studying texts. *Child Development, 49,* 1076–1088.

Brown, R. (1970). Psychology and reading: Commentary on chapters 5 to 10. In H. Levin & J. P. Williams (Eds.), *Basic studies on reading.* New York: Basic Books.

Bruner, J. S., & O'Dowd, D. (1958). A note on the informativeness of parts of words. *Language and Speech, 1,* 98–101.

Bruning, R. H. (1968). Effects of review and testlike events within the learning of prose material. *Journal of Educational Psychology, 59,* 16–19.

Buswell, G. T. (1922). *Fundamental reading habits, a study of their development.* Chicago: Chicago University Press.

Buswell, G. T. (1937). *How adults read.* Chicago: Chicago University Press.

Cairns, H. S. (1984). Current issues in research in language comprehension. In R. Naremore (Ed.), *Recent advances in language sciences.* San Diego: College Hill Press.

Calfee, R. C. (1977). Assessment of independent reading skills: Basic research and practical applications. In A. S. Reber & D. L. Scarborough (Eds.), *Toward a psychology of reading.* Hillsdale, NJ: Erlbaum.

Calfee, R. C., Chapman, R., & Venezky, R. (1972). How a child needs to think to learn to read. In L. W. Gregg (Ed.), *Cognition in learning and memory.* New York: John Wiley & Sons.

Calfee, R. C., & Pointkowski, D. C. (1981). The reading diary: Acquisition of decoding. *Reading Research Quarterly, 16,* 346–373.

Canney, G., & Schreiner, R. (1977). A study of the effectiveness of selected syllabication rules and phonogram patterns for word attack. *Reading Research Quarterly, 12,* 102–124.

Caplan, D. (1972). Clause boundaries and recognition latencies for words in sentences. *Perception & Psychophysics, 12,* 73–76.

Caramazza, A., & Zurif, E. B. (1976). Dissociation of algorithmic and heuristic processes in language comprehension: Evidence from aphasia. *Brain and Language, 3,* 572–582.

Carducci-Bolchazy, M. (1977). A survey of reading readiness practice. *Reading Horizons, 17,* 255–259.

Carey, S. (1978). The child as a word learner. In M. Halle, J. Bresnan, & G. Miller (Eds.), *Linguistic theory and psychological reality.* Cambridge, MA: The MIT Press.

Carillo, L. W. (1976). *Teaching reading: A handbook.* New York: St. Martin's Press.

Carpenter, P. A., & Daneman, M. (1981). Lexical retrieval and error recovery in reading: A model based on eye fixations. *Journal of Verbal Learning and Verbal Behavior, 20,* 137–160.

Carpenter, P. A., & Just, M. A. (1975). Sentence comprehension: A psycholinguistic processing model of verification. *Psychological Review, 82,* 45–73.

Carpenter, P. A., & Just, M. A. (1977a). Integrative processes in comprehension. In D. LaBerge & J. Samuels (Eds.), *Basic processes in reading: Perception and comprehension.* Hillsdale, NJ: Erlbaum.

Carpenter, P. A., & Just, M. A. (1977b). Reading comprehension as eyes see it. In M. A. Just & P. A. Carpenter (Eds.), *Cognitive processes in comprehension.* Hillsdale, NJ: Erlbaum.

Carpenter, P. A., & Just, M. A. (1981). Cognitive processes in reading: Models based on readers' eye fixations. In A. M. Lesgold & C. A. Perfetti (Eds.), *Interactive processes in reading.* Hillsdale, NJ: Erlbaum.

Carpenter, P. A., & Just, M. A. (1983). What your eyes do while your mind is reading. In K. Rayner (Ed.), *Eye movements in reading: Perceptual and language processes.* New York: Academic Press.

Carpenter, P. A., Just, M. A., & McDonald, J. L. (1984). *Reading and processing differences between dyslexic and normal college students* (Technical Report). Pittsburgh: Carnegie-Mellon University, Department of Psychology.

Carroll, J. B. (1964). *Language and thought.* Englewood Cliffs, NJ: Prentice-Hall.

Carroll, J. B. (1971). Measurement properties of subjective magnitude estimates of word frequency. *Journal of Verbal Learning and Verbal Behavior, 10,* 722–729.

Carroll, J. B. (1972). Defining language comprehension: Some speculations. In R. O. Freedle & J. B. Carroll (Eds.), *Language comprehension and the acquisition of knowledge.* Washington, DC: Winston & Sons.

Carver, R. P. (1971). *Sense and nonsense in speed reading.* Silver Springs, MD: Revrac Publications.

Cattell, J. M. (1885). The inertia of the eye and brain. *Brain, 8,* 295–312.

Chafe, W. L. (1972). Discourse structure and human knowledge. In R. O. Freedle & J. B. Carroll (Eds.), *Language comprehension and the acquisition of knowledge.* Washington, DC: Winston & Sons.

Chall, J. S. (1967). *Learning to read: The great debate.* New York: McGraw-Hill.

Chase, W. G., & Ericsson, K. A. (1982). Skill and working memory. In W. G. Bower (Ed.), *The Psychology of Learning* (Vol. 16). New York: Academic Press.

Chase, W. G., & Simon, H. A. (1973). The mind's eye in chess. In W. G. Chase (Eds.), *Visual information processing.* New York: Academic Press.

Chiesi, H. L. Spilich, G. J., & Voss, J. F. (1979). Acquisition of domain-related information in relation to high and low domain knowledge. *Journal of Verbal Learning and Verbal Behavior, 18,* 257–274.

Chomsky, N. (1957). *Syntactic structures.* The Hague, the Netherlands: Mouton.

Chomsky, N., & Halle, M. (1968). *The sound pattern of English.* New York: Harper & Row.

Cirilo, R. K., & Foss, D. J. (1980). Text structure and reading time for sentences. *Journal of Verbal Learning and Verbal Behavior, 19,* 96–109.

Clark, H. H. (1975, June). Bridging. In R. Schank & B. Nash-Webber (Eds.), *Theoretical issues in natural language processing.* Proceedings of a conference at the Massachusetts Institute of Technology, Cambridge, MA.

Clark, H. H., & Clark, E. V. (1977). *Psychology and language.* New York: Harcourt Brace Jovanovich.

Clark, H. H., & Sengul, C. J. (1979). In search of referents for nouns and pronouns. *Memory & Cognition, 7,* 35–41.

Clay, M. M. (1972). *The early detection of reading difficulties: A diagnostic survey with recovery procedures* (2nd ed.). Auckland, New Zealand: Heinemann.

Cofer, C. N. (1977). On the constructive theory of memory. In I. C. Uzgiris & F. Weizmann (Eds.), *The structuring of experience.* New York: Plenum Press.

Collins, A. M., & Loftus, E. F. (1975). A spreading activation theory of semantic processing. *Psychological Review, 82,* 407–428.

Collins, A. M., & Quillian, M. R. (1969). Retrieval time from semantic memory. *Journal of Verbal Learning and Verbal Behavior, 8,* 240–248.

Coltheart, M. (1978). Lexical access in simple reading tasks. In G. Underwood (Ed.), *Strategies of information processing.* New York: Academic Press.

Coltheart, M. (1979). When can children learn to read—and when should they be taught? In T. G. Waller & G. E. MacKinnon (Eds.), *Reading research: Advances in theory and practice* (Vol. 1). New York: Academic Press.

Conrad, R. (1964). Acoustic confusions in immediate memory. *British Journal of Psychology, 55,* 75–84.

Conrad, R. (1977). The reading ability of deaf school-leavers. *British Journal of Educational Psychology, 47,* 138–148.

Cooper, W. E., & Walker, E. C. T. (1979). *Sentence processing: Psycholinguistic studies presented to Merrill Garrett.* Hillsdale, NJ: Erlbaum.

Corbett, A. T. (1984). Prenominal adjectives and the disambiguation of anaphoric nouns. *Journal of Verbal Learning and Verbal Behavior, 23,* 683–695.

Corbett, A. T., & Chang, F. R. (1983). Pronoun disambiguation: Accessing potential antecedents. *Memory & Cognition, 11,* 283–294.

Corbett, A. T., & Dosher, B. A. (1978). Instrument inferences in sentence encoding. *Journal of Verbal Learning and Verbal Behavior, 17,* 479–491.

Craik, F. I. M., & Lockhart, R. S. (1972). Levels of processing: A framework for memory research. *Journal of Verbal Learning and Verbal Behavior, 11,* 671–684.

Craik, F. I. M., & Tulving, E. (1975). Depth of processing and the retention of words in episodic memory. *Journal of Experimental Psychology: General, 104,* 268–294.

Critchley, M., & Critchley, E. A. (1978). *Dyslexia defined.* London: William Heinemann Medical Books, Ltd.

Cronbach, L. J. (1957). The two disciplines of scientific psychology. *American Psychologist, 12,* 671–684.

Cronbach, L. J. (1975). Beyond the two disciplines of scientific psychology. *American Psychologist, 30,* 116–127.

Crossman, E. R. F. W. (1959). A theory of the acquisition of speed-skill. *Ergonomics, 2,* 153–166.

Cunningham, P. M. (1975). Investigating a synthesized theory of mediated word identification. *Reading Research Quarterly, 11,* 127–143.

Cunningham, P. M. (1977). Supplying the missing links from consonant substitution to "real reading." *Reading Horizons, 17,* 279–282.

Cunningham, P. M. (1979). A compare/contrast theory of mediated word identification. *Reading Teacher, 32,* 774–778.

Cunningham, P. M., Cunningham, J. W., & Rystrom, R. C. (1981). A new syllabication strategy and reading achievement. *Reading World, 20,* 208–214.

Curtis, M. E. (1980). Development of components of reading skill. *Journal of Educational Psychology, 72,* 656–669.

Dale, E., & Razik, T. (1963). *Bibliography of vocabulary studies* (2nd ed.). Columbus, OH: Bureau of Educational Research and Service, Ohio State University.

Daneman, M., & Carpenter, P. A. (1980). Individual differences in working memory and reading. *Journal of Verbal Learning and Verbal Behavior, 19,* 450–466.

Daneman, M., & Carpenter, P. A. (1983a). *Developmental differences in reading and detecting semantic inconsistencies* (Technical Report). Pittsburgh: Carnegie-Mellon University.

Daneman, M., & Carpenter, P. A. (1983b). Individual differences in integrating information between and within sentences. *Journal of Experimental Psychology: Learning, Memory and Cognition, 9,* 561–584.

Dansereau, D. F. (1978). The development of a learning strategy curriculum. In H. F. O'Neil, Jr. (Ed.), *Learning strategies.* New York: Academic Press.

Dansereau, D. F. (1983). *Learning strategy research* (Technical Report). Fort Worth: Texas Christian University.

Dansereau, D. F., Brooks, L. W., Spurlin, J. E., & Holley, C. D. (1982). *Headings and outlines as processing aids for scientific text* (National Institute of Education, Final Report, NIE-G-79-0157). Fort Worth: Texas Christian University.

Darnton, R. (1984). The origins of modern reading. *The New Republic, 190*(8), 26–33.

Davelaar, E., Coltheart, M., Besner, D., & Jonasson, J. T. (1980). Phonological recoding and lexical access. *Memory & Cognition, 6,* 391–402.

Davis, F. B. (1944). Fundamental factors in reading. *Psychometrika, 9,* 185–197.

Davis, F. B. (1968). Research in comprehension in reading. *Reading Research Quarterly, 3,* 499–545.

Davis, F. B. (1972). Psychometric research on comprehension in reading. *Reading Research Quarterly, 7,* 628–678.

Dearborn, W. F. (1906). The psychology of reading. *Archives of Philosophy, Psychology and Scientific Methods, 4,* 7–132.

deBeaugrande, R., & Dressler, W. (1981). *Introduction to text linguistics.* London: Longman.

Dee-Lucas, D., Just, M. A., Carpenter, P. A., & Daneman, M. (1982). What eye fixations tell us about the time course of text integration. In R. Groner & P. Fraisse (Eds.), *Cognitive processes and eye movements.* Amsterdam: Deutscher Verlag der Wissenschaften.

Deighton, L. C. (1959). *Vocabulary development in the classroom.* New York: Teachers College Press.

Denckla, M. B., & Rudel, R. G. (1976). Rapid 'Automatized' Naming (R.A.N.): Dyslexia differentiated from other learning disabilities. *Neuropsychologia, 14,* 471–479.

Dennis, M. (1983). The developmentally dyslexic brain and the written language skills of children with one hemisphere. In U. Kirk (Ed.), *Neuropsychology of language, reading, and spelling.* New York: Academic Press.

deVilliers, P. A. (1974). Imagery and theme in recall of connected discourse. *Journal of Experimental Psychology, 103,* 263–268.

Dixon, T. R., & Horton, D. L. (Eds.). (1968). *Verbal behavior and general behavior theory.* Englewood Cliffs, NJ: Prentice-Hall.

Dixon, W. R. (1951). Studies of the eye movements in reading of university professors and graduate students. In W. C. Morse, F. A. Ballantine, & W. R. Dixon (Eds.), *Studies in the psychology of reading.* Ann Arbor: University of Michigan Press.

Doctor, E. A., & Coltheart, M. (1980). Children's use of phonological encoding when reading for meaning. *Memory & Cognition, 8,* 195–209.

Dolch, E. W., & Bloomster, M. (1937). Phonic readiness. *Elementary School Journal, 38,* 201–205.

Dooling, D. J., & Lachman, R. (1971). Effects of comprehension on retention of prose. *Journal of Experimental Psychology, 88,* 216–222.

Downing, J. (1967). *Evaluating the initial teaching alphabet: A study of the influence of English orthography on learning to read and write.* London: Cassell.

Downing, J. (1968). i.t.a. and slow learners: A reappraisal. *Educational Research, 11,* 229–231.

Downing, J. (1973). *Comparative reading.* New York: Macmillan.

Downing, J. (1977). The probability of reading failure in i.t.a. and t.o. *Reading, 11,* 3–12.

Dowty, D. R., Karttunen, L., and Zwicky, A. M. (1985). *Natural language parsing: Psychological, computational, and theoretical perspectives.* New York: Cambridge University Press.

Drewnowski, A., & Healy, A. F. (1977). Detection errors on *the* and *and:* Evidence for reading units larger than the word. *Memory & Cognition, 5,* 636–647.

Drewnowski, A., & Healy, A. F. (1982). Phonetic factors in letter detection: A reevaluation. *Memory & Cognition, 10,* 145–154.

Drum, P. A., Calfee, R. C., & Cook, L. K. (1981). The effects of surface structure variables on performance in reading comprehension tests. *Reading Research Quarterly, 16,* 486–514.

Dubin, R., & Taveggia, T. C. (1968). *The teaching-learning paradox.* Eugene: University of Oregon Press.

Durkin, D. (1974–75). A six year study of children who learned to read in school at the age of four. *Reading Research Quarterly, 10,* 9–61.

Durkin, D. (1976). *Teaching word identification.* Boston: Allyn and Bacon.

Durkin, D. (1978–79). What classroom observations reveal about reading comprehension instruction. *Reading Research Quarterly, 14,* 481–533.

Durkin, D. (1984). Do basal manuals teach reading comprehension? In R. C. Anderson, J. Osborn, & R. J. Tierney (Eds.), *Learning to read in American schools: Basal readers and content texts.* Hillsdale, NJ: Erlbaum.

Durrell, D. D. (1980). Letter-name values in reading and spelling. *Reading Research Quarterly, 16,* 159–163.

Dykstra, R. (1966). Auditory discrimination abilities and beginning reading achievement. *Reading Research Quarterly, 1,* 5–34.

Edfelt, A. W. (1960). *Silent speech and silent reading.* Chicago: University of Chicago Press.

Ehrlich, E. (1963). Opinions differ on speed reading. *National Education Association Journal, 52*, 45–46.

Ehrlich, K., & Rayner, K. (1983). Pronoun assignment and semantic integration during reading: Eye movements and immediacy of processing. *Journal of Verbal Learning and Verbal Behavior, 22*, 75–87.

Eisenberg, L. (1978). Definitions of dyslexia: Their consequences for research and policy. In A. Benton & D. Pearl (Eds.), *Dyslexia: An appraisal of current knowledge*. New York: Oxford University Press.

Engin, A. W. (1974). The relative importance of the subtests of the *Metropolitan Readiness Tests* in the prediction of first grade reading and arithmetic achievement criteria. *Journal of Psychology, 88*, 289–298.

Epstein, W. (1961). The influence of syntactical structure on learning. *American Journal of Psychology, 74*, 80–85.

Erickson, D., Mattingly, I. G., & Turvey, M. T. (1977). Phonetic activity in reading: An experiment with Kanji. *Language and Speech, 20*, 384–403.

Feigenbaum, E. A., & Simon, H. A. (1963). Performance of a reading task by an elementary perceiving and memorizing program. *Behavioral Science, 8*, 72–76.

Feitelson, D. (1973). Israel. In J. Downing (Ed.), *Comparative reading*. New York: Macmillan.

Feitelson, D. (1980). Relating instructional strategies to language idiosyncracies in Hebrew. In J. F. Kavanagh & R. L. Venezky (Eds.), *Orthography, reading, and dyslexia*. Baltimore: University Park Press.

Feitelson, D., Tehori, B. Z., Levinberg-Green, D. (1982). How effective is early instruction in reading? Experimental evidence. *Merrill-Palmer Quarterly, 28*, 485–494.

Feldman, J. (1975). Bad-mouthing frames. In R. Schank & B. L. Nash-Webber (Eds.), *Tinlap conference proceedings*. Cambridge, MA: The MIT Press.

Feynman, R. P. (1985). *"Surely you're joking, Mr. Feynman!"* New York: Bantam Books.

Fillmore, C. J. (1968). The case for case. In E. Bach & R. T. Harms (Eds.), *Universals of linguistic theory*. New York: Holt, Rinehart, and Winston.

Fillmore, C. J. (1971). Verbs of judging: An exercise in semantic description. In C. J. Fillmore & D. T. Langendoen (Eds.), *Studies in linguistic semantics*. New York: Holt, Rinehart, and Winston.

Findler, N. V. (Ed.). (1979). *Associative networks: Representation and use of knowledge by computers*. New York: Academic Press.

Firth, I. (1972). *Components of reading disability.* Unpublished doctoral dissertation, University of New South Wales, Australia.

Fischler, I., & Bloom, P. (1979). Automatic and attentional processes in the effects of sentence contexts on word recognition. *Journal of Verbal Learning and Verbal Behavior, 18*, 1–20.

Fisher, D. L. (1978). *Functional literacy and the schools.* Washington, DC: National Institute of Education.

Fisher, D. L. (1981). Functional literacy tests: A model of question-answering and an analysis of errors. *Reading Research Quarterly, 16*, 418–448.

Fishman, J. (1977). Advances in the creation and revision of writing systems. In J. Fishman (Ed.), *Advances in the creation and revision of writing systems*. The Hague, the Netherlands: Mouton.

Fleisher, L. S., Jenkins, J. R., & Pany, D. (1979). Effects on poor readers' comprehension of training in rapid decoding. *Reading Research Quarterly, 15*, 30–48.

Fodor, J. A. (1983). *The modularity of mind.* Cambridge, MA: Bradford.

Fodor, J. A., Bever, T. G., & Garrett, M. F. (1974). *The psychology of language: An introduction to psycholinguistics and generative grammar.* New York: McGraw-Hill.

Fodor, J. A., & Garrett, M. (1967). Some syntactic determinants of sentential complexity. *Perception & Psychophysics, 2*, 289–296.

Ford, M. (1983). A method for obtaining measures of local parsing complexity throughout sentences. *Journal of Verbal Learning and Verbal Behavior, 22*, 203–218.

Forster, K. I. (1970). Visual perception of rapidly presented word sequences of varying complexity. *Perception & Psychophysics, 8*, 215–221.

Forster, K. I. (1976). Accessing the mental lexicon. In R. J. Wales & E. Walker (Eds.), *New approaches to language mechanisms*. Amsterdam: North-Holland.

Forster, K. I. (1979). Levels of processing and the structure of the language processor. In W. Cooper & E. Walker (Eds.), *Sentence processing: Psycholinguistic studies*. Hillsdale, NJ: Erlbaum.

Forster, K. I., & Chambers, S. M. (1973). Lexical access and naming time. *Journal of Verbal Learning and Verbal Behavior, 12*, 627–635.

Forster, K. I., & Ryder, L. A. (1971). Perceiving the structure and meaning of sentences. *Journal of Verbal Learning and Verbal Behavior, 10,* 285–296.

Foss, D. J. (1970). Some effects of ambiguity upon sentence comprehension. *Journal of Verbal Learning and Verbal Behavior, 9,* 699–706.

Foss, D. J. (1982). A discourse on semantic priming. *Cognitive Psychology, 14,* 590–607.

Foss, D. J., & Ross, J. R. (1983). Great expectations: Context effects during sentence processing. In G. B. Flores d'Arcais & R. Jarvella (Eds.), *The process of language understanding.* New York: Wiley.

Frazier, L., & Rayner, K. (1982). Making and correcting errors during sentence comprehension: Eye movements in the analysis of structurally ambiguous sentences. *Cognitive Psychology, 14,* 178–210.

Frederiksen, J. R. (1978). Assessment of perceptual, decoding, and lexical skills and their relation to reading proficiency. In A. M. Lesgold, J. W. Pellegrino, S. D. Fokkema, & R. Glaser (Eds.), *Cognitive psychology and instruction.* New York: Plenum Press.

Frederiksen, J. R. (1981). *A componential theory of reading skills and their interactions* (Report No. 4649). Arlington, VA: Office of Naval Research.

Fredrick, W. C., & Walberg, H. J. (1980). Learning as a function of time. *Journal of Educational Research, 73,* 183–194.

Frege, G. (1960). On sense and reference. In P. T. Geach & M. Black (Eds. and Trans.), *Philosophical writing of Gottlob Frege.* Oxford: Blackwell. (Originally published in 1892.)

Frith, U. (Ed.). (1980). *Cognitive processes in spelling.* New York: Academic Press.

Frith, U. (1985). Beneath the surface of developmental dyslexia: Are comparisons between developmental and acquired disorders meaningful? In K. E. Patterson, J. C. Marshall, & M. Coltheart (Eds.), *Surface dyslexia: Neuropsychological and cognitive studies of phonological reading.* Hillsdale, NJ: Erlbaum.

Garvey, C., & Caramazza, A. (1974). Implicit causality in verbs. *Linguistic Inquiry, 5,* 459–464.

Gelb, I. J. (1963). *The study of writing* (rev. ed.). Chicago: University of Chicago Press.

Gentner, D., & Stevens, A. L. (Eds.). (1983). *Mental models.* Hillsdale, NJ: Erlbaum.

Geschwind, N. (1962). The anatomy of acquired disorders of reading. In J. Money (Ed.), *Reading disability: Progress and research needs in dyslexia.* Baltimore: Johns Hopkins Press.

Geschwind, N. (1979). Specialization of the human brain. *Scientific American, 241*(3), 180–201.

Gibson, E. J. (1969). *Principles of perceptual learning and development.* New York: Meredith Corporation.

Gibson, E. J. (1970). The ontogeny of reading. *American Psychologist, 25,* 136–143.

Gibson, E. J., Gibson, J. J., Pick, A., & Osser, H. (1962). A developmental study of the discriminability of letter-like forms. *Journal of Comparative and Physiological Psychology, 55,* 897–906.

Gibson, E. J., & Levin, H. (1975). *The psychology of reading.* Cambridge, MA: The MIT Press.

Gibson, E. J., Osser, H., Schiff, W., & Smith, J. (1963). An analysis of critical features of letters, tested by a confusion matrix. In *Final Report on a Basic Research Program on Reading* (Cooperative Research Project No. 639). Ithaca, NY: Cornell University and U.S. Office of Education.

Gipe, J. P. (1978). Investigating techniques for teaching word meanings. *Reading Research Quarterly, 14,* 624–644.

Glanzer, M., & Ehrenreich, S. L. (1979). Structure and search of the internal lexicon. *Journal of Verbal Learning and Verbal Behavior, 18,* 381–398.

Glaser, R. (1963). Instructional technology and the measurement of learning outcomes: Some questions. *American Psychologist, 18,* 519–521.

Glaser, R., & Bond, L. (1981). Testing: Concepts, policy, practice, and research. *American Psychologist, 36,* 997–1000.

Glass, A. L., Holyoak, K. J., & Santa, J. L. (1986). *Cognition* (2nd ed.). New York: Random House.

Gleitman, L. R., & Gleitman, H. (1970). *Phrase and paraphrase: Some innovative uses of language.* New York: W. W. Norton & Company.

Gleitman, L. R., & Rozin, P. (1973). Teaching by use of a syllabary. *Reading Research Quarterly, 8,* 447–483.

Gleitman, L. R., & Rozin, P. (1977). The structure and acquisition of reading I: Relations between orthographies and the structure of language. In A. S. Reber & D. L. Scarborough (Eds.), *Toward a psychology of reading.* Hillsdale, NJ: Erlbaum.

Glushko, R. J. (1979). The organization and activation of orthographic knowledge in reading aloud. *Journal of Experimental Psy-*

chology: Human Perception and Performance, 5, 674–691.

Golinkoff, R. (1978). Phonemic awareness skills and reading achievement. In F. B. Murray & J. J. Pikulski (Eds.), *The acquisition of reading: Cognitive, linguistic and perceptual prerequisites.* Baltimore: University Park Press.

Goodenough, C., Zurif, E., & Weintraub, S. (1977). Aphasics' attention to grammatical morphemes. *Language and Speech, 20,* 11–19.

Goodglass, H., & Kaplan, E. (1972). *The assessment of aphasia and related disorders.* Philadelphia: Lea & Febiger.

Goodlad, J. I. (1966). *School, curriculum and the individual.* Waltham, MA: Blaisdell.

Goodman, K. S. (1965). A linguistic study of cues and miscues in reading. *Elementary English, 42,* 639–643.

Goodman, K. S. (1967). Reading: A psycholinguistic guessing game. *Journal of the Reading Specialist, 6,* 126–135.

Goodman, K. S. (1969). Analysis of oral reading miscues: Applied psycholinguistics. *Reading Research Quarterly, 5,* 9–30.

Gordon, B. (1985). Subjective frequency and the lexical decision latency function: Implications for mechanisms of lexical access. *Journal of Memory and Language, 24,* 631–645.

Gough, P. B. (1972). One second of reading. In J. F. Kavanagh & I. G. Mattingly (Eds.), *Language by ear and eye.* Cambridge, MA: The MIT Press.

Graesser, A. C. (1981). *Prose comprehension beyond the word.* New York: Springer-Verlag.

Graesser, A. C., Hoffman, N. L., & Clark, L. F. (1980). Structural components of reading time. *Journal of Verbal Learning and Verbal Behavior, 19,* 135–151.

Gray, S. W., & Klaus, R. A. (1970). The early training project: A seventh-year report. *Child Development, 41,* 909–924.

Gray, W. S. (1956). *The teaching of reading and writing: An international survey.* Paris: UNESCO.

Green, T. R. G. (1979). The necessity of syntax markers: Two experiments with artificial languages. *Journal of Verbal Learning and Verbal Behavior, 18,* 481–496.

Grimes, J. E., & Gordon, R. G., Jr. (1980). Design of new orthographies. In J. F. Kavanagh & R. L. Venezky (Eds.), *Orthography, reading, and dyslexia.* Baltimore: University Park Press.

Guthrie, J. T. (1973). Reading comprehension and syntactic responses in good and poor readers. *Journal of Educational Psychology, 65,* 294–299.

Guthrie, J. T. (1978). Principles of instruction: A critique of Johnson's remedial approaches to dyslexia. In A. Benton & D. Pearl (Eds.), *Dyslexia: An appraisal of current knowledge.* New York: Oxford University Press.

Haas, W. (1970). *Phonographic translation.* Manchester: Manchester University Press.

Haberlandt, K., Berian, C., & Sandson, J. (1980). The episode schema in story processing. *Journal of Verbal Learning and Verbal Behavior, 19,* 635–650.

Haddock, M. (1978). Teaching blending in beginning reading instruction *is* important. *Reading Teacher, 31,* 654–658.

Hakes, D. T. (1972). Effects of reducing complement constructions on sentence comprehension. *Journal of Verbal Learning and Verbal Behavior, 11,* 278–286.

Hakes, D. T., & Cairns, H. S. (1970). Sentence comprehension and relative pronouns. *Perception & Psychophysics, 8,* 5–8.

Hakes, D. T., Evans, J. S., & Brannon, L. L. (1976). Understanding sentences with relative clauses. *Memory & Cognition, 4,* 283–290.

Hakes, D. T., & Foss, D. J. (1970). Decision processes during sentence comprehension: Effects of surface structure reconsidered. *Perception & Psychophysics, 8,* 413–416.

Halff, H. M., Ortony, A., & Anderson, R. C. (1976). A context-sensitive representation of word meanings. *Memory & Cognition, 4,* 378–383.

Halliday, M. A. K., & Hasan, R. (1976). *Cohesion in English.* New York: Longman.

Hanna, P. R., Hodges, R. E., & Hanna, J. S. (1971). *Spelling: Structure and strategies.* Boston: Houghton Mifflin.

Hansen, D. M. (1975). *A discourse structure analysis of the comprehension of rapid readers.* Unpublished doctoral dissertation, Brigham Young University, Provo, UT.

Harper and Row Publishers (1980a). Places and puzzles: Lesson plans. In *Reading basics plus.* New York: Harper & Row.

Harper and Row Publishers (1980b). Rain and riddles: Lesson plans. In *Reading basics plus.* New York: Harper & Row.

Harper and Row Publishers (1980c). Socks and secrets: Lesson plans. In *Reading basics plus.* New York: Harper & Row.

Harris, Louis, & Associates. (1970). *Survival literacy: Conducted for the National Reading Council.* New York: Louis Harris and Associates.

Hartmann, G. W. (1946). Further evidence on the unexpected large size of recognition vocabularies among college students. *Journal of Educational Psychology, 37,* 436–439.

Hayes, J. R., & Flower, L. S. (1980). Identifying the organization of writing processes. In L. W. Gregg & E. R. Steinberg (Eds.), *Cognitive processes in writing.* Hillsdale, NJ: Erlbaum.

Hayes, P. J. (1977). *Some association-based techniques for lexical disambiguation by machine.* Unpublished doctoral thesis, University of Rochester, Computer Science Department, Rochester, NY.

Healy, A. F., & Drewnowski, A. (1983). Investigating the boundaries of reading units: Letter detection in misspelled words. *Journal of Experimental Psychology: Human Perception and Performance, 9,* 413–426.

Hebb, D. O. (1949). *The organization of behavior: A neuropsychological theory.* New York: John Wiley & Sons.

Heilman, K. M., & Scholes, R. J. (1976). The nature of comprehension errors in Broca's conduction and Wernicke's aphasics. *Cortex, 12,* 258–265.

Heilman, K. M., & Valenstein, E. (Eds.). (1985). *Clinical neuropsychology.* New York: Oxford University Press.

Henderson, L. (1982). *Orthography and word recognition in reading.* New York: Academic Press.

Herber, H. L. (1970). *Teaching reading in content areas.* Englewood Cliffs, NJ: Prentice-Hall.

Hermann, K. (1959). *Reading disability: A medical study of word-blindness and related handicaps.* Springfield, IL: Charles C. Thomas.

Hilgard, E. R., & Bower, G. H. (1975). *Theories of learning* (4th ed.). Englewood Cliffs, NJ: Prentice-Hall.

Hinshelwood, J. (1917). *Cogenital word-blindness.* London: Lewis.

Hirst, W., & Brill, G. A. (1980). Contextual aspects of pronoun assignment. *Journal of Verbal Learning and Verbal Behavior, 19,* 168–175.

Hochberg, J. (1970). Components of literacy: Speculations and exploratory research. In H. Levin & J. P. Williams (Eds.), *Basic studies on reading.* New York: Basic Books.

Hollan, J. (1975). Features and semantic memory: Set-theoretic or network model. *Psychological Review, 82,* 154–155.

Holley, C. D., Dansereau, D. F., McDonald, B. A., Garland, J. C., & Collins, K. W. (1979). Evaluation of a hierarchical mapping technique as an aid to prose processing. *Contemporary Educational Psychology, 4,* 227–237.

Holm, W. (1980). Learning to read and write in Navajo. In J. F. Kavanagh & R. L. Venezky (Eds.), *Orthography, reading, and dyslexia.* Baltimore: University Park Press.

Holmes, V. M., & O'Regan, J. K. (1981). Eye fixation patterns during the reading of relative clause sentences. *Journal of Verbal Learning and Verbal Behavior, 20,* 417–430.

Horton, D. L., & Turnage, T. W. (1976). *Human learning.* Englewood Cliffs, NJ: Prentice-Hall.

Howes, D., & Solomon, R. L. (1951). Visual duration thresholds as a function of word probability. *Journal of Experimental Psychology, 41,* 401–410.

Huey, E. B. (1968). *The psychology and pedagogy of reading.* Cambridge, MA: The MIT Press. (Originally published by Macmillan in 1908.)

Hung, D. L., & Tzeng, O. J. L. (1981). Orthographic variations and visual information processing. *Psychological Bulletin, 90,* 377–414.

Hunt, E. B. (1978). Mechanics of verbal ability. *Psychological Review, 85,* 199–230.

Hunt, E. B., Frost, N., & Lunneborg, C. (1973). Individual differences in cognition: A new approach to intelligence. In G. H. Bower (Ed.), *The psychology of learning and motivation: Advances in research and theory* (Vol. 7). New York: Academic Press.

Hunt, E. B., & Love, T. (1972). How good can memory be? In A. W. Melton & E. Martin (Eds.), *Coding processes in human memory.* Washington, DC: Winston & Sons.

Hunt, E. B., Lunneborg, C., & Lewis, J. (1975). What does it mean to be high verbal? *Cognitive Psychology, 2,* 194–227.

Hyde, T. S., & Jenkins, J. J. (1973). Recall for words as a function of semantic, graphic, and syntactic orienting tasks. *Journal of Verbal Learning and Verbal Behavior, 12,* 471–480.

Ijiri, Y., & Simon, H. A. (1977). *Skew distributions and the sizes of business firms.* Amsterdam: North-Holland.

Ingram, T. T. S., Mason, A. W., & Blackburn, I. (1970). A retrospective study of 82 children with reading disability. *Developmental Medicine and Child Neurology, 12,* 271–281.

Jackson, M. D., & McClelland, J. L. (1975). Sensory and cognitive determinants of reading speed. *Journal of Verbal Learning and Verbal Behavior, 14,* 565–574.

Jackson, M. D., & McClelland, J. L. (1979). Processing determinants of reading speed. *Journal of Experimental Psychology: General, 108,* 151–181.

Jarvella, R. J. (1971). Syntactic processing of connected speech. *Journal of Verbal Learning and Verbal Behavior, 10,* 409–416.

Javal, E. (1879). Essai sur la physiologie de la lecture. *Annales D'Oculistique, 82,* 242–253.

Jensen, A. R., & Rohwer, W. D. (1966). The Stroop color-word test: A review. *Acta Psychologica, 25,* 36–93.

Johnson, D. J. (1978). Remedial approaches to dyslexia. In A. Benton & D. Pearl (Eds.), *Dyslexia: An appraisal of current knowledge.* New York: Oxford University Press.

Johnson, D. D., & Baumann, J. F. (1984). Word identification. In P. D. Pearson, R. Barr, M. Kamil, & P. Mosenthal (Eds.), *Handbook of reading research.* New York: Longman.

Johnson, D. D., & Pearson, P. D. (1978). *Teaching reading vocabulary.* New York: Holt, Rinehart, and Winston.

Johnson, W., & Kieras, D. E. (1983). Representation-saving effects of prior knowledge in memory for simple technical prose. *Memory & Cognition, 11,* 456–466.

Jorm, A. F. (1983). Specific reading retardation and working memory: A review. *British Journal of Psychology, 74,* 311–342.

Jorm, A. F., & Share, D. L. (1983). Phonological recoding and reading acquisition. *Applied Psycholinguistics, 4,* 103–147.

Judd, C. H., & Buswell, G. T. (1922). Silent reading: A study of the various types. *Supplementary Educational Monographs, 23.* Chicago: University of Chicago.

Juola, J. F., Ward, N., & McNamara, T. (1982). Visual search and reading rapid, serial presentations of letter strings, words, and text. *Journal of Experimental Psychology: General, 111,* 208–227.

Just, M. A., & Carpenter, P. A. (1971). Comprehension of negation with quantification. *Journal of Verbal Learning and Verbal Behavior, 10,* 244–253.

Just, M. A., & Carpenter, P. A. (Eds.). (1977). *Cognitive processes in comprehension.* Hillsdale, NJ: Erlbaum.

Just, M. A., & Carpenter, P. A. (1978). Inference processes during reading: Reflections from eye fixations. In J. W. Senders, D. F. Fisher, & R. A. Monty (Eds.), *Eye movements and the higher psychological functions.* Hillsdale, NJ: Erlbaum.

Just, M. A., & Carpenter, P. A. (1980). A theory of reading: From eye fixations to comprehension. *Psychological Review, 87,* 329–354.

Just, M. A., & Carpenter, P. A. (1984). Using eye fixations to study reading comprehension. In D. E. Kieras & M. A. Just (Eds.), *New methods in reading comprehension research.* Hillsdale, NJ: Erlbaum.

Just, M. A., & Carpenter, P. A. (1985). Cognitive coordinate systems: Accounts of mental rotation and individual differences in spatial ability. *Psychological Review, 92,* 137–172.

Just, M. A., Carpenter, P. A., & Masson, M. E. J. (1982). *What eye fixations tell us about speed reading and skimming* (Technical Report). Pittsburgh: Carnegie-Mellon University.

Just, M. A., Carpenter, P. A., & Woolley, J. D. (1982). Paradigms and processes in reading comprehension. *Journal of Experimental Psychology: General, 111,* 228–238.

Just, M. A., Carpenter, P. A., & Wu, R. (1983). *Eye fixations in the reading of Chinese technical text* (Technical Report). Pittsburgh: Carnegie-Mellon University.

Just, M. A., & Clark, H. H. (1973). Drawing inferences from the presuppositions and implications of affirmative and negative sentences. *Journal of Verbal Learning and Verbal Behavior, 12,* 21–31.

Just, M. A., & Thibadeau, R. H. (1984). Developing a computer model of reading times. In D. E. Kieras & M. A. Just (Eds.), *New methods in reading comprehension research.* Hillsdale, NJ: Erlbaum.

Kandel, G. L., & Tsao, Y. (1981). Implications of neuropsychological findings for the reading instruction of boys and girls. In A. Ansara, N. Geschwind, A. Galaburda, M. Albert, & N. Gartrell (Eds.), *Sex differences in dyslexia.* Towsend, MD: The Orton Dyslexia Society.

Kaplan, R. (1973). A general syntactic processor. In R. Rustin (Ed.), *Natural language processing.* New York: Algorithmics Press.

Karlgren, B. (1929). *Sound and symbol in Chinese.* London: Oxford University Press.

Katona, G. (1940). *Organizing and memorizing: Studies in the psychology of learning and teaching.* New York: Columbia University Press.

Katz, J. J. (1972). *Semantic theory.* New York: Harper & Row.

Kaufman, N. L. (1980). Review of research on reversal errors. *Perceptual and Motor Skills, 51,* 55–79.

Kavanagh, J. F., & Mattingly, I. G. (Eds.). (1972). *Language by ear and by eye: The relationships between speech and reading.* Cambridge, MA: The MIT Press.

Keenan, J. M., Baillet, S. D., & Brown, P. (1984). The effects of causal cohesion on comprehension and memory. *Journal of Verbal Learning and Verbal Behavior, 23,* 115–126.

Keenan, J. M., MacWhinney, B., & Mayhew, D. (1977). Pragmatics in memory: A study of natural conversation. *Journal of Verbal Learning and Verbal Behavior, 16,* 549–560.

Keil, F. C., & Carroll, J. J. (1980). The child's conception of "tall": Implications for an alternative view of semantic development. *Papers and Reports on Child Language Development, 19,* 21–28.

Kieras, D. E. (1982). A model of reader strategy for abstracting main ideas from simple technical prose. *Text, 2,* 47–82.

Kieras, D. E., & Just, M. A. (Eds.). (1984). *New methods in reading comprehension research.* Hillsdale, NJ: Erlbaum.

Kimball, J. P. (1973). Seven principles of surface structure parsing in natural language. *Cognition, 2,* 15–47.

Kintsch, W. (1974). *The representation of meaning in memory.* Hillsdale, NJ: Erlbaum.

Kintsch, W. (1977). On comprehending stories. In M. A. Just & P. A. Carpenter (Eds.), *Cognitive processes in comprehension.* Hillsdale, NJ: Erlbaum.

Kintsch, W., & Greene, E. (1978). The role of culture-specific schemata in the comprehension and recall of stories. *Discourse Processes, 1,* 1–13.

Kintsch, W., & Keenan, J. (1973). Reading rate and retention as a function of the number of propositions in the base structure of sentences. *Cognitive Psychology, 5,* 257–274.

Kintsch, W., Kozminsky, E., Streby, W. J., McKoon, G., & Keenan, J. M. (1975). Comprehension and recall of text as a function of content variables. *Journal of Verbal Learning and Verbal Behavior, 14,* 196–214.

Kintsch, W., & van Dijk, T. A. (1978). Toward a model of text comprehension and production. *Psychological Review, 85,* 363–394.

Kirkpatrick, E. A. (1891). The number of words in an ordinary vocabulary. *Science, 18,* 107.

Klare, G. R. (1963). *The measurement of readability.* Ames: Iowa State University Press.

Kleiman, G. M. (1975). Speech recoding in reading. *Journal of Verbal Learning and Verbal Behavior, 14,* 323–339.

Klima, E. S. (1972). How alphabets might reflect language. In J. F. Kavanagh & I. G. Mattingly (Eds.), *Language by ear and by eye: The relationships between speech and reading.* Cambridge, MA: The MIT Press.

Koen, F., Becker, A. L., & Young, R. E. (1969). The psychological reality of the paragraph. *Journal of Verbal Learning and Verbal Behavior, 8,* 49–53.

Kolers, P. A. (1976). Buswell's discoveries. In R. A. Monty & J. W. Senders (Eds.), *Eye movements and psychological processes.* Hillsdale: NJ: Erlbaum.

Koriat, A., & Levy, I. (1979). Figural symbolism in Chinese ideographs. *Journal of Psycholinguistic Research, 8,* 353–365.

Kosslyn, S. M. (1980). *Image and mind.* Cambridge, MA: Harvard University Press.

Krueger, T. H. (1976). *Visual imagery in problem solving and scientific creativity.* Derby, CT: Seal Press.

Kucera, H., & Francis, W. N. (1967). *Computational analysis of present-day American English.* Providence, RI: Brown University Press.

Kuo, W–F. (1978). A preliminary study of reading disabilities in the Republic of China. *Proceedings of the School of Education, National Taiwan Normal University, 20,* 57–78.

Kyostio, O. K. (1980). Is learning to read easy in a language in which the grapheme-phoneme correspondences are regular? In J. F. Kavanagh & R. L. Venezky (Eds.), *Orthography, reading, and dyslexia.* Baltimore: University Park Press.

LaBerge, D., & Samuels, S. J. (1974). Toward a theory of automatic information processing in reading. *Cognitive Psychology, 6,* 293–323.

Laird, J. E., & Newell, A. (1983). A universal weak method: Summary of results. In *Proceedings of IJCAI-83.* Los Altos, CA: Kaufmann.

Lakoff, G. (1970). Linguistics and natural logic. *Synthesis, 22,* 151–271.

Langley, P., & Neches, R. (1981). *PRISM User's Manual* (Technical Report). Pittsburgh: Carnegie-Mellon University, Department of Psychology.

Larkin, W., & Burns, D. (1977). Sentence comprehension and memory for embedded structure. *Memory & Cognition, 5,* 17–22.

Lavin, D. E. (1965). *The prediction of academic performance.* New York: Russell Sage Foundation.

Leech, G. N. (1969). *Towards a semantic description of English.* London: Longman.

Lehnert, W. G. (1981). Plot units and narrative summarization. *Cognitive Science, 5,* 293–331.

Lenneberg, E. H. (1967). *Biological foundations of language.* New York: Wiley.

Leong, C. K. (1973). Hong Kong. In J. Downing (Ed.), *Comparative reading.* New York: Macmillan.

Lerner, B. (1981). The minimum competence testing movement: Social, scientific, and legal implications. *American Psychologist, 36,* 1057–1066.

Lesgold, A. M., & Curtis, M. E. (1981). Learning to read words efficiently. In A. M. Lesgold & C. A. Perfetti (Eds.), *Interactive processes in reading.* Hillsdale, NJ: Erlbaum.

Lesgold, A. M., DeGood, H., & Levin, J. R. (1977). Pictures and young childen's prose learning: A supplementary report. *Journal of Reading Behavior, 9,* 353–360.

Lesgold, A. M., Levin, J. R., Shimron, J., & Guttmann, J. (1975). Pictures and young children's learning from oral prose. *Journal of Educational Psychology, 67,* 636–642.

Lesgold, A. M., Resnick, L. B., & Hammond, K. (1985). Learning to read: A longitudinal study of work skill development in two curricula. In G. Waller & E. MacKinnon (Eds.), *Reading research: Advances in theory and practice* (Vol. 4). New York: Academic Press.

Levin, H., & Kaplan, E. L. (1970). Grammatical structure and reading. In H. Levin & J. P. Williams (Eds.), *Basic studies on reading.* New York: Basic Books.

Levy, B. A. (1977). Reading: Speech and meaning processes. *Journal of Verbal Learning and Verbal Behavior, 16,* 623–638.

Levy, B. A. (1978). Speech analysis during sentence processing: Reading versus listening. *Visible Language, 12,* 81–101.

Levy, B. A. (1981). Interactive processes during reading. In A. M. Lesgold & C. A. Perfetti (Eds.), *Interactive processes in reading.* Hillsdale, NJ: Erlbaum.

Liberman, I., & Shankweiler, D. (1979). Speech, the alphabet, and teaching to read. In L. Resnick & P. Weaver (Eds.), *Theory and practice of early reading* (Vol. 2). Hillsdale, NJ: Erlbaum.

Liddle, W. (1965). *An investigation of the Wood reading dynamics method.* Unpublished doctoral dissertation, University of Delaware, Newark, DE.

Lindsay, P. H., & Norman, D. A. (1977). *Human information processing: An introduction to psychology* (2nd ed.). New York: Academic Press.

Lorayne, H., & Lucas, J. (1974). *The memory book.* New York: Stein and Day.

Lorge, I., & Chall, J. (1963). Estimating the size of vocabularies of children and adults: An analysis of methodological issues. *Journal of Experimental Education, 32,* 147–157.

Louis Harris and Associates. *See* Harris, Louis, and Associates.

Lovell, K., Shapton, D., & Warren, N. S. (1964). A study of some cognitive and other disabilities in backward readers of average intelligence as assessed by a non-verbal test. *British Journal of Educational Psychology, 34,* 58–64.

Lukatela, G., Popadic, D., Ognjenovic, P., & Turvey, M. T. (1980). Lexical decision in a phonologically shallow orthography. *Memory & Cognition, 8,* 124–132.

Lukatela, G., & Turvey, M. T. (1980). Some experiments on the Roman and Cyrillic alphabets of Serbo-Croatian. In J. F. Kavanagh & R. L. Venezky (Eds.), *Orthography, reading, and dyslexia.* Baltimore: University Park Press.

Luria, A. R. (1970). The functional organization of the brain. *Physiological psychology: Readings from* Scientific American. San Francisco: W. H. Freeman.

Lyons, J. (1968). *Introduction to theoretical linguistics.* Cambridge: The University Press.

McCarthy, D. (1954). Language development in children. In L. Carmichael (Ed.), *A manual of child psychology* (2nd ed.). New York: John Wiley & Sons.

McClelland, J. L. (1979). On the time relations of mental processes: An examination of systems of processes in cascade. *Psychological Review, 86,* 287–330.

McClelland, J. L., & Rumelhart, D. E. (1981). An interactive activation model of context effects in letter perception: Part 1. An account of basic findings. *Psychological Review, 88,* 375–407.

McClelland, J. L., Rumelhart, D. E., and the PDP research group. (1986). *Parallel distributed processing: Explorations in the microstructure of cognition* (Vol. 2). Cambridge, MA: Bradford Books.

McClusky, H. Y. (1934). An experiment on the influence of preliminary skimming in reading. *Journal of Educational Psychology, 25,* 276–282.

McConkie, G. W., & Rayner, K. (1975). The span of the effective stimulus during a fixation in reading. *Perception & Psychophysics, 17,* 578–586.

McConkie, G. W., & Zola, D. (1981). Language constraints and the functional stimulus in reading. In A. M. Lesgold & C. A. Perfetti (Eds.), *Interactive processes in reading*. Hillsdale, NJ: Erlbaum.

McConkie, G. W., Zola, D., Blanchard, H. E., & Wolverton, G. S. (1982). *Perceiving words during reading: Lack of facilitation from prior peripheral exposure* (Technical Report No. 243). Urbana-Champaign: University of Illinois, Center for the Study of Reading.

McCracken, D. (1978). *A production system version of the Hearsay II speech understanding system*. Unpublished doctoral dissertation, Carnegie-Mellon University, Pittsburgh.

McCusker, L. X., Hillinger, M., & Bias, R. G. (1981). Phonological recoding and reading. *Psychological Bulletin, 89*, 217–245.

McDonald, J. L. (1984). *The mapping of semantic and syntactic processing cues by first and second language learners of English, Dutch and German*. Unpublished doctoral dissertation, Carnegie-Mellon University, Pittsburgh.

McDonald, J. L., & Carpenter, P. A. (1981). Simultaneous translation: Idiom interpretation and parsing heuristics. *Journal of Verbal Learning and Verbal Behavior, 20*, 231–247.

McGinnies, E., Comer, P. B., & Lacey, O. L. (1952). Visual-recognition thresholds as a function of word length and word frequency. *Journal of Experimental Psychology, 44*, 65–69.

McKoon, G., & Ratcliff, R. (1981). The comprehension processes and memory structures involved in instrumental inference. *Journal of Verbal Learning and Verbal Behavior, 20*, 671–682.

McLaughlin, G. H. (1969). Reading at "impossible" speeds. *Journal of Reading, 12*, 449–454, 502–510.

Macnamara, J. (1967). The linguistic independence of bilinguals. *Journal of Verbal Learning and Verbal Behavior, 6*, 729–736.

Macnamara, J. (1972). The cognitive basis of language learning in infants. *Psychological Review, 79*, 1–13.

Macnamara, J. (1982). *Names for things: A study of human learning*. Cambridge, MA: The MIT Press.

McNamara, T. P., & Sternberg, R. J. (1983). Mental models of word meaning. *Journal of Verbal Learning and Verbal Behavior, 22*, 449–474.

MacWhinney, B., Bates, E., & Kliegl, R. (1984). Cue validity and sentence interpretation in English, German, and Italian. *Journal of Verbal Learning and Verbal Behavior, 23*, 127–150.

Makita, K. (1968). The rarity of reading disability in Japanese children. *American Journal of Orthopsychiatry, 38*, 599–614.

Mandler, G. (1979). Organization and repetition: Organization principles with special reference to rote learning. In L. Nilsson (Ed.), *Perspectives on memory research: Essays in honor of Uppsala University's 500th anniversary*. Hillsdale, NJ: Erlbaum.

Mandler, J. M. (1978). A code in the node: The use of a story schema in retrieval. *Discourse Processes, 1*, 14–35.

Mandler, J. M., & Johnson, N. S. (1977). Remembrance of things parsed: Story structure and recall. *Cognitive Psychology, 9*, 111–151.

Manelis, L., & Yekovich, F. R. (1976). Repetition of propositional arguments in sentences. *Journal of Verbal Learning and Verbal Behavior, 15*, 301–312.

Marcel, A. J., & Patterson, K. (1978). Word recognition and production: Reciprocity in clinical and normal studies. In J. Requin (Ed.), *Attention and performance 7*. Hillsdale, NJ: Erlbaum.

Marchbanks, G., & Levin, H. (1965). Cues by which children recognize words. *Journal of Educational Psychology, 56*, 57–61.

Marcus, M. P. (1980). *A theory of syntactic recognition for natural language*. Cambridge, MA: The MIT Press.

Markman, E. M. (1977). Realizing that you don't understand. *Child Development, 48*, 986–992.

Marsh, G., Desberg, P., & Cooper, J. (1977). Developmental changes in reading strategies. *Journal of Reading Behavior, 9*, 391–394.

Marsh, G., & Mineo, R. J. (1977). Training preschool children to recognize phonemes in words. *Journal of Educational Psychology, 69*, 748–753.

Marsh, G. P. (1872). Cited in Seashore, R. H., & Eckerson, L. D. (1940). The measurement of individual differences in general English vocabularies. *Journal of Educational Psychology, 31*, 14–38.

Marshalek, B. (1981). *Trait and process aspects of vocabulary knowledge and verbal ability* (Technical Report 15). Stanford, CA: Stanford University, School of Education.

Marshall, J. C., & Newcombe, F. (1973). Patterns of paralexia: A psycholinguistic approach. *Journal of Psycholinguistic Research, 2*, 175–199.

Marslen-Wilson, W., & Tyler, L. K. (1980). The temporal structure of spoken language understanding. *Cognition, 8*, 1–71.

Mason, M. (1975). Reading ability and letter search time: Effects of orthographic structure defined by single-letter positional frequency. *Journal of Experimental Psychology: General, 104,* 146–166.

Mason, M. (1978). From print to sound in mature readers as a function of reading ability and two forms of orthographic regularity. *Memory & Cognition, 6,* 568–581.

Mattis, S. (1978). Dyslexia syndromes: A working hypothesis that works. In A. L. Benton & D. Pearl (Eds.), *Dyslexia: An appraisal of current knowledge.* New York: Oxford University Press.

Mattis, S., French, J. H., & Rapin, I. (1975). Dyslexia in children and young adults: Three independent neuropsychological syndromes. *Developmental Medicine and Child Neurology, 17,* 150–163.

Meyer, B. (1975). *The organization of prose and its effect on recall.* Amsterdam: North-Holland.

Meyer, D. E., & Schvaneveldt, R. W. (1971). Facilitation in recognizing pairs of words: Evidence of a dependence between retrieval operations. *Journal of Experimental Psychology, 90,* 227–234.

Meyer, D. E., Schvaneveldt, R. W., & Ruddy, M. G. (1974). Functions of graphemic and phonemic codes in visual word-recognition. *Memory & Cognition, 2,* 309–321.

Mezynski, K. (1983). Issues concerning the acquisition of knowledge: Effects of vocabulary training on reading comprehension. *Review of Educational Research, 53,* 253–279.

Miller, G. A. (1951). *Language and communication.* New York: McGraw-Hill.

Miller, G. A. (1956). The magical number seven, plus or minus two: Some limits on our capacity for processing information. *Psychological Review, 63,* 81–97.

Miller, G. A., & Gildea, P. M. (1985). *How to misread a dictionary.* Unpublished manuscript, Princeton University, Princeton, NJ.

Miller, G. A., & Johnson-Laird, P. N. (1976). *Language and perception.* Cambridge, MA: Harvard University Press.

Minsky, M. (1975). A framework for representing knowledge. In P. H. Winston (Ed.), *The psychology of computer vision.* New York: McGraw-Hill.

Mischel, W. (1968). *Personality and assessment.* New York: Wiley.

Moeser, S. D., & Bregman, A. S. (1972). The role of reference in the acquisition of a miniature artificial language. *Journal of Verbal Learning and Verbal Behavior, 11,* 759–769.

Morais, J., Cary, L., Alegria, J., & Bertelson, P. (1979). Does awareness of speech as a sequence of phones arise spontaneously. *Cognition, 7,* 323–332.

Mori, K., & Moeser, S. D. (1983). The role of syntax markers and semantic referents in learning an artificial language. *Journal of Verbal Learning and Verbal Behavior, 22,* 701–718.

Morphett, M. V., & Washburne, C. (1931). When should children begin to read? *Elementary School Journal, 31,* 496–503.

Morrison, F. J. (1984). Reading disability: A problem in rule learning and word decoding. *Developmental Review, 4,* 36–47.

Morrison, F. J., & Manis, F. R. (1982). Cognitive processes and reading disability: A critique and proposal. In C. J. Brainerd & M. I. Pressley (Eds.), *Verbal processes in children: Progress in cognitive development research.* New York: Springer-Verlog.

Morton, J. (1969). Interaction of information in word recognition. *Psychological Review, 76,* 165–178.

Murdock, B. B., Jr. (1971). A parallel-processing model for scanning. *Perception & Psychophysics, 10,* 289–291.

Myklebust, H. R., & Johnson, D. J. (1962). Dyslexia in children. *Exceptional Children, 29,* 14–25.

Nagy, W. E., & Anderson, R. C. (1984). How many words are there in printed school English? *Reading Research Quarterly, 19,* 304–330.

Naidoo, S. (1972). *Specific dyslexia.* London: Pitman.

Naidoo, S. (1981). Teaching methods and their rationale. In G. Th. Pavlidis & T. Miles (Eds.), *Dyslexia research and its applications to education.* New York: John Wiley & Sons.

Nas, G. (1983). Visual word recognition in bilinguals: Evidence for a cooperation between visual and sound based codes during access to a common lexical store. *Journal of Verbal Learning and Verbal Behavior, 22,* 526–534.

National Assessment of Educational Progress. (1973, July). *Reading: Released exercises* (Report 02-R-20). Denver: Education Commission of the States.

National Assessment of Educational Progress. (1975). *Functional literacy: Basic reading performance: Technical summary of an assessment of in-school 17-year-olds in 1974.* Denver: Education Commission of the States.

Neale, M. D. (1966). *Neale analysis of reading ability.* London: Macmillan.

Neely, J. H. (1977). Semantic priming and retrieval from lexical memory. Roles of inhibitionless spreading activation and limited-capacity attention. *Journal of Experimental Psychology: General, 106,* 226–254.

Neisser, U. (1967). *Cognitive psychology.* New York: Appleton.

Newell, A. (1980). Harpy, production systems and human cognition. In R. Cole (Ed.), *Perception and production of fluent speech.* Hillsdale, NJ: Erlbaum.

Newell, A., & Rosenbloom, P. S. (1981). Mechanisms of skill acquisition and the law of practice. In J. R. Anderson (Ed.), *Cognitive skills and their acquisition.* Hillsdale, NJ: Erlbaum.

Newell, A., & Simon, H. A. (1972). *Human problem solving.* Englewood Cliffs, NJ: Prentice-Hall.

Nezworski, T., Stein, N. L., & Trabasso, T. (1982). Story structure versus content in children's recall. *Journal of Verbal Learning and Verbal Behavior, 21,* 196–206.

Ninness, C. (1979, April). *The effect of elimination of subvocalization with electromyographic feedback.* Paper presented at the meeting of the Southwestern Psychological Association, San Antonio, TX.

Nurss, J. R. (1979). Assessment of readiness. In T. G. Waller & G. E. MacKinnon (Eds.), *Reading research: Advances in theory and practice* (Vol. 1). New York: Academic Press.

Nurss, J. R., & McGauvran, M. E. (1976). *Metropolitan Readiness Tests, teachers manual (Level II, Form P) Part 1: Directions for administering.* San Diego: Harcourt Brace Jovanovich.

Omanson, R. C. (1982). The relation between centrality and story category variation. *Journal of Verbal Learning and Verbal Behavior, 21,* 326–337.

O'Regan, J. K. (1975). *Structural and contextual constraints on eye movements in reading.* Unpublished doctoral dissertation, University of Cambridge, Cambridge.

O'Regan, J. K. (1979). Moment to moment control of eye saccades as a function of textual parameters in reading. In P. A. Kolers, M. E. Wrolstad, & H. Bouma (Eds.), *Processing of visible language* (Vol. 1). New York: Plenum Press.

O'Rourke, J. P. (1974). *Toward a science of vocabulary development.* The Hague, the Netherlands: Mouton.

Orton, S. T. (1925). "Word-Blindness" in school children. *Archives of Neurology and Psychia-* *try, 14,* 581–615.

Orton, S. T. (1937). *Reading, writing and speech problems in children.* New York: W. W. Norton.

Otto, W., Wolf, A., & Eldridge, R. G. (1984). Managing instruction. In P. D. Pearson, R. Barr, M. L. Kamil, & P. Mosenthal (Eds.), *Handbook of reading research.* New York: Longman.

Paap, K. R., Newsome, S. L., & Noel, R. W. (1984). Word shape's in poor shape for the race to the lexicon. *Journal of Experimental Psychology: Human Perception and Performance, 10,* 413–428.

Palincsar, A. S., & Brown, A. L. (1984). Reciprocal teaching of comprehension-fostering and comprehension-monitoring activities. *Cognition and Instruction, 1,* 117–175.

Paradis, E. E. (1974). The appropriateness of visual discrimination exercises in reading readiness materials. *The Journal of Educational Research, 67,* 276–278.

Patterson, K. E., & Marcel, A. J. (1977). Aphasia, dyslexia, and the phonological coding of written words. *Quarterly Journal of Experimental Psychology, 29,* 307–318.

Patterson, K. E., Marshall, J. C., & Coltheart, M. (Eds.). (1985). *Surface dyslexia: Neuropsychological and cognitive studies of phonological reading.* Hillsdale, NJ: Erlbaum.

Pavlidis, G. Th., & Miles, T. R. (Eds.). (1981). *Dyslexia research and its applications to education.* New York: John Wiley & Sons.

Pearson, P. D., Barr, R., Kamil, M. L., & Mosenthal, P. (Eds.). (1984). *Handbook of reading research.* New York: Longman.

Pearson, P. D., Hansen, J., & Gordon, C. (1979). The effect of background knowledge on young children's comprehension of explicit and implicit information. *Journal of Reading Behavior, 11,* 201–209.

Peeck, J. (1974). Retention of pictorial and verbal content of a text with illustrations. *Journal of Educational Psychology, 66,* 880–888.

Pepper, J. (1981). Following students' suggestions for rewriting a computer programming textbook. *American Educational Research Journal, 18,* 259–269.

Perfetti, C. A. (1983). Individual differences in verbal processes. In R. Dillon & R. Schmeck (Eds.), *Individual differences in cognition.* New York: Academic Press.

Perfetti, C. A. (1985). *Reading ability.* New York: Oxford University Press.

Perfetti, C. A., Finger, E., & Hogaboam, T. (1978). Sources of vocalization latency differences between skilled and less-skilled young readers. *Journal of Educational Psychology, 70,* 730–739.

Perfetti, C. A., Goldman, S. R., & Hogaboam, T. W. (1979). Reading skill and the identification of words in discourse context. *Memory & Cognition, 7,* 273–282.

Perfetti, C. A., & Hogaboam, T. (1975). The relationship between single word decoding and reading comprehension skill. *Journal of Educational Psychology, 67,* 461–469.

Perfetti, C. A., & Lesgold, A. M. (1977). Discourse comprehension and sources of individual differences. In M. A. Just & P. A. Carpenter (Eds.), *Cognitive processes in comprehension.* Hillsdale, NJ: Erlbaum.

Perfetti, C. A., & Roth, S. (1981). Some of the interactive processes in reading and their role in reading skill. In A. M. Lesgold & C. A. Perfetti (Eds.), *Interactive processes in reading.* Hillsdale, NJ: Erlbaum.

Petty, W. T., Herold, C. P., & Stoll, E. (1968). *The state of knowledge about the teaching of vocabulary.* Urbana, IL: National Council of Teachers of English.

Pirozzolo, F. J., & Rayner, K. (1979). The neural control of eye movements in acquired and developmental reading disorders. *Studies in Neurolinguistics, 4,* 97–123.

Pitman, I. J. (1961). Learning to read: An experiment. *Journal of the Royal Society of Arts, 109,* 149–180.

Pollatsek, A., Bolozky, S., Well, A. D., & Rayner, K. (1981). Asymmetries in the perceptual span for Israeli readers. *Brain and Language, 14,* 174–180.

Posner, M. I., Boies, S., Eichelman, W., & Taylor, R. (1969). Retention of visual and name codes of single letters. *Journal of Experimental Psychology Monographs, 79*(1, Pt. 2.).

Posner, M. I., & Mitchell, R. F. (1967). Chronometric analysis of classification. *Psychological Review, 74,* 392–409.

Posner, M. I., & Snyder, C. R. (1975). Attention and cognitive control. In R. L. Solso (Ed.), *Information processing and cognition: The Loyola symposium.* Hillsdale, NJ: Erlbaum.

Postman, L. (1964). Short-term memory and incidental learning. In A. W. Melton (Ed.), *Categories of human learning.* New York: Academic Press.

Potter, M. C., & Faulconer, B. A. (1979). Understanding noun phrases. *Journal of Verbal Learning and Verbal Behavior, 18,* 509–522.

Potter, M. C., Kroll, J., & Harris, C. (1980). Comprehension and memory in rapid sequential reading. In R. Nickerson (Ed.), *Attention and Performance VIII.* Hillsdale, NJ: Erlbaum.

Potts, G. R. (1972). Information processing strategies used in the encoding of linear orderings. *Journal of Verbal Learning and Verbal Behavior, 11,* 727–740.

Propp, V. (1968). *Morphology of the folktale* (2nd ed.). Austin: University of Texas Press.

Pryzwansky, B. (1972). Effects of perceptual-motor training and manuscript writing on reading readiness skills in kindergarten. *Journal of Educational Psychology, 63,* 110–115.

Purves, A. C., Harnisch, D. L., Quirk, D. L., & Bauer, B. (1981). *Reading and literature: American achievement in international perspective* (NCTE Report No. 20). Urbana, IL.: National Council of Teachers of English.

Pyrczak, F. (1972). Objective evaluation of the quality of multiple-choice items designed to measure comprehension of reading passages. *Reading Research Quarterly, 8,* 62–72.

Quillian, M. R. (1968). Semantic memory. In M. L. Minsky (Ed.), *Semantic information processing.* Cambridge, MA: The MIT Press.

Quine, W. V. O. (1960). *Word and object.* Cambridge, MA: The MIT Press.

Quine, W. V. O. (1974). *The roots of reference.* La Salle, IL: Open Court.

Rabin, C. (1977). Spelling reform—Israel 1968. In J. Fishman (Ed.), *Advances in the creation and revision of writing systems.* The Hague, the Netherlands: Mouton.

Rader, N. (1975). *From written words to meaning: A developmental study.* Unpublished doctoral dissertation, Cornell University, Ithaco, NY.

Ransom, G. A. (1978). *Preparing to teach reading.* Boston: Little, Brown.

Rasco, R. W., Tennyson, R. D., & Boutwell, R. C. (1975). Imagery instructions and drawings in learning prose. *Journal of Educational Psychology, 67,* 188–192.

Ratcliff, R., & McKoon, G. (1978). Priming in item recognition: Evidence for the propositional structure of sentences. *Journal of Verbal Learning and Verbal Behavior, 17,* 403–418.

Rauch, S. J. (1971). Speed reading: How to debunk numbers. *Journal of Reading, 15,* 63.

Rawson, M. B. (1968). *Developmental language disability: Adult accomplishments of dyslexic boys.* Baltimore: Johns Hopkins Press.

Rayner, K. (1975). The perceptual span and peripheral cues in reading. *Cognitive Psychology, 7,* 65–81.

Rayner, K. (1976). Developmental changes in word recognition strategies. *Journal of Educational Psychology, 68,* 323–329.

Rayner, K. (Ed.). (1983). *Eye movements in reading: Perceptual and language processes.* New York: Academic Press.

Rayner, K., & Bertera, J. (1979). Reading without a fovea. *Science, 206,* 468–469.

Rayner, K., Carlson, M., & Frazier, L. (1983). The interaction of syntax and semantics during sentence processing: Eye movements in the analysis of semantically biased sentences. *Journal of Verbal Learning and Verbal Behavior, 3,* 358–374.

Rayner, K., Inhoff, A. W., Morrison, R. E., Slowiaczek, M. L., & Bertera, J. H. (1981). Masking of foveal and parafoveal vision during eye fixations in reading. *Journal of Experimental Psychology: Human Perception and Performance, 7,* 167–179.

Rayner, K., & Pollatsek, A. (1981). Eye movement control during reading: Evidence for direct control. *Quarterly Journal of Experimental Psychology, 33A,* 351–373.

Rayner, K., Well, A. D., & Pollatsek, A. (1980). Asymmetry of the effective visual field in reading. *Perception & Psychophysics, 27,* 537–544.

Reddy, D. R. (1980). Machine models of speech perception. In R. A. Cole (Ed.), *Perception and production of fluent speech.* Hillsdale, NJ: Erlbaum.

Reddy, D. R., & Newell, A. (1974). Knowledge and its representation in a speech understanding system. In L. W. Gregg (Ed.), *Knowledge and cognition.* Hillsdale, NJ: Erlbaum.

Reder, L. M. (1983). What kind of pitcher can a catcher fill? Effects of priming in sentence comprehension. *Journal of Verbal Learning and Verbal Behavior, 22,* 189–202.

Reder, L. M., & Anderson, J. R. (1980). A comparison of texts and their summaries: Memorial consequences. *Journal of Verbal Learning and Verbal Behavior, 19,* 121–134.

Reder, S. M. (1973). On-line monitoring of eye position signals in contingent and noncontingent paradigms. *Behavior Research Methods & Instrumentation, 5,* 218–228.

Reed, S. K. (1982). *Cognition: Theory and applications.* Monterey, CA: Brooks/Cole.

Reicher, G. M. (1969). Perceptual recognition as a function of meaningfulness of stimulus material. *Journal of Experimental Psychology, 81,* 274–280.

Reiser, B. J., Black, J. B., & Lehnert, W. G. (1985). Thematic knowledge structures in the understanding and generation of narratives. *Discourse Processes, 8,* 357–389.

Resnick, D. P., & Resnick, L. B. (1977). The nature of literacy: An historical exploration. *Harvard Educational Review, 47,* 370–385.

Resnick, L. B. (Ed.). (1976). *The nature of intelligence.* Hillsdale, NJ: Erlbaum.

Resnick, L. B., & Beck, I. L. (1976). Designing instruction in reading: Interaction of theory and practice. In J. T. Guthrie (Ed.), *Aspects of reading acquisition.* Baltimore: Johns Hopkins Press.

Resnick, L. B., & Weaver, P. A. (Eds.). (1979). *Theory and practice of early reading* (Vols. 1, 2, 3). Hillsdale, NJ: Erlbaum.

Reynolds, A. G., & Flagg, P. W. (1983). *Cognitive psychology* (2nd ed.). Boston: Little, Brown.

Rich, E. (1983). *Artificial intelligence.* New York: McGraw-Hill.

Rieger, C. (1979). Five aspects of a full scale story comprehension model. In N. V. Findler (Ed.), *Associative networks.* New York: Academic Press.

Rigney, J. W., & Lutz, K. A. (1976). Effect of graphic analogies of concepts in chemistry on learning and attitude. *Journal of Educational Psychology, 68,* 305–311.

Rips, L. J. (in press). Mental muddles. In M. Brand & R. M. Harnish (Eds.), *Problems in the representation of knowledge and belief.* Tucson: University of Arizona Press.

Robinson, F. P. (1970). *Effective study.* New York: Harper & Row.

Rosch, E. (1975). Cognitive representations of semantic categories. *Journal of Experimental Psychology: General, 104,* 192–233.

Rosenbloom, P. S. (1980). *Experimental activation production system.* Unpublished manuscript, Carnegie-Mellon University, Pittsburgh, PA.

Rosenshine, B., & Stevens, R. (1984). Classroom instruction in reading. In P. D. Pearson, R. Barr, M. L. Kamil, & P. Mosenthal (Eds.), *Handbook of reading research.* New York: Longman.

Roth, E. M., & Shoben, E. J. (1983). The effect of context on the structure of categories. *Cognitive Psychology, 15,* 346–378.

Roth, S. F., Perfetti, C. A., & Lesgold, A. M. (1979, May). *Reading ability and children's word identification processes.* Paper presented at the Midwestern Psychological Association Meeting, Chicago.

Rothkopf, E. Z. (1968). Two scientific approaches to the management of instruction. In R. M. Gagne & W. J. Gephard (Eds.), *Learning research and school subjects.* Itasca, IL: F. E. Peacock.

Rothkopf, E. Z. (1970). The concept of mathemagenic activities. *Review of Educational Research, 40,* 325–336.

Rothkopf, E. Z., & Bisbicos, E. E. (1967). Selective facilitative effects of interspersed questions on learning from written material. *Journal of Educational Psychology, 58,* 56–61.

Rothkopf, E. Z., & Kaplan, R. (1972). Exploration of the effect of density and specificity of instructional objectives on learning from text. *Journal of Educational Psychology, 63,* 295–302.

Rourke, B. P. (1978). Neuropsychological research in reading retardation: A review. In A. Benton & D. Pearl (Eds.), *Dyslexia: An appraisal of current knowledge.* New York: Oxford University Press.

Royer, J. M., & Cable, G. W. (1976). Illustrations, analogies, and facilitative transfer in prose learning. *Journal of Educational Psychology, 68,* 205–209.

Rozin, P., & Gleitman, L. R. (1977). The structure and acquisition of reading II: The reading process and the acquisition of the alphabetic principle. In A. S. Reber & D. L. Scarborough (Eds.), *Toward a psychology of reading.* Hillsdale, NJ: Erlbaum.

Rozin, P., Poritsky, S., & Sotsky, R. (1971). American children with reading problems can easily learn to read English represented by Chinese characters. *Science, 171,* 1264–1267.

Rubenstein, H., Garfield, L., & Millikan, J. A. (1970). Homographic entries in the internal lexicon. *Journal of Verbal Learning and Verbal Behavior, 9,* 487–494.

Rubenstein, H., Lewis, S. S., & Rubenstein, M. A. (1971). Homographic entries in the internal lexicon: Effects of systematicity and relative frequency of meanings. *Journal of Verbal Learning and Verbal Behavior, 10,* 57–62.

Rumelhart, D. E. (1975). Notes on a schema for stories. In D. G. Bobrow & A. M. Collins (Eds.), *Representations and understanding: Studies in cognitive science.* New York: Academic Press.

Rumelhart, D. E. (1977a). Understanding and summarizing brief stories. In D. Laberge & S. J. Samuels (Eds.), *Basic processes in reading: Perception and comprehension,* Hillsdale, NJ: Erlbaum.

Rumelhart, D. E. (1977b). Toward an interactive model of reading. In S. Dornic (Ed.), *Attention and performance VI.* Hillsdale, NJ: Erlbaum.

Rumelhart, D. E., & McClelland, J. L. (1982). An interactive activation model of context effects in letter perception: Part 2. The contextual enhancement effect and some tests and extensions of the model. *Psychological Review, 89,* 60–94.

Rumelhart, D. E., McClelland, J. L., and the PDP research group. (1986). *Parallel distributed processing: Explorations in the microstructure of cognition* (Vol. 1). Cambridge, MA: Bradford Books.

Rumelhart, D. E., & Siple, P. (1974). The process of recognizing tachistoscopically presented words. *Psychological Review, 81,* 99–118.

Rutter, M. (1978). Prevalence and types of dyslexia. In A. L. Benton & D. Pearl (Eds.), *Dyslexia: An appraisal of current knowledge.* New York: Oxford University Press.

Rutter, M., Tizard, J., & Whitmore, K. (Eds). (1970). *Education, health, and behaviour.* London: Longman.

Rutter, M., & Yule, W. (1973). Specific reading retardation. In L. Mann & D. Sabatino (Eds.), *The first review of special education.* Philadelphia: Buttonwood Farms.

Rutter, M., & Yule, W. (1975). The concept of specific reading retardation. *Journal of Child Psychology and Psychiatry and Allied Disciplines, 16,* 181–197.

Rutter, M., Yule, B., Quinton, D., Rowlands, O., Yule, W., & Berger, M. (1975). Attainment and adjustment in two geographical areas. III. Some factors accounting for area differences. *British Journal of Psychiatry, 126,* 520–533.

Ryan, J. W. (1980). Linguistic factors in adult literacy. In J. F. Kavanagh & R. L. Venezky (Eds.), *Orthography, reading, and dyslexia.* Baltimore: University Park Press.

Sachs, J. S. (1967). Recognition memory for syntactic and semantic aspects of connected discourse. *Perception & Psychophysics, 2,* 437–442.

Saffran, E. M., & Marin, O. S. (1977). Reading without phonology: Evidence from aphasia. *Quarterly Journal of Experimental Psychology, 29,* 515–525.

Sailor, A. L., & Ball, S. E. (1975). Peripheral vision training in reading speed and comprehension. *Perceptual and Motor Skills, 41,* 761–762.

Samuels, S. J., Dahl, P., & Archwamety, T. (1974). Effect of hypothesis/test training on reading skill. *Journal of Educational Psychology, 66,* 835–844.

Samuels, S. J., LaBerge, D., & Bremer, D. (1978). Units of word recognition: Evidence for developmental changes. *Journal of Verbal Learning and Verbal Behavior, 17,* 715–720.

Samuels, S. J., & Turnure, J. E. (1974). Attention and reading achievement in first-grade boys and girls. *Journal of Educational Psychology, 66,* 29–32.

Sanford, A. J., & Garrod, S. C. (1981). *Understanding written language: Explorations in comprehension beyond the sentence.* New York: John Wiley & Sons.

Sasanuma, S. (1975). Kana and Kanji processing in Japanese aphasics. *Brain and Language, 2,* 369–383.

Schallert, D. L. (1980). The role of illustrations in reading comprehension. In R. J. Spiro, B. C. Bruce, & W. F. Brewer (Eds.), *Theoretical issues in reading comprehension: Perspectives from cognitive psychology, linguistics, artificial intelligence, and education.* Hillsdale, NJ: Erlbaum.

Schank, R. C. (1972). Conceptual dependency: A theory of natural language understanding. *Cognitive Psychology, 3,* 552–631.

Schank, R. C. (1975). *Conceptual information processing.* Amsterdam: North-Holland.

Schank, R. C. (1979). *Reminding and memory organization: An introduction to MOPS* (Technical Report No. 170). New Haven, CT: Yale University, Department of Computer Science.

Schank, R. C. (1982). *Dynamic memory: A theory of reminding and learning in computers and people.* New York: Cambridge University Press.

Schank, R. C., & Abelson, R. P. (1977). *Scripts, plans, goals and understanding: An inquiry into human knowledge structures.* Hillsdale, NJ: Erlbaum.

Schank, R. C., Lebowitz, M., & Birnbaum, L. (1980). An integrated understander. *American Journal of Computational Linguistics, 6,* 13–30.

Schneider, W., & Shiffrin, R. M. (1977). Controlled and automatic human information processing: I. Detection, search, and attention. *Psychological Review, 84,* 1–66.

Schonell, F. J. (1961). *The psychology and teaching of reading.* New York: Philosophical Library.

Seashore, R. H., & Eckerson, L. D. (1940). The measurement of individual differences in general English vocabularies. *Journal of Educational Psychology, 31,* 14–38.

Seidenberg, M. S., & Tanenhaus, M. K. (1979). Orthographic effects on rhyme monitoring. *Journal of Experimental Psychology: Human Learning and Memory, 5,* 546–554.

Seidenberg, M. S., Tanenhaus, M. K., Leiman, J. M., & Bienkowski, M. (1982). Automatic access of the meanings of ambiguous words in context: Some limitations of knowledge-based processing. *Cognitive Psychology, 14,* 489–537.

Shallice, T., & Warrington, E. K. (1975). Word recognition in a phonemic dyslexic patient. *Quarterly Journal of Experimental Psychology, 27,* 189–199.

Shankweiler, D., & Liberman, I. Y. (1972). Misreading: A search for causes. In J. F. Kavanagh & I. G. Mattingly (Eds.), *Language by ear and by eye: The relationships between speech and reading.* Cambridge, MA: The MIT Press.

Sharkey, N. E., & Mitchell, D. C. (1985). Word recognition in a functional context: The use of scripts in reading. *Journal of Memory and Language, 24,* 253–270.

Sheldon, A. (1974). The role of parallel function in the acquisition of relative clauses in English. *Journal of Verbal Learning and Verbal Behavior, 13,* 272–281.

Shepard, R. N. (1975). Form, formation and transformation of internal representations. In R. Solso (Ed.), *Information processing and cognition: The Loyola symposium.* Hillsdale, NJ: Erlbaum.

Shibles, B. H. (1959). How many words does a first grade child know? *Elementary English, 31,* 42–47.

Shiffrin, R. M., & Schneider, W. (1977). Controlled and automatic human information processing: II. Perceptual learning, automatic attending, and a general theory. *Psychological Review, 84,* 127–190.

Slowaiczek, M. L., & Clifton, C. (1980). Subvocalization and reading for meaning. *Journal of Verbal Learning and Verbal Behavior, 19,* 573–582.

Smith, E. E., Shoben, E. J., & Rips, L. J. (1974). Structure and process in semantic memory: A featural model for semantic decisions. *Psychological Review, 81,* 214–241.

Smith, F. (1971). *Understanding reading.* New York: Holt, Rinehart, and Winston.

Smith, M. E. (1926). An investigation of the development of the sentence and the extent of vocabulary in young children. *University of Iowa Studies in Child Welfare, 3*(5), 92.

Smith, M. K. (1941). Measurement of the size of general English vocabulary through the elementary grades and high school. *Genetic Psychology Monographs, 24,* 311–345.

Smith, N. B. (1963). *Reading instruction for today's children.* Englewood Cliffs, NJ: Prentice-Hall.

Snowling, M. J. (1980). The development of grapheme-phoneme correspondence in normal and dyslexic readers. *Journal of Experimental Child Psychology, 29,* 294–305.

Spache, G. D. (1963). *Diagnostic reading scales (Examiner's manual).* Monterey: California Test Bureau.

Spearritt, D. (1972). Identification of subskills of reading comprehension by maximum likelihood factor analysis. *Reading Research Quarterly, 8,* 92–111.

Spelke, E., Hirst, W., & Neisser, U. (1976). Skills of divided attention. *Cognition, 4,* 215–230.

Spencer, H. (1968). *The visible word* (2nd ed.). New York: Hastings House.

Sperling, G. (1963). A model for visual memory tasks. *Human Factors, 5,* 19–31.

Spilich, G. J., Vesonder, G. T., Chiesi, H. L., & Voss, J. F. (1979). Text processing of domain-related information for individuals with high and low domain knowledge. *Journal of Verbal Learning and Verbal Behavior, 18,* 275–290.

Spring, C., & Capps, C. (1974). Encoding speed, rehearsal, and probed recall of dyslexic boys. *Journal of Educational Psychology, 66,* 780–786.

Stabler, E. P., Jr. (1983). How are grammars represented? *The Behavioral and Brain Sciences, 6,* 391–421.

Stanners, R. F., Jastrzembski, J. E., & Westbrook, A. (1975). Frequency and visual quality in a word-nonword classification task. *Journal of Verbal Learning and Verbal Behavior, 14,* 259–264.

Stanners, R. F., Neiser, J. J., & Painton, S. (1979). Memory representation for prefixed words. *Journal of Verbal Learning and Verbal Behavior, 18,* 733–743.

Stanovich, K. E. (1980). Toward an interactive-compensatory model of individual differences in the development of reading fluency. *Reading Research Quarterly, 16,* 32–71.

Stanovich, K. E., & West, R. F. (1979). Mechanisms of sentence context effects in reading: Automatic activation and conscious attention. *Memory & Cognition, 7,* 77–85.

Stanovich, K. E., & West, R. F. (1981). The effect of sentence context on ongoing word recognition: Tests of a two-process theory. *Journal of Experimental Psychology: Human Perception and Performance, 7,* 658–672.

Stanovich, K. E., & West, R. F. (1983). The generalizability of context effects on word recognition: A reconsideration of the roles of parafoveal priming and sentence context. *Memory & Cognition, 11,* 49–58.

Stein, N. L., & Glenn, C. (1979). An analysis of story comprehension in elementary school children. In R. Freedle (Ed.), *New directions in discourse processing.* Norwood, NJ: Ablex.

Stein, N. L., & Nezworski, M. T. (1978). The effect of organization and instructional set on story memory. *Discourse Processes, 1,* 177–193.

Stein, N. L., & Trabasso, T. (1981). What's in a story: Critical issues in comprehension and instruction. In R. Glaser (Ed.), *Advances in the psychology of instruction* (Vol. 2). Hillsdale, NJ: Erlbaum.

Sternberg, R. J. (Ed.). (1982). *Advances in the psychology of human intelligence* (Vol. 1). Hillsdale, NJ: Erlbaum.

Sternberg, R. J. (Ed.). (1984). *Advances in the psychology of human intelligence* (Vol. 2). Hillsdale, NJ: Erlbaum.

Sternberg, R. J. (Ed.). (1985). *Advances in the psychology of human intelligence* (Vol. 3). Hillsdale, NJ: Erlbaum.

Sternberg, R. J., & Powell, J. S. (1983). Comprehending verbal comprehension. *American Psychologist, 38,* 878–893.

Stevens, G. L., & Oren, R. C. (1963). Characteristic reading techniques of rapid readers. *Reading Teacher, 17,* 102–108.

Stevenson, H. W., Stigler, J. W., Lucker, G. W., Lee, S., Hsu, C., & Kitamura, S. (1982). Reading disabilities: The case of Chinese, Japanese and English. *Child Development, 53,* 1164–1181.

Sticht, T. G. (1972). Learning by listening. In J. Carroll & R. Freedle (Eds.), *Language comprehension and the acquisition of knowledge.* Washington, DC: Winston & Sons.

Sticht, T. G. (1977). Comprehending reading at work. In M. A. Just & P. A. Carpenter (Eds.), *Cognitive processes in comprehension.* Hillsdale, NJ: Erlbaum.

Sticht, T. G., & James, J. H. (1984). Listening and reading. In P. D. Pearson, R. Barr, M. L. Kamil, & P. Mosenthal (Eds.), *Handbook of reading research.* New York: Longman.

Stolz, W. A. (1967). A study of the ability to decode grammatically novel sentences. *Journal of Verbal Learning and Verbal Behavior, 6,* 867–873.

Sutherland, Z., Monson, D. L., & Arbuthnot, M. H. (1981). *Children & Books* (6th ed.). Glenview, IL: Scott, Foresman.

Swinney, D. A. (1979). Lexical access during sentence comprehension: (Re)consideration of context effects. *Journal of Verbal Learning and Verbal Behavior, 18,* 645–659.

Taft, M. (1979). Lexical access via an orthographic code: The basic orthographic syllabic structure (BOSS). *Journal of Verbal Learning and Verbal Behavior, 18,* 21–39.

Taft, M., & Forster, K. I. (1975). Lexical storage and retrieval of prefixed words. *Journal of Verbal Learning and Verbal Behavior, 14,* 638–647.

Taft, M., & Forster, K. I. (1976). Lexical storage and retrieval of polymorphemic and polysyllabic words. *Journal of Verbal Learning and Verbal Behavior, 15,* 607–620.

Tanenhaus, M. K., Leiman, J. M., & Seidenberg, M. S. (1979). Evidence for multiple stages in the processing of ambiguous words in syntactic contexts. *Journal of Verbal Learning and Verbal Behavior, 18,* 427–440.

Tauli, V. (1977). Speech and spelling. In J. A. Fishman (Ed.), *Advances in the creation and revision of writing systems.* The Hague, the Netherlands: Mouton.

Taylor, S. E. (1962). An evaluation of forty-one trainees who had recently completed the "Reading Dynamics" program. In E. P. Bliesmer & R. C. Staiger (Eds.), *Problems, programs, and projects in college adult reading.* Milwaukee, WI: National Reading Conference.

Taylor, S. E. (1965). Eye movements in reading: Facts and fallacies. *American Educational Research Journal, 2,* 187–202.

Teuber, H., Battersby, W., & Bender, M. (1960). *Visual field defects after penetrating missile wounds of the brain.* Cambridge, MA: Harvard University Press.

Theios, J., & Muise, J. G. (1977). The word identification process in reading. In N. Castellan, D. Pisoni, & G. Potts (Eds.), *Cognitive theory* (Vol. 2). Hillsdale, NJ: Erlbaum.

Thibadeau, R., Just, M. A., & Carpenter, P. A. (1982). A model of the time course and content of reading. *Cognitive Science, 6,* 157–203.

Thomas, E. L. (1962). Eye movements in speed reading. In R. G. Stauffer (Ed.), *Speed reading: Practices and procedures* (Vol. 10). Newark: University of Delaware, Reading Study Center.

Thomas, E. L., & Robinson, H. A. (1972). *Improving reading in every class: A sourcebook for teachers.* Boston: Allyn and Bacon.

Thompson, G. B. (1981). Semantic context and graphic processing in the acquisition of reading. *British Journal of Educational Psychology, 51,* 291–300.

Thorndike, R. L. (1973). Reading as reasoning. *Reading Research Quarterly, 9,* 135–147.

Thorndyke, P. W. (1977). Cognitive structures in comprehension and memory of narrative discourse. *Cognitive Psychology, 9,* 77–110.

Thorne, J., Bratley, P., & Dewar, H. (1968). The syntactic analysis of English by machine. In D. Michie (Ed.), *Machine intelligence* (Vol. 3). New York: Elsevier.

Thurstone, L. L. (1946). Note on a reanalysis of Davis' reading tests. *Psychometrika, 11,* 185–188.

Tierney, R. J., & Cunningham, J. W. (1984). Research on teaching reading comprehension. In P. D. Pearson, R. Barr, M. L. Kamil, & P. Mosenthal (Eds.), *Handbook of reading research.* New York: Longman.

Tinker, M. A. (1958). Recent studies of eye movements in reading. *Psychological Bulletin, 55,* 215–231.

Torgeson, J. K., & Houck, D. J. (1980). Processing deficiencies of learning-disabled children who perform poorly on the digit span test. *Journal of Educational Psychology, 72,* 141–160.

Townsend, D. J., & Bever, T. J. (1978). Interclause relations and clausal processing. *Journal of Verbal Learning and Verbal Behavior, 17,* 509–522.

Townsend, J. T. (1974). Issues and models concerning the processing of a finite number of inputs. In B. H. Kantowitz (Ed.), *Human information processing: Tutorials in performance and cognition.* Hillsdale, NJ: Erlbaum.

Trabasso, T., Secco, T., & van den Broek, P. (1984). Causal cohesion and story coherence. In H. Mandl, N. L. Stein, & T. Trabasso (Eds.), *Learning and comprehension of text.* Hillsdale, NJ: Erlbaum.

Treiman, R., Freyd, J. J., & Baron, J. (1983). Phonological recoding and use of spelling-sound rules in reading of sentences. *Journal of Ver-*

bal Learning and Verbal Behavior, 22, 682–700.

Tryk, H. E. (1968). Subjective scaling and word frequency. *American Journal of Psychology, 81,* 170–177.

Tufte, E. R. (1983). *The visual display of quantitative information.* Cheshire, CT: Graphics Press.

Tuinman, J. J. (1973–74). Determining the passage dependency of comprehension questions in 5 major tests. *Reading Research Quarterly, 9,* 206–223.

Tuinman, J. J., & Brady, M. E. (1974). How does vocabulary account for variance on reading comprehension tests? A preliminary instructional analysis. In P. L. Nacke (Ed.), *Interaction: Research and practice for college-adult reading, Twenty-third Yearbook of the National Reading Conference.* Clemson SC: The National Reading Conference.

Tzeng, O. J. L., & Hung, D. L. (1980). Reading in a nonalphabetic writing system: Some experimental studies. In J. F. Kavanagh & R. L. Venezky (Eds.), *Orthography, reading, and dyslexia.* Baltimore: University Park Press.

Tzeng, O. J. L., & Hung, D. L. (1981). Linguistic determinism: A written language perspective. In O. J. L. Tzeng & H. Singer (Eds.), *Perception of print: Reading research in experimental psychology.* Hillsdale, NJ: Erlbaum.

Tzeng, O. J. L., Hung, D. L., & Wang, W. S-Y. (1977). Speech recoding in reading Chinese characters. *Journal of Experimental Psychology: Human Learning and Memory, 3,* 621–630.

Ultan, R. (1969). Some general characteristics of interrogative systems. *Working Papers in Language Universals* (Stanford University), *1,* 41–63a.

van Daalen-Kapteijns, M. M., & Elshout-Mohr, M. (1981). The acquisition of word meanings as a cognitive learning process. *Journal of Verbal Learning and Verbal Behavior, 20,* 386–399.

van Dijk, T. A. (1972). *Some aspects of text grammars.* The Hague, the Netherlands: Mouton.

van Dijk, T. A., & Kintsch, W. (1983). *Strategies of discourse comprehension.* New York: Academic Press.

Vellutino, F. R. (1979). *Dyslexia: Theory and research.* Cambridge, MA: The MIT Press.

Vellutino, F. R., Smith, H., Steger, J. A., & Kaman, M. (1975). Reading disability: Age differences and the perceptual-deficit hypothesis. *Child Development, 46,* 487–493.

Vellutino, F. R., Steger, J. A., Harding, C. J., & Phillips, F. (1975). Verbal vs. non-verbal paired-associates learning in poor and normal readers. *Neuropsychologia, 13,* 75–82.

Vellutino, F. R., Steger, J. A., & Kandel, G. (1972). Reading disability: An investigation of the perceptual deficit hypothesis. *Cortex, 8,* 106–118.

Venezky, R. L. (1970). *The structure of English orthography.* The Hague, the Netherlands, Mouton.

Venezky, R. L. (1976). Prerequisites for learning to read. In J. R. Levin & V. L. Allen (Eds.), *Cognitive learning in children: Theories and strategies.* New York: Academic Press.

Venezky, R. L. (1978). Reading acquisition: The occult and the obscure. In F. B. Murray & J. J. Pikulski (Eds.), *The acquisition of reading: Cognitive, linguistic, and perceptual prerequisites.* Baltimore: University Park Press.

Venezky, R. L. (1980). Overview: From Sumer to Leipzig to Bethesda. In J. F. Kavanagh & R. L. Venezky (Eds.), *Orthography, reading, and dyslexia.* Baltimore: University Park Press.

Venezky, R. L., Chapman, R. S., Seegal, J., Kaam, M., & Leslie, R. (1971). *The prereading skills program: Evaluation of the first tryout* (Working Paper No. 81). Madison: Wisconsin Research and Development Center for Cognitive Learning.

Voss, J. F., Fincher-Kiefer, R. H., Greene, T. R., & Post, T. A. (1985). Individual differences in performance: The contrast approach to knowledge. In R. J. Sternberg (Ed.), *Advances in the psychology of human intelligence* (Vol. 3). Hillsdale, NJ: Erlbaum.

Walcutt, C. C., & McCracken, G. (1981a). Exploring. In *Lippincott basic reading B.* New York: Harper & Row.

Walcutt, C. C., & McCracken, G. (1981b). Reaching higher. In *Lippincott basic reading C.* New York: Harper & Row.

Walcutt, C. C., & McCracken, G. (1981c). Starting out. In *Lippincott basic reading A.* New York: Harper & Row.

Wallach, M. A., & Wallach, L. (1979). Helping disadvantaged children learn to read by teaching them phoneme identification skills. In L. B. Resnick & P. A. Weaver (Eds.), *Theory and practice of early reading* (Vol. 3). Hillsdale, NJ: Erlbaum.

Waller, T. S., & MacKinnon, G. E. (Eds.). (1981). *Reading research: Advances in theory and practice* (Vol. 2). New York: Academic Press.

Wang, W. S.-Y. (1973). The Chinese language. *Scientific American, 228,* 50–60.

Wang, W. S.-Y. (1981). Language structure and optimal orthography. In O. J. L. Tzeng & H. Singer (Eds.), *Perception of print: Reading research in experimental psychology.* Hillsdale, NJ: Erlbaum.

Wanner, E., & Gleitman, L. R. (Eds.). (1982). *Language acquisition: The state of the art.* Cambridge: Cambridge University Press.

Wanner, E., & Maratsos, M. (1978). An ATN approach to comprehension. In M. J. Halle, J. Bresnan, & G. A. Miller (Eds.), *Linguistic theory and psychological reality.* Cambridge, MA: The MIT Press.

Watts, G. H., & Anderson, R. C. (1971). Effects of three types of inserted questions on learning from prose. *Journal of Educational Psychology, 62,* 387–394.

Welford, A. T. (1976). *Skilled performance: Perceptual and motor skills.* Glenview, IL: Scott, Foresman.

Werner, H., & Kaplan, E. (1952). The acquisition of word meanings: A developmental study. *Monographs of the Society for Research in Child Development, 15,* 190–200.

West, R. F., & Stanovich, K. E. (1978). Automatic contextual facilitation in readers of three ages. *Child Development, 49,* 717–727.

Westheimer, G. H. (1954). Eye movement responses to a horizontally moving visual stimulus. *Archives of Opthamology, 52,* 932–943.

Whaley, C. P. (1978). Word-nonword classification time. *Journal of Verbal Learning and Verbal Behavior, 17,* 143–154.

Whaley, W. J., & Kirby, M. W. (1980). Word synthesis and beginning reading achievement. *The Journal of Educational Research, 73,* 132–138.

Wheeler, D. D. (1970). Processes in word recognition. *Cognitive Psychology, 1,* 59–85.

Wiener, M., & Cromer, W. (1967). Reading and reading difficulty: A conceptual analysis. *Harvard Educational Review, 37,* 620–643.

Wijk, A. (1966). *Rules of pronunciation for the English language.* Oxford: Oxford University Press.

Wilensky, R. (1980). *Points: A theory of story content* (Technical Report No. UCB/ERL M80/17). Berkeley: University of California, Berkeley.

Winograd, T. (1972). A program for understanding natural language. *Cognitive Psychology, 3,* 1–191.

Winograd, T. (1983). *Language as a cognitive process.* Reading, MA: Addison-Wesley.

Winston, P. H. (1975). Learning structural descriptions from examples. In P. H. Winston (Ed.), *The psychology of computer vision.* New York: McGraw-Hill.

Winston, P. H. (1977). *Artificial intelligence.* Reading, MA: Addison-Wesley.

Wittgenstein, L. (1953). *Philosophical investigations.* New York: Macmillan.

Wood, E. N. (1960). A breakthrough in reading. *Reading Teacher, 14,* 115–117.

Wood, G. (1983). *Cognitive psychology: A skills approach.* Monterey, CA: Brooks/Cole.

Woods, W. A. (1973). An experimental parsing system for transition network grammars. In R. Rustin (Ed.), *Natural language processing.* Englewood Cliffs, NJ: Prentice-Hall.

Wright, P. (1977). Presenting technical information: A survey of research findings. *Instructional Science, 6,* 93–134.

Yee, C. (1973). *Chinese calligraphy: An introduction to its aesthetic and technique* (3rd ed.). Cambridge, MA: Harvard University Press.

Yekovich, F. R., & Walker, C. H. (1978). Identifying and using referents in sentence comprehension. *Journal of Verbal Learning and Verbal Behavior, 17,* 265–277.

Young, A. W., & Ellis, A. (1981). Asymmetry of cerebral hemisphere function in normal and poor readers. *Psychological Bulletin, 89,* 183–190.

Yule, W., Rutter, M., Berger, M., & Thompson, J. (1974). Over- and under-achievement in reading: Distribution in the general population. *British Journal of Educational Psychology, 44,* 1–12.

Zaidel, E. (1978). Auditory language comprehension in the right hemisphere following cerebral commissurotomy and hemispherectomy: A comparison with child language and aphasia. In A. Caramazza & E. B. Zurif (Eds.), *Language acquisition and language breakdown: Parallels and divergences.* Baltimore: Johns Hopkins Press.

Zhou, Y. G. (1978). To what degree are the "phonetics" of present-day Chinese characters still phonetic? *Zhongguo Yuwen, 146,* 172–177.

Zigmond, N. (1978). Remediation of dyslexia: A discussion. In A. Benton & D. Pearl (Eds.), *Dyslexia: An appraisal of current knowledge.* New York: Oxford University Press.

Author Index

Subject Index